Flows and Practices

Flows and Practices:

The Politics of Integrated Water Resources Management in Eastern and Southern Africa

Edited

by

Lyla Mehta, Bill Derman and
Emmanuel Manzungu

Published by Weaver Press, Box A1922,
Avondale, Harare. 2017
<www.weaverpresszimbabwe.com>

All the chapters in this book were first published by
Water Alternatives: 9:3
<www.water-alternatives.org>
and reproduced here with their permission.

Typeset by Weaver Press, Harare, Zimbabwe
Cover Design by Danes Design, Harare, Zimbabwe
Front cover photograph © Kristi Denby
Back cover photograph © Barbara van Koppen
Printed and bound in Great Britain by
Clays Ltd, St Ives, plc.

ISBN: 978-1-77922-314-2

Contents

Contributors

Rossella Alba

Governance and Sustainability Lab, Trier University, Trier, Germany; <alba@uni-trier.de>

Jeremy Allouche

Institute of Development Studies at the University of Sussex, Brighton, UK; <j.allouche@ids.ac.uk>

Alex Bolding

Water Resources Management group, Wageningen University, Wageningen, The Netherlands; <alex.bolding@wur.nl>

Bill Derman

Norwegian University of the Life Sciences, Department of International Environment and Development Studies, Aas, Norway; <bill.derman@nmbu.no>

Kristi Denby

Department of Environment and Development Studies (Noragric), Norwegian University of Life Sciences, Aas, Norway; <kristidenby@gmail.com>

Raphaëlle Ducrot

CIRAD, Département Environnement et Sociétés, UMR G-EAU, Montpellier, France; and IWEGA, Faculdade de Agronomia e Engenharia Florestal, Universidade Eduardo Mondlane, Maputo, Mozambique; <raphaele.ducrot@cirad>

Takunda Hove

Ateg Resources Environmental Consultants, Harare, Zimbabwe; <takunda.ateg@gmail.com>

Emmanuel Manzungu

University of Zimbabwe, Department of Soil Science and Agricultural Engineering, Harare, Zimbabwe; <emmanuelmanzungu@gmail.com>

Lyla Mehta

Institute of Development Studies at the University of Sussex, Brighton, UK; and Department of Environment and Development Studies (Noragric), Norwegian University of Life Sciences, Aas, Norway; <l.mehta@ids.ac.uk>

Synne Movik

Department of Urban and Regional Planning, Norwegian University of Life Sciences; <Synne.Movik@nmbu.no>

Alan Nicol

International Water Management Institute, Ethiopia Office, Addis Ababa (at the time of the project); GWI East Africa, CARE <a.nicol@cgiar.org>

William Odinga

Uganda Science Journalists Association, Kampala, Uganda; <wbodinga@hotmail.com>

Preetha Prabhakaran

Institute of Development Studies, University of Sussex, Brighton, UK; <preethapb@gmail.com>

Philip Mathew Sumuni

Sokoine University of Agriculture, Morogoro, Tanzania; <philipsumuni@yahoo.com>

Andrew K.P.R. Tarimo

Sokoine University of Agriculture, Morogoro, Tanzania; <andrewtarimo2@yahoo.co.uk>

Aurelia van Eeden

Dept of Environment and Development Studies (Noragric), Norwegian University of Life Sciences, Aas, Norway; <aureliave@me.com>

Barbara van Koppen

International Water Management Institute (IWMI), Southern Africa Regional Programme, South Africa; <b.vankoppen@cgiar.org>

Acknowledgements and preface

This book presents findings of the Research Council of Norway-funded project 'Flows and Practices: The Politics of Integrated Water Resources Management (IWRM) in Africa'. We are grateful to the Research Council of Norway for their generous financial support. All the chapters in this book were first published by *Water Alternatives*: 9:3 <www.water-alternatives. org> and reproduced here with their permission. For that we are grateful to the managing editors, especially François Molle.

At Weaver Press, we thank Irene Staunton and Murray McCartney for their patience and support. We also thank all the members of the Flows and Practices project for their hard work, patience and commitment during the research and publication process and all the countless people across eastern and southern Africa and beyond whom we interviewed and who shared their knowledge and insights with us. We acknowledge the support received from our institutions the Department of Environment and Development Studies (Noragric) at the Norwegian University of Life Sciences, the Institute of Development Studies, UK and the University of Zimbabwe. Finally, we thank Kristi Denby for her outstanding research assistance throughout the process and her substantial help with putting this volume together.

We dedicate the volume to the invisible users and managers of water as well as the smallholder farmers of southern and eastern Africa whose voice and rights are too often missed in official water management policies and discourses.

Lyla Mehta, Bill Derman and Emmanuel Manzungu

Brighton, Oslo and Harare
April 2017

1

Introduction – Flows and Practices: The Politics of Integrated Water Resources Management (IWRM) in Eastern and Southern Africa[1]

Lyla Mehta

Synne Movik

Alex Bolding

Bill Derman

Emmanuel Manzungu

ABSTRACT: For the past two decades, IWRM has been actively promoted by water experts as well as multilateral and bilateral donors who have considered it to be a crucial way to address global water management problems. IWRM has been incorporated into water laws, reforms and policies of southern African nations. This chapter provides a conceptual framework to study: the flow of IWRM as an idea; its translation and articulation into new policies, institutions and allocation mechanisms, and the resulting practices and effects across multiple scales – global, regional, national and local. The empirical findings of the complexities of articulation and implementation of IWRM in South Africa, Zimbabwe, Mozambique, Tanzania and Uganda form the core of this book. We demonstrate how Africa has been a laboratory for IWRM experiments, while donors as well as a new cadre of water professionals and students have made IWRM their mission. The case studies reveal that IWRM may have resulted in an unwarranted policy focus on managing water instead of enlarging poor women's and men's access to water. The newly created institutional arrangements tended to centralise the power and control of the State and powerful users over water and failed to address historically rooted inequalities.

KEYWORDS: IWRM, water policies and reform, access to water, donors, southern Africa

Introduction

For the past two decades, Integrated Water Resources Management (IWRM) has

1 First published in *Water Alternatives* 9(3): 489-411.

been considered the dominant paradigm in water resources management. It is one of the most influential policy models currently being implemented in river basins globally, including in Africa (GWP and INBO, 2009). Of the countries around the world, 80% have included IWRM principles in their water law or policies and two-thirds have developed IWRM plans (see Cherlet, 2012). While this concept has been around for a long time, its current form gained momentum at the International Conference on Water and the Environment (ICWE) in Dublin in January 1992. Since then it has been the flagship project of supranational global bodies such as the Global Water Partnership (GWP), and the World Water Council (see GWP, 2000). It is central to the European Water Framework Directive which emphasises river basins as management units, stakeholder involvement and water as an economic good (European Union, 2000). In its heyday, it was also promoted by multilateral and regional development banks (e.g. the World Bank and African Development Bank) as well as bilateral donor agencies as one of the panaceas to address the water management crisis in the global south.

The promotion by these global players has led to a quasi-global industry around IWRM manifesting itself in various forms such as Master's degrees and short courses, annual symposia such as WaterNet in southern Africa, IWRM toolkits and manuals as well as major water reform programmes and the rewriting of national policies and laws drawing on IWRM principles in a range of countries in the global South. Conca argues that IWRM "combines intuitive reasonableness, an appeal to technical authority, and an all-encompassing character of such great flexibility that it approaches vagueness" (Conca, 2006: 126-127). How such globally defined constructs of flexibility and vagueness translate into diverse political, cultural and social contexts around the world, and how and to what extent they become locally appropriate are thus key questions.

We address these issues in the context of southern Africa which has witnessed a rapid spread of IWRM in the past two decades (see Movik et al., Chapter 4). African socio-political and environmental conditions differ markedly from temperate regions and countries where IWRM originated. Africa's rivers are larger, more complex and variable, and far more prone to extreme events (Elberier and Babiker, 1998) than those in temperate zones, and there is a dearth of data on both hydrology and usage. Moreover, IWRM also emphasises decentralisation, and efforts to decentralise decision making have led to experimentation with new institutions, new procedures, new accountability standards and new planning processes. However, the capacity of national governments to ensure that these are followed remains problematic (Ribot and Larson, 2005) and often water management policies in the past have tended towards (re-)centralising power (Movik, 2010) and facilitating the rise of expert authority over locally situated knowledges and management practices (Biswas, 2004; Shah and van Koppen, 2006). Furthermore, local customary arrangements matter. African nation-states tend to have plural, overlapping and competing formal and informal legal and customary systems, and most countries in sub-Saharan Africa are characterised by primarily informal water users' practices (Biswas, 2004; Shah and van Koppen, 2006; van Koppen et al., 2005). There are also issues concerning participation, elite capture and the importance of local social, gender and power relations (van Koppen et al., 2007). It is thus important to ask whether donors, state and non-state actors rolling out water reform and IWRM take on board these ecological, socio-political and cultural complexities as well as historical legacies or whether many unintended consequences of development interventions and dominant discourses such as IWRM prevail (cf. Ferguson, 1994).

In this book, we present findings and conclusions from the research project 'Flows and Practices: The Politics of IWRM in Africa'. The project explored at various levels how ideas of IWRM, as constructed at the global and European level, have been and are being translated and adapted into narratives and practices in the countries of Mozambique, South Africa, Tanzania, Zimbabwe and Uganda.[2] All but Uganda are members of the Southern African Development Community (SADC). Specifically, the book addresses the following questions: How has IWRM as an idea travelled from Europe to southern Africa? Who have been the key actors in the varied articulations and translations of IWRM at the global and regional level and in the countries of study? Why has IWRM been so influential in southern Africa? How do abstract ideas of IWRM, which evolved in global institutions, cope with plural, overlapping and competing formal and informal legal and customary systems in Africa? Has IWRM succeeded in addressing issues concerning equity, class, race and gender? How does it contribute (or not) to wider developmental initiatives concerning poverty reduction and equitable allocation?

The following chapters explore the on-the-ground complexities of IWRM implementation, interpretations and adaptations. Grounded in social science theory and research, the book demonstrates the importance of politics, political economy, history and culture in shaping water management practices and reform. It demonstrates how Africa has clearly been a laboratory for IWRM in the past two decades. While a new cadre of water professionals and students has made IWRM their mission, we show that poor women and men may not have always benefitted from this. This is because IWRM may have resulted in an unwarranted policy focus on managing water and 'software' issues instead of enlarging access to the resource and developing water resources. In some cases, IWRM has also offered a distraction from more critical issues such as water and land grabs, privatisation, the negative impacts of water permits and a range of institutional ambiguities that prevent water allocations to small and poor water users. By critically examining the interpretations and challenges of IWRM, the book also will hopefully contribute to improving water policies and practices and making them more locally appropriate in Africa and beyond. In the rest of this introduction we focus on the conceptual and methodological underpinnings and provide some comparative insights from the country studies before concluding.

What is IWRM?

Contrary to what is commonly assumed, Integrated Water Resources Management (IWRM) is not a new concept. The idea of 'integrated' management has been practised in many forms for decades, if not centuries, and goes back to early

---

2 Uganda was added as a country of focus because it is considered to be one of the pioneers of IWRM in Africa. Even though it is in Eastern Africa, participation from Uganda is encouraged in the WaterNet network.

ideas of integrated water management in the US and Europe (Mitchell, 1990; Rahaman and Varis, 2005).[3] Conventionally dominant modes of water management have been characterised by sectoral approaches that separate out issues of water and sanitation, as well as water for food, energy, domestic supply, irrigation and floodwater management. The International Decade on Water and Sanitation (the 'Water Decade') was launched in 1981.[4] It was mainly a supply-led and government-focused initiative, in line with the thinking at the time that governments should be in the driving seat (see Nicol et al., 2012). The primary focus was on expanding and universalising coverage of drinking water supply and sanitation. In the 1990s, supply-oriented paradigms gave way to demand-led approaches in the water sector. There was an increasing emphasis on scaling back the government, slimming down public services, as well as deregulation and liberalisation in line with World Bank and International Monetary Fund led Structural Adjustment Programmes. Consequently, the early nineties saw a substantial attention and output by World Bank economists on the necessity of treating water as an economic good and using economic incentives to increase so-called water use efficiency (see World Bank, 1993; Briscoe, 1997). This period also saw the promotion of a holistic approach to water resources management, the reincarnation of IWRM[5] as well as the so-called Dublin Principles which are considered by many as the 'birth' of modern-day IWRM (see Allouche, Chapter 2).

Out of the Dublin Statement on Water and Sustainable Development (1992) emerged the four Dublin Principles which over time became considered integral to IWRM. They recognise (1) the finite nature of water and its key role in sustaining life, development and the environment (this principle has often been translated into a principle of managing water as per its resource-based boundary – i.e. the river basin); (2) the importance of participatory approaches in water development and management; (3) the central role played by women in the provision, management and safeguarding of water (see Derman and Prabhakaran, Chapter 14, for a discussion of IWRM and gender), and (4) the economic and competing values of water and the need to recognise water as an economic good (International Conference on Water and the Environment, 1992). Since Dublin, IWRM has gradually emerged as the sanctioned discourse on water resources management in both the global water domain and the national water policies and legislations of SADC and other African states (Allan, 2003; Swatuk, 2005

3 For example, the Tennessee Valley Authority, which was established in 1933 in the US, is sometimes considered to be an early example of IWRM in practice as it was set up as a river basin organisation to facilitate multipurpose management to deal with hydroelectricity, water supply, pollution, navigation, flood management and conservation (see Snellen and Schrevel, 2004; Mukhtarov, 2009; Cherlet, 2012). Still, some critical assessments of the TVA model have shown that it is different from IWRM because (1) TVA did not entail democratic forms of stakeholder participation; and (2) that the holistic management of natural resources of the Tennessee Valley was only a marginal concern to TVA which was mainly an electricity-generating outfit (see Chandler, 1984; Miller and Reidinger, 1998).

4 This was around the same time as the Southern African Development Coordination Conference (SADCC), the forerunner of SADC was being consolidated (see Movik et al., this book).

5 According to Biswas (2004), those who promoted it actively in the 1990s were not aware of its earlier incarnations.

Conca, 2006; Swatuk, 2008).

The Dublin Principles of 1992 were integrated into Agenda 21 at the United Nations Conference on Environment and Development (UNCED) and Earth Summit in Rio de Janeiro in 1992 which strongly influenced the development of IWRM (cf. Allouche, and Nicol and Odinga, this book). To put the Dublin Principles into practice, concepts such as holistic management and integration, decentralisation, participation and economic and financial sustainability are repeatedly picked up in IWRM plans and reform packages (see GWP, 2000; Xie, 2006). These concepts are of course very broad, and often difficult to implement in practice as the wide literature on IWRM reveals. Similarly, the definitions of IWRM, while very logical and sound, remain abstract even at the theoretical and conceptual level, let alone when unfolded on the ground. Hence it is safe to observe that there is no agreement on the exact definition of IWRM attributes (Molle, 2008). Yet, for the sake of conceptual clarity we will present two of its more commonly used definitions below. The most commonly used definition is the one by the Global Water Partnership (GWP, 2000) which defines it as a "process which promotes the coordinated development and management of water, land and related resources, in order to maximise the resultant economic and social welfare in an equitable manner without compromising the sustainability of vital ecosystems". Another definition by the United States Agency for International Development (USAID) says: "IWRM is a participatory planning and implementation process, based on sound science, which brings together stakeholders to determine how to meet society's long-term needs for water and coastal resources while maintaining essential ecological services and economic benefits. (...) IWRM helps to protect the world's environment, foster economic growth and sustainable agricultural development, promote democratic governance, and improve human health" (quoted in Xie, 2006).

Nobody would doubt the value of such processes, definitions and initiatives. Still as several authors such as Molle (2008) and Biswas (2004) have systematically argued, even though these definitions are impressive at face value, in reality, they are often unusable, internally inconsistent and un-implementable in operational terms. Thus, despite the very important aims of holistic and integrated approaches in water management, as the country case studies in this collection show, the concept of IWRM remains ideal-typical and is beset by contradictions, which makes it very difficult to operationalise and implement on the ground. A good case in point is the notion of integration. As Bolding et al. (2000) have argued, there are at least four possible meanings of this term, including (1) the integration of different uses of water (e.g. drinking, irrigation, ecological functions, manufacture, etc); (2) the integration of analytical perspectives and the fact that the organisation of knowledge production tends to be along disciplinary and sectoral lines, making it a challenge to integrate different disciplinary and sectoral approaches; (3) the integration of the different institutions responsible for water resources development and management and the need to break down sectoral compartmentalisation between different ministries (e.g. irrigation, rural water supply, forestry, land and so on); these raise the more general issue of how to organise stakeholder involvement in water and natural resources policy-making, planning, development and management; (4) finally, water management as integrated with ecosystem services, human health, ecological sustainability, economic growth, poverty alleviation, gender equality, employment and other aspects of human development.

Seemingly addressing all these disparate concerns around integration, IWRM provides a common framework within which to discuss water matters. The possibility of actually achieving integration makes it attractive and it has become a focal point for donors and summits, as well as national governments, almost as a 'nirvana concept' (cf. Molle, 2008). However, as Molle admits, the likelihood of achieving nirvana is low. It is thus useful to conceptualise IWRM as a 'boundary term' (Gieryn, 1999) that different actors in scientific and policy worlds interpret and deploy in different ways in accordance with prevailing political interests as well as in different ontological and epistemological points of departure. Such boundary and 'nirvana' terms help galvanise resources and action. But they also obscure the political nature of water resources management and are liable to be hijacked by particular interest groups to advance their own agendas (see the example of water grabbing in Tanzania, van Eeden et al., Chapter 12).

Problems with Integration

It is often overlooked that integration is also a political process (Saravanan et al., 2009) and we need to ask who is doing the integrating and whose interests are being represented and how contested interests should be dealt with (Merrey et al., 2005). These political and political economy aspects are often ignored because integration implicitly draws on a normative logic of Habermasian communicative rationality where different members seek to reach a common understanding and cooperative actions by consensus rather than strategic action strictly pursing their own goals (Saravanan et al., 2009). As the different country examples highlight there are often political economy concerns, relating to how to prioritise allocations and weigh trade-offs among different water uses and sectors, but these tend to not come to the fore. As with other popular approaches in development such as Elinor Ostrom's design principles (1990) and adaptive management (Pahl-Wostl et al., 2010), questions concerning power, politics and contestation are often glossed over. The IWRM emphasis on the three E's – equity, efficiency and environmental sustainability – also seems to idealise win/win scenarios and whitewash possible trade-offs and conflicts between these three goals and the resulting conflicts that usually ensue between a range of water users, decision makers as well as local people (see for example, van Koppen et al., Chapter 11).

The attractiveness of management based on river basins is evident in the European context as well. The European Water Framework Directive (WFD) was created in 2000 as a response to the fragmented legislation relating to water, and also to the mounting concerns among European citizens who perceived water pollution to be an increasing problem (Kaika, 2003). The early versions of the WFD required countries to create river basin institutions, often where none existed. However, Germany vetoed this, and the end result was that the Directive allowed countries wide latitude of discretion in terms of determining how they wished to interpret and implement the Directive. This has resulted in a variety of modes of implementation (Hedin et al., 2007). Moss (2003) has shown how it is up to each member state to set up appropriate administrative arrangements for each river basin and district. He also demonstrates how river basin management as conceptualised at the European level raises questions of 'fit' and 'compatibility' with national and sub-national institutions of water management not arranged around river basins. While river basin management seeks to manage water according to logic of ecosystems rather than political-administrative boundaries, in countries such as Germany there are problems of 'interplay' between water and other institutions (e.g. agriculture) which could be exacerbated through the creation of a different territorial unit for water management. Similar tensions have been noted in southern Africa too. Therefore the WFD has not proven effective and very limited management plans have been produced. Thus Germany is seen to practise a different form of IWRM according to Moss (2003) by choosing to stick with administrative boundaries rather than introducing new boundaries based on hydrological characteristics.

The WFD sought to move away from government 'command-and-control' styles of resources management to a more governance-oriented approach which manifests itself in different ways in different countries. Participation is one of the key principles of IWRM. But even in so-called mature democracies in Europe, public participation has been fraught with problems. Water authorities have adopted a very minimalist interpretation of public participation often taken to encompass information available in journals, newspapers and on the internet (Moss, 2003). The implementation of the WFD and the emphasis on participation has led to a shift from social contestation to consensual governance (Parés, 2011). While civil society and social movements have been able to gain access to policy-making processes, their participation has not challenged existing geometries of power (ibid.). Parés (2011) argues that new water governance arrangements are foreclosing the possibility to change the established system leading to increasing managerialism and consensual politics, a sentiment that is echoed in Swyngedouw's work on 'post-democratisation', where he explores the dynamics of de-politisation and the erosion of democracy and shrinking public spheres (Swyngedouw, 2011). A post-democratic form of governance reduces value-laden political issues to technicalities that can best be dealt with by experts.

Elsewhere in the world, Australia is considered to be the model for state-of-the-art water management and is a Mecca for courses on IWRM for officials from countries such as India and South Africa. But even here, even though states were encouraged to have legislation to support IWRM, not all of them have developed the required policies and legislation to empower catchment and watershed groups (Bellamy et al., 2002). This brief discussion in the Western context should highlight that the 'wicked' nature of water management has not been resolved through IWRM, neither in Europe through the WFD, nor in Australia, which all have a long history of engagement with IWRM related practices. If integration is so difficult here, one can imagine that the challenges in an African context are even more wicked. However, this argument might also be inverted – the lack of institutional density in many African countries may offer a wider scope for radical redesign compared to many Western settings, where a lot of institutional resistance is to be expected against any attempt to reform the way things are done. Such at least is suggested by the relatively uncontested passing of new water legislation and policies enshrining IWRM in each of the five African case study countries.

In the African context, it has also been argued that IWRM does not explicitly focus on poverty reduction issues and wider development concerns (see Swatuk, 2005). In fact, in its early years, there was an ideological tussle between those who felt that IWRM (by its focus on 'second generation issues' such as demand management and water re-allocation) could be harmful in a range of African contexts where water resources development is often more necessary than management measures and where agriculture contributes to poverty reduction and livelihood security (Merrey et al., 2005; see also Movik, Mehta and Manzungu, for SADC level debates, Manzungu et al., for Zimbabwe and van Koppen et al., for Tanzania, Chapter 11).

Conceptual approach

The 'Flows and Practices' project developed a conceptual framework that builds on three main themes: the flow of IWRM as an idea; the translation and adoption of IWRM, and the practices of IWRM across multiple scales – global, regional, national and local. In constructing such a conceptual framework, we draw on several strands of thought, namely the literature on policy processes, discourse analysis, policy diffusion and theory (flows); translation studies, donor-recipient studies, the anthropology of development (translation and adoption); and legal pluralism, anthropological and sociological analysis of community dynamics and agency (practices). By no means rigid, the chapters in this book draw either implicitly or explicitly on elements of this framework. We are fully aware though that ideas and practices reinforce each other in a constant back-and-forth process and use this heuristic to better understand why IWRM as an idea caught on so rapidly, but do not regard the notions of flows and practices as discrete or distinct in nature – rather they overlap, merge and reinforce one another in multidirectional ways. If we are successful in building a conceptual framework that will help understand how concepts travel and are taken up, we hope it will also help understand the emergence of new trends and buzzwords – such as water security, adaptive water governance and the water-energy-food nexus – and the drivers that underpin them (cf. Pahl-Wostl et al., 2010; Hoff, 2011; Cook and Bakker, 2012; Allouche et al., 2015; see also Alba and Bolding, Chapter 9).

Flows – studying the emergence and spread of IWRM as an idea

While countless studies have documented the implementation of IWRM in various guises in different country contexts, very few have been done on the spread of IWRM as a set of ideas and how these get adopted and translated. The exceptions are Mitchell, 1990; Mukhtarov, 2008, 2009 and 2014; and Cherlet, 2012.

Mukhtarov (2009) emphasises the need to combine studies of policy transfers and global networks, through what he calls Global Policy Transfer Networks, emphasising the role of epistemic communities and global networks. He has used this analysis to study IWRM in Turkey, Azerbaijan and Kazakhstan. Actor-Network Theory (ANT) maps relations that are simultaneously material (between things) and semiotic (between concepts) (Callon and Latour, 1981). Cherlet (2012) used ANT to study IWRM in Mali and showed how the 'success' of IWRM depends more on the strength of the alliance promoting it, rather than the actual paradigm itself. We build on the work of Mukhtarov and Cherlet as well as discourse-theoretic approaches to understand the rise and spread of IWRM as a dominant discourse and how it has been propagated through different networks, channels and policy processes. Allouche (Chapter 2) complements the ideas of flows with theories of policy diffusion as focusing on three key factors driving diffusion, namely coercion, cooperation, learning and emulation.[6] Our project conceptualises policy as a *process* rather than as an instrumental prescription (cf. Hajer, 1995; Shore and Wright, 1997; Fischer, 2003; Keeley and Scoones, 2003; Wester, 2008). The idea that it is possible to address a particular problem, make a well-informed decision and objectively evaluate the outcome is quite problematic, as it ignores the role of individuals, networks and 'policy entrepreneurs' (Cobb and Elder, 1979; Shore and Wright, 1997).

Useful in the analysis of this process of travel, translation and consolidation is the notion of policy levels. For the purpose of our studies we have focused on *four* policy levels, viz. the *global* policy-making level where organisations like the GWP and World Water Council (WWC) operate; the *regional* level where bodies like the SADC form key nodes informing water-policy directions of member states; the *national* policy level which constitutes the main arena for new water legislation and policy pertaining to individual states and, finally, the *local* level where policies are supposed to meet on the ground, whether this is at district, river basin or provincial scale. Our starting point is that ideas and policies that travel will always be socially constructed and subjected to contingencies and ambiguities in governance and interpretation which takes us to the issue of translations, diffusion, adoptions and transformations.

Translations, adoptions and transformations

Because (water-related) policy processes are messy, involving different sets of networks of policy actors, powerful discourses as well as politics and interests at different scales, they will always be modified and interpreted in multiple ways. The case studies (for example, Mozambique and Zimbabwe) explicitly focus on policy articulation which is the process by which "policy actors support, modify, displace and translate a policy idea as outcome that a policy or reform package becomes less or more 'real'" (Wester, 2008: 22). A "successful" policy often em-

6 Coercion and cooperation focus on the relationships and negotiation processes between external agents (like bilateral and multilateral donors, lending institutions, and outfits such as the GWP) and national governments whereas learning and emulation relate to existing practices. In this way, theories of policy diffusion encompass the ideas of flow, translation and, to some extent, practices.

anates from an unstable trajectory in which it becomes more articulated and dominant, through the enrolment of the necessary actors (cf. Latour, 1987). Intended translation occurs when there is a conscious effort to take up an idea and convert it into a form appropriate for the particular local context (see also Rørvik, 2007). For Latour, translation is the "spread in time or place of anything – claims, artefacts, goods". (Latour, 1987: 267). Policy translation has been put forward by Merry (2006), Lendvai and Stubbs (2007), Freeman (2009) and Mukhtarov (2014) as a way to look at how policies and their accompanying technologies change travel. Seen in this light, translations allow for bringing together global and local realities in understanding how ideas are adopted and implemented. Regarding the question of who is doing the translation, we need to take account of the role of donors and how national governments and donors interact. The study draws on insights from Whitfield (2009) and Whitfield and Fraser (2009) on donor-recipient relations to ask: How do current processes of negotiation between donors and recipient governments play out against the backdrop of specific historical trajectories? Rather than statist models looking at, for example, institutional fit and scale (e.g. Galaz et al., 2008) or approaches that highlight the enduring influence of 'rational-actor' models that draw on new institutional economics and game theory to explain and model client-patron relationships (see Gibson et al., 2005, for an example), we have tried to provide an account of how the ideas promoted at the global level, say in water summits, are picked up by donors and powerful state actors and negotiated in government offices and boardrooms. In several chapters, we thus explore the extent to which national governments and regional actors can exert influence and 'ownership' over these policy ideas and the processes of implementation.

Our case studies focus on the structural conditions and the economic, political and ideological factors that affect negotiating capacities of donors and recipients. As we demonstrate in Zimbabwe, Tanzania, Uganda and Mozambique, donors are key in the emergence and consolidation of the concept, as well as in the practical implementation phase, even if they may have to sometimes prematurely leave due to political reasons (as in Zimbabwe, see Derman et al. and Manzungu et al., this book). While the Foucauldian understanding of discourse risks viewing state bureaucracies, river basin officials, etc. as monoliths and absolving actors of agency and intentionality, the notion of translation also helps highlight the different ways in which national and local actors adapt, adopt and subsequently benefit from dominant discourses and interventions. This interplay of agency and structure only becomes visible through a historical sociology (Abrams, 1982) and a path dependency that we, for example, trace with respect to how IWRM became so popular in SADC (see Movik et al., this book).

Practices – Studying the implementation of IWRM in local contexts

The actual implementation or IWRM practices on the ground will be profoundly shaped by particular local histories, the donor/state negotiations discussed above as well as the prevailing social, gender and power relations. Thus, the country studies have asked: How are IWRM policies and programmes reproduced and by whom? Which historical conditions have led to diverse articulations and interpretations of IWRM? How is IWRM resisted or adapted and what changes are accepted or rejected by those organisations and institutions most vested in the promotion of IWRM? How are these shaped by issues concerning politics and political economy?

For example, while IWRM emphasises decentralisation, new accountability standards and planning processes, the capacity of national governments to ensure that these are followed often remains problematic (see South Africa cases, this book). Water bureaucracies have been particularly resourceful in maintaining their command-and-control orientation under the guise of apparently drastic institutional reforms (cf. Ferguson, 1994; McCool, 1994; Rap et al., 2004; see Mozambique and South African examples, this book). IWRM is largely made out to be apolitical and technical (cf. Derman et al., Chapter 7) but as several chapters in this book show, newly created IWRM-related institutions such as water user groups are usually power-laden, gendered and beset with conflict and factional divisions. These can thus often reproduce historically moulded axes of inequality and heterogeneous patterns of resource use based on dominance and dependence. But these issues are rarely acknowledged in the dominant IWRM literature, though fairly standard in the wider water politics literature (e.g. Mosse, 2003; Mehta, 2005; Cleaver, 2012). Finally, within the African context in particular, it is important to pay attention to the importance of customary institutions in natural resources management, and the complex matrix of institutions in which both people's lives and water management systems are located. It is also wrong to presuppose a noninteractive divide between state and customary institutions. This assumption fails to capture empirical realities in which interrelationships and overlaps link various institutional domains. In this 'messy middle', institutional arrangements may be highly contested, and beset by ambiguity and openness to divergent interpretations (Mehta et al., 1999; Cleaver, 2012). Here the study of legal pluralism especially in the water domain (Meinzen-Dick and Pradhan, 2001; van Koppen et al., 2007) will be necessary to study how IWRM will necessarily coexist with a range of pre-existing (but often invisible) customary arrangements and how diverse institutions and property regimes create different sets of cultural practices and discourses.

Methodological considerations[7]

We used a multi-sited ethnographic approach to understand how IWRM plays out in different arenas (from local to global and across bureaucracies in Europe and Africa as well as in river basins and communities). In our research we also sought to bring the global to the local and the local to the global through our interrogation of the diverse meanings, interpretations and understandings of IWRM

7 Our study consciously decided against going with one set understanding of IWRM. Instead, we sought out in the different research sites, diverse understandings and interpretations of IWRM. Also we consciously decided against just focusing on a small set of aspects of IWRM (e.g. participation or water as an economic good). We are aware that the 'anything goes' character of IWRM can pose some methodological challenges – still we believe that taking this broad approach provided the best way to study the three components of the study (flows, translations/adoption/transformations and practices).

in Europe, at the regional level and in-country studies which are presented in detail in this book. Hence our study spanned different research sites ranging from water meetings in Europe to WaterNet in southern Africa, to interviews with donors and supranational bodies in Europe and southern Africa to regional and national ministries in the countries of study to basin-level officials as well as village-level work. Multi-sited ethnography also meant following and interviewing actors/people at different levels – the people who formulated policies and have moved on; those participating in the summits, and actors in various donor organisations, government and basin officials, members of water user groups and catchment councils as well as local women and men. We also sought to trace, cross-check and triangulate key processes and events, and to analyse how particular ideas and values have carried over or been transformed in the process of translation. We also looked at key documents from various agencies, proceedings from workshops, water policies as well as grey literature were also engaged with the relevant academic literature on the topic.

We used a combination of reconstruction via historical analyses and deconstruction (e.g. policy agendas and popular narratives) whilst locating actors within both macro and micro realms. Though largely based on qualitative data, quantitative data concerning water use, extraction, withdrawals, etc. were also analysed. Additionally, the study deployed historical sources and qualitative approaches for fieldwork at the village level (e.g. ethnographic studies, semi-structured interviews, focus group discussions, participant observation). We also 'studied up' key policy actors and networks that were involved in development cooperation projects that supported the reform of water policies and the adaptation of IWRM. We also discussed our preliminary findings at national dialogues, for example in South Africa, hosted by the Water Research Commission. Finally, we were explicitly reflexive, resulting in our consortium critically engaging with our own encounters and experiences with IWRM and how these changed over time which is outlined in the chapter by Bolding and Alba.

Our research was comparative. It focused on global actors and institutions in Mozambique, South Africa, Tanzania, Zimbabwe and Uganda with an aim to rise to Wescoat's (2009) challenge to address critical water issues in the 21st century through comparative analyses, drawing on historical experiences and geographical contexts, bringing together comparisons of analyses and case studies (see also Mollinga and Gondhalekar, 2012). The case study countries were selected to complement each other and build on existing research work and familiarity. They allowed for sufficient depth and breadth of focus of the research themes across key basins, in particular around intersections between global, regional, national and local processes around conflict/hot spots. They also allowed us to investigate IWRM (and perhaps IWRM fatigue) at different stages. Four key variables were identified to guide the comparative research process: These include (1) The in-country context; (2) Water reform and policy processes/flows; (3) Uptake of IWRM at the national/regional level: translations/adoption/ transformation; and (4) IWRM practices at the basin and local level. Some key empirical findings are provided below on each of these issues which form the foundations for our conclusions. They are not a substitute for reading the rich chapters in this book that provide the contexts, depth and findings from the primary research as well as detailed accounts of how IWRM has been framed and implemented in specific river basins and at the regional level.

The Countries of Study

The contemporary southern African region was produced and consolidated through several hundred years of imperialism, colonialism, mining exploitation, racism, state building, apartheid, antiapartheid struggles, non-racialism and black nationalism (see Movik et al., this book). Our country studies reveal that in all the five countries studied, a colonial and racial history produced a divided society with the majority black population suffering alienation from water and land resources, and other resources such as minerals, at the hands of a minority white population. The alienation, which started in the late 18th to the turn of the 19th century, had, however, important differences because of the particular political dynamics in each country that produced intended and unintended consequences, which have had material effects on the transition to more equitable hydro society.

For example, both colonial and apartheid policies in South Africa confined the vast majority of the black population to 13% of the land and denied citizenship to blacks. The inequality of access to land and water has resulted in several challenges to the implementation of fairer systems of water governance and management (see Denby et al. and Movik et al., this book). The challenge of water redistribution is made complicated by the fact that South Africa is considered to be a dry and water-scarce country. Unlike the other countries in the region, it has a highly developed water infrastructure which holds and supplies water to urban, agricultural, mining and industrial uses. In Zimbabwe (previously known as Rhodesia) too, land and water rights were overwhelmingly in white hands (see Hove et al., Chapter 8). Even after independence from the British in 1980, 85% of the country's water resources continued to be used by 4500 white large-scale commercial farmers (see Manzungu and Derman, Chapter 6). Zimbabwe is a semiarid country with limited surface water and groundwater resources which have been poorly managed because of financial, human, and material challenges (see Manzungu et al., Chapter 6). The fast track land reform dramatically changed water use patterns in the country, leading to a reduction in irrigation (see Zimbabwe chapters, this book).

Mozambique achieved independence in 1975 through a combination of an armed revolution by FRELIMO and a revolutionary army coup in Portugal itself. The desire to establish a socialist nation (without a strong economic base), resulted in the nationalisation of land and water resources and a long-drawn civil war. Because of the war an indebted state sought a series of structural adjustment programmes to maintain itself from 1987 onwards. As part of the peace agreement Mozambique shifted to a formal multiparty democracy and a development strategy rooted in foreign direct investment leading to extensive land and associated water grabs. Mozambique as a downstream country, has had to enter into delicate bilateral negotiations with upstream countries, particularly South Africa, and multilateral negotiations at the regional (SADC) level. Apart from the Limpopo and Inkomati basins, water resources are abundant (see Mozambique chapters, this book). However, Mozambique tends to be negatively affected by floods, because of its downstream location, and also because it has fewer dams compared to South Africa and Zimbabwe.

Tanzania became independent in 1961 and proceeded to establish a socialist state under its founding president, Julius Nyerere. The country inherited a poorly developed agrarian economy with limited developed water resources. As all other countries studied, Tanzania nationalised her waters and land resources a few years after independence and this has given substantial leeway to the government to allocate water resources. In recent years, Tanzania has been attempting an agriculture-led economic growth strategy based upon foreign direct investment raising concerns about land and water grabbing (see van Eeden et al., Chapter 12). Tanzania has highly varied rainfall regimes and is also considered to be semiarid with highly seasonal river flows. Still, unlike other countries in the region, it has abundant water resources that are largely unexploited. Customary land tenure, including matrilineal systems, prevail and small-scale farmers utilise approximately 80% of the current water used (see van Koppen et al., Chapter 11). Like Mozambique, Uganda experienced a period of internal turmoil (in the 1980s) after the establishment of dictatorial rule by Idi Amin after it became independent from the British in 1962. Currently, the National Resistance Movement, the ruling party, has come to dominate the electoral cycle amid claims of vote-rigging and voter intimidation. The country has relatively abundant water resources and a land production system largely reliant on rain-fed farming and/or use of wetland areas although overall development has shifted from agriculture to hydrocarbons.

Flows: Water reform and policy processes

In each of the country case studies, IWRM adoption usually accompanies a water reform process where a new water policy, water law and regulatory framework are introduced, often with donor influence. In fact, the Global Water Partnership (2000) recognises policy and legal reforms as a precondition for creating an "enabling" environment for IWRM roll-out. Our country chapters analyse in detail the state of IWRM policy formulation in each country, focusing on the role of key actors such the role of the state, various government agencies and donors in the reform process and IWRM roll-out.

The State in South Africa has historically played a strong role in water resources management and continues to have formal power. South Africa is often regarded to be at the forefront of water reform with the most progressive water policies (see South African chapters, this book). The arrival of democracy in South Africa 1994 set in motion a large number of laws, policies and practices to undo apartheid with the National Water Act (NWA) of 1998 being the most significant. The progressive post-apartheid National Water Act (NWA) is the principal legal instrument related to water governance which has broadly embraced the principles of IWRM. While South Africa sought to draw on experiences from abroad when drawing up its new legislation, the seeds of IWRM were already present since the 1970s. Despite the presence of many donors (see below), South Africa has determined its own water policies and practices with a highly developed bureaucracy.

The process of drafting the NWA was a highly consultative affair with South Africa inviting in foreign advisers and also facilitating an exchange of experiences with other middle- or high-income countries such as Australia. South Africa's unique Water Research Commission (WRC) investigated a variety of institutional set-ups. A strong lobby of South African environmentalists pushed the idea of Catchment Management Agencies and the ecological reserve (see Movik et al. and van Koppen, Chapter 11). In terms of donors who supported South Africa's water policies, the UK's Department for International Development (DFID) was a strategic partner in the process of drafting the water laws and the creation of the first water allocation reform. Other donors including Danish Danida and the Deutsche Gesellschaft für Internationale Zusammenarbeit (GIZ) have been involved in IWRM experiments in particular catchments. Danida attempted a bottom-up livelihood approach in three provinces (see Movik et al. and van Koppen, this book). IWRM was a global discourse that allowed South Africa to profile itself proudly in water worlds in order to overcome its pre-1994 pariah status. However, from the very start, implementation issues and internal power struggles have been delaying the redistributive effect of the reforms. The then Department of Water Affairs and Forestry suffered from a lack of qualified staff with many qualified staff setting up shop as consultants. Facing crippling delays in the establishment of the institutional implementation vehicles (see below) and a progressive interpretation of the water use authorisation system, the Department at times struggled with even the most basic of procedures.

As the chapters by Manzungu et al., Derman et al., and Hove et al., show, in Zimbabwe, debates about equitable access to water between and within sectors, and between different races, and to some extent classes, have dominated the Zimbabwean waterscape. While Zimbabwe gained its independence in 1980, the water sector was left untouched until the mid-1990s. The belated reforms culminated in the promulgation in 1998 of the Water Act and the Zimbabwe National Water Authority (ZINWA) Act. The Water and ZINWA Acts were developed with the support of such donors as the World Bank, the Deutsche Gesellschaft für Technische Zusammenarbeit (GTZ) now known as GIZ as well as Dutch, Norwegian and British donors. The principles underlying the new acts were consistent with IWRM: user pays; decentralisation of management to Catchment and Subcatchment Councils; ensuring water for the environment and diminishing pollution. Water was to be 'owned' by the President of Zimbabwe and managed by the appropriate authorities. The country was divided into seven catchments on the basis of hydrological boundaries. Various donors undertook the funding for the catchment councils while the Dutch government and others funded the Water Resources Management Strategy team to develop the policies underlying the new water strategy. For example, the Dutch funded the formation of the Mupfure (leading to the Sanyati); the Germans the Mazowe and the Manyame Catchments; and the Swedish government the Save. Consultants from GTZ sat in the offices of the Department of Water and ZINWA to design and oversee the creation of ZINWA. ZINWA became the organisational face of user pays while the Department of Water was downsized. Permits were required to access water and expensive applications needed to be made to the catchment council. The radical land reform programme, however, led to most white landowners been forced from their farms and the donors leaving due to human rights violations. This led ZINWA and the Catchments to lose most of their funding and to struggle for survival until the present.

Like South Africa, Mozambique also legally enshrined elements of IWRM before the Dublin Principles were written and disseminated (see Alba and Bolding, Chapter 9). The 1991 Water Act promotes the role of the State in water resources management by declaring all water resources public- and state-owned. The act stresses the role of state institutions in water resources management. International agencies such as the United Nations Development Programmes (UNDP), Food and Agriculture Organisation of the United Nations (FAO) supported the formulation of the Water Act. River basin management was embraced by domestic actors due to Mozambique being a downstream nation having a strategic interest in managing water across borders at the scale of the river basin. During the 1990s, the World Bank entered the water sector and soon played a key role in shifting attention from water resources development to drinking water supply, according to neoliberal principles seeking to roll back the State. The articulation of both the 1995 and 2007 National Water Policies was supported by World Bank funds. The introduction of the IWRM policy package was further promoted by other (bilateral) donor agencies with projects such as the Pungwe River Basin project. A rather small network of Mozambican policy actors were involved in the policy reform. They were partly trained in Delft and Wageningen, the Netherlands, and were exposed to some extent to prevalent international policy ideas emanating from the Dublin and Rio conferences. This network has occupied key positions in public (water) agencies and have, more recently, established their own consultancy agencies.

In Tanzania too we see strong donor influences and also a key role played by the World Bank. In 1981, Tanzania was divided into nine river basins for development and planning purposes. From the mid-1990s onwards, the World Bank and other donors initiated new programmes on Tanzania's water resources and their management (see van Koppen et al., Chapter 11). The discourse and policy shifted from water for development to allocation of scarce water to competing users. This led to new emphases upon cost recovery, water as an economic good and an emphasis upon water scarcity. River Basin Organisations were formed in the Pangani, Rufiji and the Wami-Ruvu. Donors such as the Norwegians promoted hydropower in the Pangani and the Japanese JICA operated in the Wami-Ruvu. Tanzania's water resources management following IWRM is organised around participatory and representative forums that extend from the national level to the basin and sub-basin level (ibid.). There are five levels of water management; the nation, the basin, the catchment, the district and the community or water association level, creating uncertainties for decision-making.

Unlike the other four nations with their greater focus on irrigation, water scarcity and the legacies of settler colonialism, Uganda's water issues have revolved more around ecological concerns (see Nicol and Odinga, Chapter 13). Uganda depends heavily on its lakes and their fisheries and its wetlands. The Lake Victoria environmental programmes funded by multiple donors led by the World Bank and Nordic donors helped push IWRM and also funded a large numbers of students in relevant sciences. Technical and financial support from Danida resulted in Uganda embarking upon the world's first National Water Resources Water Action Plan (WAP) from 1993 to 1994. Uganda is considered to be an early adopter of IWRM and one of the pioneers of IWRM in Africa, not least due to the energetic efforts of Danida and policy 'entrepreneur' Torkil Jønch-Clausen from Denmark. Yet, as argued by Nicol and Odinga, several issues, including the complexities of the decentralisation process and political economy, have made IWRM to roll-out a very long and slow process.

Translations and adoption of IWRM

The specific historical context and water reforms undertaken in each country (see above) significantly influenced the translation/adoption and transformation of IWRM in each country as demonstrated by the various country papers. In all cases, we see clear trends in efforts towards decentralisation and the creation of new institutions, cost recovery and permit systems, often initiated by donors and the World Bank and usually very difficult to roll-out. All of those covered up the implications of the structural adjustment programmes and roll-back of the state as investor in infrastructure, in favour of 'market-led' neoliberalism. As we describe later, most of these initiatives have not led to favourable outcomes for smallholder water and land users.

In South Africa, IWRM centred primarily on the institutional architecture and the goal of creating 19 decentralised catchment agencies based on hydrological boundaries with Water User Associations. As demonstrated in the chapters by Movik et al., van Koppen, and Denby et al., the process of establishing the CMAs has been riddled with problems, and despite its alleged importance only two have been fully established. The democratisation of the mostly white Irrigation Boards (which were to be subsumed into the new Water User Associations) has not happened because many of them have not seen any advantage in this conversion. In a major change the original 19 CMAs were reduced to nine. These nine water management areas follow river basin boundaries but are linked to regional offices of the department of water that follow existing administrative provincial boundaries. There have been a lot of problems with institutional realignment and fragmentation; also, lack of coordination and institutional overlaps are trenchant problems. There have also been lively debates in South Africa regarding whether IWRM focuses sufficiently on local livelihoods and also on infrastructure development, so badly needed to redress historical inequities around land and water.

In Zimbabwe, like in South Africa, IWRM was initially welcomed by policy-makers but for different reasons. The adoption of IWRM was part of a package of reforms aimed at introducing market principles in the Zimbabwean social and economic space to remedy problems that had been created by the social state established at independence in 1980. From the outset major donors such as the World Bank (and IMF because water reforms were informed by Structural Adjustment Programmes), and other Western donors as well as GWP supported the introduction and implementation of IWRM. The only contestation of IWRM was from academics who criticised some of its elements mainly focusing on the limited participation of smallholder farmers in the new IWRM institutions. Other stakeholders dragged their feet; local authorities and the mining sector were unwilling participants. From 2001 until 2011 IWRM implementation entered a hiatus because of a changed political situation, epitomised by the fast track land reform programme that reduced water revenues and disturbed the operations of water institutions. In 2011 IWRM was reinstated by the World Bank as part of Zimbabwe's reengagement with the international community. This culminated in the adoption of a new Water Policy in 2013, which, however, has not seen the revival of IWRM because of focus on water supply (see Manzungu and Derman, this volme).

In Mozambique, IWRM was seen to encompass (1) shared river basins as units of governance and management, and (2) decentralised agencies that operate on principles of cost recovery. The 1991 Water Act sought to regulate and organise management of water resources based on decentralised Regional Water Administrations known as ARAs. Despite the drive for decentralisation, very limited decision-making power has devolved to lower levels. Also decentralisation has largely failed because ARAs are too large and far removed politically and administratively from most users. The State has also dominated decisions involving issuing water permits, and has tended to favour large-scale investors and decisions about major water allocations to private investors. There has been very limited stakeholder participation in the river basin committees that have only an advisory status within ARAs. Thus institutionally the water reforms have led to the reproduction of late colonial templates, reflecting a preference for hierarchical, centralised agencies which cede little say to actual users (see Alba et al., Chapter 9).

In Tanzania, IWRM has tended to mean halting infrastructure development and, instead, introducing self-financed basin institutions, permits/fees, environmental flows (and transboundary water management) (van Koppen et al., Chapter 11). However, the capacity of the State to ensure implementation of these is weak as reflected by large poorly manned and financially under-resourced basin offices. Implementation of IWRM also faces challenges from the country's drive towards 'modernising' the economy which has resulted in land- and water-grabbing and elites using IWRM-designated institutions for their own interest (see van Eeden et al., Chapter 12). Tanzania opted to transform the dormant colonial permit system into a taxation tool and implement this. This has meant that aside from water for domestic purposes, all water use requires a water permit. The Water Resources Management Act of 2009 required that all unrecorded rights be registered within two years of the act coming into force (August 1, 2009). Failure to register can result in the loss of rights and possible imprisonment. However, this part of the law has not been implemented and certainly most unrecorded rights have not been registered. By the mid-2000s, the development of the country's abundant water resources was articulated again as the primary goal. The 'D' of 'Development' was added to form Integrated Water Resource Management and Development (IWRMD). The World Bank and donors also returned to supporting irrigation development but now with stronger private-sector participation. Indeed, the private-sector's investors in large-scale land- and water-deals were the main agents to take irrigation development forward.

As discussed in the chapter by Nicol and Odinga, Uganda's experiment became an important part of the early reflexive development of the IWRM concept. By 2005, Uganda had published its Water Sector Reform Studies leading to a Strategic Investment Plan (ibid.). Shortly afterwards the Directorate of Water Resources Management was established with responsibility for developing and maintaining national water laws, policies and regulations. However, the enabling policy and legislative environment did not find an enabling 'development' environment, particularly locally, hence the slow pace of uptake and reform in practice. The process received initial push from donors, support through engagement at an international level in the wider 'knowledge environment' associated with IWRM (e.g. Uganda's pivotal role in establishing a river-basin-wide initiative on the Nile from 1999 onwards, in which there was a heavy focus on IWRM). The lack of funds to continue funding IWRM as well as the discovery of oil are likely to detract attention from IWRM. We now turn to looking at basin- and local-level impacts of IWRM practices.

IWRM PRACTICES AT THE BASIN AND LOCAL LEVEL

IWRM practices at the basin and local scales mirror the extent to which countries have managed to articulate the IWRM-based water reforms through a process that embraces broader political, social and economic challenges. There are many variations on the theme, but largely it is a story of huge gaps between IWRM rhetoric and reality.

The translation of IWRM into the South African context and, in particular, the integration of institutions related to land and water have faced many challenges due to the political nature of water and land reforms, and the tendency of governmental departments to work in silos. The chapter by Denby et al. explores the dynamics surrounding the implementation of IWRM in the Inkomati Water Management Area, the degree of integration between the parallel land and water reform processes and what the reforms mean to black farmers' access to water for their sugar cane crops at the (basin) and local levels. The empirical material highlights the discrepancies between a progressive IWRM-influenced policy on paper and the actual realities on the ground. The progressive policies and plans have failed to recognise the complex historical context, and the underlying inequalities in access to knowledge, power and resources. While there has been major progress with respect to urban water supply much less has been accomplished in providing water to black South Africans in rural areas.

One of the most pertinent local issues as far as IWRM in Zimbabwe is concerned relates to implementation of water use for domestic purposes (often known as primary water use). This does not require a permit and fits with the customary practices that no one should be denied drinking water. There is no legal protection for primary water use in this country because documentation of water use applies to commercial water use. Hence the poor 'invisible' primary water users have tended to be disenfranchised (see Hove et al., Chapter 8). This has tended to negatively affect women who rely on primary water use to irrigate gardens. Besides, very few women are in leadership positions in water institutions except in village borehole committees. The lack of IWRM at basin scale is illustrated by dysfunctional institutions as a consequence of challenges posed by the fast track land reform programme (see Manzungu and Derman; Derman and Manzungu; and Hove et al., this book). Land and water reform did not go hand in hand and, in fact, water use and irrigation cover have declined. Cost recovery has been difficult to implement and the Zimbabwe National Water Authority (ZINWA) has massive debts and has difficulty meeting its basic functions of water management.

The impact of the permit system on customary users is also a major issue in Tanzania (see van Koppen et al., Chapter 11). Aside from water for domestic purposes, all water use requires a water permit. But this law has not been implemented and certainly most local rights have not been registered because of the difficulties associated with the application process in a large basin with a small number of offices. The permit system, if implemented, is likely to be harmful to local and customary sharing arrangements as well as increasing the cost of engaging in small-scale agriculture. Moreover, permits are tradeable and provide an incentive to speculate and apply for as much water as possible. Because large-scale users usually have access to more resources and can succeed in the formal process of obtaining permits they can appropriate large amounts of water. The basin officials themselves depend on fee payments from permits. Thus they have the incentive to give out permits for as much water as possible with a strong preference to big payers. They are also biased to large users of land and water (see van Eeden et al., Chapter 12) and IWRM has inadvertently facilitated water grabs and the marginalisation of small-scale water users.

In Mozambique the 1991 Act makes a distinction between common use (*uso comun*) and private use (*uso privativo*). The former refers to the use of water for primary requirements including domestic needs, watering livestock and small-scale irrigation of up to 1 hectare of land without the use of siphoning or mechanical instruments while *uso privativo* incorporates all other uses and requires payment (Veldwisch et al., 2013). However, the multiple and widespread customary law systems that acknowledge, protect and legitimise water use at the village or local levels, are only viable through the legal construction of using water for common use purposes, and remain invisible to the State, that allocates water in favour of large-scale water users. As the Mozambique chapters argue, the winners tend to be the usual suspects, namely foreign investors and politically connected individuals. An increased presence of the State in the waterscape has not led to increased protection of access to water by smallholders. Rather, invisible water users threaten to lose their access through dispossession and issuing of water to large-scale users. This may produce detrimental effects for productivity and equity. Similarly, in Uganda the Water User Associations have tended to be dominated by politicians and civil servants. The intricacies of the decentralisation process have also delayed IWRM implementation on the ground (see Nicol and Odinga, Chapter 13). It is also paradoxical that even in water-rich Uganda, the focus was on regulating water and introducing neoliberal reform, rather than on (re)allocating water to those who needed it the most.

Concluding remarks

We return to one of the key questions raised in the book: Why has IWRM become so popular and so resilient? Why, for example, is IWRM included again in the Sustainable Development Goal 6 on water? One possible answer is that IWRM has 'something for everyone'. As it is so vague; it allows ample space for interpretation within the water sector and also unites all water professionals in negotiations with those outside the sector. Even though it means different things to different people, everybody from river-basin officials, donors and government agencies can say they are doing IWRM whilst getting on with whatever they happen to be doing at the time. Despite the problems with IWRM outlined in the previous sections it has become a ubiquitous buzzword in eastern and southern Africa spawning a massive amount of output in terms of new legislation passed, policies articulated and institutions crafted, and giving rise to reams of analysis and assessments that continue to hold a firm sway over policy-makers, practitioners and academics (see van der Zaag, 2005). In the following concluding remarks, we will address various dimensions of the travel of IWRM across the five African case study countries, such as the specific timeframe in which IWRM spread, the specificity of the water sector that facilitated its travel, the pros and cons of its travel in terms of missed opportunities, costs and access to water by particular groups in society. We end with a plea for more realistic water policies that provide renewed emphasis on water development, creating access to water for more groups in society.

The chapter by Allouche shows how, at the global level, IWRM spread from the late 1990s due to a mix of coercion on the part of donors who encouraged water reform processes around the world, as well as cooperation and learning. It was also done at a time when dams were very controversial on the international scene and global focus turned to 'soft' management issues instead of infrastructure development, which is still badly needed in southern Africa. The chapter by Movik, Mehta et al on IWRM in SADC highlights the importance of historical path dependency. It shows how the idea was picked up in SADC due to the prevalence of transboundary rivers and a long history of colonial water infrastructure development. Thus, water could be galvanised as an arena of cooperation, instead of one of conflict. Moreover, the region had strong existing institutions and donor networks mobilised for the antiapartheid struggle, on which water-related programmes and activities could be built by the Swedes, Dutch, Germans and Danes. These networks and alliances also coincided, in part, with national interests (for example, around river-basin development; ibid.). Donors were often seconded to water departments (for example, in Zimbabwe and Mozambique) and also struggled with changing fads and politics (ibid.). Yet, IWRM often served as a policy concept that allowed problems to be addressed by donors and the powerful, often corporate, interests behind them at a transboundary scale rather than at the scale of a single project or issue. The sheer scale and coordination challenge contained in a concept like IWRM provides donors and associated companies with a virtual 'carte blanche' to propose interventions and a limitless horizon of operations. Hence with hindsight, one can observe that some bilateral initiatives at making IWRM happen in, for instance, the Pungwe River in Mozambique was more interesting than proposing to build a single reservoir on a free-flowing, 'undeveloped' river (Alba et al., Chapter 9).

The Global Water Partnership and WaterNet are two successful networks that, over time, became the driving factor of IWRM in the region, linking different policy levels both in terms of policy discourse and practical push during conferences and capacity-building initiatives. These alliances of donors and dominant regional and national actors have a self-interest in sustaining themselves. When comparing the activities of such transnational lobby networks with similar organisations in different sectors, some of the specificities of the water world are borne out. Both GWP and WaterNet are networks that are dominated by actors from the sector itself rather than representatives from 'civil society'. The latter phenomenon might explain to some extent why IWRM met so little resistance, despite its contested features. While, for instance, in the environmental sector many alternative 'voices' can be heard in the shape of big transnational NGOs (e.g. Greenpeace) few such voices are rallied around a concept like IWRM. (In the water sector, civil society organises itself more around service delivery in urban areas and boreholes in rural areas.) The water world is (still?) dominated by a closely knit elite community of engineers that know each other pretty well from a limited number of grooming grounds across the globe (e.g. Alba et al., Chapter 9, report on the network of Delft-trained water engineers in Mozambique). Thus key movers across the four policy levels we distinguished for our studies, know each other well, and may even occupy various key nodes of the network during their careers. This closely-knit epistemic community of engineers forming a policy elite may warrant further study and comparison with other sectors to assess how dominant policy concepts travel. Unfortunately, such comparative perspectives are beyond the scope of this book.

IWRM as an approach has led to many important improvements in the countries studied and also in SADC. These include the need to move away from silos in the water sector, taking participation seriously and also integrating environmental, management and supply issues. It has also created a huge buzz in SADC. But it would also be fair to say that Africa has been a laboratory for IWRM in the post-cold-war world where neoliberal discourses began to reign supreme in the water sector due to influences of the World Bank and IMF that sought to privatise water services and introduce cost recovery mechanisms. While this largely took place in the domestic sector, the studies in this book show how the introduction of pricing systems and permits allowed wealthy and powerful water users to take advantage of users without permits. As discussed earlier, due to the light formal institutional frameworks in place (unlike in Europe), it was easier to create things from scratch, reinforcing the 'soft' management aspects of IWRM, as opposed to extending water infrastructure and access.

But this has come at some costs. In many parts of Africa, IWRM has stifled the water development agenda by shifting focus to the allocation of what was supposed to be a finite scarce resource when in countries such as Uganda and Tanzania this was far from the case. The focus on management tended to lose sight of the need to enlarge access to water for poor people for a range of productive purposes. Instead, much attention was directed to creating new complex institutional arrangements that largely lacked accountability and legitimacy, were prone to elite capture and tended to centralise the power and control of the State and powerful users (and the IWRM industry) over water resources. Smallholders have been made out to be 'wasteful' and 'uneconomic water users', resulting in widening inequalities and unequal power and social relations. Given the importance and numbers of smaller-scale farmers we suggest that their access to water be better protected. In our view, smallholders' own investments in water infrastructure and local water-sharing arrangements should and could be respected, protected and supported as important contributions to poverty alleviation. There should also be greater attention to socioeconomic human rights like the right to livelihood which are inextricably linked to access to water (Derman and Hellum, 2007). Where regulation is really needed in terms of pollution, then a priority entitlement would assist in conflicts over use by large-scale users.

Our studies have also shown that neoliberal trends such as water pricing and the associated introduction of permit systems have led to a bias in favour of large-scale users who require relatively large amounts of water and have the ability and the networks to apply and pay for the appropriate permits. Some of these actions have led to water grabs as discussed by van Eeden (Chapter 11; see also Mehta et al., 2012). The acquisition of large quantities of water raises the issue of whether or not such actions (real or potential) align with the broader social and anti-poverty goals that are prioritised in eastern and southern Africa. We believe there needs to be far more emphases on the issue of redress and facilitating a more equitable redistribution of water resources to support rural livelihoods. There is a need to engage local stakeholders much more effectively than has been done. One option could be to engage with long-established rural district institutions that are administratively defined rather than hydrologically. Such an approach may be more effective in redressing access to water to the marginalised.

Across the region, women's rights, that were at least partially enshrined in customary and informal arrangements, have tended to be compromised. Permits are likely to be written in the name of the male household head and often participation in water user associations by women has been largely tokenistic. As Derman and Prabhakaran (Chapter 14) have argued, IWRM implementation and roll-out such as permits, user pays principle, commodification of water and decentralisation do not address the structural and economic vulnerabilities of women. In not assessing women's specific and diverse engagements with water, Dublin Principle 3 which focuses on women has not been followed. In our research, we found it was just lumped into participation without attention to the gender implications and consequences of IWRM.

In hindsight, the focus should have been on building capacity in existing institutions and being realistic of the capacity to implement IWRM; integrating land and water reform; and integrating the rights to land, water, food and livelihoods. Future water management and development in the region thus need to respect customary arrangements and direct attention to 'primary water' for multiple uses so crucial for livelihoods and subsistence (agriculture, livestock watering, domestic supplies). Also there is the pressing need to develop water resources and create storage facilities to withstand uncertainties due to drought and increased seasonal variability. Perhaps, it is also time to just tax and monitor the large users and polluters of water, rather than getting bogged down with registering and taxing smaller informal users. Rather than recommending a uniform and bland approach to such issues we would advocate a diversified approach where every country or locality articulates its own key priorities and responds to these according to the capacity and resources available whilst developing strategies emphasising the political nature of water, linking water policies to antipoverty strategies and countering the dangers of capture on the part of powerful players.

It is interesting to note that there are signs of IWRM fatigue in Europe where dominant discourses largely focus on water and climate change, water security and the nexus between water, food and energy. Yet, IWRM has acquired a life of its own in eastern and southern Africa and is kept alive through IWRM meetings, Master's programmes as well as the activities of several generations of IWRM policy-makers, practitioners, students and consultants engaged with IWRM-related institutional and policy reforms and data-gathering exercises. How are these emerging buzzwords shaping thinking on water governance, and what will be the implications? Will these approaches supplement or be superimposed on current practices, or will they usher in whole new sets of approaches and paradigms that will eventually replace the current hegemony of IWRM as an idea? What are the implications for deeper issues of development and democracy? For instance, there is also an emerging focus on developmental water management that puts emphasis on the role of the 'developmental state' and highlights the need to move away from management to focusing on meeting people's livelihood needs, including infrastructure (van Koppen and Schreiner, 2014). We hope that our research may be drawn on to aid further investigation and study of how concepts evolve and mutate and are absorbed as well as their impacts on more deep-seated concerns of development and justice in resource distribution.

Acknowledgements

This chapter draws on Mehta and Movik (2014). We thank Barbara van Koppen, Jeremy Allouche, Peter Mollinga and Francois Molle for their very useful comments. We also thank the Research Council of Norway for making this research possible. The usual disclaimers apply.

References

Abrams, P. 1982. *Historical sociology.* Shepton Mallet: Open Books.

Allan, T. 2003. *IWRM/IWRAM: A new sanctioned discourse?* Occasional Paper No. 50. SOAS Water Issues Study Group. London: School of Oriental and African Studies, Kings College.

Allouche, J.; Middleton, C. and Gyawali, D. 2015. Technical veil, hidden politics: Interrogating the power linkages behind the nexus. *Water Alternatives* 8(1): 610: 626.

Bellamy, J.A.; Ross, H.; Ewing, S. and Meppem, T. 2002. *Integrated catchment management: Learning from the Australian experience for the Murray-Darling Basin.* Canberra: CSIRO Sustainable Ecosystems.

Biswas, A.K. 2004. Integrated Water Resources Management: A reassessment. *Water*

International 29(2): 248-256.

Bolding, A.; Mollinga, P.P. and Zwarteveen, M. 2000. Interdisciplinarity in research on integrated water resource management: Pitfalls and challenges. Paper presented at the Unesco-Wotro international working conference on 'Water for Society', Delft, the Netherlands, 8-10 November.

Briscoe, J. 1997. Managing water as an economic good: Rule for reformers. In Kay, M.; Franks, T. and Smith, L. (Eds), Water: Economics, management and demand, pp. 339-361. London: E & FN Spon.

Callon, M. and Latour, B. 1981. Unscrewing the big leviathan: How actors macro-structure reality and how sociologists help them to do so. In Knorr-Cetina, K.D. and Cicourel, A.V. (Eds), *Advances in social theory and methodology: Toward an integration of micro- and macro-sociologies,* pp. 277-303. Boston, Massachusetts: Routledge and Kegan Paul.

Chandler, W.U. 1984. *The myth of Tennessee Valley Authority.* Cambridge, Mass: Ballinger.

Cherlet, J. 2012. Tracing the emergence and deployment of the 'Integrated Water Resources Management' paradigm. Paper presented at the 12th EASA Biennial Conference, Nanterre, 10-13 July 2012, Unpublished document.

Cleaver, F. 2012. *Development through bricolage: Rethinking institutions for natural resource management.* London: Earthscan.

Cobb, R. and Elder, C. 1979. *Participation in American politics: The dynamics of agenda-building.* Baltimore: Johns Hopkins University Press.

Conca, K. 2006. *Governing water: Contentious transnational politics and global institution building.* Cambridge, MA: MIT Press.

Cook, C. and Bakker, K. 2012. Water security: Debating an emerging paradigm. *Global Environmental Change* 22(1): 94-102.

Derman, B. and Hellum, A. 2007. Livelihood rights perspective on water reform: Reflections on rural Zimbabwe. *Land Use Policy* 24(4): 664-73.

Elberier, M.O. and Babiker, A.R.A. 1998. Hazards in Africa: Trends, implications and regional distribution. *Disaster Prevention and Management* 7(2): 103-128.

European Union. 2000. Directive 2000/60/EC of the European Parliament and of the Council establishing a framework for the community action in the field of water policy. <http://ec.europa.eu/environment/water/water-framework/index_en.html> (accessed September 2016)

Ferguson, J. 1994. *The anti-politics machine: Development, depoliticization, and bureaucratic power in Lesotho.* Minneapolis: University of Minnesota Press.

Fischer, F. 2003. *Reframing public policy: Discursive politics and deliberative practices.* Oxford: Oxford University Press.

Freeman, R. 2009. What is translation? Evidence & policy. *A Journal of Research, Debate and Practice* 5(4): 429-447.

Galaz, V.; Olsson, P.; Hahn, T.; Folke, C. and Swedin, U. (2008) 'The Problem of Fit among Biophysical Systems, Environmental and Resource Regimes and Governance Systems: Insights and Emerging Challenges', in O. B. Young, L. A. King and H. Schroeder (eds.) *Institutions and Environmental Change: Principal Findings, Applications, and Research Frontiers*, Cambridge, MA. and London, UK: MIT Press:

147-187.

Gibson, C.C.; Anderson, K.; Ostrom, E. and Shivakumar, S. 2005. *The Samaritan's dilemma: The political economy of development aid.* Oxford: Oxford University Press.

Gieryn, T.F. 1999. *Cultural boundaries of science: Credibility on the line.* Chicago: University of Chicago Press.

GWP (Global Water Partnership). 2000. *Integrated water resource management.* Technical Advisory Committee Background Paper No. 4. Stockholm, Sweden: Global Water Partnership.

GWP and INBO (International Network of Basin Organisations). 2009. *A handbook for Integrated Water Resources Management in Basins.* Stockholm, Sweden: Global Water Partnership; and Paris: International Network of Basin Organisations.

Hajer, M. 1995. *The politics of environmental discourse: Ecological modernization and the policy process.* Oxford: Oxford University Press.

Hedin, S.; Dubois, A.; Ikonen, R.; Lindblom, P.; Nilsson, S.; Tynkkynen, V.P.; Viehhauser, M.; Leisk, Ü. and Veidemane, K. 2007. *The water framework directive in the Baltic Sea region countries: Vertical implementation, horizontal integration and transnational cooperation.* Nordregio Report 2007: 2. Stockholm, Sweden: Nordregio.

Hoff, H. 2011. Understanding the nexus. Background paper for the Bonn 2011 Nexus Conference: The water, energy and food security nexus. Stockholm, Sweden: Stockholm Environment Institute (SEI).

International Conference on Water and the Environment. 1992. Dublin statement on water and sustainable development. <www.gwpforum.org/servlet/PSP?iNodeID=1345> (accessed 11 June 2016)

Kaika, M. 2003. The water framework directive: A new directive for a changing social, political and economic European framework. *European Planning Studies* 11(3): 299-316.

Keeley, J. and Scoones, I. 2003. *Understanding environmental policy processes: Cases from Africa.* London: Earthscan.

Latour, B. 1987. *Science in action: How to follow scientists and engineers through society.* Cambridge Mass.; USA: Harvard University Press.

Lendvai, N. and Stubbs, P. 2007. Policies as translation: Situating trans-national social policies. In Hodgson, S.M. and Irving, Z. (Eds), *Policy reconsidered: Meanings, politics and practices* pp. 173-189. Bristol: Policy Press.

McCool, D. 1994. *Command of the waters: Iron triangles, federal water development, and Indian water.* Tucson: University of Arizona Press.

Mehta L. and Movik, S. 2014. *Flows and practices: Integrated Water Resources Management (IWRM) in African contexts.* IDS Working Paper No. 438. Brighton, UK: Institute of Development Studies. http://opendocs.ids.ac.uk/opendocs/bitstream/123456789/3523/1/Wp438.pdf (accessed July 2016)

Mehta, L.; Veldwisch, G.J. and Franco, J. 2012. Water grabbing? Focus on the (re)appropriation of finite water resources. *Water Alternatives* 5(2): 193-207.

Mehta, L. 2005. *The politics and poetics of water. Naturalising scarcity in western India.* Delhi: Orient Longman.

Mehta, L.; Leach, M.; Newell, P.; Scoones, I.; Sivaramakrishnan, K. and Way, S.A.

1999. *Exploring understanding of institutions and uncertainty: New directions and natural resource management.* IDS Discussion Paper No. 372. Brighton: Institute of Development Studies. <www.ids.ac.uk/download.cfm?objectid=DDBC-CA13-5056-8171-7B52E82693DA4E5F> (accessed June 2016)

Merry, S.E. 2006. *Human rights and gender violence: Translating international law into local justice.* Chicago: University of Chicago Press.

Meinzen-Dick, R.S. and Pradhan, R. 2001. Implications of legal pluralism for natural resource management. *IDS Bulletin* 32(4): 10-18.

Merrey, D.; Drechsel, P.; de Vries, F. and Sally, H. 2005. Integrating "livelihoods" into integrated water resources management: Taking the integration paradigm to its logical next step for developing countries. *Regional Environmental Change* 5(4): 197-204.

Miller, B.A. and Reidinger, R.B. 1998. *Comprehensive river basin development.* The Tennessee Valley Authority. World Bank Technical Paper No. 416. Washington, DC: World Bank. <http://elibrary.worldbank.org/doi/pdf/10.1596/0-8213-4308-4>

Mitchell, B. 1990. *Integrated water management: International experiences and perspectives.* London: Belhaven Press.

Molle, F. 2008. Nirvana concepts, narratives and policy models: Insight from the water sector. *Water Alternatives* 1(1): 131-156.

Mollinga, P.P. and Gondhalekar, D. 2012. *Theorising structured diversity: An approach to comparative research on water resources management.* ICCWaDS Working Paper No. 1. Bonn and London: International Center for Comparative Water and Development Studies.

Moss, T. 2003. Solving problems of 'fit' at the expense of problems of 'interplay'? The spatial reorganisation of water management following the EU water framework directive (draft). Institute for Regional Development and Structural Planning, Erkner. www.irs-net.de/workpaper3.htm (accessed September 2016)

Mosse, D. 2003. *The rule of water: Statecraft, ecology and collective action in South India.* New Delhi: Oxford University Press.

Movik, S. 2010. Return of the Leviathan? Hydropolitics in the developing world revisited. *Water Policy* 12(5): 641-653.

Mukhtarov, F. 2008. Intellectual history and current status of Integrated Water Resources Management: A global perspective. In Pahl-Wostl, C.; Kabat, P. and Möltgen, J. (Eds), *Adaptive and integrated water management: Coping with complexity and uncertainty,* pp. 167-185. Berlin and Heidelberg: Springer.

Mukhtarov, F.G. 2009. Integrated water resources management: Global water collaboration on the rise.

www.waterworld.com/articles/2009/08/integrated-water-resources.html (accessed September 2016)

Mukhtarov, F. 2014. Rethinking the travel of ideas: Policy translation in the water sector. *Policy and Politics* 42(1): 71-88.

Nicol, A.; Mehta, L. and Allouche, J. 2012. Some for all? Politics and pathways in water and sanitation. *IDS Bulletin* 43(2): 1-9.

Ostrom, E. 1990. *Governing the commons: The evolution of institutions for collective action.* Cambridge: Cambridge University Press.

Pahl-Wostl, C.; Kabat, P. and Moltgen, J. (Eds). 2010. *Adaptive and integrated water management: Coping with complexity and uncertainty.* Heidelberg: Springer Verlag.

Parés, M. 2011. River basin management planning with participation in Europe: From contested hydro-politics to governance-beyond-the-state. *European Planning Studies* 19(3): 457-478.

Rahaman, M.R. and Varis, O. (2005) Integrated Water Resources Management: Evolution, prospects and future challenges. *Sustainability: Science, Practice and Policy* 1(1): 15-21.

Rap, E.; Wester, P. and Nereida Pérez-Prado, L. 2004. The politics of creating commitment: Irrigation reforms and the reconstitution of the hydraulic bureaucracy in Mexico. In Mollinga, P. and Bolding, A. (Eds), *The politics of irrigation reform: Contested policy formulation and implementation,* pp. 57-94. London: Ashgate.

Ribot, J. and Larson, A. (Eds). 2005. *Democratic decentralisation through a natural resource lens.* London: Routledge.

Rørvik, K.A. 2007. *Trender og translasjoner: Ideer som former det 21 århundrets organisasjon,* Universitetsforlaget: Oslo.

Saravanan, V.S.; McDonald, G.T. and Mollinga, P.P. 2009. Critical review of integrated water resources management: Moving beyond polarised discourse. *Natural Resources Forum* 33(1): 76-86.

Shah, T. and van Koppen, B. 2006. Is India ripe for Integrated Water Resources Management (IWRM)? Fitting water policy to national development context. *Economic and Political Weekly* XLI.31 (31): 3413-3421.

Shore, C. and Wright, S. (Eds). 1997. *Anthropology of policy: Critical perspectives on governance and power.* London and New York: Routledge.

Snellen, W.B. and Schrevel, A.I. 2004. *IWRM, for sustainable use of water. 50 years of international experience with the concept of integrated water resources management.* Background document to the FAO/Netherlands Conference on Water for Food and Ecosystems, Alterra-report 1143. Wageningen: Alterra. <www.fao.org/ag/wfe2005/docs/IWRM_Background.pdf>

Swatuk, L.A. 2005. Political challenges to sustainably managing intra-basin water resources in Southern Africa: Drawing lessons from cases. In Proceedings of a workshop on Development and cooperation comparative perspective: Euphrates-Tigris and Southern Africa. Bonn: Centre for Development Research (ZEF).

Swatuk, L.A. 2008. Toward good water governance: Knowledge is power? 'Water for a Changing World-Developing Local Knowledge and Capacity: Proceedings of the International Symposium, Water for a Changing World Developing Local Knowledge and Capacity'. Delft, The Netherlands, June 13-15, 2007. CRC Press.

Swyngedouw, E. 2011. Interrogating post-democratization: Reclaiming egalitarian political spaces. *Political Geography* 30(7): 370-380.

van der Zaag, P. (2005) 'Integrated Water Resources Management: Relevant concept or irrelevant buzzword? A capacity building and research agenda for Southern Africa', Physics and Chemistry of the Earth, Parts A/B/C 30.11–16: 867–871

van Koppen, B. and Schreiner, B. 2014. Moving beyond integrated water resource management: Developmental water management in South Africa. *International Journal of Water Resources Development* 30(3): 543-558.

van Koppen, B.; Giordano, M. and Butterworth, J.A. (Eds). 2007. *Community-based water law and water resource management reform in developing countries.* Wallingford, UK: CABI Publishing.

van Koppen, B.; Butterworth, J. and Juma, I. 2005. African water laws: Plural legislative frameworks for rural water management in Africa. Compendium of papers presented at the International Workshop, International Water Management Institute, Johannesburg, 26-28 January.

Veldwisch, G.J.; Beekman, W. and Bolding, A. 2013. Smallholder irrigators, water rights and investments in agriculture: Three cases from rural Mozambique. *Water Alternatives* 6(1): 125-141.

Wescoat, J.L. 2009 Comparative international water research. *Journal of Contemporary Water Research and Education* 142: 1 -6.

Wester, P. 2008. Shedding the waters: Institutional change and water control in the Lerma-Chapala basin, Mexico. PhD thesis. Wageningen, the Netherlands: Wageningen University.

Whitfield, L. 2009. *The politics of aid: African strategies for dealing with donors.* Oxford: Oxford University Press.

Whitfield, L. and Fraser, A. 2009. Introduction: Aid and sovereignty. In Whitfield, L. (Ed), *The politics of aid: African strategies for dealing with donors,* pp. 1-26. Oxford: Oxford University Press.

World Bank. 1993. *Water resources management. A World Bank policy paper.* Washington, DC: World Bank.

Xie, M. 2006. *Integrated water resources management (IWRM) – Introduction to principles and practices.* New York: World Bank Institute.

2

The Birth and Spread of IWRM – A Case Study of Global Policy Diffusion and Translation[1]

Jeremy Allouche

ABSTRACT: How did the idea of IWRM emerge at the global level? Why has IWRM become so popular and so resilient, at least in discourse and policy? What has caused IWRM policies to diffuse across time and space? The principal goal of this chapter is to identify a set of concepts and mechanisms to study the global diffusion and translation of IWRM through coercion, cooperation, or learning from the ground. The chapter will also highlight the extent to which this global diffusion was contested and translated into different meanings in terms of policy orientation. Overall, IWRM was a mindset of a particular period where the water policy paradigm was evolving in the same direction as sustainable development and other related paradigms in a post-Rio moment. There were no clear alternatives at the time but now IWRM is being questioned. This IWRM fatigue is leading to other framings and discourses around the water-food-energy nexus and the green economy.

KEYWORDS: IWRM, water, policy process, global diffusion, global translation

Introduction

The water sector presents an interesting case for studying and understanding global policy diffusion and translation. In political science and international relations, there have been an increasing number of studies on global policy transfers documenting the spread of liberalism and democracy (see for e.g. Simmons et al., 2006 or Simmons et al., 2008). The question of the birth and spread of Integrated Water Resources Management (IWRM) is an interesting additional case.

As discussed in the introduction, IWRM[2] became the rallying point for inter-

1 First published in *Water Alternatives* 9(3): 414-435.

2 The most commonly used definitions include the one by the Global Water Partnership which defines it as a 'process which promotes the coordinated development and management of water, land and related resources, in order to maximise the resultant economic and social welfare in an equitable manner without compromising the sustainability of vital ecosystems' (GWP, 2000) (see Mehta et al., this book for a further discussion of the multiple meanings of IWRM).

national water policy (Conca, 2006), leading scholars such as Jeffrey and Gearey (2006: 2) to argue that it has become the orthodoxy in water resources management. The World Summit on Sustainable Development in 2002 called for all countries to draft IWRM and water efficiency strategies by the end of 2005. According to Cherlet (2012), over 80% of countries worldwide now have the IWRM principles in their water laws and two-thirds have developed a national IWRM plan. Hassing et al. (2009) reported the findings of a survey done for the 4th World Water Forum in Mexico, which showed that about three-quarters of the 95 countries for which responses were available used IWRM terminology in at least one policy or law, the vast majority of which were created after 2002. The 2012 World Water Development Report reports that more than one hundred countries have implemented IWRM (WWAP, 2012). All these facts and figures show how the concept of IWRM is very popular among governments and international organisations, and within the water expert community.

IWRM has become a ubiquitous buzzword, giving rise to reams of analysis and assessments and continuing to hold a firm sway over policy-makers, practitioners and academics (van der Zaag, 2005; Molle, 2008; Mukhtarov, 2009; Srinivasan et al., 2011). Authors such as Cherlet (2012) or Mukhtarov (2014) have shown through the Actor-Network theory or an evolutionary framework how the various mechanisms, connections and assemblages around IWRM have been established. The principal goal of this chapter is to build and complement these previous studies by going beyond coordinated diffusion mechanisms (including diffusion by learning/emulation or by translation) while at the same time clearly distinguishing between coercion and cooperation as an explanation for the global diffusion of IWRM.

The focus of this chapter is on the process of how the concept of IWRM has been diffused and translated. We understand diffusion as a process which can be defined as “the process by which an innovation is communicated through certain channels over time among members of a social system” (Rogers, 1995: 5), while translation refers to the modification of meaning and multiple interpretations of policy ideas within and across different scales (see also the Introduction, this book). Of course, there have been many studies on IWRM showing the different meanings, interpretations and contrasting practices emerging as a result of the implementation of the concept as elaborated in the Introduction. My focus is on the opposite, namely on how a seemingly common understanding emerged within and across water networks and policy processes at the global scale. Of course, we will need to deconstruct what we mean by the ‘international’ and who is part of this ‘international’. The literature on policy diffusion, as I discuss shortly, offers some interesting lenses to study this phenomenon. The idea of policy diffusion, which focuses on a consensual understanding of policy, needs to be completed with the idea of translation, showing how the ideas and policies begin to become more contested when deliberated in more detail.

This chapter is divided into two sections. Firstly, I will elaborate a conceptual framework on global policy diffusion and provide a set of key factors and contending theories that could explain the translation of the IWRM concept. Secondly, I will analyse the diffusion and translation of the concept through a three-step approach: the origins of the concept; the key discourses, and the different networks, experts and institutions linked to the diffusion of the concept.

Conceptual framework

The internationalisation of policies and policy diffusion is gaining the attention of a growing number of scholars in the field of international political economy and comparative public policy (Knill, 2005; Levi-Faur and Jordana, 2005; Simmons et al., 2007; Weyland, 2007). There are many terms associated with diffusion in social science research: convergence (Drezner, 2001); waves (Huntington, 1991); contagion (Midlarsky, 1978); imitation (Jacoby, 2000); emulation (Bennet, 1991); institutional transplantation (de Jong et al., 2002) or policy transfer (Dolowitz and Marsh, 2000). As noted by Mukhtarov (2014), each term refers to subtle differences in approaches; while 'diffusion' presumes privileging structure over agency, 'transfer' may presume the immutability of what is being 'transferred', and 'learning' may presume the cognitively sanctioned process.

There have been many ways to approach policy diffusion and translation.[3] In line with Elkins and Simmons (2005), I distinguish three large conceptual explanations of the phenomenon of policy diffusion (see Table 2.1), namely:[4]

1. Coercion[5] through soft power (including a Gramscian understanding of ideological hegemony);
2. Cooperation through technical support or epistemic communities; and
3. Uncoordinated diffusion, through learning or emulation.

Coercive diffusion involves power asymmetries where policy preferences are imposed on weaker countries. In soft coercion, dominant actors can influence others through ideational channels without exerting physical power or materially altering costs or benefits (Simmons et al., 2006). By virtue of their central positions in policy networks, more powerful countries may be influential in the framing of policy discussions (Hira, 1998). Without diminishing the importance of material power and dominance over material resources, soft coercive hegemony can be understood in terms of consent and shared beliefs with the establishment within the sphere of the internationalisation of universally accepted values (a Gramscian type of ideological hegemony).

In terms of *cooperation*, Haas's (1980) work has drawn attention to the generation of social knowledge, or "the sum of technical information and of theories about that information which commands sufficient consensus at a given time among interested actors to serve as a guide to public policy designed to achieve

3 Dolowitz and Marsh (1996) introduced a continuum of types of policy transfer that includes voluntary, coercive and negotiated forms of transfer. Evans (2009) further suggested three types of explanations to policy transfers: State-centred; transnational-organisations-centred, and policy- networks-centered.

4 Etkins and Simmons (2005) also included a fourth one on endogenous conditions within countries that lead to similar conditions (economic shock or cultural and institutional similarities).

5 Coercion entails two sets of assumptions, firstly that there is an intentional motive from powerful countries to coerce weaker ones, and secondly that weaker ones are resisting.

some social goal" (Hass, 1980: 367-8). In this approach, policy innovation spreads in the wake of the diffusion of a shared fund of often technical knowledge among elites about what is effective. Epistemic communities, networks of knowledge-based experts, are major actors in the development of social knowledge and are especially influential in the policy-making process and may contribute to the creation and maintenance of social institutions that guide international behaviour (Haas, 1992). These communities are becoming more important as a result of the expansion and professionalisation of bureaucracies and the greater technical nature of problems. These transnational epistemic communities form as a result of the diffusion of community ideas through conferences, journals, research collaborations, and a variety of informal communications and contacts.

In terms of uncoordinated diffusion, one has to distinguish between learning and emulation. Learning can be understood as a set of processes characterised by interdependent but uncoordinated decision-making (evidence and best practice), while diffusion is through emulation (theory and rhetoric serve as the basis of decision-making). In terms of emulation, work by Meyer et al. (1977) showed mass schooling expanded to all countries irrespective of political ideology, political system or level of economic development. Whereas theories related to modernisation development suggest that countries will adopt certain programmes when they are developmentally ready for them, world-polity theorists embrace new norms for symbolic reasons, even when they cannot begin to put them into practice. Thomas et al. (1987) for example, have argued that nations mimic their successful peers almost ritualistically.

In terms of learning, the learning process may not be necessarily idealistic. Uncertainties make policy choices difficult and thereby policy-makers may follow the information cascade model, where they may have no other information than the knowledge of whether others have adopted the policy. In this case, individuals may reason that they should take advantage of the accumulated wisdom of decisions of past individuals. Bikhchandani, et al. (1998) developed a model of this process, which demonstrates that choices of an entire sequence of actors can depend exclusively on the decisions of the first two or three actors. This is a typical risk reduction strategy where familiar choices may appear to be safe choices.

Whether through learning or emulation, the process of uncoordinated diffusion rests on a cooperation logic where joining a growing majority of other actors confers a degree of legitimacy (Etkins and Simmons, 2005: 39). The benefits of joining this new group is also linked to the different options in terms of available technical support. This new community of users, preferably one with skills and knowledge, and given the new policy dynamic, will be committed to refine and improve the practice.

Table 2.1 links existing theories about IWRM with those of policy diffusion. Of course, these are 'ideal-types' and some of the authors referred below on IWRM have worked across these types of diffusion and translation. In fact, these categorisations may prove to be useful to clarify and reinvigorate debates over IWRM diffusion as many of the work has moved from cooperation to coercion without much distinction. This categorisation also helps highlight how uncoordinated type of diffusion around IWRM has been neglected in current academic debates about IWRM global diffusion and translation.

Table 2.1. Mapping IWRM theories with theories for policy diffusion and translation.

Types		Diffusion		Translation
	Coordinated diffusion		Uncoordinated diffusion	
Mechanism	Coercion	Cooperation/ Adapting	Learning/ Emulation	Contestation
Key Features	Gramscian ideological hegemony	Cultural norms, reputational benefits (e.g. legitimacy), technical support (community of users), epistemic communities/IOs	Knowledge, or imperfect knowledge (information cascade)	Contestation and modification of meaning and multiple interpretations of policy ideas
IWRM is ...	a sanctioned hegemonic discourse (Allan, 2003) *** as a neo-Gramscian hegemony (Mukhtarov and Cherp, 2014). See also Cherlet (2012)	the formation of a global epistemic community and global policy standardisation and formulation (Mukhtarov, 2008)	a scientific approach and the uncoordinated spread of innovation (Wescoat, 2005)	"a house that is already in the process of deconstruction before building has been completed" (Mollinga, 2006)
	a nirvana concept so vague that it has a bit for everyone (Molle, 2005), see also (Conca, 2006; Mukhtarov, 2008)			

These three sets of explanation capture the structural or agency bias in explaining policy diffusion. While coercion and cooperation require some sort of coordination, diffusion through learning, entails that, "governments are independent in the sense that they make their own decisions without cooperation or coercion but interdependent in the sense that they factor in the choices of other governments" (Elkins and Simmons, 2005: 35). Diffusion through learning therefore entails a degree of agency of national policy-makers.

The other key debate is between the idea of diffusion versus the idea of translation. 'Translation' scholars, very much in line with constructivism, consider that policy diffusion theories follow a positivist stance, by assuming the stability of policy ideas in the process of their travel. The focus of policy diffusion literature to try and explain how actors reach, through consensus building, a common understanding of the problems and the desired action (Mehta et al., 2007; Saravanan et al., 2009), has ignored the modification of meaning and multiple interpretations of policy ideas within and across different scales. A new constructivist school of thought has therefore emerged in relation to the concept of policy translation. As explained by Lendvai and Stubbs (2007: 15),

> *policy transfer process should be seen as one of continuous transformation, negotiation, and enactment on the one hand, and as a politically infused process of dislocation and displacement ('unfit to fit'), on the other hand... Policy translation suggests the need to pay greater attention to the ways in which policies and their schemes, content, technologies and instruments are constantly changing according to sites, meaning and agencies.*

Let us then examine how policy diffusion and policy translation theories provide an interesting way to study the spread of IWRM.

The global diffusion and translation of IWRM

Very few studies have been done on the spread of IWRM as a set of ideas and how these get morphed, translated and obfuscated through processes of negotiation and transformation at the global, national and local levels (exceptions are the various pieces by Mukhtarov and Cherlet, respectively; see for example, Mukhtarov and Cherp, 2014; Mukhtarov, 2014) Mukhtarov 2008; Mukhtarov, 2009; Cherlet 2012). Farhad Mukhtarov (2008: 175) for instance provides an interesting evolutionary framework about the IWRM discourse, from bottom knowledge generation to policy standardisation and formulation at the international level to top-down diffusion. There are, of course, limits to an evolutionary theory as one could argue for the coexistence and reinforcement of these different processes. Jan Cherlet (2012) draws on Actor-Network Theory to understand how a range of actors (academics, donors, INGOs and local officials) build various alliances to support IWRM, distinguishing mediators, champions, intermediaries and larger networks (or nonhuman devices) such as the Dublin principles, and organisations such as the Global Water Partnership and the World Water Council. He thus charts how a range of actors established various connections and assemblages around IWRM. Building on and complementing these studies with additional empirical insights, this chapter aims to provide a broader range of explanations for the global diffusion of IWRM by considering diffusion by learning/emulation or by translation. Indeed, much of the preceding work focused on coordinated diffusion, and navigated between coercion and cooperation without clearly distinguishing them. Furthermore, the idea of translation was mostly applied to country case studies (e.g. Mukhtarov, 2009) rather than at the global level.

In conducting this research (through a literature review and interviews with 16 globally renowned water policy-makers and academics – see Annex), three different pathways in terms of policy diffusion with respect to IWRM were identified. For each of these pathways, we have looked at the origins of the concept and discursive shifts, and the principles and institutions in the making. The origin of concepts has not received much attention in policy diffusion debates. However, the initial understanding of how the concept emerges helps us to understand the trajectory and networks involved in policy diffusion. It also broadens the scope and understanding of what is meant by policy diffusion.

Coercion

IWRM has often been described as the sanctioned hegemonic discourse, following Allan's (2003) analysis. From this perspective, global policy diffusion occurred through a hegemonic Northern-led process imposed by the World Bank through its auxiliary, the Global Water Partnership.

Fig. 2.1. IWRM: A top-down approach? (Lankford et al., 2007: 2)

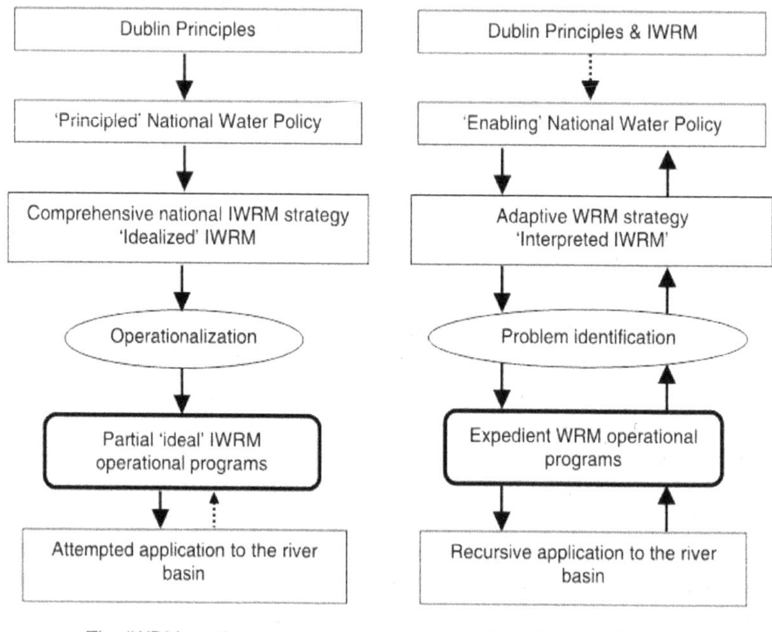

Lankford et al. (2007) shows through Figure 2.1 how IWRM was very much a top-down process in which they describe the IWRM continuum linking the Dublin principles to a national water policy and strategy. IWRM is seen as a form of coercion as it imposes a set of principles and tools to be followed. In their Working Paper, Lankford et al. (2007) proposed an alternative approach to IWRM which would focus on 'problems' on the ground rather than on IWRM principles to be articulated as it "is largely understood amongst most informed scientists; in large river basins, the constraints associated with scale, data availability, policing, knowledge, logistics, variability and systemic interfaces invalidate the pursuit of a complete 'Integrated Water Resources Management' as defined by the Global Water Partnership". (Lankford et al., 2007: 2).

The World Bank was the most active organisation promoting IWRM following the Dublin Conference and the Rio Summit (Allouche and Finger, 2001) and was key in the creation of GWP (this enthusiasm started to change in the late 1990s). Coercion was not a classical soft coercion style linked to conditionalities but rather a structural hegemonic thought pattern where no alternatives were feasible or discussed (other alternative pathways to sustainability were closed down as a policy option; see Leach et al., 2010 on pathways and closing down).

The key moment in the development of the IWRM approach was undoubtedly the Dublin principles, which some interviewees called the 'masterpiece'.[6] One can see different agendas converging at this event. On the one hand, there were a number of earlier conferences, and in particular Copenhagen, which set the tone for including economic and participatory principles. At the time, donor agencies, especially in Nordic countries and also the Netherlands and Canada, were pushing the environmental agenda in resource management. On the Canadian side, the federal and provincial governments were very much influenced by the Ontario State experience with its Conservation Authorities and by people like Jim Bruce or Frank Quinn (both from the federal civil service in Ottawa).[7] On the Dutch side, some interviews mentioned the name of Hubert Savenije (at the time International Institute for Hydraulic and Environmental Engineering, IHE – Netherlands). On the Scandinavian side, Torkil Jønch-Clausen (who sat on the Advisory Committee of the Dublin Conference) was also very active. All were advocating some of the key principles, especially in relation to finite resources, economic good and participatory forms of governance. The gender dimension was added due to pressure from civil society organisations and United Nations agency but was not central to the agenda.[8]

This shift from supply to demand management in water occurred through the World Bank's leading role in creating a new discourse around water management. Hajer (1993: 47) defines discourse coalitions as "the ensemble of a set of story lines, the actors that utter these story lines, and the practices that conform to these story lines, all organised around a discourse". In this analysis, we expand the concept of discourse coalition as a way to reflect how various discourses converge into a single agenda. One can indeed identify four key discourses in the promotion of IWRM according to those interviewed:

1. A technical solution to the imminent water-scarcity crisis,
2. An economic solution to our modern economic-growth-oriented urban society,
3. An ecosystem solution to the limits of the hydraulic mission, and
4. A social solution to the limits of not engaging communities and stakeholders.

6 See Annex.

7 Interview with Bruce Mitchell, 27 March 2013.

8 Various interviews, see Annex.

This discourse coalition, which was omnipresent in key international water conferences in the early 1990s, managed to create a new consensus. As one of my interviewees mentioned, there were plenty of conferences talking about water scarcity and the imminent crisis and that a new solution was urgently needed, from being a water supply to a water demand-driven approach.[9] And the consensus emerged, as there was recognition at the time by water specialists that current approaches were not successful and there was an urgent need for new action as a result of increasing water scarcity.

The United Nations Committee on Natural Resources (UNCNR, 1994: 73) mentions this crisis narrative in international meetings.

> *Recent international forums dealing with water resources issues have all brought about an increasing awareness of the global magnitude of a water crisis.... Although these expressions of concern may be deemed by many to be insufficient, there is a growing consensus among experts in the water resources field as to the seriousness of the situation. However, the spectre of a global water crisis has been overshadowed by concerns about other issues of manifest global proportions, such as the ozone layer, tropical forests and climate change. Internationally, the seriousness of water problems has not as yet received the recognition that warranted the situation.*

Water was believed to be misused and the chief culprit was the irrigation sector. The problem was not drinking water supply (Postel, 1992; Winpenny, 1994). A new alliance of hydrologists, environmentalists and economists was now actively pushing for policy change and writing on the topic. Two influential books that summarise the dominant thinking at the time were James Winpenny's Water as an Economic Good and Sandra Postel's Last Oasis: Facing Water Scarcity. James Winpenny, a then research fellow at the Overseas Development Institute (ODI) considered that water mismanagement was due to agriculture, industry and the 'politicisation' of water allocation and the solution was therefore to charge the real cost of water. In his final analysis, an economic approach to water management will ultimately bring both financial and environmental benefits (Winpenny, 1994). This position very much echoed the World Bank's position at the time under the leadership of Ismael Serageldin (the World Bank Vice President for Environmentally and Socially Sustainable Development) and John Briscoe (Water and Sanitation Division at the World Bank). Water as an economic good was indeed key to the 1993 World Bank Water Resource Management Strategy Paper (World Bank, 1993) and later presentations by John Briscoe and others at the World Bank in international conferences (Briscoe, 1996).

This new discourse coalition brought together economists such as Winpenny with environmentalists and conservationists such as Sandra Postel from the Worldwatch Institute. Postel (1992) also considered that the growing pressures on water resources thus called for a new approach to water resources management. She was indeed concerned by both efficiency and conservation when

9 Interview with Frank Rijsberman, 2 April 2013.

saying, for example:

> *In a sense, masking scarcity is a principal aim of water development, the collection of engineering projects and technologies that give people access to and control over nature's supply. But all too often it has proceeded without regard for harmful side-effects. We build ever more and larger projects to meet spiraling demands wherever they arise, but pay little mind to the ecological services of rivers, lakes, and wetlands that are lost in the process (Postel, 1992: 18).*

As a matter of fact, Postel follows the logic of the first Dublin principle when she says that although water is a renewable resource, it is also a finite one. Decentralisation, water pricing, the elimination of government subsidies especially for irrigation, and the active role of women are also factors that can achieve both efficiency and conservation (Postel, 1992). Again, this position was central to the Bank as illustrated through the 1993 World Bank Development Report that was focusing on Environment and Development.

Overall, sectoral policy approaches were not viable anymore as important urban centres were developing (see for e.g. Meinzen-Dick and Appasamy, 2002). Economic and social returns from urbanisation were seen in a positive light compared to irrigation development, which was criticised for being heavily subsidised. Mostafa Kamal Tolba, the Executive Director of UNEP at the time, often criticised the irrigation sector as the most subsidised sector in the world. Big water works or 'man-made' problems, mainly the widespread construction of dams and unsustainable irrigation, were also critically appraised. The hydraulic mission was called into question (Allan, 2003).

The consensus, which brought together policy-makers, environmentalist and hydrologists in the 'North' and water specialists in the 'South', was increasingly concerned with water scarcity.[10] In this respect, the spread of IWRM was the result of a particular discourse coalition promoting resource management against a more development-led concern around water supply. Indeed, the IWRM paradigm replaced the International Drinking Water Decade. This tension and shift can be seen in the meetings in the late 1980s and early 1990s (Nicol et al., 2012). In some ways, the Bruntdland Report, the Abidjan Accord and the New Delhi Statement all advocated the most basic form of 'integrated' water management: they did pay attention to both surface water and groundwater, as well as water quantity and water quality – but did not yet link water to land (erosion, floods) and the environment (Mitchell, 1990). However, the policy focus of these conferences was still on drinking water supply. This coalition of the willing was made possible since an alternative model similar to the idea of IWRM was developing in a few countries across the globe, most notably Australia, Canada, France, the Netherlands and the US.[11] New national environmental policies created increasing contradictions and the call for an integrated approach became more and more appealing. For example, there were instances in Canada where a provincial Minis-

10 Scarcity was taken as a given and it was only much later that scarcity has begun to be discursively deconstructed and politicised (see for e.g. Mehta, 2005).

11 Various interviews, see Annex.

try of Natural Resources was protecting wetlands while a Ministry of Agriculture was draining them. However, the World Bank and the GWP conceptual model for IWRM was really based on the French basin agencies after a World Bank team visit and review under the leadership of John Briscoe of the different European water management models (Finger and Allouche, 2002).

The Scandinavians, especially the Danes, were very active before the Dublin and Rio conferences. The Danish International Development Agency (Danida) took the initiative to establish a Nordic Freshwater Initiative (NFI), bringing together Denmark, Sweden, Norway and Finland, with the explicit objective to feed operational guidelines for integrated water resources planning and management into UNCED (Jønch-Clausen, 1992).[12] The NFI received a global platform at the first Stockholm Water Symposium in August 1991 (Jønch-Clausen, 1992). Several key influential Scandinavian figures were key members of IWRA (International Water Resources Association), most notably Jan Lundqvist who sat on the board of directors (1992-94) and was its Vice President (1998-2000), as well as Malin Falkenmark, who occupied the same functions in the early 1980s. Three months later, an informal consultation of the NFI in Copenhagen in November 1991 further invigorated the Nordic plea for integrated, cross-sectoral management with the Copenhagen Statement. The Statement proposed two key principles: (i) water needs to be managed at the lowest appropriate decision-making level, and (ii) it needs to be managed as a finite resource with 'an economic value' (NFI, 1992). According to some interviewed, the conference organised by the NFI was also attended by Tanzanian, Indian and West African delegates. This conference was the result of a series of meetings among Nordic countries that ran for a whole year (four or five meetings in Denmark). The initiative was supported by the Nordic governments and also involved representatives from the World Bank (most notably John Briscoe), as well as the Asian Development Bank (ADB), and the Asian Institute of Technology.

While a new sanctioned hegemonic discourse on IWRM became increasingly accepted and legitimised through Dublin and Rio meetings, the World Bank was then behind the creation of the Global Water Partnership. Ismail Serageldin, and Anders Wijkman (the Policy Director at the United Nations Development Programme – UNDP) led the initiative to create the Global Water Partnership (GWP). The leadership really came from the World Bank which then approached UNDP (rather than UNEP) due to previous collaborations around drinking water. In early 1996, there was a meeting in Stockholm when a decision was taken to translate the outcomes of the meetings in Rio and in Dublin into practice. The 'operational team' included John Briscoe, Roberto Lenton (Director of the Sustainable Energy and Environment Division at the United Nations Development Programme), Johan Holmberg (Swedish International Development Cooperation

12 The two key figures in the NFI were the Danish water professional Torkil Jønch-Clausen and the Swedish academic Jan Lundqvist. Jønch-Clausen, who was CEO of the Danish Water Quality Institute in 1993-1997 and Secretary General of IWRA in 2004-2006, was contracted by Danida to coordinate NFI. Jan Lundqvist was also a habitué of the multilateral scene, as consultant to the Swedish International Development Agency (Sida), Swedish delegate to a number of UN bodies in 1987-1992, Regional Director of IWRA in 1991-1994, and Vice President of IWRA in 1998-2000.

Agency – Sida) and Gouri Ghosh (Head of the Water, Environment and Sanitation Section, UNICEF – New York). At this meeting (which regrouped around 80 people), it was officially decided to create the GWP, and Sida offered to host the interim secretariat. The GWP was therefore the result of a small meeting in Sweden. This led to the formal creation of GWP at the Stockholm Water Week in August of 1996, when its first consultative partners' meeting was held. Besides Sida, the Overseas Development Administration (ODA) in the UK was very supportive of the GWP, both materially and intellectually.

The operational group also decided to establish an interim Technical Advisory Committee. The 'operational team' approached Torkil Jønch-Clausen (Danish Hydraulic Institute – DHI) to chair what was then called the Technical Advisory Committee (TAC, later TEC), and Torkil Jønch-Clausen played a key role in pushing the IWRM concept. Not surprisingly, one can find the same individuals at the head of the GWP, Ismail Serageldin was the first Chair and Torkil Jønch-Clausen was assigned as Chair of the GWP Technical Committee (GWP-TEC). Johan Holmberg, Assistant Director-General at Sida, served as first Secretary-General of GWP.

The institutional model of GWP was borrowed from CGIAR (the Consultative Group on International Agricultural Research) where Johan Holmberg had been active, and which was hosted by the World Bank. This model called for a light, networked organisation with a small secretariat at its centre and a heavy emphasis on scientific expertise and advice (Holmberg, 1998). GWP was quite successful in expanding worldwide. The GWP has 3000 member agencies, 85 country partnerships and 13 regional partnerships (according to their website). The light, networked organisation of GWP was cost-effective but proved difficult to manage. There was at times tension between TAC and the secretariat. As the field organisation grew, member organisations expected material support, which the centre was not resourced to provide.

Besides GWP, the most active organisation promoting IWRM was the Asian Development Bank under the leadership of Wouter Lincklaen Arriens. For some, ADB was actually much more successful in implementing IWRM compared to the World Bank.[13] Under the Water Financing Programme (WFP), ADB has committed to doubling its water investments during 2006-2010 to well over USD2 billion per year.[14] The overall target for ADB's lending under WFP 2011-2020 is USD20 billion, of which basin water investments are expected to contribute approximately 25%. Under this scenario, ADB seeks to increase basin water investments under WFP to approximately USD5 billion.[15] ADB is also active in promoting the Network of Asian River Basin Organisations (NARBO), which was established in 2003 to share knowledge and build capacity for IWRM in river basins throughout the Asia and Pacific region.

There were also other key players. Canadian Bill Cosgrove from the World Water Council also played an important role, especially in relation to the 2nd World Water Forum in the Hague, as well Mike Muller (at the time Director-General,

13 Interview with Peter Rogers, 22 March 2013.

14 www.adb.org/sectors/water/financing-program (accessed 22/08/16).

15 This is not all necessarily IWRM-related but is used as an illustration to show how water resources management is seen as an important policy priority at the ADB.

Department of Water Affairs and Forestry, Government of South Africa).

The idea of IWRM as coercion is therefore based on the idea of a hegemonic discourse that prevents any alternative. Mukhtarov and Cherp (2014) follow this view but their argument is about a key moment in time rather than the hegemonic mechanisms of its diffusion. It is not that IWRM was imposed through the World Bank as a donor conditionality but rather that it wan the ideological and political battle and was seen as the solution that the international community espoused. This was further institutionalised when IWRM was the only norm and solution as agreed at the 2002 World Summit on Sustainable Development (WSSD). This internationalisation and globalisation of IWRM, as promoted by International Organisations, transnational actors, and the internet, should not obscure the fact that this consensus was just among a rather small group of people, which became the global advocates for IWRM at a time when no other clear coalition existed.

There are a number of limits to this theory. It places too much emphasis on the soft coercive power of the GWP, which was certainly successful in spreading the concept but which had clear limits being a small network organisation. Furthermore, the World Bank, which was the key powerful actor in this story, was blowing hot and cold over IWRM.16 More fundamentally, many water specialists consider that one can trace the idea of IWRM far beyond the early 1990s and that the World Bank and the Global Water Partnership were just instrumental in implementing a growing consensus around the need for integration around water resources management.[17]

Cooperation

For other water specialists, this soft coercion idea cannot account for the global diffusion of IWRM in that it had been in existence at least since the beginning of the 20th century. In this light, IWRM is seen as a cumulative knowledge process going back before the adoption of the concept in global policy circles in the early 1990s. In this perspective, the global policy diffusion of IWRM has occurred through cooperation rather than through coercion. IWRM is seen through a 'longue durée' perspective as knowledge construction, a positivist perspective, which involves the scientific study of water systems in relation to human society and ecosystems. This creates a methodological difficulty as it is more difficult to trace and identify the mechanisms of the formation of this transnational epistemic community over such a long period.

Different experiments around integrated water management, one could argue, go back to as early as the beginning of the 20th century (if not before), notably in the US and Europe (Teclaff, 1967; Mitchell, 1990; Rahaman and Varis, 2005). The Tennessee Valley Authority (TVA), which was established in 1933 in the US, was an early example of IWRM in practice, as it was set up as a river basin organisation to facilitate multipurpose management to deal with water supply, pollution, navigation, flood management and conservation. The Ruhr River Association in Germany and the UK River Basin Authorities were other examples. For some, TVA was the first attempt to bring together social engineering, land and water

16 Interview with Alan Hall, 3 March 2014.

17 Various interviews, see Annex.

management, and regional development (Selznick, 1949; Wescoat, 1984). The TVA effort contained many elements of today's perception of IWRM: comprehensive planning of natural resource utilisation combined with economic, social and even environmental objectives (Snellen and Schrevel, 2004; Mukhtarov, 2009; Cherlet, 2012). More generally, the idea of Multi-Purpose River Valley Projects (MPRVPs) marked a new era of integrated resource management.

This so-called first generation of IWRM (1930s-1960s) was slowly replaced by the second generation of IWRM (1960s – 1990s), which integrated ecosystems and environmental concerns (Chakraborty, 2010). Scholarly advances in the general understanding of water systems and water resources helped to create ways of designing integrated water resources management policies. The breakthrough in terms of advances in knowledge really started in the 1960s. White (1961) and others started to develop key frameworks in relation to resource management, decision-making and imperfect knowledge (Simon, 1957: White, 1961; Wolpert, 1964). Another set of literature started to bring together issues of land, water and ecosystems. The driving force behind this literature was in reaction to the perceived declining quantity and quality of available freshwater (de Jong et al., 1995). The idea of water resources management as an interaction between land, resources, and the environment was well stated by Burton (1984) in his article, *The Art of Resource Management*. Burton argued for a land-use appraisal of resource use. However, even at that time, integrated management of water resources still meant *maximum* possible human use. Finally, the last set of literature focused on environmental management and water quality (see Dorfman et al., 1973).

Parallel to scholarly advances, environmental conservation around water management also began to be practised. In Canada for example, the Ontario conservation authorities were created in 1946 and later two of the authorities received the Theiss Riverprize in Australia. From the 1970s onwards, IWRM 'experiments' were established across the world. OMVS (The *Organisation pour la mise en valeur du fleuve Sénégal*; in English Senegal River Basin Development Authority)[18] is a good example of 'integrated' transboundary water cooperation. Many countries in the 'South' had also established water resources ministries (China: 1979; India: 1980) and holistic water resources management had already been practised in the 1970s in some Latin American (Argentina, Mexico) and Asian countries (Indonesia).[19] These 'experiments' around IWRM were continuously improving.

The third generation of IWRM (post-1990s) broadened the theory to include socioeconomic subsystems and the way water resources management can be connected to broader social and economic development (see, in particular, work by Mitchell, 1990). In the Netherlands, the American RAND (Research ANd Development) Corporation, in collaboration with the Delft Hydrological Institute, conducted a systems approach analysis for the government, modelling water flows and integrating the economic dimension of water management in decision-making. Frank Rijsberman, who later became Director General of the International Water Management Institute (IWMI), and then Chief Executive Officer of CGIAR

18 Initially created in 1963 as the *Organisation des Etats Riverians du Fleuve Sénégal.*

19 Interview with Roberto Lenton, 3 April 2013; and Eelco van Beek, 28 March 2013.

(Consultative Group on International Agricultural Research), was involved and heavily influenced by this approach. In Canada/US, the Great Lake 1987 agreement led to the realisation of the limits of an integrated approach and brought about ideas of defining a comprehensive and a more focused approach (Mitchell, 2008). The need to identify key areas and criteria (in this case 47 key areas of concerns according to five criteria), rather than a comprehensive overall map and health of the entire Great Lakes basin system, was established.

One interesting feature between these three generations of IWRM is the connection between them and how IWRM was diffused. One very interesting connection to the diffusion of the concept is the Harvard Water programme. Launched in the early 1950s, it resulted in the collaboration among engineers, political scientists and economists leading to the following publication in 1962: *Design of Water-Resource Systems: New Techniques for Relating Economic Objectives, Engineering Analysis, and Governmental Planning*. Many of these Harvard-trained engineers ended up at the World Bank which was a crucial actor in promoting IWRM, most notably John Briscoe but also Nagarajarao Harshadeep, John Dixon, Teddy Herman, and Gerhardt Tschannerl.

The Harvard Water Programme was just one of many water ecosystem programmes looking at the relationship among water, land and ecosystems. A slow consensus emerged across different networks and national experiences in relation to the benefits of the IWRM approach. Engineers and hydrologists were the key initial thinkers of the concept. The most active community was the optimisers, those modelling water flows using system analysis. These include people like Peter Rogers (Harvard University) or Daniel P. Loucks (Cornell University). The other key group comprised hydrologists, and most notable among them were Malin Falkenmark, Bruce Mitchell, John Burton and John Pigram to name a few.

This long tradition of working on multidisicplinarity and system analysis used the sustainable development policy momentum to bring about the IWRM concept. It is no coincidence that the concept of IWRM blossomed in the early 1990s. Although some experts, and especially Asit Biswas, claim that the UN Mar del Plata conference in 1977 was the time that the IWRM principle was endorsed internationally (see also Jeffrey and Geary, 2006; White, 1998: 23 also lists a number of UN initiatives before Mar del Plata), the policy momentum only started in the early 1990s. The emergence of the IWRM concept in the early 1990s cannot be separated from global environmental politics. Although IWRM has its particular history, the concept was linked to rising environmental awareness. The culmination of IWRM was really between 1992 and 2002 with the EU Water Initiative.[20]

Having said this, it must be stated that this epistemic community was not very successful in integrating the IWRM agenda into the sustainable development agenda. It is interesting to note that no water-related experts were involved in the Brundtland Commission. Dublin was organised by the Government of Ireland in partnership with United Nations bodies, as a pre-conference sectoral water meeting for the Earth Summit in Rio. It was not an intergovernmental meeting

20 The EU Water Initiative was a huge financial success for IWRM advocates with more than 1 billion euros available for promoting IWRM in practice in the African, Caribbean and Pacific Group of States (ACP) countries.

but was attended by government-nominated water experts. The relationship between Dublin and Rio is interesting in that many governments considered that the economic approach endorsed at Dublin by water experts was too radical. In Rio, water was considered as an economic *and* social good (Savenije and van der Zaag, 2002).

In contrast to Dublin, Rio was a political rather than a technical conference, and water did not attract the high-level regime-building negotiations that surrounded climate or biodiversity; IWRM was not high on the political agenda at that time (Conca, 2006). This had an important impact on how the policies and institutions were put in place to promote IWRM. This is very important not only in terms of different values for water but also in relation to institutional strategies; the institutions promoting IWRM were not intergovernmental but networks and partnerships (Conca, 2006). As one interviewee put it, Rio rejected the vision of water as just an economic good and the governmental route was blocked.[21] Rather than a UN-led intergovernmental body, this outcome led to the creation of two institutions: the Global Water Partnership (GWP) and the World Water Council (WWC).

Learning, information cascade and policy mimicking

Soft coercion and cooperation assume a certain level of coordination at the global level. For some policy-makers and practitioners interviewed, there was no master plan as IWRM was an ideal. IWRM was based on a 'learning from the ground' approach where it was tested and improved. The GWP was conceived as a network organisation with the objective to advocate the implementation of IWRM plans and institutions around the world and share expert knowledge. The Technical Advisory Committee (TAC) was seen as a very good way to promote and further understand the concept by bringing together an agronomist (Mohammed Aït Kadi), economists (Marian S. delos Angeles, Ramesh Prathia), a geographer (Judith Rees), engineers (Ivan Chéret, Fernando Gonzalez Villarreal, Janusz Kindler, Torkil Jønch-Clausen, Paul Roberts, Peter Rogers, and Albert Wright), an environmentalist (Anil Agarwal), a hydrologist (Malin Falkenmark), a lawyer (Miguel Solanes) and a sociologist (Sonia Davila-Poblete).[22] For some, the success of GWP lay in its TAC and its "scientific approach to water resources management" (rather than its regional networks).[23]

This theory may be supported by the fact that GWP learned a lot from the ground. It is said that Nordic countries were inspired from experiences in Africa, most notably water master plans in Tanzania.[24] Furthermore, according to Torkil Jønch-Clausen, IWRM really came from Africa.[25] In his eyes Uganda was the first country of the developing countries to try and experiment with IWRM and it was in Uganda that an interdisciplinary team of engineers and hydrologists came up

21 Interview with Tony Allan, 20 March 2013.

22 These were the initial members of the Committee, and in subsequent years the composition of the committee changed as members ended their term and new members were added.

23 Interview with Johan Holmberg, 22 March 2013.

24 Interview with Torkil Jønch Clausen, 21 March 2013.

25 Interview with Torkil Jønch Clausen, 21 March 2013.

with the three pillars so central to the IWRM doctrine, namely:

- An *enabling environment* of suitable policies, strategies and legislation for sustainable water resources development and management,

- Putting in place the *institutional framework* through which to put into practice the policies, strategies and legislation.

- Setting up the *management instruments* required by these institutions to do their job.

The Permanent Secretary of the Ugandan Ministry of Water, B.K. Kabanda, who was already involved in the Nordic Freshwater Initiative, was amongst the subscribers to the Copenhagen Statement (NFI, 1992). As a result, Danida chose to assist Uganda in developing a Water Action Plan, between January 1993 and July 1994. This plan can be considered the first African IWRM plan *avant la lettre* (Jønch-Clausen, 2004). The Danish Hydraulic Institute (DHI), a research-based not-for-profit foundation where Jønch-Clausen was Director of the Water & Environment Division, obtained the contract to develop the plan. As a result, with technical and financial support from Danida, Uganda embarked upon the world's first National Water Resources 'Water Action Plan' (WAP) from 1993 to 1994 (see Nicol, Chapter 13 for a more detailed discussion of Uganda). The water professionals of Danida felt that the approach of the Ugandan Water Action Plan was replicable and started a similar IWRM process in Central America (1997-1999), Burkina-Faso (1998-2001) and Vietnam (2004-2005).

The fact that Uganda may be the first example of IWRM in developing countries will create as many debates as there are many understandings of what IWRM means.[26] This is not really the point. This alternative theory shows that IWRM could be conceived as a bottom-up process based on learning from the ground, showing how Uganda played a critical role of the early reflexive development of IWRM. Of course, while the learning elements of the Ugandan were probably important, the bottom-up aspect could be questioned. As shown by Nicol and Odinga (Chapter 13), the Ugandan government at this particular period was more of a follower rather than a designer, as the government had become a 'donor darling', keen to show its willingness to develop policy instruments that reflected emerging mainstream aid policy.

Learning, information cascade and mimicking of IWRM are of course broader than GWP and the Ugandan experience. Wescoat (2005) gives many examples of these cultural exchanges, ranging from diplomat letters between countries across Europe, the US, Asia and the Middle East to US engineering delegations travelling to Australia, China, Egypt, Europe and India for example. Legal treaties were another form of cultural exchange. With respect to IWRM, the 'focused approach' around the Great Lake 1987 agreement led to many exchanges and

26 Mitchell, for example, mentions an IWRM project in Indonesia between 1986 and 1990. He considered the project very successful from a technical point of view but less effective on the basis of the 2nd principle to get everybody on board. In Indonesia, there were difficulties during that time in promoting a bottom-up approach. Others mention the South African experience in the late 1980s and early 1990s.

knowledge-sharing practices between Australia and Canada.[27] Models of best practice river basin organisations were another form of uncoordinated diffusion. The French model of *Agences de l'Eau* was modelled and copied across the world, including among the former Soviet states as well as Asian states that sought to institute financial self-sufficiency of River Basin Organisations (RBOs) (Mukhtarov and Gerlak, 2013). Mukhtarov and Gerlak (2013) also give the example of the Australia's Murray-Darling River Basin Commission, which has influenced developments in countries such as China, Sri Lanka, and Vietnam and contributed to the creation of the Mekong Basin Commission and its ongoing operations, as well as the International Commission for the Protection of the Rhine, which served as a model for the establishment of commissions along the Elbe, Danube, and Odra rivers. As put by Molle (2009: 491), the vogue of the IWRM concept translated into a multitude of attempts to establish RBOs, often inspired by foreign 'models', in countries such as Brazil, Indonesia, Morocco, Sri Lanka and Vietnam and promoted – among others – by the Global Water Partnership and the International Network of Basin Organisations (INBO). However, although the INBO should have played a key role, it has been limited to 'event publicity' in the words of UNESCO's International Hydrological Programme (UNESCO, 2007: 2009).

The uncoordinated diffusion of IWRM and the fact that many countries used water scarcity as a driver for water reforms could illustrate a case of policy mimicking, an issue which should deserve more research. However, one has to recognise the methodological difficulties in finding examples of policy mimicking precisely because of its uncoordinated nature. While this section is shorter than the sections on coercion or cooperation, this is not to belittle this understanding of diffusion compared to the other section but just to recognise the difficulties in researching this mechanism compared to the two previous ones.

Global policy translation: Coordination, politics and resistance

The key assumption behind these three storylines is a consensual, agreed and, to a certain extent, well-defined policy and practical agenda. In fact, what makes the Dublin Conference so significant is this apparent consensus. Abu Zeid (former minister of water in Egypt for many years throughout the 1990s), who later became instrumental in the creation of the World Water Council, played a prominent role in the Dublin Conference as the bridge maker between different epistemic communities and the policy world. As said by one of my interviewees, he 'could make things happen'.[28] Being from the 'South', he was also seen as very instrumental in convincing developing countries.

Some scholars would dispute this unified vision of IWRM policy diffusion due to IWRM's contested meaning and the institutional divisions over IWRM policies (Conca, 2006). As put by Mukhtarov and Cherp (2014: 10), "the contentious politics of water needed at least a *semblance* of consensus at a global scale" (emphasis added). Mollinga (2006: 5) states that "the so-called global water consensus, is such an amalgamation of ideas, with its own internal contradictions, and therefore not a true consensus, but more of a compromise 'sanctioned discourse'

27 Interview with Bruce Mitchell, 27 March 2013.

28 Interview with Eelco van Beek, 28 March 2013.

in the making". Furthermore, it was a consensus among few international water experts; as we have illustrated throughout this chapter, the social carriers of the concept across the world was done by a small group of people (Mollinga, 2006).

The policy translation of IWRM was more about fragmentation than consensus with the conflicting views and interests encapsulated in two organisations, the Global Water Partnership and the World Water Council. These were not limited to two organisations but they also reflected the leadership fight between international organisations (FAO, UNESCO, WMO, UNDP and World Bank) on the global water agenda.[29] The 'Dublin consensus' may have obscured some key divisions. Indeed, it is strange, to say the least, that two key global water organisations were created in the same year. While some international water experts met in Sweden in early 1996, other international key figures, most notably the IWRA president Mahmoud Abu-Zeid (also Egyptian water minister), the IWRA vice-president Aly Shady (also water advisor at the Canadian International Development Agency CIDA), and the Vice-Director of Suez Lyonnaise des Eaux René Coulomb, created the World Water Council (WWC) in 1996. The idea of the Council was established following the 1994 IWRA's VIIIth World Congress in Cairo, Egypt (Water International, 1995). As put by Salman (2003: 494), "The line of demarcation of responsibilities between the two institutions may be clear in theory. However, in practice there are areas of overlapping responsibilities, particularly with the expanding work of the Technical Advisory Committee of the Global Water Partnership and its regional offices, including the work on the strategic vision for integrated water resources management".

The World Water Council was really driven by the former World Bank irrigation adviser, previous to John Briscoe, Guy Le Moigne. A number of key people from IWRA (Asit Biswas, M. Abu Zeid, Aly Shady) were also involved. Guy Le Moigne became the first executive secretary. The French government, and then the Dutch and the Japanese governments, were the key drivers behind the Council. The Global Water Partnership was driven by another World Bank figure, John Briscoe. For some, this division reflected an internal leadership fight within the World Bank. There were many overlaps between the two organisations (WWC and GWP). An external-led evaluation of the Global Water Partnership in 2008 concluded that the demarcations between both organisations were confused and the two organisations could be seen as competitors until 2004 (Gayfer, 2008: 46). This could be primarily explained by the potential overlap of competence between the two institutions. (Salman, 2005: 50-57). For some, WWC was about a different vision of IWRM compared to the Global Water Partnership which rejected the hydraulic mission.[30] At the WWC, it was more about integrated river basin management, including engineering and construction.[31] This image was reinforced given the role the private sector was playing, especially the French multinational companies. The tension between the two organisations really came

29 Interview with Salman Salman, 22 July 2016.

30 Namely "the strong conviction that every drop of water flowing to the ocean is a waste and that the state should develop hydraulic infrastructure to capture as much water as possible for human uses" (Wester, 2009).

31 Interview with Peter Rogers, 22 March 2013; Interview with Alan Hall, 26 March 2013.

to a head at the Hague, during the 2nd World Water Forum.

However, from 2004 both institutions made a move towards collaboration with the signing of a "Framework for Cooperation between GWP and WWC". According to this framework, the Executive Director of WWC and the Executive Secretary of GWP are ex-officio members of the governing bodies of the two organisations. Provision for regular coordination meetings between the two organisations – at least two per year – was put in place. They agreed to share information and committed to avoiding overlap and maximise synergies between themselves. As put by Fromageau (2012), they have found ways to establish "pacific coexistence" among them, although a recent survey by Varady and Iles-Shih (2009: 77) shows undertones of competition between supporters of WWC and GWP, if not between the two initiatives themselves, with numerous instances of inverse scoring patterns for the two organisations by survey informants. One explanation for this potential resurgence of competition between the two organisations is that the global policy momentum over water, at least through networks and conferences, is declining, including its funding, and both organisations are fighting for their existence.

This institutional battle was just one aspect of this contestation of the fine details of the translation of the IWRM concept. The broadness of the IWRM concept, as a nirvana concept to use Molle's (2008) metaphor, made it a subject of many contestations. Molle (2008), for example, showed the tension between the precepts of equity and efficiency. Allan (2003) talks about the missing A in IWRM and shows that IWRM is void of the politics which in fact are at the core of all critical water decisions. Bolding et al. (2000) identifies how sectoral compartmentalisation between different ministries (e.g. irrigation, rural water supply, forestry, land and so on) raises more general issues of how to organise stakeholder involvement in water and natural resources policy-making, planning, development and management. Mollinga (2006) recalls the three sub-ideas of IWRM, around river basin management, participation and privatisation and shows how each of these can be in contradiction to the other. Overall, one can see how the discursive and the institutional division over IWRM implementation reveals the limits of global diffusion theories over the seemingly 'international consensus'.

Conclusion

In this chapter, I have attempted to retrace the history of the global diffusion and translation of the IWRM concept. I have focused on tracing the IWRM idea and knowledge diffusion but more work is needed to look at the political economy aspects, namely tracing back the funds among donors, institutions and IWRM programmes at the global level. Overall, institutions, and especially individuals, were key in the diffusion of this particular idea. However, this idea needs to be understood as embedded in a particular critical juncture in global environmental politics where other ideas of integration were also put forward.[32] In this respect, IWRM was just like the concept of sustainable development or integrated coastal management. It was a key concept within societies at the time, but all of them

32 Such as integrated coastal management.

proved difficult to operationalise. As put by one interviewee, it was a successful idea, but the principles were not really applied, it was the same crowd preaching to itself.[33] In fact, IWRM was not a policy, it was a mindset.[34] This is why the concept also needs to be historicised within a continuum of knowledge in which the idea of integration at the river basin level emerged. It slowly evolved when environmental considerations were taken more into account in policy circles. Conceptually this chapter broadened policy diffusion debates to constructivist ideas in that one can see how the origins of concept and ideas are so important for the study of policy translation.

Why was this idea so successful in travelling across different regions of the globe? There are many answers to this question but the key ones in my mind are as follows. The resistance to IWRM, and more particularly to the idea of water as an economic good, created an institutional pathway around networks rather than an intergovernmental route. These networks allowed for much flexibility in the diffusion and acceptance of the idea. The second most important reason is that there were no clear policy alternatives at the time to the IWRM concept. Water infrastructural development, along Mike Muller's line (Muller, 2010), was not the flavour of the day and IWRM was seen as the only solution, more specifically "the only sustainable solution" (Durham et al., 2002: 333). In fact, the alternatives to IWRM are paradoxically within IWRM itself, whether the emphasis is on a participatory approach, an ecological one or an economic one.

Finally, is there an IWRM fatigue? Are we witnessing the death of IWRM? Some have argued that IWRM is now slowly becoming replaced by other emerging concepts such as water security (Allouche et al., 2016) or the nexus (Allouche et al., 2015). Indeed, the concept may become irrelevant if one focuses on new challenges (such as adaption and climate change or the water-food-energy crises). The importance of new donors such as the BRICS countries may also challenge the concept of IWRM, as it may not fit in with their key priorities around infrastructural development. Still, as argued by Movik et al. (this book), the idea is still strong and alive and kicking in southern Africa. Despite the emergence of new fads, the Global Water Partnership and others have been quite strategic in adapting their approaches to IWRM to other challenges, for example in aligning the IWRM approach with climate change discourses and water security.

Acknowledgements

This research has benefited from the support of the Norwegian Research Council under the project Flows and Practices: The Politics of Integrated Water Resources Management in Africa. I am particularly grateful to all the key individuals that were part of the IWRM adventure for their help. I would like to thank the editors, Synne Movik and the three anonymous reviewers for their precious feedback.

33 Interview with Frank Rijsberman, 2 April 2013.

34 To use James Winpenny's word, Oxford, 19 June 2015.

References

Allan, A. 2003. *IWRM/IWRAM: A new sanctioned discourse?* SOAS Water Issues Study Group. Occasional Paper No. 50. London: School of Oriental and African Studies.

Allouche, J. and Finger, M. 2001. Two ways of reasoning, one outcome: The World Bank's evolving philosophy in establishing a "Sustainable Water Resources Management" policy. *Global Environmental Politics* 1(2): 42-47.

Allouche, J.; Middleton, C. and Gyawali, D. 2015. Technical veil, hidden politics: Interrogating the power linkages behind the Nexus. *Water Alternatives* 8(1): 610-26.

Allouche, J.; Nicol, A.; Mehta, L. and Srivastava, S. 2016. Water securities and the individual: Challenges from human security to consumerism. Pahl-Wostl, C.; Gupta, J. and Bhaduri, A. (Eds), *Handbook on water security*, pp. 59-75, Chapter 4. Camberley: Edward Elgar Publishing

Bennett, C. 1991. What is policy convergence and what causes it? *British Journal of Political Science* 21(2): 215-233.

Bikhchandani, S.; Hirshleifer, D. and Welch, I. 1998. Learning from the behavior of others: Conformity, fads, and informational cascades. *Journal of Economic Perspectives* 12(3): 151-70.

Bolding, A.; Mollinga, P.P. and Zwarteveen, M. 2000. Interdisciplinarity in research on integrated water resource management: Pitfalls and challenges. Paper presented at the UNESCO – Wotro international working conference on 'Water for Society', Delft, the Netherlands, 8-10 November.

Briscoe, J. 1996. Water as an economic good: The idea and what it means in practice. In Proceedings of the World Congress of the International Commission on Irrigation and Drainage. Cairo, Egypt, September 1996.

Burton, J.R. 1984. *The art of resource management.* Armidale: Resource Engineering Department, University of New England.

Chakraborty, S. 2010. Integrated water resource management: A human ecological perspective. *Ritsumeikan Journal of Asia Pacific Studies* 27, February.

Cherlet, J. 2012. Tracing the emergence and deployment of the 'Integrated Water Resources Management' paradigm. Paper presented at the 12th EASA Biennial Conference, Nanterre, 10-13 July 2012, Unpublished document.

Conca, K. 2006. *Governing water: Contentious transnational politics and global institution building.* Cambridge: MIT Press.

de Jong, J.; van Rooy, P.T.C. and Hosper, S.H. 1995. Living with water: At the crossroads of change. *Water Science and Technology* 31(8): 393-400.

de Jong, M.; Lalenis, K. and Virginie, M. 2002. *The theory and practice of institutional transplantation: Experiences with the transfer of policy institutions.* Dordrecht: Kluwer Academic Publishers.

Dolowitz, D. and Marsh, D. 1996. Who learns what from whom: A review of the policy transfer literature. *Political Studies* 44(2): 343-357.

Dolowitz, D.P. and Marsh, D. 2000. Learning from abroad: The role of policy transfer in contemporary policy-making. *Governance: An International Journal of Policy and Administration* 13(1): 5-23.

Dorfman, R.; Jacoby, H. and Thomas, Jr, H.A. 1973. *Models for managing regional wa-*

ter quality. Cambridge, MA: Harvard University Press.

Drezner, D.W. 2001. Globalization and policy convergence. *International Studies Review* 3(1): 55-78.

Durham, B.; Rinck-Pfeiffer, S. and Guendert, D. 2002. Integrated Water Resource Management through reuse and aquifer recharge. *Desalination* 152(1): 333-338.

Elkins, Z. and Simmons, B. 2005. On waves, clusters, and diffusion: A conceptual framework. *Annals of the American Academy of Political and Social Science* 598(1): 33-51.

Finger, M. and Allouche, J. 2002. *Water privatisation. Transnational corporations and the re-regulation of the water industry.* London, New York: Spon Press.

Fromageau, E. 2011. The Global Water Partnership: Between institutional flexibility and legal legitimacy. *International Organizations Law Review* 8(2): 367-395.

Gayfer, J. 2008. Global Water Partnership: Joint donor external evaluation. Sheffield: The Performance Assessment Resource Centre, 26 March 2008, PARC Project No. 353.

GWP (Global Water Partnership). 2000. *Integrated Water Resources Management*. GWP-TAC Background Paper 4. Stockholm: GWP.

Haas, E.B. 1980. Why collaborate? Issue-linkage and international regimes. *World Politics 32* (03): 357-405.

Haas, P.M. 1992. Epistemic communities and the international policy coordination. *International Organization* 46(1): 1-35.

Hajer, M.A. 1993. Discourse coalitions and the institutionalisation of practice. In Fischer F. and Forester, J. (Eds), *The argumentative turn in policy analysis and planning*, pp. 43-76. Durham: Duke University Press.

Hassing, J.; Ipsen, N.; Clausen, T.J.; Larsen, H. and Lindgaard-Jørgensen, P. 2009. *Integrated water resources management in action*. The United Nations World Water Assessment Programme dialogue paper. Paris: United Nations Educational, Scientific and Cultural Organization.

Hira, A. 1998. *Ideas and economic policy in Latin America: Regional, national, and organizational case studies*. Westport, Conn: Praeger.

Holmberg, J. 1998. Knowledge-intensive networks for development: The case of the Global Water Partnership. *Human Systems Management* 17(1): 39-47.

Huntington, S.P. 1991. *The third wave: Democratization in the late twentieth century*. Norman: University of Oklahoma Press.

Jacoby, W. 2000. *Imitation and politics, redesigning modern Germany*. Ithaca, NY: Cornell University Press.

Jeffrey, P. and Gearey, M. 2006. Integrated water resources management: Lost on the road from ambition to realisation? *Water Science & Technology* 53(1): 1-8.

Jønch-Clausen, T. 1992. Integrated management of land and water resources at the lowest appropriate levels: The Nordic Freshwater Initiative. In Stockholm Water Symposium (Ed), *Water Resources in the Next Century*, Proceedings of the Stockholm Water Symposium, pp. 105-18, Stockholm, Stockholm: Stockholm Vatten AB, 12-15 August 1991.

Jønch-Clausen, T. 2004. *Integrated Water Resources Management (IWRM) and water efficiency plans by 2005 – why, what and how?* TEC Background Paper No. 10. January. Stockholm: Global Water Partnership.

Knill, C. 2005. Introduction: Cross-national policy convergence: Concepts, approaches and explanatory factors. *Journal of European Public Policy* 12(5): 764-74.

Lankford, B.A.; Merrey, D.; Cour, J. and Hepworth, N. 2007. *From integrated to expedient: An adaptive framework for river basin management in developing countries.* Research Report No. 110. Colombo, Sri Lanka: International Water Management Institute.

Leach, M.; Scoones, I. and Stirling, A. 2010. *Dynamic sustainabilities: Technology, environment, social justice.* Oxford: Earthscan.

Lendvai, N. and Stubbs, P. 2007. Policies as translation: Situating trans-national social policies. In Hodgson, S. and Irving, Z. (Eds), *Policy reconsidered: Meanings, politics and practices,* pp. 172-189, Bristol: Policy Press.

Levi-Faur, D. and Jordana, J. 2005. The rise of regulatory capitalism: The global diffusion of a new order. *American Academy of Political and Social Sciences ANNALS* (AAPSS) 598(1): 12-32.

Mehta, L. 2005. *The politics and poetics of water: The naturalisation of scarcity in Western India.* Oxford: Orient Blackswan.

Mehta, L.; Marshall, F.; Movik, S.; Stirling, A.; Shah, E.; Smith, A. and Thompson, J. 2007. *Liquid dynamics: Challenges for sustainability in water and sanitation.* STEPS Working Paper No. 6. Brighton: STEPS centre.

Meinzen-Dick, R. and Appasamy, P.P. 2002. Urbanization and intersectoral competition for water. Woodrow Wilson International Center for Scholars Environmental Change and Security Project (Ed), *Finding the source: The linkages between population and water,* pp. 27-51, Washington, DC: The Woodrow Wilson Institute.

Meyer, J.W.; Ramirez, F.O.; Rubinson, R. and Boli-Bennett, J. 1977. The world educational revolution, 1950-1970. *Sociology of Education* 50(4): 242-58.

Midlarsky, M.I. 1978. Analyzing diffusion and contagion effects: The urban disorders of the 1960s. *American Political Science Review* 72(3): 996-1008.

Mitchell, B. 1990. Patterns and implications. In Mitchell, B. (Ed), *Integrated water management: International experiences and perspectives,* pp. 203-218, London: Belhaven Press.

Mitchell, B. 2008. Resource and environmental management: Connecting the academy with practice. *Canadian Geographer* 52(4): 131-145.

Molle, F. 2005. *Irrigation and water policies in the Mekong region: Current discourses and practice.* IWMI Research Report No. 95. Colombo, Sri Lanka: International Water Management Institute.

Molle, F. 2008. Nirvana concepts, narratives and policy models: Insights from the water sector. *Water Alternatives* 1(1): 131-56.

Molle, F. 2009. River-basin planning and management: The social life of a concept. *Geoforum* 40(3): 484-494.

Mollinga, P.P. 2006. IWRM in South Asia: A concept looking for a constituency. In Mollinga, P.P.; Dixit A. and Athukorala, K. (Eds), *Integrated water resources management in South Asia: Global theory, emerging practice and local needs,* pp. 21-37. Water in South Asia Series 1. New Delhi: Sage.

Mukhtarov, F. and Cherp, A. 2014. The hegemony of integrated water resources management as a global water discourse. In Squires, V.R.; Milner, H.M. and Daniell, K.A. (Eds), *River basin management in the twenty-first century: Understanding people and place*, pp. 3-21, Boca Raton: CRC Press.

Mukhtarov, F.G. and Gerlak, A.K. 2013. River basin organizations in the global water discourse: An exploration of agency and strategy. *Global Governance: A Review of Multilateralism and International Organizations* 19(2): 307-326.

Mukhtarov, F.G. 2014. Rethinking the travel of ideas: Policy translation in the water sector. Policy and politics. *Policy and Politics* 42(1): 71-88.

Mukhtarov, F.G. 2009. The hegemony of Integrated Water Resources Management: A study of policy translation in England, Turkey and Kazakhstan. Doctoral thesis. Budapest: Department of Environmental Sciences and Policy, Central European University.

Mukhtarov, F.G. 2008. Intellectual history and current status of Integrated Water Resources Management: A global perspective. In Pahl-Wostl, C.; Kabat, P. and Möltgen, J. (Eds), *Adaptive and integrated water management: Coping with complexity and uncertainty*, pp. 167-85. Berlin Heidilberg: Springer.

Muller, M. 2010. Fit for purpose: Taking integrated water resource management back to basics. *Irrigation and Drainage Systems* 24(3-4): 161-175.

NFI (Nordic Freshwater Initiative). 1992. *Copenhagen Report. Implementation mechanisms for Integrated Water Resources development and management.* Report from Copenhagen Informal Consultation, November 11-14, 1991. Copenhagen: Danida.

Nicol, A.; Mehta, L. and Allouche, J. 2012. Some for all? Politics and pathways in water and sanitation. *IDS Bulletin* 43(2): 1-9.

Postel, S. 1992. *Last oasis: Facing water scarcity*. New York & London: W.W. Norton & Co.

Rahaman, M.M. and Varis, O. 2005. Integrated water resources management: Evolution, prospects and future challenges. *Sustainability: Science, Practice & Policy* 1(1): 15-21.

Rogers E.M. 1995. *Diffusion of innovations*. New York: Free Press.

Salman, S.M. 2003. From Marrakech through The Hague to Kyoto: Has the global debate on water reached a dead end? Part one. *Water International* 28(4): 491-500.

Salman, S.M.A. 2005. Evolution and context of international water resources law. In Boisson de Chazournes, L. and Salman, S.M.A. (Eds), *Water resources and international law.* Leiden: Martinus Nijhoff.

Saravanan, V.S.; McDonald, G.T. and Mollinga, P.P. 2009. Critical review of Integrated Water Resources Management: Moving beyond polarised discourse. *Natural Resources Forum* 33(1): 76-86.

Savenije, H.H. and van der Zaag, P. 2002. Water as an economic good and demand management paradigms with pitfalls. *Water International* 27(1): 98-104.

Selznick, P. 1949. *TVA and the grass roots: A study in the sociology of formal organisation.* Berkeley, CA: University of California Press.

Simmons, B.; Dobbin, F. and Garrett, G. 2006. Introduction: The international diffusion of liberalism. *International Organization* 60(4): 781-810.

Simmons, B.; Dobbin, F. and Garrett, G. 2007. The global diffusion of public policies: Social construction, coercion, competition, or learning? *Annual Review of Sociology* 33(1): 449-72.

Simmons, B.A.; Dobbin, F. and Garrett, G. (Eds). 2008. *The global diffusion of markets and democracy*. Cambridge: Cambridge University Press.

Simon, H.A. 1957. *Models of man: Social and rational*. New York: Wiley.

Snellen, W.B. and Schrevel, A.I. 2004. *WRM, for sustainable use of water; 50 years of international experience with the concept of integrated water resources management*. Background document to the FAO/Netherlands Conference on Water for Food and Ecosystems, Alterra-Report 1143. Wageningen: Alterra.

Srinivasan, V.; Cohen, M.; Akudago, J.; Keith, D. and Palaniappan, M. 2011. Integrated Water Resources Management: A global review. Paper presented at the American Geophysical Union, Fall Meeting 2011.

Teclaff, L.A. 1967. *The river basin in history and law*. The Hague, Netherlands: Martinus Nijhoff.

Thomas, G.M.; Meyer, J.W.; Ramirez, F.O. and Boli-Bennett, J. 1987. *Institutional structure: Constituting state, society, and the individual*. Newbury Park, CA: Sage Publications.

UNCNR (United Nations Committee on Natural Resources). 1994. *Review of the progress on water-related issues. Water resources: Progress in the implementation of the Mar del Plata Action Plan and of Agenda 21 on water-related issues*. Report of the Secretary General, Geneva, Second Session, 22 February-4 March 1994 (E/C.7/1994/4), 12 January 1994.

UNESCO (United Nations Educational, Scientific and Cultural Organisation). 2007. *State of the Art Review on IWRM*. Paris: UNESCO-IHP.

van der Zaag, P. 2005. Integrated Water Resources Management: Relevant concept or irrelevant buzzword? A capacity building and research agenda for southern Africa. *Physics and Chemistry of the Earth Parts A/B/C* 30(11-16): 867-71.

Varady, R.V. and Iles-Shih, M. 2009. Global water initiatives: What do the experts think? In Biswas, A.K. and Tortajada, C. (Eds), Impacts of mega- conferences on the water sector, pp. 53-101. New York: Springer-Verlag.

Water International. 1995. Communiqué: World Water Council. *Water International* 20(2): 110-116.

Wescoat, J.L. 2005. *Water policy and cultural exchange: Transferring lessons from around the world to the western United States*. In Kenney, D. (Ed), *In search of sustainable water management: International lessons for the American West and beyond*, pp. 1-24. Cheltenham, UK and Northampton, MA, USA: Edward Elgar.

Wescoat, J. 1984. *Integrated water development*. Chicago: University of Chicago Press.

Wester, P. 2009. Capturing the waters: The hydraulic mission in the Lerma-Chapala Basin, Mexico (1876-1976). *Water History* 1(1): 9-29.

Weyland, K. 2007. *Bounded rationality and policy diffusion: Social sector reform in Latin America*. Princeton, NJ: Princeton University Press.

Winpenny, J. 1994. *Managing water as an economic resource*. London: Routledge.

White, G.F. 1961. Choice of use in resource management. *Natural Resources*

Journal 1(1): 23-40.

White, G.F. 1998. Reflections on 50-year international search for integrated water management. *Water Policy* 1(1): 21-27.

Wolpert, J. 1964. The decision process in spatial context. *Annals of the Association of American Geographers* 54(4): 537-558.

World Bank. 1993. *Water resources management.* A World Bank policy paper. Washington, DC: World Bank.

WWAP (World Water Assessment Programme). 2012. *The United Nations World Water Development Report 4: Managing water under uncertainty and risk.* Paris: UNESCO.

Annex: List of interviews

Professor Tony Allan, Emeritus Professor, Kings College London.

Mr. William Cosgrove, Former President of the World Water Council.

Dr. Peter Gleick, President and Co-founder, Pacific Institute.

Mr. Alan Hall, Senior Advisor, GWP.

Mr. Johan Holmberg, Senior Advisor, GWP.

Dr. Guy Howard, WASH Policy Team Leader, DFID.

Professor Torkil Jønch-Clausen, Chief Water Policy Adviser DHI Group.

Professor Roberto Lenton, Executive Director of the Robert B. Daugherty Water for Food Institute, University of Nebraska-Lincoln.

Professor Jan Lundqvist, Senior Scientific Advisor, SIWI.

Professor Bruce Mitchell, Professor of Geography, University of Waterloo.

Professor Peter Rogers, Gordon McKay Professor of Environmental Engineering and Professor of City and Regional Planning, Harvard University.

Dr. Salman Mohamed Ahmed Salman, former Lead Counsel with the Legal Vice Presidency of the World Bank, and the Bank's adviser on water law.

Mr. Peregrine Swan, Senior Water Advisor, DIFD.

Professor Eelco van Beek, Professor of Modelling Integrated Water Resources Management, University of Twente.

Professor Pieter van der Zaag, Professor of Integrated Water Resources Management, UNESCO-IHE.

Dr. Martin Walsh, Global Research Adviser, Oxfam.

3

The Flow of IWRM in SADC: The Role of Regional Dynamics, Advocacy Networks and External Actors[1]

Synne Movik

Lyla Mehta

Emmanuel Manzungu

ABSTRACT: This chapter explores the entry and spread of IWRM in the Eastern and Southern African Development Community (SADC) region. It traces how the idea of IWRM was promoted and sustained throughout the region by mapping key events, actors and networks that were involved in promoting the approach. It highlights the importance of regional networks in promoting IWRM and shows how regional dynamics, playing out at the interface between the global and local levels, influenced the adoption/adaptation and spread of IWRM. The chapter finds that the idea of IWRM 'hit the ground running' in SADC due to several contributing factors. These include: historical political connections between the member countries; historically rooted well-established channels and connections with bilateral and multilateral donors; the success of networks such as the Global Water Partnership and WaterNet whose mandate was to promote the concept; and the fact that two-thirds of the region's population live in transboundary basins with IWRM providing a suitable hook for transboundary cooperation, often inspired by European models. The chapter further argues that IWRM thrived because of strong donor agendas that were adapted by key SADC actors to suit strategic interests. It thus provided a platform for complex politically charged negotiations to reconcile apparently divergent goals such as infrastructure vs management and regional vs national interests. The practice of IWRM in the region is very much shaped by a conflation of regional, national and donor interests and has now acquired a life of its own, despite changing donor priorities.

KEYWORDS: IWRM, regionalisation, regionalism, SADC, southern Africa

Introduction

Ever since the International Conference on Water and the Environment (ICWE) was convened in Dublin in 1992, the idea of Integrated Water Resources Management (IWRM) has had an impressive global influence. Attention towards for-

1 First published in *Water Alternatives* 9(3): 436-457.

mulating and putting into practice the notion of integration has been a key focus of water resources managers across the globe. Still, getting to grips with, and translating, a rather abstract concept has been challenging (see Bolding et al., 2000; Biswas, 2004; Cardwell et al., 2006; Hopper, 2006; Molle, 2008; Mehta et al., 2014). Moreover, the principles themselves are broad enough to appeal universally like a kind of 'nirvana concept' (Molle, 2008) or work as a 'boundary term' (cf. Gieryn, 1999) that different actors in scientific and policy worlds interpret and deploy in different ways in accordance with prevailing political interests (see Introduction to this book for more details).

This book explores the trajectory of IWRM – its emergence and spread – as well as how it has been translated into practice (or not) in eastern and southern Africa. Allouche (this book) deals with the 'birth' and emergence of IWRM at the global level, while the country cases document how IWRM has been translated in different contexts. This chapter aims to fill the gap between these two focal areas. Between the global and national policy levels, there is another policy arena that can act as a link, fostering the downstream – or upstream – flow of policy ideas like IWRM at the regional scale. This chapter takes as its point of departure the question of how IWRM became entrenched in southern Africa with a particular focus on the Eastern and Southern African Development Community (SADC) region, which in the past two decades has witnessed much cooperation and activity around water management, and IWRM more specifically. SADC is a political and economic grouping to which practically all the mainland and island states of southern Africa belong (see below for its history and composition).

This chapter asks: (i) How did IWRM unfold in southern Africa and through which key events and actors? (ii) Why did it become so popular in the region even though its popularity is on the wane in Europe and elsewhere? and (iii) How has it been shaped and adapted in interaction with the prevailing regional dynamics?

The chapter is structured as follows. First we present some conceptual ideas on 'regions' and how ideas and policies flow within a regional space. It then provides a brief historical overview of the SADC region and water management before looking at the roll-out of IWRM in SADC and the key role of transboundary waters. The chapter then looks at the diversity of external donor perspectives and practices and the key role played by regional networks such as the Global Water Partnership (GWP) and WaterNet, a major research and capacity building regional network. The final sections analyse the mixed bag of donor-led experiences and impacts and discuss how and why IWRM became so popular in the region.

Methods

We used a mixed set of methods, combining semi-structured interviews of key informants with document analysis and internet searches to gather information on the events, processes and issues that were involved in the spread of IWRM across southern Africa. Key informants were identified through a 'snowballing' technique and we thus could map the actors who have contributed to the spread of IWRM within the region. We interviewed people through face-to-face interviews and via Skype from organisations such as the GWP, the SADC Water Division, Capacity Development in Sustainable Water Management (CapNet), the World

Bank as well as bilateral donor agencies such as Deutsche Gesellschaft für Internationale Zusammenarbeit (GIZ, formerly GTZ), Swedish International Development Agency (Sida) and the Norwegian Agency for Development Cooperation (Norad) and a range of policy-makers, consultants and academics. In all, 30 key informants were interviewed. In addition, we participated in three (2012, 2013, and 2014) annual WaterNet symposia and also interviewed several actors present there. Further, we conducted textual analysis of relevant documents such as government policies, donor strategies, academic articles, SADC, GWP documents and assessment reports to gain an understanding of the life of IWRM within SADC.

Regional integration, regionalism and external actors

Regions occupy a socio-geographical space but they are also socially constructed entities (Langeland, 2012). Much of the study on regionalisation or regional integration has tended to focus on the European context, in particular on the formation of the European Union (EU). Much less attention has been devoted to the process of regionalisation in Africa and early interest in the formation of regional organisations faded away only to re-emerge early in the 1990s (Mapuva, 2015). Studies of integration in southern Africa have largely tended to focus on the economic rationale of integration (Gibb, 2009; Mapuva, 2015) and there has been a tendency to privilege the role of states in the process of integration (Söderbaum, 2004). However, as Chan (2011) notes, the independent states that emerged in the wake of colonialism – which largely inherited the boundaries and languages of the colonisers – suffered from problems of lack of institutional capacity and legitimacy. Moving away from the fixation with state-led processes of integration, Söderbaum's (2004) study of regionalisation processes in southern Africa proposed instead to draw on the notion of the New Regionalism Approach (NRA). This approach proposes that it is not only states that play a role in the process of integration – rather, there are several processes and actors at work, both formal and informal. In the context of southern Africa, Söderbaum identifies four such processes; market integration; regime-boosting; shadow regionalism; and informal economic regionalism. Söderbaum has focussed on the multidimensional and comprehensive nature of regionalism in contemporary southern Africa. These challenge positivist approaches with their narrow focus on formal and interstate frameworks that have traditionally focused on the economic relationships between South Africa and its neighbours. In understanding regionalism, then, it is important to better understand the role of other actors, such as donors, international financial institutions and civil society as well as particular dynamics such as transboundary waters which in southern Africa have also served to promote regional integration and cooperation.

The formation of particular regional entities, such as the SADC, then, should be understood not only as a process of state-led integration, but as much a result of the workings of other informal and formal processes and actors as well. The role of external actors – such as western donors and the World Bank – has also been immense in shaping SADC and its water management trajectories. While there is a tendency to look at donor – recipient state (African) relations in rather a static and top-down way, our approach draws on Whitfield and Fraser (2009) to analyse the complex negotiations between donors, national governments and non-state actors and how policies and processes are articulated as a result. We also use a historical and diachronic approach (see Introduction) to look at how current processes and policies play out against the backdrop of specific historical, economic and political trajectories. This path dependency is critical to understanding both regional integration and the related water management processes in southern Africa. While it is beyond the scope of this chapter to provide a detailed exposition of the emergence of SADC and other historical processes, we offer a snapshot of some of the elements involved in its creation and evolution as a regional entity through a water lens. This serves as a backdrop to the ensuing portrayal of the water governance trends in the region and how the idea of IWRM came to unfold over time (also see Appendix 1 for a historic timeline of key global IWRM dates).

Colonial legacies and the emergence of SADC

The contemporary southern African region was produced and consolidated through several hundred years of imperialism, colonialism, mining exploitation, racism, state-building, apartheid, anti-apartheid struggles, nonracialism, and black nationalism (see Swatuk, 2005, 2008). The emergence of the SADC cannot therefore be understood without an appreciation of the chequered history of the region and the multidimensionality of processes of regionalisation in a historical context.

The history of South Africa is important in understanding regional dynamics. South Africa was first colonised by Dutch descendants – the Boers who, overtime, called themselves Afrikaners – and then later by the British. The two groups vied for political and economic power: the Boers finished with political power, and the British with economic affairs. Southern Africa was the core of Anglo-Saxon Africa and attracted the lion's share of British investments (Birmingham, 2008). A key ingredient in the colonisation of southern Africa was the emphasis on large-scale transboundary transport networks, such as Cecil Rhodes's idea of building a railway to connect the Cape with Cairo (which never materialised). Further, Rhodes combined three territories: southern Rhodesia, northern Rhodesia, and Nyasaland – present-day Zimbabwe, Zambia and Malawi, respectively. The Portuguese, who wielded power in the then colonies of Mozambique and Angola in particular, were also enamoured like the British, by hubristic transport projects that never materialised, e.g. the coast-to-coast network incorporating Angola, Zambia and Mozambique (see e.g. Birmingham, 2008).

Apart from physically linking territories together through large-scale infrastructure projects, a key emphasis was on economic integration. In 1910, the same year that South Africa achieved dominion status under the Commonwealth, the Southern African Customs Union (SACU) was established, the world's oldest customs union. In 1953, the Central African Federation (CAF) was created, consisting of Nyasaland and southern and northern Rhodesia, the three territories of the Zambezi valley that Rhodes had sought to dominate. Though Rhodes died in 1902, his legacy was long-lasting. Southern Rhodesia emerged as the economic, political and military powerhouse of the federation, with Nyasaland supplying cheap labour, and northern Zambia offering copper-based wealth. This union took place largely to reap the economic benefits of linking labour and wealth closer together. However, it was brought down by an increasingly disgruntled black majority in Nyasaland and Zambia only a decade later (Birmingham, 2008: Chan, 2011).

These historical trends implicitly began to pave the way towards regional integration before far more explicit political and security interests emerged. In the wake of the struggles for independence late in the 1950s and early in the 1960s, countries in the region started engaging in processes of forming political coalitions. The era of struggles for independence coincided with the Cold War, with the superpowers fighting 'proxy wars' that grew hot, particularly in Angola, Mozambique and South West Africa (Namibia). South Africa was the hegemon of the region, busily engaged in attempts to destabilise its neighbours (Chan, 2011). In 1976, a group emerged that became known as the Frontline States, making up a buffer zone against apartheid South Africa. The coalition consisted of Angola, Botswana, Mozambique, Tanzania, Zambia and eventually Zimbabwe. Thus, two diametrically opposed political, economic and security groupings existed in the region – on the one hand, there was South Africa and its homeland satellite system, and on the other there was the Frontline States (Evans, 1986). Subsequently, the latter became the driving force for the creation of the Southern African Development Coordination Conference (SADCC) in 1980, with the primary purpose of fighting against apartheid. The key elements were the mobilisation of international development assistance to the liberation movements and mobilising the international community to impose sanctions on the apartheid regime to isolate it. The Nordics and like-minded countries wholeheartedly embraced the SADCC, while the British used it as compensation for their reluctance to impose sanctions on South Africa. The Cold War came to an end at the same time as apartheid was brought to an end in South Africa.

In August 1992, the SADCC gave way to the creation of the Southern African Development Community, or SADC (Mandaza et al., 1994). Today, SADC embraces a huge area of 15 countries containing a wealth of diversity in terms of climate, topography, political, socio-economic and cultural characteristics. SADC is one of the most important networks in Africa, addressing economic, political and security and cultural issues of common interest to community members (Mapuva, 2015).

After the early 1990s, South Africa became a pivotal player in the newly emerged SADC, being the most successful in the group economically. While Mandela saw the role of the state as key for a country's development, his successor, Thabo Mbeki, was more concerned with giving the private sector a freer rein to attract foreign capital; his ambitions were not merely concerned with South Africa. His desire was to foster a new continent-wide African Renaissance, to demonstrate to the world that, in particular, South Africa and SADC were capable of becoming modern (Chan, 2011). SADC, in Mbeki's mind, was meant to be the demonstration vehicle of the African Renaissance project (ibid). The strong belief in the power of the private sector to kick-start struggling economies and to embrace neoliberal policies aligned well with global economic and political trends at the time. These in part were thwarted by Zimbabwe's economic meltdown in 2000.

The role of Western donors in the SADC region should not be underestimated. Donors were often fronting political and economic interests of their home countries – many Western countries moved from Cold War and anti-apartheid interests to emphasising the supremacy of liberal democracy, economic liberalisation, and free markets. These 'Western' interests, which are by no means homogeneous (for instance, the US and European countries have widely different aspirations when it comes to energy and resource interests in southern Africa), have had to contend with counteracting the growing influence of other emerging players such as China (Austin et al., 2008; Meierding, 2011). The net result has been a move away from state-centric policies in favour of neoliberal policies and the formation of partnerships with states, private markets and civil society actors, which echo Söderbaum's point about the need to understand the process of integration from a less state-centric vantage point.

To sum up, a multiplicity of driving factors shaped the emergence of the SADC. These included imperial interests involving large-scale transboundary transport network plans to link the territories together more tightly, economic interests, (e.g. the creation of SACU), and political and security interests in the formation of the Frontline States as a bulwark against the regime in Pretoria. These colonial and historical legacies still very much shape the cultural, linguistic and political structures of the states that make up the community membership and had a bearing on water issues also, to which we now turn.

Trends in southern African water governance

The late nineteenth and early twentieth century were characterised by the emergence of what has become dubbed the 'hydraulic mission' (Waterbury, 1979; Allan, 2003; Turton et al., 2004; Molle et al., 2009). Nation-states and colonial governments engaged in efforts to develop large-scale infrastructure to increase the assurance of water supply for various purposes, such as irrigation, energy and mining. Powerful state bureaucracies, or 'hydrocracies' (Molle et al., 2009), were created during this period. The ethos guiding such developments was often one of conquering nature, and ardent advocates tended to "preach often in hyperbolic and lyrical style, the advent of an irrigated Eden" (Molle et al., 2009: 330). One of the grandest projects in the region at the time was the Orange River project. With respect to colonial governments' engagement, the British furthered their interests through engaging in the building of the Kariba Dam in the 1950s to serve the copperbelt and expanding industries in northern and southern Rhodesia (now Zambia and Zimbabwe, respectively). The Portuguese colonial government, for its part, ordered the building of the Cabora Bassa Dam (also modelled on the TVA), which was completed in 1974.

As outlined in the Introduction to this book (see also Timeline in Appendix), in the 1990s, supply-oriented paradigms gave way to demand-led approaches. This led to the scaling back of government, the promotion of structural adjustment and the promotion of water as an economic good as well as approaches that used economic incentives to increase the so-called water use efficiency. These issues were firmly entrenched in dominant World Bank documents of the time (e.g.

World Bank, 1993; Briscoe, 1996) as well as in the so-called Dublin Principles, which are considered by many as the 'birth' of modern day IWRM (see Allouche and the Introduction, this book). However, some elements of IWRM were around earlier in the region. For instance, in South Africa, some elements of what came to be known as IWRM were already present in the 1970 Commission (Movik et al., Chapter 4). This was also the case in Mozambique where the 1991 water law included IWRM principles before Dublin (Alba and Bolding, in this book). It is also worth noting that some donors argued that they had been involved in IWRM ever since the 1960s or so.

The 1993 World Bank Water Resources Strategy promoted a particular version of IWRM based on the French/Ruhr models, which emphasised management at the river basin level and water pricing. Later that same year, the World Bank, along with the German aid organisation GTZ (later GIZ), took its strategic ideas to a meeting at Victoria Falls in Zimbabwe with the aim of pushing the rationale of economic valuation. The fact that there was a drought in the region at the time forcefully brought home the challenges of water security, and also coincided with the collapse of the Soviet Union and many countries in the region starting to 'look West instead of East' (interview with GTZ official, April 2014). Many countries started introducing market-based reforms. This brief overview shows how the initial emphasis on infrastructure and providing access to water faltered in favour of an increasing emphasis on market mechanisms and a neoliberal turn in thinking about water governance which allowed for a domination of the 1992 Dublin version of IWRM. These trends in water governance in part mirror the colonial project: from the hydraulic mission (even though this largely served the white minority) to state-led development, to the still prevailing neoliberal turn. These wider trends of course interacted with regional transboundary dynamics to which we now turn.

Rolling out IWRM in the southern African region

Transboundary waters as a catalyst for IWRM

The many shared river basins in southern Africa (SADC has 15 major river basins that are transboundary) are a (unintended) legacy from the scramble for Africa, hence the need to share water resources across nations. Today's global and national policy-makers are using the river basins to create integration in the region (see Swatuk, 2005). Transboundary issues have always been high on donor and SADC agendas. According to some authors, transboundary issues played a more forceful role than political boundaries (Asmal and Vale, 1999).

A Protocol on Shared Watercourse Systems was created in 1995 and a revised version entered into force in the 2003 Framework (SADC, 2010). It originated out of earlier work and debates on the development of regional legislation for the development of the Zambezi River Action Plan (ZACPLAN) (Granit, 2000; Mohamed, 2003). The United Nations Environment Programme (UNEP) was an important driver in the process of drafting the protocol based on the ZACPLAN experiences. The Protocol envisaged contributing to the development and management of shared international basins, suggesting equitable division and sharing of benefits. As the region's scarce water resources needed to be shared between different basin States, negotiation and cooperation were required to ensure no harm was done to any party (Mohamed, 2003).[2] The Protocol was drafted two years prior to the 1997 Helsinki protocol, and the United Nations Convention on the Law of the Non-Navigational Uses of International Watercourses strongly influenced the revision of the Protocol (Merrey, 2009).

In the words of a member of staff at the GWP-SA head office in Pretoria:

> *Transboundary issues cannot be underestimated. The SADC has fifteen transboundary basins, and many of those basins have prepared development plans, which I would say to a greater or lesser extent are based on IWRM principles. Many start with IWRM plans so we could probably say that IWRM covers about 120 million people. They cover different countries, and are not local, but international plans. Transboundary issues hence have been very important in terms of driving the IWRM agenda. For instance, the Mozambican water policy on integrated water resources management was largely driven by concerns over shared watercourses, particularly with South Africa (Interview, July 2013).*

According to a former member of the SADC Secretariat, who now works for a consultancy company in South Africa, the focus on implementing IWRM in transboundary basins clearly contributed to reducing conflicts. Even though he is critical of the concept of IWRM – perceiving it as being too broad to be of any practical use – he pointed out the beneficial ramifications of implementing IWRM plans in a transboundary basin, as these plans helped promote cooperation and defuse potential controversies between states (interview, July 2013).

The Protocol on Shared Watercourse Systems had a galvanising effect on the establishment of river basin organisations (RBOs). There was a strong donor hand in all of them. For example, the Orange-Senqu River Commission (ORASECOM), which was established in 2000, continues to receive donor funding. ORASECOM was followed by Limpopo Watercourse Commission (LIMCOM) in 2011 and by the Zambezi Watercourse Commission (ZAMCOM) also in 2011 (see Appendix 2 for further details on key transboundary institutions in southern Africa). The contribution of RBOs to fostering regional cooperation cannot be underestimated. This process however entails intense negotiation as nations also try their best to protect national interests whilst participating in regional transboundary processes.

Take the case of the Zambezi River Basin, SADC's largest (in terms of size and number of countries) and Africa's fourth largest river basin. The Central African

2 The Protocol was also revised in 2000 (SADC, 2000) to accommodate the requests of the Mozambicans with respect to the possibility offered by the original text to carve river systems up in different watercourse systems. The latter could then in theory be unilaterally developed by one riparian state, evading the possibility of other riparian states to have a say in this. Mozambique as a downstream nation of many transboundary rivers was very keen on avoiding being left out of any upstream decision-making. The revised protocol was ratified in 2005.

Federation (CAF) is engaged in its own hydraulic mission through instigating the building of the Kariba Dam on the Zambezi River between Zambia (then northern Rhodesia) and Zimbabwe (then southern Rhodesia) to supply electricity to the copper mines in Zambia and to the farms and cities of Rhodesia. Three decades later, in the mid-eighties, the donor-supported ZACPLAN initiative was launched to promote the integrated management of the Zambezi. Discussions began in 1999 and in 2004, the Zambezi River Commission (ZAMCOM) agreement was signed. Still it did not enter into force until 2011, mainly because the countries involved in the agreement were concerned about accommodating their own national infrastructure interests within the transboundary IWRM framework. Zambia, for example, was concerned that the agreement did not reflect the fact that most of the water flowing in the Zambezi originates in Zambia with up to 70.2% of the country's population of 11 million living in the basin and most of the country's electricity met from the basin's hydropower stations. In a sense, then, these protracted negotiations represent a confluence of the hydraulic mission and infrastructure development initiatives with the 'softer' aspects of creating a regional institutional platform for IWRM through ZAMCOM (see Chanda, 2004; Matemu, 2013; Gwaunza, 2014; Tauya, 2015 for more details on the ZAMCOM process). We now examine SADC's role in regional water management and also how it has dealt with and negotiated these various tensions.

The role of SADC

It can be argued that coordination and integration of the water sector were achieved in part because of the restructuring within SADC. Early on, each country was assigned a specific sector responsibility. The SADC's water agenda was driven by the Water Sector Coordination Unit (SADC-WSCU), which was set up in 1992 in Maseru, Lesotho. This approach resulted in a situation where countries pursued their own narrow interests within the sector mandate, rather than the collective good of the region (Isaksen, 2004; Söderbaum, 2004). This is why since 2001, SADC operations have been centralised at the SADC Secretariat in Gaborone, Botswana. The SADC-WSCU was dissolved in 2002 and staff relocated to Gaborone in Botswana to become SADC Water Division in the Directorate of Infrastructure and Services, one of the eight directorates.[3]

The SADC Water Division was co-responsible for the implementation of the SADC Protocol on Shared Watercourses, and water issues in the region. A year after the drafting of the 1995 Protocol, SADC decided on the necessity of developing Regional Strategic Action Plans (RSAPs) on Integrated Water Resources Development and Management (IWRM) that would provide direction and detail

3 The logic of placing water with the Directorate of Infrastructure and Services (IS) is not known to us. While housing all Secretariat activities in Botswana allowed for centralised coordination, challenges remained (Tjønneland et al., 2005). Take irrigation for example: It could easily fall in the Directorate of Food, Agriculture and Natural Resources (FANR). But the southern Africa Regional Dialogue on Agriculture found that the intention to use water for irrigation was captured in the Regional Strategic Action Plan on Integrated Water Resources Development and Management. Yet the responsibility of executing this vision rests with the Directorate of Food, Agriculture and Natural Resources. Hence, many of our interviewees lamented that irrigation seemed to fall in the crevices of the two directorates.

with respect to IWRM implementation in the region. The first RSAP was developed with support from the United Nations Development Programme (UNDP) in 1997 (SADC, 1998).[4] Under the auspices of the RSAP a regional water policy was promulgated, which sought to harmonise legal frameworks, served to consolidate policy provisions on water into one single document, and emphasised IWRM as an instrument of peace and reinforcement of regional integration (SADC, 2006). The Regional Water Policy was complemented and supported by a Regional Water Strategy (SADC, 2007).

The emphases of the various RSAPs illustrate the tension between the 'soft' water management issues promoted by donors drawing on IWRM and the 'hard' aspects concerning infrastructure and water resources development that member states favoured. In this regard, it is worth noting that IWRM under the RSAP includes (infrastructure) development, which was a hard-won concession SADC obtained from donors who were intent on the soft issues of IWRM (Swatuk, 2005). There has been what can be called a begrudging mutual acceptance on the part of donors that member countries are interested in 'hard IWRM', which includes infrastructure development.[5]

The first RSAP was all about creating an enabling environment for IWRM. This includes member states introducing water reforms and harmonising their water policies and laws. RSAP II, in addition to committing to creating an enabling environment, also boldly declared an interest in water resources development and not just water management. Infrastructure Development Support was identified as the centrepiece of the plan (SADC, 2005). RSAP III and RSAP IV have followed along similar lines. While it may appear that the move from the managerial and institutional aspects of water management towards a clearer focus on infrastructure development is not adequately supported by a concomitant surge in investments, it is important to bear in mind that RSAPs are supposed to create the enabling framework for infrastructure development. Financing infrastructure is the responsibility of national governments – they have the mandate to mobilise resources through the traditional vehicles such as the World Bank,[6] African Development Bank, and bilateral arrangements. One might however ask what exactly has been achieved by this massive focus on creating an enabling environment and what it means for people on the ground. One of the key authors of the RSAP III said:

> *Of course, we've done a lot of work to create an enabling environment in SADC, to create plans, policies and also build capacity*

4 Since then there has been a steady stream of the action plans, such as RSAP II (2000-2005), RSAP III (2010-2015) (SADC, 2005; SADC, 2010) and RSAP IV (2016-2020) which is about to be published. RSAPs are credited with defining and promoting water-related aspects of Regional Indicative Strategic Development Plan (RISDP), the overall development plan of the region. The RISDP (2015–2020) prioritises industrialisation, infrastructure development, and market integration, alongside security and peace (see Ganetsang, 2016).

5 This is despite the fact that donors have not really committed to financing infrastructure under the auspices of the RSAP.

6 Of course, the World Bank plays a double agent role of promoting IWRM using grants and offers of loans to construct dams etc. The role of China and its Exim Bank in infrastructure development is massive but beyond the focus of this chapter.

> *– but sometimes, I think the criticism is well founded. What is the point of getting locked into policies, plans, reform and building capacity, etc.; if people are still walking five miles for water? In SADC, most focus has been on getting the policy right and, of course, developing the right policies and institutions all take time. In sum, it's been a period of about ten or 15 years that has been used to create an enabling environment, but the time has come to move beyond the enabling phase to get things done on the ground and improve access to water (Interview with one of the RSAP authors, July 2013).*

A GIZ staff member who spent seven years in the region explained the need to focus on both water resources development and management:

> *I agree with the criticism that IWRM can be a distraction from infrastructure development and water resources development. This is why we always made sure that we focused on distinct things in different phases and we also identified infrastructure needs at both the national and regional level and also went around all 15 member States at the level of the utilities. This is why the regional strategic action plans focused on both IWRM and development (Interview, April 2014).*

There is thus an IWRM conundrum in southern Africa – while infrastructure development and particularly storage are regarded as important in a region where water availability is characterised by tremendous variability and where millions still lack access to water, it is not the conventional focus of the IWRM donors, unless the focus is on small infrastructure. Rather it is individual nations that either on their own or in cooperation with other countries fund infrastructure projects. This is illustrated by the fact that all infrastructure development projects are undertaken under the auspices of bilateral arrangements.[7]

There is also the wider political economy of SADC which cannot be underestimated. Due to its dependence on donor funding SADC can often struggle to implement its own priorities, which as outlined earlier, are by no means uniform given the diversity of its member states. Of the SADC funding 79% comes from donors (Ganetsang, 2016) with only 21% coming from member states[8] and one can imagine that much of that funding is spent on personnel, travel and so on, leaving much less for programmatic activities. SADC needs an estimated USD500 million over the next few years to fund the current Regional Indicative Strategic Development Plan (RISDP). There are calls to reduce dependency on donor funding and develop financial sustainability as articulated by the current Chair of SADC, Botswana's President Ian Khama, in August 2015: "While we recognize the support of our international partners, it is necessary for SADC to find other ways of financing our regional agendas" (quoted in Ganetsang, 2016). The next section continues the focus on donor priorities and perspectives.

7 The Lesotho Highlands Project is a good case in point.

8 The level of contribution depends on the size of the economy with South Africa accounting for 20% of the SADC budget, followed by oil-rich Angola (Ganetsang, 2016).

Donor perspectives and projects

In this section, we highlight some of the perspectives held by former and existing, mostly bilateral, donor representatives on the role they played in IWRM roll-out in the region. While this is by no means a comprehensive account of all existing donor-led projects and views, we use this material to offer an insight into how IWRM took on meaning and momentum in the region. As stated earlier, donor presence has been critical in water management in SADC, both around regional-level initiative to guide the reform of policies and laws in national contexts and in the establishment of River Basin Organisations and transboundary programmes. As we now outline, some donors were inspired by water management systems in their own countries and used those ideas in their work; others were starting de novo and were excited about the challenges of working both with national governments and other donors to kick-start new programmes.

In the early 1990s, some donor representatives were seconded to ministries, such as the case for the Germans and Dutch in Zimbabwe (Manzungu and Derman, Chapter 6) and the Dutch in Mozambique (Alba and Bolding, Chapter 9). One of our key informants, a German who worked in Zimbabwe for many years in what was then the National Coordinating Committee for Water, Sanitation and Hygiene remarked that "the Zimbabwean government definitely felt a sense of ownership over the programme; there were not many foreigners in the Ministry working on the policy side of things" (interview, April 2014). He explicitly said that they drew on German experiences, particularly regarding groundwater regimes but did not use the vocabulary of IWRM when working in Zimbabwe.

A Dutch academic who has been in and out of the region since the mid-1990s reflected on the Dutch influence on IWRM and water management in the region (see also Alba and Bolding, Chapter 9).

> *In the good old days before aid was tied, we had fantastic programmes around water supply and river basin organisations. Our experts were seconded to Ministries in African countries. I know some people in the World Bank think that the Dutch have promoted soft options in Africa while building dykes back home. But this is not true. Working under the umbrella of IWRM should not be seen to mean that water resources are not developed. Given all the challenges from climate change and seasonal variation, we need smart ways to enhance storage whilst reducing environmental costs. The Dutch impact in the region through WaterNet has also been immensely successful (Interview, November 2014).*

Some would disagree and contend that IWRM pushed by the donors such as the Dutch in the region has led to the prioritising of environmental and management issues over infrastructure concerns. Other donors like the Danish had more diverse conceptualisations of IWRM. With regard to Danida's role in supporting IWRM in SADC, there seemed to be quite a heated debate within the organisation about what IWRM actually constituted. According to a key informant who was working with Danida at the time:

> *Danida supported IWRM and the SADC regional programme.*

> *However, the problem was that anything that had anything to do with water was considered to be IWRM. It could be irrigation, it could be crop rotation, it could be anything. The broad scope of IWRM led to it having a lot of meaning, it was like a religion, and Torkil [Jønch-Clausen] was one of the preachers (...) He was very stubborn and very pushy. But it was admirable too as he put in a lot of energy and travelled around the world. The bottom line is that you would not have an agenda without such individuals (Interview, April 2013).*

As discussed by others in this book, Torkil Jønch-Clausen emerged as someone who wielded a great deal of influence, both at the Dublin conference itself and also through his work in Uganda in the 1990s (Allouche, Chapter 2; Nicol and Odinga, Chapter 13). Apart from this high-level strategic work, Danida also associated the IWRM concept with local-level livelihood generation projects and initiated a series of IWRM pilot projects in southern Africa (see Movik et al., Chapter 4) that took IWRM to the ground, focusing explicitly on local-level water management issues. This was done together with the International Water Management Institute (IWMI) which has been prominent in advancing a livelihoods and African smallholder perspective on IWRM (see Merrey et al., 2005; Van Koppen, 2007; Merrey, 2008).

The Norwegians, through Norad, had a long history of engagement in water management in southern and Eastern Africa, particularly focusing on drinking water and hydropower schemes. In Tanzania, Norad had been involved in supporting various hydropower schemes such as Kidatu (1979), Mtera (1980) as well as Pangani Falls (1995), largely drawing on their competence from building hydropower at home (see also Van Koppen et al., Chapter 11). According to one of our interviewees, a former Norad employee who now works for the Norwegian Water Resources and Energy Directorate, IWRM was something they had been doing 'all along' (interview, April 2013). Norad was a keen supporter of IWRM until about the end of the 1990s, when political support within Norway for water as a development theme waned.

In contrast, Sweden, through Sida, chose to take an explicitly regional focus in addition to funding some smaller projects, such as catchment councils in Zimbabwe. In 1995, Sida developed a strategy to guide its support for water resources management in the SADC region that emphasised two focal areas. One was competence in building and awareness-raising about the interconnected nature of water resources, and the other area concerned the need for IWRM-infused collaborative governance on shared watercourses as a means to avert potential conflicts (Granit and Johansson, 1995). The strategy states that "to ensure that the needs of all actors are met, integrated management of the drainage basin is the only point of departure for planning water resources utilisation" (Granit and Johansson, 1995: 10, authors' translation) and calls for "neutral support to regional river basin commissions" (ibid: 12). The strategy highlights how the idea of IWRM has developed over a long period of time, drawing attention to the overarching framework for management of shared rivers present in the report of the Helsingfors committee (ibid). The collaboration between three Nordic donors supported the development of the ZACPLAN.

Sweden has had a long-term involvement in water resources management in the SADC region, building on well-established contacts as highlighted by a key informant from Sida based in Harare at the time:

> *There were already well-established networks in the region – it was very dynamic and very supportive.... there were already strong partners present, and a good dialogue. The main focus was on transboundary, rather than national-level IWRM, and there was a lot of activity in the late 1990s and the early 2000s with a lot of buzz and training (Interview, April 2013).*

The Germans through GIZ (then known as GTZ) also focused on transboundary IWRM, in addition to working with national governments. One German key informant worked with SADC on transboundary issues for seven years (interview, April 2014). He helped set up the SADC Water Division in 2006 and was also involved in setting up the SADC Transboundary Water Management programme.[9] The programme had three tiers: macro (SADC); meso (river basin); and micro (national).[10] He also coordinated bilateral and multilateral donor efforts in the water sector in SADC amongst all International Cooperating Partners (ICPs) to monitor who was doing what around IWRM and in which country. All this work took place under the umbrella of IWRM – as he put it "like all other forms of development cooperation, we had to follow the Zeitgeist and the Zeitgeist then was IWRM". He related how the greater part of the GIZ-led programme got its funding from the Australians and the British and how there were a diversity of actors involved – NGOs, private companies as well as RBOs in Africa, Europe and Australia with a lot of cross learning. For example, the ORASECOM was directly influenced by the models followed in the Danube, Rhine and also Mekong cases.

As for multilateral donors, the World Bank exercised a great deal of influence in particular at the national level (see, e.g. Derman and Manzungu for Zimbabwe, and Alba and Bolding for Mozambique, this book). The Bank has long emphasised regional integration in its strategies (SADC-WD et al., 2008; World Bank, 2010) and one outcome of this emphasis was the establishment of the multi-donor trust fund Co-operation for International Waters in Africa (CIWA) in 2011, in partnership with the Nordic donors (Sweden, Denmark, Norway) as well as the Netherlands and the UK. CIWA's focus is on fostering growth, strengthening institutions, and facilitating investments for transboundary water resources management, drawing on the Bank's technical expertise on international waters.

9 This was a GIZ technical cooperation programme between the German Bundesministerium für Wirtschaftliche Zusammenarbeit (BMZ, the German Federal Ministry for Economic Development Cooperation) and SADC.

10 Macro or SADC level; meso at the river basin level inspired by German transboundary river systems, which had successful twinning programmes between southern Africa and Europe; and finally, micro at the national level. When asked, he acknowledged that the 'local' - or community level - was missing from the 'micro' level apart from a few IWRM pilot projects focused at the village level that were led by the Danes. He also said: "In the early days it had been 'a one-man show' with 5 million Euros but when I left it had 10 staff members and a budget eight times bigger".

The African Development Bank (AfDB) has also played a role in promoting IWRM. It launched its IWRM strategy in 2000, and IWRM continues to be emphasised in its long-term strategy (2013-2022). In an independent evaluation of the Bank's policy over a ten-year period (2000-2010), it is stated that though the policy is still relevant, it needs to be updated and adjusted to reflect the new challenges facing the continent, such as climate change, food security and inclusive growth. It appears that the AfDB's focus has very much been on single infrastructure projects, mainly drinking water supply with emphasised issues such as cost recovery and water pricing, a good case in point for which is Harare's water supply reform. When asked whether the emphasis had shifted from water resources management and development to water supply and sanitation, the official said that IWRM was still the guiding principle which allowed donors to (1) integrate water and sanitation rather than just look at water; as well as (2) build capacity and institutional structures in-country; and (3) create better policies and facilitate a water reform process (interview with AfDB official, 1 November 2012).

The impressions we get from the submissions of donor representatives point towards a mixed bag of experiences. Some donors had close bilateral relations with particular countries, having worked, for instance, on water and sanitation and hydropower projects (such as Norad in Tanzania) or being seconded to water ministries as experts, such as the case for the Germans in Zimbabwe and for the Dutch in Mozambique. Many of the Dutch experts seconded to line ministries were there as a result of historical precedent, for reasons of solidarity with Mozambique and Zimbabwe in the anti-apartheid struggle. Some individuals played key roles as 'policy entrepreneurs' spreading the idea of IWRM. Some, such as the Swedes and Germans, chose to work at 'both ends', not only offering support at the national level, but also taking an explicitly regional view of water resources management. This resulted in a split between the national-level IWRM piloting and support projects and the more explicitly regional-level IWRM transboundary approach espoused by UNDP, Sida and GIZ among others. These efforts at transboundary institution-building were often couched in somewhat instrumentalist terms as promoting peacebuilding and reducing the risk of conflicts.

SADC played the role as a conduit for donor funds to set up the various River Basin Commissions as well as coordinating policy and legal reforms. It may be argued that while the early stages of support might have seen more leaning towards the advisory roles and direct government placements, the donor focus has increasingly become centred on SADC as a means of channelling donor funds, regional networks and transboundary commissions. These efforts reflected donor agendas and the prevailing zeitgeist of the times. The next section will explore in greater detail two of the most important regional networks in promoting IWRM, namely the Global Water Partnership (GWP) and the WaterNet.

The role of implementing agents: GWP and Waternet

In 1996, the same year as SADC's WSCU was set up, the Global Water Partnership (GWP) was created. GWP regional networks were established all over the world, one of the more dynamic ones being the Southern African network (GWP-Southern Africa, GWP-SA for short). GWP-SA was established in 2000 and was the first regional branch of GWP in Africa to be launched. In the 1990s, GWP-SA's regional head office was in Harare in Zimbabwe until it was moved to Pretoria in the early 2000s to be hosted by the International Water Management Institute (IWMI). The GWP and its Technical Advisory Committee (TAC) played a key role in incorporating the Dublin principles on IWRM in SADC states and coordinated donor efforts in this area (see Savenije and van der Zaag, 2000).

Among GWP-SA's main activities are the SADC Water Day and the Annual Water Research Symposium, hosted together with the Water Research Fund for Southern Africa (WARFSA) and WaterNet, which also offers training in IWRM (see below). GWP-SA was appointed by SADC as an implementing agent for stakeholder participation and RBOs dialogue under RSAP II. In this way, GWP-SA works closely with the SADC Water Division in supporting regional water-related processes by ensuring stakeholder involvement and raising awareness of the importance of IWRM in regional development.[11] A recent review of GWP (2008) brought to light a number of challenges, including high administrative costs, and the perception that regions are too autonomous and are not seen to follow the recommendations from the Secretariat.

Over the years, GWP-SA has grown rapidly into a regional network of over 350 Partner Organisations that, in turn, have formed a number of Country Water Partnerships (CWP), and 12 out of the 15 SADC countries now have their own CWP. The Partnership enjoys multi-donor support (e.g. from the Swedes, Danes, Germans and Dutch), contributions by governments and voluntary contributions from many partners to ensure a coordinated approach to water management and development.

Apart from mobilising regional and national multi-stakeholder platforms in national development planning processes, identifying IWRM training needs and target groups, and informing IWRM research priorities and policy content, a key activity of the GWP-SA is to provide technical expertise in regional/national water policy development and implementation processes. A key informant at the GWP-SA head office said that:

> *As GWP we advise governments to develop both IWRM plans and also enshrine them in policies; otherwise, it will be left to the whims of the current government. We are only an advisory body and we build the capacity of various members to roll out IWRM and to capture lessons from other countries for learning and sharing. But of course, there are challenges. Developing an IWRM plan*

11 It is also the executing agency for Canadian International Development Agency (CIDA)-funded Partnership for Africa's Water Development (PAWD). PAWD focuses on support to national IWRM frameworks, institutional development of multi-stakeholder national and regional water partnerships and the integration of water into PRSPs (CIDA, 2009).

in isolation of a national institution makes no sense – e.g. a catchment can cross three districts. Small countries do better than larger ones. Zimbabwe was a real success story in the 1990s due to its excellent policies at the catchment level, which however changed in the 2000s due to land reform; otherwise, it would still be the shining star of IWRM (....). In the beginning there was a sense that a Western idea was being rolled out but over time, people moved away from that viewpoint. The World Summit on Sustainable Development (Rio+10) in Johannesburg in 2002 changed that because in southern Africa we made a conscious decision to promote IWRM in the region. Water Ministers also welcomed the principle but it has been more difficult to get agriculture and irrigation ministers on board (Interview, July 2013).

In response to the question whether IWRM was too abstract, the same informant said:

We are criticised for only staying at the planning level and some say we need to move to the ground – but we don't have the resources to help with implementation. The key challenge is the lack of capacity amongst the various stakeholders. Also countries may not have the financial resources to undertake the change. In Botswana, it was only when the Minister of Finance had bought in the idea that things began to take off (Interview, July 2013).

Another key factor in the promotion of IWRM has been the technical and professional training provided by WaterNet, which has the status of a SADC subsidiary institution responsible for IWRM capacity building with a secretariat based at the University of Zimbabwe in the Civil Engineering Department in Harare. The largely Dutch (but also Swedish)-funded network has more than 70 members, most of whom are tertiary-level training institutions. The flagship for WaterNet is the regional IWRM Masters' degree programme. Core modules are offered at the University of Zimbabwe and University of Dar es Salaam with specialisations offered at other SADC institutions.[12] It is thus a quite unique regional programme as institutions offer course modules in which they have comparative strength (see Jonker et al., 2012). WaterNet seeks to "produce sufficient well-trained specialists as well as new type of generalists in water resources (...) expected to constitute the 'middle ground' in integrated water resources development and management" (Jonker et al., 2012: 4227). Between 2003 and 2011, 251 students from 18 African countries graduated with Master's theses on water and many of these are presented at WaterNet conferences (ibid). The Water Research Fund for Southern Africa (WARFSA), which was initially funded by Sida, has complemented WaterNet activities (Krugmann, 2002).[13] Its main objective is very specific to

12 Such as the Polytechnic of Namibia (Water supply and sanitation), the University of the Western Cape in South Africa (Water and society), University of Malawi (Water and environment), University of KwaZulu Natal (GIS and Earth Observation), and University of Botswana (Water and land).

13 This explains the annual symposium dedicated to promoting IWRM in the region and known as the WaterNet/WARFSA/GWP symposium.

IWRM, namely to "promote and facilitate the implementation of multidisciplinary research projects in integrated water resources management in the [SADC] region" (Krugmann, 2002).[14]

Dutch academics have played key roles in the establishment of WaterNet. According to one of them:

> *The Maseru Statement highlighted the need for capacity building in the region. We used this to argue to our then Foreign Minister to justify the creation of WaterNet. In 2000, WaterNet was launched at Victoria Falls by the Prince of Orange, now King [Willem-Alexander]. We decided to focus at the Master's level and offer one integrated degree drawing on different perspectives rather than different disciplines. IWRM appeared to be the easiest way to organise this degree and nobody was against it then. The Prince had been influenced by the Dublin Principles, because he had been there. I consider myself as 'integrated' given my mixed educational background. From the beginning, I've been critical of the concept of IWRM and have always tried to find local equivalents. WaterNet links 65 departments and institutions in southern and eastern Africa. Apart from the Master's degree, it offers a platform for water professionals in the region to get together annually. The journal 'Physics and Chemistry of the Earth' does one special issue every year on southern African water issues and the papers are derived from the symposium. This journal includes 15% of all research on water in southern Africa. Thus, WaterNet has encouraged academics in southern Africa to get on with publishing in an international journal, something they were not encouraged to do earlier (Interview, November 2014).*

Anybody who has attended a WaterNet symposium will agree that it is an inclusive network that encourages and builds research capacity and collaboration between senior and junior researchers who present their research in a collaborative way at the annual meeting. It also serves as an important vehicle to bring policy-makers and researchers together. However, it must be said that the scientific quality varies. IWRM is also used very loosely and rather vaguely for all sessions and papers, be they on hydrology, water quality, water and socio-economic development, climate change, modelling or on gender issues.[15]

There is no doubt that WaterNet and GWP-SA have promoted IWRM in the region and have had a lot of influence reflected in the fact that water laws, policies and institutions have been changed in line with IWRM in many southern African countries. What all this means to poor women and men on the ground will be the

14 An evaluation undertaken in 2002 found positive outcomes such as the involvement of over 100 researchers (including young professionals) and the funding of many important research projects. The evaluation also found little collaboration across the region (only two out of 23 projects had aspects of collaboration with most funding going to Zimbabwe) and not much on the multidisciplinary aspects of IWRM (see Krugmann, 2002).

15 The 16th WaterNet symposium in Mauritius in October 2015 was the first that dropped IWRM from its title - instead, 'water security' figured in the programme heading.

focus of the country chapters in this book.

Discussion

This chapter analysed both policy development and interview material to ask why IWRM became so popular in the southern African region. We have highlighted the role of both formal and informal actors and processes as well as the role of non-State and external actors such as donors who facilitated the spread of IWRM. We have demonstrated that interpretations of IWRM differ in many ways, not least with respect to the role of infrastructure for development within IWRM. Also countries in SADC have approached IWRM in different ways and have progressed in different ways. Generally, however, policy, legislation and strategy are ahead of implementation. Only Zambia and South Africa have made real headway with regard to integrating water planning with broader economic development planning frameworks, and even there, there are challenges in integration as demonstrated in the South African cases in this book.

The regional strategies of the SADC, while first concentrating on 'soft' issues of institutions and policies, have recognised the importance of 'hardware' within the IWRM framework. Infrastructure development is clearly a key regional interest, which explains the inclusion of 'D' in IWRM in SADC documents, which as Swatuk has highlighted, represented a triumph on the part of SADC to ensure that IWRM did not exclude infrastructure development, which donors were not keen on (2005). It is, however ironical that the 'D' is silent because instead of IWRDM, it is IWRM which is emblazoned on SADC documents. This illustrates the delicate negotiations regarding IWRM in the SADC region where there is much dependence on donors. The multiplicity of transboundary river basins in the region has also been very important for the spread of IWRM which also adds yet another layer of complexity. While countries have had to share hydrological information and also cooperate on infrastructure development as in the case of the Orange, Komati and Zambezi basins, all these have been characterised by intense political negotiations. This is why commissions have taken long to come into force as illustrated by events in the Zambezi where it took two decades for ZAMCOM to come into force (see Chanda, 2004; Tauya, 2015). For downstream countries such as Mozambique, the entry point to IWRM was through transboundary concerns (see Alba and Bolding, this book) and IWRM transboundary-style, was driven far more by internal concerns rather than being imposed from outside by donors and regional networks such as the GWP. In contrast, upstream riparian countries did not necessarily share the same interest in cooperation.

While national interests determined how particular trajectories of negotiations played out in specific river basins and in the various national spaces, the role of external actors in the form of bilateral and multilateral donors has been immense. The already extensive collaborative bilateral and multilateral networks existing in the region, partly due to the historical legacies of supporting anti-apartheid and decolonisation struggles, facilitated the activities of the donors in terms of promoting the IWRM message. According to several key informants, it was just a matter of using existing channels to promote a new message rather than forging new grounds of collaboration, which would have been much more time-consuming.

The global shift to neoliberal policies in the water sector from 1992 also chimed well with IWRM roll-out and its emphasis on water permits, licences, etc. The involvement of external agents was further facilitated through the emergence and consolidation of the establishment of a defined political and economic identity through the formation of first the SADCC, and then the SADC. The SADC's explicit aim of engaging donors actively ensured that a vibrant network was established, which created the rudimentary infrastructures and nodes on which other initiatives could piggyback, as several of the informants from donor agencies have highlighted. This facilitated a form of both formal and informal integration, through the establishment of regional networks and nodes that were geared towards promoting water resources management. In a sense then, the SADC could perhaps be viewed as a donor construct that facilitated the spread of a particular discourse on IWRM. Donors also played a key role in reforming water legislations and policies, on creating the 'right' institutions, and building capacity and networks across basins and countries. Many Western water academics, for their part, seem to play a dual role. Despite being very critical of the concept, they are also at times part of the IWRM bandwagon, not least due to the opportunities offered to teaching in Master's programmes and being a part of the WaterNet fraternity (see Bolding and Alba, Chapter 15, for reflections).[16]

While it may be true that the concept was first introduced as something imported from the global north, the impression among many of our interviewees was that it is no longer perceived as an imposed concept. Instead, it has become internalised and is seen as a means of promoting better water management, and overcoming fragmented legislation.

> *The SADC experience shows IWRM can work and has opened the eyes of a lot of people in the region. It's wrong to say that it's just because of donor money. Of course, I am aware that development cooperation has the tendency to lose itself in papers, workshops, etc. If you do this, then there is no meaning at the grassroots. Regardless of the label, it is important to work in a multidisciplinary way and bring in the best people and address the key priorities of the people, member states and local communities. Overall though, we have moved from the early days when we wanted a 'one size fits all kind of solution' to now acknowledging that context matters, i.e. IWRM plans must address the particular country and also need to be relevant (Interview, November 2014).*

Many of the donors as well as southern African policy-makers interviewed also saw IWRM as a set of principles and an approach rather than a blueprint. Despite the many problems associated with the framework, it is still held as a widespread attraction. They also pointed out to the positive spin offs, for example, the increased cooperation on transboundary rivers in the region, the increased accep-

16 For downstream countries such as Mozambique, the entry point to IWRM was through transboundary concerns (see Alba and Bolding, Chapter 9) and IWRM transboundary-style, was driven far more by internal concerns rather than being imposed from outside by donors and regional networks such as the GWP. In contrast, upstream riparian countries did not necessarily share the same interest in cooperation.

tance of interdisciplinary approaches, and generally raising the profile of water in the various countries through reform processes.

However, many interviewees did acknowledge the problems with donor fads:

> *IWRM is still alive and kicking in southern Africa even though it may be dead in Europe with its obsession with Nexus, etc. We are at different levels with Europe. We had a meeting on the nexus, and a politician said – 'we are just grasping IWRM and now you are saying that donors want the nexus! What is the difference? And we haven't even sorted out IWRM as yet!' And of course, we have donors coming to us and saying 'give us a project on the nexus', and because we don't have the money, we have to find one (…) it's the same with climate change (Interview with GWP-SA representative, July 2013).*

The donors we spoke to also echoed similar sentiments: "Everything is now climate change but I still make sure we are still talking about access to water" (interview, April 2014). While donors are moving onto other fads (such as water security, the green economy and so on), one wonders what will come next. Will the region be left to get on with its own concerns, or will it again have to negotiate and make sense of new fashions as they are mediated by donor-recipient relations and regional processes?

A recurrent sentiment among many of our interviewees, both from the GWP, WaterNet, SADC and donors, was the notion that "I wish we could have 30 years to prove ourselves, not just ten". Many other informants say that it's only been about ten years of reform, and that it is too early to say what the on-the-ground impacts are.

Conclusion

In this chapter, we have demonstrated that regional dynamics have played a key role in IWRM's trip from the global level to southern Africa. The particular economic, political and colonial processes outlined in this chapter have led to a kind of path dependency that has shaped both regionalism in southern Africa and also allowed for donor-led initiatives to build on existing networks, some that go back to the anti-apartheid struggle. The geography of 15 river basins facilitated both cooperation amongst member states and attracted donor interventions which drew on the global zeitgeist of neoliberal water policies. National governments, for their part, were no passive spectators but often used IWRM to promote national interests in diverse ways, which often led to a tussle between the 'soft' and 'hard' aspects of IWRM. IWRM caught on in SADC due to the regional processes outlined in this chapter as well as strong donor agendas that were often aligned with existing national interests. While this is partly a story of an externally imposed concepts promoted through donor-funded processes, networks, fads and new and weak institutions propped up by donor money, it is also a story of negotiation and adaptation to accommodate different and, often, diverging interests. Consequently, IWRM has now acquired a life of its own in southern Africa, despite shifting global trends and changing donor interests.

Acknowledgements

We are very grateful to our colleagues in the Flows and Practices project for their stimulating ideas and research which inspired and informed the analysis presented in this chapter and to the Research Council of Norway for their financial support. We would like to thank Alex Bolding and Alan Nicol as well as three anonymous reviewers for their useful comments. We must also sincerely thank all those we interviewed, who are too many to name or whom we leave anonymous. The usual disclaimers apply.

References

Allan, A.J. 2003. IWRM/IRWAM: A new sanctioned discourse? Kings College London. University of London. In *Occasional Papers No. 50*. SOAS Water Issues Study Group. School of Oriental and African Studies. London: University College London.

Asmal, K. and Vale, P. 1999. *Water in southern Africa – The path to community and security*. South Africa. Cited in Mohamed (2003).

Austin, A.; Bochkarev, D. and van der Geest, W. 2008. *Energy interests and alliances: China, America and Africa*. EastWest Institute, Policy Paper 7/2008.

Birmingham, D. 2008. *The decolonization of Africa*. London: Routledge.

Biswas, A.K. 2004. Integrated water resources management: A reassessment. *Water International* 29(2): 248-256.

Bolding, A.; Mollinga, P.P. and Zwarteveen, M. 2000. Interdisciplinarity in research on integrated water resource management: Pitfalls and challenges. Paper presented at the Unesco-Wotro International Working Conference on Water for Society. Delft, the Netherlands, 8-10 November 2000.

Briscoe, J. 1996. Water as an economic good: The idea and what it means in practice. In *Proceeding of the World Congress of the International Commission on Irrigation and Drainage*. Cairo, Egypt: World Bank.

Cardwell, H.; Cole, R.; Cartwright, L. and Martin, L. 2006. Integrated water resources management: Definitions and conceptual musings. *Journal of Contemporary Water Research & Education* 135(1): 8-19.

Chan, S. 2011. *Southern Africa: Old treacheries and new deceits*. London: Yale University Press.

Chanda, A. 2004. Zambia delays signing as it seeks national consensus. www.sardc.net/en/ southern-african-news-features/zambia-delays-signing-zamcom-as-it-seeks-national-consensus/ (accessed 30 July 2016)

CIDA (Canadian International Development Agency). 2009. *Canada's role in the creation of the World Water Council*. Ottawa: Canadian International Development Agency.

Evans, M. 1986. *The front-line states, South Africa and Southern African security: Military prospects and perspectives* (Vol. 474). Harare: University of Zimbabwe.

Ganetsang, G. 2016. Funding headache for SADC. Sunday Standard, March 3, 2016.

www.sundaystandard.info/funding-headache-sadc (accessed August 2016)

Gibb, R. 2009. Regional integration and Africa's development trajectory: Meta-theories, expectations and reality. *Third World Quarterly* 30(4): 701-721.

Gieryn, T.F. 1999. *Cultural boundaries of science: Credibility on the line.* Chicago: University of Chicago Press.

Granit, J. 2000. *Swedish experiences from transboundary water resources management in southern Africa.* Publications on Water Resources No. 17. Stockholm: Swedish International Development Agency (Sida).

Granit, J. and Johansson, B. 1995. *Vattenresurser i Södra Afrika (SADC).* Rapportert kring vattenresurser nr. 2. Stockholm: Sida.

Gwaunza, M. 2014. Parly approves hosting of ZAMCOM. www.bh24.co.zw/parly-approves-hosting-of-zamcom/ (accessed 30 July 2016)

Hopper, B. 2006. Integrated water resources management: Governance, best practice, and research challenges. *Journal of Contemporary Water Research and Education* 135(1): 1-7.

Isaksen, J. 2004. *SADC in 2003: Restructuring and progress in regional integration.* CMI report series 2004: 3. Bergen: Christian Michelsens Institute.

Jonker, L.; van der Zaag, P.; Gumbo, B.; Rockstrom, J.; Love, D. and Savenije, H.H.G. 2012. A regional and multi-faceted approach to postgraduate water education: The WaterNet experience in southern Africa. *Hydrology and Earth System Sciences* 16(11): 4225-2012.

Krugmann, H. 2002. Water research fund for southern Africa (WARSA): Project evaluation. Sida Evaluation 02/2002.

Langeland, O. 2012. Regioner og regionalisering. In Hanssen, G.S.; Klausen, J.E. and Langeland, O. (Eds), *Det regionale Norge 1950 til 2050*, pp. 25-39. Oslo: Abstrakt forlag.

Mandaza, I.; Tostensen, A. and Maphanyane, E.M. 1994. Southern Africa. *In Search of a common future: From the conference to a community.* Gaborone, Botswana: SADC.

Mapuva, J. 2015. Skewed rural development policies and economic malaise in Zimbabwe. *African Journal of History and Culture* 7(7): 142-151.

Matemu, S.A. 2013. First workshop on river basin commissions and other joint water bodies for transboundary water cooperation: Legal and institutional aspects, 23-24 September, Geneva, Switzerland. www.unece.org/fileadmin/DAM/env/water/meetings/jointbodies/presentations/ 3.2.twm_presentation_geneva_sept.pdf (accessed 30 July 201)

Mehta, L.; Alba, R.; Bolding, A.; Denby, K.; Derman, B.; Hove, T.; Manzungu, E.; Movik, S.; Prabhakaran, P. and Van Koppen, B. 2014. The politics of IWRM in southern Africa. *International Journal of Water Resources Development* 30(3): 528-542.

Meierding, E. 2011. Energy security and sub-Saharan Africa. International Development Policy [Online] 2 (2011). http://poldev.revues.org/744 (accessed on 23 November 2015)

Merrey, D.J.; Drechsel, P.; Penning de Vries, P. and Sally. H. 2005. Integrating "livelihoods" into integrated water resource management: Taking integration paradigm to its logical next step for developing countries. *Regional and Environmental Change* 5(4): 197-204.

Merrey, D.J. 2008. Is normative integrated water resources management implementable? Charting a practical course with lessons from southern Africa. *Physics and Chemistry of the Earth Parts A/B/C* 33(8-13):899-905.

Merrey, J.D. 2009. African models for transnational river basin organisations in Africa: An unexplored dimension. *Water Alternatives* 2(2): 183-204.

Mohamed, A.E. 2003. *Joint development and cooperation in international water resources.* International Waters in Southern Africa, pp. 209-247. Tokyo [ua]: United Nations University Press (Water resources management and policy series).

Molle, F. 2008. Nirvana concepts, narratives and policy models: Insight from the water sector. *Water Alternatives* 1(1): 131-156.

Molle, F.; Mollinga, P.P. and Wester, P. 2009. Hydraulic bureaucracies: Flows of water, flows of power. *Water Alternatives* 2(3): 328.

SADC (Southern African Development Community). 1998. *Regional strategic action plan on integrated water resources development and management, 2.* Gaborone, Botswana: SADC.

SADC. 2000. *Revised protocol on shared watercourses.* Namibia: Windhoek.

SADC. 2005. *Regional strategic action plan on integrated water resources development and management.* Annotated strategic plan, 2005-2010. Supported by United Nations Development Programme (UNDP) and European Union (EU). Gaborone, Botswana: SADC.

SADC. 2006. *Regional water policy.* Gaborone, Botswana: SADC.

SADC. 2007. *Regional water strategy.* Supported by Belgian Development Cooperation, InWEnt and GWP southern Africa. Gaborone, Botswana: SADC.

SADC. 2010. *Regional strategic action plan on integrated water resources development and management, 2.* Gaborone, Botswana: SADC.

SADC-Water Division, Zambezi River Authority, Swedish International Agency for Development, Danish International Development Assistance, Norwegian Embassy (Lusaka). 2008. *Integrated water resources management strategy and implementation plan for the Zambezi river basin.* Lusaka, Zambia.

Savenije, H.H.G. and van der Zaag, P. 2000. Conceptual framework for the management of shared river basins; with special reference to the SADC and EU. *Water Policy* 2(1-2): 9-45.

Söderbaum, F. 2004. *The political economy of regionalism: The case of southern Africa.* New York: Palgrave Macmillan.

Swatuk, L.A. 2008. A political economy of water in southern Africa. *Water Alternatives* 1(1): 24-47.

Swatuk, L.A. 2005. Geographies of cooperation: Water resources management in sub-Saharan Africa. Paper prepared for presentation at the 6th WaterNET/Warfsa meeting, Mbabane, Swaziland, November 2005.

Tauya, E. 2015. The ZAMCOM process, a worthwhile journey. www.sardc.net/en/southern-african-news-features/the-zamcom-process-a-worthwhile-journey/ (accessed 30 July 2016)

Tjønneland, E.N.; Isaksen, J. and Le Pere, G. 2005. SADC's restructuring and emerging policies. Options for Norwegian Support. In *CMI Report R 2005: 7*. Bergen: Christian Michelsens Institute.

Turton, A.; Meissner, R.; Mampane, P.M. and Seremo, O. 2004. A hydropolitical history of South Africa's international river basins. In *WRC report 1220/1/04*. Pretoria: AWIRU, University of Pretoria.

van Koppen, B. 2007. Dispossession at the interface of community-based water law and permit systems. In van Koppen, B.; Giordano, M. and Butterworth, J. (Eds), *Community-based water law and water resource management reform in developing countries*, pp. 46-64. Wallingford, UK: CABI.

Waterbury, J. 1979. *The hydropolitics of the Nile Basin*. Syracuse: Syracuse University Press.

Whitfield, L. and Fraser, A. 2009. Introduction: Aid and sovereignty. In Whitfield, L. (Ed), *The politics of aid: African strategies for dealing with donors*, pp. 1-26. Oxford: Oxford University Press.

World Bank. 1993. *Water resources management: A World Bank policy paper*. Washington, DC: The World Bank.

World Bank. 2010. *The Zambezi River Basin: A multi sector investment opportunities analysis*. Summary Report, Vol. 1. Washington, DC: World Bank.

Appendix 1: IWRM timeline

The timeline contains the key dates for some global key events, regional policy and strategies, as well as a selected overview of some key policies and laws from the countries studied in this book.

Period	Activity	Who/What
1950s	Hydraulic mission (e.g. building of Kariba)	National governments and colonial administrations
1960s	Independence struggles and Cold War by proxy	
1970s	Commission report in South Africa	
1980s	SADCC created	
	Start of Structural Adjustment Programmes	
	Start of Drinking Water Supply and Sanitation Decade	
1991	Mozambique: Lei de Agua	

Period	Activity	Who/What
1992	ICWE Dublin Conference	
	UN Conference on Environment and Development Rio Earth Summit	
	The SADCC becomes the SADC	
1993	World Bank Water Resources Strategy	
	World Bank Meeting Victoria Falls	
1994	Lake Victoria Environmental Management Programme (LVEMP)	
1995	Protocol on Shared Watercourses in SADC region	
	Uganda Water Statute	
	Sida Water Strategy	
1996	SADC sets up WSCUs – Water Sector Coordination Units	Set up in Maseru, Lesotho, but then moved to Gaborone, Botswana in 2002
	Council of Water Ministers decides to draw up fist Regional Strategic Plan	Each country asked to come up with national situation report – SADC's development partners financed several of these studies. Funded by UNDP
	Global Water Partnership (GWP) created	
	Initiation of CapNet	
1997	EU-SADC Conference on Shared River Basins, Maseru, May 1997.	UNDP support.
	UN Convention on non-navigational uses of watercourses	
	South Africa Water Services Act	
	Uganda Water Act	
	1st World Water Forum	
1998	South Africa National Water Act	
	Zimbabwe Water Act	
	(UNDP Roundtable in Geneva)	
1999	Expert workshop in Maseru	
	First SADC (Water Division) Regional Strategic Action Plan I (1999-2004)	
	WSRG formed at the initiative of UNDP	

Period	Activity	Who/What
2000	WaterNet and WARFSA created	
	GWP-Southern Africa (GWPSA) launched, 1st regional arm of GWP	
	1st WaterNet/WARFSA/GWPSA symposium	
	Revised Protocol on Shared Watercourses in SADC region	
	AfDB published IWRM strategy	
	2nd World Water Forum – World Water Vision	
2001	DANIDA water strategy	
2002	World Summit on Sustainable Development held in Johannesburg	Renewed commitment to IWRM and agreement that countries should draft national IWRM plans
	CapNet launched	Integrated water resources management and water efficiency plans by 2005
2003	IWRM figures as key issue in World Water Forum (and river basin management)	
	Revised Protocol enters into force	
2004	South Africa: 1st National Water Resources Strategy (NWRS) published	
2005	SADC Regional Water Policy	
	RSAP II	
2008	Conference on IWRM in South Africa	
	GWP assessment of IWRM status and progress in SADC	
2009	Tanzania Water Resources Management Act	
2011	CIWA established	The Cooperation in International Waters in Africa (CIWA) is a multi-donor trust fund established in 2011 and represents a partnership between the World Bank and the governments of Denmark, Norway, Sweden, the Netherlands, and the United Kingdom
	RSAP III	3rd RSAP emphasised and groundwater management

Appendix 2. Timeline of transboundary river commissions, authorities and agencies

1969	Kunene Permanent Joint Technical Commission (PJTC)	
1983	Inco-Maputo Tripartite Permanent Technical Committee	The Tripartite Permanent Technical Committee (TPTC) was established in 1983 and is collaboration between three SADC member states namely, South Africa, Mozambique and Swaziland. The committee manages the water flow of the Inkomati River and Maputo River specifically during times of drought and flood, and for recommending measures to protect and develop these water resources.
1994	The Permanent Okavango River Basin Water Commission (OKACOM) agreement signed	Sida heavily involved (through The Every River Has Its People Project).
1999	International Commission of Congo-Oubangui-Sangha (CICOS)	AfDB
2000	ORASECOM signed	Danube, Rhine, Mekong as models. GTZ heavily involved.
2003	LIMCOM	
	Botswana, Mozambique, South Africa and Zimbabwe,	
2004	ZAMCOM agreement signed	ZAMCOM IWRM strategy supported by Norad, Danida and Sida
2008	Lake Tanganyika Authority	UNDP

4

Emergence, Interpretations and Translations of IWRM in South Africa[1]

Synne Movik

Lyla Mehta

Barbara van Koppen

Kristi Denby

ABSTRACT: South Africa is often regarded to be at the forefront of water reform, based on Integrated Water Resources Management (IWRM) ideas. This chapter explores how the idea of IWRM emerged in South Africa, its key debates and interpretations and how it has been translated. It maps out the history, main events, key people, and implementation efforts through a combination of reviews of available documents and in-depth semi-structured interviews with key actors. While South Africa sought to draw on experiences from abroad when drawing up its new legislation towards the end of the 1990s, the seeds of IWRM were already present since the 1970s. What emerges is a picture of multiple efforts to get IWRM to 'work' in the South African context, but these efforts failed to take sufficient account of the South African history of deep structural inequalities, the legacy of the hydraulic mission, and the slowness of water reallocation to redress past injustices. The emphasis on institutional structures being aligned with hydrological boundaries has formed a major part of how IWRM has been interpreted and conceptualised, and it has turned out to become a protracted power struggle reflecting the tensions between centralised and decentralised management.

KEYWORDS: IWRM, interpretations, institutions, historical legacies, South Africa

Introduction

Integrated Water Resources Management (IWRM) has been the dominant water management paradigm since the 1990s emerging out of the recognition of the dysfunctions of sectoral approaches to water management (GWP, 2000; Jonker,

1 First published in *Water Alternatives* 9(3): 458-474.

2007; Molle, 2008). Still, as argued by the authors in this book, there is a lot of ambiguity around what IWRM actually is and how it should be interpreted and practised (cf. Mehta et al., Chapter 1). It is a 'boundary concept' (Gieryn, 1999), as it offers something for everyone. How does such an influential idea emerge and get a foothold? How does it continue to hold sway over people in widely different geographical and political contexts? Tracing the emergence and spread of IWRM is as much an exercise in the history of ideas as it is in understanding trends in water management (see Mehta et al., Chapter 1, Allouche, Chapter 2).

This chapter explores how the idea of IWRM emerged in South Africa, the key debates and interpretations and how it has been translated. It maps out the history, main events, key people, and implementation efforts. South Africa was in the vanguard of water policy and practice in the 1990s and underwent its own reform of the water sector as part of the wider political changes after 1994. Its constitution was one of the first to recognise the human right to water and food (RSA, 1996: section 27 (b); Gleick, 1998). The translation of the constitution into water policy was executed by key South African thinkers, drawing on the advice and expertise of international experts. South Africa holds a unique position in African and global water management for a variety of reasons. These include its size, progressive constitution and water policies, the nature of inequality, interactions of race, class and historical legacies, and also institutional reform processes such as decentralisation and catchment management agencies. These reasons coupled with the fact that the National Water Act of 1998 as well as the 1997 White Paper not only wholeheartedly embrace an IWRM approach (see also Denby et al., Chapter 5) but are some of the most progressive water policies in the world, making South Africa an interesting case to explore in IWRM terms.

While there have been many papers written about IWRM in South Africa (e.g. Jonker, 2007; Funke et al., 2007; Goldin et al., 2008) most of them tend to be case studies looking at specific localities, or analysing particular dimensions of IWRM. This chapter, in contrast, seeks to understand the life of the idea of IWRM at different sites and scales in the country. The main question that we explore is how (and by whom) IWRM was brought in and conceptualised in the South African policy, legislation and implementation? In particular, we focus on the main debates around catchment management, and how these have been translated into practice. These questions were addressed by studying the actors and key policy events that were associated with the introduction of IWRM in South Africa. This involves mapping the existing literature on the subject, including grey material and unpublished documents, and doing in-depth interviews with key people who have played active roles in the process of propagating IWRM in South Africa. A particular emphasis is placed on understanding the institutional ramifications of IWRM, and how the ideas have targeted the institutional landscape that forms the backbone of South African water management.

How IWRM emerged in South Africa: The 1998 National Water Act Foundations

In order to appreciate South Africa's water governance, it is necessary to understand its unique position in historical and political economy terms. South Africa has had a multiplicity of governance forms through the course of its history – tribal kingdoms, the Dutch East India Company, the British Empire, the Union of South Africa, and the apartheid and post-apartheid republics, representing the whole gamut from authoritarian, semi-authoritarian and democratic state forms. Over time, water policy, law and institutions came to reflect the increasingly complex needs of multiple actors represented by different political regimes. A common feature has been the central role of the state (Swatuk, 2008).

The Union State played a particularly important role in terms of investing in large-scale infrastructure development to boost white agriculture in what was the South African version of the 'hydraulic mission'. The needs of urban areas and mines were mainly catered to through the financial investments of the mining houses, or self-financed by local municipalities, mainly targeted towards white communities, while neglecting the needs of the black majority (Turton and Henwood, 2002; Turton et al., 2004; Schreiner and Hassan, 2011). Interbasin transfers were an integral part of the hydraulic mission, but the ecological and social implications of such schemes have not been sufficiently addressed (Snaddon et al., 1998; Gupta and van der Zaag, 2008; see also Movik et al., Chapter 3). What the hydraulic mission represented was an effort at gaining control over the water resources, a control that was vested in the hands of the white minority, leaving the black population with no control at all. This is reflected in the distribution of water use, as registered in the Water Authorisation and Registration Management System database. In rural areas, 1.2% of the people use 95% of the water. The other 98.8%, most of whom depend on agriculture-based livelihoods, access only 5% of the water. This corresponds to a Gini coefficient of 0.99 (Cullis and van Koppen, 2008).

In addition to the investments in water infrastructure engineering, there was the grand-scale social engineering experiment set in motion, accelerated by the National Party once it came to power in 1948, to create a country neatly divided into segregated 'homelands' for the indigenous populations in order to foster what was euphemistically termed 'segregated development' (Terreblanche, 2002). The process of creating such homelands meant uprooting more than 3.5 million people, forcibly splitting up families and clans and resettling them in marginal areas with poor soils (Platzy and Walker, 1985; Levin and Weiner, 1997). The apartheid era efforts at carving up the country according to skin hues, ethnicity and race are still visible in modern day South Africa. The former homelands are very much part of the landscape – for example, in the area where the former homeland of KaNgwane used to be, now part of Mpumalanga, cattle grids mark subtle boundaries between former homeland territories and commercial farmlands. Despite post-1994 efforts to get rid of homeland legacies, systems established during colonialism and apartheid have not been done away with (King, 2005). People are still residing in overcrowded areas as a result of a staggeringly skewed land distribution. As Hall (2004: 219) notes, "the extent of land dispossession in colonial and apartheid South Africa dwarfs that of other southern African states". Inequitable land access also inevitably shapes access to water – in the Olifants Basin, for instance, 95% of the water was in the hands of white farmers and miners (Cullis and van Koppen, 2007).

The 1956 Water Act was associated with a patchwork of institutional, legal and regulatory arrangements emanating from the Act and its many amendments. A central tenet was the riparian doctrine – i.e. that water rights were appurtenant to owning land along a river – while groundwater was considered private property. Under the Apartheid regime, the homelands were supposed to become self-governing states, but only four accepted self-governance. Only one, Bophuthatswana, had its own water law. In the other homelands the republic's law was still valid.

Late in the 1960s, the Apartheid Government became increasingly concerned about water scarcity and pollution and a Commission of Enquiry into Water Matters was set up to address the issues. In 1970, the Commission Report was published, introducing a range of ideas that resembled the later concept of IWRM. It recognised water pricing, the environment as an important user in its own right, and launched the concept of wastewater discharges to mitigate pollution from industries and mines, and also promoted the idea of 'catchment committees'. Moreover, there were permits for forestry and arrangements to compensate for negatively affected downstream water users (van Koppen and Schreiner, 2014).

After a couple of decades of political turbulence, the early 1990s offered a more optimistic outlook, and in 1994 came the major transition from the apartheid republic to a democratic state. The country went from being an isolationist siege economy to a nonracial democracy and a global world player (Terreblanche, 2002). The political transition warranted a new water law to translate the new constitution in the water field. This also opened up space for reform that had been initiated by the Apartheid government. The policy networks that formed around the time of the drafting process were characterised by a set of strong personalities. Kader Asmal was a powerful figure, who emphasised the human rights aspect of water, fittingly enough with a background as a human rights lawyer. The White Paper of 1997 set out the principles of the water reform (RSA, 1997). In 1997, the Water Services Act was passed, followed a year later by the 1998 National Water Act (NWA). As there were major political reforms taking place at the same time as the water reform process was unfolding, there was a critical mass in terms of redrawing the maps and doing a systematic institutional design exercise, including bringing to life the IWRM idea of basin institutions. But it also meant major overhauls of the government administration, with the rolling out of new local municipalities to replace the old structures of apartheid. It was going to take some time before the local municipalities would be able to shoulder their new responsibilities. In the meantime, therefore, the Department of Water Affairs and Forestry (DWAF) was given the responsibility of tackling backlogs in domestic water supplies until local government structures were fully operational (Eales, 2011).

The drafting of the Act was done by a team of South Africans, led by Minister

Kader Asmal, with extensive public participation. A number of international experts were also invited to share their experiences with water reform, from FAO and countries like Zimbabwe, Australia, Namibia, the US, Finland (as donor), the UK, France and other European countries, New Zealand and Mexico. However, donor influence was not considered to be massive, as expressed by a water specialist working in a donor agency in Pretoria: "I would struggle to think that IWRM is externally imposed in South Africa; in other African countries where water ministries were set up by donors about 15 years ago, that may be the case; but not in South Africa" (Interview, April 2014).

In terms of creating the new legislation, water professionals across the world considered South Africa to be ahead of the game in many respects, particularly relating to the human right to adequate drinking water as enshrined in the Constitution, and the concept of the 'Reserve'. The Reserve basically entailed setting aside a certain amount of water in-stream, in order to be able to meet basic human and ecological needs. This further expanded on the notion of environmental needs that were already on the agenda in the 1970s Commission Report. Some environmentalists thought that if you take care of the environment, including wetlands and biodiversity, this would also help alleviate poverty.[2] The influence of the environmentalists in the drafting process remained so strong that some argue that the NWA was 'hijacked' by environmentalists (De Coning, 2006; Movik, 2012; Muller, 2014). The National Water Act also shifted to a nationwide licensing system for new water uptake, while recognising the apartheid era's highly unequal Existing Lawful Uses as continuing to be lawful until a process of area-wide compulsory licensing was complete.

A key aspect of the NWA was the emphasis on redressing past inequalities. It was recognised that the NWA itself did not provide sufficient detail on how to go about achieving a more equitable distribution, and hence the Water Allocation Reform (WAR) process was set in motion in 2003, resulting in the publication of the WAR position paper in 2006, which was later revised in 2008. However, very little progress has been made with respect to reallocation, due both to political and technical issues, and the emergence of particular 'allocation discourses' which emphasised the risks of redistribution (see Movik, 2012).

These trends need to be seen in the context of larger political changes and ideological struggles. From the early post-1994 days, South Africa's water sector was caught in an ideological struggle with respect to rights-based approaches embedded in the Reconstruction and Development Policy (RDP). Dealing with the backlog in water services formed a key component of the RDP, while in all other domains cost-recovery aims prevailed in line with the institutional recommendations of development banks and some donors. This has been a contested issue plaguing the water sector, and compromising issues of access to water (Mehta and Ntshona, 2004; Eales, 2011; Dugard, 2012). The African National Congress (ANC) governing party since 1994, underwent a radical change from a socialist development discourse to a neoliberal consensus; from growth through redistribution and meeting basic needs, to redistribution through growth achieved

2 Interview with member of water law drafting team, 22 April 2013.

through neoliberal expert orientation (Peet, 2007). The Growth, Employment and Redistribution (GEAR) policy was a strategy that endorsed liberalism and deregulation, and by implication a scaled-down role for the State (Villa-Vicencio and Ngesi, 2003). In particular, the deregulation of the agricultural sector meant that there was a shift towards more high-value commercial crops, which according to Hall (2004) served to increase the gap between 'winners' and 'losers'.

Another phenomenon that unfolded during this period was the veritable 'brain drain' from a number of departments. The Department of Water Affairs and Forestry lost many of its most experienced and senior staff, who chose to start afresh in the consultancy sector rather than stay with a job they found increasingly frustrating.[3]

Interpretations of IWRM: Debating what should be integrated and how?

Having thus set the scene in terms of the South African water governance context, we now move on to look at the idea of IWRM in more detail and how it was interpreted in different settings and at different levels. In 1997, a workshop was organised to present case studies and lessons from other countries, including Mexico, France, Australia, Britain, Malaysia, India and Zimbabwe. Australia constituted an important source of influence during the drafting of the National Water Act, as it was argued that it was very similar to South Africa in geophysical terms. According to one member of the drafting team, the model of Catchment Management Agencies (CMA) was drawn from Australia.[4] While the term IWRM is not mentioned explicitly in the NWA itself, the ideas associated with IWRM are clearly present.

> *Our whole National Water Act is, as far as I'm concerned, about IWRM. It is all about local institutions and getting people involved and it is also about balancing environment, social and development aspects of water. All this is IWRM. Biswas and others say that IWRM is not workable in South Africa. But it is no blueprint. It should be interpreted as best practice and something to work towards. We can take what suits us in South Africa; it comes from our White Paper, from Rio and from South African democracy (Interview with water department official, July 2013).*

However, how IWRM should be interpreted was clearly a matter of debate. The Water Research Commission, which is an important knowledge hub on water governance in South Africa, saw itself as playing a key role in shaping the understanding of IWRM. The Commission was established in 1971 and is South Africa's major think tank on national water issues and has initiated numerous research projects with IWRM as the main theme. According to several informants within the Water Research Commission (WRC), it was the WRC that brought IWRM to South Africa early in the 1990s.[5]

3 Personal communication with water consultant, 17 July 2013.

4 Interview with WRC (Water Research Commission), 10 August 2006.

5 Interview with WRC, 16 July 2013.

> *IWRM was en vogue internationally then – it was intellectually appealing to many of us in South Africa who were agonising and debating about similar issues. We had a charismatic Minister and a progressive government then and having outsiders endorse new policies etc. which boded well for the time. Progressive South African thinkers thought this was the best practice of the time (Interview with WRC, July 2013).*

Early on, officials and the people at the WRC spent a lot of time debating and trying to define what IWRM was. It started off with Integrated Catchment Management (ICM), and then this evolved into Integrated Water Resources Management. However, it was unclear what was meant by 'integration'. For instance, one issue was whether or not water resources and water services should be integrated, which did not occur. The operational elements of water services were ring-fenced into a separate Act. This in turn gave rise to an institutional set-up that separated the water services aspect from the water resources, where Europe pushed the IWRM bit, and America and the World Bank pushed the water services sector. The fact that two Acts were created was influenced by the then Director-General's opinions on the distinction that needed to be made between water in pipes and water as a resource. He referred to the Constitution, which makes this distinction. However, there was no consensus with respect to such a division, and some people argued that there was "no proper integration which is what IWRM calls for" (Interview, June 2013). The related institutional mandates were debated as well. One key informant argued that the department did not have the capacity to implement water services. Moreover, the ANC wanted to bring the government closer to the people, and hence the responsibility for service delivery was vested in local governments. The problem with local governments is that they are often quite cash-strapped and lacking in capacity. Provincial governments are supposed to deal with noncompliance regarding service delivery but "they have no clue" (Interview with water official in Pretoria, June 2013). DWA cannot implement directly because the national government cannot normally intervene locally. Another issue relating to integration was the initial lack of coordination between the land and water reforms, which meant that the debates about integration within the water realm, and in particular water allocation, did not link up to the political processes playing out with respect to land reform (Movik, 2012: 120; see also Denby, 2013; Denby et al., Chapter 5).

The first National Water Resources Strategy (NWRS), which was published in 2004, draws on the Global Water Partnership (GWP) definition of IWRM and states the importance of linking domestic water use/needs, sanitation and health issues to IWRM. The necessity of integrating local planning instruments, such as the Integrated Development Plan (IDP) with water supply and sanitation services is also underscored by Pollard and Du Toit (2008).

> *Even though our Water Act is all-encompassing, we have these two separate legislations (...) there was always a discussion in terms of IWRM, with respect to the separation into resources and services – there was a white paper for resources, and a separate one for*

> *water supply, which I think was too compartmentalised (...). There were research reports written on 'how to integrate', and the perennial question was – what are we trying to integrate, is it vertical, is it horizontal – what would perfect integration look like? (Interview with WRC, July 2013).*

According to the WRC informants, when the principle of IWRM was 'sort of established', it seemed a little bit too idealistic – in the sense that it did not really acknowledge the context. For instance, in South Africa the whole system is based on interbasin transfers, there are some 375 interbasin schemes across the country, and if half of the water is transported out of the basin in seven of the nine provinces, the question arises – what then is left to deal with? Because the South African system is so complex, it makes trying to adopt IWRM principles very complex too. Basically, it is an engineered system that one wants to transform into a people-centric basin management system. Still, as one of the interviewees said, "in the beginning it was so clear, it was just so clear that with the subsidiarity principle (...) you have layers of authority; you had a clear comprehensive picture of what the landscape would look like" (Interview, July 2013), adding that this was probably naïve. An important point was that the CMAs needed enough revenue and autonomy to do their job. The challenge consisted of figuring out the layers of hydrological boundaries and administrative boundaries, which were largely translated in planning instruments such as the Integrated Development Plans created bottom-up by the municipalities. Implementing IWRM was first and foremost a concern with getting the institutional set-up right.[6]

Parallel with the focus on services, environmental concerns were a key issue on the agenda as well. One adviser to the water law review team pointed out that research in the Kruger National Park in the 1970s raised concerns over the fact that the perennial Sabie River was drying up, and an emerging issue was how to deal with this. The idea of creating environmental rights surfaced already at an early stage as well.[7] The emphasis on determining what the Ecological Reserve should be in each basin was a major contributor to the licensing and the process of Water Allocation Reform (Movik, 2012), as it is so difficult to determine what it should be and close to impossible to monitor (Bourblanc, 2015).

These diverse understandings and implications of IWRM are reflected in the following quote:

> *IWRM makes sure that decision making integrates services and management issues, i.e. demand side and also how to deal with growing water services and delivery. It also highlights the need to 'value' the resource and conserve. It helps to go against silo thinking and facilitates joint planning. Of course, it is a mantra like gender. But whether departments actually work together and integrate is another matter. I would hate to dismiss it totally but not sure it is actually happening (Interview, April 2014).*

While the WRC's understanding of IWRM seemed to follow the conventional

6 Interview with WRC, 17 July 2013.

7 Interview with water law drafting team adviser, 22 April 2014.

ideas around basin management and grappling with the question of institutional integration at the national and regional levels, another version of IWRM was pursued by a donor-initiated 'pilot' exercise led by Danida. As part of a five-country pilot project on IWRM, it launched a project in three provinces in South Africa in 2000, the Crocodile West-Marico in the Northwest Province, the Mvoti to Mzimkulu in KwaZulu-Natal and the Olifants-Doorn in the Western Cape Province. The basic idea of the Danida IWRM pilot projects was an interpretation of IWRM as being about participatory bottom-up water management; about local people's access to water for livelihoods. Hence, the projects focused on small-scale water users – farmers and other small nonagricultural users – in the three regions. The programme was run in partnership with the Department of Water Affairs (DWA), the South African Local Government Association (SALGA) and aimed to support the creation of CMAs in the regions. The project used donor funds to 'do things differently rather than to do more of the same'. The focus was on poverty reduction and on using IWRM to achieve the MDGs. However, the approach was controversial. One of the people who had been involved in the project talked about how Danida's strategies in the first five to six years tended to focus on IWRM strategies at the national level, which he called 'paper stuff'. He felt it was too vague, and that one needed to take IWRM 'to the ground' and to try to help people with real water problems in their villages, which is what Danida then did. The idea was to address local people's water needs holistically without separating domestic and irrigation needs, which is conventionally the case. The project also sought to consider both the social and economic factors involved, assess whatever infrastructure was needed, and undertake the necessary steps and include everything related to water. That, essentially, was taking a bottom-up holistic approach. The main desire was to leave the national-level strategies and get to the real problems, whilst still acknowledging the need for strategies as such.

A similar 'livelihoods-based' approach to IWRM was pursued by a research programme organised by WaterNet,[8] in cooperation with UNESCO-Delft and the Consultative Group of International Research (CGIAR) Challenge Program on Water and Food in the Olifants catchment in South Africa. It focused on improving rural livelihoods and interpreting 'integration' to mean better integration of 'green' and 'blue' water, and arguing for a "new IWRM-based water governance from village to basin scale" (Love et al., 2004: 1). The idea was to develop guidelines for catchment management and scale it up to a needs-based IWRM framework for sustainable water for food development at the basin scale. Though the approach is a bottom-up, needs-based and livelihoods-centred one, the idea of the 'basin scale' is still very much present there as well.

Indeed, the idea of basin-scale management emerges as a central feature in the South African discourse on IWRM. The concept of Catchment Management Agencies (CMAs) is seen to provide an arena for stakeholder participation and negotiations. Anderson (2005) outlines ways in which historically disadvantaged

8 Southern African regional network for academic capacity building on IWRM. WaterNet established a node in Western Cape University and, from 2009 onwards, a chair in IWRM. Two of the yearly symposia were held in South Africa (see Movik et al., Chapter 3 for a detailed analysis of WaterNet).

individuals can be engaged in CMA planning processes, using the Inkomati Water Management Area as a case study. She argues that "a key criterion for successful IWRM should be the degree to which the approach empowers disadvantaged and marginalised communities" (Anderson, 2005: 1). She highlights the challenges of legitimate representation, accessibility, information/communication and the challenges of arriving at a shared consensus in a context of power imbalances. Pollard and Du Toit (2011) pick up on the latter issue, highlighting the challenges inherent in having a diverse array of stakeholders, to arrive at a shared vision of how water will be used in a specific hydrological region. They argue for the usefulness of what they call 'mental models' in order to overcome the differences in understandings and meanings among stakeholders in a context of ongoing power struggles.

CREATING INSTITUTIONS ACCORDING TO HYDROLOGICAL BOUNDARIES

Problems with creating CMAs

A key feature of the National Water Act was the idea of creating new institutions, CMAs, based on hydrological boundaries, referred to as Water Management Areas (WMA) in South Africa. The NWA states that all water resources need to be managed in an integrated manner, and where appropriate, management functions should be decentralised and delegated to the regional or catchment level to enable stakeholder participation. Section 73(4) of the NWA states that "the Minister must promote the management of water resources at the catchment management level by assigning powers and duties to catchment management agencies when it is desirable to do so" (RSA, 1998: 8). This structure was seen as quasi-federal by some commentators (Simeon and Murray, 2009) whereas others would describe it as 'co-operative government' (Constitutional Court, cited in Muller, 2014).

The notion of hydrological boundaries and catchments was present in the 1970 Commission report, but these ideas were mainly used as a basis for developing infrastructure to transfer water out of the basin, rather than for the purpose of governing water resources in accordance with basin boundaries per se. So, even though the idea was not entirely new, the concept of CMAs created much confusion, as well as uncertainty about the intentions of DWA among water users (Jonker et al., 2010). There was a lot of thinking, and it was also a case of looking at the viability of all the originally proposed 19 CMAs in terms of revenues. With respect to the widespread practice of interbasin transfers and how to deal with this from a catchment perspective, the recipient catchment would have to pay the water management charge to the donor catchment.[9]

A Water Law Review Task Team was set up, and for CMA proponents within this team, IWRM was a fortunate, internationally prestigious principle to invoke for making their case. IWRM as a term was profusely used in the task team's discussion documents. Integrated Catchment Management was seen as a key el-

9 Interview with WRC, 16 July 2013.

ement of IWRM, and it should be further developed as an approach (van Koppen and Schreiner, 2014).[10] The task team also considered devolution of central responsibilities to the provincial and local governments that were being established, but rejected this option as they were 'political'. Moreover, the argument was that they lacked constitutional powers and experience. Interventions during the negotiations of a new Constitution made sure that political federalisation of river management did not happen, as it would have involved the allocation of water resource functions to sub-sovereign levels (Muller, 2014). The approach to river management in subsequent legislation also avoided introducing 'basin federalism', the allocation of powers and functions to administrative units based on basin boundaries. The CMAs in the new South Africa were to serve a double role of upward and downward accountability. In 1999, after the 1998 NWA had come into force, the Department established a new directorate, called 'Catchment Management', and later Water Management Institutions Governance, which subsequently became the Chief Directorate for Institutional Oversight with five members of staff. The idea was to support and guide the process of establishing CMAs. A CMA task team was put together, and given the mandate to produce guidelines and tools in order to guide the setting up of CMAs in the Water Management Areas. In spite of seeing CMAs as adhering to the subsidiarity principle of management at the lowest appropriate level, CMAs retain a strong upward accountability to the Minister, conforming to the national mandate and the need to coordinate the extensive infrastructure networks which run across provincial, basin, and national boundaries. The initial functions of CMAs prescribed in section 80 of the NWA are light: to investigate and advise in water use; to develop a Catchment Management Strategy; to coordinate the related activities of water users and of the water management institutions; to promote the coordination of its Catchment Management Strategy implementation with the implementation of any applicable development plan established in terms of the Water Services Act, 1997; and to promote community participation in water use. When CMAs 'mature', the Minister can delegate or assign more functions, in particular licensing and planning and also allocating responsibilities for the funding, development, operation and maintenance of catchment-level water resources infrastructure either by other institutions or directly.

Members of the Regional DWAF staff were expected to be transferred to CMAs. From the outset, the major differences between the country's catchments were appreciated, including the fact that less wealthy areas would not be able to establish a fully self-financed CMA, based on water use charges. The resource intensity of CMAs was recognised, but no specific state funding was negotiated. "CMAs were to focus on the most problematic and conflict-ridden catchments facing water scarcity and pollution, where government cannot solve the issues alone" (Interview, July 2013).

Particularly, environmentalists found an appreciated opportunity to approach water resources as integrated eco-habitats within the (assumed) proper hydrological boundaries of a catchment (WMA). Integration for consensus seeking

10 See link for details of approach: http://inkomaticma.co.za/publications/icma-documents.html

would be across vertical layers, as well as water protection, development and utilisations, and land uses. In terms of promoting equity, other than ensuring equitable and demographic participation and board representation, redress was not an explicit goal and it was not further operationalised. There was a realisation that attempting to reallocate water within the framework of a CMA would be too politically sensitive. The task team members realised that CMAs based on partnership and consensus seeking would not be adequate for water allocation decisions in South Africa at that point in time.

One of the staff members employed in the Institutional Oversight unit recounted the early experiences with rolling out the CMAs, stating that the first four or five years were spent intensely focused on policies and guidelines, and "when looking back, I see that we were incredibly naïve" (Interview, August 2013). Further, he stated that:

> *What was intriguing, was that in the early days it was the 'tail wagging the dog', some of the people in the regions started to work on proposals while we were still trying to get the guidelines in place. It was a bizarre moment when they were running ahead of us (Interview, August 2013).*

The same staff member in the Institutional Oversight Department felt that the main reason that two CMAs had actually been established by 2015 – the Inkomati (in 2004) and the Breede-Overberg (in 2005) – is the tenacity of champions in the regions. There was generally a lot of resistance from the regions; many people did not see the point in establishing CMAs, and areas such as the Free State, the North-West Province and Gauteng were not very cooperative. The Eastern Cape was coming around to the idea. At the time, the Directorate staff thought "this was just something that the regions had to do, that we would develop the guidelines and then they would set about doing it. But like I said, we were incredibly naïve" (Interview, August 2013), and the Directorate staff did not appreciate the fact that there were going to be power struggles in the regions; they just thought that the regions would be supportive; that they would get on with it; and thus did not really engage with those discussions. There was a belief that the processes would take care of themselves. In hindsight, it is clear that much more preparatory work was necessary. These observations conform to what Funke et al. (2007) observed, that, while IWRM was official policy, it had yet to be 'officially' accepted in practice.

In the participatory processes leading up to the establishment of the CMAs, deep power imbalances persisted, in combination with a lack of decisiveness that negatively affected the processes. There were power struggles both among stakeholders and within the bureaucracy responsible for implementation, and eventually a paralysis in setting up the CMAs (see Denby et al., Chapter 5 for a detailed analysis of the Inkomati experience). An issue was that "you are basically asking staff from the government public sector to join a parastatal with the associated resistance and instability".[11] And regardless of whether the CMAs happened or not, they would still receive their bonus, which prompted the question of "how

11 Interview with task team member, 23 August 2013.

can you regulate someone whose salary is three times your own? Then there is the decentralisation discussion that we are having now. If we decentralise, we are probably getting an even more skewed society."[12] CMAs would be liable to be captured by local interest groups. By contrast, Water Boards could maintain a national voice and would not get captured by local issues/interests to the same extent.[13]

> *There was a change of leadership in the directorate in charge of institutional oversight and then the whole process of institutional re-alignment began. The task team worked closely together, but in the new director's opinion, the team was way beyond what it could do and there were simply too many institutions. From a pragmatic point of view, it was understandable that there was a need to reduce the number of CMAs. However, the current set-up was very logical from a governance point of view. When he (the new director) said 'it is not about governance, but about me telling you how many institutions there should be', that was the day I decided it was time to leave (Interview, August 2013).*

Institutional realignments

In 2002, when the first National Water Resources Strategy (NWRS) was developed, the focus was on developing 19 CMAs, but over time it was realised how complex the process was, resulting in a mere two CMAs being established in 2004 and 2005. This led to a process of soul searching, and a review of the institutional landscape.

> *The review revealed that there simply were too many entities reporting to the Minister. There were 279 irrigation boards, water boards, CMAs, etc. and their roles and responsibilities were overlapping and not clear. There was also the question of financial viability. This is when we decided to focus on consolidation – it is also easier when both administrative and hydrological boundaries are somewhat aligned. Change has also happened too slowly. The irrigation boards are still the stronghold of white farmers and the water reform process is rolling out so slowly, so change is not happening (Interview at DWA, July 2013).*

Another aspect that led to a re-examination of current set-ups was the presence of participation fatigue. The long establishment process has eroded the social capital gains and undermined the trust of the stakeholders involved in the participatory processes to form the CMA.

> *In South Africa water management is done with 'public participation'; even the pricing strategy is done by consulting NGOs, communities, Electricity Supply Commission (ESCOM), etc. But nobody thinks of whether people have the capacity to participate and what the implications of all this participation are. We also underestimat-*

12 Interview with WRC employees, 16 July 2013.

13 Interview with DWA employee, 17 June 2013.

> *ed the time, money and effort required for public participation. We overdid it and tried to get everybody on board. You can't consult everybody. This is why institutional alignment will be better (Interview with DWA, July 2013).*

In assessing the overall viability and capacity of the 19 WMAs, the minister announced in March of 2012 that in order to improve IWRM, the 19 WMAs must be consolidated into nine WMAs. The Inkomati Water Management Area (IWMA) must merge with Mhlatuze-Usuthu WMA to form the Inkomati-Usuthu WMA. As stated by a water expert in Pretoria:

> *We started with so many naïve visions of what the CMAs would have done. We need to be more pragmatic now regarding decentralisation and what is possible. In hindsight, maybe it is positive that we tripped and fell with IWRM. We can now be more realistic of what is possible. We also need an incubation process and soul searching exercise to really bring people together to figure out what is actually possible (Interview, July 2013).*

So it was back to the drawing board, with a deep sense of pragmatism. This pragmatism is coloured by an increasing disillusionment with IWRM among other members of staff at the WRC.

Discussion

The previous sections have highlighted how IWRM emerged and how it has been interpreted in diverse ways in South Africa. The South African situation is unique and differs from many other countries in the region in two major ways. The long reign of colonialism and apartheid meant that the majority of the population were squeezed into small marginal portions of the vast country, which had long-term implications for the productive potential of these areas. The 'hydraulic mission' meant that the water resources were highly developed, and the water resources system is currently rapidly approaching the 'closed' stage (Grey and Sadoff, 2006).

So, how is one to understand the emergence of IWRM against this backdrop? One important dimension was the environmental concerns, which were also an aspect in the Commission Report of the 1970s that contained many ideas that were similar in nature to those touted by modern-day IWRM advocates. When the time finally came around for opening up the country for democratic rule, the most pressing needs were certainly doing something about the backlog of water services, which was not least influenced by the human rights-background of the then Minister. The split that occurred at this time in terms of two separate Acts later became a focal point in the debates on what should be 'integrated' in IWRM, because some viewed the strict separation of services and resources as going against the grain of the 'I' in IWRM. A further pressure exacerbating this debate is the fact that in the post-apartheid era there has been an increasing trend of migration towards the urban centres, and peri-urban and squatter settlements putting further pressures on an already overstretched infrastructure.

When it came to the aspect of resources management, environmentalists and conservationists were still a force to be reckoned with. Hence, despite the emphasis on redressing past injustices and reallocating water, the concept of IWRM seemed ideally fit to serve the purpose of the environmental lobby.[14] Water as a means for poverty eradication, though implicitly a goal, was not really well thought out – as a lawyer who was instrumental in the water law drafting process later admitted (personal communication to co-author van Koppen).

South Africa's past government's early strong focus on water control meant large-scale movement of water between basins to meet the needs of the (white) mines, energy, urban centres and agricultural areas, which necessitated huge investments in infrastructure. The development of large-scale infrastructure projects, including the establishment of a supporting bureaucracy, has had significant implications for what IWRM would look like in the South African context, mainly in terms of how it has facilitated large-scale interbasin transfers.

For instance, the presence of powerful irrigation boards, as a result of the long history of investing in the (white) agricultural sector through generous subsidies and infrastructure support schemes, meant that the attempts at creating a new set of tiered governance according to hydrological boundaries did not start from scratch. The lowest tier of Water Users Associations (WUAs), was envisioned by some as emerging out of the across-the-board conversion of the existing Irrigation Boards, and to make them more representative and inclusive in the process. That project was met with much resistance and dragging of feet on the part of the already established commercial farmers, and hence the speed at which Irrigation Boards were converted into the new, more democratic WUAs, was extremely low – also with a lot of window-dressing taking place when it in fact did happen (Faysse and Gumbo, 2004; Movik, 2012), adding another dimension to the debate on decentralisation. While there was clear direction early on that the ultimate intent was to follow through with the idea of the 'subsidiarity principle' in IWRM and delegate responsibility down to the 'lowest appropriate level', this was clearly fraught with difficulty in the South African context. One consequence was the fact that the DWA did not relinquish its powers to issue licences to the ICMA until 2015, which created confusion among many water users regarding who was actually in charge (Movik, 2010; IUCMA, 2015; also Denby et al., Chapter 5). This reinforces the claim made by one of the experts tasked with setting up the CMAs, namely, that South Africa just wasn't ready for that kind of decentralisation effort, as it was far too political, and would risk getting tied up in power struggles on the ground. However, at the time of finalising this chapter, it is clear that CMAs have more power now than in the past, including making final proposals on licence allocations for approval by the head office (Senior water policy consultant, personal communication).

A further feature that sets South Africa apart from the other case studies in this book is the presence of the Water Research Commission (WRC), funded from levies on water use. Set up in 1971 after a period of severe water shortages and expanding demand by an industrialising white economy that underscored the necessity of better knowledge, its main aim was to facilitate research and generate

14 However, as pointed out by an anonymous reviewer, the requirements of the reserve have also hardly been met in the functional CMAs.

water knowledge and technologies. As mentioned, studies by the WRC supported the drafting of the National Water Act (1998). As a national knowledge hub, the WRC was also key in studying implementation projects along IWRM lines, and facilitating national and international debate on possible meanings of IWRM as relevant for the South African context. While the WRC and others were struggling to get to grips with what IWRM was and how it should be interpreted, certain donors set out to develop their own interpretations and operationalising of IWRM in selected localities of the country. Hence, there emerged a situation where there was a national stance on IWRM at the level of national policy documents (such as the National Water Resources Strategy), while the CMAs had their own Catchment Management Strategies alongside the diverse interpretations followed by donors. For instance, the Danida project took a more bottom-up view and stirred up debates on IWRM. Their efforts emphasised the participatory and poverty aspects of IWRM and the need to integrate land and water issues in a bottom-up way. These experiments thus serve to illustrate the myriad of ways in which integration can be understood, as reflected in the ongoing debates within the research community as well. What is interesting is the 'parallel lives' of diverse sets of IWRM interpretations.

Institutional arrangements became a focal point around which many of the IWRM debates played out, both within the WRC and the wider water research community. A key issue that resurfaces is the ideal-typical notion of institutions and the naïveté that coloured much of the thinking in terms of institutions. The new institutional set-up was being rolled out on an existing set of institutional structures and power constellations, and not on a blank surface that could be moulded into some technical ideal way of governing resources. While the WRC was hard at work trying to come to terms with what IWRM was – taking ICM as the point of departure – a sense was crystallised that IWRM was first and foremost about getting the institutions for river basin management right. This focus on the river basin does not explicitly come through in any of the Dublin principles or the GWP definition, but it is still what many people think about when they think of IWRM. Strikingly, in many of the countries of SADC, not just South Africa, there is an emphasis on the river basin aspect, but as in Germany and elsewhere it was hard to focus on ecological and hydrological boundaries (see Movik et al., Chapter 3). Hence, the logic of revisiting the idea of nine CMAs to be partly aligned with hydrological boundaries and partly with the administrative units of DWA's regional offices in each province. This brought to the fore the inherent tensions existing around devolving power to the regions, reflecting an intrinsic tension in the very idea of IWRM between a centralised 'holistic' approach and the desire to decentralised management at lower levels. The issue of the lack of actual decentralisation in the South African context was raised by one of the external experts, Hector Garduño, to which the Director General retorted "you don't understand South Africa" (Interview, November 2013). More broadly, the institutional set-up brought out how beset by power struggles the issue was, and particularly the relative autonomy of the regional offices. This underscored the point of the GWP southern Africa officer in South Africa that even though they were based in Pretoria, they had no influence on South Africa's policies.

Rolling out the idea of setting up 19 CMAs proved to be a long-winded uphill struggle. One issue was simply due to capacity constraints while the government was trying to do everything at once (Schreiner and Hassan, 2011) but also because of unforeseen regional resistance, looming tensions of centralisation/decentralisation, and the stickiness of water allocation reform.

> *We need to get the governance structure right which affects IWRM delivery on the ground. We also need stronger regulation processes – regulation is not enforced and unlawful water use is a big problem. We don't have the capacity to deal with this. IWRM has helped us to enhance and address equity. Transformation takes time and cannot be done in ten years despite all the best intentions. We also spent a lot of time in time-consuming activities such as compulsory licensing, verification, and validation – to achieve equity we thought we needed to know who had what so that reallocation could take place. But perhaps we spent too much time and money tracking down small users instead of only going after the big guys. But you learn from experience. Initially you want to be perfect and register everybody. But looking back we don't need to get to 80% – we could stop at about 60%. With this pragmatism in place, we should start again. I still believe in the future! (Interview, July 2013).*

However, the regions resisted the attempts of foisting upon them IWRM-based institutional novelties such as the CMAs. This resistance was not anticipated by the task team mandated to 'roll-out' the CMAs, and led to a protracted and resource-intensive struggle to establish such hydrological-based institutions across the board, but with only two CMAs being operational 15 years after the promulgation of the act – largely thanks to regional champions. The main reason for delays now in establishing the other seven CMAs are human resource/staffing issues and delegation of powers i.e. licensing remains a contentious topic. Added to all this were the complexities of trying to coordinate the different institutional set-ups at the regional and local levels. The resulting messiness and intractability rendered the idea of practising IWRM a moving target, given all the urgent issues around redistribution of land and water and the entrenched power patterns in the region.

Conclusion

IWRM emerged on the global scene a little before South Africa emerged as a new rainbow nation, keen to liberate itself from the legacies of the past. Water was seen as one of the key areas of inequality and the resulting new legislation and constitutional processes were truly radical, progressive and ahead of the time. IWRM was integrated into these processes by South Africans and foreign experts who were keen to engage with 'best international practice'. In many ways South Africa was way ahead of its time, not just in water and sanitation services, but also in water management, e.g. through the concept of the Reserve. But some of the ideas developed to maturity in the 1998 National Water Act were already nascent in the Commission Report of the 1970s and thus the emergence of IWRM was not as novel and progressive as it might seem at first glance.

Our study has shown that IWRM in South Africa has been understood in different ways across scales and regions. The institutionalisation of arrangements based on IWRM principles, i.e. Catchment Management Agencies, engendered a level of institutional complexity at the regional and local levels that did not manage to break down the 'silos', particularly of land and water (cf. Denby et al., Chapter 5). The level of ambition and the amount of time and resources spent led to a profound sense of reform fatigue and left many historically disadvantaged individuals feeling even more excluded and angry. A particularly poignant point is that the implementation process did not fully appreciate the historical legacies and skewedness of land and water access. Thus the rather 'ideal-typical' institutional arrangements layered over the deeply embedded geographies of inequality and power imbalances and the infrastructures of the hydraulic mission project that characterised much of the apartheid era. The failure to properly integrate the land and water reforms further reinforced the disconnect between the socio-geographical landscapes and the attempts at setting up river basin institutions and implementing IWRM (see Denby et al., Chapter 5). The CMAs were not given full powers, but were kept reined in by the national department, largely to avoid these institutions being captured by the most powerful players at the basin level. The existing water boards are also quite powerful organisations, and there was a concern that the newly created CMAs should not become such 'monsters'. Thus, the aim of decentralisation was not really carried through, and there is a constant centralisation-decentralisation tension present in the water sector. There were also different understandings of what should be the focal point and modus operandi of IWRM implementation. Some saw it as a natural evolution of the ICM approach, whereas others took the participatory and poverty dimension to mean that people should be empowered through adopting a livelihoods-focused, bottom-up approach.

Our study suggests that the main emphasis was the focus on the need to get the institutional structures right. This was characterised, as many of our interviewees described, by a sense of naïve optimism in terms of what could be achieved. There was a certain degree of hubris involved in the planning to prepare for the establishment of 19 new institutions that did not conform to the existing administrative boundaries, but that would be created according to a logic of hydrology as the natural boundary. What the implementers had not foreseen was the resistance on the part of the regions, the protracted power struggles, and the smouldering tensions with respect to how authority should be parcelled out between the national department and the new basin-level organisations. In short, they didn't factor in the political contestations that would follow in the wake of this endeavour. The process became a costly, bureaucratic exercise, leaving those involved with a profound sense of disillusionment. Many early champions have left the government in favour of joining the private consultancy sector, characterised by some as a veritable 'brain drain'. But some of these consultants still continue to dip in and out of the ongoing processes and are considered as colleagues by some of their counterparts in the government.

Moreover, the efforts failed to engage with the ongoing processes of land reform and also the even more protracted process of reallocating water to redress past injustices, and the lack of coordination between land and water reform processes (see Denby et al., Chapter 5). This was further underscored by the regional and local institutional hierarchies that failed to coordinate their activities adequately.

But IWRM is not totally irrelevant as Biswas may say. Also, it is not a donor-driven externally imposed process in South Africa unlike in other African countries. It has believers who feel that it is an 'approach' not a 'blueprint' that can guide and help, even if it is not implementable or workable in practice. This is despite the lack of evidence that it has helped enhance access and despite the fact that in reality local people may have been at best untouched and at worst badly affected by all the costly and bureaucratic institutional reform processes. Radical reform and reallocation processes have not taken place despite all the good intentions and structural inequalities that still persist.

Still, most of the people we interviewed[15] continue to have hope and are keen to learn from the experiences of the past decade. They are less idealistic and more pragmatic of what is possible but still look to their progressive constitution and policies and hope for more equitable water futures in South Africa.

Acknowledgements

We would like to thank the team members of the project Flows and Practices: The Politics of IWRM in Southern Africa for providing a stimulating arena for discussions. Particular thanks are due to Bill Derman, Alex Bolding, Alan Nicol and Jeremy Allouche and to the anonymous reviewers for their constructive comments. We also thank the Research Council of Norway for making this research possible.

References

Anderson, A.J. 2005. Engaging disadvantaged communities: Lessons from the Inkomati CMA establishment process. Paper presented at African Water Laws: Plural Legislative Frameworks for Rural Water Management in Africa, Johannesburg, South Africa, 26-28 January 2005.

Bourblanc, M. 2015. The South African 'ecological reserve' a travelling concept. *Politikon South African Journal of Political Studies* 42(2): 275-292.

Cullis, J. and van Koppen, B. 2007. *Applying the Gini coefficient to measure inequality of water use in the Olifants River water management area, South Africa.* IWMI Research Paper No. 113. Colombo: International Water Management Institute.

Cullis, J. and van Koppen, B. 2008. Applying the Gini coefficient to measure the distribution of water use and benefits of water use in South Africa's provinces. Unpublished report. Pretoria: Department of Water Affairs and Forestry and International Water Management Institute.

De Coning, C. 2006. Overview of the water policy process in South Africa. *Water Policy* 8(6): 505-528.

15 It must however be stated that the people we interviewed for this article are not marginalised people lacking access but largely movers and shakers of water policies and programmes in the country.

Denby, K. 2013. Institutional integration and local level water access in the Inkomati catchment management area, South Africa. MSc thesis. Norwegian University of Life Sciences, Aas, Norway.

Dugard, J. 2012. Urban basic services in South Africa: Rights, reality and resistance. In Langford, M.; Cousins, B.; Dugard, J. and Madlingozi, T. (Eds), *The role and impact of socio-economic rights strategies in South Africa: Symbols or substance*, pp. 275-309. New York: Cambridge University Press.

Eales, K. 2011. Water services South Africa 1994-2009. In Schreiner, B. and Hassan, R. (Eds), *Transforming water management in South Africa: Designing and implementing a new policy framework*, pp. 33-73. London, New York: Springer Science and Business Media.

Faysse, N. and Gumbo, J. 2004. *The transformation of Irrigation Boards into Water User Associations in South Africa: Case studies of the Umlaas, Komati, Lomati and Hereford Irrigation Boards.* IWMI Working Paper No. 73, Volume 2. Colombo, Sri Lanka: International Water Management Institute.

Funke, N.; Oelofse, S.H.H.; Hattingh, J.; Ashton, P.J. and Turton, A.R. 2007. IWRM in developing countries: Lessons from the Mhlatuze catchment in South Africa. *Physics and Chemistry of the Earth* 32(15-18): 1237-1245.

Gieryn, T.F. 1999. *Cultural boundaries of science: Credibility on the line.* Chicago: University of Chicago Press.

Gleick, P.H. 1998. The human right to water. *Water Policy* 1(5): 487-503.

Goldin, J.; Rutherford, R. and Schoch, D. 2008. The place where the sun rises: An application of IWRM at the village level. *Water Resources Development* 24(3): 345-356.

Grey, D. and Sadoff, C. 2006. Water for growth and development. In Thematic Documents of the IV World Water Forum. Mexico City: Comisión Nacional del Agua.

Gupta, J. and van der Zaag, P. 2008. Interbasin water transfers and integrated water resources management: Where engineering, science and politics interlock. *Physics and Chemistry of the Earth Parts A/B/C* 33(1-2): 28-40.

GWP (Global Water Partnership). 2000. *Integrated Water Resource Management.* Technical Advisory Committee Background Paper No. 4. Stockholm, Sweden: Global Water Partnership.

Hall, R. 2004. A political economy of land reform in South Africa. *Review of African Political Economy* 31(100): 213-227.

IUCMA (Inkomati-Usuthu Catchment Management Agency). 2015. IUCMA and our functions. Presentation to the water use verification information meetings. Nelspruit, Mpumalanga, South Africa.

Jonker, L. 2007. Integrated water resources management: The theory-praxis-nexus, a South African perspective. *Physics and Chemistry of the Earth Parts A/B/C* 32(15-18): 1257-1263.

Jonker, L.; Swatuk, L.A.; Matiwane, M.; Mila, U.; Ntloko, M. and Simataa, F. 2010. Exploring the lowest appropriate level of water governance in South Africa. WRC Report No. 1837/1/10. Pretoria, South Africa: Water Research Commission.

King, B.H. 2005. Spaces of change: Tribal authorities in the former KaNgwane homeland, South Africa. *Area* 37(1): 64-72.

Levin, R. and Weiner, D. 1997. *No more tears: Struggles for land in Mpumalanga, South*

Africa. Trenton, NJ and Asmara, Eritrea: Africa World Press.

Love, D.; Jonker, L.; Rockström, J. and van der Zaag, P. 2004. The challenge of integrated water resource management for improved rural livelihoods in the Limpopo basin – An introduction to WaterNet's first network research program. Paper presented at the5th WaterNet/WARFSA Annual Symposium, 2nd-4th November 2004, Windhoek, Namibia.

Mehta, L. and Ntshona, Z. 2004. *Dancing to two tunes? Rights and market-based approaches in South Africa's water domain*. Sustainable Livelihoods in Southern Africa (SLSA). Research Paper No. 17. Brighton, UK: Institute of Development Studies.

Molle, F. 2008. Nirvana concepts, narratives and policy models: Insights from the water sector. *Water Alternatives* 1(1): 25-38.

Movik, S. 2010. Return of the Leviathan? Hydropolitics in the developing world revisited. *Water Policy* 12(5): 641-653.

Movik, S. 2012. *Fluid rights: South Africa's water allocation reform*. Cape Town: HSRC Press.

Muller, M. 2014. Allocating powers and functions in a federal design: The experience of South Africa. In Garrick, D.E.; Anderson, G.R.M.; Connell, D. and Pittock, J. (Eds), *Federal rivers: Managing water in multi-layered political systems*, pp. 179-194. Cheltenham, UK: Edward Elgar.

Peet, R. 2007. *Geography of power: Making global economic policy*. London: Zed Books.

Platzky, L. and Walker, C. 1985. *The surplus people: Forced removals in South Africa*. Johannesburg: Ravan Press.

Pollard, S. and Du Toit, D. 2008. Integrated water resource management in complex systems: How the catchment management strategies seek to achieve sustainability and equity in water resources in South Africa. *Water SA* 34(6): 671-679.

Pollard, S. and Du Toit, D. 2011. Towards adaptive integrated water resources management in southern Africa: The role of self-organisation and multi-scale feedbacks for learning and responsiveness in the Letaba and Crocodile catchments. *Water Resources Management* 25(15): 4019-4035.

RSA (Republic of South Africa). 1996. Constitution of the Republic of South Africa. Constitutional Court, South Africa.

RSA. 1998. National Water Act (Act No. 36 of 1998). Government Gazette 398, No. 19182. Cape Town, South Africa.

Schreiner, B. and Hassan, R. 2011. *Transforming water management in South Africa: Designing and implementing a new policy framework*. London, New York: Springer Science and Business Media.

Simeon, R. and Murray. C. 2009. Reforming multi-level government in South Africa. *Canadian Journal of African Studies/La Revue Canadienne des Études Africaines* 43(3): 536-571.

Snaddon, C.D.; Wishart, M.J. and Davies, B.R. 1998. Some implications of inter-basin water transfers for river ecosystem functioning and water resources management in southern Africa. *Aquatic Ecosystem Health and Management* 1(2): 159-182.

Swatuk, L. 2008. A political economy of water in southern Africa. *Water Alternatives* 1(1): 24-47.

Terreblanche, S. 2002. *A history of inequality in South Africa 1652-2002*. KwaZulu-Natal: University of KwaZulu-Natal Press/KMM Review Publishing.

Turton, A. and Henwood, R. 2002. *Hydropolitics in the developing world: A southern African perspective*. Pretoria: African Water Research Unit.

Turton, A.; Meissner, R.; Mampane, P.M. and Seremo, O. 2004. A hydropolitical history of South Africa's international river basins. In WRC report 1220/1/04. Pretoria, South Africa: Water Research Commission.

van Koppen, B. and Schreiner, B. 2014. Moving beyond Integrated Water Resources Management: Developmental water management in South Africa. *International Journal of Water Resources Development* 30(3): 543-558.

Villa-Vicencio, C. and Ngesi, S. 2003. South Africa: Beyond the 'miracle'. In Doxtader, E. and Villa-Vicencio, C. (Eds), *Through fire with water: The roots of division and the potential for reconciliation in Africa*, pp. 267-304. Trenton, NJ and Asmara, Eritrea: Africa World Press.

5

The 'Trickle Down' of Integrated Water Resources Management: A Case Study of Local-Level Realities in the Inkomati Water Management Area, South Africa[1]

Kristi Denby

Synne Movik

Lyla Mehta

Barbara van Koppen

ABSTRACT: The historical legacy in South Africa of apartheid and the resulting discriminatory policies and power imbalances are critical to understanding how water is managed and allocated, and how people participate in designated water governance structures. The progressive post-apartheid National Water Act (NWA) is the principal legal instrument related to water governance which has broadly embraced the principles of Integrated Water Resources Management (IWRM). This translation of IWRM into the South African context and, in particular, the integration of institutions related to land and water have faced many challenges due to the political nature of water and land reforms, and the tendency of governmental departments to work in silos. The chapter explores the dynamics surrounding the implementation of IWRM in the Inkomati Water Management Area, and the degree of integration between the parallel land and water reform processes. It also looks at what these reforms mean to black farmers' access to water for their sugar cane crops at the regional (basin) and local levels. The empirical material highlights the discrepancies between a progressive IWRM-influenced policy on paper and the actual realities on the ground. The chapter argues that the decentralisation and integration aspects of IWRM in South Africa have somewhat failed to take off in the country and what 'integrated' actually entails is unclear. Furthermore, efforts to implement the NWA and IWRM in South Africa have been fraught with challenges in practice, because the progressive policy did not fully recognise the complex historical context, and the underlying inequalities in knowledge, power and resource access.

1 First published in *Water Alternatives* 9(3): 475-494

KEYWORDS: Land and water reform, IWRM, equity, water access, Inkomati, South Africa

Introduction

The widespread global water scarcity concerns and the increasing attention to sustainable development have prompted reforms of water legislation in favour of the highly influential Integrated Water Resources Management (IWRM) (see Introduction, this book; Brown, 2011; Movik, 2012). The concept of IWRM emphasises that water should not be managed sectorally or in isolation from the wider environment, and endeavours to integrate the management of land, water and related resources, taking into consideration the wider economic, environmental and equity-related aspects (GWP 2000).

The idea of IWRM emerged in Europe and North America, and was later spread and translated in the African context as best practice through external and internal channels (Funke and Jacobs, 2010; Mehta and Movik, 2014; Mutondo et al., 2016; Movik et al., Chapter 4). These efforts of implementing IWRM in sub-Saharan African countries have been met with challenges linked to representation and participation in newly formed decentralised institutions; the complexity of river basins (interbasin transfers, scarce water supply, international river basins etc.); power imbalances and plural legal systems; and lack of human capacity and poor financial resources (see van Koppen, 2000; Wester at al., 2003; Swatuk, 2005; Anderson et al., 2008; Funke and Jacobs, 2010; Brown, 2011; van Koppen and Schreiner, 2014b; Mutondo et al., 2016). This chapter focuses specifically on the South African experience, in particular the Inkomati Water Management Area (IWMA). The South African case is particularly interesting because its 1998 National Water Act is considered one of the most progressive pieces of IWRM legislation in the world (see Schreiner, 2013), and the 1997 White Paper embraces an IWRM approach (see Movik et al., Chapter 4). There have, however, been significant challenges on the ground, and this chapter explores some of these through case studies in the Inkomati.

The ambitious post-apartheid South African water policy and legislation were developed on the basis of extensive public participation, and were informed by experiences and expertise of other countries (i.e. Australia and Mexico) and the principles of IWRM (Schreiner and Hassan, 2011; Movik, 2012; ICMA, 2014; Movik et al., this book). The National Water Act (NWA) (RSA, 1998) is the principal legal instrument related to water management. It placed a strong emphasis on the efficiency of water use and management, on redressing past imbalances and the sustainable use of water to ensure water access for all South Africans, while preserving its ecosystems (DWA, 2012b). The deep historic roots of apartheid, especially with regards to access to land and water, continue to be negotiated in democratic South Africa. The Native Land Act (1913, 1936) and the Bantu Authorities Act2 of 1951 of the apartheid regime provided the legislation to restrict

2 When the National Party came to power in 1948, they set out to create a country divided into segregated homelands or bantustans for the majority of the Black population (Terreblanche, 2002). To move towards a segregated development of South Africa, the Bantu Authorities Act of 1951 officially recognised the tribal authority as the rulers of the ten bantustans of South Africa (Movik, 2012).

property rights from the black majority, and led to the forced removals of over 3.5 million people to 'tribal' reserves, formerly called homelands or bantustans (Bate and Tren, 2002; Movik, 2012, Woodhouse, 2012). As a result of these discriminatory apartheid policies the majority of black farmers in South Africa were struggling and lacked support when the country emerged independent in 1994. These people are referred to as potential or emerging farmers or 'historically disadvantaged individuals' (HDIs) because they lack sufficient water authorisations (white commercial farmers held the majority), strong networks, and planning and management skills to run a high-input irrigated farm (Woodhouse, 2012).

In order to redress the problems from the past, post-apartheid South Africa has prioritised getting the institutional set-up right (Movik, 2012; Movik et al., Chapter 4). The goal was to form Catchment Management Agencies (CMA) according to hydrological boundaries that would eventually be responsible for managing water resources at the basin level. At the local level, it was envisaged that the Irrigation Boards (IBs) from the apartheid era would be converted to more inclusive Water User Associations (WUA; RSA, 1998; DWA, 2012a). Despite, the progressive NWA, challenges persist especially with regard to water reallocation and the setting-up of decentralised water management organisations (CMAs and WUA); and the lack of integration of key institutions has continued to hamper and delay implementation (Ashton et al., 2006; Funke and Jacobs, 2010; Denby, 2013; Mehta et al., 2014). Within the IWRM-influenced water policy, a paradox exists where the holistic and integrated approach to water management is at odds with the emphasis on the decentralisation and participatory aspects of IWRM. Another complication relating to integration in the context of IWRM is that the water and land reforms in South Africa were largely drafted, and are being implemented independently of each other (Funke and Jacobs, 2010; Movik, 2012; Woodhouse, 2012). Moreover, the slow progress of both water and land reforms reflects the persisting inequalities in income distribution and access to resources, which remain strongly correlated with race, gender and location (i.e. former homelands) (May, 2000; Lahiff, 2007).

It has been more than 20 years since the end of apartheid, and the inequalities in access to water for productive purposes and the participation in designated water governance structures (DWA, CMA, IBs, WUA) have not significantly changed (King, 2005; Schreiner et al., 2010; Schreiner, 2012; DWA, 2012b; Brown, 2014). It is, therefore, critical to examine how various interpretations, challenges and outcomes surrounding the implementation of the water reform are understood and affect people, in particular black farmers at the local level, namely in rural areas and the former homelands.

In this chapter, we will examine how the efforts at implementing IWRM translate into practice, and the dynamics surrounding management and access to water at the regional (basin) and local levels. The focus is on the Inkomati Catchment Management Agency (ICMA), the first established CMA in South Africa, and home of some of the largest land claims in South Africa. In 2006, the Inkomati CMA (ICMA) was formally established after seven years of negotiations and a controversial and complex participatory process over the scarce water resources in the basin (Anderson, 2005). At the time of conducting research, it was the only one of two operational CMAs in the country which makes it an interesting case. This chapter highlights the diverse understandings of IWRM at the regional and local levels; how IWRM implementation in the Inkomati is unfolding; and how the progressive policies have influenced black farmers' access to water. Furthermore, how the parallel land and water reforms are playing out in the Inkomati are used to study the degree of integration and coordination between institutions linked to water, agriculture and land reform. We draw on case studies of sugar-cane farmers in Nkomazi (formerly the KaNgwane homeland) that explore the challenges black farmers face in relation to access to water and the discrepancies between the IWRM-influenced policy on paper and the actual realities on the ground (i.e. the trickle down of IWRM).

Study area

The Inkomati Water Management Area (IWMA) is located in Mpumalanga and a small portion of Limpopo Province, and is comprised of three major catchments with rivers that all flow into the Inkomati River system: the Sabie-Sand, Crocodile and Komati. The Inkomati River originates in South Africa, passes through Swaziland, back through South Africa, then Mozambique where it finally drains into the Indian Ocean. The basin covers roughly 31,230 square kilometres (km2) with irrigated agriculture in the IWMA utilising approximately 57% of the total available water, also referred to as the water requirement (DWA, 2012b). The IWMA is water-stressed with a growing water deficit in the basin resulting from frequent water restrictions, growing demands from emerging black farmers, international treaty obligations, and widespread concern regarding water quality and the ecological reserve (DWA, 2007; Woodhouse, 2012; DWA, 2012a). There is a deficit[3] in water yield with three of the four sub-catchments, the Komati, Sand and Crocodile all being over-allocated, and the reserve and international requirements not being met (Schreiner, 2012).

The IWMA spans through three former homelands: KaNgwane, Lebowa and Gazankulu, and has the largest number of historically disadvantaged and emerging black farmers in South Africa (ICMA, 2010). The farmer groups in the study areas can be considered as follows: (1) communal farmers (often referred to as small-scale growers living in the former homelands that are today often referred to as the communal areas); (2) land reform farmers who are beneficiaries of the redistribution and restitution from the land reform programme (often referred to as emerging farmers) and (3) commercial farmers (mainly white farmers). Both communal farmers and land reform farmers will also be referred to as Historically Disadvantaged (HD) farmers in this chapter. It must be noted that discrepancies exist between HD farmers (especially the rural poor, and women) with regard to participation and access to water (see Movik, 2012). All farmers interviewed lived in Nkomazi (local municipality in Mpumalanga Province), which lies in the former KaNgwane homeland in the Komati-Lomati River system (sub-catchment of the IWMA). At the time of the research in 2012, the formal demand for water authorisations among emerging farmers was far greater than the water available in the IWMA. We chose to focus on sugar-cane farms because it is an important

3 Approximately 165 million m^3/annum (DWA, 2012a).

export crop in the IWMA requiring irrigation, and a domain where water and land reforms overlap.

Fig. 5. 1: Inkomati Water Management Area[4] (Brown, 2014).

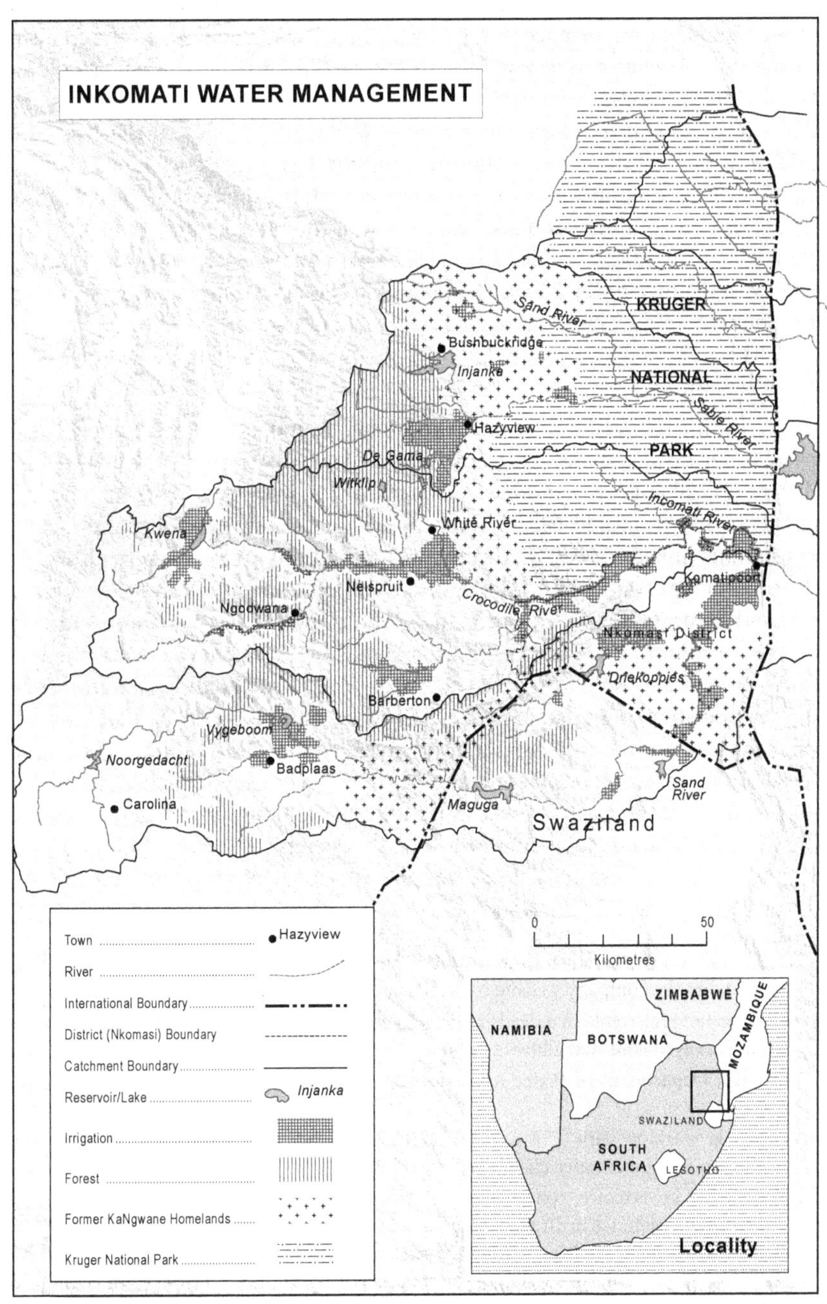

4 IWMA has expanded and is now called the Inkomati-Usuthu Water Management Area.

The catchment area of the Komati River and its tributaries, mainly the Lomati River is approximately 11,210 km2. The Lower Komati is located in Nkomazi, northeast of the Swaziland border and west of Mozambique where it meets the Crocodile River. This area is "considered to be one of the most fertile agricultural regions in South Africa" (Waalewijn, 2005: 186). Sugar cane, in particular, gained significant importance in the lower Komati catchment when the first sugar cane mill was built near Malelane (Nkomazi) in 1965 by TSB sugar holding[5] (Movik, 2012). Commercial agriculture and TSB and Malelane mills remain key pillars in the province of Mpumalanga and Nkomazi economy, currently producing over 30% of South Africa's total sugar output. Historically, the Lomati River, a tributary of the Komati served as a natural boundary between the black farmers on the right side of the river bank, and the white commercial farmers on the other side (Waalewijn, 2005; Movik, 2012). There are many black sugar-cane farmers residing in the former KaNgwane homeland in Nkomazi that have no formal land titles, but where the chief issues a Permission to Occupy (PtO).[6]

Methodology

The research employed a qualitative approach to understand the complex realities of water management and water access. Data collection included reviews of relevant official and 'grey' literature (documents, reports, minutes from meetings, etc.) and semi-structured interviews with 40 key staff at the national and regional departments linked to land and water, including Department of Agriculture, Rural Development and Land Affairs (DARDLA), Department of Rural Development and Land Reform (DRLR), Department of Water Affairs[7] (DWA), Water Allocation Reform consultant, Inkomati Catchment Management Agency (ICMA), the NGO LIMA[8], Lomati and Komati Irrigation Boards, TSB sugar holdings, South African Sugar Association, Mpumalanga Cane Growers and Nkomazi Farmers Association. Interviews at the institutional level provided key information regarding the institutional landscape and highlighted the complexities and challenges in managing and allocating water at the basin level. Attending water- and land-related stakeholder meetings, conferences and workshops,[9] provided many valuable insights. Data was also collected through participant observation and informal conversations with the attendees.

5 TSB stands for Transvaal Suiker Beperk. The translation in English is Transvaal Sugar Limited, but the company website refers to the company as TSB sugar holdings.

6 A PtO is not registrable in a deeds registry, but is rather a personal right over certain rural and unsurveyed land that allows a family/person to occupy or use the land.

7 In 2014, Department of Water Affairs became the Department of Water and Sanitation (DWS).

8 LIMA is working with TSB and DRDLR. They work with rural development, social facilitation and governance challenges. www.lima.org.za

9 Freshwater governance conference in Drakensberg; Inkomati Day of the Freshwater governance conference in Drakensberg; MCCAW meeting in Nelspruit, ICMA stakeholder meeting in White River; Mpumalanga Land Reform Development Committee in Nelspruit; Mumpalanga Provincial workshop on Framework and indicator for monitoring and auditing water allocation reform in Nelspruit; Mill cane committee meeting at TSB Malelane; NWRS2 consultation meeting in White River.

At the local level, a case study approach was adopted, in order to bring out the complexities and issues relating to farmers' access to water and IWRM in practice. The main means of information-gathering at the local level was participatory observation and in-depth semi-structured interviews. In Nkomazi, 56 sugar-cane farmers (20 females, 36 males) from nine sugar-cane projects or cooperatives were interviewed in the communal areas. We interviewed sugar-cane farmers (mostly managers or ex-owners) from seven land reform farms, one redistribution farm and six restitution farms. Multiple interviews of the same stakeholders or institutional staff were used as a means of triangulating the findings, and served as a way to cross-check and revisit key issues among the respondents.

Background

Post-apartheid historical legacy

The historical legacy of South Africa including the discriminatory policies and the imprint of apartheid in spatial planning are critical in understanding the material realities of rural residents today (King, 2005). The riparian water right doctrine[10] (see Movik et al., Chapter 4), in combination with the discriminatory Land Act of 1913 formed the foundation of a long-standing effort to deprive the black majority of South Africans access to land and water resources (van Koppen and Schreiner, 2014a). Since the end of apartheid, the boundaries of the homelands have been erased in theory; however, the legacy of apartheid and discriminatory spatial planning is still reflected in the landscape, and continues to shape many rural residents' socioeconomic realities (King, 2005; 2007). Despite the progress, black farmers, many of whom live in the former homelands, still suffer and struggle from the apartheid era evictions from their land, poverty, and underdevelopment; and the inequality of support and resource allocations under the Apartheid Government (Perret, 2002; van Koppen et al., 2009; Schreiner et al., 2010).

The adoption of IWRM: The National Water Act of 1998

South Africa is considered a predominantly semiarid country, and the water sector is characterised by "scarce water supplies, increasing water demand, exhausted infrastructure development and intensive competition among water uses and users" (Backeberg, 2005: 108). The country was in a constant state of change at the end of apartheid, with substantial new policy and legislation that have broadly taken on the principles of IWRM (Perret, 2002; Backeberg, 2005; ICMA, 2014; Movik et al., this Book). When drafting the policy, the government recognised that access to water resources was a key element in enabling many of the rural poor or historically marginalised to break out of poverty. The 1998 National Water Act (NWA) aimed to decentralise and integrate water management; redress past inequalities in access to water; create new local and regional institutions; promote participation and equal representation; and register and license water use and facilitate a market to trade water rights (Perret, 2002; van Koppen et al.,

10 Water rights were granted reasonable use of water adjacent to water or a river bank according to landownership (Movik, 2012).

2003; Backeberg, 2005). Another key priority of the NWA was to implement the ecological 'Reserve' which is defined as the amount of water in-stream that must be set aside in order to be able to meet the basic human and ecological water needs.

The NWA designated the state as the custodian of water, and adopted the principle of subsidiarity (taking decisions at the lowest appropriate level) with the goal to achieve the equity and sustainability of water management resources through the involvement of various stakeholder groups (environment, agriculture, land reform, health, etc.) in the decision-making process (ICMA, 2014). One of the guiding principles of the transformation and reform of water resources management was the legal requirement for public participation and the creation of new decentralised institutions to manage all aspects related to water (DWA, 2012a).

The creation of decentralised institutions (CMAs, WUAs) at the basin level was considered a key factor in the implementation of the NWA, and a basis to achieve the goals of the implementation strategy and framework for water governance, the National Water Resource Strategy (NWRS) (RSA, 2004). The CMAs should optimally be responsible for all basin-level water management planning, coordination, and water-related stakeholder engagement (Schreiner and van Koppen, 2002; Anderson, 2005). WUAs are essentially supposed to function as cooperative associations for water users, with equal representation, that take on water-related activities for the mutual benefit of the members (Perret, 2002).

Delegating water governance functions to the CMAs was considered groundbreaking, even though it created major delays in getting the institutional set-up 'right' and created widespread confusion among water users regarding which institution was in charge (Jonker et al., 2010). Despite the progressive water policy, the Department of Water Affairs (DWA) has acknowledged that "little substantive progress on the NWA pillar of equity (redress of race and gender water allocations for productive economic use) has been achieved since its promulgation" (DWA, 2012b: 67). This lack of redress can be attributed to the fact that the politics of resistance surrounding water was not sufficiently acknowledged, among other factors. Thus, the NWRS 2 has recognised these challenges and the slow progress in implementing the water policy in South Africa, and has moved away from a blanket IWRM approach and has prioritised IWRM activities with a strong focus on the contextual and development needs of South Africa (van Koppen and Schreiner, 2014a).

Detached and parallel water and land reforms

The redistribution of water through the Water Allocation Reform (WAR) from the 'haves' to 'have nots' greatly increased the political risks and expectations attached to implementing IWRM in South Africa (Woodhouse, 2008; Movik, 2012). In 2006, with the scarce water supply, economic prosperity and equitable distribution priorities in mind, South Africa published the Water Allocation Reform (WAR) policy. WAR aimed to "overcome the ongoing race and gender imbalances in access to water resources" (Greenberg, 2010: 10, see also Movik, 2012). The priorities of WAR were to reallocate water to implement the ecological 'reserve' and redistribute from the haves to the have-nots, primarily through a process of Compulsory Licensing (CL)[11] in water-stressed basins. Since 1994, the provision of safe drinking water has greatly improved among the rural poor; however, little has changed in the provision of access to water for productive purposes (Schreiner et al., 2010). More importantly, to date the land reform programme has been a more significant contributor to the reallocation of water, and has the ability to empower black farmers over and above the Water Allocation Reform agenda (Schreiner, 2012). Estimates indicate that between 24 and 34% of water allocations will be transferred into black hands through the completion of the land reform process in the Inkomati (ICMA, 2010).

South Africa's land reform has three different pillars: Redistribution, restitution and tenure reform. Redistribution involved government grants and programmes based on the 'willing buyer, willing seller' principle with an aim to transfer white-owned farmland to black farmers. Restitution aimed to address the evictions from the 1913 discriminatory land laws and to transfer land back to the communities, families or individuals evicted. Tenure reform is aimed at improving tenure security among the 17 million people living in the former homelands (Woodhouse, 2012). All the redistribution and restitution farms are titled, must come with a water authorisation, and are bought through the Department of Rural Development and Land Reform (DRDLR) at the provincial level, and then beneficiaries are selected or have placed a respective claim on the land. Governance issues are a major challenge – e.g. in 1918 one white farmer owned the farm where, now, 500-5000 people are beneficiaries of the same farm. Many white commercial farmers still manage their old farms that were bought by the land reform programme due to the sheer number of beneficiaries taking over a farm, and their lack of management skills and experience in running a highly commercialised farm. For these reasons many beneficiaries of the land reform programme are not involved in the farming operations, and thus do not participate in the water governance structures.

Greenberg's (2010) report on the progress of land reform in South Africa states that water allocation and land transfers must be connected at an institutional level because the links between land reform, agricultural support and provision of water resources are weak. The post-apartheid water policies, especially WAR, have not sufficiently acknowledged the necessary coordination of policies and programmes with the land reform and agricultural departments. Regardless of the interconnected nature and historical embeddedness of land and water, these reform processes have largely occurred as detached and parallel processes (Funke and Jacobs, 2010; Woodhouse, 2012; Movik, 2012). Land and water in South Africa are governed with overlapping mandates and goals, but are managed by different governmental policies, institutions and funding schemes.

---

11 CL is the main process outlined in the NWA (section 43) that must be implemented to authorise all water users, then reallocate water. This requires the verification of water use, a Catchment Management Strategy (CMS), Water Allocation Plan (WAP) and other allocation criteria to be completed first (IUCMA, 2015).

The catchment and local-level: The Inkomati Water Management Area

The complexity of setting up 19 functioning CMAs, as outlined in the NWA, was underestimated and, in 2012, these boundaries were downsized to nine WMAs, and required the merging and set-up of a total of nine CMAs (ICMA, 2014; see Movik et al., this book). In May 2014, the Inkomati WMA formally merged with the adjacent Mlhatuze-Usuthu WMA to form the Inkomati-Usuthu WMA and CMA.[12] However, the consequences of the extension of the catchment boundaries are unclear, but "may compromise the future manageability of the CMA in the interests of supposed efficiency" (Brown, 2014: 6).

The intention of DWA is to ultimately delegate full powers to the ICMA in order to institutionalise the principle of subsidiarity and to ease the national department´s administrative burden. Section 57(2) of the NWA states that water use charges must be made payable to the relevant water management institution (ICMA). The idea of administrative water use rights, or licences, is an important pillar of the NWA and is how the ICMA should be ultimately funded. A licence is one of four broad categories of water use rights – the others being schedule one (small-scale use of negligible impact), general authorisations (larger, but still low-impact use rights that can be offered to a specified group or in a specified geographical locality), Existing Lawful Use (ELU) and licences. ELU is a temporary water entitlement that allows people or organisations who were lawfully using water prior to the 1998 NWA to continue to do so, until the process of CL is completed. A key focus of the Inkomati Catchment Management Strategy (CMS) is a process of validation (checking the use) and verification (checking the lawfulness) of ELUs (ICMA, 2010). In the Inkomati, the delegation of many key legislative mandates was drawn out and politically contested. Finally, in January 2015 the Minister delegated the ICMA the legislative functions to license water use, complete the verification of existing water users and to control water use charges (ICMA, 2014; IUCMA, 2015).

Institutional set-up: Land, agriculture and water

At the regional level, the DWA Regional Office and the ICMA are responsible for the management of water resources. At the time of the research, the ICMA focused on mobilising, empowering and consulting water users and stakeholders, in particular women and the rural poor. At the lower institutional level, the 27 Irrigation Boards (IBs) formed under the apartheid government still largely managed water and collected water use charges on behalf of DWA. These were meant to be disbanded and converted to a more inclusive and representative Water User Association (WUA) (Brown, 2014). To date, few WUAs have been established due to the strict gender and race representation criteria and other complications such as transferring of assets and their inability to have paid staff in the Inkomati (see ibid.). Many people felt that DWA had unrealistic expectations in regard to the composition of WUAs, leading to the IBs distancing themselves from the trans-

12 In this chapter, we will refer to the Inkomati WMA and CMA because the research for this chapter was conducted prior to the institutional realignment.

formation process and causing some conflict with DWA (ibid.). As per the NWA, DWA envisioned that the CMA and WUA would take over all legislative mandates in regard to the management of water resources. Progress has been extremely slow, and it took DWA approximately ten years to hand over key legislative mandates since the establishment of the ICMA.

Many other regional departments have a say in water resources management to varying degrees, such as the provincial departments of the Department of Rural Development and Land Reform (DRDLR) and the Department of Agriculture, Rural Development and Land Administration (DARDLA). There was a major reshuffle of ministries and departments as a result of a change in administration led by Jacob Zuma in 2009 and 2014. Where earlier there had been the Department of Agriculture (DoA) there was an intention to more clearly demarcate the departments that were involved in production, and keep them separate from land reform and rural development issues. This strict separation between production and land reform issues has been criticised, see e.g. Hall (2004), and goes against the grain of integration.

In 2009, DRDLR was created to have one department dedicated to the social and economic development of rural South Africa, and it set out to define what 'rural development' should be and how it should be achieved, leading to the creation of the Comprehensive Rural Development Programme (CRDP). DARDLA, (formerly DoA) focuses on developing comprehensive strategies linked to land and agrarian reform and food security, such as the Comprehensive Rural Development Strategy. DARDLA holds the water authorisations for the bundles of small-scale farmers in the former KaNgwane. When drafting the NWA, the government chose to keep the water allocations with DARDLA, retaining a vestige of the old system of management in the communal areas. This may have seemed logical at the time; however, the duality of the apartheid persists with two sets of rules and institutions, one for the communal farmers and the other for the rest of the farmers.

Institutional integration and water access

The Inkomati CMS and the NWRS 2 are full of references to IWRM and the need for an integrated approach. Despite this recognition, challenges persist with institutional coordination, institutional memory and the shuffling of staff within the government. It was mentioned that "every time there is a new minister of land or water affairs they forget the lessons learnt".[13] A senior manager at the ICMA noted that the provincial institutions and their mandates "are not known by us".[14] An ICMA employee commented that there is a lot of overlap amongst the institutions, but senior officials pass the blame or hide or do not take responsibility.[15] The lack of alignment of the various governmental programmes for the benefit of communal and land reform farmers is a key issue, and the working relations are fraying at the edges.

A senior DRDLA employee commented:

13 Interview, LIMA, 15 November 2012.

14 Interview, ICMA, 6 December 2012.

15 Interview, ICMA, 9 November 2012.

> *Water allocation cannot be done in isolation from other departments because it has an impact on the other departments, (...) programmes must be put in place to make it easier for black farmers to get access to water and to understand the water policy. There is a legislative and constitutional basis in terms of developing the lives of black people; however, the pace is slow on the part of the government and we lack partnerships to collaborate.*[16]

The question of how to work together is a key challenge when so many layers and mandates exist. At the regional level, all departments interviewed mentioned something about the lack of cooperative governance between departments linked to land and water, and the importance of aligning programmes. An ICMA employee commented that "there seems to be a gap and we are lacking cooperation".[15] At the time of the research there was a complete lack of communication between DRDLR and DWA, and very little incentive or political will to collaborate. A senior staff member of DRDLR recognised that to improve the conditions for black farmers it is essential that these two institutions collaborate and align their programmes and mandates, but no plan of action to facilitate this integration was ever outlined.[17]

Accessing wet vs. paper water

Water is dynamic and fluid in nature, which can be challenging to access as compared to a static natural resource, such as land. The formal routes to access water in South Africa other than a Schedule One, General Authorisation or ELU consists of obtaining a paper licence from DWA or a water lease or transfer from the Irrigation Board (IB). This is often referred to as 'paper water', and the channels and infrastructure needed to access the water to actually irrigate the farmers' crops are known as 'wet water' (van Koppen, 2012). The channels of water access in which farmers have legally applied for or hold a government registered water authorisation under the NWA is referred to as the formal water governance system.

The lack of clarity surrounding the NWA, and slow pace of WAR have led to a lack of confidence and trust in DWA, the ICMA and the overarching formal water governance system. This high degree of distrust in the formal system prevails in Nkomazi and stems from a continuation of the norms practised during apartheid. Moreover, overlaps and confusion exist regarding water policy and governance arrangements among the various institutions and stakeholders in Inkomati. At the ICMA stakeholder meeting (15 November 2012) the HD farmers that attended expressed major concerns with accessing both wet water and paper water (licences). Many of the farmers (both women and men) spoke up and were upset about the slow pace of WAR and the lack of redress. A farmer in the meeting said in an angry tone, "(...) even if you are given a licence, how can you help me abstract the water to my farm?" The ICMA responded that the issue with access to irrigation infrastructure is not an ICMA authorised expenditure, but rather a shared problem between DARDLA and DWA. The ICMA recognised the problem with accessing paper water and the fact that getting a licence does guarantee HD

16 Interview, DRDLA, 24 November 2012.

17 Interview, DRDLR, 6 November 2012.

farmers access to water.

HD farmers were often misinformed and lacked the capacity, time, money, trust and effort it took to apply for water authorisation or get a transfer/lease from the IBs to obtain paper water. The proportion of the value of the water used and the costs associated with applying for a water licence favours large-scale users; and often leaves small-scale users at a disadvantage when forced to spend money and take time to travel long distances with no promise of obtaining the small water entitlement (see van Koppen and Schreiner, 2014a). Moreover, paper water authorisations cannot be fully utilised unless the HD farmers have well-developed water storage and conveyance infrastructure, which is often not the case among sugar-cane projects in Kangwane. Another common challenge among HD farmers is when a farmer has enough paper water, but is unable to properly pump the water due to poor or broken irrigation infrastructure, theft, financial issues or high Eskom (electricity) tariffs. In this case, the farmer must pay for the water regardless of whether they are able to use it, and often the farmers suffer with poor yields. The beneficial water use narrative is strong among the departments interviewed where many supported the creation of a 'if you don't use it, you lose it' policy. This narrative of beneficial water use was used to serve and protect economically and politically important export crops like sugar cane. The concept of beneficial water use was being discussed in stakeholder meetings at the institutional level as a way to encourage or push farmers to efficiently use their water allocations, but there was no formal policy at the time of the research.

The Inkomati is over-allocated (more water use authorisations allocated than the available supply), and until the complex process of CL is completed, which has no clear end date, there is likely to be widespread uncertainty of water delivery amongst farmers and the institutions. As a result, there are very few new water authorisations available and applying via the formal system offered little opportunity for black farmers to expand their existing irrigation systems or start a new irrigated farming operation. Due to the long and expensive process of obtaining a paper water authorisation, farmers often resorted to finding alternative or informal channels of accessing water. For example, the Ngogolo cooperative, located in Nkomazi, had poorly designed canals built by the KaNgwane government. The canals and balancing dams were leaking and the infrastructure needed to be upgraded. The water licence for the Ngogolo Cooperative was 400 ha; however, over the years the farm has expanded a few hectares at a time and at the time of research they were irrigating an unlicensed area of 150 ha. As a strategy to obtain more wet water the cooperative had a 'gentleman's agreement' with a neighbouring leather farm. DARDLA was working with the farm to upgrade the canals, and the chairman Ngogolo Cooperative was bothered by the many false promises from DARDLA/DWA, and urgently wanted to know how to access more water. Several farmers interviewed used a mix of formal and informal channels to access water. In some cases, this was achieved through a mix of the paper water through formal channels and negotiated agreements through informal networks to gain access to the wet water.

An emerging challenge: Water debt

In 2012 and 2013, water use debt was an emerging issue in Nkomazi among both communal and land reform farmers. The water debt stemmed from unpaid water use charges to the IBs and DWA (however, as of 2015, the burden of this challenge has been sitting with the ICMA which is responsible for collecting water use charges). Most farmers or sugar-cane projects have water meters and/or are charged for the volume of water resources pumped for irrigation purposes, which corresponds to their water use authorisation. Regardless of the fact that a farmer is using the water or not, she or he must pay the water bills until a water transfer is coordinated through the IB. With regard to transfers or leasing water, only a small percentage of farmers are participating or benefitting from such processes, as the well-informed commercial farmers or land reform farms and communal sugar-cane projects (funding provided by DRDLR) do, with mentors or joint ventures. In addition, if a farmer has water debt, the debt must be paid before the IB can facilitate a transfer. The majority of the HD farmers interviewed stated that they are sceptical of leasing their water rights because they mistrust the system and think their water will be taken away, further contributing to the problem of water debts. Most of the water debts began to emerge as a problem when the sugar-cane projects had fallow fields or decreasing yields, resulting from a combination of one or more challenges such as financial problems, lack of capacity and institutional support, governance challenges, infrastructural malfunctions and theft.

At the end of apartheid much of the agricultural support given to the black farmers involved in the irrigation schemes in Nkomazi was withdrawn. This led to the degradation and collapse of many of the irrigation schemes in the former homelands (Shah et al., 2002; Perret, 2002). The Tikhontele sugar-cane project (242 ha) is one of these irrigation schemes started in the late 1980s by the KaNgwane Homeland government. From 2007 until the time of the research in late 2012, the fields of the Tikhontele sugar-cane project were fallow due to enduring governance, financial and water access challenges. During this time the project accumulated 300,000 South African Rand (approximately US$35,500) of water debt. A key informant from TSB commented:

> *How can [Tikhontele] resuscitate the farm with that debt. They are aware that they have to pay the bills and they just left them and the bills kept coming with interest. If they were aware they could have leased the water and could have made money. Now DWA is finally in discussion with them about the repayment of the bills. These bills are killing projects.*[18]

In response to the water debt challenge, a DWA director said that the monthly water use bills and letters outlining outstanding water use charges were sent to the IBs, but DWA was not sure if the farmers were simply not paying the bills or the bills and notification letters were not being sent. Nonetheless, nobody was taking leadership to investigate why the bills were not being paid or to enforce that the debt was settled. He described this situation as risky and that DWA/IBs

18 Interview, TSB social facilitator, 21 December 2012.

lack human capacity and sufficient time to enforce the payment of water charges. Many of the HD farmers were unaware of the trading or leasing policies because they were not participating in water governance structures or the representatives attending the IB meetings were not passing the key messages down. In the case of the Tikhontele project, there should have been some sort of intervention or assistance in facilitating a temporary lease of the water authorisation before the water debt became such a large burden. On a positive note, Tikhontele is located on communal land so the farm cannot be auctioned off by the bank. By contrast, Land Reform (redistribution) farms that have a title can be repossessed by the bank. In some cases, farms claimed only ten years ago are being auctioned, and oddly enough are bought back by Land Reform (DRDLR) to meet the department's redistribution targets.

According to DRDLR, land reform farmers should have water authorisations that come with the farm. But in reality, the beneficiaries often lack funds, support and the skills to manage the farm. In many cases the beneficiaries cannot work the land right away or the farm is not in operation when they receive the land, resulting in the water use charges building up with no intervention or support. Furthermore, TSB, LIMA and extension officers were not aware of the debt linked to the farms before this emerged as a huge problem. The Inyathi restitution farm in Nkomazi, owned by the Mhlaba trust faces severe water debt challenges. The managers were unaware of the procedure to lease water rights and had very little knowledge regarding the formal water governance system. The managers of the project feared that leasing their water authorisations would result in their water rights being taken away, largely due to their mistrust in the government. Cases also existed where white commercial farmers incurred a substantial amount of water debt right before the transfer of land to Land Reform, creating financial and bureaucratic obstacles in the transfer of the farm to its beneficiaries.

At the regional level in Nelspruit, DRDLR (Land Reform) views the water debt problem "as reversing the gains of freedom (...) We have obtained political freedom, but there is a cry for economic freedom".[19] A strong feeling emanates among DRDLR that DWA and the IBs are not aligning programmes or informing farmers of their rights. According to DWA, certain IBs are withholding information from them, and DRDLR are not reporting new owners/beneficiaries of farms, so the information they have in their system is not representative of the situation on the ground. In contrast, DWA and the ICMA said that DRDLR is not communicating or sharing important data linked to land claims, and in turn they lack pertinent information to assist or engage with these particular farmers. The Komati IB attributes the water debt problem to sloppy land reform transfers, in which DRDLR is not checking the water debt linked to the land before they buy the farm, and to DWA for not following through or enforcing payment of bills. From the viewpoint of TSB nobody is really taking responsibility for informing farmers about leasing or trading water rights. The IB also expressed in interviews that they try to ensure the black farmer representatives in the meetings are reporting back pertinent

19 Interview, DRDLR, 6 November 2012.

information to other farmers in the communities, but information is not filtering down, especially in regard to important tenants of IWRM policy such as leasing or trading water authorisations.

The case of the water debt is complex and it showcases the deep scepticism and skewed power dynamics rooted in the post-apartheid water governance system. Each institution made excuses or blamed another department, and there was little incentive to collaborate and break free of the funding silos to solve the emerging water debt issue. This disconnect between key land and water institutions has further jeopardised the rural small-scale farmers ability to access water, participate in meetings and, most importantly, break free from poverty.

Discussion

Integration or (dis)integration of land and water reforms and institutions

The NWA aims to manage water in an 'integrated' manner which suggests the obvious interconnection between land and water institutions. However, it has proven difficult to integrate these and overcome the divide because often two or more government agencies are assigned authority over land and water (Meinzen-Dick and Nkonya, 2007). The formation of new water rights institutions can aid in social and economic development and protect crucial ecosystems, but these initiatives to improve water allocations may be deemed inadequate, "unless grounded in a good understanding of social institutions that shape rights to water, a careful assessment of the options available for improving water management and a willingness by those involved to experiment, adapt and learn from experience" (ibid: 8).

The lack of an 'integrated' approach among the departments with overlapping mandates has led to issue-based communication, lack of active participation in key stakeholder meetings by certain departments, nonalignment of projects, competition (animosity), silos, a general lack of accountability, and poor information flow between institutions. The question then arises as to why there is very little integration between institutions with overlapping mandates, despite the recognition by all the interviewees of the importance to coordinate. The answer is not easy. First, there are no incentives or enforced legislation to facilitate the necessary collaboration and ways to break free of funding silos. Second, for integration to become a reality in the Inkomati it requires the acknowledgement of the "diverse multi-actor landscape and consequent diverging interests and perceptions that make up the water allocation and land reform" (Funke and Jacobs, 2011: 82). At the policy and institutional level there has been a failure to recognise the full impact of the historical context and power imbalances in implementing IWRM in South Africa. Third, the integration debates in the water sector did not sufficiently align with the political negotiations surrounding land reform. This lack of coordination at a policy level between land and water reforms was made worse by the marked lack of sufficient incentives or political will within regional and local institutions to collaborate. Moreover, a few employees at DRLR noted that cooperative governance legislation exists, but believed it was a combination of a lack of political will and human capacity to implement and enforce these Acts at the regional level. The legislation is therefore in place, such as the Development Facilitation Act, or the Inter-Government Relations Act, but lacks the financing, capacity, and perhaps the political will to enforce and put incentives (i.e. bonuses, funding, recognition etc.) in place to facilitate institutional integration in such a complex historical landscape.

The 2013 National Water Resource Strategy 2 has recognised the livelihoods impacts of water allocation and the importance of collaboration (RSA, 2013). However, elevating the public and political profile of the WAR programme "requires linkages to broader government and private sector programmes of redress in land, agriculture and business" (DWA, 2012b: 67). The word 'integrated' is inherently subjective and was mentioned 35 times in the NWRS 2 ranging from 'integrated' planning, governance, solutions, implementation, and development. However, the strategy fails to specifically outline the criteria to achieve integration or coordination and to define what 'integrated' actually means in the South African context. This parallels the various debates surrounding the meaning and interpretations of the integration in IWRM. This may be because integration can be interpreted and understood in many ways (Movik et al., this book).

The ability of the South African governmental institutions to commit to integration is fuzzy, vague and open to interpretations, which reflect the criticisms of IWRM as a concept (see Allan, 2003; Biswas, 2004; Molle, 2008). Additionally, it has been observed by water analysts that there is an unwillingness or inability of policy-makers to commit to the integration aspect in southern Africa (see Swatuk, 2005; Jonker, 2007). Furthermore, deeper issues exist surrounding the disconnect between land and water reforms. For example, the Ministry of Water responsible for the implementation IWRM has little control over other important processes and departments linked to water, such as agriculture and land reform (Hübschen, 2011).

This disintegration of institutions and poor diffusion of key water policy information has contributed to the challenges farmers face as outlined in the cases studies. Despite the progressive reforms, water allocation still remains a profoundly political issue due to the historical context of South Africa, the economic importance of water, and the many complex needs of multiple stakeholders from differing departments, socioeconomic classes and political regimes. Moreover, in practice the water policy and corresponding institutions have neglected the real issues plaguing the most marginalised, i.e. water reallocation, agricultural support, power imbalances, and challenges to realising participation alongside persisting poverty.

Participation and power

The widespread emphasis on devolving power and increasing participation in resource management approaches has led many decision makers to assume that the benefits of participation and decentralisation outweigh the costs (Brown 2006, 2011; Jonker et al., 2010; Holmes and Scoones, 2000). However, evidence suggests "that the poor and oppressed are less able to utilise a variety of institutional channels and therefore suffer double marginalisation; remaining vulnerable and resource poor" (see Odgaard, 2002; Benjaminsen and Lund, 2003: Cleaver et al., 2005: 14). Therefore, positive interactions and effective engagement with marginalised individuals in society are crucial to improving water access and livelihoods.

The racial divide and power differences among various actors greatly affect the ability of the more marginalised groups to participate and access water through the formal system. In Nkomazi, large imbalances in knowledge and power have resulted in the majority of the black farmers lacking a 'voice' or the 'ability' to participate in formal governance structures (Denby, 2013). Both land reform and communal farmers are present at water governance meetings, but largely lack a voice to influence decisions. HD farmers felt that the meetings/forums were just about discussing, and their pertinent questions were not being answered or addressed. So, participating in these water governance stakeholder meetings etc. offered the farmers little benefit beside a free lunch. Further aggravating the problem is the lack of important functions of the ICMA, and the presence of DWA is limited on the ground and information regarding NWA and IWRM is not properly filtering down to the lowest levels.

Creating new water management institutions is a highly political exercise, something Waalewijn et al. (2005) draws attention to in his study of the processes of creating new institutions and infrastructure in the Inkomati; highlighting how there has been little mutual collaboration in terms of problem-setting and agreeing on directions and structures. Hence, the idea of 'participation' which is so important to much of the IWRM thinking seems to be a rather thinly applied concept in practice. When drafting the Water Act, not enough consideration was placed on addressing the possible challenges with farmers paying for water, and the fact that breaking into the formal water governance system requires a fundamental shift in cultural values. As evidenced by the experience of establishing the ICMA, building legitimate, decentralised institutions, capacity and effective participation takes time, and HD farmers must see their participation resulting in more than just 'talking'.

Institutional accountability

The challenges with participation, integration, water access, and water debt are all linked to flawed departmental accountability in some way or another. It can be argued that new channels of governance were required in the South African context in moving away from hierarchies and centralised control of water to a new mode of hybrid governance (see Rhodes, 1996; Teisman and Hermans, 2011). However, the slow progress in establishing the non-hierarchal governance structures promoted by IWRM has led to a lack of accountability and transparency which are key to building trust and confidence in water institutions (Frewer, 2003). The creation of new decentralised institutions (ICMA, WUA) parallel to existing governmental water institutions (DWA) brought up questions of who ultimately is in charge, who is accountable or holds the mandate to solve my water access challenges? Further complicating the integration aspect of IWRM is the tension between decentralising according to the principles of IWRM and the urge to centralise the power in DWA. This not only led to a lengthy ten year process to hand over key legislative mandates (licensing and billing) to the ICMA, but flawed the institutional legitimacy of the ICMA, and greatly slowed the ICMA's ability to take action on pressing local-level issues.

IWRM and local-level realities

Large discrepancies in power and knowledge persist between commercial growers and the many small-scale black farmers, especially women. IWRM has not really worked in practice due to the failure of the water policies to fully recognise the historic complexities and the underlying inequalities in South Africa. As in the case of the Inkomati, the growing competition for scarce resources is often felt by the most impoverished in comparison to the "high-volume, non-poor water users [that have] acquired the socio-political power to assure their permanent access to water and where poor people are generally excluded from water management institutions" (Schreiner and van Koppen, 2002: 970). Water policies must recognise the social fabric of society and not neglect the real issues on the ground. In short, an effective water rights system can substantially improve marginalised members of society access to water (Bruns and Meinzen-Dick, 2005). Major challenges on the ground persist due to the lack of institutional presence, including the flawed knowledge and mistrust in the formal water management system. Much of the 'buy in' across socioeconomic classes and racial groups has largely been lost to the delays in deciding the correct institutional arrangements to govern water instead of implementing and following through with promises (see Jonker et al., 2010).

Formal policies can be published overnight, but the informal rules and norms gradually change over time, and communities' access to water is embedded in the particular historic, social and environmental context (North, 1995). At the local level large disparities exist in relation to power and water access, and the economic and domestic water needs of the majority of black farmers are not being met (ICMA, 2010). Due to the high demand for water and the bureaucratic process of obtaining a paper licence, alternative channels are being forged in the Inkomati. Hence, when state-based water rights systems are imposed at a fast pace and differ from local water rights systems, the local arrangements are destroyed and the policy cannot become effective and be legitimate on its own (van Koppen, 2003).

Other challenges also persist related to an imposed water rights system where a paper water licence is useless if farmers are unable to access the actual wet water. "Many governments recognise this and are the first to stipulate in their water laws that they reject any legal responsibility for actually delivering the water 'promised' in the allocated formal right" (van Koppen, 2003: 1052). Ensuring water authorisations are actually met is largely underfunded – e.g. DWA's Resource Poor Farmer Programme is not sufficiently meeting the demands of the farmers. Furthermore, the high cost and demand to allocate water licences to the huge numbers of small farmers in the rural areas have created long waits and burdens on the budgets, and leave less time to regulate large-scale water users (van Koppen and Schreiner, 2014a).

Breaking into the formal water governance system and accessing both wet and paper water is clearly a cornerstone in successful sugar-cane projects and improved livelihoods in Nkomazi. The successful sugar-cane projects in Nkomazi had a combination of efficient and well-designed irrigation systems, extension or management support/skills and a sufficient water authorisation. However, the lack of access to water, rising input costs (electricity) and theft have made it more difficult for small-scale sugar-cane farmers to make a healthy profit. DRDLR saw sugar cane as 'green gold' but without access to sufficient water many black farmers were excluded from breaking into sugar-cane farming. Despite the evidence of the many positive livelihood impacts and relative efficiencies of small-scale growers, the economies of scale, export capabilities and neoliberal model of commercial agriculture dominate the water and land reforms, and political discourses in Southern Africa (Lahiff, 2003; also see Kleinbooi, 2009). Regardless of the water scarcity and progressive water policy in the Inkomati, a water consumptive crop such as sugar cane remains a political and economic powerhouse, and holds a large percentage of water authorisations, many of which are pre-1998 with existing lawful use entitlements. Thus, many black farmers are faced with challenges in accessing water, struggle to make a profit due to the economies of scale in sugar cane production, and have few options in switching crops due the difficulties in assessing new markets, the huge costs and the economic power of the sugar-cane industry in Nkomazi.

Conclusion

Efforts to implement the NWA and IWRM in South Africa have been fraught with challenges in practice. This is largely because the progressive policy did not fully recognise the complex historical context, and the underlying inequalities in knowledge, power and access to resources. The power imbalances and large disparities in access to natural resources have influenced the outcomes of the water policy, water access and the way people participate in water governance structures today. In rural areas, large discrepancies continue to persist (Funke et al., 2007; DWA, 2012b; Schreiner, 2012; Brown, 2014), and these inequalities are further reinforced when well-informed and powerful commercial farmers use them to their advantage. The empirical cases highlight the many discrepancies between the progressive IWRM-influenced policy on paper and the actual realities on the ground. In addition, the cases discussed the many challenges related to the integration of institutions linked to water, agriculture, and land reform.

Although IWRM and the NWA promote integration as a solution to inter-sectoral conflict and improved governance, evidence from the research notes that coordination is not always an easy task and silos continue to persist between sectors, reform processes and funding mandates. This chapter argues that the decentralisation and integration aspects of IWRM are lacking in the Inkomati, and there are few incentives encouraging the institutions to integrate to improve access to water for HD farmers. Currently, many HD farmers are losing faith in the formal system because of the institutional disintegration, flawed accountability, and the slow pace of Water Allocation Reform. It is widely understood in South Africa that the success of WAR is largely dependent on collaboration between all sectors, especially land reform. For these reasons there is an urgent need for a coherent water and land reform vision to counter the failed past integration attempts.

In the Inkomati, IWRM is more of an academic concept with very little empirical life in Nkomazi (i.e. the policy is not trickling down to, or understood at, the lowest levels) (van Koppen, 2012; Denby, 2013). In South Africa, IWRM is seen as a process to achieve goals; however, the fuzzy conceptualisation often favours one dimension of IWRM over another (see Biswas, 2004; Mollinga et al., 2007). There is also little consensus in South Africa on the definition of integration, and how to balance equity, efficiency and sustainability aspects of IWRM.

The NWA and WAR have also not sufficiently addressed the inequalities stemming from apartheid, and have neglected many of the issues plaguing black farmers and the rural poor at the local levels. For these reasons it can be stated that IWRM has not really worked in practice. Regardless of the NWA's focus on equity and decentralisation, DWA and the ICMA cannot ignore the pressing issues at the local-level, and must also recognise that access to water for productive purposes is crucial to improving livelihoods in the rural areas and former homelands (Schreiner et al., 2010: 13). In addition, there is a huge demand for more inclusive and pro-poor solutions through the allocation of water and the development of water infrastructure in South Africa (see Schreiner et al., 2010). We suggest that the ICMA should drive these pro-poor solutions and integration efforts in order to build capacity across institutions, improve institutional performance and, most of all, improve the conditions for black farmers in the Inkomati. And finally, water policies in South Africa must have a stronger emphasis on equity and the developmental aspects of water in improving livelihoods through coordinated and targeted reallocation approaches.

Acknowledgements

We appreciate the support from the Research Council of Norway for funding the Flows and Practices: The Politics of Integrated Water Resource Management in Africa. We are very grateful for the comments and insights from the anonymous reviewers and the entire project team when crafting this chapter, especially Bill Derman and Emmanuel Manzungu. Finally, we are ever so thankful for the people in South Africa that contributed their time, thoughts and experiences to this research project.

References

Allan, T. 2003. *IWRM/IWRAM: A new sanctioned discourse?* Occasional Paper No. 50. SOAS Water Issues Study Group. London: School of Oriental and African Studies, Kings College.

Anderson, A.J. 2005. Engaging disadvantaged communities: Lessons from the Inkomati CMA establishment process. In *Proceeding of International Workshop on African water laws: Plural legislative frameworks for rural water management in Africa,* pp. 2628. Johannesburg, South Africa, 26-28 January 2005.

Anderson, A.; Karar, E. and Farolfi, S. 2008. Synthesis: IWRM lessons for implementation. *Water SA* 34(6): 665-669.

Ashton, P.J.; Turton, A.R. and Roux D.J. 2006. Exploring the government, society, and science interfaces in integrated water resource management in South Africa. *Jour-*

nal of Contemporary Water Research & Education 135(1): 28-35.

Backeberg, G.R. 2005. Water institutional reforms in South Africa. *Water Policy* 7(2005): 107-123.

Bate, R. and Tren, R. 2002. *The cost of free water: The global problem of water misallocation and the case of South Africa.* Johannesburg, South Africa: The Free Market Foundation.

Benjaminsen, T.A. and Lund, C. (Eds). 2003. *Securing land rights in Africa.* London: Frank Cass.

Biswas, A.K. 2004. Integrated water resources management: A re-assessment. *Water International* 29(2): 248-256.

Brown, J. 2006. *A cautionary tale: A review of the institutional principle in practice, with reference to the Inkomati WMA, South Africa.* Manchester: Institute for Development Policy and Management, University of Manchester.

Brown, J. 2011. Assuming too much? Participatory water resource governance in South Africa. *The Geographical Journal* 177(2): 171-185.

Brown, J. 2014. Evaluating participatory initiatives in South Africa not just processes but outcomes too. *SAGE Open* 4(2): 1-16.

Bruns, B.R. and Meinzen-Dick, R. 2005. Frameworks for water rights: An overview of institutional options. In Bruns, B.R., Ringler, C. and Meinzen-Dick, R. (Eds), *Water rights reform: Lessons for institutional design*, pp. 3-25. Washington: International Food Policy Research Institute.

Cleaver, F.; Franks, T.; Boesten, J. and Kiire, A. 2005. *Water governance and poverty: What works for the poor.* Bradford, UK: University of Bradford, Bradford Centre for International Development.

Denby, K. 2013. Institutional integration and local level water access in the Inkomati catchment management area, South Africa. MSc thesis. Norwegian University of Life Sciences, Aas, Norway.

DWA (Department of Water Affairs). 2012a. *Business case for the Inkomati-Usuthu Catchment Management Agency.* Pretoria, South Africa.

DWA. 2012b. Proposed National Water Resource Strategy 2: Summary. Prepared by Nkondo, M.N.; van Zyl, F.C.; Keuris, H. and Schreiner, B. Pretoria, South Africa.

DWA. 2007. *Principles to guide the development of a framework for water allocation: Develop a framework for water allocation to guide compulsory licensing in the Inkomati water management area.* Pretoria, South Africa.

Frewer, L.J. 2003. Trust, transparency and social context: Implications for social amplification of risk. In Pidgeon, N.; Kasperson, R.E. and Slovic, P. (Eds), *The social amplification of risk*, pp. 123-137. Cambridge: Cambridge University Press.

Funke, N.; Nortje, K.; Findlater, K.; Burns, M.; Turton, A.; Weaver, A. and Hattingh, H. 2007. Redressing inequality: South Africa's new water policy. *Environment: Science and Policy for Sustainable Development* 49(3): 10-23.

Funke, N. and Jacobs, I. 2010. Integration challenges of water and land reform – A critical review of South Africa. In Uhlig, U. (Ed), *Current issues of water management*, pp. 81-106. InTech.

GWP (Global Water Partnership). 2000. *Integrated Water Resource Management.*

Technical Advisory Committee Background Paper No. 4. Stockholm, Sweden: Global Water Partnership.

Greenberg, S. 2010. *Status report on land and agricultural policy in South Africa 2010.* Research Report No. 40. Cape Town: University of the Western Cape, Programme for Land and Agrarian Studies.

Hall, R. 2004. A political economy of land reform in South Africa. *Review of African Political Economy* 31(100): 213-227.

Holmes, T. and Scoones, I. 2000. *Participatory environmental policy processes: Experiences from North and South.* IDS Working Paper 113. Brighton, UK: Institute for Development Studies.

Hübschen, K. 2011. *Integrated water resources management as a governance challenge for countries of the Middle East with special focus on Yemen, Jordan and Syria.* Logos Verlag Berlin: GmbH.

ICMA (Inkomati Catchment Management Agency). 2010. *The Inkomati Catchment Management: A first generation catchment management strategy.* Nelspruit, Mpumalanga, South Africa.

ICMA. 2014. 2013/2014 *Inkomati catchment management agency annual report.* Nelspruit, Mpumalanga, South Africa.

IUCMA (Inkomati-Usuthu Catchment Management Agency). 2015. IUCMA and our functions. *Presentation to the water use verification information meetings.* Nelspruit, Mpumalanga, South Africa.

Jonker, L. 2007. Integrated water resources management: The theory-praxis-nexus, a South African perspective. *Physics and Chemistry of the Earth, Parts A/B/C* 32(15-18):1257-1263.

Jonker, L.; Swatuk, L.A.; Matiwane, M.; Mila, U.; Ntloko, M. and Simataa, F. 2010. Exploring the lowest appropriate level of water governance in South Africa. WRC Report No. 1837/1/10. Pretoria, South Africa: Water Research Commission.

King, B.H. 2005. Spaces of change: Tribal authorities in the former KaNgwane homeland, South Africa. *Area* 37(1): 64-72.

King, B.H. 2007. Developing KaNgwane: Geographies of segregation and integration in the new South Africa. *The Geographical Journal* 173(1): 13-25.

Kleinbooi, K. 2009. *The private sector and land reform.* Bellville, South Africa: University of Western Cape, Institute for Poverty, Land and Agrarian Studies (PLASS).

Lahiff, E. 2003. The regional implications of the crisis in Zimbabwe: Rationale and principles of regional support for land. In Cornwell, R. (Ed), *Zimbabwe's turmoil: Problems and prospects*, pp. 77-85. Monograph No. 87. Pretoria: Institute for Security Studies.

Lahiff, E. 2007. Willing buyer, willing seller: South Africa's failed experiment in market-led agrarian reform. *Third World Quarterly* 28(8): 1577-1597.

May, J. (Ed). 2000. *Poverty and inequality in South Africa: Meeting the challenge.* Cape Town, South Africa: David Philip Publishers.

Mehta, L.; Alba, R.; Bolding, A.; Denby, K.; Derman, B.; Hove, T.; Manzungu, E; Movik, S.; Prabhakaran, P. and van Koppen, B. 2014. The politics of IWRM in Southern Africa. *International Journal of Water Resources Development* 30(3): 528-542.

Mehta, L. and Movik, S. 2014. Flows and practices: Integrated water resource management in Africa contexts. IDS Working Paper No. 438. Brighton, U.K: Institute of Development Studies.

Meinzen-Dick, R. and Nkonya, L. 2007. Understanding legal pluralism in water and land rights: Lessons from Africa and Asia. In van Koppen, B.; Giordano, M. and Butterworth, J. (Eds), *Community-based water law and water resource management reform in developing countries*, pp. 12-27. Wallingford, UK: CAB International.

Molle, F. 2008. Nirvana concepts, narratives and policy models: Insights from the water sector. *Water Alternatives* 1(1): 25-38.

Mollinga, P.P.; Meinzen-Dick, R. and Merrey, D.J. 2007. Politics, plurality and problemsheds: A strategic approach for reform of agricultural water resources management. *Development Policy Review* 25(6): 699-719.

Movik, S. 2012. *Fluid rights: Water Allocation reform in South Africa.* Cape Town, South Africa: HSRC Press.

Mutondo, J.; Farolfi, S. and Dinar, A. 2016. *Water governance decentralization in Sub-Saharan Africa: Between myth and reality.* London: Springer.

North, D.C. 1995. The new institutional economics and third world development. In Harriss, J.; Hunter, J. and Lewis, C. (Eds), *The new institutional economics and third world development*, pp. 17-26. London: Routledge.

Odgaard, R. 2002. Scrambling for land in Tanzania: Processes of formalisation and legitimisation of land rights. *European Journal of Development Research* 14(2): 71-88.

Perret, S. 2002. Water policies and smallholding irrigation schemes in South Africa: A history and new institutional challenges. *Water Policy* 4(3): 283-300.

RSA (Republic of South Africa). 1998. *National Water Act. Act No. 36 of 1998.* Pretoria: Government Printers.

RSA (Republic of South Africa). 2004. *National water resource strategy.* Pretoria: Government Printers.

RSA. 2013. *National water resource strategy: Water for an equitable and sustainable future.* Pretoria: Government Printers.

Rhodes, R.A.W. 1996. The new government: Governing without governance. *Political Studies* XLIV: 652-667.

Schreiner, B. 2013. Viewpoint - Why has the South African national water act been so difficult to implement? *Water Alternatives* 6(2): 239-245

Schreiner, B. 2012. Issues of balancing international, environmental and equity needs in a situation of water scarcity. In Dinar, A. and Albiac, J. (Eds), *Policy and strategic behaviour in water resource management*, pp. 207-230. London: Earthscan.

Schreiner, B. and Hassan, R. 2011. *Transforming water management in South Africa: Designing and implementing a new policy framework.* London: Springer.

Schreiner, B.; Tapela, B. and van Koppen, B. 2010. Water for agrarian reform and rural poverty eradication: Where is the leak? In *Proceedings of the conference on Overcoming Inequality and structural poverty in South Africa: Towards inclusive growth and development, pp. 1-23.* Johannesburg, South Africa, 20-22 September 2010.

Schreiner, B. and van Koppen, B. 2002. Catchment management agencies for poverty eradication in South Africa. *Physics and Chemistry of the Earth Parts A/B/C* 27(11): 969-976.

Shah, T.; van Koppen, B.; Merrey, D.; de Lange, M. and Samad, M. 2002. *Institutional alternatives in African smallholder irrigation: Lessons from international experience with irrigation management transfer*. IWMI Research Report No. 60. Colombo, Sir Lanka: International Water Management Institute.

Swatuk, L.A. 2005. Political challenges to implementing IWRM in Southern Africa. *Physics and Chemistry of the Earth* 30(11-16): 872-880.

Teisman, G. and Hermans, L. 2011. Perspectives on water governance: Synthesis and conclusions. In van der Valk, M.R. and Keenan, P. (Eds), *Principles of good governance at different water governance levels*, pp. 1-87. Delft, the Netherlands: UNESCO.

Terreblanche, S. 2002. *A history of inequality in South Africa 1652-2002*. KwaZulu-Natal: University of KwaZulu-Natal Press/KMM Review Publishing.

van Koppen, B. 2000. *From bucket to basin: Managing river basins to alleviate water deprivation*. Colombo, Sri Lanka: International Water Management Institute.

van Koppen, B. 2003. Water reform in Sub-Saharan Africa: what is the difference? *Physics and Chemistry of the Earth Parts A/B/C* 28(20-27): 1047-1053.

van Koppen, B. 2012. Personal Communication. On the phone. November 2012.

van Koppen, B.; Jha, N. and Merrey, D.J. 2003. *Redressing racial inequities through water law in South Africa: Revisiting old contradictions?* Comprehensive Assessment Research Paper No. 3. Colombo, Sri Lanka: International Water Management Institute.

van Koppen, B.; Sally, H.; Aliber, M.; Cousins, B. and Tapela, B. 2009. *Water resources management, rural redress and agrarian reform*. Development Planning Division Working Paper Series (7). Halfway House, South Africa: Development Planning Division, Development Bank of South Africa.

van Koppen, B. and Schreiner, B. 2014a. Priority general authorisations in rights-based water use authorisations in South Africa. *Water Policy* 16(2014): 1-19.

van Koppen, B. and Schreiner, B. 2014b. Moving beyond integrated water resource management: Developmental water management in South Africa. *International Journal of Water Resources Development* 30(3): 543-558.

Waalewijn, P.; Wester, P. and Straaten, K. 2005. Transforming river basin management in South Africa: Lessons from the Lower Komati River. *Water International* 30(2): 184-196.

Wester, P.; Merrey, J.D. and De Lange, M. 2003. Boundaries of consent: Stakeholder representation in river basin management in Mexico and South Africa. *World Development* 31(5): 797-812.

Woodhouse, P. 2008. *Water rights in South Africa: Insights from legislative reform*. BWPI Working Paper. Manchester: Brooks World Poverty Institute.

Woodhouse, P. 2012. Reforming land and water rights in South Africa. *Development and Change* 43(4): 847-868.

6

Surges and Ebbs: National Politics and International Influence in the Formulation and Implementation of IWRM in Zimbabwe[1]

Emmanuel Manzungu

Bill Derman

ABSTRACT: In the 1990s, the Government of Zimbabwe undertook water reforms to redress racially defined inequitable access to agricultural water. This chapter analyses how a water reform process, seemingly informed by a clear political economy objective, was hijacked by efforts directed at implementing Integrated Water Resources Management (IWRM). It uses the notion of policy articulation to analyse why and how IWRM 'travelled' to and in Zimbabwe and with what outcomes. The chapter shows that attempts at introducing and implementing IWRM in Zimbabwe have had a chequered history. The efforts of Zimbabwe in pioneering implementation of IWRM in southern Africa, have subsequently waned, and prospects for resurrecting IWRM in its original form are low. Introduced in the 1990s when Western donors jumped on the bandwagon of the liberal economic agenda inspired by the IMF/World Bank, it declined between 2000 and 2009 due to a combination of poor economic performance, national-level politics and international isolation. In 2011 IWRM was reintroduced as the country re-engaged with the international community. The re-emergence of IWRM, however, seems to be largely rhetorical as the focus is now on fixing a crisis-ridden water sector, with a new political dispensation adding another layer of complexity. The chapter concludes that the development of IWRM in Zimbabwe mirrors broader national-level socio-political processes and their complex relationship with the international community.

KEYWORDS: Water reform, IWRM, policy (dis)articulation, Zimbabwe

Introduction

In the 1990s, the Government of Zimbabwe (GoZ) embarked on a water reform process because of the need to redress racially defined inequitable access to agricultural water in a country in which agriculture dominates the economy. This was an enormous challenge, given 90 years of colonialism. From 1890 when

1 First published in *Water Alternatives* 9(3): 495-514.

Zimbabwe (then known as Rhodesia) became a British colony until it gained independence in 1980, land, water and mineral resources, and other levers of economic power, were systematically entrenched in a white minority population to the disadvantage of the black majority. The result was that, until the reforms were legislated in 1998, close to two decades after independence in 1980, 85% of the water resources of the country were still being used by 4500 white large-scale commercial farmers (Manzungu, 2001). The belated reforms culminated in the repeal of the 1976 Water Act (Rhodesia, 1976), and promulgation in 1998 of the Water Act (GoZ, 1998a) and the Zimbabwe National Water Authority (ZINWA) Act (GoZ, 1998b). The 1976 Act was a revision of the 1927 Water Act (Rhodesia, 1927), which heralded the birth of an agriculture-oriented water legislation and state control of water resources (Vincent and Manzungu, 2004).

In this chapter we explore how a water reform process, seemingly informed by a clear political economy objective, was hijacked by efforts directed at implementing Integrated Water Resources Management (IWRM) as stated in the most recent (2013) water policy:

> *The reforms were undertaken primarily to redress the inequitable access to the country's water resources that has been enshrined into the 1976 Water Act and to embark on key principles of Integrated Water Resources (IWRM) on the basis of which the Water and ZINWA Acts were developed (GoZ, 2013a: 9).*

Zimbabwe is a good test case to understand why and how IWRM 'travelled' from the North to the global South (Mehta et al., 2014). It was the first southern African country to (try) to implement IWRM (Manzungu, 2004).[2] The question is: given the country's political history and hydrological characteristics, was/is IWRM part of the solution to the country's water challenges? Zimbabwe is a semi-arid country with limited surface water and groundwater resources that are, to make matters worse, poorly managed because of financial, human, and material challenges (GoZ, 2013a). Its economy is water-dependent: there is a close relationship between annual rainfall and annual Gross Domestic Product (GDP) because of the importance of rainfall-dependent agricultural and hydro-electricity production to the economy, which also affects industry, mining and tourism (GoZ, 2013a). On average, agriculture uses 82% of surface water while urban and industry use 14% and mining 3% (Davis and Hirji, 2014). Throughout the colonial and post-colonial history, debates around equitable access to water between and within sectors, and between different races and, to some extent,

2 Implementation here refers to when IWRM was explicitly stated officially as the guiding approach in water management and when steps were taken to that effect. It does not refer to when some elements of IWRM, which predated the official introduction of IWRM, were implemented. In this regard, Zimbabwe can claim to be the first southern country to implement IWRM because, although both South Africa and Zimbabwe enacted new pro-IWRM water laws in 1998, Zimbabwe proceeded to institute the enunciated principles, by for example, setting up water management institutions according to hydrological boundaries (catchment and sub-catchment councils) within a year of the enactment of the law while South Africa prevaricated and changed the number of catchment management agencies (CMAs) and only set up the first CMA in 2004, some 6 years after the enactment of the law (see Movik et al., this book).

classes, have dominated the Zimbabwean waterscape. This explains the various water reform cycles, with the present day IWRM-informed reforms being the latest (GoZ, 2013a).

A few years after the 1998 water reforms were enacted into law, questions were raised regarding the relevance of a neoliberal water reform agenda drawing on global paradigms, such as IWRM in Zimbabwe (see Manzungu, 2001, 2002). The new water law accorded a smaller role for the state in the planning and management of water resources and water financing. The expectation was that commodification of water and related services, through the application of the user pays principle, would pay for the planning and management of water resources. But the social, political and economic conditions in the country have dramatically changed since the time when the reforms were enacted. Some of the important changes, which are expanded in later sections of this chapter, include: transferring ownership of agricultural land from the white minority to the majority black population; a significant shrinking of the economy; increasing volatility of the political environment; and the deterioration of social conditions, such as poverty levels.

Against this backdrop it is important to examine whether IWRM was and is still relevant to Zimbabwe. This is important because the GoZ, as captured in the 2013 National Water Policy (see above), still continues to frame its water management approach along IWRM lines, epitomised by the user pays principle and realignment of water management institutions from politico-administrative (following local government structures) boundaries to hydrological ones. The Government believes the difficult conditions that prevailed in the country between 2000 and 2008 negatively affected implementation of IWRM (GoZ, 2013a). This chapter poses the fundamental question as to why the implementation of IWRM was chosen as the vehicle for delivering the stated political economy objective of equitable water use, and what the prospects for its successful implementation were.

The chapter uses the notion of policy articulation to analyse why and how IWRM 'travelled' to and in Zimbabwe and with what outcomes. The economic and political conditions under which IWRM was formulated and implemented are highlighted, as well as how this was shaped by the IMF/World Bank-sponsored liberal economic agenda which was complemented by Western donors eager to promote IWRM (Manzungu, 2001, 2002; Derman and Manzungu, this book). In this chapter, implementation of IWRM refers to steps taken to operationalise one or more of Dublin principles or Global Water Partnership (GWP) IWRM principles. It does not suggest wholesale adoption of IWRM or IWRM principles to the letter.

Approach of the Study

In our view, understanding why and how IWRM 'travelled' to and in Zimbabwe, or any country for that matter, is not helped by the popular definition of IWRM as the process which promotes the development and management of water, land and related resources, in order to maximise the resultant economic and social welfare in an equitable manner without compromising the sustainability of vital ecosystems (GWP, 2000). This popular definition of IWRM conjures up the notion of an apolitical and instrumentalist activity, and by so doing depoliticises the (political) choices that are inherent in the formulation and implementation of IWRM. Instead we prefer to refer to IWRM as a political project, to denote the politics inherent in resource management decisions made up of everyday politics, politics of policy-making, hydropolitics and global politics (Mollinga, 2001). Such a viewpoint rejects the idea of policy-making and implementation as a linear process and activity (Mollinga and Bolding, 2004). In this chapter we draw insights from the politics of policy-making to try and understand the IWRM journey to and in Zimbabwe (Wester, 2008; see also the Introduction to this book).

Due to the internationalisation of IWRM, we widen our scope of analysis to include international institutions that played a role in exporting IWRM to Zimbabwe, and how these interacted with national-level players. We use the notion of policy articulation to try and understand the political dynamics that were involved. Policy articulation is defined as the process by which policy actors support, modify, displace and translate a policy idea with the outcome that a policy or reform package becomes less or more real (Wester, 2008). We also talk of policy disarticulation to refer to a situation where a policy is not merely supported, modified, displaced or translated but discarded or ignored to the extent that it loses its currency in the contemporary discourse.

The evidence that will be presented in this chapter will show that articulation of IWRM was due to the IMF and World Bank and other Western donors, and was disarticulated because of national-level politics. We also show that it was the same actors who articulated IWRM in the first instance who came back to (try to) resuscitate it. We also discuss the agency of the various actors involved in the implementation of IWRM (see Cherlet and Venot, 2013). Consequently, we argue that, although there was influence from outside, the GoZ had some leeway to adopt and implement IWRM (see below).

This study was undertaken between 2011 and 2014, and involved a number of steps. First, we analysed the main pieces of water legislation (Water and ZINWA Act), and water policy (2013 National Water Policy) where our interest was to assess how IWRM was formulated and how it was to be implemented. We also examined related documents, namely consultancy reports of studies sponsored by the World Bank, which fed into the development of the 2013 National Water Policy.

Secondly we followed national-level political processes, which we reckoned to have had a material effect on the water reforms. Of particular importance was the entry in 1999 of a strong opposition political party on the political scene in the shape of the Movement for Democracy (MDC). It contested the 2000, 2005, 2008 and 2013 elections and posed a serious electoral challenge to the dominant party, the Zimbabwe National African Union Patriotic Front (ZANU PF), which by itself or in alliance with another political party had ruled the country since independence in 1980.

Lastly, we interviewed and interacted with past and present key actors in the water sector, which included architects of the water reforms. Our interest was to understand the negotiations between and among the key Zimbabwean and international actors, such as the World Bank, which promoted IWRM in Zimbabwe.

Drivers and triggers of IWRM in Zimbabwe

A good starting point to understand the IWRM journey in Zimbabwe is to identify what drove and triggered the water reforms in general and IWRM in particular. In this section we do so by providing an overview of water reforms from 1890, when the country was first colonised until independence in 1980, right up to the present day. Table 6.1 shows the major laws that regulated access to land and water resources during the colonial period. As can be seen from Table 6.1, there was a systematic disenfranchisement of blacks as far as access to land and water was concerned.

Due to their privileged position, white settlers actively participated in all issues pertaining to water management unlike the black population (Bolding et al., 1999). While the colonial water law provided for the Minister to appoint persons to represent black water users (Mtisi, 2011) this was more on paper than on anything else. The racist water agenda was helped by cheap finance which ensured that white settlers could install water infrastructure on their farms (Manzungu and Machiridza, 2009).

Up to 1998 when the new Water Act was enacted, the post-colonial state seemed reluctant to disturb white commercial agriculture, which formed the backbone of the country's economy. As already stated, a large proportion of developed water resources (85%) was still being used by 4500 white large-scale commercial farmers (Manzungu, 2001). Events in the land sector support this conclusion. The government, for the first ten years of independence, abided by the Lancaster House constitution,[3] which stipulated that for the first decade after independence land reform would proceed on a willing buyer-willing seller basis (see Hove et al., in this book). After the expiry of that clause the government passed the Land Acquisition Act in 1992 which provided for compulsory land acquisition, but this remained largely unimplemented.

Table 6.1. Major highlights of laws regulating access to land and water resources in Zimbabwe during the colonial period.

Date	Event/Activity	Objectives in relation to land and water resources
1890	Beginning of colonialism under British South African Company (BSAC) rule on behalf of the British Empire (Phimister, 1987)	Maximising profits through exploitation of the colony's natural resources, particularly mineral deposits (Manzungu and Machiridza, 2009). Mining sector accorded priority vis-à-vis allocation of land and water resources to the exclusion of indigenous blacks.

3 This was the constitution that the liberation movements and the British Government agreed to in negotiations leading up to independence in 1980. The liberation movements had reluctantly agreed to the land clause.

Date	Event/Activity	Objectives in relation to land and water resources
1898	Native Reserves Order	Blacks moved to arid and infertile areas in the 'Native Reserves' (Kramer, 1997) A once vibrant indigenous agriculture, which had supplied early white settlers with surplus produce, was fundamentally undermined (Ranger, 1985).
1913	Water Ordinance	Provided generous riparian water rights* to owners of adjacent or overlying lands to address wrangling among white settlers on how best to allocate agricultural water. Blacks not included because they were not landowners (Vincent and Manzungu, 2004).
1920	Amendment of the 1913 Water Ordinance	Instituted the priority date system.°
1923	BSAC pulled out of the colony in 1923	Insignificant profits and loss of support among white settlers resulting in a responsible government.^
1927	Water Act	Sought to improve the Water Ordinance which could not solve water disputes and devised a system that addressed agricultural water use (Chereni, 2007).
1930	Land Apportionment Act	Act legalised racial segregation of agricultural land that had begun in the 1900s. Fertile half of the total agricultural land was reserved for the minority white population. White settlers accorded full land rights while blacks were disenfranchised.
1969	Land Tenure Act	Strict racial access to agricultural land (Palmer, 1977).
1976	Water Act	State assumes ownership of water through abolishment of generous rights of riparian landowners. In addition to the priority date system, water rights were issued in perpetuity. Agriculture enjoyed a lower status than water for mining and urban use. Basic water needs catered for through the provision of primary water rights.

*This conferred 'reasonable use of water' to owners of adjacent or overlying lands.

° The system provided for priority of accessing water to those with senior water rights based on date of application, which further marginalised black farmers who by law could not hold water rights in their own right (Hellum and Derman, 2005).

^An all-white electorate voted to be ruled by a responsible government rather than be part of the Union of South Africa as had been favoured by the British Government.

But the strategy of not disturbing the white-run economy by, among other things, not undertaking significant land and water reforms could not be sustained for long, thanks to worsening economic conditions and the worst drought in living memory. While the economy had grown by 14.4% and 12.1% after the first two years after independence, a lacklustre performance characterised the next decade (ECA et al., 2013). This explains why, towards the end of the first decade of independence, the country was forced to engage with the IMF and World Bank for an economic bailout. This signalled the start of a complex relationship with these two institutions (and the major Western block countries that wield influence over them). But the immediate trigger of the water reforms was the 1991/1992 drought, the worst in the country's history, which reduced the country's GDP by 25% (Benson and Clay, 1998). These factors opened a window of opportunity for donors to bring in IWRM through a donor-funded Water Resources Management Strategy (WRMS) Unit. The Unit operated semi-autonomously and did the groundwork for the new water reforms in which elements of neoliberal agenda featured prominently. In the early stages IWRM was, however, not mentioned by name.[4]

Efforts at Introducing and Institutionalising IWRM

Introduction of IWRM

Beginning in 1990, the government began to implement the IMF/World Bank-sponsored Economic Structural Adjustment Programme (ESAP), a liberal economic blueprint the government had reluctantly agreed to adopt. Reluctantly is the operative word here. The country had flirted with socialism in the first few years of independence in 1980 but gradually abandoned it in the wake of poor economic performance and resorted to sponsorship of IMF/World Bank. The minister responsible for water could not have been more explicit on the relationship between the World Bank/IMF economic philosophy which the country had adopted, and the IWRM-inspired water reforms when she said:

> *With such a background (too much government involvement and cost) government decided in May 1994 to form the Zimbabwe National Water Authority which amalgamates the functions of Regional Water Authority and those of the Department of Water Resources and to operate on commercial lines. The proposal for the formation of ZINWA is in line with the objective of the Economic Structural Adjustment Programme (ESAP), to streamline civil service operations and promote economic efficiency.*[5]

She was keen to show that this was part of a global neoliberal movement and not an isolated Zimbabwean project:

> *More and more throughout the world it is becoming evident that*

4 It is only in the 2013 National Water Policy that IWRM is mentioned by name, and effort is made to explain it.

5 Joice Mujuru, Minister of Water Development and Rural Resources (Press Conference at Valley Dam on the 17th November, 1997).

> *provision of water as opposed to the planning of water resources should be on commercial lines. Indeed, our neighbours are currently involved with changing the status of their respective Water Departments to commercial ventures. Botswana, Malawi, Namibia, South Africa and Zambia have either commercialised or are currently in the process of commercialisation.*[6]

Given the timeline of Zimbabwean water reforms, it is not amiss to conclude that the Dublin principles guided the Zimbabwean water reforms, which were later adopted as IWRM principles by the GWP (see Mehta et al., this book; Allouche, this book).[7] In documents produced post-1998, particularly the Water Resources Strategy and later the National Water Policy, there is more explicit reference to the Dublin/IWRM principles as follows:

1. Freshwater is a finite and vulnerable resource, essential to sustain life, development and the environment;
2. Water development and management should be based on a participatory approach, involving users, planners and policy-makers at all levels;
3. Women play a central part in the provision, management and safeguarding of water; and
4. Water has an economic value in all its competing uses and should be recognised as an economic good (GoZ, 2013a).

As a consequence, water management in Zimbabwe was to be based on the following principles:

1. Water as part of the same hydrological cycle with surface water and groundwater being part of one management system;

1. Water management areas demarcated along hydrological boundaries (known as catchment and sub-catchment councils) instead of politico-administrative boundaries since water does not respect such boundaries;

2. Stakeholder participation based on democratic elections;

3. User pays principles for all commercial water use buttressed by a water permit based on a 20-year period rather than water rights issued in perpetuity and on the priority date system;

4. The environment as a legitimate water user (which introduced the notion of environmental flow requirements); and

6 Joice Mujuru, Minister of Water Development quoted in Hansard Vol. 23, No. 8, 15 September 1998. However, Zimbabwe went much further down the road of commercialisation than the other southern African countries were prepared to go.

7 GWP endorsed the Dublin principles by asserting that, while there were numerous general principles, approaches and guidelines relevant to IWRM, the Dublin principles were particularly useful (GWP, 2000).

5. Polluter pays principle (GoZ, 2000).

In our documentation of implementation of IWRM we shall focus, in the next section of this chapter, on principles one and four, and to some extent five and six. The two chapters, one by Derman and Manzungu and the other by Hove et al., in this book adequately deal with principles two and three.

Attempts at institutionalising IWRM – The Integrated Water Resources Management Strategy for Zimbabwe

Some two years after aspects of IWRM were included in the Water and ZINWA Acts, the WRMS Secretariat produced a document, titled 'Towards Integrated Water Resources Management: Water Resources Management Strategy for Zimbabwe' (GoZ, 2000) to which was appended the National Water Resources Policy and the National Water Pricing Policy and Strategy. While the title refers to IWRM, nowhere in the document is IWRM defined. A close examination shows that the Strategy was produced in the same year GWP put out its famed IWRM definition as attested by the minister in her foreword:

> *Water took a centre stage at the Second World Water Forum in The Hague in March 2000. The Ministers of Water (of which I was privileged to be one) declared that water is vital for life and health of people and ecosystems and a basic requirement for the development of nations* (GoZ, 2000).

This reveals, as argued by other authors in this volume, the massive donor- and international-influenced adoption of IWRM in southern Africa. In Zimbabwe, the Strategy was never formally adopted by cabinet for reasons that are not clear. Interestingly, the WRMS Secretariat was already proposing to amend the Water Act to pave the way for a third tier of water governance (below sub-catchment councils) to be known as water user boards, which had been scrapped in the lead up to the enactment of the legislation because of the fear that it would entrench the power of white farmers (Moyo, 2004). It is not clear how the secretariat proposed to diminish the political power of white farmers who, at the time, were still on the farms.

The Strategy proposed a National Water Resources Policy and not a National Water Policy, which is the exact opposite to the new 2013 Water Policy which devotes considerable attention to water supply. The Strategy thus reflected the mood of the day, namely that water reform was about how the water resource was to be managed. Water supply fell under local government and was not considered to be in a crisis. This is why issues concerning water supply, which were important to rural communities, had been an irritation to white farmers during sub-catchment council meetings. The repair of boreholes, which were an important and sometimes the only source of water for rural communities was considered to be peripheral to the weighty issues of water resources management (Kujinga and Manzungu, 2004). Things however changed in the second coming of the IWRM in the 2000s when water supply, and in particular the privatisation of urban water supply, began to dominate the water sector in Zimbabwe (see below).

UNRAVELLING OF IWRM: 2000-2009

Political context

In this section we examine the challenges that confronted the implementation of IWRM between 2000 and 2009. Table 6.2 shows a selection of the most important events which had a significant impact on IWRM implementation. As can be seen from the Table 6.2, the events related to economic challenges, national-level politics and the country's international isolation.

Table 6.2. Important national political events that affected implementation of IWRM in Zimbabwe between 2000 and 2009.

Year	Event	Results	Outcomes
2000	The ruling ZANU PF party-sponsored national referendum on new constitution is rejected	Ruling ZANU PF allows war veterans to invade white commercial land in protest heralding the start of the fast track land reform programme•	Agricultural production declines; donors withdraw financial support from the water sector; start of economic downturn, which resulted in government defaulting on loans; beginning of international isolation
	National elections	Opposition MDC party wins 57 out of 120 seats	Ruling ZANU PF party is unsettled and promotes fast track land reform
2002	Presidential elections	President Mugabe wins elections and cements his power	Ruling party continues its land policy which dislocates water reforms by diminishing water revenue and disregarding existing irrigation systems
2005	National elections	Opposition MDC wins only 41 out of 120 seats	Ruling ZANU PF party becomes confident and does not change policy. Economic crisis deepens giving rise to hyperinflation
2008	National elections	Opposition MDC wins parliamentary majority by 110 out of 210 seats. Ruling ZANU PF loses parliamentary majority and its presidential candidate (Robert Mugabe) loses in the first round and wins a disputed second-round election	International isolation is enhanced; country cannot access lines of credit and donor funds; hyperinflation worsens; political dialogue starts in September to resolve the political impasse
		Worst cholera outbreak in Africa in the last 15 years infects 92,000 people in 2008/2009 and results in over 4000 deaths (Mason, 2009)	International community offers water supply and sanitation support as part of humanitarian assistance

Year	Event	Results	Outcomes
2009	Political settlement culminating in a National Unity Government in February 2009	International recognition resulting in some level of international engagement	Humanitarian assistance continues and diversified from short-term intervention into long-term intervention in the form of rehabilitation of water supply and sanitation infrastructure mainly in urban areas; GDP growth of 6% registered in 2009 and over 10% in the following two years
2013	National elections	ZANU PF regains parliamentary majority and its leader (Robert Mugabe) wins presidential elections putting an end to the national unity government	Western donors and multilateral institutions continue to engage government on development programmes

• The widely held interpretation is that while the ruling party in public accepted the result it was rattled and allowed the land invasions which began in early 2000 and in time came to be known as the fast track land reform programme, which was characterised by unlawful and violent seizure of white commercial farms.

As described later, the international re-engagement paved the way for the development of the new 2013 Water Policy, which essentially tried to resurrect IWRM. For now, we turn to the implementation challenges between 1998 (when the water reforms were introduced) and 2013, until introduction of the new policy when there was another attempt to operationalise IWRM principles.

Unintegrated water management

Illusion of a unified water allocation system and integrated water management

The Water Act provides for one unified water allocation system on the basis that all water is part of the same hydrological cycle (GoZ, 1998a). Theoretically therefore, surface water (in rivers and stored in dams) and groundwater should be allocated by catchment councils with the help of the catchment manager who is a ZINWA employee (GoZ, 1998a). Allocation is ideally based on the water permit system which is supposed to keep a record of all water use and also forms the basis for charging for water.

The vision of a unified water allocation system did not materialise for a number of reasons. First, because of the fast track land reform, it was not possible to keep a record of who was cultivating which land and who was using how much water where and when. Second, water in government dams, continued to be allocated and sold by ZINWA and remained outside the remit of catchment councils as provided in law (Davis and Hirji, 2014).[8] This was justified on the grounds

8 It appears that ZINWA does not want to let go of this responsibility, which is understandable given not only the lack of capacity among catchment councils but also that this is perhaps a

that the government had invested public money in building the dams. Such water is managed by ZINWA and accessed by farmers who enter into agreement with ZINWA to purchase a defined volume of water per year. This is why it is called agreement water. Once allocated this water has to be paid for irrespective of whether it is used or not since the water cannot be reallocated to someone else. It is also worth noting that the water is sold at the national blend price that takes into account the recovery of a hypothetical loan annuity payment over 40 years and the operation and maintenance costs of the dams (GoZ, 2013a). It is more expensive than water abstracted from rivers and groundwater.

The distinction between the two 'waters' is operationally complex for two reasons. First, water released by ZINWA from dams goes through rivers, which raises the practicality of separating water flowing in rivers and water in government dams. Second, since water in rivers is cheaper[9] the result was that many water users apply for abstracting water from rivers with the full knowledge that this would be water released from government dams (Manzungu, 2011; Hove et al., in this book).

There were also other factors that complicated water allocation. First, many of the new water users were ignorant of the law, and sometimes defied/circumvented of the law. Second, authorities, when it suited them, violated some provisions of the law. For example, some black farmers were issued with water permits despite the fact that there were no catchment outline plans in place as required by law (GoZ, 1998a). The plans were only published in 2011, and were poorly conceptualised in terms of process and content (Mabiza, 2013). Third, the inability to pay for water due to low profitability of agriculture, as well as due to unresolved ownership/usage arrangements regarding the use of water in dams, irrigation infrastructure, undermined implementation of the permit system (Manzungu, 2011).

Complexities in integrating land and water

IWRM prides itself in 'the development and management of water, land and related resources', implying a seamless development of the two. In Zimbabwe this was not the case but was, in fact, far from it. Land and water reforms were undertaken separately (see Hove et al., in this book and the case of South Africa, in this book). The two reforms could not attract the attention of donors at the same time. In the early 1980s land reform was more visible in the discourse and was funded by Western donors (Thomas, 2003) while water became more visible in the discourse in the 1990s and was also funded by Western donors (see Derman and Manzungu in this book). But from the late 1990s into the early 2000s, land reform became more prominent and its implementation derailed water reform as it was envisaged (Mtisi and Nicol, 2003).

---

major revenue stream for ZINWA.

9 Water abstracted from a public stream and groundwater only attracts a water and sub-catchment levy which used to be in the region of USD3/ML but has been reduced to USD1/ML.

Deficiencies in environmental protection of water resources

Another integration challenge was how to ensure environmental protection of water resources, which depended on having in place a system that integrated the management of water quality and water quantity (which includes environmental flow releases). There were a number of challenges. First, monitoring of water quality was separated from monitoring of water quantity. ZINWA lost the mandate for monitoring water quality to the Environmental Management Agency (EMA) on the basis that enforcement of all environmental phenomena should fall under one body (EMA). A related challenge is that ZINWA's database on water quantity is based on hydrological boundaries while EMA's database on water quality is based on political-administrative boundaries. In the second instance ambient water-quality monitoring and discharge licences, which are critical for enforcing the polluter pays principle, are poorly implemented because EMA lacks human and financial capacity (Naome et al., 2012). There are also no resources for ensuring compliance with the conditions of the licences. Third, ZINWA has not implemented environmental flow releases because of capacity constraints (GoZ, 2013a).

User pays principle falters

In this section we show that the mantra of water as an economic good, as represented by the user pays principle, came unstuck because of differences in hydrological realities, diminishing water use and political pragmatism and rent seeking.

Hydrological realities

As already reported above, water revenue comes from either permits granted to abstract surface water and groundwater or from water stored in government dams. By policy, revenue from flow water is the only revenue stream for sub-catchment councils while ZINWA sells water in government dams. Therefore, sub-catchments located in high rainfall areas can sell more water unlike in dry sub-catchments where rivers dry up for a greater part of the year. As such in drier catchments there is very little revenue even if irrigation is taking place and is using 'agreement water'.

Sub-catchments where there are many boreholes can also raise significant revenue. This is the case in urban areas where, because of shortcomings in the urban water supply, residents have turned to drilling boreholes (Manzungu et al., 2016). Such is the case in Upper Manyame Subcatchment Council in which the Greater Harare, the largest metropolitan area of the country is found, which accounts for 16% of the country's population (Manzungu et al., 2016). But all sub-catchments are, in general, financially disadvantaged because they levy a relatively smaller percentage of water resources in the country – it is estimated that only 16% of the water permits are flow permits which sub-catchments can levy. The result is that there are many financially unviable sub-catchments, whose operations have been crippled since they are solely funded by water revenue. But even in those that are potentially financially viable, diminishing water use has become a challenge as described below.

Diminishing water use

All sub-catchments and ZINWA were negatively affected in large part due to the impacts of the fast track land reform programme. Revenues from irrigation significantly dwindled because of reduced irrigation activity (Manzungu, 2011; Mtisi, 2011). The consequence was a huge decline in water revenue across all the catchments (Fig. 6.1).[10]

The reduced water revenues negatively affected the operations of ZINWA and sub-catchment councils. This was not helped by poor economic performance, and uncertainties about land tenure, and drought. This situation was also worsened by donors, who had supported catchment and sub-catchment councils, and had stopped doing so because of political issues in Zimbabwe.

The net result was that water resources management was negatively affected in three dimensions. First, there was inadequate information gathering and monitoring worsened by a deteriorating infrastructure. Second, ZINWA virtually stopped dam safety inspections. Third, there were limited silt and sediment surveys.

Political manoeuvrings, pragmatism and rent seeking

In this section we provide more evidence of amputation of the 'user pays principle' or 'water is an economic good' in general terms. First it is worth noting that the price of water is the same across all the catchments. This went against the liberal economic paradigm. Calls were made for the blend price to be dispensed with and for water tariffs to vary per catchment to reflect the varying (market) demand for water, which was rejected on the grounds that the blend price protected public interest in water (MWRDM, 2012).

Fig 6.1. Status of agricultural water use in Zimbabwe's catchment areas as of 2011.

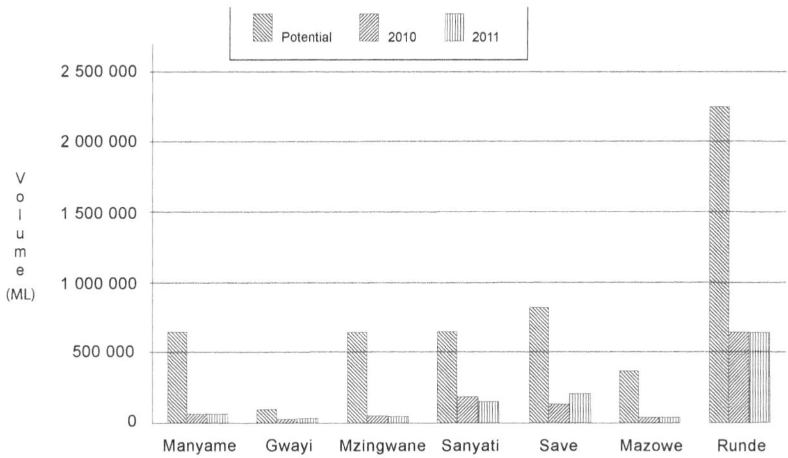

Source: Manzungu, 2011.

10 The high water sales in the Runde Catchment was because of the large commercial sugarcane estates in the southeastern Lowveld where irrigation was not disrupted much.

The user pays principle could also not be implemented to the letter because of socio-political considerations. Irrigation water is charged differently for different water users, with the government subsidising smallholder farmers (Table 6.3). There was also tension between individual farmer interests (who now include the who is who in Zimbabwe) and public interest. Water institutions favoured high water levies because these equalled more revenue while farmers lobbied for low water levies. In the end, farmer interests prevailed because in 2013 water levies across the country were reduced to USD1/megalitre from USD3.[11] The argument was that this would boost agricultural production. A closer examination of Table 6.3 shows that the level of subsidy for the poor farmers (categories 5, 6 and 7) is the same as that for the middle class farmers (category 3). Moreover, the reduction of water to the poor farmers was only useful if the farmers had access to irrigation infrastructure. Many do not.

There are also policy areas that have been left grey, which have allowed some users to benefit from hidden subsidies. A World Bank-sponsored paper found that some people paid for storing water (storage permits) while others do not and yet others paid at a rate or lower price than abstracting water from a public stream on the understanding that farmers would have invested in storage facilities (Manzungu, 2011).

But by far the biggest subsidy went to the government, which refused to pay for storage permits for all ZINWA dams. By law, sub-catchment councils can charge ZINWA for storing water in their areas of jurisdiction as ZINWA, like any other applicant, is issued a storage permit for each dam. But the government refused arguing that this would mean paying for stored water which was not being used.

Table 6.3. Water tariffs for raw water secured under agreement water in Zimbabwe

Consumer category	Water use	USD/ML	2016 price (USD/ML)	% price reduction
1	Industry	13.17	9.45	28.2
2	Commercial Agriculture-Estate	12.68	12.00	5.4
3	Commercial Agriculture-A2 Farmers	12.19	5.00	59.0
4	Local authorities	11.17	6.00	46.3
5	A1 farmers	7.80	3.00	61.5
6	Communal pumped	5.00	2.00	60.0
7	Communal gravity	5.00	2.00	60.0

Source: Manzungu, 2011; GoZ, 2016.

11 A high ranking ZINWA official revealed that there was no statutory instrument for this. This was through a ministerial pronouncement.

Political favours also compromised the market thrust of the reforms. This was epitomised by Greenfuel, a company involved in sugar-cane production for ethanol production in the southeast part of the country. It managed to get a discount on the price of water through a ministerial intervention and not through ZINWA or catchment councils, which are the relevant formal channels. A well-placed source revealed that it was not even paying the discounted price! The circumstances are so sensitive that the details of the irregular dealings were not available. We can add that the company was never far from controversy. After the 2013 elections when a ZANU PF government was in power it managed to secure mandatory blending of petrol with ethanol (Zhangazha, 2015), which had been opposed by the minister who hailed from the opposition (see below). Yet another controversy related to allegations of the company taking land from the local community (Mutopo and Chiweshe, 2014) and its contribution to pollution of local rivers (The Standard, 2014).

Resuscitating IWRM: Formulation of the Zimbabwe National Water Policy (2011-2013)

IWRM was resuscitated in Zimbabwe largely through the Zimbabwe National Water Policy which we focus on in detail below. It is important to state that in parallel, there was another process to rehabilitate the water supply and sanitation infrastructure in urban and rural areas, which had deteriorated significantly between 2000 and 2008 (which caused the cholera outbreak that killed over 4000 people in late 2008 and early 2009 (Mason, 2009). The international support resulted in two main financial facilities, the Unicef Water, Sanitation and Hygiene Project and the Zimfund Urgent Water Supply and Sanitation Rehabilitation Project, which was launched in 2010 and administered by the African Development Bank (AfDB). Huge figures are involved. For example, the 2015 Zimbabwean government budget statement notes that development partners were supporting the Unicef administered facility to the tune of USD83 million between 2013 and 2016 of which USD53 million was earmarked for urban areas and the balance for rural areas (MFED, 2015). Meanwhile there was practically no money pledged for traditional IWRM-related activities such as water resources management that could be used to support the activities of ZINWA, catchment and sub-catchment councils.

Justification of a new Water Policy: 2011-2013

The return of IWRM into the public policy discourse in Zimbabwe can be linked to the country's re-engagement with the international community, which was a consequence of the Government of National Unity formed in 2009 following the disputed elections of 2008. The improved political climate provided an opportunity for Western countries to widen their support beyond humanitarian relief, which was the only permissible support under the Western sanctions that were imposed on the country. For that to happen a new cooperation framework that would permit developmental assistance was needed. In the water sector this took the shape of developing a new water policy meant to provide direction for the development and management of water resources in the short, medium, and the long term.

Since the World Bank could not use its own funds in Zimbabwe, it coordinated donor funds through a new entity called the Analytic Multi Donor Trust Fund (AMDTF), which was not a lending programme but a facility for providing technical and policy support. One of the important tasks of the Trust Fund was to develop a new National Water Policy. The Bank mobilised funding to develop a draft policy that the Ministry would use to engage stakeholders. The process was meant to be participatory and was coordinated by the National Action Committee (interministerial committee responsible for coordinating the water sector). However, the short time frame made this an impossible task.[12]

In terms of process, a number of issue papers, authored by local and international consultants, were produced between September and December 2011 under the guidance of local and international World Bank staff. The papers were integrated into a background paper by the Bank. This was then refined into a policy discussion document produced by two Zimbabwean consultants. Oversight of the process and content were provided by the Ministry of Water Resources Development and Management. The draft Water Policy went through a number of discussions involving representatives of stakeholder groups. It was adopted on December 12, 2012 and officially launched in March 2013.[13] The commitment to IWRM is evident:

> *Zimbabwe enacted the 1998 Water and ZINWA Acts based on universally accepted principles of Integrated Water Resources Management (IWRM) and following wide consultative processes from 1995 to 2000. Although the vision of this legislation has not yet been fully realised, the principles of IWRM applied are relevant for Zimbabwe today and in the future. Besides being universally applicable, most of the principles are already imbedded in Zimbabwe's policies and legislation, including the unpublished 2004 Water Policy, the EMA Act of 2002, Water Resources Management Strategy of 2000 and 2009 National Environmental Policy and Strategies (GoZ, 2013a: 18, emphasis added).*

The policy reiterates that IWRM is the approach that maintains the integrity of the water resource so that water can be used productively for present and future water users based on 1) integrating the management of the whole water cycle, 2) decentralising responsibility of water management to the river catchment level, 3) promoting stakeholder participation in decision-making processes involving water management, and 4) treating water as a social and an economic good (GoZ, 2013a: 18).

12 The whole process from production of technical papers to production of the draft policy document took about 8 months.

13 The National Water Policy was approved by the government on 12 December 2012 and publicly launched on World Water Day, March 22, 2013 in Victoria Falls by the Deputy Prime Minister, Ms. T. Khupe. The policy was presented by the Permanent Secretary, Mr. R.J. Chitsiko at the Third Zimbabwe Water Forum held on 30 January, 2013 with Mr. Zeb Murungweni, Water Resources Development and Management Specialist and Mr. Ousmane Dione, Sector Manager, East Asia, World Bank as discussants.

Reincarnation of neoliberalism and prominence of water supply

The Policy did not suggest anything new as far as water resources management was concerned except to appeal for more funding to ensure that catchment and sub-catchment councils and ZINWA discharged their respective mandates effectively. There was also a suggestion to streamline the relationship between Department of Water (DWD), catchment and sub-catchment councils and ZINWA.

However, the Policy made a strong pitch for privatising urban water supply. As a way of preparing the groundwork for water privatisation, a new institutional architecture for water supply and sanitation was mooted. Local authorities would act as service authorities that would engage service providers with an independent Water and Wastewater Services Regulatory Unit acting as the arbiter. Revenue from water sales would be ring-fenced so that it would finance water-related activities and not operate as a general fund (MWRDM, 2012).

The new policy is weak on social agenda, which was a surprising omission given the debate about the human right to water during the consultations of the new constitution between 2009 and 2013. The new 2013 constitution provides for clean drinking water as a basic human right (GoZ, 2013b). The Policy provides that in rural areas primary water shall be given the first and higher priority. In urban areas, primary water needs were to be based on lifeline tariffs, and it is only in cases where people cannot afford to pay, that a free life-saving water per household of 10 m^3 per month can be supplied (GoZ, 2013a). Since it was realised it would be difficult to establish who could not pay, there was the provision of a two- or three-stage rising block tariff regime (GoZ, 2013a). This position was a compromise because urban municipalities had argued this would constitute a substantial revenue loss on their part.

World Bank as an honest broker?

According to the Zimbabwean authors of the draft water policy, the process involved complex negotiations between and within government departments and the donor community represented by the World Bank. Within government departments there was a begrudging cooperation from the agricultural and water supply sub-sectors. They were interested in developing their own sectoral policies. The agricultural ministry was developing an irrigation policy while the water supply and sanitation subsector was interested in developing a sanitation and hygiene policy to support the strategy that was already in place.

The water ministry argued that the National Water policy was meant to be broader than a sectoral policy. In his foreword, the Minister stated that the National Water Policy was based on international best practice, and would include sub-sectoral policies for both urban and rural water supplies and sanitation, water resources management and development, the environment and agricultural water use (GoZ, 2013a: i).

Given the contentious nature of the issues, it was left to the World Bank staff to steer the discussion. In this process they played their cards strategically by not appearing to lead the process while actually leading it. They played the role of a broker between and within government departments. This shrewd political game guaranteed that the new policy would gain legitimacy. In some cases, this meant endorsing disputable facts. For example, the country's irrigation potential is given in the policy as 2 million hectares (ha) at the insistence of the Ministry of Agriculture when, in fact, the widely quoted figure is around 600,000 ha (Manzungu, 2011; GoZ, 2013a). On its part, the World Bank got pretty much what it wanted – the Bank once again managed to sell a neoliberal approach to water management.

PROSPECTS FOR IMPLEMENTING IWRM

The Zimbabwe National Water Policy promised a renewal and revival of IWRM in Zimbabwe. The question is: what are the prospects for its successful implementation? The Policy was developed under the watch of an MDC-T minister who has since left office after the disputed July 2013 elections won by ZANU-PF. This is worth mentioning because the international isolation has continued albeit with some modification. As described above, donors did not return to water resources management.

The Policy suggests that Zimbabwe needs to urgently prepare an implementation strategy for the recovery of the water sector and emphasises water supply and sanitation services unlike the WRMS document. This was to be achieved through a review, amendment and synchronisation of legislation and regulations, and coordinating activities of relevant agencies. Some of the proposed changes include revisiting the role of the catchment manager, unbundling ZINWA into strategic business units, and moving the non-commercial aspects of water (referred to as statutory functions) away from ZINWA.

It was observed that three years later nothing had materialised. The government does not seem to be channelling money towards IWRM. The Director of Water Resources acknowledged that since the approval of the new policy, there has been little progress because of financial constraints, worsened by the fact that there is no longer any donor support – the support was now being channelled toward physical infrastructure in the water supply and sanitation subsector. He lamented the fact that the focus has been on small efforts that did not require significant amounts of money. He also observed that the Water Act would have to be reviewed to cater for the policy changes and the new constitution.

Despite the apparent lack of progress, the IWRM rhetoric does not seem to be dying anytime soon. The Director claimed that IWRM guides water management in the country, pointing to the existence of the concept of catchment, which illustrated decentralised water management. But one has to read in between lines. We wonder if there was a real intent to ensure decentralisation, which comprises openness, participation and accountability, takes hold (Batterbury and Fernando, 2006). History matters and commitments to local governance in Zimbabwe remain suspect (Makumbe, 1996). It appears what is being suggested is decentralised revenue collection in pursuit of the notion of water as an economic good. The fact that there is no longer a stand-alone ministry of water has also diminished prospects for implementing the policy. The whole water sector has been reduced to one of three sub-sectors in the new Ministry of Environment, Water and Climate.

Discussion and conclusion

This chapter sought to understand why Zimbabwe's water reforms, undertaken in the mid-1990s, and seemingly motivated by a clear political economy objective of trying to redress 90 years of racially motivated inequitable access to agricultural water, was hijacked by efforts directed at implementing IWRM. The chapter focused on the formulation, implementation and reformulation of IWRM, which was anything but linear as implied in the standard definition of IWRM. This is because IWRM meant different things to different actors, living up to its billing as a nirvana concept (Molle, 2008). For example, the Government of Zimbabwe first introduced and saw it as a means to fix a government cash flow problem, which differed materially from some academics and World Bank staffers who saw it as a solution to Zimbabwe's water management challenges (Chenje et al., 1998; Davis and Hirji, 2014). Thus the government and donors were still able to claim that they were implementing IWRM when actually they were pushing different agendas. The various narratives, influenced by different interests, resulted in a chequered history of IWRM in Zimbabwe. We highlight below a few critical factors that explain this chequered history. To this end we analyse what happened in the first articulation (the first surge), the dis-articulation (the ebb) and re-articulation of IWRM (the second surge) in that order.

The first IWRM surge occurred in the 1990s when Western donors complemented the IMF/World Bank-inspired liberal economic agenda, which Zimbabwe had signed up to in 1990. Thus to a domestic water reform agenda was added a neoliberal agenda, which was part of a wider liberalist economic philosophy whose roots can be traced to the structural adjustment programmes that many African countries, including Zimbabwe, underwent in the 1980 and 1990s. And unfortunately, just like the structural adjustment programmes, IWRM in Zimbabwe has failed and is failing the majority of the population.

The Government of Zimbabwe's initial enthusiasm of IWRM was followed by a decade of what could be construed as the lowest ebb in IWRM implementation as illustrated by paralysis in the implementation of IWRM (Feresu, 2010). This was because of a combination of poor economic performance (due to poor or wrongly implemented social and economic policies), national-level politics as political parties jostled for power, as well as waning international support due to poor international creditworthiness, and donor withdrawal at the behest of Western countries on allegations of democratic and human rights violations in the country. During this period land reform proved to be the most disruptive to IWRM implementation (see Hove et al., in this book). The dis-articulation of IWRM demonstrated that water resources management decisions were made up of everyday politics, politics of policy-making, hydropolitics and global politics (Mollinga, 2001). The end result was that operationalisation of IWRM became difficult if not impossible to achieve as attested by challenges of implementing a unified water allocation system, integrating land and water, and implementing the user pays principle.

The return of IWRM on the Zimbabwean scene in 2009 showed the link between politics and IWRM – it needed a political settlement between the political players in Zimbabwe (in the shape of the unity government between ZANU PF and MDC) for IWRM to once again appear on the radar. Meanwhile the World Bank still believed that IWRM could have succeeded were it not for the 'extraneous political issues'. But this Habermasian perspective of IWRM, which emphasises that IWRM implementation can succeed if communicative rationality is applied (Saravanan et al., 2009), has no empirical basis as illustrated by various articles in this book.

From the above we can observe that the nature of IWRM articulation, dis-articulation and re-articulation was inherently political as argued by others in this book (see also Mollinga, 2001; Wester, 2008). It was through cooperative and sometimes conflicting relationships between the Zimbabwean state and donors that we see delicate negotiations at play, which by no means were static. Thus, the fortunes of IWRM in Zimbabwe reflected the competing and sometimes irreconcilable narratives between the main protagonists – the international community on the one hand and the Zimbabwean state on the other. IWRM was a bargaining chip but of course not the only one. Where the (political) interests between the two protagonists converged, as was the case at the start when World Bank 'sold' the Economic Structural Adjustment Programme to Zimbabwe, which Zimbabwe 'bought' because of the need to fix the economy, IWRM flourished in the form in which it was defined. But when the interests diverged IWRM began to unravel. The international community suspended promoting IWRM because it wanted to implement IWRM in an 'acceptable' political environment. The Zimbabwean state could only provide this environment as long as it lined up with its own political interests, which was informed by continuing in power. In this game, discarding IWRM was a small price to pay. By acting thus, the Zimbabwean state opted for strategic acquiescence (to a limited extent though) where it selectively embraced those aspects that mostly met its political objectives. Thus, the government resisted attempts to go further down the IWRM road when its political interests were in jeopardy. The IWRM bandwagon could move as long as the IMF/World Bank and the Government of Zimbabwe agendas were mutually self-reinforcing. Once that mutuality stopped IWRM could no longer be sustained. National-level events and processes also provided another dimension to implementation of IWRM (see Tables 2 and 3). But politics was not confined to the national level – interdepartmental interests led to implementation challenges as illustrated by the clash between ZINWA and EMA over water-quality issues and the foot-dragging by the agricultural and water supply and sanitation sub-sectors during the formulation of the 2013 National Water Policy.

In conclusion we make the observation that the articulation, dis-articulation and re-articulation of IWRM resulted in Zimbabwe having in its cupboard an IWRM skeleton, maintained more by inertia than by design. Having set up catchment and sub-catchment councils and the other IWRM trappings, such as establishing self-financing water institutions, the government could not be drawn into dismantling them at least in explicit terms. So IWRM in Zimbabwe is likely to be continuously invoked by different actors when it suits their purposes.

Acknowledgements

This chapter is based on research from a Norwegian Research Council-funded project, Flows and Practices: The Politics of IWRM in Africa. We are grateful to the Norwegian Research Council for the generous support.

References

Batterbury, S. and Fernando, J. 2006. Rescaling governance and the impacts of political and environmental decentralization: An introduction. *World Development* 34 (11): 1851-1863.

Benson, C. and Clay, E. 1998. *The impact of drought on sub-Saharan African economies: A preliminary observation*. IMF/World Bank paper. Washington, DC: World Bank.

Bolding, A.; Manzungu, E. and van der Zaag, P. 1999. A realistic approach to water reform in Zimbabwe. In Manzungu, E.; Senzanje, A. and van der Zaag, P. (Eds), *Water for agriculture in Zimbabwe: Policy and management options for the small-holder sector*, pp. 225-253. Harare: University of Zimbabwe Publications.

Chenje, M.; Sola, L. and Paleczny, D. (Eds). 1998. *The state of Zimbabwe's environment.* Harare, Zimbabwe: Government of the Republic of Zimbabwe, Ministry of Mines, Environment and Tourism.

Chereni, A. 2007. The problem of institutional fit in integrated water resource management: A case study of Zimbabwe's Mazowe catchment. *Physics and Chemistry of the Earth* 32(15-18): 1246-1256.

Cherlet, J. and Venot, J. 2013. Structure and agency: Understanding water policy changes in West Africa. *Water Policy* 15(3): 479-495.

Davis, R. and Hirji, R. 2014. *Climate change and water resources planning, development and management in Zimbabwe: An issues paper.* Washington, DC: World Bank.

ECA (Economic Consulting Associates); Dorsch International Consultants and Brian Colquhoun; Hugh, O. and Donnel and Partners. 2013. *Zimbabwe: Water sector investment analysis.* Working Paper No. 5 – Water-development growth and development. London: Report to the World Bank, Economic Consulting Associates Limited.

Feresu, S.B. (Ed). 2010. *Zimbabwe environment outlook: Our environment, everybody's responsibility.* Harare, Zimbabwe: The Ministry of Environment and Natural Resources Management.

GoZ (Government of Zimbabwe). 1998a. *Water Act [Chapter 20: 24]*. Harare: Government Printers.

GoZ. 1998b. *Zimbabwe National Water Authority Act. [Chapter 20; 25].* Harare: Government Printers.

GoZ. 2000. *Towards integrated water resources management: Water resources strategy for Zimbabwe.* Harare, Zimbabwe: Ministry of Rural Resources and Water Development.

GoZ. 2013a. *National water policy*. Harare, Zimbabwe: Ministry of Water Resources and Development.

GoZ. 2013b. *Constitution of Zimbabwe Amendment (No. 20).* Harare: Government Printers.

GoZ. 2016. Zimbabwe National Water Authority (Raw Water Tariffs), Chapter 20: 25 Statutory Instrument 48 of 2016, Harare, Government Printers.

GWP (Global Water Partnership). 2000. *Integrated water resources management.* TAC Background Paper No. 4. Stockholm: Global Water Partnership.

Hellum, A. and Derman, B. 2005. Negotiating water rights in the context of a new political and legal landscape in Zimbabwe. In von Benda-Beckmann, F.; von Benda-Beckmann, K. and Griffiths, A. (Eds), *Mobile people, mobile law: Expanding legal relations in a contracting world,* pp. 177-198. Aldershot and Burlington, VT: Ashgate.

Kramer, E. 1997. The early years: Extension in peasant agriculture in colonial Zimbabwe, 1925-1929. *Zambezia* 24(2): 159-179.

Kujinga, K. and Manzungu, E. 2004. Enduring contestations: Stakeholder participation in water resource management in the Save catchment area, Eastern Zimbabwe. *Eastern Africa Social Science Review* 20(1): 67-92.

Mabiza, C. 2013. IWRM, institutions and livelihoods under stress: Bottom up perspectives from Zimbabwe. PhD thesis. Delft University, Delft, the Netherlands.

Makumbe, J. 1996. *Participatory development: The case of Zimbabwe.* Harare: University of Zimbabwe Publications.

Manzungu, E. 2001. A lost opportunity: An analysis of the water reform debate in the fourth parliament of Zimbabwe. *Zambezia* 28(1): 97-120.

Manzungu, E. 2002. Global rhetoric and local realities: The case of Zimbabwe's water reform. In Chikowore, G.; Manzungu, E.; Mushayavanhu, D. and Shoko, D. (Eds), *Managing common property in an age of globalisation: Experiences from Zimbabwe,* pp. 31-44. Harare: Weaver Press.

Manzungu, E. 2004. Water for all: Improving water resource governance in southern Africa. *Gatekeeper Series* 113: 1-24.

Manzungu, E. 2011. *Reviving irrigation development and management.* Thematic Paper No. 3 for Background Paper on Water Resources Development and Management to support Zimbabwe National Water Policy. Washington, DC: World Bank.

Manzungu, E. and Machiridza, R. 2009. Economic-legal ideology and water management in Zimbabwe. *Economics, Management and Financial Markets* 4(1): 66-102.

Manzungu, E.; Mudenda-Damba, M.; Madyiwa, S.; Dzingirayi, V. and Musoni, S. 2016. Bulk water suppliers in the City of Harare – An endogenous form of privatisation of urban domestic water supply in Zimbabwe. *Water Alternatives* 9(1): 56-80.

Mason, P.R. 2009. Zimbabwe experiences the worst epidemic of cholera in Africa. *The Journal of Infection in Developing Countries* 3(2): 148-151.

Mehta, L.; Alba, R.; Bolding, A.; Denby, K.; Derman, B.; Hove, T.; Manzungu, E.; Prabhakaran, P. and van Koppen, B. 2014. The politics of IWRM in Southern Africa. *International Journal of Water Resources Development* 30(3): 528-542.

MFED (Ministry of Finance and Economic Development). 2015. 2016 National Budget Statement. Harare.

Molle, F. 2008. Nirvana concepts, narratives and policy models: Insights from the water sector. *Water Alternatives* 1(1): 131-156.

Mollinga, P.P. 2001. Water and politics: Levels, rational choice and South Indian canal irrigation. *Futures* 33(8-9): 733-752.

Mollinga, P.P. and Bolding, A. (Eds). 2004. *The politics of irrigation reform: Contested policy formulation and implementation in Asia, Africa and Latin America.* Aldershot, UK: Ashgate.

Moyo, M. 2004. Participation dynamics in integrated water management in the Mazowe watershed. In Moll, H.; Leeuwis, C.; Vincent, L. and Manzungu, E. (Eds), *Agrarian institutions between policies and local action: Experiences from Zimbabwe*, pp. 109-126. Harare: Weaver Press.

Mtisi, S. 2011. *Water reforms during the crisis and beyond: Understanding policy and political challenges of reforming the water sector in Zimbabwe.* Working Paper No. 333. London: Overseas Development Institute.

Mtisi, S. and Nicol, A. 2003. Caught in the act: New stakeholders, decentralisation and water management processes in Zimbabwe. Sustainable Livelihoods in Southern Africa: Institutions, Governance and Policy Processes, Research Paper Series No. 14. www.ids.ac.uk/slsa (accessed 22 July 2016)

Mutopo, P. and Chiweshe, M. 2014. Large scale land deals, global capital and the politics of livelihoods: Experiences of women smallholder farmers in Chisumbanje, Zimbabwe. *International Journal of African Renaissance Studies* 9(1): 84-99.

MWRDM (Ministry of Water Resources Development and Management). 2012. Water resources development and management background paper. *Towards a water secure Zimbabwe: Improving governance and utilization of water resources for the national water policy.* Harare, Zimbabwe.

Naome, R.; Rajah, D. and Jerie, S. 2012. Challenges in implementing integrated environmental management approach in Zimbabwe. *Journal of Emerging Trends in Economics and Management Sciences* 3(4): 408-414.

Palmer, R. 1977. *Land and racial domination in Rhodesia.* London: Heinemann.

Phimister, I.R. 1987. *Economic and social history of Zimbabwe, 1890-1948: Capital accumulation and class struggle.* London: Longmans.

Ranger, T. 1985. *Peasant consciousness and guerrilla war in Zimbabwe.* London: James Currey.

Rhodesia. 1927. *Water Act, No. 41.* Salisbury: Government Printers.

Rhodesia. 1976. *Water Act.* Salisbury: Government Printers.

Saravanan, V.S.; McDonald, G.T. and Mollinga, P.P. 2009. Critical review of integrated water resources management: Moving beyond polarised discourse. *Natural Resources Forum* 33(1): 76-86.

The Standard. 12 October 2014. Greenfuel poisoning the environment.

http://allafrica.com/stories/201410120104.html (accessed 22 July 2014)

Thomas, N.H. 2003. Land reform in Zimbabwe. *Third World Quarterly* 24(4): 691-712.

Vincent, L. and Manzungu, E. 2004. Water rights and the availability of water in the Lower Odzi watershed in the Save catchment. In Moll, H.; Leeuwis, C.; Vincent, L. and Manzungu, E. (Eds), *Agrarian institutions between policies and local action: Experiences from Zimbabwe*, pp. 127-163. Harare: Weaver Press.

Wester, P. 2008. Shedding the waters: Institutional change and water control in Lerma-Chapala basin, Mexico. PhD thesis. Wageningen University, Wageningen, the Netherlands.

Zhangazha, W. 2015. Local fuel costly despite blending. *Zimbabwe Independent,* 7 August 2015.

www.theindependent.co.zw/2015/08/07/local-fuel-costly-despite-blending/ (accessed 22 July 2016)

7

The Complex Politics of Water and Power in Zimbabwe: IWRM in the Catchment Councils of Manyame, Mazowe and Sanyati (1993-2001)[1]

Bill Derman

Emmanuel Manzungu

ABSTRACT: In the mid-nineties Zimbabwe formed participatory institutions known as catchment and sub-catchment councils based on river basins to govern and manage its waters. These councils were initially funded by a range of donors anticipating that they could become self-funding over time through the sale of water. In this chapter, we explore the origins of three of the councils and the political context in which they functioned. The internal politics were shaped by the commercial farming elites who sought to control the councils with a 'defensive strategy' to keep control over water. However, external national political processes limited the possibilities for continued elite control while simultaneously limiting water reform. Despite significant efforts to alter the waterscape, fast track land reform which began in 2000 led to the undermining of the first phases of IWRM and water reform and to the privileging of land over water. The economic foundations for funding the new participatory institutions were lost through the withdrawal of donors, the loss of large-scale farmers able to pay for water and the economic and political crises that characterised the period from 2000 to 2010.

KEYWORDS: IWRM, power, water reform, catchment councils, Zimbabwe

Introduction

Underlying water management and central to debates on IWRM is the question: what forms of power do their implementation rely upon and what are the broader structures of power that help shape decisions on water governance? We use an eclectic approach to power focusing on systemic inequalities and questions of control over water, the resources to make large amounts of water available for particular purposes and the knowledge to do so (cf. Foucault, 2001; Chabal,

1 First published in *Water Alternatives* 9(3): 515-532.

1994; Lukes, 2005). It is not immediately obvious at what levels and what issues are actually subject to participation by water users. For example, despite the emphasis upon participation in IWRM, its actual design and implementation are most often carried out in the absence of participation and consultation by water users (Goldin, 2013). Moreover, the agenda for the creation of new institutions is at least, partially controlled, by international donors. IWRM like other forms of technical and non-political ways to improve water distribution and management calls for the analysis of who actually controls the resources and what might be needed to challenge and undo such control (Li, 2007). One central mechanism for attempting to remove water management from political considerations was utilising ecological boundaries (watersheds or river basins) as the new units of management and participation. This presumably would detach water governance from mainstream or dominant political concerns.[2] We are particularly interested not only in the exercise of power within catchment councils but also in the field of power outside of catchment councils and water governance more generally.

In this chapter, we explore the formation and operation of catchment councils that were to be the foundations of participatory and decentralised water governance in Zimbabwe in the 1990s. They were intended to include all users, rural and urban, and all occupations. In this examination, we find that the framing of water governance and management as technical issues rather than political ones by the World Bank, Gesellschaft für Technische Zusammenarbeit (GTZ),[3] and by the government which supported, unintentionally, the efforts by farming elites to continue their control of Zimbabwe's waters. Concurrently, the efforts to alter water governance and reform need to be placed in the context of how the state and ruling party held and used its power.[4] It is surprising that in the promotion of water resources management by international donors they expected decentralisation and participation could be practiced in the water sector unlike other state sectors. Zimbabwe (as noted in the other chapters in this book) was ruled by a dominant party which operated in a highly centralised manner.

Zimbabwe provides a relevant case for examining the absence of the analysis of power and the role of political and commercial elites in the design and implementation of IWRM. The obstacles that this version of decentralisation would face, given Zimbabwe's historical experiences with the ruling party's version of decentralisation, should have been evident (Brand, 1991; Mutizwa-Mangiza, 1991; Derman et al., 2000).[5] However, we do not conclude that a better-designed

2 The World Water Forum in 2012 located the 'water crisis' as largely a governance crisis as did the second World Water Development report (UNESCO, 2006). According to the Global Water Partnership (2002) water governance refers to the range of political, social, economic, and administrative systems that are in place to develop and manager water resources, at different levels of society.

3 They are now known as GIZ - German Corporation for International Cooperation.

4 Water reform in the Zimbabwe context refers to the processes leading up to the passage of two acts: The Water Act, 1998, its associated statutory instruments, and the Zimbabwe National Water Act, 1998.

5 There are multiple discussions and analyses of Zimbabwe's efforts to decentralise local government functions involving wildlife and forestry management. There is not enough space here to describe them. We are not considering them in this chapter because the

approach taking power into account, would have led to a successful and different water reform. Considered an early success story in the conceptualisation and implementation of IWRM (see Manzungu and Derman, this book), it is worth re-examining its history in order to consider how power shaped the process. This should in turn assist us in reflecting on the future of IWRM in Zimbabwe (see the other articles on Zimbabwe in this book) and in the region more generally.

The World Bank water intervention in southern Africa marks an important turning point in how water should be governed and managed with an emphasis upon the correct pricing of water. It is also central in lining up donors to fund the strategy for and implementation of water resources management (see Manzungu and Derman, this book). Still, Zimbabwe had its own national priorities for water reform to which were added the initiatives of catchment councils. In this chapter, we consider the formation and history of these new institutions in three catchments or river basins, the Mupfure (which was folded into the Sanyati), the Mazowe and the Manyame. These three catchments were selected because of their agricultural importance and the location of their headwaters which were in or near the capital city of Harare. Two of the catchments served as pilots for the water reform and the third was the heart of irrigated wheat production (and is discussed in Hove et al., Chapter 8).[6]

The chapter is organised as follows: In the first section after a brief discussion of methods, we examine some critical dimensions of participation, power and political processes in integrated water resources management as it entered Zimbabwe and was reshaped there. In the second, we examine three catchment councils – the Mupfure, the Mazowe and the Manyame – how they were formed and how they grappled with water issues.[7] In the third section, we discuss how Zimbabwe's early experiences with the adoption and implementation of IWRM raise broader issues of water governance and the continued relevance of IWRM.

Methods

Part of the material for this chapter is drawn from a research programme on water reform in Zimbabwe and Malawi during the period 1998-2002.[8] The rest of the material is drawn from the Flows and Practices project (Mehta et al., in the Introduction to this book) in which we interviewed key actors in the water reform process, members of the Manyame catchment council, the lower, middle and upper Manyame sub-catchment councils, the Mazowe Catchment Council and employees of the Zimbabwe National Water Authority. In the earlier research

implementation of IWRM sought to bypass local government institutions.

6 The World Water Forum in 2012 located the 'water crisis' as largely a governance crisis as did the second World Water Development report (UNESCO, 2006). According to the Global Water Partnership (2002) water governance refers to the range of political, social, economic, and administrative systems that are in place to develop and manage water resources, at different levels of society.

7 Its origins were part of the broader research portfolio of the Centre for Applied Social Sciences (CASS) of the University of Zimbabwe on natural resources management which included grazing areas, wildlife, forestry, fisheries, and water (Nhira and Derman, 1997).

8 The research was carried out in collaboration with the Centre for Applied Social Sciences at the University of Zimbabwe.

project Bill Derman attended meetings of the Mupfure, Mazowe and Manyame catchment councils (and selected committee meetings) from 1998 to 2001. He also attended meetings to publicise the Water Act of 1998 held by the Water Resources Management Strategy. The purpose was to gain a full understanding of how the new acts (Water and ZINWA) were rolled out, how the new institutions understood their roles, how they acted and whose interests were privileged in the process. To understand the continuities and discontinuities between the initial period and 2010-2014 we interviewed farmers, the former Permanent Secretary for Water, the Director of the Ministry of Environment, Water and Climate in charge of water, the former Permanent Secretary for Irrigation, and several donors including Australian Aid, the World Bank, the African Development Bank, and The Deutsche Gesellschaft für Internationale Zusammenarbeit (GIZ). In both projects, we reviewed and analysed international documents and policy statements on water resources and the policy and project documents and laws of the Government of Zimbabwe. Drawing on material from earlier research has provided a longitudinal perspective which has given us first-hand knowledge of how IWRM came to Zimbabwe, who the actors were, how the new institutions functioned, and in general the promises of the water reform. Our more recent research enables us to examine what happened, the inability of the councils to function productively in the subsequent decade and the overall loss of much of the original intentions. This chapter fills in some of the details of the broader process that we describe in Manzungu and Derman (Chapter 6) and Hove, Derman and Manzungu (Chapter 8).

Participation, Power and Political Processes in Water Governance

In an agrarian settler economy like Zimbabwe, the waters were overwhelmingly allocated to the white-dominated agriculture sector.[9] However, in the period considered in this chapter there appears to be consensus that the new water management institutions were dominated by large-scale commercial farmers (overwhelmingly white), water engineers, and water specialists funded by donors (Sithole, 2001; Chikozho, 2001, 2008; Latham, 2002; Tapela, 2002; Swatuk, 2002; Manzungu, 2002a,b; Mtisi and Nicol, 2003; Hellum and Derman, 2005). The concerns of small-scale farmers, i.e. the communal area residents were limited and the voices of women virtually absent. In addition to participation, what constituted the limits and boundaries of water-related issues that could be taken up by these new institutions (Mtisi 2011; Mapedza and Geheb 2010; Manzungu and Dzingirai 2012)?

9 The Land Tenure Commission Report (1994) (sometimes known as the Rukuni Commission) directly linked the great inequality in land to inequalities in water use and access. Research Study number 6 of the commission was a critical review of Zimbabwe's water resources management system whose purpose was "to study and evaluate Zimbabwe's water resources and master plan with a view of examining the constraints and potential solutions to water distribution and utilisation in communal and resettlement areas" (1994, 3: 77-78). During most of the 1990s water reform was pursued without substantially increasing allocations to communal areas.

Decentralisation of water governance and management was part of a more general pattern of natural resources decentralisation in Zimbabwe including wildlife and forestry. Unlike the other domains, the most powerful actors in the water sector were white commercial farmers living on privately owned land. A number of researchers sought to understand how catchment and sub-catchment councils would operate. They found that stakeholders who were participating in the new institutions were highly skewed toward those who already had access to water (Sithole, 2001; Swatuk, 2002; Manzungu, 2002a, b; Mtisi and Nicol, 2003; Stalgren, 2006). Hellum and Derman (2005) found that the interests of smaller water users were dismissed from consideration at meetings. Power and knowledge asymmetries existing in the water sector were not sufficiently addressed in the new institutions (Derman et al., 2000; Manzungu, 2002a,b; Chikozho, 2008). In general, little attention, if any, was paid to the social inequalities that were part of multi-stakeholder platforms (Faysse, 2006). On the other hand, Mabiza (2013) documents how the water interests of small-scale farmers and communal area residents are still ignored by the Zimbabwe National Water Authority (ZINWA) as they formulated the catchment plan for the Mzingwane Catchment (which partially includes the city of Bulawayo).

Lastly, the historian Musemwa (2008) contends the command of water figured in the ruling party's strategy to keep control of Zimbabwe's urban population. He examines the shift from the focus on rural waters to urban water and the efforts by the national government to take water supply and sanitation away from cities now governed by the opposition party, Movement for Democratic Change (MDC). The parastatal, ZINWA did not remain as an independent self-financing water entity. The national government changed ZINWA's mission from providing raw water to providing urban water supply to Zimbabwe's cities. A directive instructed ZINWA to take over the management of urban water supply and sanitation and from all the urban local authorities which had voted for the opposition party.[10] Musemwa (2008: 10) observes the state treated ZINWA as an agent that could regain lost control and influence over urban areas and capture substantial revenues thereby weakening urban authorities.

Turning to the first issue of the domains of power and the realm of the political, the government was controlled until 2009 by a single dominant party (see Manzungu and Derman, Chapter 6). The party set the rules of the 'political game' and was able to control the agenda. In addition, it could prevent citizen or group demands from becoming political issues or even being made to the power holders (cf. Lukes, 2005: 40).[11] However, there was a bureaucratic autonomy for the water reform process because at least some of its elements fitted with major objectives of government. Two of these objectives were to undo the highly unequal distribution of Zimbabwe's water to large-scale commercial farmers (GoZ, 1994, 2000a) and reduce the number of civil servants by creating a new commercial parastatal to manage water and shift state employees to ZINWA. This new institution was to be self-funding and thus reduce state expenditures (Manzungu and

10 This position was reversed when it became clear that ZINWA failed to improve the image of the government and the ruling party because of its failure to solve water problems.

11 This is part of what Lukes terms the three-dimensional view of power.

Derman, Chapter 6, provide the background).

However, it is unclear the extent to which the ruling party agreed with or indeed understood other elements of the reform. For example, to shift water governance away from current political boundaries to one based solely on ecological criteria was debated and seen as workable by the affected ministries. The purpose of the new water management units was intended to remove water governance from political debates and place it in the hands of technocrats and catchment and sub-catchment councils. As indicated in Manzungu and Derman, the cabinet controlled completely by ZANU-PF did not turn the WRMS report into the national water policy. In practice, it also placed the waters in the hands of those who had been managing the rivers until then. While in principle all water users had the 'right' to come to meetings and participate in discussions, the structures favoured large users because they were the ones with the knowledge, experience and resources. In addressing issues of participation, the ruling party did not support new organisations of communal area residents outside of the party.[12] Thus the lack of participation in new water institutions (other than in the Mupfure Sub-Catchment, see below) is not surprising. In the formation and creation of catchment and sub-catchment councils, the Zimbabwe Farmers' Union ostensibly represented communal area farmers while Rural District Councillors represented their residents. Again, with the exception of the Mupfure Sub-Catchment council communal area residents were not directly consulted. The Dutch government that funded the Mupfure Pilot Catchment (and also research in eastern Zimbabwe on small-scale irrigation) directly sought to engage communal area men and women to express their water needs and formulate project proposals to meet them (Taylor et al., 1996; personal conversations with Alex Bolding, a consultant on the project).

What is the political?

In keeping with viewing IWRM as an apolitical or non-political activity most participants in the water reform process sought, in relying on the best practices of water management, to keep 'politics' out of water.[13] The large-scale commercial farmers' strategy toward IWRM in the context of Zimbabwe can be understood as a 'defensive one'. It was the means by which the farm-owning elite could attempt to keep control over this critical resource and side-line debates over larger political and economic questions. What commercial farmers did can be thought of as the use of 'defensive power' (Salverda, 2011, 2013). It was a strategy of a 'racial' minority to keep their waters and stay out of an increasingly tense political

12 A clear example of Lukes' (2005) notion of the second dimension of power, the power to set the agenda and who could and could not represent water users.

13 This phrase repeated in many of the meetings attended by Bill Derman in 1999 and 2000 to keep references of land and other political issues like the opposition party out of the official meetings of councils and sub-councils even though it was the context in which meetings were being held. Perhaps the irony was that one rationale for water reforms, ensuring equitable water access, was political. Nonetheless participants in the new institutions brought together by politics were supposed to be apolitical and an apolitical strategy favoured large users.

situation.[14] The farmers certainly viewed themselves as under threat and sought to demonstrate that they were essential to Zimbabwe's economy (Pilosof, 2012). They sought accommodation with the internationally approved and nationally legislated water reform process. In Lukes' terms, they had lost power over, and sought the power to control the decision-making process over waters. Not surprisingly, they argued for the autonomy of the new water institutions. However, the outcome of new struggles for water was short-circuited by other political processes and the effort by the presidency to redefine what constituted the political. The use of defensive power could not be sustained in the face of violence and executive power.

The president transformed the meaning of what 'the political' is. President Mugabe stated that land and all related land issues were 'political' which had the unique meaning that land issues (but not including water issues) were outside the consideration of the courts, police and any others who sought to object to the land occupations and the acquisition of land by government. In what can be seen as an exercise in 'power over and power to'.[15] President Mugabe bypassed all normal procedures at least until he was able, for example, to remove the Chief Supreme Court Justice who had initially decided that farm occupations and the accompanying violence violated the rights of farm owners, and farm employees.[16] In claiming what was 'political', the President sought to create a new form of knowledge and to render illegitimate any other considerations of land issues. It was the exercise of executive power that could not be challenged and certainly not by the water sector.[17] In practice, it ruled any discussion of land issues illegitimate in the context of water governance making meaningless notions of IWRM since most water was used for irrigation. In sum, the emphasis upon participation, who did participate and who did not while very important, misses the broader picture of water governance and how it responds to and helps shape the exercise of power. Framing our analysis in this way assists in explaining why IWRM has struggled in Zimbabwe.

Zimbabwe's political reform period

In the mid- and late 1990s, new political spaces opened up in several arenas. These included trade unions, the expansion of nongovernmental and human rights organisations, demands for a new constitution and a new national political opposition party, the Movement for Democratic Change (Hammar et al., 2000;

14 Salverda analyses the case of the Mauritian white elite and their strategies in the face of their loss of power.

15 Lukes, 2005; Gaventa, 2006.

16 On 14 December 2000, President Mugabe, speaking at his party's congress, disowned the courts. With reference to the land issue, he said, "The courts can do what they want. They are not courts for our people and we shall not even be defending ourselves in these courts". President Mugabe's statement followed the invasion of the Supreme Court "by close to two hundred war veterans and followers, which was nothing but disgraceful. ...They stood on chairs, benches and tables, in a gesture of absolute contempt for the institution of the courts as the third essential organ of a democratic government" (Gubbay, 2009). Gubbay was the former Chief Justice of the Supreme Court forced out of office in 2001.

17 Meredith, 2002 ; Blair, 2002 ; Chan, 2002; Alexander and McGregor, 2013.

Raftopoulos and Mlambo, 2009). This opening also influenced the possibilities for water reform, which permitted open discussion and debates around the country after the formation of the Water Resources Management Strategy group (see below) which sought public discussion of new water acts and water policies. This political opening closed after the referendum on the new proposed constitution drafted by the ruling party in 2000 produced a 'no' vote (Bratton, 2014). The referendum defeat was followed by the violent farm occupations and a highly contested and violent parliamentary election. In addition to the wider political considerations were the economic constraints placed upon these water institutions by the state and by donors who withdrew from the water sector. It is also important to consider the limited power or influence that the Ministry of Water Resources and Rural Development (the name in that era, now the Ministry of Environment, Water and Climate) and the newly created Zimbabwe National Water Authority had over the national purse. In general, most budgetary resources for water were used for government dams (GoZ, 2000a).

The World Bank and international donors

In July of 1993 one year after the adoption of the Dublin Principles, the World Bank sponsored a workshop at Victoria Falls[18] to bring together international and national experts for the purpose of 1) Creating programmes of national and regional actions which could enhance the region's capacity to manage water resources and recommendations and 2) Developing specific follow-up activities to implement the new programmes. Based upon water resources management the timing of the workshop, July 1993, was close in time to the formation of a Zimbabwean Board to Review Zimbabwe's Water Act convened in June of 1993. The Bank's meeting contended that water was an economic good and water policies and management had to be adjusted to this 'fact'. The presentations were by Mr. Le Moigne, the Senior Water Resources Advisor of the Bank, an engineer trained at the University of Paris and Cornell; Dr. North, a specialist in water resources economics; Mr. Gabriel Tibor, also from the Bank; Mr. Harvey Garn, economic advisor in the Bank and lastly one environmentalist, Malin Falkenmark well known for analyses of water scarcity.

The thrust of the World Bank interventions was to emphasise the economic dimensions of water and that the key to effective water management was pricing policies.[19] There was no discussion or analysis of the fact that most Zimbabweans (and other southern Africans) lacked access to water for agriculture and water

18 Workshop on *Water Resources Management in Southern Africa: Proceedings of the Workshop*, Victoria Falls, Zimbabwe, July 5-9, 1993. It was organised by the Water Resources Branch of the United Nations Department of Economic and Social Development, the Training Centre for Water and Sanitation of the University of Zimbabwe and the Department of Water, Ministry of Lands, Agriculture and Water Development, Government of Zimbabwe. Sponsors were the World Bank, the Commonwealth Secretariat, the United Nations (UNDP and UNEP) and the Canadian International Development Agency.

19 For example Tibor's statement: "Water is an increasingly scarce resource: it is often treated as a public good when in fact it is anything but free. More so, for many uses water has all the properties of an exclusive economic good, which is just the opposite of a public good" (IBRD, 1993: 1 Annex 4-IV).

for drinking. (While we covered some of these same issues in Manzungu and Derman, Chapter 6, here we are describing in greater detail how IWRM came to Zimbabwe and how it fitted with some national priorities.)

Shortly after the World Bank workshop, the Zimbabwe Government launched a review of its own Water Act (1976). The terms of reference[20] for the Water Act Review Board (chaired by Dr. S.S. Mlambo from the Ministry of Lands, Agriculture and Water Development) emphasised the examination of the principle of granting of water rights in perpetuity by the use of priority dates in determining water allocation. While water was, in the main, not privately owned, landowners could obtain rights to access specific amounts of water in perpetuity through application to the Department of Water. The allocation of water in a river would be determined by when the applicant received the right. The other major item on the agenda was the need to change the pricing policy for water.

Unlike the World Bank meeting, the land-water nexus was highlighted in the findings and observations of the Water Review Board. The board commented on the lack of access to water by communal and small-scale farmers. They concluded that charging for all water should be considered as a means of increasing the efficient use of water while there should be specific programmes to bring water to communal areas and small-scale farmers. At the time of the Review Board, communal area residents could not obtain water rights on their own but only through Rural District Councils, an unchanged legacy from the colonial dual property system. Residents of commercial farming areas could obtain water rights in their own names. In addition, the Review Board observed that participation in water management was highly skewed. River Boards that oversaw the distribution and use of water were composed only of water-rights holders who were almost exclusively white commercial farmers. The Review Board also accepted the continued division of primary and commercial water.[21] Primary water or water for domestic purposes in communal areas was to remain free while commercial water was to have a price collected by the government. Commercial water is defined as water used for business purposes and it has been prioritised in water resources management.

The World Bank workshop and the national review process led to the creation of a new advisory group to lead the development and implementation of new water laws and policies and to fill in the links that led to the donors' support for the water sector. This group was located outside of the Department of Water and its ministry. Moreover, as an indication of ambivalence it was called the Water Resources Management Strategy but no title afterwards to indicate its status. WRMS

20 The terms of reference were as follows: 1. Review the existing Water Act, its subsequent amendment and any relevant background information; 2. Examine the principle and basis for granting water rights; 3. Examine and determine the extent of efficient and effective usage of water rights by those holding them; 4. Review principle of riparian use; 5. Determine principle of priority dates; 6. Determine pricing policy; 7. Solicit people's farmers and ordinary citizens' views on the subject of water rights; 8. Determine the principle to be adopted in allocation of water in the light of the existing one; 9. Determine the necessity for the formation of river boards; 10. Produce report and recommendations.

21 Draft Report of the Water Act Review Board, official minutes January 1994, typed. We thank Dr. Alex Bolding for making these available to us.

and the Department of Water were tasked with writing new water legislation. In parallel with the writing of the new water laws, WRMS began operation in 1996 and ended in 2000 with the publication of their final report.[22] While WRMS got underway the Royal Dutch Embassy and the German development agency, GTZ, funded the Mupfure Pilot Catchment and the Mazowe Catchment Council, respectively. GTZ then began funding the Manyame Catchment. In addition, other donors had begun funding other catchment councils including the Save, and the Runde. In terms of new national policies, the most important change during this period was the creation of the Zimbabwe National Water Authority and the downsizing of the Department of Water. This transition was funded by GTZ including substantial technical and personnel support.

Examining the WRMS project more closely

The two bills – the Water Bill and the ZINWA Bill were placed in the public domain in November 1997. At that time water, land and the environment were to be closely linked. For example, in an effort to define what constituted catchment planning Hugh Williams (WRMS, 1998: 8), a member of WRMS provided a definition: "An integrated land and water resources development and management plan, that is capable of being implemented". Another planner for WRMS, Shepherd Sithole (WRMS, 1998: 9) emphasised the importance of linking land use and water and critiqued those using only a mono-disciplinary approach. Maintaining the division of Zimbabwe's waters into three categories (Primary, Commercial and Urban, Industrial and Mining). The WRMS group contended that: "Allocation of water shall take cognizance of the fact that water for primary purposes has priority over all other uses and any person is entitled to use water for primary purposes" (WRMS, 1998: 13). However, despite this assertion there is no discussion on how to ensure that this 'right' was to be maintained. Other than primary uses all other water uses required permits obtainable only from catchment councils.[23]

The environment featured centrally in WRMS concerns with major efforts to limit and control pollution. It was argued, consistent with IWRM, that preserving water quality combined with water for environmental purposes are best served through using ecological boundaries of water (this is discussed in Manzungu and Derman, Chapter 6). The major innovation of the water reform and in compliance with decentralisation was to create new institutions based upon ecological boundaries and high user participation known as catchment and sub-catchment councils.[24] Between them they would be responsible for the following:

22 *Towards Integrated Water Resources Management* (GoZ 2000a), the WRMS policy document was put forward by the Ministry to the cabinet but it was never adopted. Thus, it never became official policy.

23 This was changed to enable the Catchment Manager to approve permits where there was no controversy. While seemingly just bureaucratic, it increased the power of the manager.

24 The precise legal functions of catchment councils are to be found in Government of Zimbabwe (2000b). The legal functions of sub-catchment councils are put forward in Government of Zimbabwe (2000c).

1. Allocate water within the framework of the catchment plan.
2. Monitor water use in accordance with the allocations.
3. Monitor groundwater levels and abstraction of water.
4. Monitor water quality.
5. Protect the catchment from degradation.
6. Raise and collect levies (levies are separate from the sale of water).
7. Maintain user discipline.

Two pilot catchments were formed to determine how these new institutions should function. The empowerment of the two pilot catchments – the Mazowe and Mupfure (to become the Sanyati) with donor funding – led to their efforts to take over water management from central authority.[25] With the creation of ZINWA, a new set of conflicts arose over the powers of the newly created catchment managers. Catchment councils were constituted by two elected members from each sub-catchment council within the catchment. There was, and is, no salary for members of the councils although their transport and a sitting allowance were paid through donor funding. It was assumed that when the donors withdrew sub-catchment councils would pay allowances from their water revenues while the Water Fund, created by the ZINWA Act would use levies imposed on water permit holders to support catchment councils.[26] The catchment councils were to be technically supported by a catchment manager appointed, hired and paid by ZINWA. Catchment managers were all trained engineers and were to carry out the secretarial duties on behalf of the Council. Following the Dublin Principles, the WRMS reports (and later the published strategy) women were to participate and be represented at all levels of decision-making. There were no measures enacted to ensure that this occurred and there was little evidence that this took place (Hellum and Derman, 2005). Land and water were to 'be integrated' in the eyes of WRMS but what happened is described in Hove et al., Chapter 8. For example, WRMS had to adjust to the expression of power by a highly centralised state and the councils could not address what to do about the division of land between the communal sector with no individual water rights and the commercial sector with individual water rights.

Catchment councils and sub-catchment councils: The new participatory institutions

In this section we will briefly describe the formation of three catchment councils and their early operations. We start with the Mupfure and the Mazowe councils to be followed by the Manyame. The latter two catchments were to be 'pilot' projects and the intent was that they would run for three years before the implementation

25 Field notes of Bill Derman 1997-2000.

26 Most sub-catchment councils had difficulty funding their activities over time while the water fund was not used to support catchment councils.

of the Water and ZINWA Bills to permit modifications or amendments along with designing the statutory instruments to implement them effectively. This was to be a major departure from past governmental policy decisions and to provide an empirical context in which to assess the efficacy of the new institutions of water management.

Joice Mujuru, then Minister of Water Development and Rural Resources, contended that the water sector would become responsive to stakeholder management and "with the government playing only the role of regulatory authority" (Darby, 2000: 20). According to the Minister the pilot catchments would be "tested and verified before nation-wide replication is undertaken" (ibid). She emphasised that the pilot projects were to provide a learning experience for the development of effective stakeholder institutions at catchment level" (ibid).

However, this process was not permitted to run its course.

The Mupfure Catchment

The Mupfure River originates just south of Harare and ends in Lake Kariba. It is approximately 224 kilometres long and drains an area of 11,866 square kilometres. It was made up of four subunits each (termed CUFs which is not an acronym) each of which would manage a subsection of the river. It was anticipated that the Mupfure pilot catchment council would be merged into the much larger Sanyati Catchment in 1999-2000 and the Mupfure would become a sub-catchment. The purpose of this new catchment authority was "the establishment of an effective and efficient system for sustainable water resources management in the Mupfure Catchment, which takes into account the management of water at the lowest appropriate level and the full representation of all interest groups" (Taylor et al., 1996: 11). This pilot catchment was funded by the Dutch government and was intended to serve as a model for the more equitable distribution of water (1996: 12). Moreover, unlike the other two catchment councils the specific object of this project was "to support disadvantaged communities to improve their opportunity to represent themselves in water management issues, and to give preference to the protection of the environment" (1996: 20). While the document notes that women will be major beneficiaries since they are the ones who are involved in fetching drinking water, food crop agriculture and firewood collection there are no specific recommendations as to how women should be included in all dimensions of the project. Project activities with a budget allocation included water allocation guidelines, a hydro-information system, catchment outline plans, catchment protection plans, water quality and a financing system for the catchment and sub-catchment authorities. In addition, the new Mupfure Catchment Council was to work in coordination with WRMS and the drafters of the new Water Bill. There were to be two community development officers modelled on the early phase of the project whereby Dutch consultants with members of the Department of Water to have villagers prioritise what kinds of water projects they wanted. The project drew up budgets for the proposed priorities and in several instances implemented them. This was done to create a demand for the new catchment institutions. Moreover, these village projects focused on primary water – boreholes or water for cattle – and not on commercial water. This emphasis was not duplicated subsequently.

In one of the many workshops held by WRMS in the Mupfure, the following indicates some of the major difficulties. The workshop was held at the Chegutu Hotel in September 1997.[27] The workshop was to explain the new water bill and institutional structures and was chaired by Dr. Sakupwanya and Mrs. Matiza, a WRMS economist. The priority areas identified by the people attending were as follows:

1. Water availability and the need for dams in catchments without permanent rivers.
2. Water rights. Getting access to water and costs involved.
3. Awareness and training on dealing with water.
4. Conservation of rivers and adjoining stream banks.

There was a heavy participation by small-scale farmers, resettled farmers and communal area residents in this meeting as well as large-scale farmers. There was substantial interest in obtaining more water especially for irrigation and also worries about the new costs associated with the water reform. With the passage of the Water and ZINWA Acts and their implementation in 1999, the Mupfure Catchment was absorbed into the Sanyati Catchment.

In general, the Mupfure Catchment Council before it became the Sanyati took decentralisation and water resources management seriously. The issues were local which was consistent with the intent of the Water Act. They included the possibility of a new dam located in a communal area, to stop the city of Chegutu from polluting the Mupfure River, and to have the donor (the Dutch Government) provide their funds directly to the Council rather than through WRMS. With the formation of the Sanyati Catchment Council, it contended that communal area concerns for small dams and boreholes were beyond their mandate. This disconnected communal area residents from the Catchment Councils.

Many of the most active commercial farmers on catchment and sub-catchment councils found their farms occupied and then resettled. They then dropped out of water management. Discussion of the land occupations and the violence accompanying them were not permitted in council and sub-catchment council meetings. They were to be about water alone! The Dutch government withdrew from funding the Sanyati that crippled its activities after 2001.

After Dutch funding ended, the council saw little or no reason to continue the emphasis upon participation (Hellum and Derman, 2002). The funding for small-scale farmers to participate evaporated. In general, the size of the Sanyati Catchment discouraged participation without funding for transport. The meetings became irregular and many sub-catchments stopped functioning.

27 The account of the meeting is from the field notes of Bill Derman who attended it as part of the CASS research.

The Mazowe Catchment

Before it became a pilot project, big water users had formed the Mazowe River Catchment Development Company, which was made up of seven River Boards[28] operating under its umbrella. The purpose of this company was to maximise the profitable use of the Mazowe's waters that initially excluded those without water rights. As part of the water reform, the new catchments had to expand the area and create new sub-catchments which meant the incorporation of communal areas. The first three years of the project (1996-1998) focused on creating functioning council and sub-catchment councils. The Mazowe pilot Water Management Project prepared its own studies including one on how to allocate water rather than the priority date system. The study focused on improved equity of access through a proportional allocation system that, in the end, was not adopted by either ZINWA or the Department of Water Development (DWD). Politically, the management of the pilot catchment recognised that without black Zimbabwean ownership of the process it would fail. To this end, they recruited the Chair of a Rural District Council, a member of the upper echelons of the ruling party and a farmer to become Chair of Mazowe Catchment Council. In addition, other politically important black Zimbabweans became part of the Mazowe Catchment Council. However, despite their efforts to protect themselves politically they could not stop the farm occupations and seizures.

From its inception, the catchment council leadership emphasised that the Mazowe Catchment Council should devote most of its time to promoting and/or mobilising finance for development within the catchment and they created a formal committee on development. What form the development should take was an area of disagreement (Darby, 2000: 24). In general, it meant the expansion of commercial agriculture and greater use of water by 'new users'. The leadership contended that the Ministry of Water Resources and Rural Development and ZINWA should be willing under decentralisation to give up central planning and central decision-making (Darby, 2000: 24). Mazowe and Mupfure attempted to shift real power to the catchment and sub-catchment councils. To accommodate new users the Mazowe Catchment Council proposed setting aside 10% of the rivers' waters for them. To remain committed to the principle of subsidiarity, they promoted a third tier of management which they termed water user boards. They suggested that Water User Boards (WUBs) with substantial commercial use provide funding for WUBs with mainly primary water use. As noted earlier, this third tier, has not been recognised in the formal governance structures because it is not included in the Water Act

The Mazowe project sought to locate all existing dams, potential small dam sites, quantify the number of wells and boreholes and to promote involvement of water users in the planning process. They found substantial resistance from the Department of Agriculture for data on land use. Large-scale farmers were asked to confirm abstraction points, locations of all existing dams and boreholes and to identify potential dam sites. The farmers were unwilling to provide the infor-

28 River Boards were composed of water rights holders only. In the Water Act, they were to be replaced by sub-catchment councils.

mation because they suspected the data would be used to tax them or restrict their water use. In sum, it was not possible to collect the needed data. In 2000, the Mazowe Catchment Council suggested writing a simplified catchment outline plan rather than a more complex one in line with available resources, time and expense. These plans were not completed until 2009-2010.[29]

A consultant noted in a Development Committee meeting that there was need to revisit the definition of irrigation since informal irrigation is more important to small-scale farmers than formal irrigation.[30] She pointed out that in Musami (a water user board in the upper Mazowe area) there were approximately 5,000 hectares of land under informal irrigation. She suggested that this meant there was an important need to include it in catchment planning. In response, the catchment planner told the members that he was trying to incorporate gender issues into his planning but the women were not taking the opportunity to be involved in catchment planning. He claimed that women refused to participate and were engaged in erosion-producing stream bank cultivation. This was one of the very few discussions of women and it was cut-off before it began. Returning to the question of garden irrigation she said that gardens are going to impact on water usage and hence there is a need to include them in catchment planning. Mr. Wood (a water and irrigation consultant) replied that gardens are only found in wet areas and there is very little potential for them to expand since there were very few wet areas without gardens left in the whole catchment. Therefore, the male expert succeeded in blocking any further discussion and analysis.[31]

The Council sought to improve information on pollution and who had water rights. The council contended that the Ministry did not have up-to-date and easily accessible information on the water rights in order to covert the rights into permits. Efforts to install new flow monitoring equipment were frustrated due to lack of resources. There was no capacity in ZINWA to assess water quality and water pollution and to implement its programme to reduce water pollution. It was anticipated that with payment for water there would be increased funding to make the new system work.[32]

The Mazowe Catchment Council was potentially the richest. Mr. Lang of GTZ who sometimes attended meetings prepared a document with estimates of levies that were likely to be collected in the Mazowe catchment. His conclusion was that one could anticipate the figure to be 14-15 million Zimbabwean dollars (ZWD). (At the time USD1.00 was worth ZWD54.00.) He also believed that given this scenario, Mazowe would not face serious financial constraints in its operations. One Council member asked him whether he had also considered

29 According to the Water Act, a catchment council could not offer permits until after its plan was approved by ZINWA. However, ZINWA did not provide the technical expertise to do the plan.

30 Bill Derman field notes on Mazowe Valley Catchment Planning Subcommittee Held at Agritex Offices, Marondera, 9 October 1997.

31 Official Minutes of the Mazowe Valley Catchment Planning Subcommittee Held at Agritex Offices, Marondera on 9 October 1997 and personal notes taken by Bill Derman.

32 Field notes from Mazowe Catchment Council meetings in 1997 and 1998 in possession of Bill Derman.

the extent of the impact of the farm invasions and how much this was going to lower or increase the number of permits from which levies could be collected. He said he had not taken that into account because no one can accurately predict or calculate those changes at the moment.[33] At least for the Mazowe, it could have been self-supporting as the designers of the water reform had hoped.

The Manyame Catchment[34]

Much of Zimbabwe's tobacco and wheat was grown on the large-scale commercial farms located in this catchment. These farmers were usually members of river boards and had substantial knowledge of irrigation and water management. Unlike the other two catchments, there was no pilot catchment but rather the government insisted that the river boards, farmers and other representatives form sub-catchment councils. The Manyame river basin was divided into sub-catchments (mainly following the old River Board boundaries) and the District Administrator called for meetings in each area to form them. The only group to be well represented aside from the government was the commercial farmers who had excellent communication networks (Latham, 2002). People at the meeting who came from named stakeholder groups in the new Water Act became members of the sub-catchment council and selected two of their own to be part of the Manyame Catchment Council.[35]

Across the country in 2000, other catchment and sub-catchment councils were rapidly formed ensuring there would be no inclusion of the results and experiences from the pilot projects. At the full council meeting of the Manyame, the Chief of Guruve, the late Chief Bepura was elected as chair of the Council while Piers Nicolle, one of the largest farmers in the catchment was elected as vice-chair. The actual functioning of the council was tenuous due to the land occupations. Very quickly, two of the sub-catchments were convulsed by land occupations and meetings by the sub-catchment councils were abandoned. In a third, area conflicts between supporters of the then opposition party MDC and ruling party supporters made meetings and cooperation virtually impossible. By 2002, only the Lower Manyame, Middle Manyame and Upper Manyame sub-catchment councils were functioning with GTZ funding their activities.

Prior to 2002 the following were the main issues: Payment for water and levies and what would be done with the monies, the shift from the priority date system to one of proportional allocation of water stored in privately built and owned water works and how to convert old water rights to time-limited permits. However, this could not be done until the writing and acceptance of what is called a catch-

33 Mazowe Catchment Council Meeting 23 January 2001, Harare at Kurima House. Bill Derman field notes.

34 Hove et al. (Chapter 8) describe what happens to the waters of the Middle Manyame Sub-Catchment after the land reform.

35 Stakeholders are the following: large-scale commercial farmers, indigenous large-scale commercial farmers, communal land farmers, small-scale commercial farmers, resettlement farmers, industry and commerce, local government, large-scale miners and small-scale miners.

ment outline plan.[36] All meetings saw a discussion of sitting allowances, transport allowances and meeting the costs of meetings. Another major issue was that the sub-catchment council was to be designated as the agency to collect the levies by ZINWA. ZINWA proposed to pay 2.5% of the levies back to sub-catchment councils for services rendered while Manyame Catchment Council was proposing 25% as an initial but negotiable figure. While the Water Act only specified two levels of institutions – catchment and sub-catchment councils – Manyame (like Mazowe and Sanyati) wanted a third tier of user representation contending that they would be much closer to water users. Lastly, there was substantial emphasis upon the need for educating all water users on the new laws, the new administration of water and the purposes of water reform. The chair of Manyame Catchment Council went to inform traditional leaders and headmen of the new Water Act focusing on why people needed to pay for water.

Each catchment, including the Manyame, noted the absence of a third and fourth tier of water users. The council observed that it was at the lower levels that the actual management of water took place and yet they were not properly represented on the sub-catchment council or catchment council nor were they supported through the new levy system. In a bid by commercial farmers to keep their land, they raised the issue of Biri Dam. Biri Dam was a major infrastructure project on the Manyame River just south of Chinhoyi City. It was partly funded by commercial farmers and the National Social Security Authority (NSSA). Biri Dam was to be a multipurpose dam supplying water for Chinoyi, water for irrigation, and storing enough water to permit Harare to increase the amount of water it withdrew from the headwaters of the Manyame River. In a meeting with the governor of Western Mashonaland, Peter Chanetsa at his office (27 February 2001)[37] one of the largest farmers in the catchment, Piers Nicole raised the issue that 60% of farms who had invested in Biri Dam were to be acquired for land reform. He attempted unsuccessfully to delist farmers who had contributed to the dam. In the end, most of the farmers who had contributed to the dam were indeed removed from their farms.

Discussion

The Dublin Principles and IWRM while never discussed in general were always present in the issues discussed by the council and sub-councils. We will briefly discuss three crosscutting themes that we have identified: first, power; second, water for development and third, gender.

Power

Catchment and sub-catchment councils attempted to gain power and control over these new institutions. This included not only white farmers but also black Zimbabweans who had become the chairpersons of Mazowe and Manyame Catchment Councils. Council members sought to govern and manage the waters on

36 In fact, the catchment outline plan was not written until 2009 and it is unclear if it has ever been finalised.

37 Meeting notes from Jim Latham in possession of Bill Derman.

their own. ZINWA, in their view, was to serve them and not vice-versa. They took subsidiarity seriously and sought to control their institutions. In addition, they sought engagement and service from the Catchment Managers who were caught by surprise at these developments. The exception was the Catchment Manager for Sanyati (formerly of Mupfure) who understood the major shifts in how water was to be managed. The councils refused to accept the low percentages of monies they would receive for collecting the levies for ZINWA. They sought to influence some dimensions of the Water Act and attempted to have a third tier added to legal entities that made up the new institutions.

The institutions of water governance enjoyed their freedom from the already existing political units. Following ecological boundaries (more or less), they were not engaged with provinces, districts and rural district councils. They were deeply engaged with ZINWA but this was seen to be, until it was given municipal waters to sell, as a non-political institution. This was important since water supply was a function of Rural District Councils and water provision also rested in the provinces. How this might have changed over time, we cannot know.

However, as has been clear throughout the three Zimbabwe chapters in this book, the newly empowered catchment and sub-catchment councils could not influence land reform. Indeed, they engaged in self-censorship trying to protect themselves by claiming that they could only discuss water in their meetings despite the fact that to produce catchment outline plans they needed information on land. It was a strategy that failed. Land reform proceeded with neither little or no consideration of water governance and management nor the economy of water reform. It is doubtful given the power of the president to declare that land could not be debated and that challenging fast track was not politically possible. The new weakness of commercial farmers was manifest as their farms were occupied and they were chased out of them. Their strategy of defence thus failed.

Development

One of the critiques of IWRM has been its lack of focus on socioeconomic development. In the case of Zimbabwe, economic development and the more efficient use of water were to come through the better pricing of water. The emphasis at the national level and in ZINWA has been the user pays principle. However, at the catchment level water users recognised the importance of water for development. Still, they were not supportive of higher prices for water and were extremely conscious of who had and who did not have water rights. In the case of the Mupfure Catchment, a strong effort was made to engage communal area residents in formulating their water needs. Water was identified as a real constraint upon development. When the Mupfure merged into the Sanyati, those communal area projects were ended and the emphases shifted to pollution from mining, pollution of the Mupfure River by Chegutu Town, and planning for a new dam in Mhondoro Communal Land to provide new water for irrigation. In general, there was a shift in emphasis from small waters to big waters. In the Mazowe Catchment they formed a development committee whose task was to propose to the whole council how increasing access and use of water by 'new users' (a euphemism for discussing black Zimbabweans in communal areas) could be accomplished. The

Chair of the committee was passionate in his claim that water reform was purposeless without development.[38] By development, they meant figuring out how to run the river fairly, allocate water for new users and subsidise their use for up to five years. Unlike the other two catchments, the Manyame Council did not focus much on communal areas which were located at the bottom of the catchment with nothing but commercial farms above. In part they came into being much later than the other two and had less time to organise and plan before the farm occupations. The catchment councils did not, unlike the national government, lose sight of the development part of water reform.

Gender

In all three catchments, the Dublin Principle on the importance of women was ignored (see Derman and Prabhakaran, Chapter 14). Despite some attention to gender issues in WRMS (GoZ, 2000a: 81-84) it was neglected by all catchment and sub-catchment councils. While the Mazowe Catchment did recognise the importance of primary (domestic) water use they did not ask, nor did any other council focus on who was engaged in small-scale irrigation. Nor did they concern themselves with who supplied domestic water to the household. The one exception as noted above in the Sanyati Catchment was the pilot Mupfure Catchment where the consultants refused to hold meetings on community needs in water without large numbers of women present. They sought a method to ensure that women's voices were heard in discussions and possible projects about water. This was followed up by hiring community development officers who were female and supposed to continue the focus on women and water. However, the positions disappeared when the Dutch donor left.

Part of the reason why women were not included had to do with the division between commercial and primary water. The catchment and sub-catchment councils along with ZINWA focused upon commercial water, water that had to be paid for. Thus people who used and relied upon primary water were, for the most part, absent from councils' concerns. In addition, the world of commercial farming was overwhelmingly white men.

Concluding observations

With the decentralisation of water, catchment councils attempted to expand their powers and test the limits of what they could do. It did not take them long to understand that they could exert greater control over this key resource in a decentralised system. They were exercising their agency and taking decentralisation seriously. Despite some efforts to include land, at least in shaping their plans, the councils powers were circumscribed. They were circumscribed in four ways: The first was the lack of acknowledgment of how dependent they were upon donor-support and -funding. The second was the lack of political influence, in part, because the water reform attempted to construct new non-political boundaries for its institutions thus challenging directly and indirectly already existing insti-

38 Field notes from the Development Sub-Committee of Mazowe Catchment Council by Bill Derman, 1999 and 2000.

tutions. The third was the visible and hidden powers of the ruling party that over time sought to control the actions of the new water institutions including what could and could not be discussed. Fourth, and last, was the fast track land reform that undermined the economic base for supporting water reform. Thus this initial period of water governance and management experimentation still referred to as the water reform process, was in contradiction to, in addition to being in tension with, the other major reforms of that era.

After the donors withdrew, the new institutions of catchment and sub-catchment councils lacked monies and were unable to collect funds from new farmers. Despite promises, ZINWA did not provide funding for the catchment and sub-catchment councils. In addition, the land reform did not include an assessment of farms' water resources and how the waters could be best utilised with a change of ownership and settlement patterns (Hove et al., Chapter 8). To generalise from Zimbabwe's mixed and to-date mainly unsuccessful efforts to implement IWRM at the catchment levels is problematic given the other events and processes at work after 2000 which are discussed in detail in Manzungu and Derman, Chapter 6 The major processes that altered the path of water reform consist of the loss of its major funding base combined with the withdrawal of international donors that had been supporting the process. In its casual disregard of water resources, water management and water infrastructure, the fast track land reform process undermined the irrigation infrastructure in place on the former commercial farms. While IWRM and water reform attempted to operate outside of the politics of land, and the power behind it, this turned out to be impossible. Thus an effort was made to have water be a 'technical issue' that could be discussed and debated in what were supposed to be apolitical and representative participatory institutions. In order to keep the meetings apolitical only water issues could be discussed. Indeed, discussions and debates about water allocation, distribution and reform did take place with a mix of water engineers, catchment managers, ZINWA officials, commercial farmers, representatives of small-scale commercial areas, chiefs, representatives of donor organisations and academics. More generally, without far stronger political support, IWRM cannot resist the exercise of strong state power or economic and political elites. The new institutions were left to fund and manage themselves in a harsh social, economic and political environment. The vision of participatory institutions made up of representatives of all water users ran aground on the political terrain in which they tried to function.

Acknowledgements

This chapter is based on research from the project Flows and Practices: The Politics of IWRM in Africa, funded by the Norwegian Research Council, to which we are grateful for its generous support. We thank the anonymous reviewers and Lyla Mehta for their careful reading and helpful comments on our chapter.

References

Alexander, J. and McGregor, J. 2013. Introduction: Politics, patronage and violence in Zimbabwe. *Journal of Southern African Studies* 39(4): 749-763,

Blair, D. 2002. *Degrees in violence: Robert Mugabe for power in Zimbabwe.* London and New York: Continuum.

Brand, C. 1991. Will decentralization enhance local participation? In Gasper, D.R.; Brand, C. and Wekwete, K.H. (Eds), *Decentralization in Zimbabwe: Essays on the decentralization of government and planning in the 1990s*, pp. 79-96. The Hague: Institute of Social Studies.

Bratton, M. 2014. *Power politics in Zimbabwe.* Boulder: Lynne Rienner.

Chabal, P. 1994. *Power in Africa: An essay in political interpretation.* New York: St. Martin's Press.

Chan, S. 2002. *Robert Mugabe: A life of power and violence.* Ann Arbor: University of Michigan Press.

Chikozho, C. 2001. *Restructuring the commons: Water reforms in Southern Africa in the context of global water resources management paradigm shifts.* Harare: Center for Applied Social Sciences, University of Zimbabwe.

Chikozho, C. 2008. Stakeholder participatory processes and dialogue platforms in the Mazowe river catchment, Zimbabwe. *African Studies Quarterly* 10(2&3). http://africa. ufl.edu/asq/v10/v10i2a2.htm (accessed on March 17, 2014)

Darby, B. 2000. *History and lessons learned from the formation of the Mazowe Catchment Council, Zimbabwe.* Harare: Deutsche Geselleschaft für Technische Zusammenarbeit (GTZ).

Derman, B.; Ferguson, A. and Gonese, F. 2000. *Decentralization, devolution and development: Reflections on the water reform process in Zimbabwe.* Draft No. 3. Harare, Zimbabwe: Centre for Applied Social Sciences, University of Zimbabwe. http://pdf.usaid.gov/pdf_docs/Pnacl415.pdf (accessed 10 August 2014)

Faysse, N. 2006. Troubles on the way: An analysis of the challenges faced by multi-stakeholder platforms. *Natural Resources Forum* 30: 219-229.

Foucault, M. 2001. *Power* (The Essential Works of Foucault, 1954-1984, Vol. 3, edited by Faubion, J.). New York: New Press.

Gaventa, J. 2006. Finding the spaces for change: A power analysis. *IDS Bulletin* 37(6).

Goldin, J. 2013. Propositions for a sector toolkit: Addressing the gap between policy and practice through the use of a multi-dimensional poverty framework. *Water Policy* 15: 309-324.

GoZ. (Government of Zimbabwe). 1994. *Report of the Commission of Inquiry into Appropriate Agricultural Land Tenure Systems.* Three volumes. Harare: Government of Zimbabwe.

GoZ. 2000a. *Towards Integrated Water Resources Management.* Harare: The Government Printers.

GoZ. 2000b. *Statutory Instrument 33, Water (catchment councils) Regulations of 2000.* Harare: Government Printers.

GoZ. 2000c. *Statutory Instrument 47, Water (sub-catchment councils) Regulations of 2000.* Harare: Government Printers.

Gubbay, A. 2009. The progressive erosion of the rule of law in independent Zimbabwe. Third International Rule of Law Lecture, London. <www.kubatana.net/Html/archive/legal/091209ag.asp?sector=LEGAL&year=2009&range_start=1> (accessed 10 August 2014)

Hammar, A.; Raftopoulos, B. and Jensen, S. 2000. Zimbabwe's unfinished business. Harare: Weaver Press.

Hellum, A. and Derman, B. 2002. Neither tragedy nor enclosure: Are there inherent human rights in water management in Zimbabwe's communal lands? *The European Journal of Development Research* 14(2): 31-50.

Hellum, A. and Derman B. 2005. Negotiating water rights in the context of a new political and legal landscape in Zimbabwe. In von Benda-Beckmann, F.; von Benda-Beckmann, K. and Griffiths, A. (Eds), *Mobile people, mobile law: Expanding legal relations in a contracting world,* pp. 177-198. Aldershot and Burlington: Ashgate.

IBRD (International Bank for Reconstruction and Development) (World Bank). 1993. *Workshop on water resources management in Southern Africa.* Victoria Falls, Zimbabwe, 5-9 July, 1993.

Latham, J. 2002. Catchment management: A case study of the Manyame catchment. In Manzungu, E. (Ed), *The processes and dynamics of catchment management in Zimbabwe*, pp. 21-44. Harare: Save Africa Trust.

Li, T. 2007. *The will to improve: Governmentality, development, and the practice of politics.* Durham: Duke University Press.

Lukes, S. 2005. *Power: A radical view.* London: Palgrave-MacMillan.

Mabiza, C. 2013. Integrated water resources management, institutions and livelihoods under stress: Bottom-up perspectives from Zimbabwe. PhD thesis. Delft University of Technology, Delft, the Netherlands.

Manzungu, E. 2002a. Global rhetoric and local realities: The case of Zimbabwe's water reform. In Chikowore, G.; Manzungu, E.; Mushayavanhu, D. and Shoko, D. (Eds), *Managing common property in an age of globalisation: Experiences from Zimbabwe,* pp. 31-44. Harare: Weaver Press.

Manzungu, E. 2002b. More than a headcount: Towards strategic representation in catchment management in South Africa and Zimbabwe. *Physics and Chemistry of the Earth* 27 Issues 11-22: 927-933.

Manzungu, E. and Dzingirai, V. 2012. Towards empowered stakeholder participation in water resource management in Zimbabwe. *Journal of Social Development in Africa* 27: 85-108.

Mapedza, E. and Geheb, K. 2010. Power dynamics and water reform in the Zimbabwean context: Implications for the poor. *Water Policy* 12(4): 517-527.

Meredith, M. 2002. *Our votes, our guns: Robert Mugabe and the tragedy of Zimbabwe* New York: Public Affairs.

Mtisi, S. 2011. *Water reforms during the crisis and beyond: Understanding policy and political challenges of reforming the water sector in Zimbabwe.* Working Paper No. 333. London: The Overseas Development Institute.

Mtisi, S. and Nicol, A. 2003. *Caught in the act: New stakeholders, decentralisation and water management processes in Zimbabwe.* Sustainable livelihoods in southern Africa.

Research Paper 14. Brighton, UK: Institute of Development Studies.

Musemwa, M. 2008. *Politics of water in post-colonial Zimbabwe, 1980-2007*. Leiden: The African Studies Centre. www.ascleiden.nl/pdf/papermusemwa.pdf? origin= publication detail (accessed on 12 March 2014)

Mutizwa-Mangiza, N. 1991. Decentralization and local government administration: An analysis of structural and planning problems at the rural district level. In Helmsing, A.H.J.; Mutizwa-Mangiza, N.; Gasper, D.; Brand, C.M. and Wekwete, K.H. (Eds), *Limits to decentralization in Zimbabwe: Essays on the decentralization of government and planning in the 1980s*, pp. 51-78. The Hague: Institute of Social Studies.

Nhira, C. and Derman, B. 1997. *Toward reforming the institutional and legal basis of the water sector in Zimbabwe: Current weaknesses, recent initiatives and their operational problems.* Harare: CASS Occasional Paper.

Pilosoff, R. 2012. *The unbearable whiteness of being: Farmers' voices from Zimbabwe.* Harare: Weaver Press

Raftopoulos, B. and Mlambo, A. 2009. *Becoming Zimbabwe: A history from the pre-colonial period to 2008.* Harare: Weaver Press.

Salverda, T. 2011. Embodied signs of elite distinction: Franco-Mauritians' white skin colour in the face of change. *Comparative Sociology* 10(4): 548-570.

Salverda, T. 2013. In defense: Elite power. In Abbink, J. and Salverda, T. (Eds), *The Anthropology of elites: Power, culture and the complexities of distinction*, pp. 113-138. New York: Palgrave Macmillan.

Sithole, B. 2001. Participation and stakeholder dynamics in the water reform process in Zimbabwe: The case of the Mazowe Pilot Catchment Board. *African Studies Quarterly* 5(3): 19-40.

Stalgren, P. 2006. Worlds of water: Worlds apart. How targeted domestic actors transform international regimes. PhD thesis. University of Gothenburg, Gothenburg, Sweden.

Swatuk, L. 2002. Water reforms in Zimbabwe: Some observations based on the Save catchment experiences and suggestions for ways forward. In Manzungu, E. (Ed), *The processes and dynamics of catchment management in Zimbabwe*, pp. 45-68. Harare: Save Africa Trust.

Tapela, B. 2002. The challenge of integration in the implementation of Zimbabwe's new water policy: Case study of the catchment level institutions surrounding the Pungwe-Mutare water supply project. *Physics and Chemistry of the Earth* 27(11): 993-1004.

Taylor, P.; Chatora, C. and Hoevenaars, J.P. 1996. *Project formulation: Mupfure catchment integrated water management.* Harare: Royal Netherlands Embassy.

UNESCO (United Nations Educational Scientific and Cultural Organization). 2006. *World Water Development Report 2: Water, a shared responsibility.* New York: United Nations.

WRMS (Water Resources Management Strategy). 1998. Report of the Water Resources Management Strategy Second National Workshop held at Brondesbury Park Hotel, Juliusdale, 25-27 March, 1998. Prepared by the WRMS Technical Secretariat on behalf of the Ministry of Rural Resources and Water Development.

8

Land, Farming and IWRM: A Case Study of the Middle Manyame Sub-Catchment[1]

Takunda Hove

Bill Derman

Emmanuel Manzungu

ABSTRACT: Zimbabwe's water reforms that were undertaken in the 1990s were meant to redress the colonially inherited inequalities to agricultural water, increase water security against frequent droughts, improve water management, and realise sustainable financing of the water sector. They were underpinned by the 1998 Water and Zimbabwe National Water Authority Acts, which were based on Integrated Water Resources Management (IWRM) principles. This chapter describes how IWRM has been implemented against a backdrop of an ever-evolving land reform programme and a struggling agricultural sector. We examine how water is accessed and used in and around three water sources in the Middle Manyame Sub-Catchment, one of the seven sub-catchments of the Manyame Catchment. The Sub-Catchment is of particular significance because there was significant agricultural production on white-owned large-scale farmers, which have now been extensively allocated to small black farmers. The study demonstrated that while the land reform has, in theory, broadened access to water, irrigation water usage has remained low because of a depressed agricultural sector, shortage and high costs of electricity, and lack of capital needed to restore damaged or stolen irrigation equipment. The findings indicate that the assumption of a self-financing water sector, based on a well-functioning agricultural sector, which is the largest water user, has not been realised, and this has negatively affected implementation of IWRM in the Middle Manyame area in particular, and in Zimbabwe in general.

KEYWORDS: Water reform, land reform, agriculture, IWRM, Zimbabwe

Introduction

Zimbabwe's water reforms were undertaken in the 1990s for internal and external reasons. Historically, Zimbabwe's developed water resources were mainly

1 First published in *Water Alternatives* 9(3): 533-550.

used by large-scale commercial farmers (overwhelmingly white) to irrigate a wide variety of crops at the expense of the majority black population (Manzungu and Derman, Chapter 6). This explains the intention by government to redress this skewed and unequal access to water (Manzungu, 2001). At the same time, the World Bank and other donors promoted a neoliberal agenda, which among other things tried to institutionalise the notion of water as an economic good (Derman and Manzungu, and Manzungu and Derman, Chapter 6). Thus the water reform process was at a crossroads – how to reallocate water to black farmers while maintaining water revenue from white farmers who were on the land. Another conundrum was how to factor in land reform into the water reform process. The fast track land reform ignored the new units of water management – catchment and sub-catchment councils – which among other dimensions had responsibility for water allocation, monitoring water use, billing water and catchment protection (Derman and Manzungu, Chapter 7).

For this and other reasons (see Manzungu and Derman, Chapter 6) the promise of Integrated Water Resources Management (IWRM) water was stalled. For example, concerning integrating land and water, there was a failure to build upon the Water Resources Management Strategy (WRMS) document that had proposed to link water and land (GoZ, 2000a). The document was meant to operationalise water reforms as captured in the Water Act (GoZ, 1998a) and the Zimbabwe National Water Authority (ZINWA) Act of 1998 (GoZ, 1998b). In this chapter, we focus on water access and water use by the new settlers who received land under the land reform programme and some white farmers who have remained. More specifically, we focus on whether the new settlers were able, not just to access water, but to use it for agricultural production. We also wanted to know if the past water revenues from agriculture would be maintained, because they were critical to self-financing water sector in accordance with the IWRM principles enunciated in the Water Act.

Most of the water used in Zimbabwe is surface water, of which 45% is stored in government dams and the remaining 55% in some 5,700 dams in former large-scale commercial farming areas, on mines and on plantation estates (GoZ, 2000a). Underground water, representing about 10% of the total water use in Zimbabwe, is tapped mainly through boreholes. Records show that there were over 24,300 boreholes in the country (GoZ, 2000a).[2] While the country has a total developed irrigated area of approximately 206,000 hectares (ha) and a potential irrigable area of 1,500,000 ha (Madiya and Zawe, 2013: 8),[3] the former figure has substantially decreased since 2000 because of aged and outmoded equipment, limited working capital, poor management, the collapse of social institutions and their poor placement (Anseeuw et al., 2012). Another reason has

2 The number of boreholes has dramatically increased with the collapse of the Harare (capital city of Zimbabwe) water supply system (Manzungu et al., 2016) and some farmers opting to use cheap groundwater (see below).

3 Manzungu (2011: 16) citing FAO figures, estimates a lower figure. "On the basis of available water resources the irrigation potential of the country is estimated at 365, 000 ha on the basis of the available internal renewable water resources and not on water from the Zambezi and Limpopo border rivers and such sources". It is fair to say that there is need for new research to revisit the irrigation potential of Zimbabwe.

been the failure to irrigate because of the transition to fast track land reform. As Matondi (2012: 213) writes:

> *The wastage in terms of infrastructure was phenomenal. The irrigation systems were idle, either because the pumps or pipes had been stolen or damaged, or because the new settlers lacked the necessary skills to run them. Tractors and other farming equipment were appropriated from farms through illegal means and were literally driven into the ground due to lack of care and maintenance.*

This explains why much of the water that remains in dams is unused. Agriculture, which had previously used over 80% of the water resources for irrigation is depressed. Our focus is the Middle Manyame Sub-Catchment (MMSC), one of the hubs of white large-scale commercial agriculture that witnessed two types of agricultural resettlement for black farmers: A1 village based farms and A2 commercial farms. A1 farms are organised into village-like farms with each member receiving 1-70 ha of land (depending on the agro-ecological region) divided into residential, farming land (arable) and grazing land.[4] The purpose of A1 farms is to lift small farmers out of poverty and to decongest communal areas in contrast to the commercial orientation of the A2 model. A2 farms were supposed to be given to individuals who had resources and sought to become commercial farmers. They range in size from 2-1000 ha depending upon the agro-ecological region. Our chapter examines how IWRM fared in the midst of agricultural and land reform. It provides evidence to highlight the inability of IWRM to accommodate changes in other sectors, particularly agriculture and energy. As argued by Mapedza et al., in the midst of a political, social and economic crisis IWRM has few prospects for success (Mapedza et al., 2016). By casting water reform as a technical process, and abandoning its political economy roots, the stage was set for a water reform, which achieved neither its neoliberal objectives nor the political economy of promoting a vibrant black agriculture.

The chapter is organised as follows: After a short discussion of methodology, we discuss Zimbabwe's land reform and a transformed agriculture in this sub-catchment. We then turn to the details of agriculture and water use in the Middle Manyame and how water users gain access to water. We note the central place that payment for water takes from the perspective of ZINWA, and the catchment and sub-catchment councils. The chapter concludes by examining how the Zimbabwean emphasis upon commercial water and user pays has limited IWRM and the use of water for development purposes.

For the field research portion of this study, we selected three dams, the Biri, Mazvikadei, and Kingston.[5] These enabled us to study the different uses of water and the variation of water access and use within the sub-catchment. The study adopted a case study research design. We selected the Middle Manyame

4 Matondi (2012: 55) describes the A1 model as "comprising small, integrated communities using locally evolved norms and rules to manage resources and people". Scoones et al (2011) observe that the average size for A1 farms in 37 ha incorporating arable and grazing land while that of A2 is 328 ha.

5 For a more detailed consideration of the methods see Hove, 2012.

Sub-Catchment (MMSC) because it was one of the centres of large-scale white commercial agriculture, had an extensive irrigation sector and contributed a significant proportion of the nation's tobacco, wheat and maize production. In addition, we could build on earlier research on the formation of the catchment and sub-catchment councils (see Derman and Manzungu, Chapter 7). Lastly, it gave us the opportunity to study the water use and irrigation patterns on the resettlement farms. We interviewed people who were using or had used the waters in the past and the present water users.[6] In addition to water users and farmers, we interviewed representatives from ZINWA, Manyame Catchment Council, Middle Manyame Sub-Catchment Council, Rural District Councillors, Ministry of Water, Environmental Management Agency, Parks and Wildlife Authority, Department of Agriculture and Rural Extension, Ministry of Lands and water users' associations.

LAND, WATER AND AGRICULTURE IN ZIMBABWE: A BRIEF HISTORICAL OVERVIEW

Zimbabwe's agrarian history has been characterised by the division of lands which saw the colonists claiming by 1970 45% of the land with approximately 40% in Native Reserves reserved for blacks (Palmer, 1977). At that time, there were approximately 5,310,000 blacks and 255,000 whites (Palmer, 1977). White or European lands, which became the large-scale farming sector after independence, occupied the more fertile lands and possessed the better water sources. Undoing this inequality in land and water has been a major goal of the Zimbabwe government since its independence in 1980. In addition, historically whites benefited from state support for agriculture, irrigation and water supply (Herbst, 1990). In the meanwhile, black Zimbabweans were forced into the more marginal lands (Palmer, 1977; Ranger, 1985; Manzungu and Machiridza, 2009). The Native Land Husbandry Act (1951) sought to make blacks resident in the Tribal Trust Lands and choose between subsistence agriculture and full-time urban or industrial employment. This had a net effect of undermining black agriculture. In addition, the Southern Rhodesian government[7] of the day sought to reduce the number of cattle owned by blacks. This effort resulted in fierce resistance and ultimately the programme was abandoned but not before generating severe unrest (Duggan, 1980; Alexander, 2006).

To correct the historic land imbalances, the newly independent Government of Zimbabwe planned to redistribute 5 million ha of land located mainly in the less-favoured agro-ecological regions and which tended to be farms abandoned during the war of liberation (Kinsey, 2000) because of the willing seller/willing buyer basis. During the 1980s, the government resettled 56,000 households on 3,324,880 ha (Moyo, 1995: 121). There were a variety of models of land reform but the most common was Model A that gave a family 5 ha of land for cultivation, 10 ha of grazing land and 0.5 ha for their homes. The present A1 model is based upon this older form. In sum, the first phases of land reform did not involve the

6 We note that several A2 farmers coming from the security sector were not open to being interviewed.

7 Southern Rhodesia was the colonial name of present-day Zimbabwe.

best lands or satisfy the larger need for land reform. Most white farmers and corporations' lands were left untouched.

During the 1990s, while water reform was initiated and implemented, the pressures for land reform were building. Despite the Land Acquisition Act of 1992, which ended the restrictions of the Lancaster House Constitution on acquiring land for resettlement, there was little movement until 1997 when the government announced it would acquire 1804 large-scale commercial farms (Moyo, 2000a: 73). This was followed by a major donor conference in 1998, which sought to provide a framework for land reform. The conference failed in its objectives and some 1471 farms were listed to be acquired by government for redistribution. This process of acquisition stalled in the courts as landowners objected to their farms being listed (Moyo, 2000b; UNDP, 2002; Alexander, 2006).

In 2000, the government embarked on the Fast Track Land Reform Programme (Matondi, 2012; Moyo, 2013; Moyo and Yeros, 2013), whose motives and results are subject to highly divergent opinions. Proponents of the programme saw it as part of a potential revolutionary strategy towards black economic emancipation. According to Moyo (2004) market-assisted land redistribution in the first two decades of independence had done little either to level out ownership disparities between the large-scale farming sectors and black farmers, or to restructure the rural landscape. However, opponents saw it as a strategy by an increasingly unpopular (ZANU PF) party to use the redistribution of land to retain power (Alden and Anseeuw, 2009; Compagnon, 2010; Maunganidze, 2015). They point to the launch of farm invasions right after the government suffered its first ever electoral defeat when the government-proposed draft constitution was rejected in the February 2000 referendum. With parliamentary elections looming, a national opposition party growing, the claim is that the government-sponsored the violent takeover of white farms spearheaded by war veterans to prevent farm workers from voting or assisting the opposition party, and to reward war veterans, party officials and government officials with land (Hellum and Derman, 2004; Kriger, 2003; Compagnon, 2010).

The Fast Track Land Reform Programme produced two types of resettlement farms as mentioned earlier, A1 and A2. The majority of the people resettled under A1 model scheme were communal residents, urban unemployed, followed by war veterans, military, and civil servants (James, 2015). By 2011, 145,775 people had benefitted from the land reform on about 5.8 million ha (Matondi, 2012). In general, as highlighted below, A1 farmers have struggled to balance cash crops (tobacco, vegetable gardens and contract farming) with food production (mainly maize). The challenges also arise from the fact that, because A1 farmers come from different areas, some communal and some urban, they have struggled to build new and viable institutions to manage water (and other resources) for productive and domestic purposes. This is an area that requires new research because the leadership of A1 villages has tended to fall on war veterans who led the Committees of seven but are now subject to local variations. A2 farmers, on the other hand, were expected to be commercial farmers with farms ranging from 2-2000 ha, depending on location and the agro-ecological region.

The A2 model is administered under the Agricultural Land Settlement Act

(Chapter 20: 01). In the A2 model, altogether 16,386 beneficiaries had accessed approximately 2.9 million ha of land by 2009 (Matondi, 2012). In essence, these newly resettled farmers represented an emerging group of water users, but with little or no history of institutional access to water (Derman and Gonese, 2003; Hove, 2012). A few white commercial farms remained on the land, usually with their farms diminished in size but maintaining their irrigation systems and infrastructure. By 2009, the Government of Zimbabwe had acquired about 10.8 million ha of land for the entire resettlement programme out of a total of 12.3 million ha of commercial farmland (Ministry of Land Reform and Resettlement (MLRR) cited in Matondi, 2012)

While there is widespread agreement on Zimbabwe's need for land reform and for providing access to black Zimbabweans, there are disagreements as to how successful it has been and who has benefitted from it and its long-term implications. On one side of the debate is the view that many more (black) farmers participating have entered into the agriculture sector and have contributed to either an actual increase in agricultural production or else the potential to do so (see Scoones et al., 2010; Hanlon et al., 2013; Moyo, 2013). On the other side is the view that there remain significant challenges relating to secure land tenure and agricultural production (Marongwe, 2011; Zamchiya, 2011; Cliffe et al., 2011; Matondi, 2012) before the outcomes of the fast track will lead to a strong rural economy.

We will not enter into the debates in this chapter. Suffice to say for the time being, food insecurity remains a part of the Zimbabwe landscape. While there was an increase in food security and maize production in 2013-2014, 2015-2016 was a poor year due to drought in some parts of the country.[8] This has not been helped by a weak economy, the loss of jobs in the formal sector, and high unemployment. The International Monetary Fund notes that Zimbabwe's economy remains in a weak state, with an unsustainably high external debt, massive de-industrialisation, informalisation of the economy and high rates of unemployment. While Zimbabwe's Gross Domestic Product (GDP) grew at an average of 7.5% from 2009 to 2012 it is now slowing down rapidly. This economic slowdown is due to continued de-industrialisation, liquidity challenges (the lack of, and high cost of, capital, revenue underperformance and bank weaknesses), outdated technologies, structural bottlenecks that include power shortages and infrastructure deficits, corruption and a volatile and fragile global financial environment (African Development Bank, 2014). This is the backdrop against which agriculture has been practised in Zimbabwe since 2000.

Post-fast track agriculture in the Middle Manyame Sub-Catchment has seen the transformation of its agriculture from large scale to medium and small-scale

8 The Famine Early Warning System (FEWS) has a series of reports on Zimbabwe. They say that Poor households relying on food purchases will continue to face livelihood protection deficits and food gaps even with ongoing safety-net programmes and a near-normal start to the 2016/17 cropping season. National cash shortages are expected to limit economic and livelihood activities, such as agricultural and nonagricultural labour, and self-employment. Worst-off areas may face Emergency (IPC Phase 4) outcomes during the peak of the lean season. www.fews.net/sites/default/files/documents/reports/Aug%202016_FAOB.pdf (accessed on August 22, 2016)

farms. Most of the large-scale commercial farms, which dominated the landscape, are now locations of resettlement. Up until 2001-2002, the Middle Manyame area was the centre of winter wheat production, which depended upon a reliable supply of irrigation water. The situation has dramatically changed. For example, wheat production across the country has fallen from 250,000 tons in 1999-2000 to 30,000 tons in 2010 and has remained more or less at that level (Anseeuw et al., 2012: 38).[9] According to the Financial Gazette (24 July 2014) the 10,000 to 12,000 tonnes expected in 2014 were enough for one week's supply of flour for bread. This means Zimbabwe would have to import at least 440,000 tonnes to meet the shortfall in national demand, paying close to USD220 million for wheat imports at an import parity price of USD468 to USD500 per tonne.

The Middle Manyame Sub-catchment: A Description

The Middle Manyame Sub-Catchment is one of the seven sub-catchments that make up Manyame Catchment (Fig. 8.1). It covers a large part of Zvimba District and small parts of Makonde, Mazowe, and Chegutu districts (Latham, 2002a,b; Hove, 2012). There are four major rivers that drain the catchment, namely the Manyame, Mukwadzi, Muzare and Munene. The average annual rainfall for the sub-catchment is 802.3 mm while the mean annual runoff (MAR) is 123 mm. The percentage coefficient of variation is 110.

Our study focused on three different sites around three dams, Mazvikadei, Biri and Kingston. Construction of the Mazvikadei Dam located north of Banket town on the Mukwadzi River was funded by the Zimbabwean government. An Italian company undertook the construction. It was completed in 1985 to supply water for irrigation. Over time, it has become the site for luxury cottages and water-based recreation activities.

Biri Dam is located on the Manyame River about 120 km northwest of Harare, Zimbabwe's capital city and approximately 20 km from Chinhoyi Town. Its surface area is 2,300 ha and has a storage capacity of 345,000 mega litres (ML). Apart from being a source of irrigation water, the dam also supplies water to Chinhoyi town. It was built by a consortium of about 70 white and black large-scale commercial farmers, and the National Social Security Authority (NSSA) contributing 22.5%, which makes it the single largest shareholder. The ownership of the dam is contentious – the government through ZINWA is now the owner after the government nationalised all large dams in the aftermath of the Fast Track Land Reform Programme. NSSA[10] and the other farmers who contributed financially, insist that they still have co-ownership, until they are bought out by ZINWA.

Kingston Dam was built by a white farmer (Mr. Robin Smith) in 1972, and he is the owner of the dam.[11] Located on Pindipark farm near Chinhoyi, the dam was

9 We focus on wheat since it was a major user of irrigation water. Other grains while declining have been rebounding since 2009 relying mainly on the rain.

10 As far as NSSA is concerned it can ill afford to lose the money that belong to pensioners.

11 Mr. Smith is one of the few white commercial farmers who has managed to remain on land. He is the ZANU-PF councillor for Zvimba Rural District Council Ward 31 and has held that position for 32 years.

built at the confluence of the Chitawe and Msengi rivers. It has a capacity of 3600 ML of water, below ZINWA's cut-off point (5000 ML) for being designated a national dam. There are five farmers who use its water for irrigation; Mr. Smith and four resettled A2 farmers. Mr. Smith is a very experienced commercial farmer, who grows barley under contract from Delta Beverages for beer-making as well as tobacco, potatoes and soybean. He has been farming in this area since 1965 and had 250 ha of land under irrigation. After the land reform, he is now left with 91 ha. The other four A2 farmers have land ranging from 5 ha to 60 ha under irrigation, and grow soybean, wheat, maize, potatoes and tobacco. Wheat is now being grown on a lesser scale because of the delay by the state-owned Grain Marketing Board (GMB) to pay and the high cost of electricity to irrigate, coupled with massive load-shedding[12] and billing.[13] In general, most farmers are shunning growing wheat due to these two reasons. The decline in wheat cultivation has had an impact on the revenue that accrues to the sub-catchment. According to an official from Middle Manyame Sub-Catchment, this has left it in a precarious financial position because of depressed revenue from water.

Tobacco is fast becoming the most important cash crop for A1 and A2 farmers because the price is not regulated as that of maize and wheat. It is sold either using the auction system whereby it is sold to a buyer who pays the best price or increasingly through a contract system where the costs of production are provided by a tobacco company and then deducted from the sale. The fortunes of soybean are also better – unlike maize and wheat there are many private players who compete for it.

Small gardens specialising in semi-commercial vegetable production are found usually close to water sources around the three sites. These gardens measure around 1000 m^2 and are irrigated using small diesel pumps or manually by buckets. The gardens are run on a family basis though around Biri Dam some gardens are run on a cooperative basis. Gardens are a way of supplementing A1 farmers' incomes especially during the dry season. Fishery owners, mainly at Mazvikadei, have also established gardens as a way of supplementing their income, especially during winter when there is a decreased catch of fish. Crops grown in the gardens include vegetables like rape, covo and tomato. The produce is sold to the nearby communities, visitors who come to Mazvikadei Resort, as well as to Gold Dust Township, Chinhoyi and Banket towns.

Water use in middle Manyame

Irrigation water

The fast track land reform led to substantial changes in irrigation in the sub-catchment. A good case in point is the Ghost Acre Irrigation Consortium that, at one time, was the largest water user from Mazvikadei Dam. It comprised six farms

12 A major difficulty for farmers has been load-shedding by the national electricity company – ZESA (Zimbabwe Electrical Supply Authority) combined with high rates.

13 For example, one A2 farmer was worried about the legitimacy of a US$28,000 Zimbabwe Electricity Supply Authority (ZESA) electricity bill that he had just received given how often he did not have electricity.

Fig. 8.1. Sub-catchments of Manyame Catchment

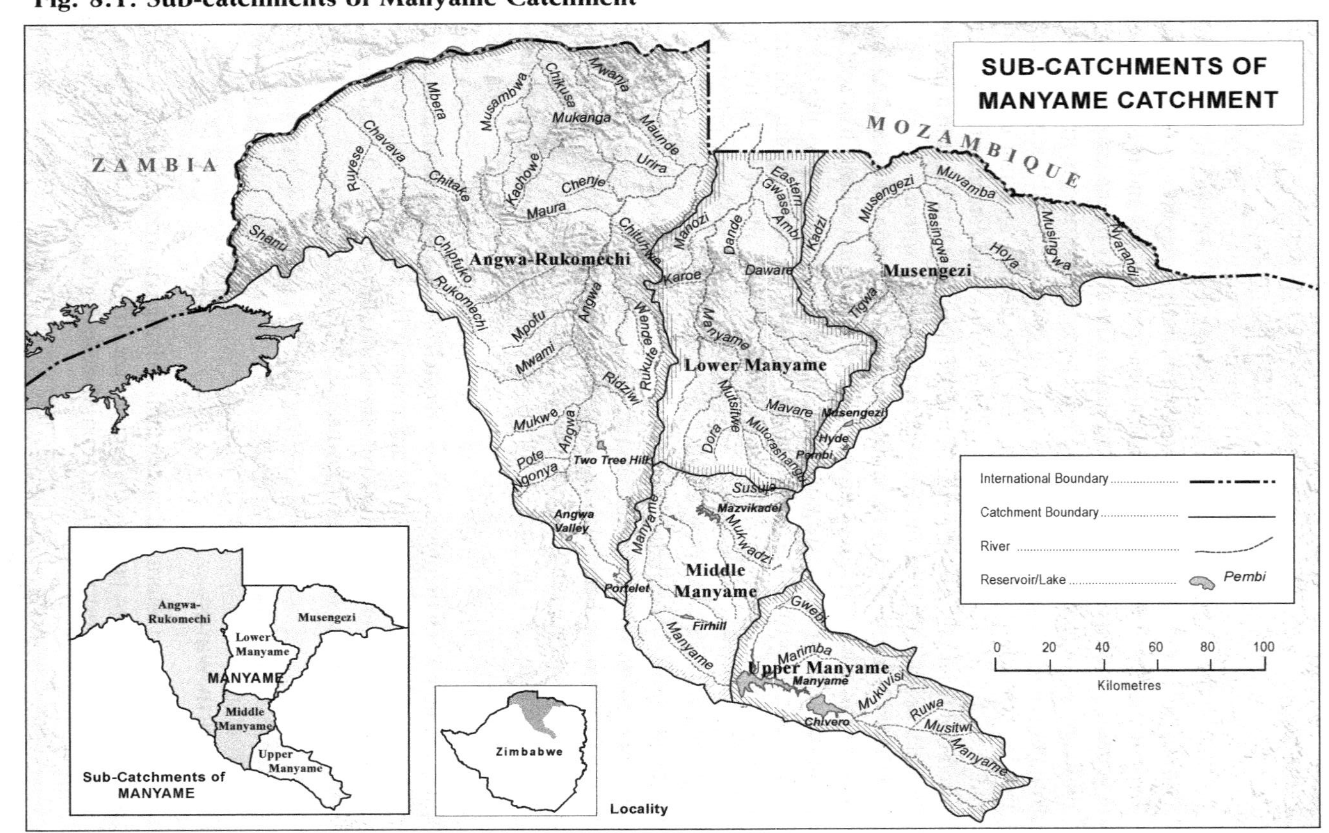

that were linked through a single irrigation system. Water was pumped from Mazvikadei Dam into Ghost Acre Dam and then onto individual farm reservoirs (Zawe, 2006).[14] Each farm had its own pumping station and had a consistent supply of electricity. The farmers shared the main pipelines, main pumping system and security of the irrigation equipment. Each farm was managed individually. The farms had varied cropping emphases such as wheat, maize seed, and soybean and, often, changed crops depending upon market conditions.

In the aftermath of the fast track land reform, these farms were designated as A2 farms. The new owners included a managing director of a local bank, an army major, a university associate professor (who had just become a judge), and the Zimbabwe Ambassador to the United Nations. Ghost Acres Farm moved from being one large farm to seven A2 farms. The new A2 farmers were not able to cooperate to undertake irrigation as has been the case before because they came to the farms at different times, and had different expectations, experiences and resources (Zawe, 2006). In the end, the old irrigation system was not utilised resulting in pipes being sold or unrepaired. The other problem, which was common to the A1 and A2 settlers, was that they became irrigation farmers overnight and in most cases they lacked the capacity to keep the irrigation systems functional (Zawe, 2006). There are also challenges regarding access to water. As can be seen from Table 1 the majority of farmers were not irrigating and as low as 8% irrigated from a dam because dam water is more expensive.

Table 1: Methods and proportion of A2 farmers accessing irrigation water.[15]

Method of water access	Proportion of A2 farmers accessing water (%)
Irrigating direct from a dam	8
Irrigating from a private borehole	18
Irrigating from a river	31
Not irrigating	43

The remaining white commercial farmers showed resilience. About 62% of the remaining white commercial farmers were irrigating the land and had applied for permits (GoZ 2001). Their stay on farms is tenuous given the continued general hostility to 'white' farmers and thus complying with the law is essential for being permitted to remain on their farms.

A similar story of underutilising irrigation infrastructure was also unfolding in the A1 sub-sector. Tendai Murisa described another case involving A1 farmers settled on what had been the Dalkeith Farm. Here the 73 settlers received pipes and sprinklers from the government. According to Murisa (2011: 1115):

> *The Chidziva Farmers' Association was established to improve the farming capacities of the members and to contribute towards bet-*

14 This account is based on Conrade Zawe's PhD thesis. Zawe had also been an irrigation engineer in the Department of Irrigation and, currently, he is the Director of Irrigation Development Division in the Ministry of Agriculture, Mechanization and Irrigation Development. The division has been grossly underfunded.

15 Data from Middle Manyame Sub-catchment Council Records obtained by Takunda Hove.

> *ter lives through collectively seeking for farm inputs, markets and introducing other income generating projects. The initial focus of the association was on irrigated winter wheat, and specifically on securing inputs and coordinating both household and hired labour. The leadership of the group successfully requested assistance for farm implements from the Government of Zimbabwe after the co-existence deal with the former farm owner had collapsed. The government issued them with two brand new 125 horsepower water pumps and some of the pipes required for irrigation and the Government of Zimbabwe insisted that the group should produce wheat for resale to the Grain Marketing Board. However, by 2008 the group members were yet to use the new equipment due to the nonavailability of electricity.*[16] *The reasons cited by A1 farmers are varied. One major reason was the shortage of capital to acquire, for example, water pumps. The lack of cooperation among A1 farmers worsened the situation as evidenced by their failure to pool resources to secure two water pumps needed after water pipes and sprinklers were provided by the government at Dalkeith farm. Instead of the pipes being used for the prime purpose of irrigation, some people were stealing and selling them. This prompted the Village Development Committee Chairperson to ask every farmer to come and collect their share of pipes and keep them for themselves because of the risk of keeping them in a central location.*

According to the current chairperson of the MMSCC, Mrs. Biri, they have been centralised again and the villagers are now hopeful of receiving two pumps from the government in an effort to revitalise the irrigation sector.[17] In general, we did not see the capacity in agricultural extension to advise A1 farmers on either the appropriate technology or appropriate group structures to do irrigation.

Overall, the decline in water usage in dams, because of lack of irrigation, has resulted in a situation where most dams within the Middle Manyame are almost full at the end of the dry season. Mazvikadei Dam, the largest in the sub-catchment, was almost 90% full in August 2016 despite the drought. This was not the case before fast track when most dams would be less than 50% full by October because of irrigation by commercial farmers. Thus, although the land reform broadened users' access to water through opening up water sources traditionally meant for white farmers, there has been no concomitant use of irrigation water.

Gardening

Irrigated gardens usually found close to the dams are irrigated by hand or by diesel pump. The gardens range in size from about an eighth of a hectare to one hectare. A1 farmers gain access to garden land in two ways: Firstly, for farmers living close to dams, they move closer to the dam and establish gardens claiming

16 Murisa recounts a second case study of an A1 farm which saw initial success of irrigated wheat and then its significant decline. The area under irrigated wheat production declined from 40 to just 3 ha (Murisa, 2011: 1161).

17 Interview at Chinoyi, August 2013.

that it is their land. These actions can result in the garden owners being fined by the Environmental Management Agency (EMA) for cultivating within 30 m of a watercourse. Secondly, Village Development Committees also allocate land for gardens within their area of jurisdiction.[18] The main crops grown are green mealies (maize), tomatoes, and vegetables (rape, covo, cabbages, onions, sweet potatoes and spinach). Where gardens are hand-irrigated, a large majority of the participants are women whereas in gardens irrigated by pumps, men tend to participate more (Hove, 2012). Women typically sell the produce to the local communities as well as in nearby towns, Banket and Chinhoyi.

In the Mazvikadei area, people involved in fishing tend to establish their homes near the dam[19]and also utilise land adjacent to their homes as gardens. Fisher-folk do this to supplement their income, especially during winter when there is a decreased catch of fish. No one allocates them land for gardens; it seems like an unwritten rule that a fishery owner has the right to establish a garden adjacent to his fishery.

An employee of the MMSCC commented that the sub-catchment council does not charge for water used for irrigating land less than a hectare because this is considered primary water use. In principle, the use of a pump would trigger payment for water. However, in practice, farmers are not charged for using water in gardens. A local ZINWA employee when asked if a farmer using a pump was paying for water, the response was loosely translated "For that one, we all agreed to let him prosper first before we can start levying him".[20]

Domestic water

Access to water for domestic water varies across different groups. The white farm-owners supplied their farm workers with drinking and domestic water from boreholes.[21] With the farm occupations and transfer of ownership to A1 farmers, boreholes that relied on electricity for pumping broke down or the electricity was cut off because new farmers could not afford to pay. In addition, the government did not support the new farmers to maintain water infrastructure. Water shortages therefore currently affect the majority of the resettled farmers, particularly A1 farmers. Some farmers have been able to install manual pump technology to replace the electric pumps.

Mining

The Middle Manyame Sub-Catchment includes small-scale and large-scale mines.

18 We did not establish the criterion used to allocate land.

19 In Zimbabwe, the dam refers to both the dam itself and the waters behind the dam. In wider usage one could say lake or the waters behind the dam.

20 Interview at Middle Manyame Sub-catchment Council official, Chinhoyi, 28 February 2013.

21 A1 farmers forced the farm workers out of their homes and then occupied them. The farm workers are now doing piece jobs for the A1 farmers in return for clothes, milk, soap and any other commodity that the A1 farmers have. It is through the establishment of this working relationship that former farm workers may be allowed to obtain water from the few boreholes together with A1 farmers (Rutsate et al., 2015).

There are large-scale mines of chrome, gold, and dolomite as well as numerous small-scale mines that are dotted across the sub-catchment. Some A1 farmers are complaining that they are no longer able to use water from Mukwadzi River (which is downstream of Mazvikadei Dam) because of cyanide contamination from Ayrshire mine's leaking slimes dam.[22] This complaint was supported by the Councillor of the area who called for the Environmental Management Agency (GoZ 2002) to levy stiffer penalties on mining companies that pollute the environment. Asked to respond to these allegations, an Ayrshire mine official disputed the A1 farmers' claims and said they should instead thank the mining company for making water available during periods of scarcity when Ayrshire asks ZINWA to open the valves of Mazvikadei Dam for the downstream commitments.

Some A2 farmers have raised concern over the encroachment of small-scale miners known as *Korokozas* on to their farms. These miners leave open pits, trenches and shafts, which are a danger to livestock. To add to that, many small-scale miners pan in the watercourses especially along the Chitawe River. This leads to increasing rates of siltation in dams downstream and potential pollution by mercury. Kingston Dam, for example, is located downstream of panning at the confluence of Chitawe and Msengi rivers.

Operationalising the User Pays Principle[23]

While the water reform was intended to emphasise the various elements of IWRM such as monitoring water use in line with allocations, we found in 2012 and 2013 in interviews with ZINWA and with the Chairperson of the MMSC that the focus was largely on increasing the amount of revenues from the sale and on payment for water. In one typical interview we asked an A2 farmer the following:

> Q. Are you aware of Middle Manyame Sub-Catchment Council?
> A. Yes we are aware of it.
> Q. What is its role in water management?
> A. I am not sure but I only see them when they come to drop their invoices.
> Q. Are you ever consulted on issues relating to water management or have you ever been invited to participate in water resources management meetings?
> A. We have never been consulted. Like I said the only time we hear about them is when they drop off their invoices.

Thus irrigation has become important in the sub-catchment, not just because it stabilises and increases crop yields, but because it generates revenues for ZINWA

22 A slimes dam or slimes is for storing the materials left over after separating gold from the ore.

23 In the National Water Policy there can and should be flexibility. The policy states: "Water pricing: To achieve efficiency, water prices will be based on the user pays and polluter pays principles and be socially acceptable to different interest groups in the water sector. Subsidies will be targeted to users who are not in a position to pay the full cost of the service provider or where national interests would be compromised". (GoZ, 2013: 20). As of October 2016, there are no provisions for supplying water to users who cannot pay the full cost although the cost of water has been reduced (see Manzungu and Derman, Chapter 6).

and MMSCC.[24] Payment for water is based on either a permit to abstract river water or groundwater, which is issued by the Catchment Council, or an agreement between the farmer and ZINWA for accessing water stored in government dams. As reported by Manzungu and Derman (Chapter 6) agreement water (water from government dams) is much more expensive (up to 10 times) than water abstracted from rivers or underground.

To simplify their revenue collection the MMSC based payment for water on the size of the land under cultivation and the crops being grown.[25] For wheat it was estimated that it required 7.5 ML/ha until it reaches maturity. For other crops a value of 7 ML/ha was used. The sub-catchment makes a site visit to one's farm to determine the type of crop under cultivation as well as the size of the land in question, before they can bill for water.

As highlighted below, the user pays principle has not been accepted by many water users, particularly farmers nor did they know much about the functions of catchment and sub-catchment councils (Kujinga and Jonker, 2006; Mtisi, 2002, 2008, 2011). The resistance to pay in combination with a failure to pay has resulted in the incapacitation of water management institutions, i.e. catchment and sub-catchment councils, and ZINWA. But farmers were not the only problem. As of August 2016, ZINWA was owed USD133 million by local authorities, irrigating farmers and government. As a consequence, ZINWA has had great difficulty in meeting its payroll.[26] The remaining white commercial farmers were at the forefront recording a 62% payment rate followed by A2 farmers with 26%. There was nothing significant from A1 farmers. A caveat is however, needed. Many A1 farmers do not irrigate using permit or agreement water. Most families have resorted to gardens where water is not charged and in terms of legal categories it is regarded as 'primary water' (water for domestic use, see Derman and Manzungu, Chapter 7).

Across the board, the amount of legal water requested for irrigation is low. The former Chair and the current Chair of the MMSCC, the Catchment Manager of the Manyame and current farmers all assert that much less water is being requested and being used for irrigation than in the past. Unlike Mazvikadei and Biri Dams, the waters from Kingston Dam are, in percentage terms, more heavily used because the water is cheaper.

In general there is a growing trend of farmers 'running away from agreement water' and preferring to pay for actual water use (flow water) because of the

24 When we began our research, a nationally known accountant was chairperson of the sub-catchment. He also owneda farm in the sub-catchment. He was replaced by a woman who worked in the Department of Agriculture and who had also received a farm in the sub-catchment.

25 The capacity for determining actual water used has been lost with no monitoring of borehole use for irrigation and for lack of measurement of water pumped onto a farm.

26 Zinwa chief executive officer Jefter Sakupwanya told the Parliamentary Portfolio Committee on Lands that the water utility was facing financial problems, with its 2000 workforce being owed a total of USD11 million in salary arrears which accrued over the past seven months. The biggest debtors are local authorities owing USD36 million, irrigators USD37 million, other small farmers owing USD5 million and the government owing the rest (Newsday June 22, 2016).

desire to access cheaper water (see also Manzungu and Derman, in Chapter 6). In some cases this means playing the system. Most of the farmers, particularly around Biri Dam are drawing water from Manyame River as opposed to drawing directly from the dam. Further, most interviewed farmers favour water from their farm dams which are ungazetted hence only attract a water levy (US$1.06/ML) and the sub-catchment rate (USD1/ML) annually. This is different from drawing water directly from the Biri Dam where a farmer will, in addition to the aforementioned charges, also incur agreement water charge of USD12.68 (plus VAT)/ ML/year. The large town of Chinhoyi, including a district hospital and university, rely on water from the Manyame River. Rather than drawing its water from behind the dam, Chinhoyi Municipality obtains it from the river below. This way the town is charged for flow water as opposed to agreement water.[27] In order to make the waters available at the lower rates, ZINWA opens the dams' valves for Chinoyi.

The same applies for most A2 farmers and white commercial farmers who opt to draw water from Manyame River directly rather than from Biri Dam so as to be charged for flow water and not agreement water charge. In 2014 Chinhoyi Municipality's water abstraction per day was about 20 ML which translates to 600 ML of water per month and about 7200 ML per year. The Municipality is supposed to be paying for water at the municipal rate of USD11.71 per ML per year plus a water levy of USD1.06 per ML plus the sub-catchment rate of USD1 per ML. The total if this occurred would be USD111,790 per year. Instead, the Municipality is only paying the water levy (USD1.06 per ML) plus the sub-catchment rate (USD1 per ML) equalling USD2.06 per ML. This means that for the whole year, Chinhoyi Municipality is only paying USD2.06 multiplied by 7200 ML which equates to about USD14,832.

As the owner of Zimbabwe's dams larger than 5000 ML, ZINWA is mandated by law to inspect and maintain them. They are currently facing financial and human resource challenges to effectively exercise their mandate. In the MMSC we observed the deterioration of the Biri Dam as well the malfunctioning of one of the dam valves as a result of lack of maintenance. In a visit to the dam wall we found leaking valves, a leaking maintenance boat, the absence of a rope to climb to the water level of the control tower, lack of documentation of water quality and, in general, lack of support of the two ZINWA employees who are tasked with dam maintenance as well as with collecting levies on behalf of ZINWA.

The story is the same around the Mazvikadei Dam. Five of 18 farmers interviewed prefer to irrigate from their private boreholes as opposed to drawing more expensive water from the dam. In general, farmers do not pay for borehole water. The unregulated drilling and use of borehole water throughout Zimbabwe has undermined the 'user pays' principle and the notion of the indivisibility of water.

Most farmers are aware there is legislation that compels them to pay for commercial use of water but above half (53%) of the A1 farmers interviewed are not prepared to pay for water even if they irrigate, contending that water is a free God-given resource and nobody should force people to pay. One farmer remarked

27 Even so, Chinhoyi Municipality has difficulty in paying ZINWA.

"ZINWA has not put any cent on this dam, so why should it force people to pay".[28] But, some 20% of the A1 farmers professed ignorance about the Water Act and its provisions. They expressed surprise when informed that any commercial usage of water must be done through a water permit.

The unwillingness or inability to pay was also evident among A2 farmers. Some 57% of the 18 A2 farmers interviewed are irrigating. However, of them 74% are not keen on paying for water. While other A2 farmers are willing to pay, they cannot afford to because of the delay by Grain Marketing Board (GMB) to pay them for the produce delivered. This is further exacerbated by massive electricity load-shedding which has affected most farmers who rely on electric pump yields. Some farmers claim that electricity is now too expensive and hence it becomes uneconomic to irrigate. Some black commercial farmers who were part of the consortium of about 70 large-scale commercial farmers that built the Biri Dam, refuse to pay saying they built the Biri Dam and hence cannot pay for water from the said dam. One black commercial farmer had this to say, "the government gave us permission to build this dam and we have got the papers to confirm that".[29]

One of the reasons cited is the laxity in enforcement of the Water Act. Farmers will only pay when their lack of payment attracts the attention of ZINWA. The laxity of legal enforcement was confirmed by ZINWA who cited lack of resources to properly monitor water usage and curb illegal abstractions. Some A2 farmers said they cannot pay for water to irrigate yet the land they are irrigating was given to them by the government for free. These sentiments were also echoed by Derman and Manzungu (Chapter 7) and Mtisi (2011) when they reported that farmers are refusing to pay for water arguing that they got land for free from the government. The same gesture should be extended to water access. In addition, most respondents claim that the most politically well-connected A2 farmers were not paying and ZINWA personnel were often reluctant to even enter their farms.[30]

Discussion and conclusions

This study sought to understand if and how IWRM has been sustained in the context of an ever-evolving land reform programme, a struggling agriculture sector and poorly resourced institutions. The situation that we found in 2013 is vastly different from what existed in 2000 (see Derman and Manzungu, Chapter 7). In 2000, irrigation water was scarce at the height of the dry season. Winter wheat and many other crops were irrigated through an array of large dams, small farm dams, and boreholes. Primarily large-scale white commercial farmers who had invested heavily in irrigation controlled the waters. Farmers were paying for water at a nationwide set price and paying a small levy for the operation of a River Board. While there were issues with electricity supply in the 1990s, farmers were, in general, able to rely on electricity for their irrigation pumps whose supply was far more regular in the 1990s than after 2000. Water revenue flowed into state coffers until fast track land reform forced large-scale farmers off their farms.

The water reform envisaged commercial farmers remaining on their farms.

28 Interview conducted by Takunda Hove, July 17, 2012.

29 Interview, Urundi Farm, 24 October 2012.

30 For security of respondents, it is not possible to name them.

However with fast track the envisaged water revenues for the sale of agricultural water dried up, which severely hindered the operations of ZINWA, catchment and sub-catchment councils despite attempts by ZINWA and councils to mobilise financial resources.

While land reform has broadened people's access to agricultural resources, which could not be achieved under the neoliberal water reform (see Manzungu and Derman, Chapter 6) the transition to a viable agriculture sector is proving challenging. In place of relatively large commercial farms there are now new A1 villages and smaller but commercial A2 farms (Matondi, 2012; Moyo, 2013). Many A1 and A2 farmers lack irrigation infrastructure some of which was vandalised during the fast track land reform, some of which was sold and others with poor crop pricing. As a result, water revenues declined. Many new farmers have resisted paying for water for reasons including: they cannot afford to pay, they are ignorant of the law or refuse to pay. Some farmers express the opinion that since they got land from the government for free the same gesture should hold for water. Our findings are corroborated by Mtisi (2011) who found that land reform gave birth to new water users, which posed challenges of how the available water resources could meet both the social and economic objectives of the reforms. There are also issues related to the land reform – insecure tenure has led to some farmers doubting whether they would remain on farms against the backdrop of land being vested in the state. Government could arbitrarily cancel the offered letter or the 99-year lease which reduced some investments (Matondi and Dekker, 2011). To date, the 99-year leases have not been accepted by financial institutions as guarantee of loans which has meant lack of funding for investments. Without loans it is difficult for farmers, even with the best of intentions, to maintain their infrastructure.

There are also cultural issues at play. The user pays principle of commercial water is in conflict with the customary notion that water is a God-given resource that is available for all. Establishing a user-pays principle has gone against notions of fairness (Derman and Hellum, 2007; Hellum and Derman, 2005; Chikozho and Latham, 2005). In customary law, a distinction is made between drinking water where there is usually a norm of sharing and water for irrigation.[31] Water for irrigation has had to be paid for since the 1990s and only rarely does it involve customary sharing arrangements. An exception has been hand-dug wells for gardens in communal areas. In general, many A1 farmers come from communal areas where water has always been managed by local institutions under the legal notion of primary water but under the belief that water comes from God and that hence it is for free (Derman and Hellum, 2003).

It is not enough to observe that the two reforms undertaken by the government with a view to address inequalities in access to both land and water resources were incompatible and compromised the goals of both reforms. We instead need to ask why was this obvious connection between land and water reforms missed? We suggest that the answer may lie in the politics of water and land reform.

31 Rutsate et al. (2015) have found that this does not ordinarily extend to farm workers and former farm workers on resettled farms.

Within the Government of Zimbabwe there have been two major constraints to supporting IWRM: the first has to do with government resources to respond to farmers' needs and requirements of water; the second is the lack of communication and policy coherence between the ministries of water and agriculture. When ZINWA was created large numbers of the Department of Water's personnel moved to the new institution. However, because of the loss of revenues and lack of state support, ZINWA struggled to maintain essential services. The Ministry of Agriculture, on the other hand, was driven politically to focus on nationalising all private farms, resettling them and providing for resettled farmers and not communal areas ones. IWRM, no longer donor-supported, was not among the priorities at any level of government or in ZINWA except for one dimension – water as an economic good. However, the better resourced Ministry of Agriculture did not provide sufficient resources for the maintenance and support of existing irrigation systems.

This study has shown that while water reform has potential to enhance access for small- and large-scale farmers and enhance livelihoods, it is difficult to realise such benefits if the reforms are not carried out in recognition of the redistribution of land which coincided with water reforms. The rural landscape has been dramatically altered through fast track and land reform. Rather than having a few large-scale commercial farms in the MMSCC there are now hundreds of new A1 farmers, and many new A2 farmers. The water management system was designed for large-scale, not smaller-scale and small-scale farmers and thus it requires significant new resources to alter previous irrigation systems. ZINWA and the catchment councils have been unsuccessful in convincing resettled farmers (Models A1 and A2) what services they will receive if they pay for water. Water users do not value the role of the catchments and sub-catchment councils who from the current perspective are rent-seeking organizations. The national government provides little support to ZINWA while owing it large amounts of money. Donors have re-entered as described by Manzungu and Derman (Chapter 6), but with an emphasis upon urban water supply, infrastructure and sanitation increasing ZINWA's reliance upon 'selling' water. Most users at this point in time seek to pay as little as possible and preferably nothing. Only councils that have substantial amounts of permitted water will be able to sustain themselves.

In July 2016 the government launched a new programme called Command Agriculture. The USD500 million Command Agriculture Programme launched by Vice President Mnangagwa aims to have farmers produce two million tonnes of maize on 400, 000 ha of land. Government's decision to embark on the programme was necessitated by the rise in national food insecurity from about 12% in 2011 to 42% this year. Zimbabwe, like several other SADC countries, had to rely on imports to supplement its meagre grain harvest this season. The Zimbabwe Vulnerability Assessment Report said four million people need food aid this year because of an El-Niño-induced drought.[32] This marks the importance

32 www.thezimbabwedaily.com/top-stories/64179-500m-maize-scheme-on-cards.html (accessed September 1, 2016). It has also been reported in The *Herald*, the government's national newspaper in a series of articles. For example, www.herald.co.zw/command-agric-nets-300-000ha/ (accessed September 7, 2016).

of irrigation but how the water will be provided and who will pay for it remains unknown.

However, the program has been centrally decided in the absence of sufficient resources. It has bypassed catchment and sub-catchment councils. As emphasized by Manzungu and Derman in Chapter 6, we find little reason to be optimistic about a broad and holistic conception of IWRM in Zimbabwe. There is now a 15 year history of radical land reform's failure to create a holistic program. The water sector has become donor reliant and contemporary priorities have changed. Given the lack of economic support for the Ministry of Environment, Water and Climate, and the severe economic difficulties of ZINWA, water resources management has a low priority. It is hard to envision ZINWA or the Ministry re-investing in IWRM because it does not promise quick monetary returns from the sale of water. There was no strategy or policy guidance on how the transformation of agriculture in the Middle Manyame Sub-catchment would support IWRM to improve the efficiency, equity and environment. In the current economic and political climate of Zimbabwe the resumption of IWRM seems highly unlikely.

Acknowledgements

This chapter draws on ongoing research from a Norwegian Research Council-funded project, Flows and Practices: The Politics of IWRM in Africa. We are grateful to the Norwegian Research Council for their generous support. We thank Lyla Mehta and the anonymous reviewers for their comments on the chapter.

References

African Development Bank. 2014. Zimbabwe Economic Outlook. www.afdb.org/en/countries/southern-africa/zimbabwe/zimbabwe-economic-outlook/ (accessed on 2 August 2015)

Alden, C. and Anseeuw, W. 2009. *Land, liberation and compromise in southern Africa.* London: Palgrave Macmillan.

Alexander, J. 2006. *The unsettled land: State-making and the politics of land in Zimbabwe 1893-2003.* Oxford, Harare, Athens: James Currey, Weaver Press, Ohio University Press.

Anseeuw, W.; Kapuya, T. and Saruchera, D. 2012. *Zimbabwe's agricultural reconstruction: Present stage, ongoing projects and prospects for reinvestment.* Working Paper Series No. 32. Pretoria: Development Bank of southern Africa.

Chikozho, C. and Latham, J. 2005. Shona customary practices in the context of water sector reforms in Zimbabwe. In van Koppen, B.; Butterworth, J.A. and Juma, I.J. (Eds), *African water laws: Plural legislative frameworks for rural water management in Africa,* . Proceedings of a workshop. Johannesburg, South Africa, 26-28 January 2005. Pretoria: International Water Management Institute. http://projects.nri.org/waterlaw/AWLworkshop/CHIKOZHO-C.pdf (accessed on 25 November 2015).

Cliffe, L.; Alexander, J.; Cousins, B. and Gaidzanwa, R. 2011. An overview of fast track land reform in Zimbabwe: Editorial introduction. *Journal of Peasant Studies* 38(5): 907-938.

Compagnon, D. 2010. *A predictable tragedy: Robert Mugabe and the collapse of Zimbabwe.* Philadelphia: University of Pennsylvania Press.

Derman, B. and Gonese, F. 2003. Water reform in Zimbabwe: Its multiple interfaces with land reform and resettlement. In Roth, M. and Gonese, F. (Eds), *Delivering land and securing rural livelihoods: Post-independence land reform and resettlement in Zimbabwe,* pp.287-307. CASS, University of Zimbabwe, Land Tenure Centre, University of Wisconsin-Madison.

Derman, B. and Hellum, A. 2003. Neither tragedy nor enclosure: Are there inherent human rights in water management in Zimbabwe's communal lands? In Benjaminsen, T. and Lund, C. (Eds), *Securing land rights in Africa,* pp. 31-50. London: Frank Cass.

Derman, B. and Hellum, A. 2007. Livelihood rights perspective on water reform: Reflections on rural Zimbabwe. *Land Use Policy* 24(4): 664-673.

Duggan, W.R. 1980. The Native Land Husbandry Act of 1951 and the rural African middle class. *African Affairs* 79(315): 227-239.

Herbst, J. 1990. *State politics in Zimbabwe.* Harare: University of Zimbabwe Publications.

GoZ (Government of Zimbabwe). 1998a. *Water Act Chapter 20: 24.* Harare: Government Printers.

GoZ. 1998b. *Zimbabwe National Water Authority ZINWA Act Chapter 20: 25.* Harare: Government Printers.

GoZ (Government of Zimbabwe). 2000a. *Towards integrated water resources management: Water resources strategy for Zimbabwe.* Harare, Zimbabwe: Ministry of Rural Resources and Water Development.

GoZ (Government of Zimbabwe). 2000b. *Statutory Instrument 47, Water Sub-catchment Councils Regulations of 2000.* Harare: Government Printers.

GoZ (Government of Zimbabwe). 2001. *Statutory Instrument 206, Water Permits Regulations of 2001.* Harare: Government Printers.

GoZ (Government of Zimbabwe). 2002. *Environmental Management Act* [Chapter 20: 29]. Harare: Government Printers.

GoZ (Government of Zimbabwe). 2013. *National Water Policy.* Harare: Ministry of Water Resources Development and Management.

Hanlon, J.; Manjengwa, J.M. and Smart, T. 2013. *Zimbabwe takes back its land.* Sterling, VA: Kumarian Press.

Hellum, A. and Derman, B. 2004. Land reform and human rights in contemporary Zimbabwe: Balancing individual and social justice through an integrated human rights framework. *World Development* 32(10): 1785-1805.

Hellum, A. and Derman, B. 2005. Negotiating water rights in the context of a new political and legal landscape in Zimbabwe. In von Benda-Beckmann, F.; von Benda-Beckmann, K. and Griffiths, A. (Eds), *Mobile people, mobile law: Expanding legal relations in a contracting world,* pp. 177-198. Aldershot and Burlington, VT: Ashgate.

Hove, T. 2012. Land reform and the right to water in Middle Manyame Sub-Catchment: Unravelling users' access to water in the face of socio-political dynamics. MSc thesis. University of Zimbabwe, Harare.

James, G. 2015. Transforming rural livelihoods in Zimbabwe: Experiences of fast track land reform, 2000-2012. PhD thesis. University of Edinburgh.

Kinsey, B. 2000. The implications of land reform for rural welfare. In Bowyer-Bower, T.A.S. and Stoneman, C. (Eds), *Land reform in Zimbabwe: Constraints and prospects*, pp. 103-132. Aldershot, UK: Ashgate.

Kriger, N. 2003. War veterans: Continuities between the past and the present. *African Studies Quarterly* 7(2&3): 113-137.

Kujinga, K. and Jonker, L. 2006. An analysis of stakeholder knowledge about water governance transformation in Zimbabwe. *Physics and Chemistry of the Earth Parts A/B/C* 31(15-16): 690-698.

Latham, C.J.K. 2002a. The Manyame Catchment Council: A review. *Physics and Chemistry of the Earth Parts* A/B/C 27 (11-22): 907-917.

Latham, C.J.K. 2002b. Catchment management: A case study of the Manyame Catchment. In Manzungu, E. (Ed), *The processes and dynamics of catchment management in Zimbabwe*, pp. 21-44. Harare: Save Africa Trust.

Manzungu, E. 2001. A lost opportunity: An analysis of the water reform debate in the fourth parliament of Zimbabwe. *Zambezia* 28(1): 97-120.

Madyiwa, S. and Zawe, C. 2013. A historical analysis of smallholder irrigation development in Zimbabwe: Cases of Fuve Panganai C and Rupike Irrigation schemes. Consultancy Report for International Water Management Institute. Pretoria: International Water Management Institute.

Manzungu, E. 2011. *Reviving irrigation development and management.* Thematic Paper No. 3. Water Resources Development and Management Consultancy Reports. Harare: World Bank.

Manzungu, E. and Machiridza, R. 2009. Economic-legal ideology and water management in Zimbabwe. *Economics, Management and Financial Markets* 41: 66-102.

Manzungu, E.; Mudenda-Damba, M.; Madyiwa, S.; Dzingirayi, V. and Musoni, S. 2016. Bulk water suppliers in the City of Harare – An endogenous form of privatisation of urban domestic water supply in Zimbabwe. *Water Alternatives* 9(1): 56-80.

Mapedza, E.; Manzungu, E.; Rosen T.; Ncube, P. and van Koppen, B. 2016. Decentralized water governance in Zimbabwe: Disorder within order. *Water Resources and Rural Development* 8: 1-11.

Marongwe, N. 2011. Who was allocated fast track land and what did they do with it? Selection of A2 farmers in Goromonzi District, Zimbabwe and its impacts on agricultural production. *Journal of Peasant Studies* 38(5): 1069-1092.

Matondi, P.B. and Dekker, M. 2011. *Land rights and tenure security in Zimbabwe's post-fast track land reform programme: A synthesis report.* Harare: Ruzivo Trust.

Matondi, P.B. 2012. Zimbabwe's *fast track land reform.* London and New York: Zed Books.

Maunganidze, L. 2015. Zimbabwe: Institutionalized corruption and state fragility. In Olowu, D. and Chanie, O. (Eds), *State fragility and state building in Africa: Cases from eastern and southern Africa*, pp. 39-60. Heidelberg: Springer.

Moyo, S. 1995. *Land question in Zimbabwe (Southern Africa Political Economy).* Harare: SAPES Books.

Moyo, S. (Ed). 2000a. *Zimbabwe environmental dilemma: Balancing resource inequities.* Harare: Zimbabwe Environmental Research Organization.

Moyo, S. 2000b. The political economy of land redistribution in the 1990s. In Bowyer-Bower, T.A.S. and Stoneman, C. (Eds), *Land reform in Zimbabwe: Constraints and prospects*, pp. 73-82. Aldershot, UK: Ashgate.

Moyo, S. 2004. *The politics of land distribution and race relations in southern Africa identities*. Research Institute for Conflict and Cohesion Programme Paper No. 10. New York: United Nations.

Moyo, S. 2013. Land reform and redistribution in Zimbabwe since 1980. In Moyo, S. and Chambati, W. (Eds), *Land and agrarian reform in Zimbabwe: Beyond white settler capitalism*, pp. 29-78. Dakar: CODESRIA.

Moyo, S. and Yeros, P. 2013. The Zimbabwe model: Radicalisation, reform and resistance. In Moyo, S. and Chambati, W. (Eds), *Land and agrarian reform in Zimbabwe: Beyond white settler capitalism*, pp. 331-358. Dakar: CODESRIA.

Mtisi, S. 2002. Livelihoods and water reforms, emerging issues for new stakeholders. In Manzungu, E. (Ed), *The process and dynamics of catchment management in Zimbabwe*, pp. 109-142. Harare: Save Africa Trust Publications.

Mtisi, S. 2008. Zimbabwe's water reform and effects on local level water management processes and rural livelihoods: Evidence from Lower Save East Sub-Catchment. PhD thesis. University of Manchester, Manchester, UK.

Mtisi, S. 2011. *Water reforms during the crisis and beyond: Understanding policy and political challenges of reforming the water sector in Zimbabwe.* Overseas Development Institute Working Paper 333. London: Overseas Development Institute.

Murisa, T. 2011. Local farmer groups and collective action within fast track land reform in Zimbabwe. *The Journal of Peasant Studies* 38(5): 1145-1166.

Palmer, R. 1977. *Land and racial domination in Rhodesia*. London: Heinemann.

Ranger, T. 1985. *Peasant consciousness and guerrilla war in Zimbabwe: A comparative study.* London: James Currey.

Rutstate, E.; Derman, B. and Hellum, A. 2015. A hidden presence: Women farm workers right to water and sanitation in the aftermath of the fast track land. In Hellum, A.; Kameri-Mbote, P. and van Koppen, B. (Eds), *Water is life: Women's human rights in national and local water governance in southern and eastern Africa*, pp. 420-456. Harare: Weaver Press.

Scoones, I.; Marongwe, N.; Mavedzenge, B.; Mahenehene, J.; Murimbarimba, F. and Sukume, C. 2010. *Zimbabwe's land reform: Myths & realities*. Woodbridge: James Currey/Boydell & Brewer.

Scoones, I., Marongwe, N., Mavedzenge, B., Murimbarimba, F., Mahenehene, J., and Sukume, C. 2011. Zimbabwe 's land reform: A summary of findings. Institute of Development Studies, Brighton.

UNDP (United Nations Development Programme). 2002. Zimbabwe land reform and resettlement: Assessment and suggested framework for the future. http://eisa.org.za/PDF/zimlandreform.pdf (accessed on 2 August 2015)

Zamchiya, P. 2011. A synopsis of land and agrarian change in Chipinge District, Zimbabwe. *Journal of Peasant Studies* 38(5): 1093-1122.

Zawe, C. 2006. Reforms in turbulent times. A study in the theory and practice of three irrigation management policy reform models in Mashonaland, Zimbabwe. PhD thesis. Wageningen University, Wageningen, the Netherlands.

9

IWRM *Avant la Lettre*? Four Key Episodes in the Policy Articulation of IWRM in Downstream Mozambique[1]

Rossella Alba and Alex Bolding

ABSTRACT: The first substantive piece of water legislation ever adopted in Mozambique, the Lei de Águas of 1991, was crafted before IWRM (Integrated Water Resources Management) was endorsed as the newly emerging global consensus on water governance. Yet, the Lei de Águas already incorporated the river basin concept and its decentralised water management, making Mozambique a case of IWRM 'avant la lettre'. In this chapter, we reconstruct the drivers behind four key policy episodes that shaped the travel of IWRM to Mozambique, viz. the Lei de Águas 1991, the SADC Water Protocol, the National Water Policy 1995, and the 2007 national reforms and regulations, drawing from the experiences of two Mozambican river basins, the Limpopo and the Pungwe. In terms of process, we observe that domestic concerns, a small Mozambican water policy elite nurtured by international donors, and the agenda of financial institutions highly shaped the articulation of IWRM. In terms of outcomes, several contradictions emerge: i.e. centralised State management seems to have become further entrenched, stakeholders have virtually no say in water matters and the most powerful and wealthy stakeholders use payments to secure water cheaply at the expense of unregistered smallholder users who depend for their livelihoods on primary water.

KEYWORDS: IWRM, policy articulation, elite, stakeholder participation, Mozambique

Introduction

The first and only piece of water legislation ever approved by the Mozambican parliament, the *Lei de Águas* of 1991 (GoM, 1991), was crafted and formulated before the Integrated Water Resources Management (IWRM) paradigm and its principles were endorsed as key elements of the newly emerging global consensus on water governance. The Water Act already emphasised the management of water on the basis of (transboundary) river basins, instituted a legal framework for water allocation and water pricing, and introduced a form of decentralisation of water resources management through Regional Water Administrations (*Ad-*

1 First published in *Water Alternatives* 9(3): 551-570.

ministrações Regional de Aguas, ARAs) and River Basin Management Units (*Unidades de Gestão de Bacia*). The translation of a set of dominant IWRM principles, viz. seeing water as an economic good rather than as a public good, and opening up the water sector for private service providers was, however, only hastily inserted during the formulation of the 1995 National Water Policy (Serra, 2011).

Since the promulgation of the 1995 National Water Policy, several reforms have sought to strengthen the implementing capacity of the decentralised agencies in regulating bulk and drinking water use, diminish the bureaucratic power of government departments, foster the role of water pricing in both allocation and cost recovery, and strengthen Mozambique's position as downstream water user in internationally shared river basins (GoM, 2007a; GoM, 2007b; Manjate, 2010). Meanwhile, several donor-funded projects, like the Pungwe joint IWRM project, the PRIMA project in the Incomati, and continued support for ARA-Sul (*Administração Regional de Águas do Sul*) through Dutch bilateral aid, have sought to operationalise and implement IWRM policy in a number of key river basins (RoM/RoZ/Sida, 2006; van Woersem et al., 2007).

Through the 1991 law, policies and projects mentioned above, a new 'water architecture' (Swatuk, 2002) based on IWRM ideas/principles has been introduced in Mozambican water policies and articulated in everyday water management practices. Building on the overall framework presented in the introduction, this chapter aims at analysing how IWRM ideas 'travelled' to Mozambique and how such ideas were articulated in policies and practices. Several studies analyse and discuss the state of implementation of the IWRM-inspired policies, given the institutional and legal framework provided by the Water Act and the National Water Policies (van der Zaag, 2010; Gallego-Ayala and Juízo, 2011, 2012; Inguane et al., 2014). Rather than assessing the degree of implementation of IWRM-based reforms, this chapter first traces the origins of Mozambican water reforms and discusses the endorsement of IWRM ideas in light of domestic and international drivers. Second, it discusses how some IWRM articulations have influenced practices in Limpopo and Pungwe river basins resulting in new forms of water allocation and stakeholder participation on the ground. A second chapter included in this book further elaborates on the case of Limpopo and the politics of water payments and stakeholder participation (Alba et al., Chapter 10).

IWRM here is understood as a comprehensive 'policy package' comprising three major shifts in water governance, according to Bolding (2004): (1) from administrative (province) to resource-based water governance (river basin); (2) from centralised state to decentralised stakeholder-based governance through the creation of local water administrations and river basin committees; and (3) from public to private and market-based forms of water governance (i.e. introduction of water pricing). Even though the earliest form of recognised integrated river basin management dates back to the early 1930s in the shape of the Tennessee Valley Authority (TVA) experiment (Miller and Reidinger, 1998; Biswas, 2004), the endorsement of the so-called 'Dublin Principles' is often referred to as a turning point in bringing together the IWRM package (Mehta et al., 2014). IWRM resulted in an umbrella framework involving a number of policy ideas (i.e. decentralisation, participation, demand management mechanisms, and so on) endorsed as the way to improve Water Resources Management (WRM) everywhere.

For the case of Mozambique, this chapter illustrates how the different elements associated with IWRM have received fluctuating attention serving both the domestic agenda and international donors' requests. Furthermore, the contradictory outcomes of internationally endorsed shifts in water governance are discussed. Whilst the IWRM package aims at making water accessible to all, and managing it in a sustainable, democratic and (cost)-effective way, the outcomes of the reforms in Mozambique seem to move towards a different direction: Centralised State management has become further entrenched and stakeholders have virtually no say in water matters. Meanwhile, the introduction of a water rights framework has led to a situation where the most powerful and wealthy water users (e.g. private sugar estates) use water licences to secure water at the expense of those unregistered smallholder users who depend for their livelihoods on primary water (Van der Zaag et al., 2010; Alba et al., this book). This points at the need to appreciate locally available repertoires of governance, State histories and existing divergent cultures of governing (e.g. technocratic versus customary rule) that inevitably shape the articulation of policy ideas into practices. Particularly for Mozambique, many authors have pointed at the lack of any tradition of democratic rule (Mamdani, 1996; Alexander, 1997) and the great dependency on foreign aid (Hanlon and Smart, 2008).

In the rest of this chapter, we first outline our conceptual approach towards policy process analysis. The second section describes the context of the study and the methodology. Then, the historical trajectory of the policy process is analysed, followed by insights on the articulation of IWRM on the ground by drawing from the cases of Limpopo and Pungwe river basins. Finally, in the conclusions, we present and discuss the main findings.

How does policy travel? (Policy network and policy articulation)

Drawing from Wester's study on the decentralisation of irrigation management in Lerma-Chapala Basin in Mexico, we use the term '*policy articulation*' to define the dynamic process "by which policy actors support, modify, displace and translate a policy idea" into something 'real' (Wester, 2008: 24). The idea works as a 'form of connection' that makes a whole of different elements (Hall, 1996 cited in Li, 2000), like how IWRM brings together land, water, people, livelihoods, donor organisations, and so on. Meanwhile, the articulation of these elements translates the idea into material practices. Thus, scrutinising the articulation of IWRM is about investigating how abstract ideas such as volumetric water pricing, decentralisation and stakeholder participation, are translated into contextualised practices (e.g. setting water prices, creating river basin authorities and committees).

Our view on policy processes is partly inspired by the actor-network theory as a descriptive tool that seeks to explain 'how' relations assemble (Law, 2009). Indeed, rather than framing policy as a linear process, moving rationally from formulation to implementation to outcomes, 'policy articulation' looks at the practices as the contingent outcome of the assemblage of heterogeneous elements such as people, ideas, interests, events and objects that constitute the '*policy network*' (cf. Long and van der Ploeg, 1989; Mosse, 2004). The articulation of these elements translates the idea into material practices through uneven and unpredictable policy pathways. Such articulation is inherently political as it represents the outcome of the struggle between different interests, priorities and objectives that are continuously negotiated and contested by policy actors (see Mollinga, 2008).

As policy ideas travel through different networks they engage in a transformative process where ideas are translated and transformed while they move around and are confronted with local circumstances and interest groups. Indeed, as Mukhtarov (2009) discusses in his insightful analysis of IWRM translation, in travelling, policies are not just transferred but translated across places and times. He points at scales, contingency and modification on meanings as important elements in the translation of IWRM in England, Turkey and Kazakhstan (Mukhtarov, 2009). Similarly, but with a different geographical focus, the analysis proposed here and in Mehta and Movik (2014) considers how different countries and/or river basins with their history, resources and people actively and have recursively shaped the articulation of IWRM ideas.

While we call such transformations and reinterpretations a form of policy articulation, Wedel et al. (2005) suggest looking at policy transformations as 'chemical reactions'. In her study on Western aid to Eastern Europe, Wedel (2001) describes aid policies as a series of reactions that "begin with the donor's policies but are transformed by the agendas, interests, and interactions of the donor and recipient representatives at each stage of implementation and interface" (Wedel et al., 2005: 39). Likewise, IWRM principles have been transformed by local, regional and national agendas and through the interplay between donors, banks and local interest groups (Mehta et al., 2014). As in chemical reactions, the articulation of policy ideas involves experts, instruments and laboratories. Water professionals, bureaucrats and academics within one or several epistemic communities represent the experts; national laws, documents, strategies, guidelines, the instruments and river basins or pilot projects represent the 'laboratories of practices' (cf. Latour, 1987).

Research methodology

The chapter brings together the main findings of a number of studies on the case of Mozambique (Bolding, 2004; Praagman, 2013; Alba, 2013; Bolding and Alba, 2013) conducted under the Flows and Practices research project. For the case of Mozambique, the flow of IWRM ideas is analysed focusing on the recursive interaction of different actors in policy-making fora at river basin, regional, national and international levels (Table 9.1) and four key moments, so-called 'policy episodes' (cf. Wester, 2008), each corresponding with the endorsement of key policies and legislations (the *Lei de Agua* 1991, the National Water Policy 1995, the 1995 and 2005 SADC Water protocol and the 2007 national reforms and regulations). Meanwhile, the experiences of Limpopo and Pungwe river basins provide insights from the field on the articulation of IWRM into practices.

The research methodology is illustrated below.

Table 9.1. Overview of the actors involved in each policy area.

Policy arena	Actor
International	Global Water Partnership and other global water-related initiatives
	Donor agencies and international financial institutions (i.e. World Bank, International Monetary Fund)
Regional	SADC and transnational river basin commissions (i.e. Limpopo Water-course Commission, LIMCOM)
National	National Directorate of Water (Direcção Nacional de Água, DNA) under the Ministry of Public Works and Housing
	National Water Council
	National Water Regulatory Council (Conselho de Regulacão do Abasteci-mento de Agua, CRA)
River Basin	Regional Water Administrations (i.e. ARA-Sul, ARA-Centro)
	River Basin Management Units (i.e. Limpopo River Basin Management Unit, UGBL)
	River Basin Committee (Comité da Bacía, CdB)
	Water Users (i.e. individual smallholder farmers, large-scale ones, irriga-tion schemes, etc)

At regional and national level, the water reform process that unfolded in the 1990s was 'studied up' (Nader, 1972) through a literature review, study of secondary documents retrieved from the National Water Directorate library and a total of 23 interviews with key policy actors. Interviewees included senior engineers and staff working for the National Water Directorate, the ARAs, Limpopo River Basin Management Unit, and the Water Regulatory Board and independent consultants. Interviews were carried out also with academics and Dutch policy actors operating with the Development Cooperation Agencies. At local level, due to their history, geographical characteristics and recent developments, Limpopo and Pungwe river basins were selected (Fig. 9.1).

Although providing an in-depth presentation of the two basins is beyond the scope of this chapter (see Alba et al., this book; van der Zaag and Bolding, 2009; Praagman, 2013), here we clarify the main motivations behind the selection of the two basins. Limpopo provides an interesting example of a transboundary river basin; indeed, the basin comprises a shared watercourse between Zimbabwe, South Africa, Botswana and Mozambique, with only 20% of the total river basin surface belonging to Mozambique. The downstream Mozambican stretch of the basin has been an important area for agricultural production since colonial times and, today, most of the water demand is concentrated on irrigated agriculture (van der Zaag et al., 2010; Ducrot, 2011). Furthermore, the proximity of the basin to Maputo, the capital of Mozambique, made it one of the first testing grounds for the establishment of new river basin-based institutions, following the Mozambican tendency of

Fig. 9.1. The different Regional Water Administrations (ARAs) and the location of the Limpopo and Pungwe river basins.[2]

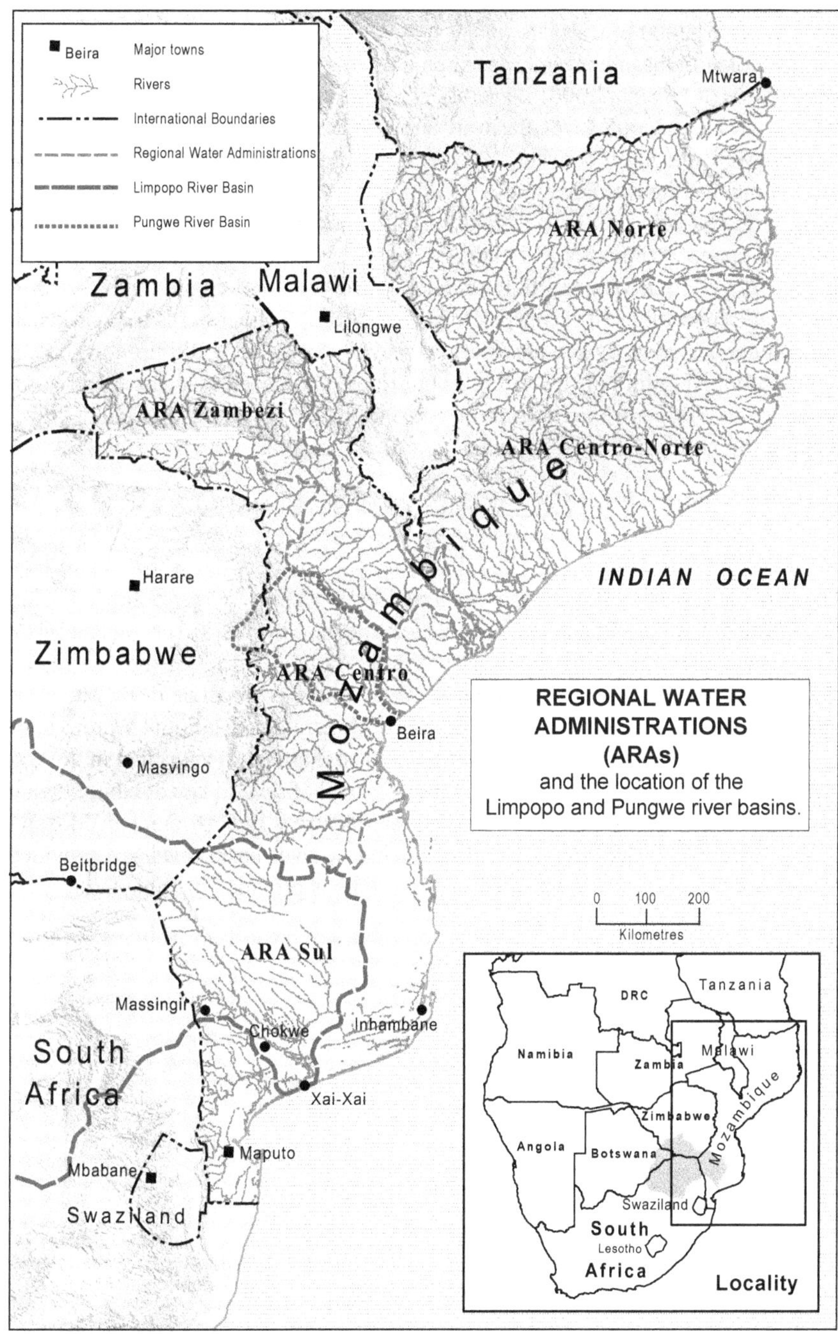

2 Source: Adapted from http://america.pink/images/2/7/0/5/3/4/9/en/2-list-rivers-mozambique.jpg

geographical spread of policy implementation from the capital outwards to the rest of the country. Meanwhile, the Pungwe River was selected given its role as a testing ground for a Swedish consortium of donor agencies (including Sida and SWECO) from 2000 onwards to 'make IWRM happen' through the formulation of a joint IWRM management and development strategy and subsequent investment phase (RoM/RoZ/Sida, 2006). Several field visits were carried out in different locations in the Limpopo River Basin in 2012 and 2013; and in three locations in the Pungwe River Basin between 2005 and 2007.Semi-structured interviews were carried out in English, Portuguese or Changana (the vernacular language), the latter with the help of a field assistant, using snowballing as a method to select the participants. While archival material and interviews with senior water professionals proved to be very useful in understanding the unfolding of the policy process, some limitations in reconstructing the politics of the process also surfaced. We managed to identify key negotiations and conflicts, but could produce only a limited understanding of the details about them. Moreover, it seems there was a tendency to edit contradictions and contestations out of the historical narrative, making the policy narrative 'too neat'.

Articulating IWRM in policy networks: Drivers and timelines

The articulation of IWRM ideas is analysed by focusing on four policy episodes (cf. Wester, 2008) defined around policies and key events in the Mozambican water sector. The first episode focuses on the Water Act, the second centres on the process that led to the SADC Shared Watercourse Protocol of 1995. The third episode considers the formulation of the first Mozambican National Water Policy (1995). The fourth episode describes the impulse that IWRM ideas had in the water sector during the 2000s leading to the approval of several key documents that constitute the current framework for water resources management in Mozambique. Insights on the development occurring at river-basin level are provided along with the episodes. A timeline of key events is provided in Table 9.2.

Table 9.2. Overview of key policy episodes and resulting policies, regulations and institutions.

Policy episodes	Key events
Policy episode one – 1980s until 1991	Water Act (GoM, 1991)
Policy episode two – 1982 until 2005	SADC Shared Watercourse Protocol of 1995 Ratified in 2005
Policy episode three –1990s	National Water Policy (GoM, 1995) National Water Tariff Policy (GoM, 1998)
Policy episode four – 2000s	Consultation GTA for renewal of the National Water Policy and Act New National Water Policy (GoM, 2007b) National Water Resource Management Strategy (GoM, 2007a) Regulation for Licences and Concessions Water Policy (GoM, 2007c)

Policy episode one: The emergence of IWRM ideas

Occurring at the height of the civil war and with the end in sight, the Water Act (1991) represents the only legislation concerning water formally approved by the Mozambican parliament to date. It puts together socialist ideas with new 'modern' ideas in water resources management that later became part of the IWRM paradigm. It stresses the role of State institutions in water resources management and declares all water resources public- and State-owned. The Act sets the distinction between common use (*uso comun*) and private use (*uso privativo*). The former refers to the use of water for primary requirements such as domestic needs, watering livestock and small-scale irrigation of up to 1 hectare (ha) of land without the use of siphoning or mechanical instruments while the latter refers to all other uses (Veldwisch et al., 2013). From a rather fragmented and non-integrated water sector, the Act promised regulated and organised management of water resources based on decentralised Regional Water Administrations (ARAs) and river basin management.

Three main issues steered the formulation of the Act: the lack of a legal framework for water allocation, the national and international impulse for decentralisation of water resources management and the need to deal with transboundary issues seeking to secure a minimum water allocation to the downstream nation of Mozambique, while protecting its populous urban centres in the delta from devastating floods. To properly understand the context in which the Act was crafted, we need to step back in time.

Before the approval of the Water Act, legislation on water resources management was scattered in several texts dating to the colonial times, without apparent coordination (Caponera, 1983). As a result, the legislation was "either unknown or ignored" (ibid: 15). Since the early 1980s the Government of Mozambique (GoM) had established collaboration with the Food and Agriculture Organisation of the United Nations (FAO), the United Nations Educational, Scientific and Cultural Organisation (UNESCO) and, later on, with the United Nations Development Programme (UNDP) for assistance in the development of water-related legislation (Caponera, 1983; Solanes, 1989). As Dante Caponera, one of the key figures in the Act formulation process wrote in his Mozambique mission report for the FAO legal branch: "there was a sincere desire from all concerned to secure the most rational use of available waters and, for these purposes, to introduce a water policy, and set up an adequate legal institutional framework" (Caponera, 1983: 4). Several interviewees mentioned a panel meeting held in Maputo in 1984 as a key moment in the development of the Water Act. During the meeting, a group of Mozambican and international engineers coming from different sectors (e.g. Agriculture, Water Management, Electricity), including experts from the TVA, Thames Water and Dutch engineers from the Delft University, concluded that Water Resources Management in Mozambique should be based on an integrated and multifunctional approach (DNA, 1984).

The ideas discussed within the FAO and UNDP reports and the experiences of the TVA and European countries in water resources management informed the deliberations of a new generation of Mozambican engineers. As students, most of these young Mozambican engineers, spent a semester or more in the Netherlands and studied at the Technical University of Delft. Otherwise, they were trained at the Engineering Faculty of Eduardo Mondlane University by Mozambican professors who in turn were trained in the Netherlands or by Dutch experts. During their education, they were exposed to new ideas on WRM, particularly river basin management that they eventually brought into the national policy arena. After Independence, "despite the leaving of Portuguese technicians, DNA became a strong institution with the incorporation of young Mozambican technicians and with the support of the cooperation of different countries, mainly of the Netherlands, Italy and Bulgaria" (Carmo Vaz, 2003: 67). During the 1970s and 1980s several young professionals from socialist countries came to Mozambique to support the newly created Mozambican revolutionary State (e.g. the Soviet Block, the Netherlands, Italy, Cuba). Among others, several students, recently graduated from Dutch universities, were recruited through solidarity groups. Known as 'cooperantes', they were employed by the Mozambican government. In the water sector, several (Dutch) students from Delft Technical University and Wageningen University worked at DNA or as engineers in large-scale irrigation schemes. Since most donors left the country in the late 1980s or were severely constricted in their development efforts due to the intensifying civil war, these young and highly educated engineers became key policy actors in the formulation of the Water Act and subsequent policies in the water sector (Alba, 2013).

A second element that influenced the policy process was the ongoing decentralisation of water resources management. Since the 1960s, several experiments based on river basin planning and management had been taking place in Mozambique. As a report written by a Dutch group of engineers working at DNA observes "with the construction of three dams [Pequenos Limbobos, Corumana and Massingir] in the South of the country the necessity to define regional water supply policies gained again impetus" (WaterGroup, 1988: 14). Among others, the Unidade de Direcção de Aproveitamento Hidráulicos (UDAH) was created in order to coordinate the construction works of the first two dams (Pequenos Limbobos and Corumana dams) providing water to Maputo. UDAH offered the institutional template for the creation of the first regional water administration (ARA-Sul) and the subsequent ones. With regard to water pricing, an early experiment was instituted involving the introduction of bulk water tariffs paid by those benefitting from the use of water stored in the dams in Umbeluzi and Limpopo river basins (Manjate, 2010). Yet, water tariffs became a key concern only later, at the end of the 1990s, when new legislation was introduced and put into practice. Then, new experiments with water payments were introduced at basin level, as we discuss below for the case of Limpopo.

Eventually, the developments occurring at regional level provided further impetus for the definition of a clear framework for the management of national water resources. In particular, a framework for water rights allocation (e.g. water licences) provided a way for accounting for existing water demand at river basin level. Indeed, while water supply was increasingly regulated through the construction of hydraulic infrastructure, high uncertainty surrounded water demand. This becomes relevant in relation to the downstream position of Mozambique and the increasing competition for water at the international level. The next policy episode further illustrates how Mozambican policy actors and concerns in the transboundary Incomati River Basin shaped the articulation of IWRM ideas.

Policy episode two: The definition of 'shared water course'

While at the national level the institutional and legislative framework inspired by IWRM was emerging, at the regional level the attention was concentrated on the SADC Shared Watercourse Protocol claimed by Mozambican and other southern African policy actors as the 'Mozambican SADC Protocol'. Mozambican downstream concerns regarding sharing water of the Incomati River with Swaziland and South-Africa played a key role in the policy process that led to the definition of 'shared water courses' in the regional agreement (Carmo Vaz and Lopes Pereira, 2000). Several tripartite agreements between these countries on sharing Incomati water paved the way to the ultimate SADC revised protocol signed in 2005.

The first agreement between South Africa and Portugal about rivers of mutual interest was signed in 1964, and was known as the Cunene Agreement (named after a dam in southern Angola). The agreement introduced a number of principles, which recurred in later bilateral and trilateral agreements over the sharing of the Incomati River. The first principle emphasised 'best joint utilization' in developing the river's water resources. Secondly, cooperation should take place through sharing (hydrological) information and performing joint studies. Thirdly, these two principles should form the basis for diplomatic negotiations over mutual interests (van der Zaag and Carmo Vaz, 2003).

Despite these auspicious beginnings during the colonial era, it was, however, only by 1982 in the wake of a terrible drought, which reduced the inflow of water in the Incomati River at the Mozambican end of the border to zero, when representatives from the water sector of South Africa, Mozambique and Swaziland met again. They established the Tripartite Permanent Technical Committee (TPTC) that would advise their ministers responsible for water on the uses of the water resources of common interest, i.e. the Maputo and Incomati River basins, in February 1983 (van der Zaag and Carmo Vaz, 2003). All three riparian countries had big plans with regard to developing a dam in their part of the river basin. The consultations took place in a tense political climate: FRELIMO government supported the African National Council (ANC) against the South African government of the day while South Africa supported RENAMO forces that fought against the Mozambican government. This represented a case of interstate hydro-politics (Mollinga, 2001) and showed that at times of strained diplomatic relations between the countries, the management of international waters became one of the few possibilities for negotiation. Interestingly enough, the water- based negotiations led to a breakthrough on the diplomatic front rather than on the water front, when the then president of Mozambique, Samora Machel, promised to evict the ANC from Mozambican territory in exchange for apartheid South Africa withdrawing its support of RENAMO. This diplomatic Incomati Agreement of 1984 did unfortunately not secure the peace Mozambique had hoped for.

On the water front, the World Bank, through a team of Dutch experts, established that Mozambique had suffered heavily from upstream water developments in South Africa. Swaziland required Mozambique's no objection to the construction of the Maguga Dam in order to receive World Bank funds towards its construction. Furthermore, South Africa demanded a no objection from Mozambique for the construction of the Driekoppies Dam, which Mozambique was only prepared to give as long as a minimum inflow into the Mozambican end of the Incomati was guaranteed. These developments paved the way for the Piggs Peak Agreement of February 1991 in which South Africa guaranteed a minimum inflow of 2m3/s (van der Zaag and Carmo Vaz, 2003). The Piggs Peak agreement led to subsequent joint studies in the Incomati that eventually resulted in the SADC Shared Watercourse Protocol of 1995. This was ratified by Mozambique on the condition that its definition of shared water courses was expanded to shared rivers, preventing the practice of South Africa to strike separate (bilateral) deals with Swaziland over sharing the headwaters of both the Maputo and Incomati rivers without including Mozambique.

The expanded definition of shared rivers was included in the second SADC protocol, which was ultimately ratified by Mozambique in 2005; hence, the reference to the 'Mozambican SADC protocol'. Of further note is that the ongoing discussion between the Governments of Mozambique, Swaziland and South Africa over the joint management of the Maputo and Incomati rivers, made the Mozambican engineers very conscious of the river basin concept. The contest over water-related disasters (droughts and floods) with its upstream apartheid neighbour, probably resulted in the innovative and modern use of the river basin concept in the Lei de Aguas as highlighted in policy episode one above.

Policy episode three: The neoliberal turn

The third episode centres on the endorsement of IWRM ideas in the national policy arena. The episode demonstrates the influence of Mozambican post-war concerns and neoliberal, market-inspired International Monetary Fund (IMF)/ World Bank (WB) agenda in the formulation of the National Water Policy (NWP) and the water sector as a whole.

In the 1990s, the country witnessed great changes in the political scene that inevitably influenced the entire Mozambican society and economy (Pitcher, 2002). In 1992, FRELIMO and RENAMO signed a peace agreement, and in 1994 the first multiparty elections took place. Mozambique was worn out by years of conflict, several natural disasters and a severe drought and famine (1991-1992). Reconstruction and poverty alleviation were the main objectives of the government, that soon became an 'exemplary client' for the WB and the IMF (West, 1997; Hanlon and Smart, 2008; Hanlon, 2010). Meanwhile, "[n]early all donors made aid conditional on the recipient having programmes with the IMF and World Bank" (Hanlon, 2010: 86), thus pushing the Mozambican government to follow an economic structural adjustment programme. Within the water sector, the agenda focused on improving (or creating) basic services such as water supply in both urban and rural areas.

The drafting of the National Water Policy started before the Peace deal was signed, received a lot of attention after 1992 and was approved by the Council of Ministers in August 1995 (GoM, 1995). The NWP endorsed IWRM (Gestão integrada de recursos hídricos in Portuguese) and promoted the decentralisation of water management and the participation of water users in planning, implementing, managing and financing of water infrastructure. The NWP, however, focused on Water Supply and Sanitation leaving little space to water resources management concerns. This shift should be understood in the context of the low water coverage rate that characterised post-war Mozambique (Coppel and Schwartz, 2011), the international attention towards providing safe drinking water (e.g. the International Drinking Water Decade) and the IMF/WB agenda mentioned above.

Furthermore, the NWP diverges from the 1991 Law as it emphasises the definition of water as an economic good and promotes public-private partnerships in the provision of drinking water. Following the adoption of the NWP, the Water Tariff Policy (in Portuguese *Política Tarifaria de Águas*) was approved in 1998. The document contains guidelines for the introduction of water charges following cost-recovery, user-pays and polluter-pays principles. As Alba (2013) reports, the shifts towards increased participation of the private sector and market-based reforms did not come without contestations that resulted in the definition of water as an economic as well as a social good. Nevertheless, the intervention of Bretton Woods institutions was seen as a good option (if not the only) to obtain financial support required for reconstruction.

Informed by the emerging IWRM paradigm, new forms of stakeholder participation were introduced at river basin level. The southern region and Limpopo River Basin were again the main focus: in 1993, ARA-Sul was established, followed by the creation of the Limpopo River Basin Management Unit and the Limpopo River Basin Committee that met for the first time in 1998. The Committee still represents the arena for discussion and participation of stakeholders at river basin level. The experience of ARA-Sul served as an example for the other four regional administrations (ARAs) created between 1993 and 2007 (see Fig. 9.1). The decentralisation process was rather slow, characterised by a lack of political and institutional commitment to transfer of authority from the central administration to new decentralised administrations and a lack of human resources (Inguane, 2010). Indeed, during the 1990s the water sector was characterised by an outflow of skilled people from the central administration (i.e. the National Water Directorate) to either newly created agencies dealing with water supply or to the private sector (i.e. consultancy companies). This only slowed down the establishment of the ARAs, but the sector as a whole, since the formulation of water policies, became increasingly shaped by skilled engineers and water management working for consultancy companies with ties in the government.

It can be observed that the three shifts in water governance described in the introduction were articulated and endorsed in Mozambican policy documents in the 1990s. From centralised management, decentralised water administrations and river basin units and new forms of stakeholder participation, were created (however stunted they functioned in practice); water was formally defined as an economic and social good and new water pricing mechanisms coupled with increased private sector participation were introduced. The events highlighted above, however, suggest that the globally endorsed IWRM discourse was not the main driver behind these shifts. National concerns regarding post-war reconstruction and lack of public finance guided the articulation of IWRM ideas. Indeed, during the 1990s, water resources management was not the core concern of the GoM as attention was diverted to drinking water supply and increased attention towards economic instruments for WRM. The role of water charges was enhanced both as a way to pursue cost-recovery and as an instrument to promote rational use of water and environmental protection. Yet, it seems that the definition of water as an economic good and the introduction of the Water Tariff Policy have produced only limited effects at river basin level (Alba, 2013).

Policy episode four: Promotion and acceleration of implementation

In 2007, another key moment occurred when the Council of Ministers approved the new National Water Policy, the National Water Resources Management Strategy, the Regulations on Water Licenses and Concessions and the Water Tariff for the southern region. Following the World Summit on Sustainable Development, held in Johannesburg in 2002, which called on all countries to develop IWRM plans (Jønch-Clausen, 2004), in Mozambique IWRM-based water governance was further promoted and great efforts were devoted to the conversion of IWRM-inspired policies into practices.

The Policy and the Strategy came about as a result of a participatory consultation process started between 2001 and 2002 financed by the World Bank. A stakeholder forum (Grupo de Trabalho Alargado – GTA) was created with participants representing donors, the private sector, NGOs, university and governmental institutions. According to one of the participants, the whole process was quite exceptional in terms of participation of a wide range of stakeholders and quality of the discussion, "for the first time, even the environmental NGOs were involved".[3] The consultation was organized into eight thematic sections or building blocks. For each block a consultancy was in charge of an inventory of the situation and strategy development that subsequently were both discussed and presented to the whole GTA. Within the consultation process, a failed attempt to revise and amend the Water Act took place. It is not clear what reasons were behind the non-approval of the proposed amendments of the Law. Some interviewees mentioned disagreements about the allocation of responsibilities among different ministries as a possible reason, particularly between the increasingly powerful Ministry of Natural Resources and Energy and the Ministry of Public Works and Housing. On top of the revisited Policy and Strategy a much more elaborate and specific World Bank country WRM strategy was published which attached funds and projects/programmes to Mozambique's stated ambitions. If the renewed NWP and the Strategy outlined the principles in WRM, the World Bank country strategy set the agenda by defining the priority areas of investment for the bank and the donors (World Bank, 2007).

Approved in 2007, the Regulations on Water Licenses and Concessions set the basis for achieving financial sustainability on the part of the ARAs. Together with the 1991 Act, the document sets the framework for water rights in Mozambique including the procedures regarding the granting of water rights, in the form of

3 Interview by Rossella Alba with a senior consultant, Maputo, Mozambique, June 2013.

a licence or a concession, and the collection of water taxes. Over time, more and more staff and energy have been devoted at river basin level to the establishment of decentralised administrations, passing of licences and collection of tariffs. During the 2000s, the last regional water authority was formally created (ARA-Norte in 2006), while several river basin committees were set up (Inguane, 2010). The operational decentralisation of water resources management and the financial autonomy of Regional Water Administrations received great attention from the GoM and from the ARAs themselves. In order to improve fee collection, within the ARA-Sul several measures were undertaken including the development of a business plan, the creation of a commercial department and the amendment of a new bulk water tariff for the southern region. Rules and regulations were translated in local practices giving rise to new experiments that fit local contexts. Insights from Limpopo and Pungwe river basins presented in the next section provide some examples of the articulation of water rights and stakeholder participation on the ground.

This episode shows how IWRM ideas were further articulated within a new round of policy-making resulting in the introduction of several policy documents in 2007. The policy episode reveals the role of both State bureaucracies and consultancy companies in shaping the articulation of IWRM ideas While the creation of the GTA reinforced the consensus around the policy process by promoting dialogue among different institutions, we have limited knowledge on how the voices of different stakeholders have been incorporated in the policies. It has also become clear that IWRM policy discourse has become more influential in shaping policy regulations and strategies, if only because these are indirectly or directly supported by sector funding agreed with donor organisations.

Insights from the field: Water rights and stakeholder participation in Limpopo and Pungwe River basins

On the ground, policy ideas have been translated into several heterogeneous practices depending on local geographical and sociopolitical circumstances and the presence of international donors. In the Limpopo River Basin, the shift from central to decentralised water administrations, stakeholder participation and the introduction of payments for water, have been shaped by the number of users and the magnitude of their water use as well as their political importance both at national and local level (see Alba et al., this Book). In the Pungwe River 'laboratory', where events on the ground were heavily influenced by the Swedish-financed Pungwe River Basin Joint Water Resources Management and Development Strategy (RoM/RoZ/Sida, 2006), the lack of big water users, except for a sugar estate owned by a South African company and an urban water supply company (*Águas de Beira*) both located in the downstream end of the river, has resulted in a definite focus on hydrological dam studies and water development scenarios at the expense of an active engagement with stakeholders and their water management concerns (GoM/GoZ/Sida, 2005a, 2005b). We briefly review below the emergence of new water governance forms in the two basins.

The introduction of water permits and charges

Based on the Water Act (GoM, 1991) and the Regulation of Licensing and Concession (GoM, 2007c), all water uses should be registered in a cadastre and legal permits granted for private water uses. As soon as a user formally obtains a licence, he or she is required to pay for the volume of water abstracted. The process for obtaining a licence is rather long (taking up to one year) and bureaucratic. The user has to present several documents (i.e. information about the abstraction point and the technology used, the method for measuring the volume abstracted, a copy of the land right) and these need to be verified by the river basin authorities with a field visit. The length of the registration process is also due to the limited availability of human and financial resources at the disposal of ARAs. For instance, in early 2013 only two persons were in charge of registration of users within the whole Limpopo River Basin. In order to deal with these and other local challenges, water rights frameworks have been (or had to be) dovetailed.

In the Limpopo Basin, formal provisions in relation to water users' registration have been translated into two main local 'arrangements': Large-scale water users enjoy tailor-made agreements (memorandum); meanwhile, smallholder farmers scattered along the river banks have been organised into water users' groups represented by 'Focal Points' (see Alba et al., this Book). The memorandum represents the outcome of ad-hoc negotiations between the river basin management unit and large-scale agricultural users. For instance, HICEP, the agency managing the Chokwe Irrigation Scheme, negotiates a yearly memorandum with UGBL/ARA-Sul while in early 2013 negotiations were taking place between the regional water administration and the large-scale water user agency present in the downstream Baixo Limpopo, RBL-EP, and MAI, the commercial water user in the upstream end of the basin.

Water charges have also been recontextualised into local practices. Depending on the opportunities to actually measure the volume of water abstracted from the river, water charges are calculated in different ways. In the case of the Chokwe Irrigation Scheme water charges are calculated according to the volume of water abstracted (with a discount of 40% on the official water rate). This is due to the physical feature of the irrigation scheme, namely the presence of one intake that allows for volume measurements. Instead, given the high transaction costs involved with measurement of the volumes of water abstracted and the physical difficulties in calculating the volume, the water charges in the case of the smallholder users are calculated in relation to the area cultivated.[4] Local farmers representing their neighbours, so-called Focal Points, are in charge of both establishing the amount of land cultivated by each user and collecting the fees, in exchange for keeping part of the collected fees as reward (Alba et al., this Book).

In the Pungwe River Basin, the matter of water use licences became an issue for ARA-Centro (Administração Regional de Águas do Centro) only as a result

4 In 2013, a flat fee was charged per hectare. Depending on the location of the land in the Limpopo River Basin either 12,000 m^3 (upper part) or 21,500 m^3 (middle and lower part) of water were assumed to be used per hectare (the difference reflects climatological variation as calculated in crop water requirements, see Alba, 2013: 54).

of the IWRM project's attempts to mobilise and register actual water use stakeholders in the river basin. Hence, what started in March 2003 as a stakeholder 'mobilisation' exercise to shape and articulate stakeholder participation in IWRM soon turned into an opportunity to "increase the number of water use licences" (GoM/GoZ/Sida, 2005a: 3-2).This motive for stakeholder participation, viz. providing a source for cost recovery of ARA-Centro, soon became the overriding legitimation for stakeholder engagement, besides the initial claims that stakeholder participation formed a 'building block' of IWRM and that such participation was "of paramount importance" as "input to the work of the Consultants, and in order to get feedback on certain issues" related to scenario and strategy development (GoM/GoZ/Sida, 2005a: 2-1).

The outcome of five stakeholder mobilisation workshops held at administrative district level in 2003-2004 was the realisation that: (1) users were not aware of the need to have water permits, partly because the Water Act was unknown; (2) the procedure to get a water permit should be simplified and accessible at district level (rather than only at the ARA-Centro office in Beira); (3) stakeholder participation had to be organised per subbasin rather than per administrative unit; and that (4) a limited number of local actors, named 'elementos', were key in establishing effective links between the multitude of water users and the ARA-Centro office (GoM/GoZ/Sida, 2005a, annexes on stakeholder mobilisation workshops). These 'elementos' can be seen as precursors of the 'Focal Points' that were later instituted in the Limpopo.

Ultimately, the outcomes with regard to water permits and cost recovery were not very different in the Pungwe River Basin from those observed later in the Limpopo River Basin. It was basically a 'game of overwhelming numbers' whereby the transaction costs of charging a multitude of smallholder users exceeded the administrative costs and potential rewards of registration. By July 2004, only 90 stakeholders had been registered while another 44 had been identified, making up a total of 134 stakeholders in a river basin the size of the Netherlands (GoM/GoZ/Sida, 2005a: 3-7). A study to identify existing smallholder irrigation schemes in seven districts in central Mozambique, of which five fall in the Pungwe River Basin, found a total of over 10,000 ha under irrigation in at least 320 different systems (Beekman, 2011; Beekman et al., 2014). In 2005, a staff member of ARA-Centro indicated that rather than registering and charging each and every smallholder user, the stakeholder registration liaison officer would limit his scope to the few big water users in the Pungwe River, who signed annual agreements on monthly water payments (at discounted fees) irrespective of their actual (volumetric) water use.[5] It is unclear whether the collection of water fees from smallholder water users through Focal Points, as instituted in the Limpopo recently, is presently also rolled out for the Pungwe River Basin, particularly in the wake of the renewed emphasis since 2007 on fee collection.

Decentralization and stakeholder participation

In the Pungwe Basin, the Swedish-funded IWRM project initially made a substantive effort to shape and articulate stakeholder participation, which the project

5 Interview with staff member of ARA-Centro by Alex Bolding, Beira, 27 September 2005.

considered weak and limited in Mozambique when compared to the role accorded to stakeholders in Zimbabwe's National Water Authority (ZINWA) and Catchment Councils. It was observed that stakeholders in Mozambique, united in the Basin Committee, only played an advisory role in decision-making processes that were the prerogative of ARAs and other government agencies. Also, stakeholders played only a limited role on the management boards of ARAs, according to the 1991 Water Act. In a bold move, the Pungwe Basin Committee was constituted in July 2004 as an integral part of ARA-Centro, whereas the constitution of the latter agency was only formally approved in August 2004 (after its legal creation by Ministerial Decree in 1997!) (GoM/GoZ/Sida, 2005a: 3-14). The internal regulations of the Pungwe Basin Committee were primed on existing regulations for basin committees that were already operational under the wings of ARA-Sul with one crucial difference – the operational costs of the Pungwe Basin Committee (PBC) would be borne by ARA-Centro.[6] Rather than electing the 18 stakeholder representative members of the Pungwe Basin Committee (together with one representative of ARA-Centro), it was decided to have them appointed by ARA-Centro, because it was a function of the PBC to 'give voice' to stakeholders rather than 'giving a vote'. The latter was not considered in accordance with the Water Law's stipulations on stakeholder participation (GoM/GoZ/Sida, 2005a: 3-15, 3-16).

In the Limpopo Basin, the introduction of stakeholder participation reflects local circumstances and power relations where a seat in the River Basin Committee is guaranteed to all large-scale water users and only one member of the Committee represents hundreds of smallholder farmers (Praagman, 2013). Furthermore, representatives of smallholder users' groups (Focal Points) have not been invited to attend meetings of the basin committee, since they are only a "tool in establishing a payment system for water use" according to the chairman of the Limpopo Basin Committee (Praagman, 2013: 69).

Both the Pungwe and Limpopo Basin Committees function as a purely advisory and consultative body to "optimise the water use in the basin, minimise damages and conserve the environmental balance in the basin" (GoM/GoZ/Sida, 2005a: 3-16). The Pungwe Basin Committee met twice a year, on average (with the exception of the 2007-2008 period) and the issues discussed at their meetings were often of an informative nature (flood warning) or to do with information needs of ARA-Centro with regard to new infrastructural developments. The topics discussed at the twice annual meetings of the Limpopo Basin Committee are also mostly of an informative nature to do with weather forecasts, basin hydrology, finances and water tariffs. Furthermore, future large-scale agricultural developments of the basin are only presented to the members of the committee who have no decision-making power in this respect. This is the case of Massingir Agro-Industrial (MAI) who at the time of the research planned to abstract 682 million m3/year water for irrigating a large sugar cane estate in the upstream

6 This promise proved conditional, as was borne out by the fact that funds for organising meetings of the Pungwe Basin Committee ran out when the IWRM project was negotiating a second phase and its funding dried up for two years. During those years (2007-2008) no Basin Committee meetings were held, emphasising the donor-pushed nature of this element of water governance.

end of the basin (see Alba et al., Chapter 10). Van der Zaag et al. (2010) have demonstrated that such a large water concession may seriously impair the existing water use by downstream irrigators in Chokwe and Baixo Limpopo. However, the potential negative impact on water access for downstream water users was only partly discussed during the Committee's meetings. The MAI representative later commented that his presentation in the meeting was only for the benefit of future relations with other stakeholders, and not to solicit their approval for the water concession, which in his view was a matter for decision-makers at the highest level only (Praagman, 2013: 70).[7]

These local arrangements represent different 'translations' of the policy into practices. They offer an example of how policy ideas are transformed in the day-to-day management of water resources. The articulation of the policy into practices seems, in the end, influenced by local circumstances and the action of local policy actors. Both users and water authorities with their interests and concerns contribute to the creation of a particular 'local' version of the policy process. Equally indicative of the influence of previously existing cultures of governance is the concentration of decision-making power in the hands of a small policy elite, who jointly with big investors and large-scale (foreign) water users, decide on the allocation and distribution of the 'water cake'. The way stakeholder participation has been shaped in both the Pungwe and Limpopo policy 'laboratories' bears a heavy imprint of previously existing Portuguese centralised and authoritarian forms of governance, where legally recognised authorities jointly with corporate business make decisions on behalf of the masses of 'beneficiaries', reviving romantic notions associated with the Salazar-coined Estado Novo.

Discussion and conclusions

Even though ideas concerning river basin management, decentralisation and demand-management were present in Mozambique before the 1990s making it a case of Integrated Water Resources Management (IWRM) 'avant la lettre', IWRM as a policy package was endorsed only with the 1995 National Water Policy. The key policy ideas associated with IWRM such as volumetric water pricing, stakeholder participation and decentralisation had to be dovetailed with the existing legal framework and institutional organisations introduced by the Water Act to the extent that they often seem grossly at odds with it. For instance, whereas in the Water Act it is stated that the State plays a key role in water supply and management, in the Water Policy that same State will withdraw from any involvement in the provision of water. According to the Policy, the State and its organs should be reduced to an agency that sets priorities and acts as a policy regulator and monitor, determining minimum levels of service, and promoting private-sector involvement. This very shift in the role of the State from being the key development agency to a mere regulator, reflects an evolution of national policies in line with the simultaneous transformation of the dominant party FRELIMO from a socialist- to a capitalist-oriented movement. The contradiction between the Act and subsequent Policies has remained intact, because no new water legislation

7 Ultimately the water concession for MAI was approved by ARA-Sul. In July 2016, the MAI project was at a standstill (email communication, R. Ducrot, 10.08.2016).

has been passed since 1991 (i.e. since the introduction of multiparty elections in 1994).

Furthermore, the shift from central to decentralised water resources management was built upon the early post-colonial efforts in river basin planning as well as upon existing institutions and institutional formats. The decentralisation process led to the creation of tailor-made institutions in the Mozambican water sector, the regional water administrations, dealing with water resources management from a position between the central State and the river basin. At the lower policy level, management units and river basin committees were created. Nevertheless, the newly created decentralised administrations have been endowed with only limited decision-making power and financial autonomy. This politics of decentralisation has resulted in a limited mandate of the river basin units and committees: managerial for the former and consultative for the latter.

The articulation of IWRM ideas did not follow one linear path, but passed through different rounds of policy-making illustrated by the four episodes: 1) emergence; 2) international influences; 3) neoliberal transformation; and 4) donor-funded promotion and acceleration of implementation. The analytical framework proposed in this chapter and by the Flow and Practices project as a whole (see the Introduction), centring around the concepts of policy package, articulation and networks, allows the unpacking of the key drivers and elements responsible for the translation of the idea of IWRM into a number of concrete practices of water management on the ground, though one may wonder who, and at which point in time, made the crucial translation from Dublin principle into the practice on the ground. Of importance to the Mozambican case were the, often donor-funded, policy experiments in the Incomati, Limpopo and Pungwe river basins. Three main features of the policy process are discussed below: the encounter between the domestic political agenda and international one; the tensions between policies and practices; and the role of national champions in translating IWRM ideas and historical patterns that shaped the unfolding of IWRM in Mozambique.

First a considerable domestic Mozambican agenda informed the formulation of the Lei de Águas (1991). The Water Act represented the culmination of Mozambican efforts to deal with its antagonistic upstream neighbour South Africa, and the new forms of cooperation in the water field which had evolved in the Incomati River Basin informed by international experiences (e.g. TVA). The emphasis on drinking water supply and the promotion of private participation in the 1995 National Water Policy also reflects the priorities of the government at the time (e.g. addressing the huge water supply problems in the aftermath of the devastating civil war) and the requests of the World Bank/IMF. The introduction of volumetric water pricing responded to national concerns in relation to the financial sustainability of the envisaged Regional Water Administrations, rather than the global understanding of water as an economic good. The Mozambican concern was with cost recovery, not with economising the use of water according to market principles. The reference framework for water licensing remained the one included in the Water Act and the socialist imprint that characterised the wide definition of common use (primary water use) resisted, for a long time, the neoliberal transformations occurring in Mozambique.

Second, when the policies eventually reached the ground, they faced the complexities of the reality. Or better put, local water administrations dealing with the translation of the policies from documents into operational guidelines, had to face the local physical, economic and political difficulties. Then, the water bureaucrats working at the lower policy level, who Lipsky (2010) calls street-level bureaucrats, turned into key policy actors. In close interaction with the users, they reformulated the policy while translating it. Hence, the emergence in the Pungwe Basin of the so-called '*elementos*': key local actors who could act as intermediaries between actual water users and ARA-Centro. These were again later transformed into the Focal Points, collecting water fees from fellow water users, in the Limpopo River Basin (Alba et al., Chapter 10).

Third, a rather small network of Mozambican policy actors were involved in the above policy episodes. They were partly trained in Delft and Wageningen, the Netherlands, and were exposed to some extent to prevalent international policy ideas emanating from the Dublin and Rio conferences. The Dutch can be said to have played a large role in the training and support of this closely knit Mozambican policy elite through university programmes, cooperantes networks and international aid. For instance, in 2006, the Netherlands contributed 13% of the total ODA funds disbursed to the Mozambican water sector, less than the African Development Bank (with 40%) and the World Bank (with 35%), but more than the rest of all bilateral donors together (van Woersem et al., 2007: 16). This emerging water elite over time spread its wings, rotating offices of important State institutions in the water sector and at the Eduardo Mondlane University, whilst diversifying into consultancy companies making use of the burgeoning bilateral aid networks affiliating themselves with the water sector. This reveals a rather exclusive policy process where the 'power to define' (Shore and Wright, 1997) the content and the terms of reference of the water reforms is concentrated in the hands of a few well-positioned and well-connected actors.

Eventually, the study points at some historical patterns, influences and manifestations in the shaping of the water reforms. Firstly, the massive investment in hydraulic infrastructure of the Portuguese in the late colonial period (1960s, early 1970s) was accompanied by the crafting of heavily centralised, yet autonomous, regulating and managing institutions which eventually provided the institutional template for the crafting of ARAs. Secondly, the development and management of water resources constituted a key political terrain for the post-colonial State 'hydraulic mission' (e.g. the Limpopo Valley was defined as the 'breadbasket of the nation') and provided for the affirmation of Mozambique political influence within the SADC. Ultimately, the Portuguese tendency to establish top-down, hierarchically structured, and highly centralised, State-affiliated managing agencies has partly continued to the present day supported by current Mozambican governments. This is revealed by the weak forms of stakeholder participation and the discriminatory treatment of users in relation to distribution of water licences and water pricing in the Limpopo River Basin. This State authoritarian tendency has left Mozambique with little experience on how to set up a responsive, accountable, democratic and representative management agency.

Acknowledgements

The chapter draws on research from a Norwegian Research Council – funded project, Flows and Practices: The Politics of Integrated Water Resource Management (IWRM) in Africa. We would like to thank two internal reviewers (Emmanuel Manzungu and Jeremy Allouche) and three anonymous reviewers for their sincere and constructive criticism. We acknowledge support by the German Federal Ministry of Education and Research (BMBF) through project 01LN1316A.

References

Alba, R. 2013. Travelling with IWRM. The articulation of water permits and payments for water in policies and practices in Limpopo river basin, Mozambique. MSc thesis. Wageningen University, Wageningen, The Netherlands.

Alexander, J. 1997. The local state in post-war Mozambique: Political practice and ideas about authority. *Africa* 67(01): 1-26.

Beekman, P.W. 2011. Identification of the irrigation potential for smallholder horticulture in the uplands of Manica and Sofala provinces. PROIRRI Report. Maputo: Direcção Nacional de Água.

Beekman, P.W.; Veldwisch, G.J. and A. Bolding, 2014. Identifying the potential for irrigation development in Mozambique: Capitalizing on the drivers behind farmer-led irrigation expansion. *Physics and Chemistry of the Earth* Parts A/B/C 76-78: 54-63.

Biswas, A.K. 2004. Integrated water resources management: A reassessment. *Water International* 29(2): 248-256.

Bolding, A. 2004. In hot water. A study on intervention models and practices of water use in small-holder agriculture, Nyanyadzi catchment, Zimbabwe. PhD thesis. Wageningen University, Wageningen, The Netherlands.

Bolding, A. and Alba, R. 2013. 'IWRM 'avant la lettre'? Four key episodes in the policy articulation of IWRM in the downstream nation of Mozambique', conference proceeding, 14th WaterNet/WARFSA/GWP-SA Symposium 30th October-1st November, Dar es Salaam, Tanzania.

Caponera, D. 1983. Report to the Government of the People's Republic of Mozambique on Water Resources Policy, Administration and Legislation. Project 'National and International Water Law Consultancy'. Rome: FAO.

Carmo Vaz, A. 2003. Breve retrospectiva sobre a gestão da água em Moçambique. In Proceeding of SILUSBA – Simpósio de Hidráulica e Recursos Hídricos dos Países de Língua Portuguesa, pp. 59-75. Cabo Verde, 10-13 November.

Carmo Vaz, A. and Lopes Pereira, A. 2000. The Incomati and Limpopo international river basins: A view from downstream. *Water Policy* 2(1): 99-112.

Coppel, G.P. and Schwartz, K. 2011. Water operator partnerships as a model to achieve the Millenium Development Goals for water supply? Lessons from four cities in Mozambique. *Water SA* 37(4): 575-584.

DNA (Direcção Nacional de Água, in English National Directorate of Water). 1984. Panel on water resource Management with special reference to problems of Mozambique, Final Report. Maputo.

Ducrot, R. 2011. Land and water governance and pro poor mechanisms in the Mozambican part of the Limpopo basin: Baseline study. Working document, CGIAR (Consultative Group for International Agricultural Research). Challenge Programme on Water and Food. Maputo, IWEGA.

Gallego-Ayala, J. and Juízo, D. 2011. Strategic implementation of integrated water resources management in Mozambique: An A'WOT analysis. *Physics and Chemistry of the Earth, Parts A/B/C* 36(14): 1103-1111.

Gallego-Ayala, J. and Juízo, D. 2012. Performance evaluation of River Basin Organizations to implement integrated water resources management using composite indexes. *Physics and Chemistry of the Earth*, Parts A/B/C 50-52: 205-216.

GoM (Government of Mozambique). 1991. Lei de Águas (Water Law). Law No. 16/91 of August 3.

GoM. 1995. Política Nacional de Águas (National Water Policy). Resolution No. 7/95 of August 8.

GoM. 1998. Política1 tarifária de Água (Water Tariff Policy). Resolution No. 60/98 of December 23.

GoM. 2007a. Política de Águas (Water Policy). Decree No. 46/2007, of October 30.

GoM. 2007b. Estratégia nacional de gestão de recursos hídricos (National Water Resources Management Strategy).

GoM. 2007c. Regulamento de Licenças e Concessões (Regulations on Water Licenses and Concessions). Decree No. 43/2007, of October 30.

GoM/GoZ/Sida (Government of Mozambique, Government of the Republic of Zimbabwe and Sida). 2005a. Development of the Pungue River Basin joint integrated water resources management strategy. Phase 2, Pungwe river basin development scenario, Volume 2, Report on the activities of the stakeholder component February 2002-April 2005. Beira, Mozambique: Sweco in association with ICWS, SMHI, Opto, NCG, Consultec, UCM-Beira, InterConsult.

GoM/GoZ/Sida (Government of Mozambique, Government of the Republic of Zimbabwe and Sida). 2005b. Development of the Pungue River Basin joint integrated water resources management strategy. Phase 2, Pungwe river basin development scenario, Volume 3, Technical report. Beira, Mozambique: Sweco in association with ICWS, SMHI, Opto, NCG, Consultec, UCM-Beira, InterConsult.

Hall, S. 1996. On postmodernism and articulation: An interview with Stuart Hall (edited by Lawrence Grossberg). In Morley, D. and Chen, K.-H. (Eds), Stuart Hall: Critical Dialogues in Cultural Studies, pp. 131-50. London: Routledge.

Hanlon, J. 2010. Mozambique: The war ended 17 years ago, but we are still poor. *Conflict, Security & Development* 10(1): 77-102.

Hanlon, J. and Smart, T. 2008. *Do bicycles equal development in Mozambique*? UK: James Currey.

Inguane, R. 2010. Political, institutional and economic factors constraining the performance of decentralized water management in Mozambique: From the major perspective of government water functions. MSc thesis. University of Queensland, Brisbane, Australia.

Inguane, R.; Gallego-Ayala, J. and Juízo, D. 2014. Decentralized water resources management in Mozambique: Challenges of implementation at river basin level. *Phys-*

ics and Chemistry of the Earth, Parts A/B/C 67: 214-225.

Jønch-Clausen, T. 2004. Integrated water resources management (IWRM) and water efficiency plans by 2005: Why, what and how. Sweden: Global Water Partnership (GWP). Technical Committee.

Latour, B. 1987. *Science in action. How to follow scientists and engineers through society.* Cambridge, Massachusetts: Harvard University Press.

Law, J. 2009. Actor network theory and material semiotics. In *The new Blackwell companion to social theory*, pp. 141-158. London, Blackwell Publishing.

Li, T. 2000. Articulating indigenous identity in Indonesia: Resource politics and the tribal slot. *Comparative Studies in Society and History* 42(01): 149-179.

Lipsky, M. 2010. *Street-level bureaucracy: Dilemmas of the individual in public services.* New York: Russell Sage Foundation.

Long, N. and van der Ploeg, J.D. 1989. Demythologizing planned intervention: An actor perspective. *Sociologia Ruralis* 29(3-4): 226-249.

Mamdani, M. 1996. *Citizen and subject: Contemporary Africa and the legacy of late colonialism.* Princeton: Princeton University Press.

Manjate, C. 2010. Analysis of water and related laws in Mozambique. In van der Zaag, P. (Ed), What role of law in promoting and protecting the productive use of water by small-holder farmers in Mozambique?, pp. 9-29. Unpublished report of the Water rights in informal economies project (CP66), Challenge Programme for Water and Food, Pretoria, South Africa: International Water Management Institute.

Mehta, L. and Movik, S. 2014. *Flows and Practices: Integrated Water Resources Management (IWRM) in African Contexts.* IDS Working Paper No. 438. Brighton: Institute of Development Studies.

Mehta, L.; Alba, R.; Bolding, A.; Denby, K.; Derman, B.; Hove, T.; Manzungu E.; Movik, S.; Prabhakaran, P. and van Koppen, B. 2014. The politics of IWRM in Southern Africa. *International Journal of Water Resources Development* 30(3): 528-542.

Miller, B.A. and Reidinger, R.B. 1998. *Comprehensive river basin development. The Tennessee Valley Authority.* World Bank Technical Paper No. 416. Washington, D.C: World Bank.

Mollinga, P.P.M. 2001, Water and politics: Levels, rational choice and South Indian canal irrigation. *Futures* 33: 733-752.

Mollinga, P.P.M. 2008. Water, politics and development: Framing a political sociology of water resources management. *Water Alternatives* 1(1): 7-23.

Mosse, D., 2004. Is good policy unimplementable? Reflections on the ethnography of aid policy and practice. *Development and Change* 35(4): 639-671.

Mukhtarov, F. 2009. The hegemony of integrated water resources management: A study of policy translation in England, Turkey and Kazakhstan. PhD thesis. Central European University, Budapest.

Nader, L. 1972. Up the anthropologist: Perspectives gained from studying up. *Reinventing Anthropology* 1972: 284-311.

Pitcher, M.A. 2002. *Transforming Mozambique. The politics of privatization, 1975-2000.* New YorK: USA: Cambridge University Press.

Praagman, E. 2013. The political arenas of water management in the Limpopo basin,

Mozambique. Stakeholder participation at different policy levels. MSc thesis. Wageningen University, Wageningen, The Netherlands.

RoM/RoZ/Sida (Republic of Mozambique, Republic of Zimbabwe, and Sida). 2006. Pungwe river basin joint integrated water resources management and development strategy. Part 1 – The Strategy.

Serra, C.M. 2011. Colectânea de Legislação de Águas. Maputo: Ministério da Justiça, Centro de Formação Jurídica e Judiciária.

Shore, C. and Wright, S. 1997. *Anthropology of policy: Critical perspectives on governance and power.* London: Routledge.

Solanes, M. 1989. Report on a mission to Mozambique. New York: United Nations.

Swatuk, L.A. 2002. The new water architecture in southern Africa: Reflections on current trends in the light of 'Rio+ 10'. *International Affairs* 78(3): 507-530.

van der Zaag, P. 2010. What role of law in promoting and protecting the productive uses of water by smallholder farmers in Mozambique? Unpublished report of the Water rights in informal economies project (CP66), Challenge Programme for Water and Food. UNESCO-IHE Institute for Water Education, and Water Resources Section, Delft University of Technology. Delft, The Netherlands.

van der Zaag, P. and Carmo Vaz, A. 2003. Sharing the Incomati waters: Cooperation and competition in the balance. *Water Policy* 5(4): 349-368.

van der Zaag, P. and Bolding, A. 2009. Water governance in the Pungwe river basin: Institutional limits to the upscaling of hydraulic infrastructure. In Swatuk, L.A. and Wirkus, L. (Eds), *Transboundary water governance in Southern Africa. Examining underexplored dimensions*, pp. 163-78. Nomos Verlaggesellschaft, Baden-Baden.

van der Zaag, P.; Juizo, D.; Vilanculos, A.; Bolding, A. and Post Uiterweer, N. 2010. Does the Limpopo river basin have sufficient water for massive irrigation development in the plains of Mozambique? *Physics and Chemistry of the Earth* 35(13): 832-837.

van Woersem, B.; Zijlstra, P.J. and Juizo, D. 2007. Country report Mozambique. Draft report submitted for comments to the Royal Netherlands Embassy in Maputo, Mozambique.

Veldwisch, G.J.; Beekman, W. and Bolding, A. 2013. Smallholder irrigators, water rights and investments in agriculture: Three cases from rural Mozambique. *Water Alternatives* 6(1): 125-141.

WaterGroup. 1988. The Mozambican water sector. Priorities for recruitment of ex-patriates by Netherlands non-governmental organizations EMS, DOG and PSO.

Wedel, J.R. 2001. *Collision and collusion: The strange case of western aid to Eastern Europe.* New York: Palgrave.

Wedel, J.R.; Shore, C.; Feldman, G. and Lathrop, S. 2005. Toward an anthropology of public policy. *The Annals of the American Academy of Political and Social Science* 600(1): 30-51.

West, H.G. 1997. Creative destruction and sorcery of construction: Power, hope and suspicion in post-war Mozambique. *PoLAR: Political and Legal Anthropology Review* 20(1): 13-31.

Wester, P. 2008. Shedding the waters: Institutional change and water control in the

Lerma-Chapala Basin, Mexico. PhD thesis. Wageningen University, Wageningen, the Netherlands.

World Bank. 2007. *Making the water work for sustainable growth and poverty reduction. Mozambique Country Water Resources Assistance Strategy 2008-2011*. Washington, DC: World Bank.

10

The Politics of Water Payments and Stakeholder Participation in the Limpopo River Basin, Mozambique[1]

Rossella Alba

Alex Bolding

Raphaëlle Ducrot

ABSTRACT: Drawing from the experience of the Limpopo River Basin in Mozambique, the chapter analyses the articulation of a water rights framework in the context of decentralised river basin governance and IWRM-inspired reforms. The nexus between financial autonomy, service provision, stakeholder participation and the resultant allocation of water within the river basin is explored by scrutinising the newly instituted system of water permits and payments. Three cases are examined: (1) parastatal agencies managing large perimeters of irrigated land; (2) large-scale commercial companies irrigating land; and (3) so-called focal points representing groups of smallholder irrigators. The three presented cases show that structural challenges, local geographies and power relations shape the final outcome of water reforms in relation to decentralised river basin management, stakeholders' participation and accountability. Rather than improving accountability to users and securing the financial basis for sustainable infrastructure operation and maintenance, the permit system in place reinforces existing inequalities.

KEYWORDS: IWRM, policy articulation, elite, water permits, stakeholder participation, Mozambique

INTRODUCTION

Since the endorsement of the Water Act (GoM, 1991), the Mozambican water sector has experienced great transformations. Water reforms followed and partly anticipated the emergence of Integrated Water Resources Management (IWRM) as a dominant paradigm in the management of water resources (Mehta et al.,

1 First published in *Water Alternatives* 9(3): 571-589.

2014; Alba and Bolding, this book).2 The river basin became the unit for water resources management substituting existing administrative divisions, followed by the decentralisation of decision-making to river basin authorities and creation of new arenas for stakeholder participation, the river basin committees (Inguane et al., 2014). Since the mid-1990s, 13 river basins have been defined following the watershed features: five Regional Water Administrations (ARAs, Administrações Regionais de Águas) were established while river basin committees (CB, Comité de Bacía) were introduced in most of the basins. Secondly, private forms of management and market-based policies were initiated, substituting for publicly managed entities.

Drawing from the experience of the Limpopo River Basin in Mozambique, this chapter describes and analyses the challenges, opportunities and local innovations related with the introduction of formal water rights systems within the Mozambican part of the river basin. While the Mozambican articulation of IWRM-inspired reforms is analysed in the chapter by Alba and Bolding, here we concentrate on the introduction of water permits and payments for water within the Limpopo River Basin. We are particularly interested in the nexus between newly established forms of financial autonomy, service provision, stakeholder participation and the resultant allocation of water within the river basin.

In Mozambique, as in many other African countries, the introduction of a formal water rights framework (*direito de uso e aproveitamento de água*, in English: Right to use and exploit water) went hand in hand with the introduction of payments for abstracting water that (should) finance the provision of services from the Regional Water Administrations including the management of hydraulic infrastructure (e.g. dams). The basic mantra informing these new policies emphasises the beneficial effects of 'less State, more market and more users' involvement in water governance. The promise of such a move lies in substituting for lethargic, ineffective, cash-strapped public agencies with financially autonomous agencies supplying water in exchange for payment and downstream accountability. Through such a move one would shift accountability relations from predominantly upward accountability to the State treasury towards downward accountability and service provision for paying water users. Hence, in theory, the water agency becomes oriented not so much to the National Treasury but rather to the actual water users and the satisfaction of their needs in exchange for improved or even full cost recovery (see Small and Carruthers, 1991; for a critique, see Oorthuizen and Kloezen, 1995).

In theory, the newly introduced permit and payment system aims to achieve productive, equitable and sustainable use of scarce water resources. It hopes to do so by instituting a democratic and transparent mechanism of financial accountability and cost recovery. However, this chapter will show that in the case of the Mozambican part of the Limpopo River Basin, the introduction of permits,

2 For a discussion on the history and criticisms related to Integrated Water Resources Management and the conceptualisation of key elements of IWRM see the introduction to this book. For insights about the introduction of IWRM policies in Mozambique, see Gallego-Ayala and Juizo (2011, 2012) and Inguane et al. (2014).

water payments and participation in decision-making are not operating as envisaged in theory. Indeed, while large-scale water users secure their access to water by mobilising their resources (including political connections, licences and payments), small-scale users are largely ignored or are made to pay for water through the creation of so-called Focal Points, while not receiving vital services in return (see also van der Zaag et al., 2010). While IWRM as a policy concept provides the overall frame for scrutinising the interrelation between water payments and user participation in water governance, the chapter does not aim to assess how well IWRM was implemented in Mozambique; neither does it aim to compare its implementation in Mozambique with IWRM implementation in other countries.

In the remainder of this chapter we first explain the conceptual lens and applied methodology of the study, then present both the characteristics of the Mozambican part of Limpopo River Basin (water availability and use, main water users) and the key policy moves responsible for instituting a new water rights framework and its associated neo-liberal payment regime. Next we assess the new water allocation dispensation in practice by scrutinising how the Southern Region Water Administration (ARA-Sul, *Administração Regional de Águas do Sul*) has been issuing water permits and collecting fees from users located in the Limpopo Basin including (1) parastatal agencies managing large perimeters of irrigated land; (2) large-scale commercial companies irrigating land; and (3) the so-called focal points representing groups of smallholder irrigators. In the subsequent conclusion and discussion we point at the flaws in the financial autonomy model and propose alternative ways of administering water use(r)s, that are more user friendly and likely to be more effective in the Mozambican circumstances. The principles of the proposed alternatives may be equally relevant in other African river basins.

Conceptual framework

Water permits and payments

Permits refer to legal entitlements or formal authorisation issued by a state agency to a user, in the form of a licence or a concession formally recognising the user´s right to abstract a certain amount of water during a certain period of time from a source.[3] In theory, permits contribute to 'reserve' water for certain uses and make users' administratively visible as a licence formally recognises, not only the existence of a user but also her or his water requirements. Water permits introduce an administrative order mediating water and society, and in this way, they simplify the reality of the river basin and make it legible (Scott, 1998). The careful registration of permits offers an opportunity to account for the

3 In the case of Mozambique, two types of water permits exist: licence and concession. The main difference resides in the validity of the permit as the licence lasts for 5 years and then has to be renewed, while the concession lasts for 50 years (GoM, 1991). There is also a difference in application procedure, which reflects their order of magnitude – concessions being issued only in case of large abstractions (none were issued until the application by MAI in Massingir, described below in this chapter).

river discharge already committed and the water that remains available for future development/allocation within a river basin The underlying idea is that "a clear definition of who is entitled to use a certain amount of water, with the specification on when and where this is possible, will reduce uncertainty and conflicts" (Molle, 2004: 208). In neoliberal thinking, water permits are often regarded as a means for ensuring rational water use, helping to address water scarcity (Boelens and Zwarteveen, 2005).

Yet, holding a licence does not guarantee access to, and use of, water. In fact, legal permits are only one of the mechanisms of access to water resources (Ribot and Peluso, 2003). The authors also stress the importance of access to technology, capital, knowledge and authority. In the context of water rights, Boelens and Zwarteveen (2005) look at formal authorisation as one of the three dimensions constituting water rights and refer to technical infrastructure (i.e. dams, weirs gates, pumps, canal) and management tasks including decision-making processes and mobilisation of resources (i.e. money, social connections) as the other two. Furthermore, it is worth mentioning several issues that play a role in relation to allocation of water permits. First, power relations and the availability of economic resources influence users′ ability to obtain a permit and access water. Large-scale and better-off users can make use of their wealth of resources to secure access to water at the expense of other, less powerful, and less wealthy users (Franco et al., 2013). Second, in southern Africa as well as in other regions, there is a dual legal framework, *viz.* (informal) customary law systems that acknowledge, protect and legitimise water use at community level and State-backed civic and statutory law systems that are administered at national level. Official water permit systems typically work at national level and often override or mix-up customary rights. Thirdly, the institution of formal legal frameworks for water rights allocation has often been tied together with the introduction of forms of water payments such as (volumetric) water pricing (Van Koppen, 2003). Payments for water come in the form of a tax or fee over the volume of (raw) water abstracted from the river by one user or multiple users for productive uses (e.g. agricultural, industrial, drinking purposes). Registration, coupled with taxation, results in discouraging smallholder registration and keeping them 'invisible' and their uses not accounted for (Veldwisch et al., 2013). The latter may present a 'dangerous' side-effect when water that is already beneficially used by informal, invisible downstream users gets (re)issued to legally recognised upstream water users in the form of new permits (van der Zaag et al., 2010). In the section below, we further conceptualise the relation between permits and payments for water by scrutinising the relationship between financial autonomy and accountability.

Financial autonomy and accountability

The drive for reforming public agencies into semi-private, financially autonomous agencies originated from the irrigation sector in the 1980s. In that decade the debt crisis, which started with the first oil crisis in the early 1970s, came to a head: many nations in the South that relied heavily on irrigated production started to suffer from shortages of funds to both operate and maintain publicly managed irrigation schemes (see Oorthuizen and Bolding, 2010). As a result, production in these systems declined, which in turn negatively affected both government revenues derived from export crops and the willingness of farmers to pay more for their systems' upkeep. Hence, many publicly managed irrigation schemes entered a vicious cycle of decline, where poor upkeep resulted in poor service delivery (unreliable water distribution) and poor yields, which in turn affected the willingness of farmers to pay (ibid). To break this cycle several neo-liberal and neo-institutional policy recipes were tried, like the introduction of volumetric water payments, which proved difficult to implement in large-scale canal irrigation schemes (Repetto, 1986; Moore, 1989), and the transfer of irrigation management (also referred as IMT or Irrigation Management Transfer) to users through the establishment of Water User Associations and other forms of collective action (Wester, 2008; Ostrom, 1992). Drawing from the irrigation sector, we explain below how we conceptualise financial autonomy and how services, accountability and user participation are interlinked in theory.

Financial autonomy in the irrigation sector is defined as a condition where the water agency must rely on user fees for a significant portion of the resources used for operation and maintenance (O&M) including staff salaries, with the agency exercising expenditure control over the use of the funds generated from these charges (Small, 1990). In theory, in an environment of financial autonomy, irrigation performance will improve, compared to publicly managed irrigation systems, by both freeing the O&M budget from the constraints imposed by the central government's fiscal difficulties, and increasing the accountability of the irrigation system managers to the water users (Small and Carruthers, 1991).

Accountability is defined as the extent to which the performance of all managers and staff having responsibilities at different levels of an irrigation organisation is monitored and controlled by the water users (Uphoff et al., 1991). Financial autonomy improves the accountability of the agency to farmers, because it presumably transforms the position of farmers from mere water users into clients or consumers of services of the agency. Since the agency depends financially on fees collected from farmers, it has a clear stake in providing their clients with an efficient service (see Fig. 10.1). In other words, following the popular reasoning which says that 'one should not bite the hand that feeds you', financially autonomous agencies are stimulated to be accountable to their clients who want to get their money's worth. Such an agency can be expected to increase the amount of effort they put into O&M as it wishes to increase the farmers' capacity and willingness to pay fees. If fees are levied on an area basis, as is commonly done in the irrigation sector, this means that the agency has a strong vested interest in expanding the area receiving adequate irrigation service, increasing fee collection rates, and increasing farm incomes (Svendsen, 1993). Hence, financial autonomy provides strong incentives to the irrigation agency to improve the quality of its management of public systems.

Financial autonomy in theory also provides a strong incentive for cost-effective management. The agency's interest is to reduce costs to keep its budget in the black, while farmers like to keep the fees as low as possible. This mutual interest stimulates a greater efficiency in resource use and an economically rational division of tasks (Small and Carruthers, 1991).

Fig. 10. 1. Diagram depicting the relations in terms of finance and accountability between central government, bureaucracy (e.g. Regional Water Administration) and farmers.[4]

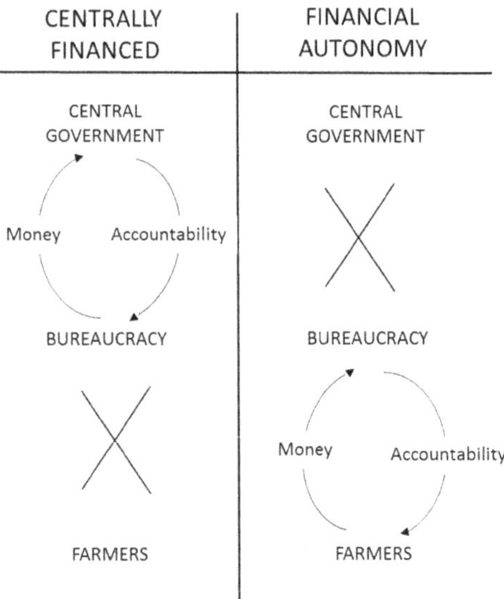

In itself, this 'money-based-farmer-empowerment-approach' is understandable and offers potential. However, increasing evidence shows that the beneficial effects of financial autonomy on State-water users relationships may not apply. In the Philippines the irrigation agency, the National Irrigation Administration (NIA), was reformed into a financially autonomous agency during the seventies. The results of this reform in terms of farmer empowerment and the quality of work of the irrigation bureaucracy are at best mixed. Oorthuizen (2003) has demonstrated that the reorientation of NIA from the central government financing to fee collection from farmers, seriously affected the performance of agency staff: they spent most of their time and effort on harassing farmers to pay their fees (which constituted a considerable part of their salaries) at the expense of actual water delivery or maintenance of the system. On the positive side, it is probably true that the withdrawal of State subsidies for irrigation management to NIA was one of the important contributing factors behind the 'transformation of the bureaucracy' into a more progressive and client-oriented agency (Bagadion, 1989). It stimulated the adoption of its widely praised participatory programme, in which farmers participate in construction activities as well as management. This indeed empowered farmers vis-à-vis the NIA in a few pilot areas (Illo, 1989), and may have had a positive impact on the overall management performance of the agency-managed systems (Svendsen, 1993; NIA, 1994). On the other hand,

4 Source: Oorthuizen and Bolding (2010)

it has been argued that the NIA's financial interests impeded the emergence of strong and viable farmer irrigators' organisations (Lauraya and Sala, 1994), and caused cuts in management expenditures which harmed the quality of irrigation management (Oorthuizen and Kloezen, 1995).

Attempts at improving irrigation management through the introduction of financial autonomy and accountability principles resonated with IWRM-inspired reforms dominating the water debate from the early 1990s onwards. Rather than the irrigation scheme, the river basin, the management of large-scale hydraulic infrastructure (in particular dams and weirs) and the presence of multiple users abstracting water directly from the river became the units of water rights reforms now aiming at improving water allocation between different uses and users while ensuring cost recovery. As van Koppen (2003) notes,

> *In the past, water rights were only well defined for localised systems such as irrigation systems, usually through a blend of customary and state law. Today, governments that declare themselves as the custodians of the nations' water resources are making the quantum jump from co-administering small schemes to regulating nothing less than the full hydrological cycle (pp. 1051).*

New legal frameworks for water rights allocation based on permits and licences were introduced in several sub-Saharan African countries and tied together with forms of payments. The notion of water as an economic good and emphasis on stakeholder participation as promoted by the Dublin Principles, further contributed to the introduction of demand-driven approaches based on financial autonomy, cost-recovery and market principles (World Bank, 1993; Savenije and van der Zaag 2002; Molle and Berkoff, 2007). In the case illustrated in the chapter, transposing the financial autonomy and accountability principles and mechanisms from the irrigation sector to water governance at river basin level ARA-Sul, as a financially autonomous institution, was supposed to maintain dams and supply water at the right place in the right amount at the right time, in exchange for a water fee that would cover its operating costs. Those water users that benefitted from water stored in infrastructure operated by ARA-Sul would pay for that water as soon as their water requirements exceeded that of *uso comum* (primary water use). However, how participation and decision-making come into this equation of financial accountability remains unclear, both in theory and in practice.

Methods

This chapter is based on a literature review, interviews and document analysis carried out in The Netherlands and Southern Mozambique between March and June 2013 (Alba, 2013). The research combined fieldwork research with an ethnographic method of engaging with policy actors called 'studying up' (Nader, 1972). The former included interviews and focus group discussions with representatives of large-scale users and smallholder ones abstracting water for agricultural use along Limpopo riverbanks. The latter, 'studying up', focused on the perspectives of the people who have influenced the policy process (i.e. the introduction of a legal framework for water rights) by setting the terms of reference and taking part in key events such as the drafting of the Water Act or the National Water Policies. Interviewees included senior and young engineers, consultants, lawyers, academics, staff of the National Water Directorate (DNA, *Direcção Nacional das Águas*) and employees of ARA-Sul.

Altogether 34 interviews were carried out by the main author of the chapter in English, Portuguese and the local *Changana* language (the latter with the help of a translator) and these were recorded as hand-written notes. In the case of smallholder users, interviews took place literally on their agricultural fields at their pump or intake points; in the case of large-scale users and policy-makers interviews were carried out in their offices in the city. Observations, analysis of the river basin cadastre (registry), and informal discussions during visits to the key hydraulic infrastructure in the Limpopo Basin (Massingir Dam, Macarretane weir and Chokwe intake) contributed to triangulate the findings. Extensive periods of fieldwork in the Limpopo River Basin and in the Pungwe River Basin of Mozambique by the two co-authors of the chapter provided background information (e.g. Ducrot, 2011).

The case study: Mozambique and Limpopo River Basin

In Mozambique, the Water Act (1991) established a formal framework for the allocation of water rights based on licences and payments for the use of bulk water. The Law differentiates between *usos comuns* and *usos privativos*. The former refers to water uses for primary needs such as domestic use, watering of livestock and irrigation of crops for plots up to one hectare (ha) without the use of siphoning or mechanical instruments. The latter concerns bulk water use for industry, agriculture and energy production. While common uses are free of charge and do not involve a licence, private ones require a licence (or concession, here also referred to as a permit) and are subjected to the payment of a *taxa de água,* in English: water tax (GoM, 1991). Regional Water Administrations are responsible for registering users, issuing water licences and the collection of fees. These activities are carried out partly within the River Basin Management Units (in Portuguese, *Unidades de Gestão de Bacía, UGB*), which are decentralised offices of the ARAs.

The Limpopo River flows through Botswana, South Africa and Zimbabwe before reaching Mozambique. In Mozambique it covers a length of 450 km over the 1460 km full length of the river (Ducrot, 2011). The main tributary river is the Elephant River that runs through South Africa and then reaches the Limpopo River in Mozambique. The Massingir Dam represents the main infrastructure used to store water and protect the lower Limpopo valley from floods. A second infrastructural work, Macarretane Weir, is positioned downstream of the confluence between the Elephant and the Limpopo to provide water to the irrigation scheme of Chokwe. As van der Zaag et al. (2010) highlight, great uncertainties exist pertaining to the availably and use of water within the river basin. This is due to uncertainties surrounding future water development in upstream countries, incomplete discharge measurements and paucity of information on the water that is currently consumed particularly for agricultural production and domestic uses.

The river offers a key source of livelihood for the communities scattered along the riverbanks, as it is the main source of water for irrigation, drinking and domestic uses (including livestock watering) and the only permanent body of water in the basin. Within the Mozambican part of the basin, most of the users abstract water for agricultural purposes, cultivating an area between four and 30 ha (van der Zaag et al., 2010). According to UGBL (*Unidade de Gestão de Bacía do Limpopo*, Limpopo River Basin Management Unit, in English) in 2013 there were around 280 registered users together with an indefinite number of so-called 'common users', but these numbers are subjected to annual fluctuations (Alba, 2013). The river is a source of water for two main irrigation schemes, located in Chokwe and in downstream Xai-Xai, respectively. Both schemes are characterised by a long history that dates back to the 1950s when they were designed for use by Portuguese settlers (Veldwisch, 2015). Recently, large-scale agro-industrial investments are emerging upstream of the Chokwe scheme (e.g. Agrisul, CAM). In 2011, the Mozambican government allocated about 37,000 ha of land directly downstream of Massingir Dam to MAI (*Massingir Agro-Industrial*) for sugar cane production that should start in 2017. When the project comes on steam, its projected water abstraction will have huge ramifications for water users downstream (van der Zaag et al., 2010).

Apart from the large water users, several smallholders and medium-size users populate the river basin. Since 2008, water users' groups, comprising mainly smallholder farmers, have been introduced into the river basin. Little information is available on the water users located along the main course of the Limpopo River flowing from Zimbabwe upstream of Macarretane weir. ARA-Sul has only started to register users in the areas of the basin where the flow of water is regularised by the presence of a dam (the Elephant River Basin downstream of Massingir) leaving out the areas that do not fall downstream of a dam (the main course of the Limpopo River upstream of the Macarretane Dam) as the irregularity of the water flow does not provide for them conditions to charge users. The Limpopo River also supplies drinking water needs for the two main cities in the basin, Chokwe and Xai-Xai.

Currently, water management follows a rather complex institutional framework where responsibilities are spread between several entities at regional, national and local levels. The scheme below shows the governance framework within the Mozambican part of the Limpopo River (Fig. 10. 2). At the regional level, SADC (Southern African Development Community) and LIMCOM (Limpopo Water Course Commission) play a role in influencing water management within the river basin. At the national level, the National Directorate of Water, within the Ministry of Public Works and Housing (MOPH, *Ministério das Obras Públicas e Habitação*), is responsible for overall water management and the implementation of the national water legislation and policies. ARA-Sul through its management unit (UGBL), manages water resources at the local level. UGBL is in charge of the management of the main infrastructure (dams and hydrometric and rainfall stations), the registration of water users, organisation of the cadastre and the collection of water fees. By managing the Massingir Dam and the Macarretane Weir, UGBL influences the quantity of water present in the river in relation to the water demand by the users. The Limpopo River Basin Committee (CBL, *Comité da Bacía do Limpopo*) serves as a consultative body for coordination between different users and institutions involved in land and water management in the river basin.

At the time of the research, the Comité was composed mainly of representatives of district administrations and large- and medium-scale agricultural users. Smallholder farmers were not directly members of the CBL but are represented by members of irrigation associations (who are not smallholder farmers themselves; see Praagman, 2013). However, even though the Committee has been set up in the name of stakeholder participation, it rather works as an information dissemination body (Praagman, 2013). The committee has the official title of advisory body to the director of UGBL, thus leaving little role for stakeholders in terms of decision-making power at the river basin level.

Fig. 10. 2. Water management in Limpopo Basin.[5]

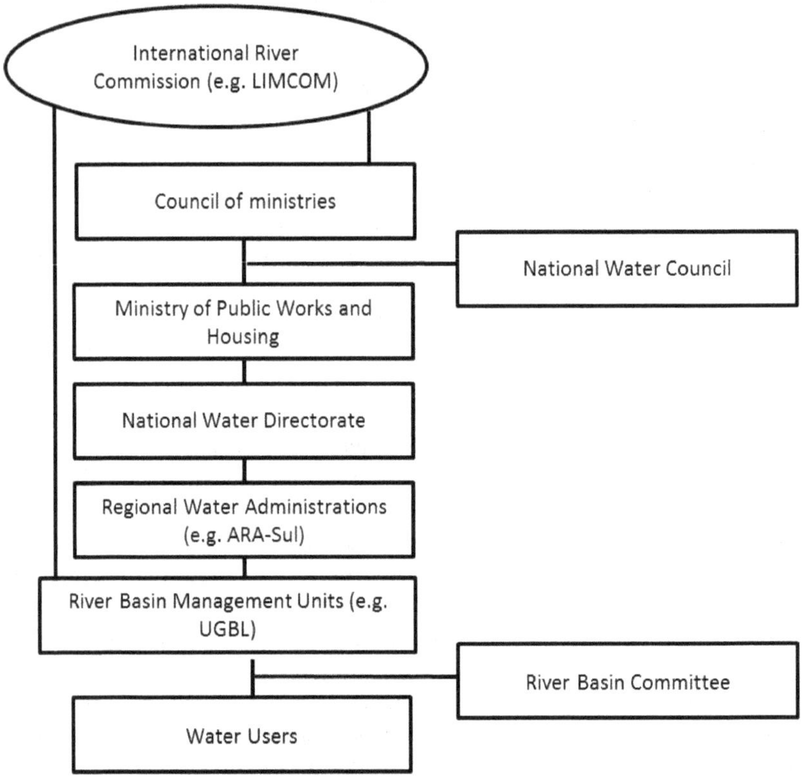

International River Commission (e.g. LIMCOM)
Council of ministries
National Water Council
Ministry of Public Works and Housing
National Water Directorate
Regional Water Administrations (e.g. ARA-Sul)
River Basin Management Units (e.g. UGBL)
River Basin Committee
Water Users

Experiments with water permits and payments

Since the late Portuguese Colonial days, the Limpopo Basin together with the Incomati and Umbeluzi basins, functioned as a catalyst for the management of water resources and the establishment of water-related administrations (Alba and Bolding, this book). Harnessing the hydraulic potential for agricultural production through the development of dams, irrigation schemes and other infrastruc-

5 Source: own elaboration, based on Ducrot, 2011.

ture, was a key concern of both colonial and post-colonial governments (Alba, 2013). Furthermore, the Portuguese have left their imprint in the way irrigation schemes have been managed in the basin involving partnerships between the State and private capital.

As mentioned in the previous section, the 1991 Water Act is the reference framework for water permits in Mozambique. Although few data were collected in relation to the articulation of water permits (Alba, 2013), their early introduction can be explained in light of two aims: water demand control and cost-recovery. First, while water supply was increasingly regulated through the construction of hydraulic infrastructure, the actual water demand was subject to high degrees of uncertainty. Water permits were introduced as a way for accounting for the existing water demand at the river basin level. This is relevant given the downstream position of Mozambique and the increasing competition over water at the international level. Second, water permits provided the basis for introducing water charges at the river basin level. Indeed, holding a permit was introduced as a prerequisite for payment.

An early experiment with the introduction of volumetric tariffs took place in Umbeluzi and Limpopo river basins in 1988 when the Ministry of Public Construction and Water approved a tax for the 'beneficiaries' of bulk water from Pequenos Limbombos and Massingir dams (Solanes, 1989). According to Manjate (2010), bulk tariffs were introduced as a way to cover maintenance costs of the dams through the income generated from the tariffs paid by those benefitting from the use of the water stored in the dams. A similar rationality lies behind the introduction of water charges for abstracting water envisaged in the Water Act (1991). Indeed, as Alba and Bolding (this book) further illustrate, water charges were introduced both as a cost-recovery mechanism and as a revenue generation exercise for the ARAs in light of the limited State finance to support new decentralised institutions. Cost-recovery represents also the guiding principle within the Water Tariff Policy (in Portuguese *Política Tarifaria de Aguas*) that was approved by the Council of Ministers in 1998 (GoM, 1998). Yet, according to the policy, the same water charges are deemed suitable to promote pollution control, environmental protection and efficient use of water resources. According to the Water Tariff Policy, users should pay for the water they consume, applying the so-called user-pays principle. At the same time, tariffs should guarantee access to basic water needs for the whole population. The Policy uses the terms *tarifa* or *taxa*, which in general refers to water charges for bulk water abstraction or for service delivery. The tariff is set according to the costs of water resources management in each river basin (e.g. administrative costs, infrastructure maintenance costs). According to the Water Tariff Policy the water fees represent the revenue of the Regional Water Authorities.

During the 2000s, the operational decentralisation of water resources management and the financial autonomy of water authorities received great attention from the GoM and the ARAs themselves. Once all ARAs were formally established, the focus shifted towards improving their financial autonomy both from the central State and from the donors, supporting their establishment, by improving their ability to collect fees from water users. Yet, until 2010, the ARAs, excluding ARA-Sul, had remained largely financially dependent on grants received from the central administration (MOPH and DNA). Inguane (2010) suggests that this financial dependence interfered negatively with their decision-making autonomy as "most of the RWAs' plans are indirectly approved by the central level in regard to what they have to do with the central-allocated budget" (ibid: 60, RWA stands for ARA in this quote). Secondly, the central government has the last word over water fees as the Council of Ministry, based on a proposal by the Regional Water Administration, approves the level of the fees. In this way, the central government maintains control over the setting of the water fees, limiting the decision-making power of the ARAs. This tension between financial autonomy and State decision-making was confirmed during interviews (Alba, 2013).

In order to improve fee collection, several measures were taken by ARA-Sul. In 2004, a Business Plan was drafted to improve the financial autonomy of ARA-Sul (GoM, 2004). The Business Plan refers to *'venda de agua bruta'* (in English, the sale of bulk water) and the concession of licences for water abstraction as one of the main ways to guarantee financial sustainability of the ARA and promote rational use of water (ibid: 3). In 2007, the commercial department of ARA-Sul was created and new bulk water tariffs were introduced for the southern region (Alba, 2013). The new tariff varies in each river basin within ARA-Sul depending on the cost for maintaining infrastructure and operational units. It also varies according to the use of water (e.g. agriculture, industry and drinking water). Since the approval of the bulk water tariff and the introduction of a regulation for licences and concessions, registration and fee collection have constituted two key activities of the local water administrations.

Post-2007 water allocation in Limpopo: Three cases

The Water Act of 1991 together with the Water Tariff Policy and the Regulations on Water Licences and Concessions (*Regulamento de Licenças e Concessões*), which were approved in October 2007, set the framework for water rights in Mozambique (GoM 2007a, 2007b). We highlight below how this regulatory framework has been articulated on the ground, drawing from three cases of fee collection in the Limpopo River Basin, each representing a different kind of user (parastatal, private companies, and smallholder irrigators). The data for these case studies were collected in 2008-2009 and 2013.

State versus State: Chokwe and Baixo-Limpopo irrigation schemes

In the Limpopo River Basin there are a few big water users. The two biggest are State enterprises under the Ministry of Agriculture: *Hidráulica de Chokwe – Empresa Publica (HICEP)* managing the Chokwe Irrigation Scheme and the *Regadio de Baixo Limpopo – Empresa Pública* (RBL-EP) managing the irrigation perimeter near Xai-Xai before the river discharges into the Indian Ocean. Due to their political importance and their linkages with the central government, these enterprises enjoy a special regime with regard to water licensing and fee collection. Both these enterprises are represented in the River Basin Committee.

HICEP was created in 1997 to manage the Chokwe Irrigation Scheme. With its 22,000 ha command area it is the largest and oldest irrigated perimeter in Mozambique offering space to commercial farming enterprises as well as smallholder and medium farmers (Pellizzoli, 2010). In 2012, nearly 12,000 farmers were occupying the scheme (Chilundo et al., 2012). However, in 2010 only 9400 ha were actually irrigated (van der Zaag et al., 2010) and during the hot season of 2011/2012 the area cultivated amounted to a mere 5781 ha (Chilundo et al., 2012). Since Independence, agricultural production in the Chokwe scheme has been decreasing together with the actual irrigated area (Veldwisch, 2015). The poor status of the infrastructure, salinisation, limited access to inputs (e.g. seeds and fertiliser), unreliable access to markets (few buyers, long distance) and lack of processing facilities represent some factors underlining the poor performance of the scheme (Veldwisch et al., 2013).

From the perspective of the UGBL, the scheme represents only one large-scale user that abstracts water from one single intake. From the intake at Macarretane, the water flows through the whole irrigation scheme and part of it returns to the river through the drainage system (Alba, 2013). Once a month, UGBL and HICEP staff meet at the intake and measure the water flow. Every three months an invoice is issued to HICEP based on the average measured water flow in the three previous months discounted by 40% (ibid). This arrangement has been introduced in order to facilitate the payment of the water charges by HICEP. Water requirements for the irrigation scheme for the whole year and the payment terms for the water charges are defined by HICEP and ARA-Sul/UGBL annually in a memorandum of understanding.

It is not clear if HICEP has ever paid for water. During interviews, several explanations for the inability of HICEP to pay were discussed (Alba, 2013). The most common explanation claims that the irrigation scheme does not 'use' the whole amount of water it takes. Due to the design of the infrastructure (gravity-led canals) a rather large amount of water is required to reach the last sector of the scheme (80 km away from the intake). However, not all that water is used for productive use, as the actually irrigated area covers less than 6000 ha. HICEP collects water fees only for the cultivated area, but it is charged by ARA-Sul for the total volume flowing through the main intake. Thus, HICEP is not able to pay ARA-Sul. Other interviewees referred to the unlikelihood that the State pays to the State. Indeed, HICEP is a State enterprise and UGBL/ARA-Sul are part of the State administration. However, the HICEP budget depends on the Ministry of Agriculture, while UGBL/ARA-Sul comes under the authority of the Ministry of Construction and Housing. Given the huge debt of HICEP towards ARA-Sul, since 2002 negotiations are taking place at ministerial level in order to find ways to settle the debt (GoM, 2004). By September 2008, the treasurer of HICEP admitted that they had incurred arrears on the ARA-Sul water bill to the tune of the equivalent of USD 2 million.[6]

The second state enterprise, RBL-EP, administers an area of 70,000 ha in the lower Limpopo including the Xai-Xai Irrigation Scheme. The scheme originally covered only an area of 12,000 ha. However, only part of the 70,000 ha is

6 Interview at HICEP, Chokwe, by Alex Bolding and others, 10 September 2008.

equipped with irrigation infrastructure (Ganho, 2013). Since 2005 a Chinese investor has been present in the perimeter (Praagman, 2013). As in the case of Chokwe, RBL-EP represents one user for the UGBL. As of June 2013, RBL-EP did not yet have a water licence. A memorandum concerning the volume of water abstracted as well as water charges, was under discussion between RBL-EP and UGBL/ARA-Sul.

Private sector versus the State: Procana and Massingir Agro-Industrial (MAI)

Starting in October 2007, ProCana, a subsidiary of a Cobalt mining company (CAMEC), announced its plans to irrigate up to 30,000 ha of land downstream of Massingir Dam. Sugar cane would be irrigated to produce ethanol in one of the biggest plants for biofuel production in Africa. ProCana was a joint venture owned by a London Stock Exchange (AIM) registered company called BioEnergy Africa Ltd (94%) and a locally owned Mozambican company called Biolimpopo limitada (in which the then President, Guebuza, was rumoured to have a stake). To reassure its shareholders ProCana managed to acquire a temporary water licence, directly through the President's office, to the tune of 750 million m3 of water per annum.[7] Whilst the recently upgraded Massingir Dam Reservoir had a storage capacity of approximately 2800 million m3, the reliable annual discharge of the Elephants River downstream of the dam was estimated at a maximum of 800 million m3 (see van der Zaag et al., 2010). The dam was further extended in 2014. At ARA-Sul senior staff were disgruntled by the issue of this huge water licence, committing 94% of the annual flow to ProCana to the possible detrimental expense of other downstream users, such as HICEP and RBL-EP. Besides this neglect of downstream interests, ARA-Sul's main concern was that it had been bypassed in the decision to allocate the water, possibly for reasons of superior political expediency.[8] This negative impact would only be partially mitigated by the promised 7000 jobs on the ProCana estate and the 10,624 ha of irrigated cane land under smallholder outgrower contract.[9]

However, in the end a number of adverse factors were responsible for the ultimate demise of ProCana and its grand plans for establishing a huge irrigated estate downstream of the Massingir Dam. First and foremost amongst these factors were not the domestic concerns of smallholder farmers who had been displaced by the newly established Limpopo National Park (whose new land for resettlement coincided with the land allocated to ProCana; see Milgroom, 2012) or the concerns of the smallholder irrigators of Marringuele Association, whose

7 AIM statement by BioEnergy Africa Ltd., entitled 'Admission to AIM', dated 1 September 2008, downloaded on 2 May 2009 from <www.bioenergyafrica-ltd.com>

8 Interview at ARA-Sul offices with senior staff, Maputo, by Alex Bolding and others, 12 September 2008.

9 The figure of 7000 jobs kept being mentioned by both the Company itself and Mozambican and international media reports, despite the admission by the ProCana director that a maximum of 2000, mostly temporary, jobs would be created in case the Company opted for the subsoil drip system with mechanised combine harvesting of cane. Interview with country director of ProCana by Alex Bolding, Maputo, 22 September 2008.

pump house and water licence had been taken over by ProCana to supply 125 ha of formerly smallholder land with water for a cane nursery (Manjate et al., 2010). After incurring losses to the tune of USD 7.7 million, reported on 29 September 2009,[10] a radical change of strategy was announced by the Company on 6 October 2009. The main reason cited was "the global economic climate and current reduced interest in non-carbon related fuel products" which would make it "difficult for the Company to raise the necessary financing required under the Massingir Investment Agreement".[11] So basically the global financial crisis, which especially hit the hedge funds on which ProCana relied for its investment capital, and the prospect of reduced oil prices in the mid to long term, meant the Company could not raise the necessary finance for the agreed investment plan. As a result, the Mozambican government nullified the issued land concession (DUAT), pulling the plug on the project.

What also played a role in the ultimate decision of CAMEC CEOs to pull out of the Massingir project were two technical factors. Firstly, there were the frustrating and protracted negotiations with ARA-Sul staff about the proposed water intake, which ultimately proved inconclusive. The Company wanted to construct its own pumping station on top of the dam abutment, rendering ARA-Sul's water releases from the main dam valves dependent on ProCana's water abstraction (effectively making ProCana a head end user on whom all other downstream users would become dependent for their own water supply). The option ARA-Sul preferred involved a pumping station along the river, downstream of the dam, which however would increase running costs for the Company, since they would have to pump the water up to the irrigated command area which was situated at a higher elevation.[12] Secondly, in May 2008 a terrible incident took place at the dam, whereby the main valves and discharge pipe were blown out, due to the raised water pressure caused by the heightened dam wall. This incident negatively affected the ability of ARA-Sul to operate the water releases from the dam.

With the exit of ProCana, Massingir Agro-Industrial (MAI), a joint venture of South African-British-Mozambican origin entered the scene. Since 2011, MAI has sought to relaunch the project for the production of sugar cane in Massingir District.[13] MAI is a joint venture consisting of Transvaal Suiker Beperk (TSB) a South African sugar company (51%) and Limpopo Agro-Industrial Investment Company (SIAL, 49%), a Mozambican company whose chairperson is a former Minister of Industry.[14] MAI plans to cultivate sugar cane on irrigated land of 37,500 ha and reserve 1000 ha for food production for the benefit of the population living near

10 AIM statement by BioEnergy Africa Ltd, entitled 'Final statement for the 23-month period ended 31 March 2009', dated 29 September 2009, downloaded on 8 November 2009 from <www.bioenergyafrica-ltd.com>

11 AIM statement by BioEnergy Africa Ltd., entitled 'Proposed adoption of investing policy and change of name', dated 6 October 2009, downloaded on 8 November 2009 from <www.bioenergyafrica-ltd.com>

12 Interview with resident engineer, ARA-Sul, by Alex Bolding, Massingir, 7 May 2009.

13 'ProCana bio-fuel project to be relaunched', 25 November 2011, source: www.esi-Africa.com/node/13887, consulted on 9 December 2011.

14 http://allafrica.com/stories/201211120298.html [last visited 10/08/13]

the project area (Borras et al., 2011).[15] At the time of the research, production was envisaged to start in 2016 (Praagman, 2013).[16]

In May 2013, MAI was in the process of obtaining a land right for 37,000 ha and a water concession. At the time of the fieldwork, negotiations with ARA-Sul around a memorandum of understanding were taking place in Maputo. According to several interviewees, the draft memorandum allowed MAI to abstract half of the water from Massingir Dam Reservoir and half from a pumping station downstream of the dam. Meters for calculation of the volume of water abstracted were seen at each intake; thus MAI assumed it would have to pay according to the volume of water abstracted.[17] MAI operated initially much more cautiously than ProCana, having to deal with the latter's negative heritage of broken promises and accusations of land theft by a number of NGOs.[18] The cautious strategy is reflected in MAI's request for a water concession (rather than a licence) which has to be approved both by ARA-Sul and the Council of Ministers thus ensuring political goodwill and avoiding a loss of face on the part of ARA-Sul staff.[19] Second, a MAI representative went to present their investment plans and water abstraction plan to the Comité da Bacía (river basin committee). This was done not to gain permission from the congregated stakeholders over their water allocation, but rather to create goodwill by informing potentially affected water users in a responsible manner (Praagman, 2013).[20]

Smallholders versus the State: Focal points

Besides the few large-scale users and the parastatal agencies supplying water to a variety of users as described above, the Limpopo and Elephant rivers supply water to hundreds of small- and medium-scale irrigators who live along the riverbanks and directly abstract water from these rivers using private or community-owned pumps. Here we refer to smallholders as users (individual or collective) who cultivate less than 30 ha of irrigated land (often only 3-4 ha).

According to the staff working for UGBL, registration and fee collection are quite challenging in remote areas that are physically difficult to reach due to dis-

15 According to the project 23,000 ha will be cultivated directly by MAI, 12,000 ha will be developed by SIAL and 2500 ha will be cultivated by local communities under an outgrowing model.

16 In July 2016 the project was at a standstill (email communication, R. Ducrot, 10.08.2016).

17 Interview with representatives of MAI by Rossella Alba, May 2013, Maputo, Mozambique (Alba, 2013).

18 Interview with project manager MAI by Rossella Alba, 14 May 2013, Maputo. The negative accusations by NGOs are reported in Manual and Salomao (2009) and in an online article by Adam Welz, entitled 'Ethanol's African Land Grab', published in March 2009 at www.motherjones.com/environment/2009/03/ethanols-african-landgrab, consulted on 25 May 2009.

19 Interview with senior ARA-Sul staff by Alex Bolding and Rossella Alba, 16 May 2013, Maputo.

20 Apparently, in 2015, a Kuwaiti group claimed it was going to restart the Procana project and/or take over the MAI project. The relationship between both is unclear. It seems TSB is still willing to invest with MAI and was supposed to start at the end of 2015 (personal communication, R. Ducrot, 3 December 2015).

tance and bad conditions of the roads (Inguane, 2010) leading to increased transaction costs for both UGBL staff and users (e.g. transport costs and time required). According to several interviewees, the lack of a culture of payment for water within the river basin further complicates the process. In order to deal with these difficulties, between 2008 and 2009 informal groups of water users led by one Focal Point (FP, in Portuguese ponto focal) were created with the support of UGBL. Often, the Focal Point is the leader of the village or a well-known and respected man (e.g. a farmer) appointed by the water users. Since 2009, 13 groups have been established in the area downstream of the Massingir Dam. The size of the group is variable as is the number of users, as illustrated in Table 10.1. Due to the difficulties in calculating the volume of water abstracted by these remote users, the water charges are calculated according to the area each user cultivates based on a study of water requirements carried out by ARA-Sul between 2004 and 2005.

The Focal Points facilitate the registration of users and the collection of water fees. In theory, they also improve communication and information exchange. Indeed, the Focal Point represents a connection link between UGBL and the users (see Figure 10.3). The Focal Point is in charge of carrying out an inventory of the amount of land that each user has planted and/or effectively cultivated in a specific area and communicates it to UGBL. On the basis of the data collected by the Focal Point, the Basin Authority calculates the water charges and issues an invoice. Then, the Focal Point is in charge of collecting the money from the users and hand it over to the Basin Authority (Alba, 2013).

Focal Points represent a network of water users that reach the community level and (should) facilitate information exchange with the river basin authority (Praagman, 2013). Yet, at the time of the research, they seemed to serve more as a means to collect water fees than as a means of disseminating or collecting information. Focal Points, and in general smallholder farmers, are not represented in the River Basin Committee and play only a limited role in decision-making. Hence their financial accountability is completely separated from any (political) decision-making power or even being informed about dam openings that are increasingly the cause for potentially devastating flash floods (that might sweep mobile pump sets away).

Figure 10.3. The Focal Point System (our elaboration).

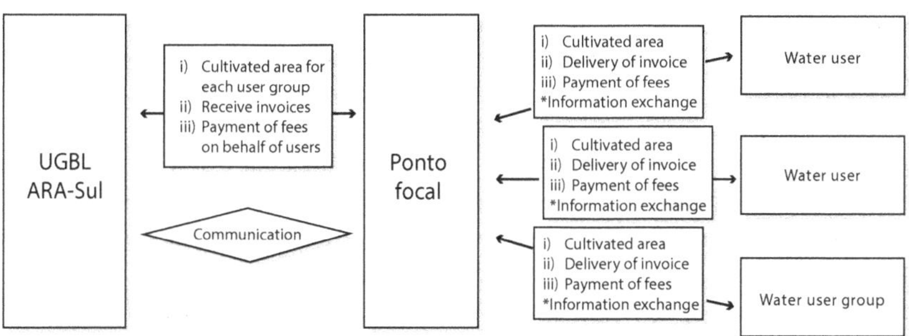

Table 10.1. Water users group in the Limpopo River Basin.

Users' group	District	Number of users	Area cultivated (ha)*
I	Massingir	7	10
II	Massingir	2	6
III	Massingir	14	37
IV	Massingir	2	4
V	Massingir	2	1.5
VI	Chokwe	15	26
VII	Chokwe	6	6

Source: own elaboration based on cadastre 2012 of ARA-Sul

Users-group	District	Number of users	Area cultivated (ha)*
VIII	Chokwe	2	2
IX	Chokwe	2	3
X	Chokwe	18	35.5
XI	Guija	40	117
XII	Chibuto	3	0
XII	Xai-Xai	0	0

*the area cultivated refers to the last trimester 2012

Source: own elaboration based on cadastre 2012 of ARA-Sul.

Analysis and Discussion

The historical reconstruction of the articulation of the new water rights framework and the practices presented above and in Alba and Bolding (Chapter 9) foresee a key role for the central State and the decentralised ARAs in the definition of water rights (the policy), in the registration of users and in the role accorded to water users in accessing water and in decision-making about these practices. Yet, structural challenges and local geographies shape the final outcome of water reforms in relation to decentralised river basin management, stakeholders' participation and accountability. The examples given above portray several differences between water users that are not equal in terms or political connections, availability of financial resources, volume of water abstracted and also position in relation to the source. Equally, the capacity of Regional Water Authorities like ARA-Sul to administer and provide water to a multitude of water users is limited, certainly when taking into account the latter's different water requirements and various points of abstraction. We analyse below the outcomes of the newly instituted water payment and permit system by assessing for each of the four different user groups how political relations undermine the financial autonomy of ARA-Sul. Finally, we provide a number of pragmatic recommendations to achieve a modicum of financial sustainability and water user registration.

Politics undercut the achievement of ARA's financial autonomy

From the case material presented above, it is observed that ARA-Sul in its attempts to administer and supply water to the existing variety of water user groups has sought to reduce the number of transaction points, while aiming to secure a steady income through the introduction of a variety of different payment systems. On the other hand, various powerful water users have sought to acquire water rights and evade volumetric water payments through negotiations with authorities at a higher political level than ARA-Sul. Both trends have resulted in an active undermining of the financial autonomy of ARA-Sul.

Whereas the theory of financially autonomous agencies has it that agency services (volumes of water) are delivered in exchange for (user) payment, thus empowering water users and making the agency independent of State power, the practice as found in the Limpopo River Basin is different. Indeed, the hypothesis that sustains the reform, namely the creation of a client/service provider relation, does not hold given the politics of water allocation and the complexity of the river basin where a few large-scale users compete with a large number of invisible and dispersed small-scale users. The large-scale users are politically too sensitive to be sanctioned on the one hand, while the feasibility of charging dispersed users is problematic (in terms of cost-effectiveness). We examine below the position of each of the four groups of water users.

In the case of the two parastatal agencies (HICEP and RBL-EP) that administer and manage the formerly publicly managed irrigation schemes of Chokwe and Baixo Limpopo, ARA-Sul has taken the view that these represent one water user that can be charged for its water through a so-called memorandum that charges them for a fixed monthly water volume against a reduced rate. However, non-payment of water bills has not resulted in suspension of the service provided by the Regional Water Authority: supply of water to the irrigation schemes. Hence, in the case of the Limpopo River, the financial accountability mechanism has been fatally undermined: the water authority lost the incentive of providing good services as it is not compensated for it by the users. In the case of the Limpopo River the reason for this must be sought in the large number of small- and medium-scale producers operating in these irrigated perimeters (whose production depends on the water) and their political importance. The Limpopo Valley can be regarded as the political heartland of the ruling Party FRELIMO (Pellizzoli, 2010). Moreover, it can be observed that the Ministry of Public Works, under which ARA-Sul operates, has failed to muster sufficient clout to exact payments from its sister Ministry of Agriculture for the services it provides to the latter. To some senior policy actors such intra-State payments may not make much sense.

Large-scale commercial water users like ProCana and MAI have secured huge water permits on the basis of political negotiations going beyond ARA-Sul's office. This way of securing water has undermined the principle of financial accountability between ARA-Sul and the Company (water user). Rather, the often personal and patrimonial interest of top policy actors (often located in the President's office) seems to override whatever relation exists between the service provider and the (foreign investment) company in question. The attempts of both ProCana and MAI to construct a pumping station on top of the Massingir Dam should be understood in the light of a desire on the part of the investment company to secure water for its estate at the expense of downstream interest in the same resource as well as securing independence from the service provider, ARA-Sul. Yet, as far as we could gather, both ProCana and MAI had to pay for the volume of water they abstracted from the river for their start-up operations. It remains unclear, however, what payments will be exacted once the full estate has been developed.

Unable to collect sufficient money from large-scale users, regional water authorities have turned to smallholder farmers who operate downstream of water infrastructural works as a potential source of cost recovery. Water users' groups were established serving more as a means to register users and collect fees, rather than as a means to disseminate information. So-called Focal Points have been mobilised to act as tax farmers, exacting payment per unit of irrigated land from fellow irrigators. However, the absence of any kind of service provision in terms of information on water releases from dams or decision-making power through a seat on the Comité da Bacía, has threatened to undermine the financial accountability mechanism. Here it is the lack of political decision-making power on the part of the water users that negatively affects the achievement of financial autonomy for ARA-Sul. In this case, the conversion of Focal Points from cash into Power Points may be a necessary step for the policy of financial autonomy to work.

Finally, there is a large group of 'informal' water users, such as those smallholder farmers located in nonregulated areas of the Limpopo River and those depending for their livelihoods on machongos close to the river estuary, making use of their primary water right (*uso comum*), who escape registration and payment. By this very act they remain 'invisible' and their water use is unaccounted for, with the risk that the apparently 'unexploited' water is awarded to new large-scale investors (see also van der Zaag et al., 2010).

Ways forward

In terms of equitable resource allocation and sustainable water management, much can be gained by recognising the unequal position of water users in sociopolitical and economic terms and the difficulties that water authorities encounter in the licensing process. In the Limpopo River Basin, water users′ groups and the Focal Points network offer the opportunity to involve small-scale users who cultivate their land outside large-scale irrigation schemes in decision-making and information exchange. Ensuring their representation in the River Basin Committee will contribute to fostering democratic practices in the management of water resources.

Recent developments in the river basin, such as agro-industrial investments (e.g. MAI) and new forms of agrarian change (see Ganho, 2013; Veldwisch, 2015), call for renewed attention for allocation of water resources (who gets the water and how) and the role of State actors. Further research on the practices related to access and allocation of water resources within Mozambican river basins is necessary. Besides the legal dimension involved with the water rights framework, technical and socioeconomic aspects should also be investigated (Boelens and Zwarteveen, 2005). These include the management and access to infrastructure and technologies that allow the users to physically access water and materialise their formal water rights, together with the ability of users to mobilise resources (e.g. money) and participate in decision-making processes.

With regard to previous attempts to cover the operating expenses of Regional Water Authorities like ARA-Sul, we would recommend to charge the large-scale water users for their water consumption, based on water measurements at the pumping station or main abstraction point, while avoiding payment by the multitude of small water users. The bulk of the water which is abstracted for productive purposes from any of the rivers in Mozambique, is used by relatively few large-scale water users, normally making up less than 10% of the total number of water users. Meanwhile, for those 'informal' smallholder water users who make use of their primary water right *(uso comum)* and make up the majority of water users, it could be better to reserve a dedicated amount of water based on demographic estimates, so as to prevent their water allocation being forfeited to large-scale users upstream. In this way, one can achieve both a form of financial accountability and a modicum of cost recovery without the presently prevailing inequities in both access and payment for water.

Acknowledgements

The chapter draws on a research project funded by the Research Council of Norway – Flows and Practices: The Politics of Integrated Water Resource Management (IWRM) in Africa. A previous version of the chapter was presented at the VI IESE conference, Maputo 26-27 August 2014. We would like to thank two internal reviewers (Emmanuel Manzungu and Barbara van Koppen) and three external reviewers for their constructive criticism.

References

Alba, R. 2013. Travelling with IWRM: The articulation of water permits and payments for water in policies and practices in Limpopo river basin, Mozambique. MSc thesis. Wageningen University, Wageningen, The Netherlands.

Alba, R. and Bolding, A. 2016. IWRM avant la lettre? Four key episodes in the policy articulation of IWRM in the downstream nation of Mozambique. *Water Alternatives*, 9(3): 551-570.

Bagadion, B.U. 1989. The evolution of the policy context: An historical overview. In Korten, F.F. and Siy, R. (Eds), *Transforming a bureaucracy, the experience of the Philippine National Irrigation Administration*, pp. 1-19. Quezon City: Ateneo de Manila University Press.

Boelens, R. and Zwarteveen, M. 2005. Prices and politics in Andean water reforms. *Development and Change* 36(4): 735-758.

Borras, Jr, S.M.; Fig, D. and Suárez, S.M. 2011. The politics of agrofuels and mega-land and water deals: Insights from the ProCana case, Mozambique. *Review of African Political Economy* 38(128): 215-234.

Chilundo, M.; Munguambe, P. and Namagina, C. 2012. Contextualização e Sintetização dos Estudos Realizados no Âmbito do Regadio de Chókwè, Relatório Final. Maputo: Faculdade de Agronomia e Engenharia Florestal, Universidade Eduardo Mondlane.

Ducrot, R. 2011. Land and water governance and pro-poor mechanisms in the Mozambican part of the Limpopo basin: Baseline study. Working Document, CGIAR (Consultative Group for International Agricultural Research) Challenge Programme on Water and Food. Maputo: IWEGA.

Franco, J.; Mehta, L. and Veldwisch, G.J. 2013. The global politics of water grabbing. *Third World Quarterly* 34(9): 1651-1675.

Gallego-Ayala, J. and Juízo, D. 2011. Strategic implementation of integrated water resources management in Mozambique: An A'WOT analysis. *Physics and Chemistry of the Earth Parts A/B/C* 36(14): 1103-1111.

Gallego-Ayala, J. and Juízo, D. 2012. Performance evaluation of River Basin Organizations to implement integrated water resources management using composite indexes. *Physics and Chemistry of the Earth Parts A/B/C* 50-52: 205-216.

Ganho, A.S. 2013. 'Friendship' rice, business, or 'land-grabbing'? The Hubei-Gaza rice project in Xai-Xai. Working Paper No. 32. Sussex: Land Deal Politics Initiative (LDPI).

GoM (Government of Mozambique). 1991. Lei de Águas. Law n. 16/91 of August 3.

GoM. 1998. Political tarifária de Água (Water Tariff Policy). Resolution n. 60/98 of December 23.

GoM. 2004. Primeiro projecto nacional de desenvolvimento de água. Fundo Nórdico de Desenvolvimento: Crédito NDF 197. Business Plan da ARA-Sul, Fase II, Tomo 1: relatório principal. Unpublished Report.

GoM. 2007a. Política de Águas (Water Policy). Decree n. 46/2007, of October 30

GoM. 2007b. Regulamento de Licenças e Concessões de Águas (Regulations on Water Licenses and Concessions). Decree n. 43/2007, of October 30.

Illo, J.F.I. 1989. Farmers, engineers and organizers: The Taisan Project. In Korten, F.F. and Siy, R.Y. (Eds), *Transforming a bureaucracy: The experience of the Philippine National Irrigation Administration*, pp. 31-60. Connecticut: Kumarian Press.

Inguane, R. 2010. Political, institutional and economic factors constraining the performance of decentralized water management in Mozambique: From the major perspective of government water functions. MSc thesis. University of Queensland, Brisbane, Australia.

Inguane, R.; Gallego-Ayala, J. and Juízo, D. 2014. Decentralized water resources management in Mozambique: Challenges of implementation at river basin level. *Physics and Chemistry of the Earth Parts A/B/C* 67-69: 214-225.

Lauraya, F.M. and Sala, A.L.R. 1994. *Alternative support systems to strengthen Irrigators' Associations in Bicol, the Philippines, after irrigation management turnover.* Sri Lanka: International Water Management Institute.

Manjate, C. 2010. Analysis of water and related laws in Mozambique. In van der Zaag, P. (Ed), *What role of law in promoting and protecting the productive use of water by small-holder farmers in Mozambique?*, pp. 9-29. Water rights in informal economies (CP66). Delft, The Netherlands: CGIAR (Consultative Group for International Agricultural Research) Challenge Program on Water & Food.

Manjate, C.; de Oliveira, E. and Sibia, O. 2010. Water rights in informal economies: The case of ASAMA, the Associação dos Agricultores de Marreguele. In van der Zaag, P. (Ed), *What role of law in promoting and protecting the productive use of water by small-holder farmers in Mozambique?*, pp. 71-88. Water rights in informal economies (CP66). Delft, The Netherlands: CGIAR (Consultative Group for International Agricultural Research) Challenge Program on Water & Food.

Manual, L. and Salomao, A. 2009. Biofuel and land rights in Mozambique – The Pro-Cana case. *Haramata* 54: 17-19.

Mehta, L.; Alba, R.; Bolding, A.; Denby, K.; Derman, B.; Hove, T.; Manzungu E.; Movik S.; Prabhakaran P. and van Koppen, B. 2014. The politics of IWRM in Southern Africa. *International Journal of Water Resources Development* 30(3): 528-542.

Milgroom, J. 2012. Elephants of democracy: An unfolding process of resettlement in the Limpopo National Park. PhD thesis. Wageningen University, Wageningen, the Netherlands.

Molle, F. 2004. Defining water rights: By prescription or negotiation? *Water Policy* 6(3): 207-227.

Molle, F. and Berkoff, J. 2007. Water pricing in irrigation: Mapping the debate in the light of experience. In Molle, F. and Berkoff, J. (Eds), *Irrigation water pricing: The gap between theory and practice*, pp. 21-93. Comprehensive Assessment of Water Management in Agriculture. Wallingford, UK and Cambridge, MA: IWMI/CABI.

Moore, M. 1989. The fruits and fallacies of neo-liberalism: The case of irrigation policy. *World Development* 11(17): 1733-1750.

Nader, L. 1972. Up the anthropologist: Perspectives gained from studying up. *Reinventing anthropology* 1972: 284-311.

NIA (National Irrigation Administration). 1994. *The impact of the participatory approach on the performance of National Irrigation Systems.* NIA consul. Quezon City: National Irrigation Administration.

Oorthuizen, J. 2003. *Water, works and wages: The everyday politics of irrigation management reform in the Philippines.* New Delhi: Orient Longman.

Oorthuizen, J. and Bolding, A. 2010. State and irrigation. In Lecture notes from the Irrigation and Development course. MSc in International Land and Water Management, Wageningen University, Wageningen, the Netherlands.

Oorthuizen, J. and Kloezen, W.H. 1995. The other side of the coin: A case study of the impact of financial autonomy on irrigation management performance in the Philippines. *Irrigation and Drainage Systems* 9(1): 15-37.

Ostrom, E. 1992. *Crafting institutions for self-governing irrigation systems.* San Francisco: Institute for Contemporary Studies Press.

Pellizzoli, R. 2010. 'Green revolution' for whom? Women's access to and use of land in the Mozambique Chókwè irrigation scheme. *Review of African Political Economy* 37(124): 213-220.

Praagman, E. 2013. The political arenas of water management in the Limpopo basin, Mozambique. Stakeholder participation at different policy levels. MSc thesis. Wageningen University, Wageningen, the Netherlands.

Repetto, R. 1986. *Skimming the water: Rent-seeking and the performance of public irrigation systems.* Research Paper No. 4. Washington: World Resource Institute.

Ribot, J.C. and Peluso, N.L. 2003. A theory of access. *Rural Sociology* 68(2): 153-181.

Savenije, H.H. and van der Zaag, P. 2002. Water as an economic good and demand management paradigms with pitfalls. *Water International* 27(1): 98-104.

Scott, J.C. 1998. *Seeing like a state: How certain schemes to improve the human condition have failed.* Yale University Press.

Small, L. 1990. *Irrigation service fees in Asia.* Irrigation Management Network Paper 90/1e. London: Overseas Development Institute.

Small, L.E. and Carruthers, I. 1991. *Farmer-financed irrigation: The economics of reform.* Cambridge: Cambridge University Press.

Solanes, M. 1989. *Report on a mission to Mozambique.* New York, United Nations.

Svendsen, M. 1993. The impact of financial autonomy on irrigation system performance in the Philippines. *World Development* 21(6): 989-1005.

Uphoff, N.; Ramamurthy, P. and Steiner, R. 1991. *Managing irrigation: Analyzing and improving the performance of bureaucracies.* New Delhi, Newbury Park, London: Sage Publications.

van der Zaag, P. 2010. *What role of law in promoting and protecting the productive uses of water by smallholder farmers in Mozambique?* Water rights in informal economies (CP66). Delft, The Netherlands: CGIAR (Consultative Group for International Agricultural Research) Challenge Program on Water & Food.

van der Zaag, P.; Juizo, D.; Vilanculos, A.; Bolding, A. and Post Uiterweer, N. 2010. Does the Limpopo river basin have sufficient water for massive irrigation development in the plains of Mozambique? *Physics and Chemistry of the Earth* 35(13-14): 832-837.

van Koppen, B. 2003. Water reform in Sub-Saharan Africa: What is the difference? *Physics and Chemistry of the Earth, Parts A/B/C* 28(20): 1047-1053.

Veldwisch, G.J.; Beekman, W. and Bolding, A. 2013. Smallholder irrigators, water rights and investments in agriculture: Three cases from rural Mozambique. *Water Alternatives* 6(1): 125-141.

Veldwisch, G.J. 2015. Contract farming and the reorganization of agricultural production within the Chókwè Irrigation System, Mozambique. *The Journal of Peasant Studies* 42(5): 1003-1028.

Wester, P. 2008. *Shedding the waters: Institutional change and water control in the Lerma-Chapala Basin*, Mexico. PhD thesis. Wageningen University, Wageningen, The Netherlands.

World Bank. 1993. Water resources management strategy. A World Bank policy paper. Washington, DC: World Bank.

11

Winners and Losers of IWRM in Tanzania[1]

Barbara van Koppen

Andrew K.P.R. Tarimo

Aurelia van Eeden

Emmanuel Manzungu

Philip Mathew Sumuni

ABSTRACT: This chapter focuses on the application of the concept of Integrated Water Resources Management (IWRM) in Tanzania. It asks: how did IWRM affect the rural and fast-growing majority of smallholder farmers' access to water which contributes directly to poverty alleviation and employment creation in a country where poverty and joblessness are high? Around 1990, there were both a strong government-led infrastructure development agenda and IWRM ingredients in place, including cost-recovery of state services aligning with the Structural Adjustment Programmes, water management according to basin boundaries and the dormant colonial water rights (permits) system. After the 1990s, the World Bank and other donors promoted IWRM with a strong focus on hydroelectric power development, River Basin Water Boards, transformation of the water right system into a taxation tool, and assessment of environmental flows. These practices became formalised in the National Water Policy (2002) and in the Water Resources Management Act (2009). Activities in the name of IWRM came to be closely associated with the post-2008 surge in large-scale land and water deals. Analysing 25 years of IWRM, the chapter identifies the processes and identities of the losers (smallholders and – at least partially – the government) and the winners (large-scale water users, including recent investors). We conclude that, overall, IWRM harmed smallholders' access to water and rendered them more vulnerable to poverty and unemployment.

KEYWORDS: Integrated Water Resources Management, water law, basin management, taxation, Tanzania

1 First published in *Water Alternatives* 9(3): 590-609.

Introduction

In the narrative of Integrated Water Resource Management (IWRM), the 3Es of Equity, Environmental sustainability and Economic efficiency, are often mentioned as three concurrent goals. However, over two decades of operationalisation and implementation of IWRM have shown that equity has hardly been achieved (WGF, 2012). This is part of the broader IWRM problematic – IWRM claims to be a universal and globally relevant concept, and yet there are key determinants vis-à-vis the fit or misfit of a standard application of IWRM in a country, in particular the level of economic development and formalisation of water provision and water business (Shah, 2007). These issues are especially relevant for low-income agrarian countries, in which most water uses are rural, small and informal. Here, states primarily tend to seek to mobilise the required resources to develop water infrastructure to promote welfare (Shah, 2007). However, little is known about the precise processes in low-income countries that represent such misfits and generate winners and losers and, if so, who they are, which was the primary focus of the study Flows and Practices: The Politics of IWRM in Africa, which informed this book. As documented by several authors in this book, this is partly due to the vagueness of the concept of IWRM itself. IWRM came with donors' funding earmarked for the training of water professionals to translate, interpret and put IWRM into practice, often paying little attention to its socioeconomic context. The donor dependency, which has given rise to a whole IWRM industry that brings together donors and water professionals who tend to gain in various ways, has tended to blunt evidence-based analysis. The present chapter seeks to make a contribution to fill this gap in Tanzania where IWRM was introduced in the early 1990s (Tarimo et al., 2014). The chapter aims to identify whether and how winners and losers emerged during the introduction ('birth'), translation and interpretation of the concept of IWRM in policy and legal frameworks as well as its early implementation at national, basin and local levels (the 'life' of IWRM). The study is based on the review of literature and policy documents and on interviews with key stakeholders at all levels.

Our definition of IWRM is derived from the study's findings that, at the abstract level, the definition of IWRM in Tanzania aligns with the global definition of the Global Water Partnership (Mutayoba, 2002). However, events and concrete activities carried out in the name of IWRM in Tanzania centred on a few typical ingredients: a new narrative of water as an economic good; the promulgation and initial implementation of new water policy and law, which stipulate basin organisations, permit systems, environmental flows, and transboundary water management. We focus on these aspects, with the exception of transboundary management, which is beyond this chapter's scope. Further, we operationalise the broad question about equity in IWRM in Tanzania by asking the question: how did IWRM affect access to water by smallholder famers?

The next section provides the rationale for the focus on smallholder farmers. The following two sections provide a chronological analysis of context and relevant events. We then discuss the context of the late 1980s just before IWRM was introduced. This shows how key aspects of IWRM already existed. We further identify the 'birth' of IWRM as a strongly donor-influenced concept and trace the 'life' of IWRM during the upscaling of that concept into national policy and law, and expanding activities to implement IWRM and Integrated Water Resource Management and Development, as it was called later, in three river basins in Tanzania. Finally, experiences during the 25 years of IWRM are assessed in terms of winners and losers, and conclusions are drawn.

Smallholders' poverty and water uses

Smallholders' poverty and engine of growth

The reason for focusing on Tanzania's rural population many of whom are smallholder farmers, as an indicator for assessing equity objectives and whether IWRM is a fit or misfit in this regard, is that they are not only the country's poorest and most numerous citizens, but also the potential engine of growth. Overall, 64% mainland Tanzanians are poor and 31.3% live in extreme poverty, according to the Multidimensional Poverty Index (UNDP and URT, 2015). Poverty is worse in rural areas, where 73% of the population live (UNDP and URT, 2015). Moreover, population growth is fastest in the rural areas. At independence in 1961, Tanzania had a population of 10.1 million and, in 2014, thanks to a population growth rate of 2.8 and 4,95 children per woman the total population had grown to almost 50 million (Index Mundi, 2014). During this period, the growth in rural population was three times as high as the growth in the urban population, in spite of massive urbanisation. For example, in Dar es Salaam, the country's capital, the population increased from 2.1 million in 2000 to 3.6 million in 2011 (Agwanda and Amani, 2014; Index Mundi, 2014).

The economic structure of Tanzania mirrored the importance of the rural sector for employment. In 2006, agriculture provided 77% of the total employment (UNDP and URT, 2015). Although cultivated area expanded, the faster population growth meant that average plot size fell from 1.3 hectares (ha) per household in the mid-1970s to 1 ha per household in 2005 (Skarstein, 2005). All the same, small-scale farming has become even more important as the mainstay of the rapidly growing rural population and, indeed, the country's potential engine of growth to overcome its current highly skewed 'jobless growth' (UNDP and URT, 2015).

However, in terms of contribution to GDP, agriculture has dropped while the agrarian structure has become more unequal. The high growth rate of 6% during the 2000s was primarily a result of foreign investors' extractive (and polluting) mining of gold, and also diamonds, iron, coal, nickel, Tanzanite, uranium and natural gas. Mining grew at an average of 13% over the 2000s and constitutes 40% of exports. Construction, manufacturing, services (especially communications and financial intermediation) and tourism also grew. The share of industry rose from 18% in 2001 to 22.1% in 2012 (UNDP and URT, 2015). The service sector is the largest sector in terms of output. For example, in 2012 it accounted for 44% of the GDP.

On the other hand, the share of agriculture to GDP fell from 29% in 2001 to

24% in 2010 (UNDP and URT, 2015). The export performance of the agriculture sector weakened, also as a result of declining global prices. The share of gross output of cash crops to GDP, mainly coffee and tobacco, fell from 6.7% in 1996 to 2.8% in 2010. The only success story is the horticulture sub-sector, which has grown at between 6 and 10% per annum with exports rising as well (UNDP and URT, 2015).

In spite of the economic growth of the 2000s, the poverty rate declined only slightly. According to the income-based poverty headcount of the 2012 Household Budget Survey, it declined from 36% in 2000/2001 to 33.3% 2007 and to 28.2% in 2012. Poverty persisted during the 2000s partly because food prices, which accounted for 44% of the cost of living for the majority of Tanzanians, rose more than prices of nonfood items. While the cheaper imported food was advantageous for poor urban net food buyers, it had the net effect of killing the markets for local producers. Poverty also persisted because, for the first time in history, the growth rates of employment shifted away from industry and services towards agriculture. The historical links between urban and rural economic growth were broken (UNDP and URT, 2015).

The agrarian structure became more skewed when the financial and food crisis of 2008 triggered large-scale foreign companies to invest in Tanzania's abundant land and related water (and mineral) resources for food and agro-fuel. By the end of 2010, they had requested over four million ha of land. By then, 70,000 ha of land had been formally leased to foreign investors (Oakland Institute, 2011). This was part and parcel of Tanzania's 'economic diplomacy', which saw the launch in 2009 of the 'Kilimo Kwanza' (Agriculture First) policy (Tarimo et al., 2014; see also van Eeden et al., Chapter 12). This policy has been criticised for favouring foreign big investors instead of the majority smallholder farmers. This is because in these land deals weaknesses in law are abused, sometimes with the complicity of politicians, government officials and unscrupulous village-level officials. As a consequence, peasant farmers and pastoralists have been sidelined, further aggravating their socioeconomic standing. Under this new large-scale production, Tanzanian wage workers risk becoming 'slaves' on their ancestors' land (Business Times, 2012). Similar large-scale land-based investments in sub-Saharan Africa have proved to become 'water grabs' at the same time (Mehta et al., 2012). Van Eeden et al. (Chapter 12) discuss how water grabbing has unfolded in Tanzania's Wami Ruvu Basin.

In this economic climate, self-employment in family farming for subsistence on smaller plots has become more important. The Tanzania Household Budget Survey records a rise in the percentage of people working on their own farms out of total employment, from 57% in 2007 to 63% in 2014. Production for own consumption also gained in importance: while the absolute level of marketed crop production has increased over the past decade, the relative proportion of non-marketed crops appears to have slightly grown. Food crop production dominates. Out of the 5.1 million ha cultivated annually, 85% is for food crops. But productivity is a challenge (UNDP and URT, 2015).

Low and stagnating productivity is reflected in low technology use. About 70% of Tanzania's crop area is cultivated by hand hoe, 20% by ox plough and 10% by tractor. The use of fertiliser in Tanzania is only 9 kg per ha compared with 27 kg in Malawi, and 279 kg in China (UNDP and URT, 2015). Above all, productivity is low because most agriculture is rain-fed and vulnerable to seasonal fluctuations, droughts and floods. These uncertainties also limit the benefits that can be derived from expensive high-yielding seeds and fertiliser for high-value crops. Hence, improved access to water through water storage and conveyance infrastructure is pivotal for increased agricultural productivity. Higher smallholder productivity would not only improve smallholders' livelihoods but also provide food for markets at lower prices. This could revive smallholder agriculture as the engine of broad-based growth (Timmer, 1988). This sets the stage for the question that is examined in the remainder of this chapter: how did IWRM affect smallholders' access to water? Next, we discuss smallholders' current water uses and the availability of water resources, as one of the conditions to expand water use.

Smallholders' underdeveloped water uses

Smallholders are not only the most numerous and the poorest citizens, but also the largest number of water users in Tanzania. Irrigation accounts for about 89% of the total water withdrawals (by volume), domestic water supply for 9% and industrial water for the remaining 2% (MoWI, 2010). The total irrigated area is about 500,000 ha (see below). About 80% of this is irrigated by smallholders, primarily as traditional informal self-managed irrigation (MoWLD, 2002). River diversions and cultivated wetlands, which are part of the traditional irrigation systems, existed well before the arrival of settlers (Hillbom, 2010). The other 15-20% are cultivated by sugar companies (Sukari, 2014), irrigated paddy enterprises and tea estates.

Tanzania has abundant water resources, which have yet to be developed. Tanzania has groundwater and surface water, inland and bordering freshwater lakes, wetlands and swamps. Total annual water withdrawal for various socioeconomic purposes is estimated to be 5184 km^3, which is 6% of the total internal renewable resources. With an estimated 2000 m^3/capita/year, the availability of the country's water resource is well above the level of 1700 m^3/capita/year set by the United Nations as denoting water stress (MoW, 2014). The issue is the variability of water during the seasons and between different parts of the country. About one third of Tanzania, mainly the central and northern parts, receives less than 800 mm of rainfall per annum, and is classified as arid or semiarid. Moreover, the dry season is long, normally extending from June to October, which results in low seasonal river flows. In contrast, in the southern, western and northern highlands, which receive more than 1000 mm/year of rainfall, rivers are perennial and flooding is frequent.

The country's irrigation potential has hardly been exploited. Out of 44 million ha suitable for agriculture, the area suitable for irrigation is estimated to be about 29.4 million ha. Out of this, 2.3 million ha are classified as high potential, 4.8 million ha as medium potential, and 22.3 million ha as low potential (MoWI, 2009). Recent estimates of total irrigated area vary between 460,000 (Kamwelwe, cited in Mugarula, 2016) and 589,254 ha (Makoye, 2013). This translates to 2% of the full potential of irrigable land. In sum, water resources for further smallholder irrigation development are available. The question is whether IWRM provides a good platform to exploit this potential.

Water management in Tanzania: Background and context

Rolling back the state

Julius Nyerere, the country's founding president, by the Arusha Declaration of 1967, ushered socialism as the country's economic philosophy. The Arusha Declaration adopted the vision of an African socialist state to spearhead state-led economic growth for self-reliance (Tarimo et al., 2014). Central to the inclusive economic growth was 'Siasa ni Kilimo' (Politics is Agriculture) based on modern technology including irrigation. It was envisaged that higher smallholder productivity would generate the surplus for autonomous industrialisation and independence from the foreign powers and markets which, otherwise, would derive disproportionate benefits and widen inequalities (FAO, 2011). The blossoming smallholder coffee and cotton cooperatives were converted into state-managed 'authorities' and became an important funding source for the ruling party. The National Food Corporation (NAFCO) led the transformation of the former irrigated estates into state farms (Tarimo et al., 2014).

The one-party state provided public education, health care, and domestic water. 80% of the dispersed population was resettled in the *'ujamaa'* villagisation from 1971 to 1974 to enable such service delivery. All land was nationalised, and managed by new village councils. There was neither place for tribal chiefs, who had become unpopular allies of the British, nor for ethnic sentiments among the over 120 ethnic groups (Tarimo et al., 2014).

A rigorous, militaristic top-down discipline co-existed with a remarkable reference to human rights and bottom-up, non-elite freedom of debate and the promotion of gender equality as enunciated in the Arusha Declaration. Top-down discipline and authority were also warranted because of the surrounding political and security uncertainties as a consequence of the country's support for the military liberation of other southern African countries. Tanzania, together with Zambia, were important springboards of the liberation movements. While the Russians provided military support and training, the Chinese also provided military and other forms of help, for example by building the railway to Zambia (Tarimo et al., 2014).

By the early 1980s, it became clear that the nationalisation and monopolisation of economic enterprises by the ruling party had not worked and was not working: productivity dropped; state enterprises became a drain on the national budget instead of contributing revenues; and funding for public services dried up. This was compounded by the global oil and debt crises and the regional Tanzania-Uganda war in 1978-1979 (UNDP and URT, 2015). The government initially reacted to the economic breakdown with self-guided adjustment efforts, but in 1985 it finally and reluctantly agreed on a Structural Adjustment Economic Recovery Programme. This adjustment was strongly influenced by the paradigm shift of the World Bank and International Monetary Fund (IMF) in the mid-1980s, and Nyerere stepped down – he could not steer the country into the new direction. The centrally planned economy by the one-party state shifted to a multi-party democracy from 1992 and a liberalised 'free market' economy followed (Wobst, 2001).

The state was 'rolled back' and many officials were retrenched. The former parastatals and state enterprises were opened up for sale to the private sector. Under its new strategy, dubbed 'economic diplomacy', the Tanzanian government launched a charm offensive to attract foreign investors. In 1997, the Tanzania Investment Centre was formed as a one-stop shop to facilitate such investments (UNDP and URT, 2015). In this process, politics and economy increasingly colluded. This was formalised in the Zanzibar Declaration of 1992, which allowed the party's politicians and civil servants to take up additional employment. This gave especially the party elite preferential access to land, water and other assets that used to be held by the state (Shivji, 2009). They also became the gatekeepers for the growing number of national and foreign investors seeking land, water and, increasingly, minerals and gas.

This collusion of political and economic power fuelled widespread corruption and bribery, which has haunted the country ever since. Nyerere had instilled a high sense of moral among civil servants through his own impeccable example, and strict, if not dictatorial, control. However, when he retired in 1985, the new president Mwinyi appeared unable to control corruption in his government. Mwinyi's successor, Mkapa's promised to tackle corruption but this did not materialise.

Stringent cost-recovery measures became the mantra in public services (Mashauri and Katko, 1993), alongside local government and line agencies that further decentralised and expanded. Districts employed professional staff from village level upwards reporting to both their national line agency and the District Executive Director (DED) under the Prime Minister's Office of Regional and Local Government. The DED and District Development Committee interacted with the political arm of elected village, ward and district councillors. Decentralising local government, free and relatively fair elections, and gradual civil awareness-raising became the new mottos for bottom-up democracy (UNDP and URT, 2015). To what extent these new democratic structures facilitate the much needed further water development for the majority of smallholder farmers is the question which we explore hereunder.

Infrastructure development for multiple uses and basin boundaries

In the 1960s the post-colonial state supported by foreign agencies set out to develop water infrastructure to meet the range of water needs, both for smallholder agriculture and the growing water needs for hydropower and urbanisation. Boundaries for planning and implementation were pragmatic – they either followed administrative or river basin boundaries. The Food and Agriculture Organisation (FAO), for example, adopted a basin perspective as far back as 1956 in a study on determining the potential for irrigation development in the Wami Ruvu River Basin (FAO, 1969).

After independence the key ministry was the Ministry of Agriculture, which also employed young Tanzanian irrigation engineers who had obtained irrigation degrees abroad. In 1975, an irrigation division was established. In the new agricultural universities, irrigation departments were set up. Administrative irrigation 'zones' were established when the growing number of cadres enabled decentralisation into more zones. On the ground, irrigation officials collaborated with the local government. However, irrigation schemes were built according to top-down modern technical insights, and those of the aid agencies, such as the FAO. However, without stakeholder consultations, there were hardly any success stories of these investments (Majule and Mwalyosi, 2003; Tarimo et al., 2008). Informal farmer-managed irrigation was not recognised.

Initially, domestic water supply services were also housed in the Ministry of Agriculture. However, urban demands in Dar es Salaam and other towns were so specific that the water supply division was moved to another ministry in 1964. After the 1970 elections, a separate ministry was established (Zephania, 2015). The single Principal Water Officer who was responsible for the registration of water rights of the entire country (see below) moved with them. Hydropower generation and mining were added to this ministry. Over time, there were many combinations of sectors with the water ministry as shown in Table 11.1.

Table 11.1. Ministries with water mandates in Tanzania since 1961.

Year	Ministry with water mandate
1961	Agriculture
1964	Lands, Housing and Water Development
1971	Water and Power
1976	Water, Electricity and Minerals
1978	Water, Energy and Minerals
1982	Water and Energy
1985	Water, Energy and Minerals
1987	Water
1990	Water, Energy and Minerals
1996	Water
2001	Water and Livestock
2006	Water
2008	Water and Irrigation Development
2010	Water
2016	Water and Irrigation

Source: https://en.wikipedia.org/wiki/Minister_of_Water_and_Irrigation

By the early 1980s, Water Master Plans were developed for larger-scale planning of irrigation, electricity, mining, and municipal uses. Foreign agencies, such as the Danish International Development Agency (DANIDA) and the Norwegian Agency for Development Cooperation (NORAD) supported this planning, motivated by a mixture of own economic interests and humanitarian development aid considerations. These master plans were based on administrative boundaries (DANIDA, 1983). Boundaries also served some degree of geopolitical interests and specialisation among the different donors (Hirji and Patorni, 1994). For example, Japan focused on the Ruvu Basin (Andersson, 1980). Considering the rapidly growing water supply requirements of downstream Dar es Salaam, they adopted a basin approach. By 1993 Japanese engineering firms for International Cooperation Agency (JICA) had compiled a basin-wide resource development master plan for the Ruvu Basin (Macha and Mwakalinga, 1994).

The river basin approach was widely adopted in hydropower planning, as downstream plants depended on upstream flows and uses. For a long time, hydropower was by far the most important source of electricity generation in the country and was provided by the nationalised parastatal Tanzania Electric Supply Company (TANESCO). Downstream in the Pangani Basin, the Hale power plant was built in 1964, followed by the Nyumba ya Mungu plant further upstream in 1969 and was supported by Norway. In the Great Ruaha tributary in the Rufiji Basin, the Mtera and Kidatu hydroplants, which function in tandem, were constructed between 1969 and 1981. This was supported by the World Bank and the Swedes. The Kihansi plant was added in 2000.

Nyerere had also envisaged the construction of the Stiegler's Gorge Dam, which would have the country's largest hydropower plant (2100 MW). The Rufiji Basin Development Authority (RUBADA) was established in 1975 for integrated planning of hydropower, smallholder agriculture and nature reserves. However, for economic and environmental reasons, the construction kept being postponed. By 2015, alternatives to hydropower had become more attractive: diesel and the recently discovered onshore and offshore gas reserves. By then, hydropower supplied only a bit more than one third of the country's energy needs (MEM, 2015). Electricity provision still favoured urban areas. In spite of recent rural electrification programmes, usage in rural areas was still only at 8%, while this was 49% in urban areas in 2014 (UNDP and URT, 2015).

Legally, the Water Utilisation (Control and Regulation) Act of 1974 mentioned Regional Water Officers and the option that the Minister "may declare any area and land to be water basin" (URT, 1974, section 7). In an amendment in 1981 (URT 1981), management according to basin boundaries was further articulated by dividing Tanzania into nine basins, as in Fig. 11.1: Pangani (I), Wami Ruvu (II), Rufiji (III), Ruvuma and Southern Coast (IV); the (transboundary) Lake Nyasa (V), the internal drainage basin (VI), Lake Rukwa (VII), Lake Tanganyika (VIII), and Lake Victoria (IX). The amendment also stipulated that each new basin has a Water Officer and a Basin Advisory Board. The national Principal Water Officer has a Central Advisory Board. In this sense, basin boundaries and the design of the governance structure of basin management, typical ingredients of IWRM, already existed in Tanzania by 1981.

Fig. 11.1. River basins of Tanzania.

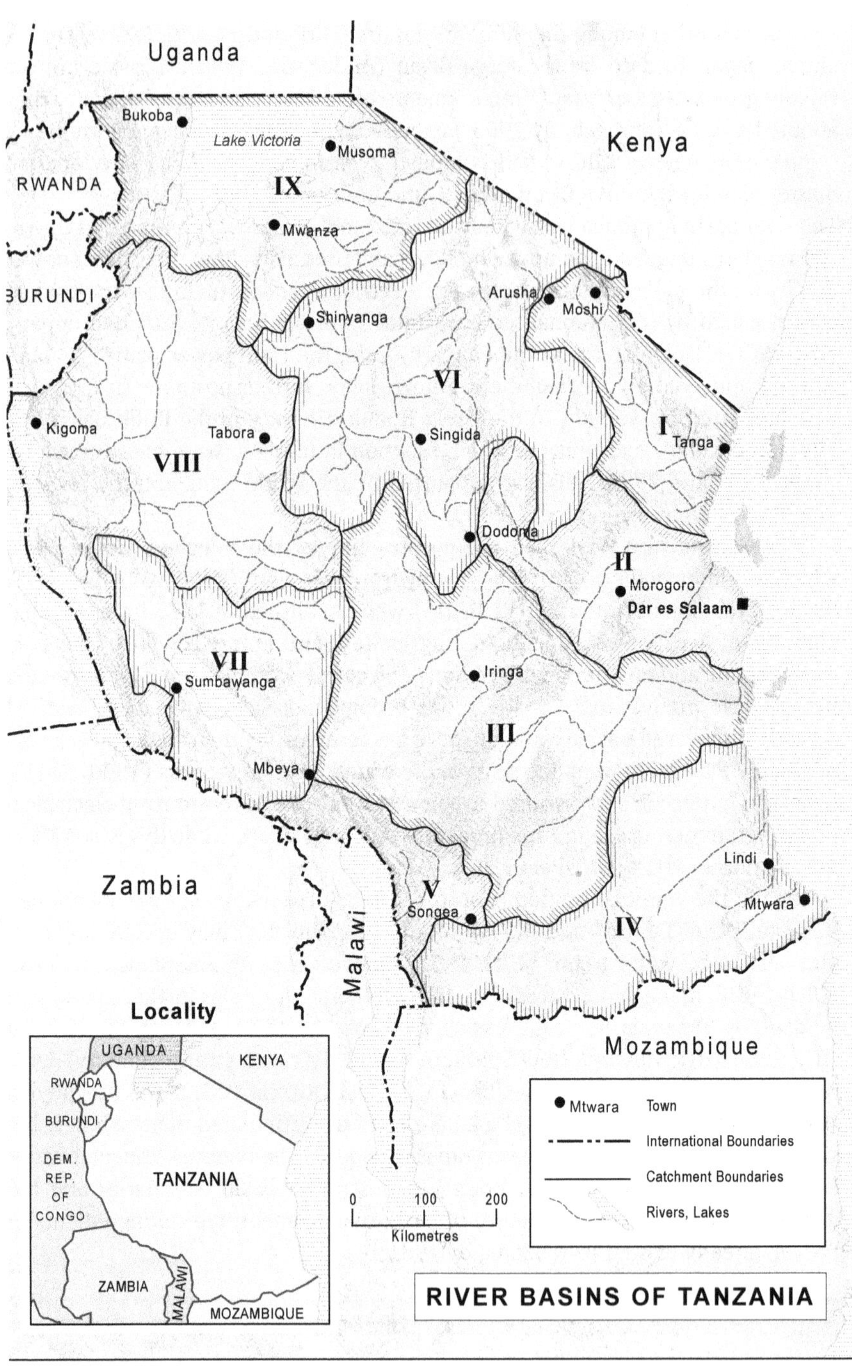

Source: MoWLD, 2004.

Water rights

The other typical aspect of IWRM is the legal system of water 'rights' (a name that changed into 'permits' in the Water Resource Management Act of 2009). Although water law reforms in the name of IWRM are often portrayed as 'an innovation', the water rights system in Tanzania dates back to 1923 and was consolidated in the Water Ordinance of 1948, chapter 257 (TUTT, 1948). This water rights system was a massive colonial water grab: section 4 states that "the entire property in water within the Territory is hereby vested in the Governor, in trust for His Majesty as Administering Authority for Tanganyika" (TUTT, 1948). Initially, only settlers could obtain a water right derived from this colonial authority. One national Water Officer meticulously registered these rights holders and their 'lawful' abstractions. Customary water arrangements were recognised as existing legal arrangements, but sections 3 and 5 of the Ordinance stipulated that only the "duly authorised representative of natives" was recognised [section 13 (9)]. Moreover, in most cases, representation was only "in addition to the District Commissioner" [section 33 (9)] (TUTT, 1948). With a stroke of the pen, all prior and future local and customary water users became losers in any competition for water, at least on paper.

The Water Ordinance of 1959 (TUTT, 1959) expanded this water right system to cover everyone in the entire territory. Instead of the few hundreds of colonial settlers with relatively larger water-dependent enterprises, the law was to apply to the 10 million at that time and, in principle, 50 million citizens today. It stipulated that *all* those who 'divert, dam, store, abstract and use water' were required to register that use with the Water Registrar (Maganga et al., 2004). At the same time, it underlined that a formal water right, let alone just a registration, was no 'right' in the sense of state-backing of any property claims: "Nothing in any such water right shall be deemed to imply any guarantee that the quantity of water thereon referred to is or will be available" (art 15 (4)). By imposing one single law across the country, customary water rights regimes were entirely annulled.

The post-independence Water Utilisation (Control and Regulation) Act of 1974 replaced 'the Governor for His Majesty' by 'the United Republic' as the entity in which water was vested (URT, 1974). Other provisions simply continued. The Principal Water Officer kept the authority to allocate water rights to any citizens who 'divert, dam, store, abstract and use' water, with conditions as he saw fit. Only abstractions of water for domestic purposes, and only if this was without construction of any works (art. 10), were a right exempted from this obligation. A collective water right could be vested in a local association of water users. Applications for water rights needed to be communicated to those who might be affected, so they could express objections. Owners and occupiers of land could abstract groundwater up to a daily volume of 22.7 cubic meters (m^3). Enforcement, on paper, was rigorous. After a written request by the Water Officer to remedy an offence, all Tanzanians developing water were declared offenders and liable to fines or imprisonment of up to two years, until they had applied for a formal water right and until the country's single Principal Water Officer had administered and approved the application. Unregistered customary and informal water arrangements became criminal.

Up to the 1990s, this water law was primarily a paper register of public water schemes and a number of individual water users. As procedures just to reach the single Principal Water Officer were long, it often took years after the construction of a public scheme before the right was finally allocated. For some uses a fee was introduced, for example for TANESCO's royalties. Public irrigation schemes also paid some amount to the Principal Water Officer. IWRM revived and transformed this largely dormant register.

The birth and life of latter day IWRM in Tanzania

This section describes the birth and life of present-day IWRM in Tanzania in terms of how it all began and was implemented. The consequences of this on the majority of smallholder farmers are described in the following section.

Two basin offices for hydropower

In 1991, before the 1992 declaration of the Dublin principles, Tanzania's first basin office was established: Pangani River Basin Office, financed by NORAD. The establishment of this office was the condition for the Pangani Falls Redevelopment Project to go ahead. Further upstream, the Lower Moshi and Ndungu Irrigation Schemes sponsored by JICA had been completed in 1987. Both JICA's irrigation schemes and the hydropower plants were reliant on certain flow rates, and the Pangani Basin's Water Officer was given the task of bringing water use under control. In this zero-sum game, informal water users became the target. The officer identified 1015 abstractions with water rights and 1881 abstractions without formal water rights that were used by smallholder farmers. A crash programme was launched to install several hundred control gates to limit the abstractions of water for farmer-managed irrigation. Most of the new control structures were, however, broken down by farmers as soon as the constructors had left (Lein and Tagseth, 2009).

In 1993, the Tanzanian government financed a second River Basin Office in the Rufiji Basin. The Mtera-Kidatu power plants, the Ruaha National Park, and the Kilombero catchment for sugar cane are in this basin. The RUBADA questioned why they could not become the basin organisation with the authority to charge water fees, but this was rejected by pointing at the national legal framework (Hirji and Patorni, 1994). The World Bank financed the opening of a subbasin office in Rujewa, primarily with the aim to implement the water rights system in the Upper Ruaha Subbasin.

In 1994, the World Bank and a few European donors, in collaboration with the Ministry of Water, Energy and Minerals, initiated a Water Sector Review and a Rapid Water Resources Assessment in four prioritised basins: Pangani, Rufiji, Ruvu and Lake Victoria (MWEM, 1995). DANIDA and the World Bank compiled a basin study for the Rufiji Basin (World Bank/DANIDA, 1995). A seminar on water resources management in Tanzania was organised to discuss the preliminary findings of this review, and other issues and international experiences relating to basin management (Hirji and Patorni, 1994). This was a first effort to synthesise the limited existing data on the availability of water resources. The seminar highlighted the need for cross-sectoral coordination, including the need for coordination among donors driven by government. Hydropower received much attention, as capable of providing an estimated 85-90% of electricity at the time (Msuya, 1994). Also, in line with the structural adjustments and dwindling government funds of the period, the need for cost-recovery of water infrastructure services was emphasised. Past practices were to be abandoned in which "social and political considerations have outweighed economic and financial considerations in the setting of water tariffs". Participants welcomed that 'water is now seen as an economic good', but this referred to a more stringent recovery of the actual costs of infrastructure and service delivery. This handful of professionals also still envisaged infrastructure development for all uses (Hirji and Patorni, 1994). This changed with the introduction of IWRM.

The concept of IWRM and its upscaling

The World Bank's next project, which started in 1996, was the River Basin Management – Smallholder Irrigation Improvement Programme (RBM-SIIP) (World Bank, 1996). The RBM-SIPP project was highly influential in translating the globally prevailing ideology of IWRM for Tanzania. The project management confirmed that the interpretation of IWRM in RBM-SIIP was "more or less the same as the definition of IWRM by the Global Water Partnership" (Mutayoba, 2002). The 1991 National Water Policy had largely focused on the need for more community participation in the design of water supply, also as a precondition for payment. Just five years later, the World Bank declared this policy as inadequate and introduced radical changes justified by a new notion of 'water as an economic good'. This had six aspects.

First, unlike the earlier agenda of developing storage and conveyance infrastructure to meet the range of growing water needs, the focus shifted to competition for water as a scarce finite resource. Implicitly, this assumed that the level of water development was bound to stay as low as it was. The assumption was that direct competition between agriculture and hydropower in a zero-sum game, as in the Pangani and Rufiji basins, was inevitable. Second, in such a competition, the highest economic value should have the priority. Hydropower got such priority over agriculture, irrespective of agriculture's role as an engine of economic growth. The emphasis on economic value was later somewhat balanced by considering the environment, narrowly interpreted as quantitative environmental flows. The environment also gained a higher priority than agriculture. Third, economic goods were to be paid for. This was not anymore just translated into cost-recovery for services provided, but there was also an obligation to pay for the use of the water resource. Fourth, as the World Bank reasoned: payment for water would support wise water use. Fifth, and most importantly, water fees collected by the Basin Water Officer would be the revenue to finance the new Basin Officers and the office's operations. The last aspect concerned the pivotal tool to achieve wise water use, namely water allocation to the highest economic value, and payment for the use of water resources to finance the new basin organisations. This tool was established by the revival and transformation of the dormant water rights system into a taxation tool.

The Smallholder Irrigation Improvement (SIIP) component of the RBM-SIIP project targeted smallholders to use less water. They should become more 'efficient' on their existing irrigated areas and certainly stop expanding new water uptake. The project constructed concrete weirs in river diversions that were supposed to enable such curtailment of water use (World Bank, 1996). The River Basin Management (RBM) component of RBM-SIIP financed the formulation and adoption of the new concept in new national policy and law. The six aspects of 'water as an economic good' were upscaled nationwide, starting the life of IWRM.

An amendment to the law in 1994 introduced a fixed once-off payment for registration of a water right of USD40, plus the so-called 'economic water users' fees' proportionate to annual volumes of water allocated [in absolute volumes (m^3) or flows (l/s)] (URT, 1994). In 1997, a Schedule of Fees for much higher amounts was promulgated (URT, 1997), with the introduction in 2002 of a more rewarding flat tariff for any small-scale uses, irrespective of factual uses (URT, 2002).

Further, Water Utilisation (General) Regulations in 1997 changed the status of the National and Basin Water Boards from advisory bodies to bodies that would oversee the work of the Central Water Officer and – still to be appointed – new Basin Water Officers. So the basin-level government officials became accountable to these boards. Moreover, membership of the Central and Basin Water Boards, given to those who used to come exclusively from government bodies, was opened up to non-State actors as well, including the private sector.

In 2002, the new water policy was promulgated, lifting the six aspects up to national policy, now also including the priority water needs of the environment (MoWLD, 2002). The policy was followed by the National Water Sector Development Strategy 2006-2015 (MoW, 2006). A new statutory water law was drafted with early drafts in 2004. It took five years before a new Water Resources Management Act in 2009 was promulgated (URT, 2009a). This confirmed the new parallel five-tier governance structure proposed in the National Water Policy (2002): national, basin, catchment, sub-catchment and water user association (the latter encompassing several wards sharing the same surface water source). A Water Supply and Sanitation Act was promulgated in the same year (URT, 2009b).

This course of events was hardly contested, partly because there was hardly any public debate on the new water policy and law. Issues were technical and complex and seemed legitimised by formal law. With the exception of a disagreement on the role of local government (see below), water officials generally accepted the World Bank's conceptual construction of physical water scarcity that ended the earlier primary focus on infrastructure development for all, promoted basin institutions, and invented a new taxation tool to finance water resource management functions by an increasingly under-sourced state to which, nevertheless, a new governance layer of tiered basin institutions was added.

The life of IWRM in the Pangani, Rufiji and Wami Ruvu basins

The two main IWRM laboratories, the Pangani and Rufiji basins, were studied by many international and national researchers (Lankford et al., 2004; Lein and Tagseth 2009). In the Pangani Basin, the International Conservation Union (IUCN) implemented the Water and Nature Initiative (WANI). The project was the first to calculate an environmental flow in Tanzania (IUCN, 2010). On its part the World Bank undertook various projects to support the implementation of the transformed water rights system.

In the Rufiji Basin, the focus was on the Mkoji Sub-Catchment and Usangu Plains in the Great Ruaha. Many stretches had always been ephemeral (Mwaruvanda, 1994), but the alarm bell was rung when the river was dry during more days than before in the dry season. This 'drying up of the Great Ruaha' was also assumed to profoundly negatively affect the downstream Ruaha National Park and the Mtera-Kidatu power plants.

The United Kingdom's Department for International Development (DFID) supported research from 1998 to 2004 to inform the water policy-makers of that period with hydrological and other scientific analyses on the causes of competition, and to advise on the drafting of the new policy and law, including environmental concerns. The research contrasted its empirical findings with the firmly entrenched views held by the various actors, who especially blamed small-scale and other irrigators. Instead, for example, it was found that the operators of the Mtera-Kidatu hydropower plants had been too optimistic in releasing water in the wetter years, and had also miscalculated inflows from other tributaries. Further, it pointed at the existing feasibility studies for a dam that would provide sufficient water to the Ruaha National Park (Lankford et al., 2004). The World Bank appreciated this nuancing of its initial IWRM narrative, but the option of water development as a long-term and win-win solution, as this research also proposed, was still hardly discussed, let alone supported. The World Wildlife Fund continued with a project to organise smallholders in Water User Association and an apex organisation with the aim of conserving and fairly distributing the limited water resources.

In 2002, the third basin office was opened: the Wami Ruvu Basin office. The Basin Water Board consisted of eight government officials and two corporate sector representatives. As the Basin Officer summarised her role in implementing IWRM, IWRM was "a step-by-step and open-ended process of managing water resources in a harmonious and environmentally sustainable way by involving stakeholders" (Kalugendo, 2012; see also van Eeden et al., Chapter 12). As in other basins, the core of officers' work centred on the implementation of permits and waste discharge permits; the collaboration with the Basin Water Board; water resources monitoring; pollution prevention; awareness raising; and coordination of the basin's IWRM and development plan (Kalugendo, 2012). Building on their earlier work, Japanese consultants, funded by JICA, compiled a remarkably thorough and extensive basin development plan between 1994 and 2013 (MoW et al., 2013). Unlike the World Bank's narrative that shifted away from infrastructure development, JICA kept focusing on water development to meet the rapidly expanding water needs of all users, especially those of industrial and urban users in downstream Dar es Salaam. JICA found that earlier assessments of environmental flows in 2008 by USAID, IUCN and Florida University (Water Action Hub Wami Ruvu Basin, 2015) were overestimated and recommended a more flexible and context-specific assessment of environmental flows. The study identified and prioritised a range of project proposals. It remains totally unclear, though, who will finance and implement these projects.

The water sector status reports of 2010 (MoWI, 2010) and 2014 (MoW, 2014) evaluated how IWRM had fared since the water sector development plan of 2006. Based on these reports and further evidence from the above-described chronology of events in the name of IWRM, we now turn to answering our question: how did IWRM affect smallholders' irrigation? Who were the winners and losers?

Winners and losers of IWRM

Losers

Stifling smallholders' access to water infrastructure

IWRM negatively affected smallholders' access to water in three ways. First, IWRM stifled Tanzania's water development agenda by shifting focus to the allocation of what was supposed to be a finite scarce resource. Winners and losers in this zero-sum game needed to be defined. Agriculture, largely consisting of smallholders, became the loser in this narrative – smallholders were the largest, most wasteful and, in the neoliberal economic model, most uneconomic water user. The water-sector reports reinforced the adverse view of smallholder farming as the thirsty overconsumer of 89% of water abstractions, complaining: "There are still a large number of traditional furrow irrigation systems that have not been improved and are responsible for high water losses because they are poorly operated and maintained" (MoW, 2014).

Competition was strengthened by adding the environment as a water user in its own right. The Water Resource Management Act (2009) consolidated a second priority to 'the environment', after domestic water uses. This is before "socioeconomic activities depending on the availability of water resources" (Water Resources Management Act 2009, Sub-section 6 (2)).

However, by the mid-2000s, the development of the country's abundant water resources was articulated again as primary goal: government's water sector reports added the 'D' of 'Development', to form Integrated Water Resource Management and Development (IWRMD). The World Bank and donors also returned to supporting irrigation development but now with stronger private-sector participation (World Bank, 2005). Indeed, the private-sector's investors in large-scale land- and water-deals were the main agents to take irrigation development forward.

While the water sector's overall budget also picked up from the mid-2000s onwards after the significant drop in foreign funding since the 1980s, the IWRMD component was marginal. Foreign funding by 19 Development Partners constituted 75% of the water sector's budget for the period 2006-2014. (Compare with 28% of foreign funding for Tanzania's overall budget (UNDP and URT, 2015)). However, the 2014 budget not only showed the marginal significance of IWRMD for government and donors, but also the continued lack of integration.

The 2014 water-sector budget consisted of four components, which were divided along the conventional subsector lines. As the smallest component, IWRMD received only 6% of the total budget. The IWRMD budget was mainly used for strategic infrastructure (from boreholes to dams), and for water resource monitoring stations. The other sectors, urban water supply, rural water supply and capacity building/staffing received 55, 32, and 7%, respectively. Thus, in spite of the strong narratives of integration, IWRMD was a subsector even *within* the water sector. Irrigation continued to be funded through the Agricultural Sector Development Plan's basket. Integration across sectors, for example with the energy sector, was even less.

Already since 2010 (MoWI, 2010), there was no funding for setting up permit systems:

> *The WRM Act (2009) requires all unrecorded rights to be registered within two years of the Act coming into force (August 1st, 2009). This is a legal requirement whose implementation requires adequate resources to implement specific activities including: awareness creation, extensive water use surveys and verifications, inventory of water uses, stakeholder consultations and engagements (with those with rights and those without water rights) through participatory processes. To implement this requirement of the Water Resource Management Act (2009) it is estimated that a total of USD4.5 million is required for all nine basins. There is, however, no allocation for this vital activity within the approved Water Sector Development Programme financing framework (MoWI, 2010: 45).*

Exclusion from basin-level water resources development planning

Second, smallholders were excluded from the new governance layer of basin institutions and their decision making about water resource planning and water allocation. Decision making about the actual implementation of the revived permit system had added a significant new mandate. While this was decentralised from the central Water Officer to nine Basin Water Officers, it represented new top-down powers.

By 2012, all nine Basin Offices and Basin Water Boards had been established, and had started water resource planning. However, while many studies were conducted, the only IWRMD plan that had been finalised by 2013 was the above-mentioned report for the Wami Ruvu Basin by JICA. American universities were leading the IWRMD plan for the Rufiji Basin. In any case, this public information fitted the needs of foreign and national investors to identify the most fertile and well-watered (and most mineral-rich) land.

Representation of smallholders in the new basin institutions was weak, if not non-existing. Basin Boards were powerful because the basin officers were accountable not only to their national superiors but also to Basin Water Board members. However, representation in the Basin Boards was more open to the corporate private sector than to smallholders. Local government remained just one of the members of the Basin Water Boards, and yet local government is both an elected bottom-up stakeholder representation and the state's most localised hub for actual investments in water development and water conflict resolution. Tanzanian officials had repeatedly contested this sidelining of local government in Basin Boards, for example in a position paper in 2003, and also before and after the promulgation of the Water Resources Management Act. However, this all remained in vain (Mwaruvanda, 2013, personal communication).

Further decentralisation of basin-level decision-making was through three more institutional layers according to hydrological boundaries that had also to be established from scratch. The bottom-up establishment of water user associations (WUA) was a non-starter because Basin Officers' primary aim of organisation was to reduce transaction costs for the collection of water fees. For example, in the Wami Ruvu Basin, 12 WUAs had been registered between 2002 and 2014 primarily to reduce transaction costs for fee collection. As found by Sumuni (2016), the roles and responsibilities of WUAs other than fee collection, remain unclear. Farmers questioned whether any other service was to be delivered and refused to pay membership fees without such service. Moreover, local water users challenged the authority of these water user associations to interfere in their local water management (Sumuni, 2016).

Thus, the acclaimed 'decentralisation' to 'participatory Basin Boards' in accordance with the 'subsidiarity principle' seems a thin cosmetic layer to further legitimise new top-down powers of Basin Board members, especially in implementing a revived and transformed water entitlement and taxation system. Basin management by basin offices opened new doors for winners in the form of large-scale users at the top. Smallholders, by all accounts, are losers as they have no practical way of being meaningfully involved, in the near future, in the new parallel governance layers.

The power of the corporate sector in water management, even beyond basin boundaries, is further illustrated by the case of the Southern Agricultural Growth Corridor of Tanzania (SAGCOT). In 2010, this partnership was forged with the aim of investing in the Rufiji Basin's land with minerals or fertile lands with ample water and mineral resources for sugar cane, maize, paddy and cassava cultivation. The main initiators were the USA, Norway, Ireland, Alliance for a Green Revolution in Africa, FAO, IFAD, World Bank, African Development Bank, the Tanzanian Agricultural Council, Tanzania Investment Centre and the Ministry of Agriculture. SAGCOT covers one third of Tanzania: the Rufiji Basin and parts of the Wami Ruvu and Lake Rukwa basins. SAGCOT recreated RUBADA as its 5% shareholder, beyond the three basin offices, with even more power to directly compete with local people's land, water and markets (SAGCOT, 2011).

Criminalising informal smallholder irrigators

Third, smallholders lost in the permit system. By 2014, 3680 water use permits (and effluent discharges and drilling permits) had been allocated across the entire country (MoWI, 2014). Thus, the overwhelming majority of informal water users in Tanzania were *de jure* criminals. Since 1974, their failure to apply for a permit can, in principle, result in imprisonment, set at a maximum of six months in the Water Resource Management Act (2009). However, even if the hundreds of thousands of smallholder irrigators had been informed about the law and had applied for a permit, state capacity would have been too limited to process even a fraction of their applications. The Water Resource Management Act recognises this by asking Basin Officers to also maintain an Unauthorised Abstractions Register (URT, 2009a).

Smallholders protested that God gave water for free to their ancestors (van Koppen et al., 2004; Mdee et al., 2014). Basically, they contested what had become a reality: the colonial 1948 Water Ordinance, which dispossessed all 'native' non-formalised water rights arrangements, in favour of a handful of colonial settlers; the 1959 Regulation which brought everyone under the principle that water uses are only lawful with a water right; and the independent State's continuation of dispossession of non-statutory legal regimes. IWRM not only revived this paper principle and enforced its implementation across the country among informal water users, but the transformation of this legal system into a taxation tool pushed its enforcement even further. At best, smallholders can invoke living customary law that they see as legitimate. Obviously, the illegal status of such local arrangements erodes any bargaining position vis-à-vis water users with permits.

The weak and unfair bargaining position of water users invoking informal and customary water rights regimes vis-à-vis permit holders plays out within communities and between small and more powerful large-scale users. We discussed the possibility that permits could be introduced in an area with extensive development of community-managed canals in the Uluguru Mountains (van Koppen et al., 2013). The ward councillor reflected on the first-come-first-serve principle of permits and the type of ad-hoc organisation required for collective permits, which would undoubtedly be led by the more powerful male elite. She predicted: 'permits will create chaos'. The villagers did consider the risks of outside 'big investors' in land and water, and proposed a solution: vest permits in local government as an already legitimate mediator in any local conflicts and as the most local, legitimate organised representation of communities and their land and water resources vis-à-vis outsiders. However, IWRM's top-down governance layer denies this authority to local government. In sum, smallholders who irrigate informally are the pertinent losers of IWRM, for the moment mainly on paper and in discourse, but with continued enforcement, increasingly in reality as well.

Winners

The winners of permit systems, which are issued on a first-come, first-serve basis, are the formal, powerful, better-connected, administration-proficient water users, both foreign and national, including state officials. The formal approval procedure of an application through the Basin Water Board is usually administrative only. The corporate sector's informal contacts with Basin Water Officers, if not their formal representation in Basin Water Boards, ensures approval. No evidence was found of a genuine public participation process in which those affected by a new water abstraction were heard to negotiate benefit-sharing arrangements, although permits formally require such a process before approval. In any case, there are only limited data about water availability for the affected downstream users and Basin Water Officer to check. So access to first-class entitlements is relatively easy.

Moreover, permits are tradable, and there is ample scope for applicants to speculate and apply for larger volumes than those immediately needed. Unused water can later be sold to another new user. Or, in case the state needs to expropriate those waters again for public interest, as the Act allows, the permit holder might well demand monetary compensation from the state. The prevailing norm that 'investors should have enough security in order for them to make the investment' further legitimises such speculative behaviour. Yet, the big promises about major land-based investments are notoriously rarely realised in practice.

Is Government empowered to better regulate water use?

Is government with its Basin Offices a winner or loser of IWRMD? Government also lost, especially as a result of permit systems as supposedly effective tool for three goals at the same time: water allocation, revenue collection, and regulation in other fields, such as pollution prevention. In allocation of water resources, permits created new problems, while no existing water-sharing problem was solved. This emerged from the evidence of the specific projects that sought to implement permits among small-scale informal water users, for example in the Rufiji Basin (van Koppen et al., 2004; Sokile, 2005; Mehari et al., 2009) and Wami Ruvu Basin (Mdee et al., 2014; Sumuni, 2016). The government's promise that permits would give better entitlements vis-à-vis competing neighbours, was attractive for small-scale users who heard first about it, in the logic of 'first come first serve'. These were usually men with close contacts with public institutions. However, this incentive disappeared once neighbours had also obtained permits. Without water control structures, and even without water monitoring structures, permits neither helped the Basin Water Officers nor the communities to mediate in times of conflict. Moreover, an average annual volume, or even a seasonal average volume is useless in periods of water scarcity when nobody can get that average. Hence, over time, Basin Water Officers wisely toned down any promise of water security. They referred to the Water Resource Management Act that repeated the same as its contents in 1959: a permit is no guarantee that water is actually available. As found in the Pangani Basin, Basin Water Officers increasingly left the thorny water-sharing issues to farmers themselves (De Bont et al., 2015). Komakech et al. (2011) also found that large flower growers avoided invoking their formal power of a permit and, instead, negotiated with upstream and downstream local users for sustainable conflict resolution and labour relations.

The new goal of permit systems as water taxation tool created further losses.. Enforcement of permitting is vital for the basin offices to raise sufficient revenue to be able to carry out its functions, and probably the major incentive to implement. However, the government lost in taxation, first because the transaction costs to collect volume-based revenue among many small-scale uses were excessive and bound to lead to net revenue losses, certainly compared to the few large-scale users. For example, Sumuni (2016) found that 960 permits had been allocated in the WamiRuvu Basin. The 30 largest permits used 89% of the total volume of water allocated. These included five permits for Mtibwa sugar estates, and two for the biofuel company SEKAB. The other 930 permit holders only used 11% of the total volume of water, corresponding to a comparable proportion of revenues raised. Net losses could have been avoided by designing a lean, well-targeted cost-effective taxation tool that could have been enforced in many ways (as other forms of tax enforcement).

Second, in demanding fees, Basin Offices lost legitimacy among small-scale water users for two more reasons than those mentioned above. When permits were introduced in the Mkoji sub-catchment (Usangu Plains) smallholders did not oppose payment, anticipating that a public service would be delivered to them in return, in particular more secure access to water. However, as explained above, that failed. When the Basin Water Officers realised their practical inability to ensure access to water through permits, they allocated temporary permits only. Holders of temporary permits had to pay but could not claim any water (Mehari et al., 2009). When smallholders realised that their fees were 'disappearing in a black hole' they stopped paying.

A second ground for disgruntlement that weakened government's legitimacy was that permits were only partially implemented (as will remain the case). As Sumuni (2016) found, those who had paid for water found it unfair that others did not pay.

Last but not least, the government lost because providing entitlements in return for the payment of fees weakened the power of the state as regulator. Again, large-scale users won: the higher payments of large-scale users to the Basin Office became a strong but perverse incentive for the officers to generously allocate water entitlements to large-scale users. This not only jeopardised any effort towards wise water use, but it lawfully 'bribed' officials to protect the water rights of the already powerful large-scale users, at still a fraction of the profits that can be made from water. It even further weakened Basin Water Officers' already limited power to impose regulatory measures, such as pollution prevention.

Conclusion

The case of Tanzania confirmed the significant neglect of Equity aspects compared to the other two Es in the narrative of IWRM (Economic efficiency and Environmental sustainability). 'Equity', which focused on access to water by smallholders to contribute to poverty alleviation and to broad-based agricultural and economic growth, was far from being realised in the IWRM dispensation. IWRM got a life as national policy and law for basin-level planning (taking forward the master plans and basin plans of the pre-1990s); as (new) basin institutions according to the (pre-1990) basin boundaries; as a (revived and transformed) colonial permit system; and as (new) environmental flows. There was no deliberate well-thought-out strategy to ensure equitable water use. After 15 years of IWRM, the government recast the concept as IWRMD to reintegrate infrastructure development in water policy discourse. After 25 years, IWRMD had only a tiny budget that was still isolated from other water-sector budget lines, and even more from other ministries and funding streams.

The water permit system perhaps epitomises inequitable water use. The design and early implementation of the transformed permit systems and basin institutions further marginalised informal smallholder irrigators. For the moment, this marginalisation is still largely discourse and paper policy and law. Yet, the evidence from the past 25 years raises new questions to address this marginalisation.

One question that needs to be addressed relates to the existing local and customary arrangements, including current and potential roles of local governments, as a starting point of rural water governance. How to protect and reconcile interests of existing local and customary uses with large-scale investors? Would local government be a good place? At higher aggregate scales, questions centre on democratic representation and lean regulation that strengthens basin offices' authority vis-à-vis powerful users. If permits are to be taken forward, questions would focus on their redesign for effective targeting, establishment of thresholds below which water uses are authorised without permit and possibly prioritised, and removal of unjust entitlements.

The more fundamental and broader question regards the rapidly growing majority of smallholders, who, often at no cost to the tax payer, invest in infrastructure to better provide for their own food security and to feed the nation. How can their potential as an engine of growth be unlocked not only by prioritising their existing water uses but also by investing in their accelerated water uptake?

Acknowledgements

This chapter is based on research and inspiring debates within the project team of the Norwegian Research Council-funded project Flows and Practices: The Politics of IWRM in Africa. We thank the Norwegian Research Council for the generous support given to us. This included the opportunity for Aurelia van Eeden and for Philip Sumuni to conduct research as part of fulfilment of their Master's dissertations. We also thank the guest editors of the Special Issue of *Water Alternatives* (9:3) and the anonymous reviewers for their excellent comments.

References

Agwanda, A. and Amani, H. 2014. *Population growth, structure and momentum in Tanzania*. Background Paper No. 7, ESRF. Discussion Paper No. 61, Dar es Salaam: Economic and Social Research Foundation

Andersson, I. 1980. *The development of water supplies in Tanzania. A study of three regions, Kilimanjaro, Shinyanga and Mwanza regions.* Lund, Sweden: University of Lund.

Business Times. 2012. The pros and cons of Kilimo Kwanza. www.businesstimes.co.tz/index.php?option=com_content&id=1967: tanzania-the-pros-and-cons-of-kilimo-kwanza&Itemid=5

DANIDA (Danish International Development Agency). 1983. Water master plans for Iringa, Ruvuma and Mbeya regions. Socio-economic studies. Village Participation on Water and Health Volume 13. United Republic of Tanzania Danish International-al Development Agency. Dar es Salaam and Copenhagen: Institute of Resource Assessment. University of Dar es Salaam and Center for Development Research.

De Bont, C.; Veldwisch, G.J.; Komakech, H.C. and Vos, J. 2015. The fluid nature of water grabbing: The on-going contestation of water distribution between peasants and agribusinesses in Nduruma, Tanzania. *Agriculture and Human Values* (ahead-of-print): 1-14. http://link.springer.com/article/10.1007%2Fs10460-015-9644-5

FAO (Food and Agriculture Organisation of the United Nations). 1969. *Report to the Government of Tanzania. Water development planning and soils aspects of irrigation development.* Rome: Food and Agriculture Organization of the United Nations and United Nations Development Programme. No. Ta 2718.

FAO. 2011. *Sub Saharan Africa's unfolding tragedy in mega land deals for agro-investments with lessons from Tanzania.* Bede Lyimo, Dar es Salaam, Tanzania. Rome: FAO.

Hillbom, E. 2010. Institutional continuity and change. A century of smallholders' water rights in Meru, Tanzania. Paper presented at evaluating the 20th century in Africa: Linking Colonial and Post-Colonial Economic Development, ASAUK Biennial conference, 16-19 September 2010, Oxford.

Hirji, R. and Patorni, F.-M. (Eds). 1994. Water resources management in Tanzania. Proceedings of the seminar Tanga, September 12-16, 1994. Washington, DC: The Economic Development Institute of the World Bank.

Index Mundi. 2014. Tanzania Demographics Profile 2014. www.indexmundi.com/tanzania/demographics_profile.html

International Union of Conservation of Nature (IUCN). 2010. *The Wami basin: A situational analysis.* IUCN Eastern and Southern Africa. https://portals.iucn.org/library/efiles/documents/2010-035.pdf

Kalugendo, P. 2012. Powerpoint presentation made at Water Utilities Conference September 2012 Dar es Salaam. www.esi-africa.com/wp-content/uploads/Praxeda_Kalugendo1.pdf

Kamwelwe, I. 2016. Deputy Minister of Water and Irrigation. Cited In Mugarula, F.; Tanzania: Government plans irrigation scheme for every district. Tanzania Daily News. 8 August 2016. www.dailynews.co.tz/index.php/home-news/52477-government-plans-irrigation-scheme-for-every-district

Lankford, B.; van Koppen, B.; Franks, T. and Mahoo, H. 2004. Entrenched views or insufficient science? Contested causes and solutions of water allocation: Insights from the Great Ruaha River Basin, Tanzania. *Agricultural Water Management* 69(2): 135-153.

Lein, H. and Tagseth, M. 2009. Tanzanian water policy reforms – Between principles and practical applications. *Water Policy* 11(2009): 203-220.

Macha, M. and Mwakalinga, I.E. 1994. Ruvu basin development plan and management. In Hirji, R. and Patorni, F.-M. (Eds), *Water resources management in Tanzania*, Chapter 5. Proceedings of the seminar Tanga, September 12-16, 1994. Washington, DC: The Economic Development Institute of the World Bank.

Maganga, F.P.; Kiwasila, H.L.; Juma, I.H. and Butterworth, J.A. 2004. Implications of customary norms and laws for implementing IWRM: Findings from Pangani and Rufiji basins, Tanzania. *Physics and Chemistry of the Earth* 29 (15-18): 1335-1342.

Makoye, K. 2013. Tanzania adopts irrigation law to help farmers battle climate change. Thomson Reuters Foundation. http://news.trust.org//item/20130904190945-6crok/ (accessed August 2016)

Mashauri, D.A. and Katko, T.S. 1993. Water supply development and tariffs in Tanzania: From free water policy towards cost recovery. *Environmental Management* 17(1): 31-39.

Mdee, A. with Harrison, E.; Mdee, C.; Mdee, E. and Bahati, E. 2014. *The politics of small-scale irrigation in Tanzania: Making sense of failed expectations.* Working Paper No. 107. Brighton: University of Sussex, Mzumbi University and Future Agricultures. www.future-agricultures.org

Mehari, A.; van Koppen, B.; McCartney, M. and Lankford, B. 2009. *Unchartered innovation? Local reforms of national formal water management in the Mkoji sub-catchment, Tanzania. Physics and Chemistry of the Earth Parts A/B/C* 34(4-5): 299-308.

Mehta, L.; Veldwisch, G.J. and Franco, J. 2012. Introduction to the Special Issue: Water grabbing? Focus on the (re)appropriation of finite water resources. *Water Alternatives* 5(2): 193-207.

Ministry of Energy and Minerals. 2015. *The draft national energy policy.* Dar es Salaam: Ministry of Energy and Minerals.

MoW (Ministry of Water). 2006. National Water Sector Development Programme (2005-2025) Consolidated Document. Dar es Salaam: Ministry of Water.

MoW (Ministry of Water). 2014. Water sector development program. The water sector status report 2014. Marking the End of Water Sector Development Plan Phase-I. Dar es Salaam: Ministry of Water.

www.maji.go.tz/sites/default/files/u12/WaterSectorStatusReport %202014. pdf

MWEM (Ministry of Water, Energy and Minerals). 1995. *Rapid water resources assessment*, Volumes 1 and 2. Dar es Salaam: Ministry of Water, Energy and Minerals in collaboration with the World Bank.

MoWI (Ministry of Water and Irrigation). 2009. The National Irrigation Policy Draft. Dar es Salaam: Ministry of Water and Irrigation.

MoWI (Ministry of Water and Irrigation). 2010. Water Sector Status Report 2010. Dares Salaam: Ministry of Water and Irrigation.

MoWLD (Ministry of Water and Livestock Development). 2002. *National water policy.* Dar es Salaam: Ministry of Water and Livestock Development.

MoW et al. (Ministry of Water, Japanese International Cooperation Agency, Earth System Science Co, Ltd.; Japan Techno Co. Ltd.; Oriental Consultants Co, Ltd). 2013. The study on water resources management and development in Wami Ruvu basin in the United Republic of Tanzania. Dar es Salaam: Ministry of Water.

Msuya, M.O.Y. 1994. Rapid water resources assessment. In Hirji, R. and Patorni, F.-M. (Eds), *Water Resources Management in Tanzania*, Chapter 4. Proceedings of the Seminar Tanga, September 12-16, 1994. Washington, DC. The Economic Development Institute of the World Bank.

Mutayoba, W.N. 2002. Management of water resources through basin management. Paper presented at the 3rd WaterNet/Warfsa Symposium, Dar es Salaam, 29-31 October 2002.

Mwaruvanda, W. 1994. Rufiji basin management. In Hirji, R. and Patorni, F.-M. (Eds),

Water Resources Management in Tanzania, Chapter 6. Proceedings of the seminar Tanga, September 12-16, 1994. Washington, DC. The Economic Development Institute of the World Bank

Oakland Institute. 2011. Understanding land investment deals in Africa. Country Report Tanzania. Oakland: Oakland Institute. www.oaklandinstitute.org/understanding-land-investment-deals-africa-tanzania

SAGCOT (Southern Agricultural Growth Corridor of Tanzania). 2011. Investment blueprint.www.sagcot.com/uploads/media/Invest-Blueprint-SAGCOT_High_res.pdf

Shah, T. 2007. Issues in reforming informal water economies of low-income countries: Examples from India and elsewhere. In van Koppen, B.; Giordano, M. and Butterworth, J. (Eds), *Community-based water law and water resource management reform in developing countries*, pp. 65-95. Comprehensive Assessment of Water Management in Agriculture Series 5. Wallingford, UK: CABI Publishers.

Shivji, I.G. 2009. *Where is Uhuru? Reflections on the struggle for democracy in Africa.* UFAHAMU Books, Pambazuka Press.

Skarstein, R. 2005. Economic liberalization and smallholder productivity in Tanzania. From promised success to real failure, 1985-1998. *Journal of Agrarian Change* 5(3): 334-62. Cited In United Nations Development Programme and United Republic of Tanzania, 2015.

Sokile, C.S. 2005. Towards improvement of institutional frameworks for intersectoral water management. The case of Mkoji Sub Catchment of the Great Ruaha River in the Rufiji basin, Tanzania. PhD thesis. University of Dar es Salaam

Sukari. Sugar Board of Tanzania. 2014. An overview of the Tanzania sugar industry. Powerpoint presentation.

Sumuni, P.M. 2016. Influence of institutional set-up on performance of traditional irrigation schemes, a case study of Nyandira Ward, Mvomero District Tanzania. Master thesis, Sokoine University of Agriculture, Morogoro, Tanzania.

TUTT (Tanganyika United Trust Territory). 1948. Water Ordinance of 1948, Chapter 257. Dar es Salaam: Government Printers.

TUTT. 1959. The Water Ordinance of 1959. Dar es Salaam: The Governor of Tanganyika.

Tarimo, A.K.P.R.; Kihupi, N.I.; Bjerkholt, J.T.; Mkoga, Z.J. and Gomani, L.M. 2008. Evaluation of the effectiveness of proportioning water division weirs in Herman Canal Farmer Managed Irrigation Scheme, Usangu Plains Tanzania. *Journal of Agricultural Science* 9: 40-53.

Tarimo, A.K.P.R.; van Koppen, B. and Sumuni, P.M. 2014. Integrated Water Resources Management in Tanzania. Unpublished project report.

Timmer, C.P. 1988. The agricultural transformation. In Chenery, H. and Srinivasan, T.N. (Eds), *Handbook of development economics,* Volume 1, pp. 275-331. Amsterdam: Elsevier Science Publishers.

UNDP and URT (United Nations Development Programme and United Republic of Tanzania). 2015. Tanzania Human Development Report 2014. Economic Transformation for Human Development. Dar es Salaam: Economic and Social Research Foundation.

URT (United Republic of Tanzania). 1974. *Water Utilisation (Control and Regulation)*

Act No. 42 of 1974. Dar es Salaam: The United Republic of Tanzania.

URT. 1981. *Water Utilization (Control and Regulation) (Amendment) Act, 1981 (Act No. 10)*. Dar es Salaam: The United Republic of Tanzania.

URT. 1994. *Subsidiary Legislation [Government Notice No. 347 of 1994 under section 38(2) of the Water Utilization (Control and Regulation) Act No. 42 of 1974]*. Dar es Salaam: The United Republic of Tanzania.

URT. 1997. *Water Utilization (General) Regulations of 1997*. Dar es Salaam: The United Republic of Tanzania.

URT. 2002. *Water Utilization (General) (Amendment) Regulations. 2002*. Dar es Salaam: The United Republic of Tanzania.

URT. 2009a. *The Water Resources Management Act no. 11*. Dar es Salaam: Government Printer.

URT. 2009b. *The Water Supply and Sanitation Act no. 11*. Dar es Salaam: Government Printer.

van Koppen, B.; Sokile, C.; Hatibu, N.; Lankford, B.; Mahoo, H. and Pius, Y. 2004. *Formal water rights in Tanzania: Deepening a dichotomy?* IWMI Working Paper No. 71. Colombo, Sri Lanka: International Water Management Institute.

van Koppen, B.; Tarimo, A.; Sumuni, P. and Shimiyu, K. 2013. Uluguru Mountains Field Study 31 May-3 June 2013. Unpublished Report. Pretoria: International Water Management Institute.

Water Action Hub Wami Ruvu Basin. 2015. Documents. UN Global Compact.

https: //wateractionhub.org/regions/view/16/basin-document/

WGF (Water Governance Facility). 2012. *Human rights-based approaches and managing water resources: Exploring the potential for enhancing development outcomes*. WGF Report No. 1. Stockholm: Stockholm International Water Institute.

Wobst, P. 2001. *Structural adjustment and intersectoral shifts in Tanzania*. A Computable General Equilibrium Analysis. Washington, DC: International Food Policy and Research Institute.

World Bank. 1996. Staff appraisal report, Tanzania. In *River Basin Management and Smallholder Irrigation Improvement Project*. Report No. 15122-TA. Washington: Agriculture and Environment Operations, Eastern Africa Department.

World Bank. 2005. Tanzania – Agricultural Sector Development Program Project. Washington, DC: World Bank.

http://documents.worldbank.org/curated/en/458491468116661828/Tanzania-Agricultural-Sector-Development-Program-Project.

World Bank/DANIDA. 1995. Water resources management in the Great Ruaha Basin: A study of demand driven management of land and water resources with local level participation. Prepared for the Rufiji River Basin Office by the Study of Integrated Water and Land Management.

12

Whose Waters? Large-Scale Agricultural Development and Water Grabbing in the Wami-Ruvu River Basin, Tanzania[1]

Aurelia van Eeden

Lyla Mehta

Barbara van Koppen

ABSTRACT: In Tanzania like in other parts of the global South, in the name of 'development' and 'poverty eradication' vast tracts of land have been earmarked by the government to be developed by investors for different commercial agricultural projects, giving rise to the contested land grab phenomenon. In parallel, Integrated Water Resources Management (IWRM) has been promoted in the country and globally as the governance framework that seeks to manage water resources in an efficient, equitable and sustainable manner. This chapter asks how IWRM manages the competing interests as well as the diverse priorities of both large and small water users in the midst of foreign direct investment. By focusing on two commercial sugar companies operating in the Wami-Ruvu River Basin in Tanzania and their impacts on the water and land rights of the surrounding villages, the chapter asks whether institutional and capacity weaknesses around IWRM implementation can be exploited by powerful actors that seek to meet their own interests, thus allowing water grabbing to take place. The chapter thus highlights the power, interests and alliances of the various actors involved in the governance of water resources. By drawing on recent conceptual insights from the water grabbing literature, the empirical findings suggest that the IWRM framework indirectly and directly facilitates the phenomenon of water grabbing to take place in the Wami-Ruvu River Basin in Tanzania.

KEYWORDS: Integrated Water Resource Management (IWRM), water grabbing, development policies, agricultural development, water governance, Tanzania

1 First published in *Water Alternatives* 9(3): 610-628.

Introduction

As discussed by van Koppen et al. (Chapter 11), Integrated Water Resources Management (IWRM) was introduced in Tanzania in the early 1990s and was then incorporated into the national water policy in 2002 and water law in 2009. In recent years, national development policies have been actively promoting commercial agricultural investment (Cotula et al., 2009; Cotula, 2011). From the late 2000s onwards, foreign investors began tapping into Tanzania's land and water resources, giving rise to the heavily contested 'land grab' phenomenon whereby vast tracts of land have been allocated to investors for commercial agriculture (Cotula et al., 2009; Cotula, 2011; Matondi et al., 2011; Matondi and Matupo, 2011). While suitable land has been the driving force behind these investments, recent evidence has indicated that water has been the missing dimension in debates on land grabbing (Bossio et al., 2012; Bues and Theesfeld, 2012; Mehta et al., 2012).

In Tanzania, conflicts between communities, government and investors have been on the increase (see van Eeden, 2014). Land and water grabs have led to new forms of water and food scarcities for local communities and the manner in which land deals have been implemented has meant that some communities that used to have access to water and other resources connected to the land, are now excluded from using these resources (ibid). Furthermore, the physical aspects of water allocation are also notoriously complicated in Tanzania where rivers and river basins are complex and highly variable (see Lankford and Mwaruvanda, 2007). These issues have questioned the ability of the IWRM framework as implemented in Tanzania, to efficiently and equitably allocate water among water users in a river basin. While IWRM seeks to reconcile goals of economic efficiency, social equity and environmental sustainability, clearly these goals are often "antagonistic (...) and trade-offs are necessary but hard to achieve in such situations" (Molle, 2008: 133; Franco et al., 2013).

Central to the working of IWRM is the granting of water permits whereby a certain amount of water is allocated to a water user for a specific purpose (van Koppen et al., 2007; van Eeden, 2014). However, since water allocation is both physically complex and intrinsically a political and power-laden process, it can entail the potential reallocation of water to those 'priority uses' with the supposedly highest economic value that, in turn, tend to have detrimental impacts on the lives and livelihoods of local communities (Mehta et al., 2012; Veldwisch et al., 2013). The water permit application process in Tanzania and other parts of sub-Saharan Africa has also been criticised for being too rigid, complicated and favouring the 'administrative-proficient' (van Koppen et al., 2007; Franco et al., 2013: 1665). Therefore, concerns have been mounting over the visibility of small-scale farmers who, failing to acquire water use permits, lack the legal footing to stand their ground against large-scale water users in any water conflict (ibid).

Since IWRM is the major water governance framework in both Tanzania and the world, it is important to ask how it deals with these tensions and conflicting interests in a river basin and the particular situation of small-scale users. This chapter thus explores how the IWRM governance framework is used to manage the competing interests of diverse water users in a river basin. It asks whether institutional and capacity issues can be exploited by powerful actors that seek to meet their own interests, thus allowing water grabbing to take place (Franco et al., 2013). Specifically, this chapter addresses how IWRM manages the diverse priorities and interests of both large and small water users in the midst of foreign direct investment in commercial agricultural projects in the Wami-Ruvu River Basin (WRRB), Tanzania. After a short conceptual framework, the chapter provides a background of water and land development in Tanzania. It then looks at how IWRM has been implemented in the Wami-Ruvu River Basin. We focus on two sugar companies and a surrounding village at each of the companies' operations: Mtibwa Sugar Estate (MSE) and Lukenge Village, upstream in the Wami River, and EcoEnergy and Matipwili Village situated downstream. These cases were chosen as the two commercial sugar farms are the largest users of water in the WRRB, abstracting water from the Wami River. Also, their position relative to one another, one being upstream and the other downstream, makes for a vibrant study of the power relations not just between the two of them, but also between them and the villages that surround each of them.

The research was conducted over a 5-month period in Tanzania and pursued a qualitative methodology. It used the Case Study Method[2] (CSM) approach (see Stake, 2005: Creswell, 2007; Berg and Lune, 2012). The study utilised/resorted to multiple sources of enquiry including; semi-structured interviews, focus group discussions, seminars and forums, stakeholder observation at various levels, reports, policy and media reviews as well as informal communication. Both case studies operated within a politically charged arena and had sensitive aspects to their operations that at the time made regular headlines of Tanzanian news. Thus, in preparation of the interviews a question guide was prepared with key topics and questions in line with the objective of the study.

Individual interviews were held with various employees, consultants and advisors of the two sugar estates; officials of the Wami-Ruvu River Basin Office, District and Ward offices; employees of NGOs and Ministry officials.

Through the empirical evidence derived from this research study, the chapter highlights the power and interests of the various actors involved in the governance of water resources and argues that the IWRM framework indirectly and directly facilitates the phenomenon of water grabbing to take place in these two areas in the Wami-Ruvu River Basin. This also suggests that the IWRM approach may not be really suitable in a country like Tanzania where thousands of smallholders, for multiple reasons, never gain access to permits and thus their rights will lie outside of the 'official' water governance framework (see also van Koppen et al., Chapter 11).

2 Berg and Lune (2012) defines the CSM approach as a method to collect enough data in a systematic way to effectively understand how a certain social setting, person, group or event operates or functions (Berg and Lune, 2012).

Fig. 12.1. Wami-Ruvu River Basin, Tanzania

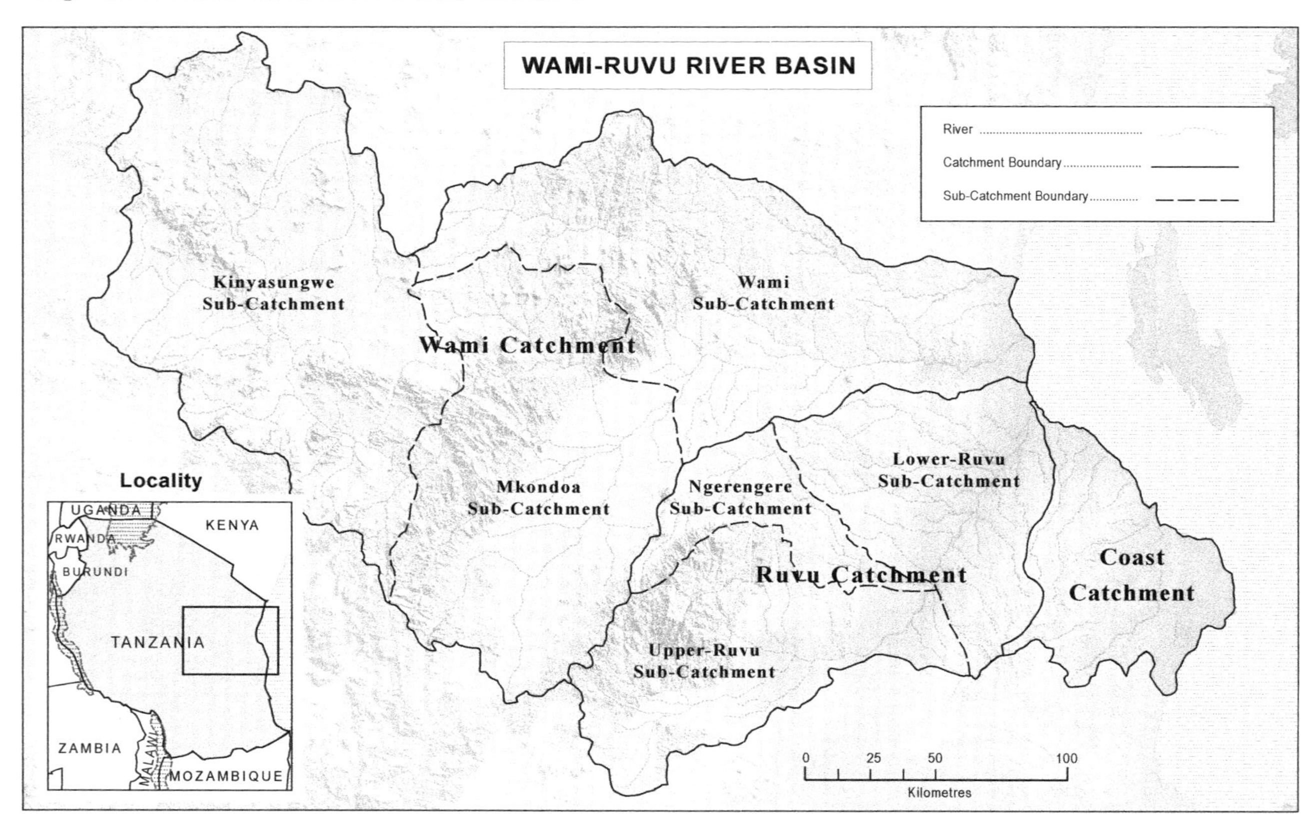
WAMI-RUVU RIVER BASIN
River
Catchment Boundary
Sub-Catchment Boundary
Kinyasungwe Sub-Catchment
Wami Sub-Catchment
Wami Catchment
Mkondoa Sub-Catchment
Ngerengere Sub-Catchment
Lower-Ruvu Sub-Catchment
Ruvu Catchment
Upper-Ruvu Sub-Catchment
Coast Catchment
0
25
50
100
Kilometres
Locality
UGANDA
KENYA
RWANDA
BURUNDI
TANZANIA
ZAMBIA
MALAWI
MOZAMBIQUE

Theoretical points of departure

The Tanzanian government's development policies such as 'Development Vision 2025' and 'Kilimo Kwanza' (Swahili for *agriculture first*) are perhaps the highest-profile attempts to eradicate poverty through economic development. A significant feature of these initiatives is the development of large-scale commercial agriculture where vast tracts of land have been earmarked by the government to be developed by investors for different commercial agricultural projects. However, allowing investors to gain access to land has meant that others, especially local communities, have been excluded from decisions regarding their own land now earmarked for agricultural investments or from having access to resources which are key to sustain their livelihoods. This is why scholars note that many development programmes designed to eradicate poverty can, in fact, create poverty for some (Li, 2007; Hall et al., 2011).

The recent wave of large-scale resource appropriation is being justified by governments and the private sector by promoting narratives that consider water and land wasted if it is not developed or fully utilised for commercial purposes (Mehta et al., 2012). Vast tracts of 'marginal' or 'unused' lands have been made available by governments to investors for productive purposes. However, many scholars have debated that these 'marginal' or 'unused' resources are in fact not unused but rather belongs to villages and smallholders with customary rights over the resource (van Koppen et al., 2004; Kiishweko, 2012; Mehta et al., 2012).

Resource grabbing is "the appropriation of natural resources, including land and water and the control of their associated uses and benefits, with or without the transfer of ownership, usually from poor and marginalised to powerful actors" (see Mehta et al., 2012: 195; Fairhead et al., 2012). The growing body of empirical research that underpins the phenomenon of the global 'land-grab' is broadly based on Harvey's notion of 'accumulation by dispossession' (Harvey, 2005), a concept that highlights the transfer of property from public to private ownership which serves the interests of the state or a few capitalist elites (Harvey, 2005). The term 'grabbing' is intentionally used to 'grab' attention to memories of past and present-day injustices of resource enclosures and dispossessions (Mehta et al., 2012).

While power and control over water resources do not constitute a new concept, the water grab phenomenon "draws attention to the involvement of new capitalist players and stakeholders in water resources management and the rise of new political and economic power relations through diverse trajectories of neo-liberalism" (Mehta et al., 2012: 198). The process of water grabbing is much more 'slippery' than land grabbing, not least due to the nature of water (Mehta et al., 2012). Water is fluid in nature and by implication its governance (through IWRM) requires the continued, active measuring and monitoring of water resources and allocations (Hodgson, 2004). However, this is extremely difficult due to the limited human and financial resource capacity of water governance agencies. Secondly, the fluidity of water implies that its availability fluctuates over space and time, which may further complicate decisions concerning water allocations. A third crucial aspect is that downstream users are deeply affected by upstream users' abstractions and other uses (Arduino et al., 2012; Sosa and Zwarteveen, 2012) and this affects both the quantity and quality of water available to users in a river basin (ibid).

We take a social justice perspective to the term 'water allocation' following the water grabbing literature that has been presented in a past special issue of *Water Alternatives* (see Special Issue on water grabbing; Mehta, et al., 2012). We also acknowledge that equity in allocation is notoriously difficult to judge and is not the same as equality (see Lankford, 2013). There are also many physical issues around water allocation that lead to inequalities in distribution, especially in Tanzania where river systems and river basins are complex and highly variable. These include physical problems in using fixed weirs when allocating water down a gravity-fed river (see Lankford and Mwaruvanda, 2007) or the fact that water flows are notoriously difficult to measure and that water allocation policies and their delivery are both badly thought through and poorly implemented (Hooper and Lankford, 2016). Due to these reasons, Tanzania offers a context in which ad hoc and licensed misappropriation can run high, also contributing to powerful players resorting to water grabs.

Access to both land and water is crucial for rural livelihoods as well as for the pursuit of a wide range of development objectives (Hodgson, 2004). In Tanzania, this relationship becomes increasingly critical as investments in land (as well as donor-driven projects) for large-scale commercial agricultural ventures continue to rise, causing growing tension among villagers, pastoralists, investors and the government. Yet, the manner in which the policy, regulatory and administrative frameworks to govern these resources have evolved in isolation from one another reflects the adoption of sectoral priorities over that of an integrated approach (ibid). In the case of Tanzania, the lack of harmonisation and coordination between the various sectoral policies has had detrimental social, economic and environmental consequences: from reinforcing exclusion of marginalised groups from resources, to the exploitation of resources for a few elites' economic gains (Hodgson, 2004; Lein and Tagseth, 2009).

A focus on the concept of 'exclusion' of Hall et al. (2011) is important for our study. 'Exclusion' is defined as the "ways in which people are prevented from benefiting from things" (Hall et al., 2011: 7), and is the inversion of Ribot and Peluso's (2003) definition of access as "the ability to benefit from things" (Ribot and Peluso, 2003: 153). Hall et al.'s (2011) four 'powers' that give way to exclusion and shape how different actors are prevented from accessing land provide a logical framework to discuss the complexities pertaining to exclusion. These include the powers of regulation, force, the market and legitimisation (ibid). Through regulation, exclusion happens by delineating land and setting terms of use within certain boundaries, for certain uses and for certain purposes; this is useful in the context of this study to describe how the Tanzanian government appropriates land for commercial agriculture and thereby excludes communities. The power of market on the other hand, drives exclusion through setting a price tag on resources and making it unaffordable for some (Myers, 2012). It drives the demand for land, as well as the price thereof in line with certain uses and markets; as in this case a 'boom crop' such as sugar cane for biofuels. The power of force describes instances where harm will come to those who try to access land and water resources (Harms, 2011), and is useful to describe instances where the Government of Tanzania (GoT) removed villagers or pastoralists from land earmarked for commercial agricultural production. However, it also includes the power of force imposed on people from actors other than the state, such as fellow villagers, investors and private companies. Legitimisation is further used to describe the rationale used by the state to justify the exclusion of some people, and also hinges on normative ideas of what is the 'right' or 'wrong' way to use resources and for what purposes it 'should be' used (ibid). This last concept of legitimisation is useful to discuss the current water governance framework in Tanzania that centres on water permits, and to discuss the complexities pertaining to the exclusion of the majority of the water users in the country who are still unregistered and 'informal'.

The complexities surrounding legal pluralism in Tanzania have highlighted the weaknesses of IWRM to effectively allocate water through the water permit system (Maganga et al., 2003; van Koppen et al., 2004). Legal pluralism is the coexistence of multiple legal orders, including statutory law and customary law, and thus the management and regulation of natural resources such as land and water by different institutions and pieces of legislation (Maganga et al., 2003). A major challenge of IWRM implementation in the global South concerns integrating plural legal management systems (Maganga et al., 2003; van Koppen et al., 2007). This is also the case in Tanzania when policy-makers adopted unitary, rigid property rights in order to establish formal legal regimes and formalise informal customary arrangements (van Koppen et al., 2004). In doing so, customary users of land and water have been rendered invisible, especially in the context of increasing foreign direct investments (FDIs) in commercial agriculture and despite being legally recognised in national policies and laws (Maganga et al., 2003; van Koppen et al., 2004). Furthermore, the permit system tends to favour those who have the time and financial resources to apply for permits, while excluding a large portion of rural water users who lack these resources (Hodgson, 2004).

There are multiple avenues by which powerful players can take control of, and gain access to, water resources. For the purpose of this study, these avenues are broadly categorised as 'new alliances' formed and 'acts of dispossession' (Islar, 2012). These avenues range from new coalitions of interest that can take on the form of newly created state agencies that are specifically geared for assisting investors to appropriate land (e.g. the Tanzanian Investment Centre), to business coalitions or new alliances between bureaucrats or politicians and private companies all of which have interests in large-scale agricultural investments. In her study on the privatised hydropower development in Turkey, Islar (2012) argues that although sometimes regulated, transformations in land and water property regimes can result in exclusive rights that have unequal distributional outcomes, resulting in the exclusion or marginalisation of communities. Also the blurring of boundaries between state actors, private companies and financial actors makes it difficult for local communities to benefit (ibid). Similar to the findings of Islar (2012), we also show how affected communities struggle to make their claims heard as they have no clear legal or institutional framework on which to base their claims to water rights (ibid). In these cases, conflicts have emerged where local communities seek to both protect and legitimise their uses of water (Islar, 2012; van Eeden, 2014). The chapter will tease out these various alliances in the context of the Wami-Ruvu Basin and demonstrate how they result in water-grabbing processes that favour the large users of land and water.

Overview of water resources management in Tanzania

Tanzania's water resource management policies centre on the water use permit system, and has served to implement the priorities of colonial and national policies over the years (van Koppen et al., Chapter 11). This agenda has, as early as 1923, enabled displacement of Africans to make way for large-scale colonial estates. Tanzania's water and land sector reform can be roughly divided into four major periods: From colonial to independence (1923 – 1961), *ujamaa* (familyhood in Swahili) and *villagisation* (1968 – 1975), economic liberalisation (1980 – 1989), and the foreign investment promotion period (1990 to the present).

While Tanzania's water resources are managed by the National Water Management Act of 2009 (URT, 2009), this Act revised the Water Utilisation (Control and Regulation) Act No. 42 of 1974 (URT, 1974) which was the first water governance act after gaining independence. Alongside the villagisation programme, full power was delegated to the Prime Minister to issue directions over village land use as he saw fit (Land Utilisation Act of 1973 and the Village Act of 1975, respectively). Furthermore, the introduction of the Water Utilisation (Control and Regulation) Act No. 42 vested all water resources in the United Republic of Tanzania instead of the colonial rulers, which is still the case today. The Water Utilisation (Control and Regulation) Act No. 42 further stipulates that all Tanzanians need to apply for a water right in order for their productive water use to be considered legitimate (Maganga et al., 2003). This implied that any water use should be declared illegal if unregistered (van Koppen et al., 2004).

While the water right application process was introduced by the Water Ordinance of 1948, Section 7, the process has evolved to also obliging all customary[3] productive water users to apply for a water right, which, under the Water Resources Management Act of 2009 has changed the term into 'permits'. This was underpinned by the National Water Policy (NAWAPO) of 2002 (URT 2002; van Koppen et al., 2004). Along with the application and subsequent approval of a water permit, the water permit holder needs to pay a once-off registration fee, as well as an annual volumetric water user fee as set out in the Water Utilisation (Control and Regulation) Act No. 42 of 1974 and especially in its subsequent amendments[4] (Lein and Tagseth, 2009). This fee was introduced on the recommendation of the Rapid Water Resources Assessment in 1994/1995 by the Min-

3 The Water Ordinance of 1959 Section 11, 12 and 14 made voluntary provisions for customary water practices to register for a water right (Van Koppen et al., 2004; Lein and Tagseth, 2009).

4 In 1994 the Subsidiary Legislation [Government Notice No. 347 of 1994 under section 38(2) of the Water Utilisation (Control and Regulation) Act No. 42 of 1974] was promulgated to introduce the annual fee structure for water rights (Van Koppen et al., 2004). In 1997, a Schedule of Fees was promulgated in the Water Utilisation (General) Regulations of 1997, and later revised in the Water Utilisation (General) (Amendment) Regulations, 2007.

istry of Water, Energy and Minerals in collaboration with the World Bank and DANIDA (MWEM 1995), and the subsequent World Bank's Staff Appraisal Report in 1996 (World Bank 1996). The aforementioned assessment and report found that the country was experiencing immense water user conflicts and that water resources were deteriorating due to exploitation, misuse and uncoordinated management mechanisms (URT, 1995; van Koppen et al., 2004; Hillborn, 2012; see also van Koppen et al., Chapter 11). It was believed that the introduction of the fee and managing water as an economic good would deter water wastage and alleviate the challenges that the newly appointed water basin officials and water boards were facing in having to be financially self-sustainable (URT, 1995; van Koppen et al., 2004; Hillborn, 2012).

The National Water Policy of 2002 framed these recommendations and primarily focused on decentralisation through river basin organisations in order to use water to alleviate poverty and for economic development. However, ironically as will be demonstrated in this chapter, the investment promotion period (1990 to the present) which was initially aimed to resurrect the country from its economic slump during the 1980s, has instead resulted in major resource grabs by investors that, in turn, have resulted in heightened tension and conflicts among villagers over limited water and land resources. During this period, in February 1990, Tanzania adopted its first investment policy, the Investment Promotion Policy which was an extension of the Agricultural policy in that it also emphasised modernisation by allocating land to commercial farmers (Sundet, 2004). This policy was soon followed by the National Investment Promotion Protection Act (NIPPA) of 1990 which gave the directive to establish the Investment Promotion Centre (IPC) to facilitate, monitor and approve foreign direct and local investments (ibid).

These developments have opened up for numerous investments in the country's agriculture sector, especially in the form of land acquisitions for commercial farming. It is, however, important to note that the relationship between land and water is equally significant for realising development objectives, as well as for rural livelihoods. This relationship becomes increasingly critical as the investments in land for large scale commercial agriculture continue to rise. Sadly, the isolated manner in which land and water policy and administrative frameworks evolved, prioritising the government's drive for development through foreign investments, has resulted in dire social, economic and environmental consequences. These include the over-exploitation of resources for the financial gain of a few elites while already marginalised groups are being excluded from certain water and land resources (van Eeden, 2014).

Agricultural investment and land acquisition in Tanzania

A large number of multinational organisations, development banks, private-sector players as well as a few members of the local elite have taken advantage of the government's development drive. Perhaps the most controversial of these is the Southern Africa Growth Corridor of Tanzania (SAGCOT) project which was initiated at the World Economic Forum Africa summit in May, 2010. SAGCOT brings together the Tanzanian government and more than 20 multinational companies and organisations (e.g. Monsanto, YARA and the World Bank) in a public-private partnership in an effort to alleviate food insecurity through commercial agriculture (SAGCOT, 2014). SAGCOT is currently planned to span across a third of Tanzania's land, affecting livelihoods, land and water resources (ibid) of hundreds of communities.

In 2006, the GoT formed the National Biofuel Task Force (NBTF) in an effort to strengthen the policy, legal and institutional framework for biofuel development in Tanzania. In addition to this, the GoT had also passed laws and commenced with the development of a regulatory framework to allow the smooth development of biofuel projects in Tanzania, both for local landowners and the investors. These included the Tanzanian Investment Policy of 1997, the Village Land Act of 1999, the establishment of the Tanzanian Investment Centre (TIC) in 2005, as well as the Public Private Partnership Policy and Public Private Partnership Act of 2010.

The culmination of the above-mentioned efforts is manifested in the presidential initiative, Kilimo Kwanza (agriculture first) launched in 2009. This initiative focuses on the modernisation of both small and large-scale agriculture, political reform, foreign investment and public-private partnerships (Mousseau and Mittal, 2011). Through the national policy, Kilimo Kwanza, Tanzania claims it has taken a firm handle in combating food insecurity. Through actively promoting investment in Tanzania's agriculture sector, Kilimo Kwanza is the culmination of various policies discussed above that together ease the process of large-scale land acquisitions.

The increasing focus on commercial agriculture has had far-reaching implications for the governance of water, as well as for communities' access to water. Communities' access to water has in some instances literally been cut off to demarcate land for commercial agricultural purposes. Despite being critical to the successful implementation of these initiatives, the importance of water was almost negligible in the formulation and adoption of Kilimo Kwanza (van Eeden, 2014). Similarly, not much importance was given to the water governance framework and the institutions which were meant to strengthen water resources governance and management, such as the water basin offices, the introduction of volumetric pricing as well as water permits. These are now in turn being altered and shaped to fit into the national agenda of the various investment policy initiatives. We now turn to the water governance framework and the implementation of IWRM in the Wami Ruvu River Basin amidst these investment policies.

IWRM in the Wami Ruvu Basin

Since Tanzania's adoption of the river basin as the planning unit for effective and efficient water management in the Water Utilisation (Control and Regulation) Act No. 42 of 197[5], the Minister of Water, in 1989, gazetted nine river basins of which

5 The repealed Water Utilisation (Control and Regulation) Act No. 42 of 1974 introduced the concept of managing water resources based on the river basin as a planning unit. The Act was amended in 1981, 1989, 1997 and 1999 (Tobey, 2008). It was later repealed and

the Wami Ruvu River Basin was one (Tobey, 2008). Subsequently, the Government of Tanzania established the Wami-Ruvu River Basin Office (WRBO) and its Basin Water Board in 2001 (see also van Koppen et al., Chapter 11). Tanzania's water resources management is organised around participatory and representative forums that decentralise from the national to the basin and sub-basin levels (URT, 2002; Ngana et al., 2010).

This institutional framework aims to integrate various sectors such as mining, irrigation and industry across the different levels of water management to ensure that water resources are managed in a participatory and transparent manner. However, as discussed, water management among sectors happens in silos and the integration between the sectors does not often exist. This is still mainly because water for noncommercial purposes assumes a lower priority than for other sectors such as large-scale irrigation and mining.

Furthermore, water use permits are core to managing water resources under the auspices of IWRM. While the Water Resources Management Act (WRMA) of 2009 clearly stipulates the process to apply for a water use permit, water users are able to bypass these official steps through forming alliances with the government, district and water basin officials, as well as through manipulating other water users (van Eeden, 2014). Large users can thus exploit the weak capacity of the basin office to bypass legal requirements and form alliances that suit their interests. It can be argued that this is another form by which water grabbing takes place. While water may not be grabbed physically, the water permit legally allows the water user to abstract water, giving her or him a certain power over those, often smaller water users, who lack a water use permit.

Illegal water abstraction by users that exceeds their allocation as well as those abstracting water without the necessary water permit, constitute a major concern in the Wami-Ruvu River Basin as it complicates the accurate monitoring of water use in the basin. As per the new WRMA of 2009, all water users, including those who already held water permits under the previous Water Utilisation (Control and Regulation) Act No. 42 of 1974, are legally obliged to register their water abstraction points or reapply for a new permit before August 2011 (Tobey, 2008; Ngana et al., 2010). However, in November 2011, a mere 11% of the permits subject to renewal was submitted for reapplication, while only 789 of the 988 permits on the WRBO record were still active permits (JICA, 2013). It is noteworthy that out of these permits, the 30 largest permits, including five permits of Mtibwa Sugar Estate and two by Sekab (the former holding company of the EcoEnergy project), equalled 89% of the total volume of water allocated, and, hence, the proportion of fees to contribute to the costs of the WRBO and the salaries of its staff (Sumuni, 2015). In an attempt to streamline the WRBO, the Japan Investment Cooperation Agency (JICA) assisted the WRBO in updating their database and introduced a new permit database[6] that was 'user-friendly' and allowed for

replaced by the Water Resources Management Act (WRMA), No. 11 of 2009 (Ngana et al., 2010).

6 The new permit database is one of six stand-alone databases that are integrated into a main database. The other databases include information concerning Water User Associations, Hydrology, Water Quality, Hydrogeology and River Structure.

easy update of information. Despite JICA's efforts to establish the new database the officers at the WRBO still used the old Excel spreadsheet to get information and update info regarding permits (van Eeden, 2014).

In addition to the financial strain that the WRBO experiences as a result of non-payment and no financial assistance from the Ministry of Water, the office struggles to conduct their day-to-day responsibilities due to a shortage of staff. The WRBO has a work force of 78 staff members (as of August 2012) that need to collect water fees, measure water flow, evaluate water permit applications and monitor water abstraction points in the entire WRB which covers an area of approximately 66,295 km^2 (JICA, 2013; van Eeden, 2014). According to interviews with staff members, the Ministry of Water, who appoints staff for the WRBO, has stopped new recruitments for many years. This not only resulted in an enormous age gap between staff members, but also in terms of work experience. The newly appointed graduates have not yet had the chance to acquire the necessary technical and managerial skills required by their job descriptions. Not only do the young employees lack the necessary experience, but they are also ill-equipped to handle the political pressure that they are often subjected to.

The lack of capacity and financial resources hampers the productivity and efficiency at the WRBO, while it also poses opportunities for bending the formal procedures among water users and basin officials. As has been pointed out by similar research studies, underpaid staff of the public sector in developing countries develop a series of coping strategies to make up for inadequate income (World Bank, 1997; Chêne, 2009; van Eeden, 2014). In her study, van Eeden describes instances where water permits were issued, while no formal applications were submitted by water users (van Eeden, 2014). In one case, a water basin official granted a water permit to a large-scale mineral and resources company over the phone without following the stipulated procedures (van Eeden, 2014). Another example relates to an instance where a junior basin official was intimidated by a senior official to sign-off on a water permit, despite an evaluation which concluded that there was insufficient water available in the Wami River to meet the need of the specific water user (ibid). In the particular case of EcoEnergy to be described below, the company went as far as to alter the Environmental Impact Assessment report which was conducted by Orgut (2008), an independent Swedish environmental consultancy. The initial report by Orgut indicated that there were insufficient levels of water in the Wami River to support the development of 22,000 ha sugar-cane plantations (van Eeden, 2014). Despite these developments, and the subsequent withdrawal of Orgut from the project, EcoEnergy received a water permit from the Wami Ruvu River Basin. The JICA report also indicates that more water permits have been granted and more water has been allocated than the amount of water available in one of the rivers in the WRRB, having multiple implications on future water security (JICA, 2013; van Eeden, 2014).

Although the WRBO and other water management institutions have the authority to issue permits, numerous factors are preventing them from doing so. The wider literature on water grabbing has indicated how large-scale users, by colluding and forming alliances with key stakeholders and government officials can obtain water permits without necessarily following – or even ignoring altogether – the formal application process (Mehta et al., 2012; Molle, 2008; van Eeden, 2014). Even if large-scale users follow the correct procedure without undue influence, the majority of smaller water users still struggle to get water permits, either due to their lack of knowledge of the procedures to apply or due to their lack of financial capacity, while the basin offices lack the capacity to process those applications even if they were submitted. Also, there are instances where large-scale water users use their power and technical ability to gain control and access to the water resource to the detriment of other water users. These instances will be described in the following sections.

Upstream: Mtibwa Sugar Estate

Mtibwa Sugar Estate (MSE) is the single largest user of water for irrigation in the Wami Ruvu River Basin, despite collectively not holding the largest water use permit. The Wami-Ruvu Basin Office (WRBO) database indicates that MSE holds nine water permits of which some date back to 1960. However, the database does not coincide with actual abstraction points at MSE and has also not been updated with MSE's latest application for a water permit for irrigating their fields in the Dakawa Ranch (Meggison Tandberg et al., 2013; van Eeden, 2014).[7] These discrepancies have implications for future development and allocations in the WRRB, as having incorrect information can lead to overallocation and shortages for some users in the future (van der Zaag et al., 2010).

The manner in which MSE abstracts water for irrigation is particularly contentious. Upstream of the Mkindo rice scheme and Lukenge Village, MSE constructed a weir and an irrigation canal in the Diwale River that flows into the Wami River. MSE has total control over this weir and has been opening and closing the weir to meet their irrigation demand, often for months on end, regardless of the needs of downstream users (Meggison Tandberg et al., 2013; van Eeden, 2014). MSE's irrigation technician confessed that in order to irrigate their sugar-cane plantations he will need to keep the weir closed for up to two months, while there is no monitoring by the basin officials as to the amount of water actually being discharged (ibid). MSE is thus literally grabbing water from downstream water users. This has sparked major conflicts between them, i.e. downstream communities as well as pastoralists in the area.

Some of these conflicts take place within the community. Some community members, who are also employees of the Mtibwa sugar estate, are forced to stay away from work or strike against the employer in order to put pressure on the company. Many employees feel threatened by their fellow community members and also risk losing their jobs if they do not go to work (van Eeden, 2014). The situation gets even more complicated, as many of the employees are also outgrowers to the company. These outgrowers deliver a certain amount of sugar cane, which they produced on their own land, to the mill in return for compensation. Often, companies require the sugar cane from outgrowers in addition to

7 MSE applied for a water permit for irrigation purposes to the amount of 4.5 m^3/second for a dam that forms part of the expansion project in Dakawa; however, the permit was only granted for 2.5 m^3/second.

their own plantations to sustain their business. Because many employees are also outgrowers, they are forced to go on strike with fellow outgrowers because they have not received payment from Mtibwa for the sugar delivered, resulting in them not being able to repay loans for the previous season's input costs such as seeds and fertilisers.

These conflicts have partly also been the result of the WRBO's inability to monitor and service all the water abstraction points or to issue penalties and fines to those users who overuse their water allocations. Although the WRBO officials have the legal authority to issue fines, according to basin officials, they have never done so. This may be due not only to their lack of resources and capacity but also to the huge convening power of the large-scale users. Despite having an allocated abstraction amount to abide by, MSE is misusing its power over the weir to suit its own needs and interests and thus creating water-scarcity problems downstream (Komakech et al., 2011; Meggison Tandberg et al., 2013). The perceived problem of water scarcity has manifested in various ways among downstream water users in the basin. Villagers and small-scale rice farmers had no choice other than to take on a more reactive approach to manage this problem; by walking with their machetes to the weir protesting and demanding that the weir be opened once they physically experience a shortage of water downstream. Other large-scale users take on more of a proactive approach to deal with this problem as will be illustrated in light of EcoEnergy's water use and management.

Mtibwa Sugar Estate was established during Tanzania's sugar sector reform when the state-owned sugar industry was privatised from 1998 to 2001. At the time of MSE's privatisation, the company held 75% shares while 25% was retained by the GoT to be sold to interested parties in future. While this equity share arrangement was in line with contracts between the GoT and the sugar industry at the time of the reform, it shortly changed after the company's establishment in 1998. Instead of selling the remaining 25% of shares to interested parties, the GoT decided to sell their shares back to MSE, foregoing the opportunity by others, such as the Outgrower Associations to buy shares and have a stake in the company.

This ownership structure has given the GoT an excuse not to intervene in the ongoing disputes between surrounding communities, the outgrowers and MSE. According to multiple interviews conducted during this research, government officials have claimed that the GoT cannot interfere in the struggle between the various parties, leaving the outgrowers alone in their fight against the company (van Eeden, 2014). This struggle concerns hefty disputes and strikes by the outgrowers over not being paid by MSE for sugar cane that they have delivered, as well as conflicts over access to water resources and water pollution, to which we will return in the following section.

In addition to MSE's elusive ownership structure, another point of contention is the alleged stake that the ex-president of Tanzania, Mr. Benjamin William Mkapa has in the company (van Eeden, 2014). Through this relationship, MSE has been enjoying immense support from the ex-president on numerous occasions,[8] further

8 Mr. Mkapa [in turn] has been involved in many economic development initiatives in the Mtibwa ward (TDN, 2012). However, the communities around MSE have received these

aiding to sense of powerlessness of the outgrowers and communities (ibid). As indicated in the wider literature, through dissolving mergers and acquisitions, companies are able to create vagueness and confusion over their true ownership structure (Mehta et al., 2012; van Eeden, 2014). This not only implicates their accountability to the government and public but ultimately creates opportunities for companies to obtain water and land resources by obscure means. MSE's equity structure has thus given the owners of the company the leverage to misuse their power, which is in line with the wider literature on water grabbing and the power of large-scale water users (Mehta et al., 2012; van Eeden, 2014).

Downstream: EcoEnergy

In contrast to MSE's company structure, Agro EcoEnergy Ltd. (EcoEnergy) was established in Tanzania by multiple international and Tanzanian entities.[9] It was initiated in 2008, with the signing of a Memorandum of Understanding (MoU) between the GoT and SEKAB BioEnergy Tanzania Ltd. (SEKAB BT). The MoU was signed with the intention to kick-start the development of a long-term and sustainable bioenergy platform in the country (Chachage, 2010).[10] EcoEnergy's biofuel project is the first of its kind in Tanzania where the state has entered into a partnership with the investor. This model is known as the Land for Equity Policy, which was developed by the Ministry for Lands, Housing and Human Settlements Development in 2012. It is through the auspices of this policy that the GoT presented EcoEnergy with 22,000 ha of the Razaba Ranch in return for 25% equity in the biofuel project. The Land for Equity policy is, however, not without its critiques. In order for the policy to benefit investors and communities, Tanzania's land and villages need to be surveyed and demarcated before it is allocated to investors. However, 90% of Tanzania's villages do not have a land use map that clearly demarcates the boundaries and borders of the villages (Havnevik, 2012).

As in this instance, village governments and the GoT have allocated land, and

initiatives with mixed emotions. The Mtibwa Outgrowers Association (MOA) recalled the time that the ex-president was invited to open up a branch of the Bank of Africa towards the end of 2012: a news article describes this event as being a victory for rural communities as the bank was implementing the government's policy that encourages banks to go rural and to encourage people to have bank accounts and how to save and facilitate development at large (TDN, 2012). However, the ex-president made it clear that the community should be thankful to MSE for facilitating development within the community (van Eeden, 2014: 116).

9 SEKAB is 70% municipally owned and has a reputation for upholding it as it is directly accountable to Swedish tax payers (Havnevik et al., 2011). SEKAB BT comprises two entities, (1) the Tanzanian Community Finance Company (CFC), which focuses on the establishment of community-based farming to foster rural development and (2) the Swedish Ethanol Chemistry AB (SEKAB), which is the largest producer of ethanol for the Scandinavian market and owned by three Swedish public utility energy companies (Van Eeden, 2014).

10 As with MSE's elusive ownership, the dissolving of SEKAB BT and subsequent establishment of EcoEnergy has raised questions pertaining to the overall manner in which the company does business and has also created a lot of confusion amongst various stakeholders and villagers. For an in-depth discussion regarding the transition from SEKAB BT to what is now EcoEnergy, refer to van Eeden (2014), Section 6.3 p.118.

effectively water resources to EcoEnergy without the knowledge of where their village boundaries lay (van Eeden, 2014). This has resulted in intense conflicts between village communities, pastoralists and EcoEnergy as will be discussed in the sections to follow.

The Razaba Ranch in the Bagamoyo District is situated 80 km northwest of Dar es Salaam, 20 km north of Bagamoyo Town and borders the Sadaani National Park to the South. The Ranch has a long history of farmers, traders and hunters who have lived on the land for centuries up until 1974 when the GoT formally gave the ranch to the Government of Zanzibar as a livestock grazing area (Orgut, 2008). At that time, inhabitants of the area were compensated for their loss of land while 7000 head of livestock came to be stocked in that area. However, 20 years later all operations ceased due to persistent problems with tsetse flies (ibid).

Since operations ceased in 1994, various pastoralist communities brought their cattle to graze and drink from the water resources on the Razaba Ranch while other communities have also settled on the land. The activities of these communities ranged from charcoal producers, hunters, collectors of medicinal plants and farmers who cultivated paddy fields, perennial plants (sugar cane, pineapples, coconuts and citrus fruit) and annual crops (maize, rice, sweet potatoes and cassava) (Orgut, 2008). These communities had to be resettled elsewhere when the GoT allocated the entire Razaba Ranch to EcoEnergy. EcoEnergy prepared a Resettlement Action Plan (RAP) in line with the African Development Bank's Involuntary Resettlement Policy.[11] According to the survey conducted for the RAP, approximately 1200 people had to be resettled, including the villagers of Kaloleni Biga, Gobole, Gama, Bozi and 11 pastoralist families belonging to the Datooga tribe and owning 1750 head of cattle (Johansson, 2013).

When EcoEnergy acquired the Razaba Ranch as well as village land from Matipwili and Fukayosi,[12] five access ways to the Wami River were blocked off (Philemon, 2013). This has meant that pastoralists, who are dependent on the water in the Razaba Ranch as well as the Wami River, can no longer access these resources and take care of their cattle. Subsequently, pastoralists have been forced to seek alternative resources, often on village land. Villagers have complained that the influx of pastoralist and their cattle on their land have placed immense pressure on the land resources and has left their water resources depleted (Engström, 2014). As a result, these villagers now need to buy water from a tanker or cover additional distances to collect water from other water resources (ibid).

Although EcoEnergy has acquired a water use permit from the WRBO allowing them to abstract water from the Wami River to meet the irrigation demand for the full 22 000 ha, a previous study by Orgut found that there is not enough wa-

11 "[This policy] states that people are eligible for compensation for their land whether they have legal rights over the land or not. However, the GoT only recognises people who are legal residents or users of the land to be eligible for compensation (AEE, 2012b). This implied that, during government surveys of the communities in the area, pastoralist families were not accounted for, as they do according to Tanzanian law, not legally own any land. Charcoal producers were also omitted from the survey as they were deemed illegal and unauthorised, using the Razaba Ranch without permission" (AEE, 2012b: 124).

12 For an in-depth description of EcoEnergy's land acquisition and the resettlement of communities refer to van Eeden (2014) Section 6.3.

ter in the Wami River to sustain the needs of the downstream Matipwili Village, livestock and the environment (van Eeden, 2014). This required EcoEnergy to conduct another study, this time by themselves and students from the University of Dar es Salaam, concluding with a favourable amount of water for the intended uses; i.e. the plantations, communities and livestock. However, the independence and precision of this study is questionable. In line with Lankford et al. (2007), this draws attention to the inadequate and short-sighted studies conducted by basin officials and investors that give way to allocating water rights – with related fees – that favour large-scale users over that of communities (Lankford et al., 2007). Because of EcoEnergy's position in the Wami sub-catchment, situated downstream of Mtibwa Sugar Estate and other agricultural and industrial developments upstream, they are exposed to severe water shortages that directly influence the viability of their project. This has made EcoEnergy seek alternative ways of ensuring that their future water demands are met.

In their Integrated Water Resources Management Plan, EcoEnergy proposed two long-term mitigation measures that will alleviate the water shortage during the deficit months: a large-scale storage dam and assuming a seat on the Wami-Ruvu Basin Board. These solutions would direct more power to the company concerning decisions of water resources management in the WRRB (AEE, 2012a). In the short term however, EcoEnergy has resorted to a third route to ensure the security of water supply in the future. It has identified 3000 ha of land from farmers belonging to Matipwili, Gama and Kiwangwa villages (AEE, 2014) who need to organise themselves into groups who will collectively own 75-150 ha of sugar cane (ibid). Each of these groups will establish an outgrower company in accordance with the Companies Act 2002, No. 12 and have a long-term off-take agreement of 11 years with EcoEnergy (ibid). EcoEnergy envisages that 25-35 outgrower companies will be established, producing approximately 300,000-400,000 tonnes of sugar cane for the EcoEnergy sugar mill (van Eeden, 2014). The outgrower companies will also be able to apply for loans from, for instance, the Tanzanian Investment Bank through the Kilimo Kwanza initiative for smallholder farmers (AEE, 2014).

However, to obtain these loans[13] the companies require three documents: 1) a business plan including the land title deeds of their farms, 2) a sugar-cane purchase agreement (the long-term off-take agreement) between EcoEnergy and their company, as well as 3) a water use permit from the WRBO. It should be noted that water use permits are issued on a first-come, first-serve basis, which, together with MSE's expansion plans provide enough concern for EcoEnergy to ensure that they have secured water permits for their outgrowers as soon as possible, even though it will still take another few years for these to be established and operational, if this happens at all. Thus, instead of following the formal process of applying for a water permit for their outgrower scheme at the basin office, EcoEnergy requested the Bagamoyo District Officer to apply for a water use per-

13 While farmers indicated that they would like to apply for a loan, they were oblivious of the actual amount they would need to apply for, to operate an outgrower company; this is roughly estimated to be USD800,000-1.2 million payable over an 11-year period (van Eeden, 2014).

mit on behalf of the entire outgrower scheme. This was decided after EcoEnergy raised their concern with the director of the WRBO who instructed them to follow this speculative route. In sum, EcoEnergy has gained access to land and water resources through various acts of dispossession as well as through the creation of new alliances with government officials and key figures in communities. It has both followed official procedures and also used more creative ways that circumvent these official steps.

Discussion and conclusions

This chapter has illustrated how IWRM has directly or indirectly favoured the priorities of companies and investors in the Wami-Ruvu River Basin. This has started with the shift towards neoliberal water policies that strengthened statutory water permits and simultaneously neglected customary rights to water (van Eeden, 2014). Furthermore, the redefinition and creation of institutions that justify the government's drive towards 'modern' agricultural development (i.e. the TIC, Kilimo Kwanza, and the Biofuel guidelines), have also allowed investors to gain access to large amounts of water and land, which in the case studies described above, resulted in instances of water grabbing. These have resulted in the exclusions (cf. Hall et al., 2011) of small and usually poor users who have not been able to benefit from the new policies and governance frameworks. The two cases presented above will now be discussed in light of 'undue influence and new alliances' and 'acts of dispossession' (Islar, 2012).

Undue influence and new alliances

Each of the two case studies represents and involves different actors, powers and agendas that contribute to instances of undue influence and new alliances. Firstly, then, perhaps the biggest contributor to MSE's misuse of the weir, results from the positional power they enjoy from their established relationship with the ex-president. This undue influence effectively gives them the sanction power to fully control the weir and deprive downstream users of sufficient water without having to be concerned about the consequences. While MSE has the backing of the ex-president, the downstream communities can only rely on their collective social power to force MSE to open the weir and let water through.

Despite the social power that the communities have, their sense of powerlessness against MSE's misuse of the weir is compounded by them not having legal rights to water (Crawford and Andreassen, 2013; Hellum et al., 2013). This sense of powerlessness through not having a water permit to abstract water, has to some extent also surfaced in EcoEnergy's case; for the latter, the statutory permit application process to secure water rights in future worked well. EcoEnergy's alliances with the basin director and district officer among others, have given them the ability to fully exploit the IWRM framework to suit their needs.

In addition to these alliances, the Land for Equity model is another means by which new alliances are fostered between private companies and influential government officials. EcoEnergy has gained large tracts of land and access to the Wami River's waters through the myriad of alliances they have formed, by various means, with influential village members and key government officials. As Bakker elucidates, these new alliances between government and private companies imply "a more diffuse, opaque form of governance, with important and technical consequences, namely loss of transparency and accountability, and an incomplete assessment of the future economic returns and the environmental and social impacts of proposed projects" (Bakker, 1999: 228). Despite the equity model being upheld as a means whereby communities are being involved in the project and ensured of economic returns, the EcoEnergy case has illustrated how certain key individuals profit while thousands of community members are deprived of their land and water resources.

The creation of new alliances, whether it is between private companies and government officials, or with certain community members, has resulted in social exclusion among certain community members. In line with other water grabbing cases, social exclusion in this instance is the result of conflicts between those who see the opportunities that the project holds and those whose livelihoods depend on the land and water resources claimed by EcoEnergy and MSE (Dauvergne and Neville, 2010; Islar, 2012; van Eeden, 2014). EcoEnergy formed new alliances with those prominent individuals within the villages who have the authority to make decisions about village resources, such as wealthy farmers, village elders and village chairmen (van Eeden, 2014). The effect thereof is increased social divisions and mistrust between village members and EcoEnergy, as well as these key village members (ibid).

Acts of dispossession

In the cases presented above, two main factors contribute to acts of dispossession: The requirement to apply for permits and the speculative means by which powerful actors can do so; and the physical diversion or overabstraction of water by powerful actors that deprive small-scale water users of their ability to access sufficient water.

MSE enjoys both a physical and sociopolitical prominent position in the Wami-Ruvu River Basin, which gives them the upper hand to intercept and divert water away from downstream water users. While MSE contends that they are using water within the limits of their allocated amount, from the research study conducted by van Eeden (2014) it is clear that they misuse their power over the weir and deprive downstream communities from having access to sufficient water. This has multiple implications on downstream users; both those communities in the immediate surroundings that experience the effect of MSE's water grabbing more directly and instantaneously and those users located at the end of the river who are also rather concerned about future water availability and security. As mentioned above, these users have varying degrees of capabilities and support to deal with this situation. While communities need to fend for themselves, EcoEnergy enjoys the support from various key actors in government and communities to be creative in securing water rights for their development in the future.

At the onset of EcoEnergy's project, they demarcated their project land and closed off major access ways that were used by communities and pastoralists to get water from the Wami River (van Eeden, 2014). The effects of this entailed that communities and pastoralists had to go in search of water resources on other land, placing additional stress on the already water- and land-scarce environment surrounding the Razaba Ranch. This has further resulted in violent conflicts among communities and the pastoralists, as well as with EcoEnergy.

While the IWRM framework did not directly contribute to these conflicts by its ineffective implementation in Tanzania it has allowed powerful actors to manipulate the legal framework and secure water for their own use, as in the case of EcoEnergy who was able to secure water for their own operations in future, resulting in what can be argued as water grabbing. As mentioned, EcoEnergy was able to circumvent and manipulate the formal water right application process whereby the District Officer had to apply for a water right on behalf of EcoEnergy's outgrowers. This was done without the knowledge of the outgrowers and without many of them knowing what a water right and the subsequent payment for water entailed (ibid). Thus, by securing water for themselves, albeit on a piece of paper, EcoEnergy is robbing other water users who wish to abstract water from their water rights in the future. This arguably relates to acts of dispossession. The issue of water availability in future is further complicated when taking into consideration the basin officers' inability to measure current abstractions in the basin to effectively establish a baseline and allocate water accordingly.

To conclude: the institutional shortcomings of IWRM have created many difficulties for the WRBO to effectively implement IWRM in the Wami-Ruvu River Basin. This is because of major power disparities among the water users in the basin coupled with the physical and political complexities of water allocation that are rarely addressed through IWRM. The various new alliances described in this chapter have led to acts of dispossession that have excluded local users from land and water. Thus, we concur with others that the IWRM framework can be exploited by powerful actors' agendas to influence decisions regarding water allocations (see Franco et al., 2013). IWRM, as implemented in the Wami-Ruvu River Basin, is not able to allocate water among water users in a fair and equitable way. Rather water is being allocated to 'priority' users, namely commercial agricultural companies and investors with detrimental outcomes on small-scale users.

Acknowledgements

We are very grateful to our colleagues in the Flows and Practices project for their stimulating ideas and research which inspired and informed the analysis presented in this chapter and to the Research Council of Norway for their generous support. We would like to thank in particular Bill Derman as well as three anonymous reviewers for their useful comments. Finally, we thank Noragric for the support and opportunity presented to Aurelia van Eeden to conduct this research as part of the fulfilment of her Master's degree.

References

AEE (Agro-EcoEnergy). 2012a. *EcoEnergy Bagamoyo: Integrated Water Resource Management Plan, January 2012.* Dar es Salaam: Agro-EcoEnergy.

AEE. 2012b. *Executive summary of the Resettlement Action Plan.* Dar es Salaam:

Agro-EcoEnergy.

AEE. 2014. *AgroEcoEnergy outgrower programme*. Dar es Salaam: Agro-EcoEnergy.

www.ecoenergy.co.tz/outgrower-programme/the-outgrower-programme/(accessed on 31 March 2014).

Arduino, S.; Colombo, G.; Ocampo, O.M. and Panzeri, L. 2012. Contamination of community potable water from land grabbing: A case study from rural Tanzania. Water Alternatives 5(2): 344-359.

Bakker, K. 1999. The politics of hydropower: Developing the Mekong. *Political Geography* 18(2): 209-232.

Berg, B.L. and Lune, H. 2012. Qualitative research methods for the social Sciences. 8th edition, *International Education*. USA: Pearson.

Bossio, D.; Erkossa, T.; Dile, Y.; McCartney, M.; Killiches, F. and Hoff, H. 2012. Water implications of foreign direct investment in Ethiopia's agricultural sector. *Water Alternatives* 5(2): 223-242.

Bues, A. and Theesfeld, I. 2012. Water grabbing and the role of power: Shifting water governance in the light of agricultural foreign direct investment. *Water Alternatives* 5(2): 266-283.

Chachage, C. 2010. *Land acquisition and accumulation in Tanzania. The case of Morogoro, Iringa and Pawni regions*. Dar es Salaam, Tanzania: PELUM.

Chêne, M. 2009. *Low salaries, the culture of per diems and corruption*. Bergen, Norway: U4 Transparency International, Anti-Corruption Resource Centre.

Cotula, L.; Vermeulen, S.; Leonard, R. and Keeley, J. 2009. *Land grab or development opportunity? Agricultural investment and international land deals in Africa*. London/Rome: International Institute for Environment and Development/ Food and Agricultural Organization of the United Nations/ International Fund for Agriculture and Development.

Cotula, L. 2011. *The outlook on farmland acquisitions*. Rome, Italy: IIED contribution to ILC Collaborative Research Project on Commercial Pressures on Land.

Crawford, G. and Andreassen, B.A. 2013. Human rights, power and civic action. In Andreassen, B.A. and Crawford, G. (Eds), *Human rights, power and civic action. Comparative analyses of struggles for rights in developing societies*, pp. 1-21. Oxon: Routledge.

Creswell, J. W. 2007. *Qualitative inquiry and research design: Choosing among five traditions*. Thousand Oaks, California: Sage.

Dauvergne, P. and Neville, K.J. 2010. Forests, food, and fuel in the tropics: The uneven social and ecological consequences of the emerging political economy of biofuels. *The Journal of Peasant Studies* 37(4): 631-660.

Engström, L. 2014. *Too rushed? Sweden's support for sugar production in Tanzania*. Uppsala, Sweden: The Nordic Africa Institute.

Fairhead, J.; Leach, M. and Scoones, I. 2012. Green grabbing: A new appropriation of nature? *Journal of Peasant Studies* 39(2): 237-261.

Franco, J.; Mehta, L. and Veldwisch, G.J. 2013. The global politics of water grabbing. *Third World Quarterly* 34(9): 1651-1675.

Hall, D.; Hirsch, P. and Murray Li, T. 2011. *Powers of exclusion: Land dilemmas in*

Southeast Asia. Singapore: NUS Press.

Harms, E. 2011. Book review: Powers of exclusion: Land dilemmas in Southeast Asia. *The Journal of Lao Studies* 3(1): 132-134.

Harvey, D. 2005. *Brief history of neoliberalism*. Oxford: Blackwell.

Havnevik, K.; Haaland, H. and Abdallah, J. 2011. *Biofuel, land and environmental issues: The case of SEKAB's biofuel plans in Tanzania*. Tanzania: Nordic Africa Institute, the University of Agder, Norway and Sokoine University of Agricultural Sciences.

Havnevik, K. 2012. *Tanzanian land for equity policy*. Uppsala, Sweden: The Nordic Africa Institute.

Hellum, A.; Derman, B.; Feltoe, G.; Sithole, E.; Streward, J. and Tsanga, A. 2013. Rights claiming and rights making in Zimbabwe. A study of three human rights NGOs. In Andreassen, B.A. and Crawford, G. (Eds), *Human rights, power and civic action. Comparative analyses of struggles for rights in developing societies*, pp. 22-54. Oxon: Routledge.

Hillborn, E. 2012. Institutional continuity and change: A century of smallholders' water rights in Meru, Tanzania. Paper presented at the ASAUK Biennial conference. Evaluating the 20th century in Africa: Linking colonial and post-colonial economic development. Oxford, England, 16-19 September 2012.

Hodgson, S. 2004. *Land and water – The rights interface*. FAO Legislative Study No. 84. Rome, Italy: Food and Agriculture Organisation.

Hooper, V. and Lankford, B.A. 2016. Unintended water allocation; Gaining share from the ungoverned spaces of land and water transformations. In Conca, K. and Weinthal, E. (Eds), *Oxford handbook of water politics and policy*. New York: Oxford University Press, forthcoming 2016.

Islar, M. 2012. Privatised hydropower development in Turkey: A case of water grabbing? *Water Alternatives* 5(2): 376-391.

JICA (Japan International Cooperation Agency). 2013. *The study on water resources management and development in Wami/Ruvu Basin in the United Republic of Tanzania*. Dar es Salaam, Tanzania: Japan International Cooperation Agency, Water Resources Division, Ministry of Water.

Johansson, E.L. 2013. A multi-scale analysis of biofuel-related land acquisitions in Tanzania: With focus on Sweden as an investor. MSc thesis. Lund university, Department of Earth and Ecosystem Sciences, Lund, Sweden.

Kiishweko, O. 2012. Tanzania takes major steps towards curbing land 'grabs'. Guardian development network: *The Guardian*. www.theguardian.com/global-development/2012/dec/21/tanzania-major-step-curbing-land-grabs (accessed 9 April 2012)

Komakech, H.; van Koppen, B.; Mahoo, H. and van der Zaag, P. 2011. Pangani River Basin over time and space: On the interface of local and basin level responses. *Agricultural Water Management* 98(11): 1740-1751.

Lankford, B.A. and Mwaruvanda, W. 2007. A legal-infrastructural framework for catchment apportionment. In van Koppen, B.; Giordano, M. and Butterworth, J. (Eds), *Community-based water law and water resource management reform in developing countries*, pp. 228-247. Comprehensive Assessment of Water Management in Agriculture Series. London: CABI Publishing.

Lankford, B.A. 2013. Does Article 6 (Factors Relevant to Equitable and Reasonable Utilization) in the UN Watercourses Convention misdirect riparian countries? *Water International* 38(2): 130-145.

Lankford, B.A.; Tumbo, S. and Rajabu, K. 2007. Water competition, variability and river basin governance: A critical analysis of the Great Ruaha River, Tanzania. In Molle, F. and Wester, P. (Eds). *River basin trajectories: Societies, environments and development*, pp. 171-195. Oxfordshire, UK: CAB International and IWMI.

Lein, H. and Tagseth, M. 2009. Tanzanian water policy reforms – Between principles and practical applications. *Water Policy* 11(2): 203-220.

Li, T.M. 2007. *The will to improve: Governmentality, development, and the practice of politics.* Durham, North Carolina: Duke University Press.

Maganga, F.P.; Hilda, L.; Kiwasila, I.; Juma, H. and Butterworth, J.A. 2003. Implications of customary norms and laws for implementing IWRM: Findings from Pangani and Rufiji basins, Tanzania. In Proceedings of the 4th WaterNet/WARFSA Symposium Gaborone, Botswana, 15-17 October 2003.

Matondi, P.B.; Havnevik, K. and Beyene, A. 2011. *Biofuels, land grabbing and food security in Africa.* London: Zed Books.

Matondi, P.B. and Matupo, P. 2011. Attracting foreign direct investment in Africa in the context of land grabbing for biofuels and food security. In Matondi, P.B.; Havnevik, K. and Beyene, A. (Eds), *Biofuels, land grabbing and food security in Africa*, pp. 68-89. London: Zen Books.

Meggison Tandberg, E.; Denby, K. and Tomicki, S. 2013. Sugarcane farming in the Mtibwa Valley: Power dynamics and drivers in water access and management. *UMB Student Journal of International Environment and Development Studies* 3: 53-60.

Mehta, L.; Veldwisch, G.J. and Franco, J. 2012. Water grabbing? Focus on the (re)appropriation of finite water resources. *Water Alternatives* 5(2): 193-207.

MWEM (Ministry of Water, Energy and Minerals). 1995. *Rapid water resources assessment, Volumes. 1 and 2.* Dar es Salaam: Ministry of Water, Energy and Minerals in collaboration with the World Bank.

Molle, F. 2008. Nirvana concepts, narratives and policy models: Insights from the water sector. *Water Alternatives* 1(1): 131-156.

Mousseau, F. and Mittal, A. 2011. *Understanding land investment deals in Africa.* Country Report: Tanzania. Oakland, CA: The Oakland Institute.

Myers, R. 2012. Book review: Powers of exclusion antipode foundation: Antipode. https://radicalantipode.files.wordpress.com/2012/09/book-review_myers-on-hall-et-al.pdf (accessed 19 June 2014)

Ngana, J.O.; Mahay, F. and Cross, K. 2010. Wami basin. A situation analysis: Wami/Ruvu Basin Water Office. Supported by International Union for Conservation of Nature.

Orgut. 2008. *Environmental and social impact statement of the proposed bio ethanol production from sugar cane on the former Razaba Ranch, Bagamoyo District, Tanzania.* Dar es Salaam, Tanzania: ORGUT Consulting AB and Ardhi University.

Philemon, B. 2013. DC Kipozi aghast as pastoralists' lands are sold, river shut out. Dar es Salaam: IPPmedia.com. www.ippmedia.com/frontend/?l=57272 (accessed on 29 April 2014)

Ribot, J. and Peluso, N.L. 2003. A theory of access. *Rural Sociology* 68(2): 153-181.

SAGCOT (Southern Africa Growth Corridor of Tanzania). 2014. Southern agricultural growth corridor of Tanzania. www.sagcot.com/our-partners/partnership/ (accessed 26 February 2014)

Sosa, M. and Zwarteveen, M. 2012. Exploring the politics of water grabbing: The case of large mining operations in the Peruvian Andes. *Water Alternatives* 5(2): 360-375.

Sundet, G. 2004. The politics of land in Tanzania. Unpublished manuscript.

Sumuni, P.M. 2015. Influence of institutional set-up on performance of traditional irrigation schemes, a case study of Nyandira Ward, Mvomero District Tanzania. MSc. thesis. Sokoine University of Agriculture, Morogoro, Tanzania.

TDN (Tanzania Daily News). 2012. Tanzania: Banking services set to transform Mtibwa. Tanzania Daily News (TDN). http://allafrica.com/stories/201212170111.html (accessed 17 March 2014)

Tobey, J. 2008. A profile of the Wami River sub-basin Tanzanian coastal management partnership for sustainable coastal communities and ecosystems in Tanzania. Supported by the USAID.

URT (United Republic of Tanzania). 1974. *Water utilization (control and regulation) Act No. 42 of 1974*. Dar-es-Salaam: The United Republic of Tanzania

URT. 2002. *Water utilization (general) (Amendment) regulations*. Dar-es-Salaam: The United Republic of Tanzania.

URT. 2009. *The Water Resources Management Act No. 11*. Dar-es-Salaam: Government printer

van der Zaag, P.; Juizo, D.; Vilanculos, A.; Bolding, A. and Uiterweer, N.P. 2010. Does the Limpopo River Basin have sufficient water for massive irrigation development in the plains of Mozambique? *Physics and Chemistry of the Earth* 35(13): 832-837.

van Eeden, A. 2014. Whose waters: Large-scale agricultural development in the Wami-Ruvu River Basin. MSc thesis. Norwegian University of Life Science, Department of International Environmental and Development Studies, Ås, Norway.

van Koppen, B.; Sokile, C.S.; Hatibu, N.; Lankford, B.A.; Mahoo, H. and Yanda, P.Z. 2004. *Formal water rights in rural Tanzania: Deepening the dichotomy*. Pretoria, South Africa: International Water Management Institute.

van Koppen, B.; Giordano, M. and Butterworth, J.A. 2007. Community-based *water law and water resource management reform in developing countries. comprehensive assessment of water management in agriculture series*. Pretoria, South Africa: International Water Management Institute.

Veldwisch, G.J.; Beekman, W. and Bolding, A. 2013. Smallholder irrigators, water rights and investments in agriculture: Three cases from rural Mozambique. *Water Alternatives* 6(1): 125-141.

World Bank. 1996. Staff appraisal report, Tanzania. In *River Basin Management and Smallholder Irrigation Improvement Project*. Report No. 15122-TA. Washington, DC: Agriculture and Environment Operations, Eastern Africa Department.

World Bank. 1997. *Helping countries combat corruption. The role of the World Bank*. Washington, DC: World Bank.

13

IWRM in Uganda – Progress after Decades of Implementation[1]

Alan Nicol

William Odinga

ABSTRACT: Uganda lies almost wholly within the Nile Basin and is a country characterised as well-endowed with water resources. Receiving considerable inflows of aid since the early 1990s, some of this aid emerging after the 1992 Earth Summit in Rio de Janeiro enabled the country to begin a process of Integrated Water Resources Management (IWRM), taking the lead from Chapter 18 of Agenda 21. With a focus on more comprehensively managing the country's critical water endowment amidst growing pressure on the resource, bilateral technical assistance and financial support played a large part in backstopping these national efforts. Nevertheless, in spite of this support and government backing, some two decades later implementation on the ground remains thin and the exercise of IWRM in practice is limited. This paper examines the Ugandan IWRM experience and identifies complex political-economy issues lying at the heart of current challenges. It argues that rarely is there likely to be an easy fix to sustainable financing and suggests the need for stronger citizen engagement and buy-in to the wider logic of IWRM to support longer-term effectiveness and sustainability.

KEYWORDS: Water Policy, IWRM, governance, decentralisation, political economy, development, Nile, Uganda

INTRODUCTION

> *Uganda has reached far into implementation of the IWRM Framework. An IWRM process was started in Uganda in 1993, at a time when civil strife had caused the breakdown of all water monitoring and information systems, when institutional capacity was at a record low and when water policy and legislation was rudimentary. Ten years later, the IWRM framework has been built up to a degree where Uganda has asserted its role in the Nile Basin, where a consistent policy and legislation provides the guidance and rules*

1 First published in *Water Alternatives* 9(3): 629-645.

> *for priorities of water use, allocation and wastewater discharge and where stakeholder participation and decentralisation provides local involvement. The identified programme activities in the Water Action Plan 1994 has* [sic] *provided the road map for this development which has resulted, among others,* [sic] *in empowerment both at local, regional and international level* (Jønch-Clausen, 2004).

This early and optimistic portrayal of IWRM progress in Uganda ten years after its introduction came from a well-known global leader of the concept and approach, closely involved in the Global Water Partnership. More widely, this was a period of optimism, coming shortly after Rio +10 Earth Summit and its expectation that all countries would have produced IWRM plans by 2005.

The UN Conference on Environment and Development held in Rio de Janeiro in 1992 had been a defining moment in global water policy, with a shift towards 'Integrated Water Resources Management' (IWRM). This resulted from a pre-Summit meeting involving international water institutions which sought to shape the water policy narratives arising out of Rio. The 'Dublin Meeting'[2] succeeded in this task through launching a set of four core principles that would provide a foundation for water policy development at a global level (see Muller, 2011): 1) Freshwater is a finite and vulnerable resource, essential to sustain life, development and the environment; 2) Water development and management should be based on a participatory approach, involving users, planners and policy-makers at all levels; 3) Women play a central part in the provision, management and safeguarding of water; and 4) Water has an economic value in all its competing uses and should be recognised as an economic good.

Principles No. 2 and No. 4 in particular became embedded in the formulation of IWRM as a policy approach, with policy actors emphasising the notion of water management at the lowest appropriate level; in effect, meaning the engagement of local water users within catchment-level institutions. Combined together these broad concepts forged a new policy discourse at an international level with a focus on user participation and payment for water usage through the issuing of permits.

Uganda's emergence as an early adopter of IWRM (Jønch-Clausen, 2004) emerged from the new government's strong relationship to the donor community.[3] The political leadership embarked on policy development that reflected principles of democratic decentralisation, market and trade liberalisation and private-sector engagement in service provision (Crook and Manor, 1998).

The geographic location of Uganda within the Nile Basin further enhanced interest in donor engagement. Since the early 1990s, Nile countries had begun to benefit from the end of Cold War politics. This unlocked development potential, a factor seized upon by donors, including the World Bank (Nicol and Cascão, 2011), and led the World Bank and others to launch the Nile Basin Initiative

2 In full, the International Conference on Water and the Environment (ICWE) in Dublin, Ireland, held between 26 and 31 January 1992.

3 See, for example, <www.theguardian.com/society/katineblog/2009/may/26/uganda-and-poverty>

(NBI) in 1999. Entebbe, Uganda, was chosen as the base for the NBI Secretariat[4] reflecting Uganda's strong commitment to new paradigms of water management, including its willingness to support the NBI.[5]

Uganda's readiness to undertake new policy directions was also a response to the challenging legacy of preceding years of conflict. Pressing development issues included the transformation to more productive rural economies, and tackling entrenched poverty, particularly in rural areas. In these areas where over 80% of people still live (PROTOS, 2011) low input-output subsistence production remained the norm. More widely, the Ugandan economy remains dominated by the four million farming households and, until recently, was driven by the production and export of the *robusta* coffee, most of which came from smallholders in specific parts of the country. In recent years, the government has provided few, if any, inputs to improve yields and marketing opportunities (Ahmed, 2012).

The government in tackling these development challenges has achieved some successes. The percentage of people living in absolute poverty, for instance, declined from 56% in 1992/3 to 24.5% in 2009/10 (GoU, 2013). The country also has a dynamic and developing service sector, though largely confined to urban and small town areas. On a wider basket of criteria, in 2014 Uganda was still ranked 163rd out of 188 countries (UNDP, 2015) illustrating the scale of the development challenge facing the country as a whole. It is within this context that the challenge for implementation of IWRM exists, and it is a challenge that is essentially based on the complex development pathways taking place in rural areas where nonfarm employment is scarce, agricultural extensification is the norm and balancing catchment development and protection with social change and economic demands presents a complex policy challenge.

One specific challenge in Uganda is the slower decline of poverty in rural areas (Barker, 2009) based, in part, on the lack of income sources that do not rely on exploitation of natural capital – for subsistence farming, to meet energy demands, and to provide for building materials and other artisanal occupations. Up to 90% of the population in rural areas still rely on available biomass for energy sources, particularly for cooking. At around 3.3% per annum, Uganda has one of the highest population growth rates in the world leading to an anticipated doubling to 100 million by 2050.[6] This level of increase will substantially drive further competition for land and biomass energy sources, increase the exhaustion of soils, affect stream-flow and siltation and exacerbate problems of downstream

4 98% of the country lies within the basin and in 1999 Uganda was chosen as host of the new Nile Basin Initiative Secretariat, Nile-SEC, in Entebbe.

5 Though beyond the scope of this chapter, this translated into eventual disillusionment by upstream countries at the slow pace of change, a new investment environment (new players emerging) and, eventually, a shift to more unilateral project development. Whilst the NBI continues to function, it is substantially affected by tensions, particularly between Egypt and Ethiopia over the construction of the Grand Ethiopia Renaissance Dam and filling of the reservoir.

6 Source: Population Division of the Department of Economic and Social Affairs of the United Nations Secretariat, World Population Prospects: The 2012 Revision, http://esa.un.org/unpd/wpp/index.htm

flooding. Natural disasters in some parts of the country are a regular occurrence.[7] Further encroachment is likely to take place in more marginal areas including vulnerable watersheds and on heavily-forested slopes. In and around Lake Victoria, one of the key catchment zones, large population concentrations are already employed in fisheries, drawn to the lake littoral for alternative livelihoods. This contributes to rapid urbanisation around the lake which is now seriously affecting water quality and, ultimately, damaging highly-productive fish stocks and the livelihoods of many communities (Barghouti, 2006). The need to manage shared catchments in the context of such rapidly-changing pressures is growing. Reforms that Uganda has been undertaking for over two decades now need to lead to achievements on the ground so that the ideas of IWRM can be translated into practices that deliver positive development outcomes. Uganda is not alone in facing this challenge, of course, as many chapters in this book make clear. However, given the long gestation period of policy on IWRM in the country, there is a high level of expectation that it can and must deliver at ground level.

This chapter examines the experience of IWRM in Uganda from initial development of the concept in the early 1990s to current implementation across the country. It describes the progress of IWRM and assesses challenges related to translation of IWRM ideas into practice, including the complexities associated with transposition of catchment-based systems onto existing political-economic contexts. The first part of the chapter looks at the IWRM policy context to uptake and adoption in Uganda, including the country's pioneering experience after the Earth Summit. The second part then assesses the context for decentralisation in the country and the relationship to political economic change. The third section examines recent steps taken to implement IWRM, followed by an analysis of experience in the Albert Water Management Zone (AWMZ). Conclusions then focus on why the journey from ideas to implementation has taken so long, and present the argument that future success will lie in more strongly embedding the development logic of IWRM in local institutions and communities. The approach taken focused on a literature review combined with in-depth examination of experience in one catchment through field visits and key-informant interviews. These interviews were conducted during August and September 2014 in Kampala and in the AWMZ. Experts on water and natural resources management were carefully selected based on experience of the IWRM process. NGO workers and IWRM leaders or implementers at the local level were selected with the help of the Albert Water Management Zone technical office of the Directorate of Water Development.

IWRM IN POLICY DEVELOPMENT

Emerging from the Earth Summit in 1992, the key output was Agenda 21 (for water, Chapter 18) which made explicit the need to implement IWRM (see details in box below). According to Jønch-Clausen, Uganda became the first country to follow these new, internationally-agreed, principles (Jønch-Clausen, 2004), in part because of its existing engagement in the Nordic Fresh Water Initiatives, led

7 www.monitor.co.ug/News/National/Landslides-bury-five-villages-in-Bududa/-/688334/1944328/-/ji1lwz/-/index.html

by Danida, that had emerged out of an earlier Copenhagen Conference.[8]

With technical and financial support from Danida, Uganda embarked upon the first National Water Resources 'Water Action Plan' (WAP) from 1993 to 1994 before IWRM had been fully refined as a policy prescription. The now widely-accepted IWRM troika of 'enabling environment', 'institutional framework' and 'management instruments' was developed under the Ugandan WAP, and later adopted by GWP in its articulation of IWRM during the mid-1990s. Uganda's early experiment, in other words, became an important part of an internationally-emerging experience of IWRM development.

The Post-Rio Agenda: Agenda 21 – the major product of Rio – included a key chapter on water, Chapter 18.[9] The major thinking processes behind IWRM are included in the following section:

> 18.8. Integrated water resources management is based on the perception of water as an integral part of the ecosystem, a natural resource and a social and economic good, whose quantity and quality determine the nature of its utilisation. To this end, water resources have to be protected, taking into account the functioning of aquatic ecosystems and the perenniality of the resource, in order to satisfy and reconcile needs for water in human activities. In developing and using water resources, priority has to be given to the satisfaction of basic needs and the safeguarding of ecosystems. Beyond these requirements, however, water users should be charged appropriately.
>
> 18.9. Integrated water resources management, including the integration of land- and water-related aspects, should be carried out at the level of the catchment basin or sub-basin. Four principal objectives should be pursued, as follows:
>
> (a) To promote a dynamic, interactive, iterative and multi-sectoral approach to water resources management, including the identification and protection of potential sources of freshwater supply, that integrates technological, socioeconomic, environmental and human health considerations;
>
> (b) To plan for the sustainable and rational utilisation, protection, conservation and management of water resources based on community needs and priorities within the framework of national economic development policy;
>
> (c) To design, implement and evaluate projects and programmes that are both economically efficient and socially appropriate within clearly defined strategies, based on an approach of full public participation, including that of women, youth, indigenous people, and local communities, in water management policy-making and decision-making;

8 Copenhagen informal consultation on integrated water resources development and management, 11-14 November 1991.

9 See: www.earthsummit2002.org/ic/freshwater/reschapt18.html

(d) To identify and strengthen or develop, as required, in particular in developing countries, the appropriate institutional, legal and financial mechanisms to ensure that water policy and its implementation are a catalyst for sustainable social progress and economic growth.

According to officials involved at the time, Danish experts were keen on policy development and wanted separate laws and policies for water supply and water resources management.[10] Uganda decided to have one law with two sections covering Water Supply and Water Resources Management, for reasons of simplicity and institutional alignment. The WAP underpinned the sector reform process and enshrined the concept of water as an economic good with an economic value attached. This was again reflected in the Water Statute completed in 1995 and in the 1999 National Water Policy.

Under the substantial 14-document WAP published in 1995, Uganda established four sub-sectors covering rural water, urban water, water for production and water resources management (DWD/WWAP, 2005). This included preparatory work and action plans (10 out of the 14 documents). It was envisaged that in the first stage of implementation the technical unit would become a permanent WAP Implementation Unit with the following basic tasks to enable full roll out of the reforms:

- Provide general support to implementation of the WAP Action Programme.
- Formulate project proposals and support the Directorate of Water Development and the Ministry of Water and Environment (MoWE) to arrange funding from government and other sources for implementation of activities.
- Liaise with other projects to carry out monitoring functions within the water sector.
- Assist the DWD to develop a permits system for abstractions and wastewater discharge (in the absence of more permanent arrangements).
- Report to the Water Policy Committee (WPC) on progress and constraints, the WPC being the overseer within the sector.

The 12-member multi-sector Water Policy Committee (WPC),[11] also established under the Water Statute (1995), was regarded as a way of promoting IWRM

10 Interview with Patrick Kahangire, former Director, DWD, September 2014.

11 Permanent Secretary in the Ministry responsible for Water Resources; Executive Director, National Environment Management Authority; The director responsible for irrigation; The director responsible for Animal Industry and Fisheries; The commissioner responsible for Industry; The commissioner responsible for hydropower; One District Resistance Council Chairman (appointed by Minister); One Chief Administrative Officer (appointed by Minister); The Managing Director National Water and Sewerage Corporation; Two persons having special qualifications or experience relevant to the functions of the Water Policy Committee (appointed by Minister); The Director of Water Development.

nationally and would develop and guide the strategic management of water resources within Uganda. Under the plan, Catchment Management Committees would carry forward the roles and responsibilities of the Water Policy Committee at a local level. As an advisory body, the WPC, was also expected to undertake conflict resolution between national authorities where these arose in relation to water management, a challenge anticipated as new legislation was drafted and began to be implemented across a range of sectors and geographic areas.

Further impetus for IWRM came from the wider East Africa Region, particularly with the establishment of regional bodies during the 1990s. Kenya, Tanzania and Uganda individually prepared a National Environmental Action Plan (NEAP) in this period, acknowledging that Lake Victoria and its catchments required urgent action to address resource degradation through regional cooperation. The NEAPs focused on issues including water pollution, biodiversity loss, land degradation, deforestation, and damage to wetlands. Discussions to broaden regional environmental cooperation covering the Lake Victoria Basin started in late 1992 and by 1994 the three governments had agreed to jointly prepare and implement the Lake Victoria Environmental Management Programme (LVEMP), to be funded by the World Bank and the Global Environment Facility (GEF).

The programme aimed to restore a healthy, varied ecosystem addressing issues such as declining biodiversity, oxygen depletion in the lake and reduced water quality (Barghouti, 2006). In particular, LVEMP reflected the dominant ecosystem discourse coming out of the Earth Summit discourse (LVEMP, 2003). To a significant extent, LVEMPI helped to raise awareness about natural resources issues amongst Ugandans and, according to a key official at the time, "There was need to get a critical mass behind this concept [IWRM], and in Uganda and East Africa LVEMP1 had the biggest impact in building capacity and creating awareness".[12] LVMP1 was the biggest force behind IWRM in Uganda, he argues, not least because its focus on Lake Victoria included support for 50 doctorates, 100s of Masters and thousands of other [qualification] levels, many of which built on concepts of IWRM and helped instil wider consciousness of the approach.[13]

In conjunction with the arrival of IWRM in national policy, Uganda had also begun moving rapidly towards a more decentralised system of governance. In 1995 Uganda adopted a new constitution which charged the government with responsibility to hold the natural resources of Uganda in trust. This was followed in 1997 by the promulgation of the Local Governments Act. In parallel with the 'lowest appropriate level of water management', this Act enshrined governance over development processes at lower levels, with substantial stakeholder involvement. A year later the Water Resources Regulations, Water Supply Regulation, Environmental Impact Assessment Regulations, National Environmental Waste Management Regulations and the National Environment (Wetlands, River Banks and Lake Shores Management) Regulations (1999) were also completed. This draft of new legislation triggered by Rio, described as a "lot of laws in Uganda",[14] underscored the close donor engagement in Uganda's planning and poli-

12 Interview with Tom Okurut, former Executive Secretary of the LVBC, September 2014.

13 Ibid.

14 Ibid

cy-making, but also created considerable complexity. This complexity overlay an already-challenging political-economic environment in which a thrust towards greater decentralisation of government had become a centrepiece of development policy. It also, however, revealed the difficult interrelationship between governance of resources under IWRM and wider institutions of government at a local level. This political-economic challenge subsequently affected IWRM implementation in Uganda. The following section examines these factors in relation to the emergence and development of the country's decentralisation agenda.

Lessons from the decentralisation agenda

Uganda's government undertook rapid decentralisation[15] during the 1990s, reflecting prevailing democratic decentralisation discourse of the era. After Idi Amin Dada's government was overthrown in the late 1970s, governance shifted from increasingly autocratic rule by decree to governance through Local Resistance[16] Councils under the Statute of that name promulgated in 1993. This established the LC5 as the basic administrative and political unit of local government, thereafter written into the 1995 Constitution of the Republic of Uganda and enshrined in the Local Governments Act of 1997 (Steiner, 2006). Whilst this decentralised governance ostensibly meant more popular control of local affairs, in many ways it enabled the government to exert greater political control. At the time, it was described as one of the most radical devolution initiatives in an era of decentralisation and was in step with the World Bank and other agencies pursuing an agenda of smaller government, and more democratic decentralisation.

As a political strategy by the ruling party the District Council – LC5 – became the main political organ of local government. Members of the Council would be regularly elected and the executive organs at different local government levels were in charge of collecting and implementing plans from lower levels. In theory at least, these reflected higher levels of policy and planning. This bottom-up process suggested grassroots participation, but in practice proved difficult to sustain. Under this policy, national government was responsible for the provision of public goods (defence, security and foreign relations) and guiding policy-making, whilst local authorities delivered key local public services (Steiner, 2006). The major challenge lay in financing these responsibilities. Local councils needed funds, so some level of fiscal decentralisation was necessary to enable the collecting of local taxes and fees as well as receipt of conditional grants from the central level. In practice, significant challenges rendered the responsibility and (to some extent) capacity, but not the resources necessary to deliver services to local communities. Proceeds from local taxation were generally very low – not least because of the low taxation capacity of rural communities – and in most cases transfers from the centre made up the bulk of income received by local government, reaching as high as 90% in the mid-2000s (ibid). Central government continued to control local financing processes.

15 A process of devolving political, fiscal, and administrative powers to subnational units of government (Burki et al., 1999 cited in Cammack et al., 2006).

16 The term 'resistance' was with reference to their establishment within liberated areas (Cammack et al., 2006).

Resistance to relinquishing control from the centre came from different directions. Line ministries were concerned at loss of fiduciary influence (and budget), which led them to maintain direct control over decision-making under the key Poverty Eradication Action Plan (PEAP) policy. Up to 80% of funds transferred from the centre were, in fact, earmarked or conditional with ministries concerned about perceived weaknesses in local government financial decision-making and scrutiny. Another additional incentive for re-centralisation in fact came inadvertently from donors themselves. With the emergence of Sector-Wide Approaches as a way of disbursing aid under the Paris Protocols, this served to privilege decision-making and financing processes at the centre, including within the water sector.

Other processes that challenged fiscal decentralisation (and in effect impaired the whole project of decentralised government) included gradual politicisation of taxation as opposition to the government strengthened in advance of the 2005 election. This was caused by a sense of general politicisation of taxes[17] by the government, accompanied by arbitrary, regressive and sometimes forceful collection practices. In addition, there was a lack of awareness about tax collection and service delivery links, causing the collection of low overall tax returns (Steiner, 2006). Local governments were left with insufficient funds to fulfil basic provision of goods and services, a problem compounded by the growth in so-called new districts (Cammack et al., 2007). District subdivision could reward loyalty, through providing new jobs and resource allocations, in spite of the additional administrative complexity generated. It did not however, compensate for capacity needs in the new districts and frequently left new districts bereft of administrative and technical capacity.

This had the net effect of hindering emerging catchment management (Bratton and van de Walle, 1997 cited in Cammack et al., 2006). As one early proponent of IWRM implementation comments:

> *With decentralisation, now we have districts with no resources. You may also find 39 districts in a (Water Management) Zone. It is a nightmare coordinating them. You also have people with different interests within the catchment. A district environment officer may, for example, feel you are trespassing in his docket when bringing in IWRM.*[18]

This complexity of the political-economic development environment should not be underestimated in assessing the challenge of IWRM implementation and in the Uganda case, it has continued to hinder the practice of IWRM beyond the development of organisational structures and plans.

A generally poor taxation environment and dependence on central transfers was combined with low educational levels amongst councillors. Without an effective relationship between the Chief Administrative Officer (executive branch)

17 For example, the use of the subsequently-abolished graduated personal taxes for campaign purposes in the 2001 Presidential election (when the opposition had called for abolishment in their manifesto), led to widespread reluctance to pay the tax and an overall drop in collections (Steiner, 2006).

18 Interview with Mr. Patrick Kahangire, former Director, DWD, September 2014.

and the Council Chairperson (elected official), decision-making could become paralysed, as Steiner notes: "Due to the clash between these two functionaries... council meetings were not so much dedicated to development or poverty-related issues but rather to argument about the distribution of power" (Steiner, 2006: 14). These systemic and political-economic factors challenged the achievement of IWRM management at the 'lowest appropriate' level. The assumption inherent is that management at this level is relatively simple. The reality, revealed by experience in Uganda, is rather one of complex environments with demands placed on people and institutions that are difficult to address.

Even key proponents of democratic decentralisation, the World Bank, identified limitations in the process in Uganda. In 2000, an assessment team concluded that the coverage of infrastructure and services at the subnational government level posed a "considerable challenge" with coverage "far behind" the needs of the population (Obowona et al., 2000 cited in Cammack et al., 2007). Other analyses pointed to capture of political (electoral) processes by the local elite in LCs through the distribution of simple largesse, including basic household products (Francis and James, 2003 cited in Cammack et al., 2007). The conclusion reached was that at a local level decentralisation had helped to create and strengthen an elite which then managed to consume much of the "locally generated revenue as well as the non-conditional grants from central government" (Cammack et al., 2007: 39). These political-economic challenges persist and continue to grate against the capacity to mobilise effectively local populations and institutions in support of IWRM implementation at the catchment level and below.

The political ups and downs of Uganda electoral cycles led to direct politicisation of local government in 2005 when the Constituency Development Fund was introduced and a sum of USD6,000 was given to each MP to "supplement development funding by central and local government" (Cammack et al., 2006; 39). Whilst these MP funds could help support local development activities, in reality they were likely to oil further neo-patrimonial politics. With the relocation of control over finances from the centre at the same time this placed emphasis on local officials 'staying in favour' with the ruling party. This also reduced incentives to prioritise local development interests (Cammack et al., 2006). The challenges of such a situation persisting in relation to IWRM relate to the essential fragmentation that this can pose within catchments, where several districts may share a catchment, with competing political interests in different districts combined with strong neo-patrimonialism driving local-level decision-making.

With the abolition of graduated tax at a local level the link between payment of taxes and delivery of services was effectively broken. This meant that an important accountability mechanism with, and for, the local population ceased to exist, however unpopular the tax. Within this prevailing environment of decentralised administration, but financial recentralisation, it is worth questioning the logic of IWRM at 'the lowest appropriate level' and asking whether local user-driven implementation can actually survive and prosper in an environment such as that of Uganda.

THE FINAL THRUST TO IWRM IN PRACTICE – CURRENT CHALLENGES

In the early 2000s it became clear in Uganda that implementation of IWRM given capacity and other institutional constraints[19] would remain slow unless a stronger institutional framework could be created. A Water Resources Management Reform Study (led by COWI[20]) between 2003 and 2005 set in motion a shift from more centralised management to a catchment-based WRM system under which the country was divided into four Water Management Zones (WMZs – see Fig. 13.1 overleaf).

This more intensive and focused approach bridged the emerging gap in operational capacity at a local level between articulation of a sectoral policy discourse on IWRM and the hard realities of political-economic governance described above. The Ministry of Water and Environment was reorganised with the establishment of the Directorate of Water Resources Management in 2007 (Barker, 2009), part of which entailed increasing the capacity of water resources management, described by the then Director of Water Development as "institutional strengthening. In terms of skills there was now a team to promote Water Resources Management. The separation was a good ground for establishing IWRM".[21]

This new institutional environment resulted from another 'global push' to IWRM – this time as a target under the MDGs. Launched at the 'Rio+10' meeting (the World Summit on Sustainable Development held in Johannesburg in 2002) the international community called for the development of "integrated water resource management and water efficiency plans by 2005", with the promise that "support [would be] given to developing countries". This presented a further opportunity for donor engagement in and financing of IWRM as a policy objective, with a renewed emphasis from European countries under the European Union Water Initiative, reflecting the successful completion of the European Framework Directive, in which catchment management featured strongly.

By 2005, Uganda had dutifully published its Water Sector Reform Studies, analysing the four main water subsectors leading to a Strategic Investment Plan (SIP) the objective of which was to bring local government at all levels, as well as NGOs and the private sector, into the wider decentralisation context in Uganda (MOWE, 2009). This recognised explicitly that a major barrier to implementation was capacity for local operationalisation and meant moving beyond the water 'silo' whilst recognising that IWRM needed to be more embedded in local institutional environments. This bridging of water and wider governance arrangements set the scene for a complex process of policy implementation.

Shortly afterwards the Directorate of Water Resources Management (DWRM) was established with responsibility for developing and maintaining national water laws, policies and regulations, and managing, monitoring and regulating water resources through the issue of permits. It was also tasked with coordinating Uganda's engagement in Transboundary Water Resources Management

19 An FAO consultant noted that in the late 1990s, a single person was running the Water Right Administration Unit.

20 A Danish consulting firm.

21 Interview with Eng. Patrick Kahangire, then Director of Water Resources Development, September 2014.

Fig. 13.1. Water Management Zones established in Uganda*

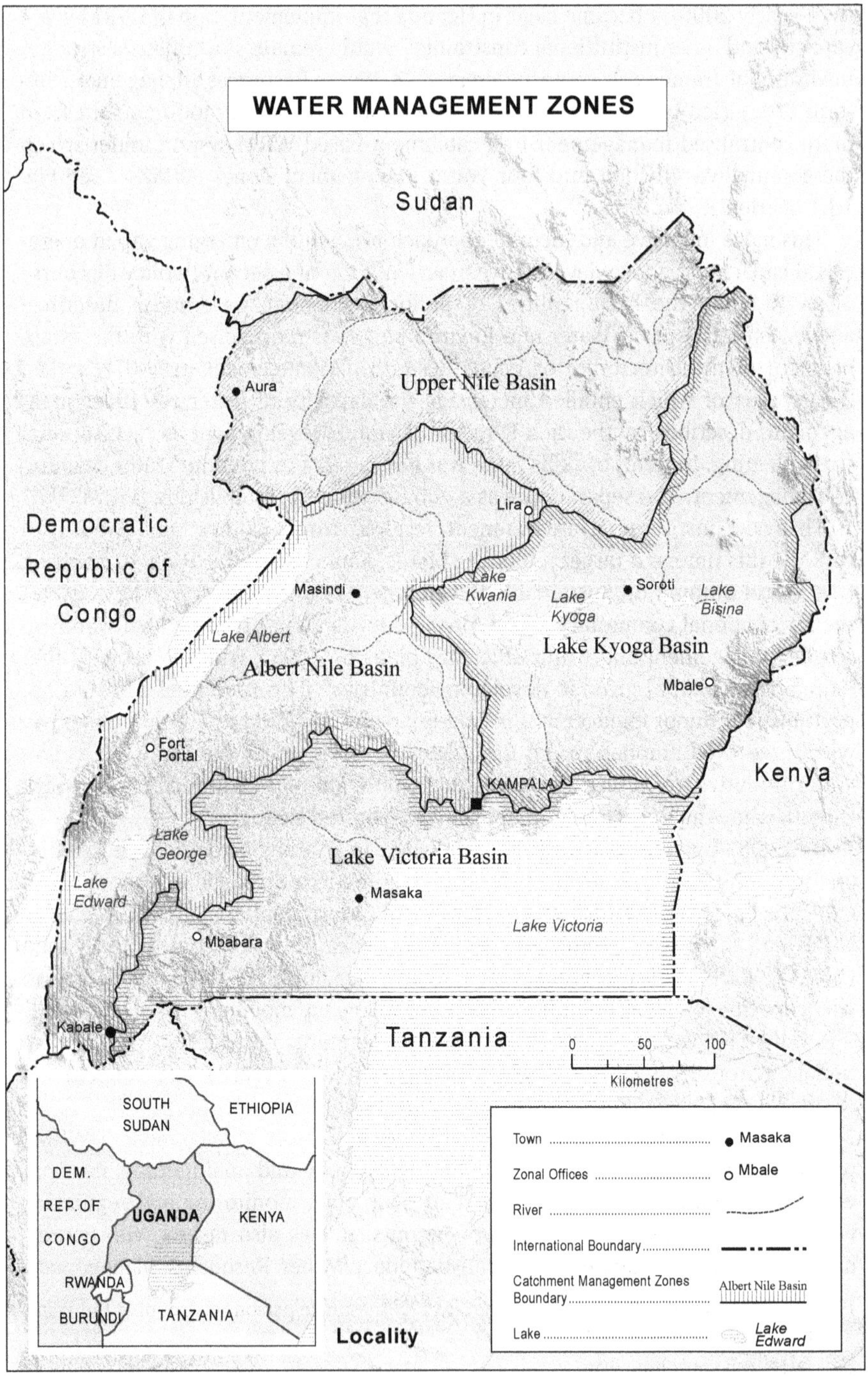

WATER MANAGEMENT ZONES

Sudan

Upper Nile Basin

Aura

Lira

Democratic Republic of Congo

Masindi

Lake Kwania

Lake Kyoga

Soroti

Lake Bisina

Lake Albert

Albert Nile Basin

Lake Kyoga Basin

Mbale

Fort Portal

KAMPALA

Kenya

Lake George

Lake Victoria Basin

Lake Edward

Masaka

Lake Victoria

Mbabara

Kabale

Tanzania

0 50 100 Kilometres

SOUTH SUDAN, ETHIOPIA, DEM. REP. OF CONGO, UGANDA, KENYA, RWANDA, BURUNDI, TANZANIA

Locality

Town — Masaka

Zonal Offices — Mbale

River

International Boundary

Catchment Management Zones Boundary — Albert Nile Basin

Lake — Lake Edward

*Source:https://cmsdata.iucn.org/downloads/status_of_catchment_based_IWRM_in_Uganda.pdf and MoWE, Uganda.

(TBWRM), particularly given the opportunities for investment that had begun to arise under the NBI. Most importantly for IWRM, the DWRM became responsible for the national pilot sub-catchment projects that were planned across the country by 2015.

This new structure was to enable "holistic planning and equitable allocation of the available water resources (in any given sub-basin/catchment) to the various demands/users to avoid conflicts and to ensure long-term sustainability" (MoWE, 2013). The four WMZs were initially Albert, Kyogo, Victoria and Upper Nile. Each WMZ comprised different catchments (some transboundary in nature[22]) spread over varying numbers of districts. Each catchment was expected to establish a Catchment Management Organisation (CMO), supported by the WMZ team.

Fig. 13.2. The structure of water resources governance in Uganda (as at 2015).[23]

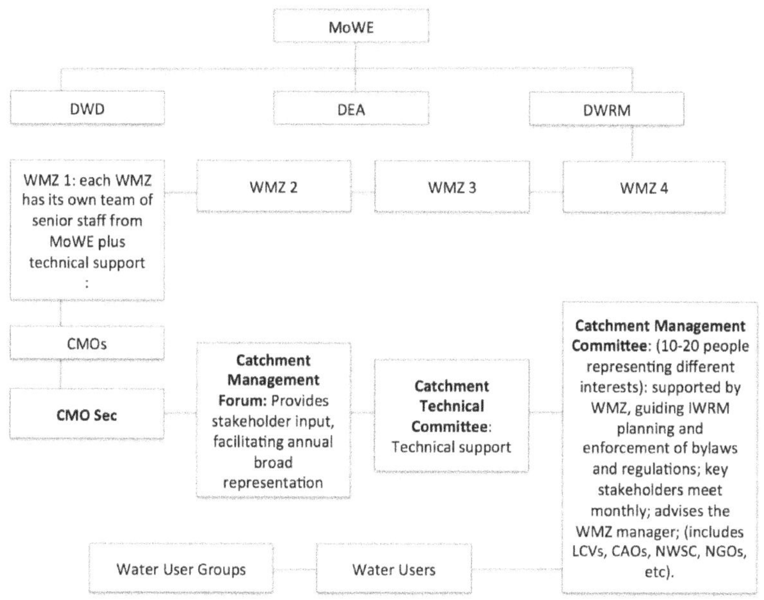

By 2015, four CMOs had been set up in the Rwizi, Albert, Mpanga and Semliki basins.[24] Each CMO has a mechanism for stakeholder coordination including the

22 In one case, this added a particular complexity in shared catchments with Democratic Republic of Congo: "We have a challenge to work with the DRC on IWRM. The problem with Congo is the administration. You have chiefs and warlords there. It is quite complicated" (Herbert Kamuhanda, Personal communication).

23 Ministry of Water and Environment (MoWE); Chief Administrative Officer (CAO); Catchment Management Organization (CMO); Directorate of Environmental Affairs (DEA); Directorate of Water Development (DWD); Directorate of Water Resource Management (DWRM); Local Council Five (LCV); Water Management Zone (WMZ); National Water and Sewerage Corporation (NWSC).

24 An additional, but smaller pilot, was established under the International Union for the

Stakeholder Forum, Catchment Management Committee, Technical Committee and Secretariat (see Fig. 13 2 above). Districts located within catchments are where activities are "to be implemented" (PROTOS, 2011), which suggests an assumption about the strength of linkages between the CMOs and district-level planning and development processes. Under this new process a number of non-governmental organisations have played a key role, particularly in the establishment of pilot projects.[25] In addition, an IWRM Working Group was established in 2013 under the Uganda Water and Sanitation Network, the official NGO water network in Uganda. The detailed structure of CMO development is captured in the Operationalisation of Catchment-based Water Resource Management (2010).

Given the growing linkage between IWRM implementation and structures of local government, the following section examines in more detail the experience of decentralisation and IWRM in one catchment and asks whether challenges encountered here have been partially responsible for the slow implementation of IWRM more widely in Uganda.

Recent experience in the Semliki catchment, Albert Water Management Zone

The Semliki River flows from Lake Edward and drains in Lake Albert, contributing 63% of the lake's inflow. The Semliki is augmented by rivers Mubuku and Nyamwamba, which flow from Mt. Rwenzori, before the river embarks on a 140 km journey to Lake Albert. Human demand for water is mainly for agriculture, much of which involves poor land management. Deforestation, fuelled by opening up increasing tracts of land for farming and an ever-growing demand for wood fuel and timber, has increased the risk of flooding and caused greater siltation of Lake Albert, including an ever-expanding delta at the outlet of the Semliki.

In July 2011, an AWMZ team of six arrived in the western Uganda town of Fort Portal from the DWRM. The team was sent to establish an office under which to facilitate implementation of IWRM in the Lake Albert catchment. The same process was ongoing in the other three WMZs in Uganda. This was part of what those involved in establishing the four WMZs called a 'big bang' approach – launching all four simultaneously.[26]

The team was given one small room at the Technical Support Unit (TSU) 6 to start work. In the Semliki River catchment the NGO WWF had already begun a pilot project on IWRM in Uganda under the Semliki River Catchment and Water Resources Management Project. This was implemented in the districts of Kasese, Ntoroko and Bundibugyo. Environment officers were the focal persons at the Local Government level. Other key groups included DWRM staff, the Uganda Wildlife Authority (UWA), National Environmental Management Authority (NEMA), National Water and Sewerage Corporation (NWSC) as well as Tronda Power and Kilembe Mines from the private sector. In 2011. they established in-

Conservation of Nature (IUCN) in Otuke District on the Awaz Sub-basin.

25 Possibly linked to the growing NGO funding available for 'climate adaptation' projects.

26 Personal communication with Patrick Kahangire, former Director, DWD.

stitutional structures starting with water user committees at village level up to parish, sub-county and district levels. The role of the newly established WMZ officers was to help move pilot activities forward on a surer footing, with the establishment of effective procedures and guidelines.[27] As explained by the District Environment Officer:

> *We tasked members to move around registering every resource user (name, activity, telephone number). They were to elect nine people among themselves to form a committee and of the nine at least three had to be women and at least one woman should hold an executive post. One of the key principles of IWRM is that women play a big role in natural resources so they have to be recognised.*[28]

The purpose of these WUAs (combining farmers, cattle keepers, brick makers, sand miners and all other water users), is to guard against activities that are detrimental to the environment while undertaking restoration practices such as tree planting on river banks. After their formation, the associations were given laws and guidelines and WWF provided funding of between Shs 10 m (USD4,000) and Shs 20 m (USD8,000). However, the end of external funding under WWF ushered in the realities: According to a number of interviewees, following up on activities became difficult even on the part of the NGO because there were no funds. According to one WUA Chairman only recently had the DWRM reached local levels, and articulated the concepts behind IWRM.[29]

One key institutional shortcoming is the lack of legal entity of WUAs under the Water Act. Hence, even if funds were available they would be unable to access them directly. This is a serious impediment given the essential principle of local action and responsiveness to local water management demands. This is also one of the reasons why the government has pursued an approach based on working with NGOs, given their local engagement and legal status.

According to Albert Orijabo, Principle Water Officer, AWMZ, "the law is being reviewed so that these new groups can be recognised and financed. But we have budget lines that, for example, support tree planting around river banks. We shall continue to work with NGOs to implement management activities". This underscores the virtually negligible budgets for natural resources management and the continued centralisation of water resources management at national level. According to one Community Development Officer, the local government provides a budget of just UGX100,000 (USD40) a year, from a total sub-county tax base of some UGX10 million (about USD4,000),[30] according to Hamda-Saadi Kibuuka, Community Development Office (CDO) Karusandara subcounty, Kasese. At the lowest end of the local government (LC1), where mobilisation for natural resources management is very critical, the system is completely broken. There

27 Personal communication with Albert Orijabo, Principle Water Officer, AWMZ.

28 Personal communication with Herbert Kamuhanda, Ntoroko District Environment Officer.

29 Personal communication with Clovis Kalegutsa, Chairman Mubuku-Nyamwamba Water User Association.

30 Personal communications with Hamda-Saadi Kibuuka, CDO, Karusandara sub-county, Kasese.

are very sparse human and financial resources and to get any kind of community action going resources need to be provided directly to the 'officials'.[31]

The challenge of sparsely-resourced institutions of management in acutely poor development environments is becoming a substantial impediment to realising the goal of management at the most appropriate level. Semliki Catchment Management Organisation, headed by the LC5 Chairman of Kabarole District, has had no impact since it was formed in 2012 according to some key informants. Clovis Kalegutsa, Chairman Mubuku-Nyamwamba Water User Association stated:

> *The political part of local leadership is a problem. They are only interested in votes. From Water User Associations we formed a catchment organisation, which is full of civil servants and politicians. It is probably because of political reasons that the Semliki Catchment Organisation has not taken off. The guidelines were that this organisation would be constituted by top civil servants and politicians. The argument was that they should own the process since they are leaders.*[32]

One of the main challenges for local leaders – political and non-political alike – is that there is acute pressure to be responsive and identify immediate solutions to pressing problems. IWRM is not set up for such responsiveness and is rather longer-term in approach. Among local leaders interviewed there was a mixture of perceptions when it came to IWRM. One key issue was the lack of understanding of the interconnectedness of water management, land restoration and development. "There is a fundamental disconnect between water supply and environmental management. Many people can't link water supply to water management. For example, it is easier for a politician to understand digging a borehole than planting trees", stated one key informant in the WMZ.[33] This was reinforced by the current Executive Director of NEMA, who stated that:

> *After the big push of LVEMP1, MoWE remained the key champion of IWRM and that is where problems came in. Right now, catchment zones are bringing other professionals on board but elsewhere people are looking at IWRM as a water affair. There is a silo structure at the top. Land use and soil conservation, for example, are not in-*

31 Personal communication with Clovis Kalegutsa, Chairman Mubuku-Nyamwamba Water User Association.

32 a) Representatives of local authorities, councils and public bodies responsible for matters relating to water resources in the catchment area;

b) Representatives of any agency, department or organisation whose area of jurisdiction or any part of it falls within the catchment area;

c) Representatives of the business community operating within the catchment area concerned;

d) Representatives of nongovernmental organisations engaged in water resources management activities within the catchment area concerned;

e) Any other person who has demonstrated competence in matters relating to management of water resources - The Water (Deconcentration of Water Resources Management) Regulations, 2012.

33 Personal communication Albert Orijabo, Principle Water Officer, AWMZ.

tegrated. We have to ask questions such as: how is the Ministry of Agriculture contributing to IWRM?[34]

Conclusions

This thing is not yet politically accepted and adequately supported.[35]

The lineage of IWRM policy development in Uganda is long, but the experience of implementation on the ground relatively short. Given the challenge of externally-generated principles and institutional structures superimposed on a complex and dynamic political-economic landscape this is perhaps not surprising. However, there is real need now to bring IWRM into effective local-level management and planning of resource use within catchments as pressures on natural capital – land, water and forest and fishery resources – continue to grow. Without effective management of resources that provide a platform for many people's livelihoods, particularly in rural areas, there will be major challenges for future livelihood security. The balance between IWRM as a resource management tool and a development approach still needs to be effectively struck and articulated locally. As one informant stated: "There is the issue of poverty and livelihood. IWRM principles are looking at conservation. You are telling people 'don't lay bricks here' but they have to pay for their children's school fees".[36]

In conclusion, the process of developing the policy framework in Uganda has taken time – over two decades. In this period the population of the country has effectively doubled and along with this increase, demand for resource access has grown, posing new institutional and governance challenges. Having been approached as a grand policy design flowing from international meetings via international agencies and government institutions, the concepts of IWRM are now meeting hard realities of local political economy and resource governance in Uganda. Not surprisingly there are challenges. Little prior consideration has been given to the embedding of catchment management institutions in local political and other processes, and this challenge remains to be adequately addressed. Two key ways forward are suggested:

First, local government needs to be brought into catchment management in a more substantial way. This is increasingly the case where local government and catchment management institutions are expected to converge and work together. Aside from (political) elite capture of the management institutions, which remains a challenge, there are wider questions of the financing relationship between local government, as implementers, and catchment organisations as planners. These processes are locally very political; catchment institutions are, to all intents and purposes, another layer of government intervening in the lives of local people and expanding the reach of the state into otherwise locally-governed natural resources spaces.

This leads to the second need, which is around the socialisation of the ideas of IWRM with the broader public so that its development logic is better appreciated

34 Personal communication Dr. Tom Okurut, Executive Director, NEMA.

35 Personal communication Patrick Kahangire, former Director, DWD.

36 ibid.

by users. It may be that narratives focusing on development rather than resource conservation and management should be used more frequently and widely. As one key informant observed:

> *Defining the environment without including human beings takes you away from the real issues because the human being is an influencing factor, for example the impact of population growth. We need to define the environment correctly to understand that IWRM brings the human being to the centre.*[37]

People matter not just as participants, but also as users of resources and derivers of livelihoods from different landscapes. Their understanding and knowledge can become keys to the success of IWRM in Uganda, as champions of the approach, and, ultimately, as those to whom the actions of catchment organisations should be accountable.

The experience of Uganda shows that IWRM can be a long process of policy-making and institution-building; but also that its real development potential requires careful navigation of power and political economy realities at local levels. One key step forward entails the embedding of IWRM's core development logic in the local communities and institutions it is supposed to serve. This large, but important, task can help ensure the future uptake and sustainability of IWRM in Uganda.

Acknowledgements

The authors would like to acknowledge the resources and intellectual contribution of the Flows and Practices research project and its members and the individuals interviewed in the preparation and completion of this chapter. We also acknowledge the very constructive and detailed comments and feedback provided by the internal and anonymous reviewers. We also acknowledge and thank the key informants in Uganda for their insights and willingness to share their experience and knowledge and the Research Council of Norway for the generous financial support.

References

Ahmed M. 2012. Analysis of incentives and disincentives for coffee in Uganda. *Technical notes series.* Rome: Monitoring and Analysing Food and Agricultural Policies (MAFAP), FAO.

Barghouti, S. 2006. *Case study of the Lake Victoria Environmental Management Project: An independent evaluation of the World Bank's support of regional programs.* Independent Evaluation Group (IEG) Working Paper Series; support of regional programs. Washington, DC: World Bank.

Barker, J. 2009. *Lake Albert Eastern Catchment Management initiatives, Uganda.* Final Evaluation Report. Kampala: WWF-Uganda Country office and WWF Norway.

Barnet, S.; Mille, S. and Loffman, M. 2008. *Case study – Uganda, mainstreaming conflict prevention – A study of EU action in ACP countries.* Brussels: The Quaker

37 Personal communication with Dr. Tom Okurut, Director, NEMA.

Council for European Affairs.

Bratton, M. and van de Walle, N. 1997. *Democratic experiments in Africa: Regime transitions in comparative perspective.* Cambridge University Press. Cambridge.

Cammack, D; Golooba-Mutebi, F.; Kanyongolo, F. and O'Neil, T. 2006. Neopatrimonial politics, decentralisation and local government: Uganda and Malawi in 2006. Working Paper No. 2. *Good governance, aid modalities and poverty reduction.* Dublin: The Advisory Board for Irish Aid.

Crook, R. and Manor, J. 1998. *Democracy and decentralisation in South Asia and West Africa – Participation, accountability and performance.* Cambridge: CUP.

DWD (Department of Water Development)/WWAP (World Water Assessment Programme). 2005. *Uganda National Water Development Report 2005.* Government of Uganda and United Nations Educational, Social and Cultural Organisation (UNESCO).

GoU (Government of Uganda). 2013. *Millennium Development Goals Report for Uganda, 2013.* Kampala: Ministry of Finance, Planning and Economic Development, September.

Hoekstra, A.Y. and Hung, P.Q. 2005. *Globalisation of water resources: International virtual water flows in relation to crop trade. Global Environmental Change* 15(1): 45-56.

Jønch-Clausen, T. 2004. *Integrated water resources management (IWRM) and water efficiency plans by 2005 – Why, what and how?* TEC Background Paper No. 10. Stockholm: Global Water Partnership.

Kilama, J.L. 2007. Power and development: Controversies over the Bujagali hydropower project along the Nile river in Uganda. Masters Thesis (unpublished), Department of Water and Environmental Studies, Linkoping University, Sweden.

Kiwanuka, M. 2012. Decentralization and good governance in Africa: Institutional challenges to Uganda's local governments. *Journal of African and Asian Local Government Studies* 1(3): 44-59.

Leefers, K. 2004. The course of political development in Uganda and its effect on economic development, *Critique*: A Worldwide Student Journal of Politics, Spring. Illinois State University. https://about.illinoisstate.edu/critique/Documents/aboutus.htm

LVEMP (Lake Victoria Environmental Management Programme). 2003. *Lake Victoria Environmental Management Project Phase 1.* Regional Stocktaking. Washington, DC, World Bank.

Maenen, S. 2013. *Obstacles and opportunities for a negotiated approach to IWRM* (chapter no. Uganda, Lake Albert Catchment). July. Kampala, Both Ends.

Magabi, E. 2004. Uganda's decentralisation policy, legal framework, local government structure and service delivery. Paper prepared for the First Conference of Regional Assemblies of Africa and Europe organised by the Regional Assembly of Tuscany under the patronage of the Italian Presidency and the United Nations Department of Economic and Social Affairs (UNDESA). September, Florence.

Manzungu, E.; Bolding, A. and Senzanje, A. 1999. Towards integrated water resource management. A conceptual framework. In Manzungu, E.; Senzanje, A. and van der Zaag, P. (Eds), *Water for agriculture in Zimbabwe*, pp. 254-264. Harare: University of Zimbabwe Publications.

Mehta, L.; Alba, R.; Bolding, A.; Denby, K.; Derman, B.; Hove, T.; Manzungu, E; Movik, S.; Prabhakaran, P. and van Koppen, B. 2014. The politics of IWRM in southern Africa. *International Journal of Water Resources Development* 30(3): 528-542.

Mehta, L. and Movik, S. 2014. *Flows and practices: Integrated Water Resource Management in Africa contexts.* IDS Working Paper No. 438. Brighton, UK: Institute of Development Studies.

Moncrieffe, J. 2004. *Uganda's political economy: A synthesis of major thought.* Report prepared for DFID Uganda, February, Final Draft. London: Overseas Development Institute.

MoWE (Ministry of Water and Environment). 2009. *Strategic sector investment plan.* Kampala: Ministry of Water and the Environment, July.

MoWE. 2013. *Uganda sector performance report.* Kampala: Ministry of Water and the Environment.

Muller, M. 2011. The challenges of implementing an African water resource management agenda. In Kondlo, K. and Ejiogu, C. (Eds), *Africa in focus – Governance in the 21st century*, pp. 146-162. Cape Town: Human Sciences Research Council Press.

Muriisa, R.K. 2008. Decentralisation in Uganda: Prospects for improved service delivery. *Africa Development* XXXII (4): 83-95. Council for the Development of Social Science Research in Africa, South Africa.

MWLE. 1999. A *national water pol*icy. Kampala: Republic of Uganda.

MWLE. 2007. Climate change – Uganda national adaptation programmes of action. Kampala: GoU, GEF and UNEP.

MWLE. 2013. *Water and environment sector performance report.* Kampala: GOU.

Nicol, A. and Cascão, A. 2011. Against the flow – New power dynamics and upstream mobilisation in the Nile Basin. *Review of African Political Economy* 39(128): 317-325.

Ojambo, H. 2012. Decentralisation in Africa: A critical review of Uganda's experience. *Potchefstroom Electronic Law Journal* 15(2).

Okidi, J.A. and Guloba, M. 2006. *Decentralization and development: Emerging issues from Uganda's experience.* Occasional Paper No. 31. Kampala: Economic Policy Research Centre.

Polak, M. 2013. Sharing experience with Integrated Water Resources Management (IWRM), water, energy, transport – IWRM Working Group. Bonn: Deutsche Gesellschaft für Internationale (GIZ).

Protos. 2005. *Study on IWRM legislation.* Final Report, April. Uganda.

Protos. 2011. Involving local communities in preparing a long term CC and IWRM action plan to enhance their adaptive capacity to CC, and integrate improved water management in the Mpanga Catchment of the Nile Basin in Uganda. Proposal prepared by PROTOS and Ministry of Water and Environment (Directorate of Water Resources Management), Uganda, June. (Unpublished).

Ribot, J. 2001. Integral local development: Accommodating multiple interests through entrustment and accountable representation. *International Journal of Agricultural Resources, Governance and Ecology* 1(34): 327-350.

Robinson, M. 2006. *The political economy of governance reforms in Uganda.* Discussion Paper No. 386. Brighton: Institute of Development Studies.

Rwakakamba, T.M. 2009. How effective are Uganda's environmental policies? *Mountain Research and Development* 29(2): 121-127.

Saxena, K.; Paul, S. and Goel, P.R. 2010. *Decentralisation in Uganda.* Kampala: National Council of Applied Economic Research, August.

Steiner, S. 2006. *Decentralisation in Uganda: Exploring the constraints to poverty reduction.* Working Paper No. 31. Transformation in the Process of Globalisation. Hamburg: German Institute of Global and Area Studies.

UNDP (United Nations Development Programme). 2015. *Work for human development. 2015 Human Development Report.* New York: United Nations.

UNEP (United Nations Environment Programme). 2004. *Water resources management, environmental degradation and human welfare: Lessons learned from the Lake Kyoga Catchment in Uganda.* Policy Brief.

UN-Water. 2006. National Water Development Report: Uganda. Prepared for the 2nd UN World Water Development Report, World Water Assessment Programme.

UN-Water. 2008. Status Report on Integrated Water Resources Management and Water Efficiency Plans, prepared for the 16th Session of the Commission on Sustainable Development, May.

World Bank. 1993. *Water resources management.* A World Bank Policy Paper. Washington, DC: The World Bank.

14

Reflections on the Formulation and Implementation of IWRM in Southern Africa from a Gender Perspective[1]

Bill Derman

Preetha Prabhakaran

ABSTRACT: While it is claimed that the founding principles of integrated water resources management are the Dublin Principles this does not appear to be the case for Principle No. 3, which underlines the importance of women in water provision, management and safeguarding. Mozambique, South Africa, Tanzania and Zimbabwe are members of SADC and have signed the SADC Protocol on Women and other international human rights instruments. However, we do not see an incorporation of these instruments and other empowerment frameworks into water policies. We find that Principle No. 3 has been sidelined in the implementation of Integrated Water Resource Management (IWRM). In examining the gender practices in these four nations of Africa, gender equality remains distant from the concerns of the water sector. We enumerate many of the commonalities among these countries in how they are marginalising women's access to, and use of, water.

KEYWORDS: Gender, IWRM, Dublin Principles, southern Africa

INTRODUCTION

This chapter focuses on one aspect of the more general Flows and Practices project: What has been the place and importance of women's equality in the rolling out and implementation of Integrated Water Resource Management (IWRM)? What have been the policies and strategies promoted and followed to ensure that women were included in all phases of the old and new institutions tasked with formulating IWRM at the various levels involved in water governance and management? How have the general gender policies of the four nations been included in the water sector? If women's management of water has not figured centrally to

1 First published in *Water Alternatives* 9(3): 646-663.

date what are the implications for their access to land and water in the context of large-scale water and land appropriation?

The IWRM discourse recognises women as important stakeholders in achieving the stated goals of efficiency, equity and environmental sustainability (GWP, 2006). It advocates for gender-sensitive approaches in the implementation of IWRM principles in order to ensure women's greater involvement in water management (ibid). But, does this focus on women address gender issues that shape differential access to water? While policy interventions to address issues of inequitable water allocation and distribution have included gender in the overall 'field of vision' (Seager, 2010), this focus has often been limited to representing women either as a separate 'add-on' category, or as a vulnerable and homogenous group with undifferentiated interests (Cornwall et al., 2007; Rathgber, 2003.). This narrow vision tends to overlook or oversimplify issues of gendered power relations, which lie at the core of inequality that determine one's access to, use of, and control over, water resources (Prabhakaran, 2013).

This chapter locates gender as a key analytical category for understanding issues of differentiation in water access and equity. The focus on gender is important because IWRM has influenced water-sector reforms around the world, where gender relations shaped within specific socio-political histories, have led to vast inequalities in access to, and distribution of, water. Policy framings on gender have emphasised gender sensitivity and gender mainstreaming. There is strong agreement as to the content of gender mainstreaming: Gender mainstreaming is:

> *The process of assessing the implications for women and men of any planned action, including legislation, policies or programmes, in all areas and at all levels. It is a strategy for making women's as well as men's concerns and experiences an integral dimension of the design, implementation, monitoring and evaluation of policies and programmes in all political, economic and societal spheres so that women and men benefit equally and inequality is not perpetuated. The ultimate goal is to achieve gender equality.*[2]

The implementation of the four Dublin Principles[3] is at the heart of IWRM although Principle No. 3 has been neglected. It reads:

Principle No. 3 – Women play a central part in the provision, management and safeguarding of water. It goes on to state:

> *This pivotal role of women as providers and users of water and guardians of the living environment has seldom been reflected in institutional arrangements for the development and management of water resources. Acceptance and implementation of this principle require positive policies to address women's specific needs and to equip and empower women to participate at all levels in water resources programmes, including decision making and implementation, in ways defined by them.*

2 www.un.org/womenwatch/daw/csw/gms.pdf Report of the Economic and Social Council for 1997 (A/52/3, 18 September 1997).

3 The Dublin Statement on Water and Sustainable Development, Dublin 1992 prepared for the Rio de Janeiro Conference on Sustainable Development.

This reads and sounds very much like gender mainstreaming and women's empowerment but yet the water sector has been strongly resistant to accomplishing this.[4] The Dublin Principles include all waters no matter how they are conceptualised and divided in law and in practice. These principles do not say that only primary or domestic water must include women but rather say that all aspects of water governance should include women (De Jong et al., 2012). Moreover, according to the Global Water Partnership, IWRM is not an end in itself but a means of achieving three key strategic objectives: efficiency to make water resources go as far as possible; equity, in the allocation of water across different social and economic groups; environmental sustainability, to protect the water resources' base and associated eco-systems. IWRM was to incorporate all Dublin Principles[5] which leads us to ask what have been the difficulties faced in recognising the importance of women and supporting their domestic, livelihood, and productive water-related activities? Furthermore, if the importance of women has been recognised, have their interests and needs been neglected and ignored in the implementation of IWRM (Prabhakaran, 2013)? IWRM has become the dominant discourse in how to analyse and resolve water issues while claiming to incorporate all the Dublin Principles.[6] According to most accounts, IWRM has not included, although this may be changing, the right to water[7] and in general the human-rights based approach to development.[8]

In the domain of gender there have been strong international pressures to support women's issues and equality. Alongside the adoption and spread of IWRM have been the signing of international human-rights instruments. These include the Convention on the Elimination of All Forms of Discrimination against Women (CEDAW), The Southern African Development Community Protocol on Women, the Covenant on Economic, Social and Cultural Rights, and many others. These often provide an important context in which international, national and local NGOs seek to improve the position of women. All four countries are members of SADC and have signed the SADC Protocol on Gender and Development (1997) and other international human-rights instruments. We have not found these other gender frameworks incorporated into water policies (Hellum et al., 2015a).

This book has discussed the ways by which IWRM has come to, and been modified and translated, in five African countries, namely South Africa, Zimba-

4 We are of course aware of the role that women play in borehole committees, and on some irrigation committees depending upon context. However here we are focusing on IWRM and its adoption by ministries of water. We also consider national water policies.

5 We recognise that the Dublin Principles have been subject to multiple and controversial interpretations.

6 World Bank's Water Resource Sector Strategy, the European Union's Water Initiative, UNEP's Water Policy Strategy Document, Asian Development Bank, the African Development Bank and the Inter-American Development Bank.

7 General Assembly Resolution (64/292 July 28, 2010) and General Comment 15 from the Committee on Economic, Social and Cultural Rights (2003) that clean drinking water and sanitation are human rights. For a multi-level account of the human right to water for domestic and productive purposes in Africa see Hellum et al., 2015b.

8 There have been several attempts to see if IWRM and the human right to water are compatible. The most thorough is Tremblay, 2014.

bwe, Mozambique, Tanzania and Uganda.[9] The various articles have discussed different aspects of IWRM implementation and roll out such as permits, user pays principle, commodification of water and decentralisation. We believe and will demonstrate in this chapter that these aspects do not address the structural and economic vulnerabilities of women. Water is inextricably connected to the construction of gender, of livelihoods and of cultural ideologies and practices. In many rural contexts, the provision of water by women and girls has material and symbolic dimensions. Clean water is essential for the health of the family. Simultaneously, women have to provide sufficient water for bathing meaning, often, a large time and energy commitment.[10] Women and girls are also mainly responsible for hand-irrigating gardens (large and small) for a more balanced diet and an income for the children's needs. Or, more broadly how gender, nature and life are intertwined (Walsh, 2015) in the multiple dimensions of water and how gender figures in all dimensions of access to, and use of, water.

All the aforementioned nations belong to SADC which has issued its own critique of water policies within SADC. In its water strategy there is a strong critique of SADC's own approach to gender in its Regional Water Strategy.[11] Furthermore, IWRM in SADC has taken little cognisance of the role that women play in water resources development, utilisation and management, and has made little effort to involve women in the decision-making processes. The challenges that exist in gender mainstreaming are highlighted by:

- Limited understanding and integration of gender sensitivity in IWRM
- Lack of recognition and appreciation of the role of women in IWRM
- Inadequate capacity by women to engage in IWRM
- Lack of opportunities for women and other disadvantaged groups to participate in IWRM at different levels. For instance, lack of child-care facilities can deny women with small children from participating in stakeholder fora
- Inadequate capacity and/or reluctance by some service providers to engage women and other disadvantaged groups in IWRM processes
- An inadequate conceptual framework to include women's productive uses of water as part of broader development strategies to increase women's access to and use of water.

---

9 Uganda is not considered in this article in part because it is not a member of SADC.

10 This perspective can be understood through the article 'A good wife brings her husband bath water' (van Houweling, 2016) which directs our attention to the multiple functions of water, the importance of domestic relations in the lives of men and women, and the differences in responsibility and caring.

11 The Regional Water Strategy for the Southern African Development Community (SADC) is "aimed at providing a strategic framework for sustainable, integrated and coordinated development, utilisation, protection and control of national and transboundary water resources in the SADC region. This strategy supports the SADC Common Agenda of socio-economic development and regional integration and improvement of the quality of life of all people in the region". www.sadc.int/files/2513/5293/3539/Regional_Water_Strategy.pdf (accessed September 1, 2016).

A systematic consideration of how women's difficulties in accessing land and land rights can limit their access to, and control of, water (SADC, 2006). Given this critical analysis of gender in the water sector, we were surprised to learn how little has been done to shift water policies and practices to systematically include gender in practices and policies.

The chapter is organised as follows: After a discussion of methods and sites of research we present four national summaries. We briefly describe national gender policies of Mozambique, South Africa, Tanzania and Zimbabwe. We select examples at the river basin or catchment level to explore gender issues. Following the country descriptions, we compare broad commonalities (and some differences) among the four nations with respect to gender policies and practices. This is followed by our conclusions.

Methods and sites of research

We have been carrying out research on IWRM in four countries: South Africa, Tanzania, Zimbabwe and Mozambique from 2011 to 2014. We were surprised by the lack of attention to gender issues in general and women's incorporation at all levels of IWRM planning and implementation in light of Dublin Principle 3. To explore the gender dimensions, we reviewed international policy documents and recommendations on gender and water, and regional documents on gender and water before turning to the relevant national documents. Where relevant we also read international donor and NGO documents and then sought to take a gender lens on our own IWRM research. Moreover, we read water-related research which used a gender focus in order to supplement our own research. Additionally, we read literature on gender and development. One caveat, this chapter is about IWRM and not about all water policies that these governments have framed, attempted or implemented. In general, much more attention has been given to gender in rural water supply than in water resources management. For example, the UK-based NGO Water Aid focuses heavily on gender in its water and sanitation work.[12] Moreover, there may be different gender outcomes for example, for water supply in contrast to irrigation water.[13]

Mozambique

Mozambique introduced IWRM as the basis of its water laws and policies in the early 1990s (Bolding and Alba, Chapter 9; Alba, 2013). With a majority of its population as rural smallholder farmers, they have managed their own waters in a complex array of customary practices and norms. As a member state of SADC and the African Ministers' Council on Water (AMCOW), Mozambique has ratified the SADC protocol on gender and development (2008) and the AMCOW Policy for mainstreaming gender in the water sector (2010) which promotes full and equal enjoyment of rights for women in all aspects in the region. Additionally, it is committed to the other regional and international legally binding documents including the Convention on the Rights of the Child (1989), the Africa Platform of

12 www.wateraid.org/uk. They have numerous papers on gender issues in general and applied to specific national contexts.

13 Who benefits and who loses more generally from IWRM is the subject of this book.

Action (1985), the Beijing Declaration and Its Platform for Action (1995) as well as the most powerful document for gender equality and women's rights being the United Nations Convention on the Elimination of All Forms of Discrimination against Women (CEDAW, 1979). With the assistance of donors, Mozambique has been active in adding a gender dimension to climate change (Ribeiro and Chauque, 2010), agriculture (Gender Unit of the Ministry of Agriculture, 2005, Republic of Mozambique. 2005), and the Ministry of Women and Social Action (2014, Republic of Mozambique 2014). What is surprising in these particular documents is the absence of water despite women's importance in agriculture and domestic work (van Houweling, 2013). This is not to deny progress in other areas.

Research in Mozambique, as in much of Africa, demonstrates women to be the primary water collectors and the major carers. Women are associated, in general, with water supply while irrigation tends to be focused on men. These generalisations ignore women's roles which vary. Nonetheless, like many other parts of sub-Saharan Africa the gender division of labour is highly unequal. Women bear the brunt of household work while men's contribution is minimal (Arora, 2015). In a detailed study of men's and women's time Arora found that women's total work per day is almost twice as much as men's work time and men enjoy more leisure, around three times that of women. According to her, gender is the most important determinant of time-poverty (ibid: 214). This begins to explain the difficulties in changing domestic patterns of labour and the importance of incorporating the domestic relationships and structures tied to water practices (Van Houweling, 2016: 1066).

The Mozambican case studies took place in two large catchments: The Inkomati and the Limpopo. As with the other countries, Mozambique has shifted from a state-managed centralised water management system to one to be decentralised and driven, in principle, by stakeholders. Simultaneously, emphasis and priority have been given to investors to promote large-scale irrigation projects based upon large-scale concessions of land (and therefore of water). In the allocation of irrigable land, water must also be allocated in order to provide water security for the large farms. As part of our research, Elke Praagman conducted research on two large-scale irrigation schemes: the first was Massingir Agro-Industrial Company and the Massingir Dam in the Limpopo Basin and the second the Irrigation Scheme of Baixo on the Limpopo River. Praagman analysed how and in what ways different categories of water users (stakeholders) engaged with the different levels of water governance. In the case of the Massingir Reservoir there were two very large proposals for using the water for vast sugar cane plantations. The first was ProCana Company who have now left the scene to be replaced by Massingir Agro-Industrial (MAI) owned by a combination of South African and Mozambican companies. She documents the focus on land while the implications and rights of water users were not discussed in approving the project.[14] In presenting the replacement of ProCana by MAI poorer members of communities were not consulted nor were they aware of what was happening. The heteroge-

14 The Mozambican Land Law of 1997 is regarded as progressive since it recognises customary land tenure and provides for communities to delimit their land and hold a certificate of occupancy (DUAT) (Tanner, 2010).

neity of water users was not recognised and those in positions to benefit from the new sugar cane plantations spoke on behalf of the 'communities'.

Without discussing the details of each case, both projects involved the appropriation of large amounts of water resources in one case for sugar cane and in the other for rice. In neither case was consideration given to upstream users, and what would happen to their access to water.[15] In the formulation of the National Water Resources Strategy 2005, stakeholders' involvement was regarded as a core element for the comprehensive strategy development process.[16] While this underlies one of the core principles of IWRM, there is no indication of the process that was followed to ensure the involvement of all categories of water users in decision making. How were women represented in this mix, and was the heterogeneity of women and their particular needs given due consideration? While the Water Act distinguished between what are termed 'common uses' and private uses, there is no legal protection for 'common uses', which are using water for drinking, cleaning, washing, watering cattle and irrigation for less than one hectare without mechanical means. In the law it is said to take priority over other uses but in practice uses are not registered and become invisible (Praagman, 2013).

The marginalisation of common water uses over private uses consequently render women's access to water potentially more difficult keeping in mind their already gendered positioning in access to water for private uses. Private uses are supposed to be registered, licences for the quantities of water set, and the user is supposed to pay the appropriate fees and costs. In Praagman's cases water was allocated without knowing the amounts of water available or its seasonality. While a process was followed to establish community landownership, water allocations were not included. In general, once the government granted large land concessions to private parties they also turned over the responsibility for community issues to the lessee.

Overall, though involvement of women in all stages of decision making and managing water resources forms one of the central pillars of IWRM and within the Water Resources Management Strategy of Mozambique, the issue of gender itself is treated as a separate subject and is articulated under the section on gender mainstreaming without demonstrating how it should be carried out. This has removed consideration of gendered uses and gendered access to water while strategising processes of water allocation in each river basin. This makes it easier to ignore the needs of different categories of women.

Common to the treaties that Mozambique has signed is the view of gender equality as a fundamental right based on non-discrimination of civil, political, economic and social rights. Article 18 of the SADC Protocol (2008: 16) pertaining to access to property and resources, categorically states that "state parties shall by

15 Upstream, because irrigators would be obliged to let water flow freely to the downstream users.

16 "One of the Act's main objectives is to progressively decentralise the responsibility for water resources management from national to regional institutions, the principal institutions being catchment management agencies. These agencies must promote participation by water users and other stakeholders in all aspects of water resources management in their areas of operation (2005:151)".

2015 review all policies and laws...to end all discrimination against women and girls with regard to water rights and property such as land and tenure". Similarly, the AMCOW (2011: 5) policy on mainstreaming gender in the water sector seeks to "ensure that gender concerns are taken into account in policy formulation in all sectors of water (...)". Furthermore, though the human right to water is not built into the design of IWRM, the fact that the country has committed to regional and international human rights treaties which includes the human right to water, should not be ignored within the national water policy. However as is seen currently, these rights are not articulated within the Mozambican national water strategy. This is in spite of the core principles in both SADC and AMCOW that the "state parties shall harmonise national legislation, policies, strategies and programmes with relevant regional and international instruments.... for the purpose of ensuring gender equality and equity" (SADC, 2008: 9; AMCOW, 2011: 5)

Tanzania

Like the other countries, Tanzania has adopted IWRM as a key framework for water resources management. In the Tanzanian National Water Policy (URoT, 2002) this integrated approach is focused on addressing participatory, multi-sectoral, multidisciplinary river basin management in order to address the challenges of managing water as a scarce resource (Lein and Tagseth, 2009). A reference to the four Dublin Principles as the basis for this new approach is made; however, the policy details only three major shifts: the holistic approach for multi-sectoral integration, the principle of subsidiarity and decentralising decision making involving stakeholder participation and water as an economic good. There is no reference to the Dublin Principle No. 3, and the roles of women are subsumed within the principle of enhancing participation in decision making without a gender focus.

Tanzania has also adopted in its constitution the human right to drinking water and sanitation. This is reflected in the national water policy in the form of water for basic needs being accorded a human rights status; however, there is no incorporation of other gender frameworks like CEDAW etc. which envision how these rights could be realised. Indeed, many other related rights would need to be realised in order to for women's human right to water to materialise in this case. For example, the water allocation system distinguishes and separates the water use permit from land title, but typically there is no indication of the process by which women can access water irrespective of not owning land. Also participation of women and men in decision-making processes is governed by power dynamics that are shaped by landownership. Therefore, by not focusing on how to increase women's access to land, women's access to water is questionable. Men too have to apply for a permit and if large-scale users are privileged then men's access to water (and their wives' and families') can also be jeopardised. The policy overall favours large-scale over small-scale users (van Koppen et al., 2004; Hepworth, 2009; Jimenez and Perez-Foguet, 2010; van Eeden et al., Chapter 12). Indeed, in a quantitative study of the amount of global water grabbing the authors have found in Africa that blue water grabbing is highest in Tanzania and Sudan (Rullia et al., 2013). In policy and in practice, commercial irrigated agriculture will take precedence over customary tenure and practices (van Eeden, 2014; van Koppen et al., Chapter 11). It does not take into account the role that living customary law plays in providing women access to land and water (Nkonya, 2008).

Our research has focused upon the upper and lower reaches of the Wami-Ruvu Catchment. The catchment contains a wide variety of water uses but numerically it is dominated by small-scale farmers. In this catchment the Tanzanian Water and Sanitation Network has found multiple obstacles and levels to access water by people living with HIV/AIDS, people with disabilities, the elderly, by children and by rural communities. The broader requirements of a human-rights-based approach to water has not been incorporated into the interpretation of IWRM (TAWASANET, 2012).

The current development strategy of providing large amounts of land to agricultural investors works against the issue of access to water for vulnerable groups (van Eeden, 2014). In her research on large-scale land investment, van Eeden observes that the institutional shortcomings of IWRM have created many difficulties for the Wami-Ruvu River Basin Water Office (WRBWO) to effectively implement its framework. Of these shortcomings, perhaps the most controversial is the failure of the framework to recognise the major power disparities among the water users in the basin as it aims to govern water in a decentralised fashion. She contends that the IWRM framework, as it is currently implemented in the Wami-Ruvu River Board (WRRB) is subject to powerful actors' agendas that are able to capture the governing process and influence decisions regarding water allocations (van Eeden, 2014: 180).

Lecoutere (2012) in her thesis on small sub-catchments in the Rufiji Catchment recounts a different story whereby irrigators and water users have had to solve their own issues and conflicts. In a fine account of legal pluralism, she conducted her research in a context of customary norms and practices. According to her research, water conflict resolution relies on pragmatic problem-solving rather than being based on well-defined institutions. The norm where she was carrying out her research was that everyone has an equal right to water. Lecoutere (2012: 106) writes:

> *It is noteworthy that none of the irrigation schemes in our case study operates with a legal water right, which implies all water appropriation is illegal according to national water laws. Still the village government intervenes in governance of 'illegally' appropriated water.*

While in most cases she found that cases of water conflict were amicably resolved at the local level there were, however, four cases of conflict that were not resolved. In these cases persons with a lower status simply gave up their claims. Of the four, three were women. As in most rural areas institutional pluralism remained important despite the formation of new institutions for water and irrigation management. Resolution, or what Lecoutere terms pragmatic problem solving is not always fair but nonetheless accepted. But from her analysis it seems clear that if powerful outsiders are able to get water rights/permits they will be able to appropriate water, and the local mechanisms for problem-resolution will most likely be lost. Water scarcity does and will produce conflict. She suggests that where there are norms of sharing and equity, scarcity does make it more difficult to comply with such norms. Those norms will become even more difficult to maintain if outside actors seek to obtain irrigation water.

As in Mozambique, it seems that to date much of Tanzania's use of IWRM relies on gender stereotyping. For example, the focus on gender is limited to improving gender participation in rural water supply programmes (Cleaver and Toner 2006). To this effect, gender finds mention primarily in the section on rural water supply in its water policy.[17] The focus on empowering women, increasing their representation and involvement in decision making in order to improve the efficiency of water supply programmes is far too limited. The limited emphasis upon water supply rather than water management relies upon gender stereotyping which categorises women as primary users and responsible for the provision and maintenance of domestic water. It does not challenge the notion of why it should be primarily women's responsibilities. Second, empowerment of women is approached as a means to improve the functioning of water supply programmes and the infrastructural investments rather than ensuring that women's multiple needs for water, which includes productive uses of water, are met. Third, the goal should be women's equality not a reinforcement of their subordinate status.

Zimbabwe

Zimbabwe like Mozambique, Tanzania and South Africa, adopted IWRM in the 1990s (see Manzungu and Derman, Chapter 6). The reforms emphasised that the waters of Zimbabwe would be managed by seven catchment councils in coordination with a new parastatal, the Zimbabwe National Water Authority (ZINWA). There was no mention in the new legislation of the importance of women in water governance, management, storage, or supply. There is a hint of Dublin Principle No. 3 being included under the principle of increasing stakeholder participation. However, representation in the sub-catchment councils which selected the catchment councils was based on economic sectors including large-scale farming, large-scale small-scale mining, etc. and did not include women. Nor were there any mechanisms set in place to ensure women's participation. The Water Act and ZINWA Act of 1998 and the statutory instruments regulating membership and elections to catchment and sub-catchment councils are all silent about the ways and means of enhancing women's participation. The majority of the members of Manyame Catchment Council and the Middle Manyame Sub-catchment Council where we did our research for many years were men.[18] While the new institutions were said to manage all water since all of Zimbabwe's waters – surface water

17 For example, in analysing gender in an irrigation scheme, Kissawike (2008: 178-79) writes: "Even though women are central in irrigated rice production, and therefore the ones to know and decide when and where to use irrigation water, very few women participate in the formal management of the scheme. There were no female representatives at any level of water users' organisations, while the various decision-making levels related to water management within the scheme exhibit a conspicuous gender imbalance. Women's absence in meetings and committees can be largely explained as resulting from traditional norms and rules, which strongly associate water management and control over water with men, but it also reflects the gender-biased pattern of plot ownership".

18 In the meetings held in May 2014 a woman was elected chair of the Middle Manyame Subcatchment Council.

and groundwater – were now owned by the president; the leadership in the new institutions contended they were doing resources management and thus drinking water and even small dams were considered outside of their remit. In this way, the catchment and sub-catchment councils ignored the water issues of the communal areas.

In a highly centralised state like Zimbabwe the existence of customary norms and institutions for the management of water were, and are, not recognised (Hellum and Derman, 2005). The exception had been the Irrigation Boards formed by commercial farmers which were disbanded when the Water Act took effect to become part of sub-catchment councils. When the seven catchment councils were formed in 1999 and began operations there was no policy to ensure that women were included. In addition, there was , for example, no department or group in ZINWA to explore how women's access to water could be expanded. There is widespread acknowledgment that much of Zimbabwe's accomplishments in the water sector deteriorated between 2000 and 2010 (see Manzungu and Derman, Chapter 6) and efforts are being made, according to the new Water Policy (2013) to first; stem the major deterioration of infrastructure and rehabilitate it and then; to build new infrastructure, especially in Harare and its surrounding areas. The suggested path forward has been traced to Zimbabwe's new water policy (GoZ, 2013).

In its reformulation of Dublin Principle No. 3 which stresses the importance of women in all aspects of water governance, women in Zimbabwe's National Water Policy are included primarily in terms of participation. Participation as a right however is not articulated but rather it is an effort to improve decisions. The full text in the appendix on the principles of IWRM is as follows:

> *Participation in decisions improves public acceptance of those decisions, improves the quality of decisions because of the greater breadth of expertise and experience, and reduces the risk that opposition from disaffected groups will delay or even stop implementation of decisions. The 1992 Dublin Principles emphasise the importance of allowing women to participate in decisions about water, given the role that women play in fetching water and managing small irrigation plots in many countries. The ability to participate in decisions is the flip side of paying for permits to use water resources* (GoZ, 2012: 34).

For instance, it is assumed in the last sentence that only people who have money and pay for permits can participate in water management. Moreover, women are viewed as those who fetch water and manage small irrigation plots but not as full irrigators or engaging in productive water use.

This is further reflected in the policy as it makes a distinction between primary water and water for commercial purposes. The policy states that "water for primary needs is a right for all Zimbabweans" and that "equity in access to water by all Zimbabweans is a right" (GoZ, 2013: 18). This continues the gender stereotyping since women's access to water or right to water is seen primarily in the context of primary needs defined as "water for direct personal consumption, personal household hygiene, and food preparation and for household productive purposes such as gardening and household stock watering, not for commercial purposes" (GoZ, 2013: 18). This makes invisible women's use of water for commercial and productive purposes through 'multiple-use systems' and the important roles that they play in commercial agriculture.

We have found a strong historical continuity which downplays the importance of small, irrigated gardens located next to a variety of water sources usually worked by women and critical for the well-being of families. Yet the new water policy also states: "Women play a pivotal role in the use, management and protection of water resources and water services and should therefore be involved fully in the decision-making processes at all levels" (GoZ, 2012: 23).

In a discussion of cross-cutting themes of the water policy it says that the policy will recognise and promote gender equity in allocation, access and utilisation of water as well as implementation of WASH (water and sanitation) activities. The policy "acknowledges the disproportionate burden placed on women and the girl child when fetching water and taking care of the sick. Targeted programming and implementation of WASH activities shall be gender-sensitive. Gender-based budgeting will be promoted" (GoZ, 2013: 25).

The policy then proposes that at least 30% of the catchment and sub-catchment councils' positions will be reserved for women and the youth. There is no comment on why these two categories are combined. In addition, at least three members of the ZINWA board will be women, youth or worker representatives. Once again why these three are grouped together remains obscure especially given the diversity among women.

Whether it is rural or urban water supply, or water for irrigation there are few indications of how to recognise women for the contributions they are making on the one hand, and to incorporate them in their unity and diversity into water policy-making, governance and participation, on the other.

As in the two previous case studies, other gender policies ratified by Zimbabwe are not integrated within its water policy. The concept of indivisible human rights as defined in CEDAW is not integrated when looking at primary water as a human right. In order to access this right to water, women's other rights (right to land, food security, credit etc) need to be realised. The distinction made between primary vs commercial waters and institutional frameworks while designed to increase stakeholder participation are in fact predicated on one's access to land which most women lack. In practice this means that women's right to participation is not integrated with their other rights.[19] Nonetheless, the current water policy at least on paper marks a considerable change from the Water and ZINWA Acts.

South Africa

In marked distinction from Mozambique, Tanzania and Zimbabwe, South Africa has a strong human rights orientation, a very active Human Rights Commission and a set of policies for rural and urban water to address the needs of the poor and of women. While IWRM is part of South Africa's water policies (Anderson

19 For a detailed consideration of women's human rights and water see the Zimbabwe chapters (10-13) in Hellum et al., 2015b.

et al., 2008; van Koppen et al., Chapter 11; Movik 2011) there are other major frameworks which include water as a human right, free basic water and a water reserve for basic human needs. These frameworks are included in major policy documents on the incorporation of gender along with the existence of the National Commission on Gender Equality and the South African Human Rights Commission (SAHRC). The SAHRC wrote an outstanding report (2014) on the Right to Access Sufficient Water and Decent Sanitation in South Africa. There are specific requirements for women to be employed at all levels in government departments and also in the yet to be completed Catchment Management Agencies. The current Minister of Water and Sanitation in South Africa is a woman. This is not to say that even now there are no major gender issues in the South African water sector.

South Africa adopted two separate acts: the Water Services Act of 1997, followed by the National Water Act of 1998, which governs water resources management of bulk supplies of 'raw' water and water for productive uses. These acts have been supplemented by new strategies and frameworks including: the Strategic Framework for Water Services (2003) addressing service delivery of 'potable' water, and most recently the National Water Resources Strategy, Second Edition (2013). The new water legislation introduced a nationwide system for legal water authorisations. These are:

- *Schedule 1* – Small volumes of water for household use only. No need to apply for a licence.
- *General Authorisations* – Larger volumes of water may be authorised for a specific type of water use or category of water user. These users need to register their use but do not need a licence.
- *Existing Lawful Use* – This allows water use that was lawfully used before the National Water Act (NWA) came into effect to continue until it can be converted into a licence using compulsory licensing.
- *Licensed Water Use* – Licences are issued under the NWA, and require approval of an application by the Department of Water and Sanitation.

In 2000, a new municipality system was initiated with the responsibilities for water supply given to them. Some DWS technical staff were seconded to local government to assist in their water responsibilities. This transition created much confusion and sometimes led to the deterioration of the water supply services that existed under apartheid. Communal areas remained literally and metaphorically at the end of the pipe (van Koppen et al., 2015).

Nonetheless, South Africa probably has the widest provision of domestic water to indigent households on the subcontinent, especially in urban areas. According to the government in their report (2013) to the United Nations, 72% of the 2.2 million indigent households received free water. The percentage however drops significantly in the provinces with those having the highest percentage of communal areas. Limpopo Province, for example, only meets the needs of 40% of its residents as does the Eastern Cape Province (RSA, 2013: 23).

Given our rural emphasis in this chapter we sketch some aspects of South Africa's communal areas. Communal areas are the former homelands of which there were ten African and six coloured. They pose multiple developmental challenges in general, and water ones in particular. In dismantling the homeland governance structures and creating a new unitary state apparatus, water supply (and sanitation) functions were given to the newly created districts and municipalities which incorporated the communal areas which at the same time are under the authority of chiefs.[20] Irrigation waters were controlled by DWS and the provincial Department of Agriculture and Rural Development.

Michael Aliber et al. (2011: 9) have estimated that there are 2,300,000 subsistence-oriented black households practising some form of agriculture along with 200,000 commercially oriented ones, nationwide. Access to water for domestic and productive use in the Limpopo Province, the most rural of South Africa's provinces remains difficult. Access to water for agriculture is based upon access to land. Land is held for the most part by men and ultimately by chiefs.[21] In the allocation of land, women (especially unmarried women and widows) have multiple difficulties in gaining access while married women have insecure rights because they gain access through their husbands.[22] While water for household purposes (including gardens) is overwhelmingly managed by women they are faced with a general scarcity of water. The scarcity in communal areas continues to be due to the appropriation of water by large-scale farmers, a general water scarcity and the need to make more water available with infrastructure in the communal areas (Rust and Hanise, 2009; Department of Water Affairs, 2012).

In terms of gender, the picture for South Africa does, however, vary considerably (Claassens, 2015). Kristi Denby (2014) reports that some projects in the communal areas such as the Recapitalisation and Development Programme (RADP), a land reform programme that required the cooperative members to allow wives and daughters of members the ability to receive the land title from the chief when their husband or father passed away. According to Denby this was an issue fraught with controversy while she was conducting her research. The Department of Land Reform made it very clear at public meetings that women must be involved often against the wishes of those at the meeting. They also stressed the importance of women participating in the cooperative meetings.

In contrast, the former homeland of Gazankulu represents how, in the Limpopo Province, some former homeland residents lost out in the shift from homeland water supply to the creation of municipalities due to the lack of proper or no attempt to increase the amount of water to be made available for rural residents at the time of transition. While the amounts of water allocated for residents of former white urban areas and water allocated for irrigated agriculture increased,

20 See van Koppen et al. (2015) and van Koppen and Schreiner (2015) on South Africa in this book. For the powers of traditional authorities in relationship to women see Claassens, 2013.

21 This is a highly contested area. For an introduction to the issues see Claassens, 2015.

22 We are speaking generally. Some projects in the communal areas such as the RADP land reform program require the cooperative to allow wives and daughters the ability to hold the land title from the chief when their husband/father passes away. In addition, the Department of Land Reform insisted on women attending meetings.

water for rural residents remained at basic water supply levels for the villages and towns of the communal area. We found no evidence that account was taken of increasing rural supply to facilitate socioeconomic development or to realise the right to clean drinking water and for domestic purposes. For example, the major source of water for Giyani and Siyandhani is the Middle Letaba Dam which is rarely full and according to DWS over-committed, over-permitted (more water was allocated than available) and there is a general deficit in the catchment.[23] No reallocation was made to increase the amount of water or to upgrade the infrastructures to provide a better flow to Giyani and its surrounding villages (Nyabeze et al., 2007).

An example of weaknesses in the transition to municipalities can be found in the research of Thoko Masangu (2007). She documented the complicated provision of water to the village of Siyandhani a few kilometres east of Giyani Town. There was no attempt made to reduce the amount of water allocated to orange plantations down river while the amount of water delivered to Giyani often did not meet the town's basic requirements. In Siyandhani, most of the households in village had yard taps installed in the 1970s and 1980s but the taps are dry most of the time. Water for the yard taps was supposed to come from the purification plant at Nsami Dam through the pipeline from the Middle Letaba Dam. Most of the households situated on the western side of the village have not had water from the taps for seven years or more while those on the eastern side get it sporadically during the rainy season. The only reliable supplies are the irrigation canals which is from where most households, most of the time, obtain their water. Women, primarily responsible for water fetching, have to walk as long as one to five hours per day to obtain drinking water from these canals. Villagers with a bit more means have turned to water vendors who carry their containers to spigots or houses with water supply and then sell them at relatively high prices to women.[24]

This is one example from one province. We do know that the areas of highest poverty in South Africa are the former homelands. And these are not precisely the areas where under IWRM principles they can afford water nor will the economic benefits be sufficient to support further infrastructure development. It would appear that IWRM reflected in South African policy has not been helpful in addressing the deep poverty in South Africa's communal areas. It has been very difficult to undo the influence of 'big users' in the allocation of water. In terms of urban users however, South Africa has made remarkable progress in making drinking water available.

23 The waters in the Middle Letaba Dam are always less than expected because of high and undocumented water abstractions (Nyabeze et al., 2007: 1043).

24 President Jacob Zuma undertook a monitoring visit to Giyani in October 2014 to assess the provision of water following recent community complaints. During the visit he opened a new water treatment plant. However, the water has yet to arrive from the long completed but still unused water from the Nandoni Dam. Why this is the case is a long story and involves conflicts among the Province's political leaders. For a recent summary see The Mail and Guardian, 13 February 2015. 'Giyani: The thirst that won't be quenched' by Sipho Kings.

Discussion and findings

In examining the commonalities among the four nations, we have found from our current research that the pivotal role of women as providers and users of water is ignored at policy levels and, most often, in the differing levels of formal institutions of water governance. Examining the understanding and implementation of IWRM in selected areas of Mozambique, Tanzania, Zimbabwe and South Africa this chapter finds that insufficient attention has been paid to the multifaceted roles that different categories of women play.

We have found that there are several commonalities in water gender policy and practice among the four nations that have all adopted IWRM. Each country relies on a distinction on the one hand between customary, informal or primary access to water and formal or licensed access to water, on the other. In general, this system of licensing water use has been through permit systems or authorisations (South Africa). The distinction between customary or primary water (non-permitted) and permitted water typically coincides with the national distinctions between domestic water (unpaid) and permitted or authorised water (paid and often mistakenly labelled productive water). Water provided through a municipal system is not permitted but ordinarily paid for.

Despite the national emphases upon commercial or permitted water being 'productive' we find that referring to domestic (or primary) uses does not mean that the water is not productive. Van Koppen has convincingly argued for a scalar or quantity approach to productive water, especially regarding rural water (van Koppen et al., 2014). The majority of water use in Mozambique, Tanzania, and Zimbabwe is informal and without formal registration. Permits are dominated by larger-scale commercial users. In South Africa most water use is indeed formalised due to the extensive water infrastructure development. Uses prior to 1998 have been formally declared as 'existing lawful use'. New large-scale (post-1998) water users have to obtain a licence. Most use in communal areas is not individually recognised but is protected under Schedule 1.[25]

The distinction between domestic and productive uses of water render women's productive uses of water invisible. Formal water rights in both South Africa and Zimbabwe under the current water reforms, are applicable only for commercial use of water (van Koppen et al., 2006). Most women in South Africa and Zimbabwe cultivate crops for commercial sale by accessing water through informal sources and networks. Since commercial water rights are based on landownership, which most women are not entitled to (op.cit.), their role as productive users of water continues to remain invisible. Similarly, the provision of limited free water for domestic purposes or for primary uses in South Africa and Zimbabwe respectively, recognises only the basic domestic needs and roles of women, without providing water for their productive activities. This separation of domestic and productive water in policies is isolated from the gendered contexts of people's livelihoods and an understanding of how people access water in their daily lives. These discourses create an artificial separation between what constitutes as productive and non-productive uses of water. This reflects the historical bias

25 The most important conditions of Schedule 1 in South Africa for this article are that people are free to take water for reasonable domestic use at the household.

that has existed in recognising women's productive roles, as work done within the domestic sphere is seen only as reproductive work, mostly done by women (Folbre, 2004), and the use of water for income-generation activities within the household is made invisible.

National policy documents incorporating IWRM articulate the need for 'integration' and an 'inter-sectoral' approach. Global understandings of integration in terms of coordination and regulation of water demand should be based on an understanding of people's multiple water needs and the ways in which they access and use water. This is important to achieve efficiency, equity and sustainability in water use which is relevant to people's lives.

South Africa and Zimbabwe voted for the General Assembly Resolution on the Human Right to water while Tanzania abstained and Mozambique was not present.[26] Nonetheless all four nations being signatories to a range of UN treaties and covenants, and the African Charter on Human and Peoples' Rights they are subject to international law on the human right to water. However, they do not make use or apply other UN instruments where the right to water features as in the Right to Health, the Child Rights Convention and the Convention on the Elimination of All Forms of Discrimination against Women (CEDAW) (Hellum et al., 2015a). Nor do water ministries cite or make use of the Protocol to the African Charter on Women's Rights which features women's empowerment and rights.

None of the four countries has provisions in its water laws and policies to recognise the existence of living customary law as a legitimate source to accessing water. This is surprising given the growing recognition of customary rights to land in Mozambique and Tanzania. Little attention is paid to how women access water under customary arrangements and whether they would lose that access and use under permit systems. In general, women are seen as a homogenous category which makes invisible the gender inequitable relations among women. The needs and interests of small-scale women farmers differ from those involved in large-scale commercial farming. This is not articulated or paid attention to in any of the policy documents.

The current water reforms focus on the use of statutory legal systems to regulate access to water resources. While each country recognises water for domestic uses, not one of these countries has a clear complaint or legal mechanism to enable residents to protect their customary rights. On the contrary, the adoption of one single legal system can formally cancel their user-rights to access land and water within customary marriage laws and kinship systems.

With the partial exception of South Africa we have been unable to find a formal, long-term plan to include women in all capacities of water governance and management. Moreover, there are other multiple sectors where water is essential including agriculture, health, forestry, environment, and mining, etc. that involve water. If women are marginal in these sectors, then the gender consequences of water management will have profound consequences for them in their multiple roles as water managers.

We have not found any national government policy and plan to address the gender stereotyping of women as domestic providers and storers of water while

26 General Assembly GA/10967, July 2010.

their productive uses are relatively ignored. On the other hand, the national water policies reinforce this gender stereotyping of water roles and practices for women and men. We have not found policies or programmes to encourage or facilitate men to share the burdens of water fetching, storage, cleaning, and general caring.

Conclusions

We have found in our research that despite the varied colonial histories and governments described in the other articles in this book, there are strong commonalities among these four countries in terms of women and water. This is not to deny that within each of the four nations there are significant and large differences in how women gain access to water and how they participate in the institutions that govern and manage water. However, every country has gender policies paying attention to the inclusion of women. Each country has been signatory to a range of human rights instruments – international and regional – which in principle should apply to the governance and management of water. It appears that the two most important ones CEDAW and the SADC Protocol on Gender have not been used in the adoption of IWRM. This observation takes on significance because despite its cross-cutting nature, water management and governance take place bureaucratically in silos. While water is essential for domestic and caring needs, agriculture, industry, health, mining, and the environment, there are few or no ways to link them in water management despite the emphasis upon integration in IWRM. The difficulties of fetching water in rural water are relatively well known but there are increasing burdens for women in obtaining water in urban areas. This has been especially true not only in Zimbabwe with the failure of municipal water systems but also in the peri-urban areas of Tanzania, Mozambique and South Africa.

While there is acknowledgment of rights to domestic water in all four nations (Schedule 1 in South Africa, primary water in Zimbabwe, common uses in Mozambique, and water for human needs in Tanzania), these have no legal protection and no way for water users to protect their customary uses. Moreover, given development strategies which are more reliant upon large-scale investment strategies rather than smaller-scale emergent farmers and smallholder irrigation this will harm women (and men) (Sitko and Jayne, 2012; Xie et al., 2014).

The discourse on participation renders invisible aspects of women's gendered participation within formal institutions which are socially embedded, with rules often set within social norms of power and gender hierarchies (O'Reilly, 2008). Participation processes are time-consuming and often the timing and location of meetings do not take into account women's reproductive and domestic tasks that exclude them from formal decision-making processes (Meinzen-Dick and Zwarteveen, 1998). Even when women do participate in formal processes, they are unable to influence decisions within unequal power relations of ownership and control of resources. Balanced against this policy emphasis upon women and gender are the overt and subtle ways by which women find themselves with weaker rights, reduced access to resources and social protections than men.

It remains to be seen if IWRM will continue to maintain its hegemonic position in water governance as water security (Lankford et al., 2013) increases its presence. However, whether it is IWRM or water security there needs to be a major change in the understanding and support of recognising the water rights and water access for the millions of small-scale multiple needs of water users. It is not just clean drinking water, or water for small-scale agriculture, or water for pastoralists' cattle but how to shift the thinking and practice underlying water governance. For women, not increasing their rights and access to water will jeopardise families' health and a weakening of human rights. The promise of IWRM to have greater integration especially with land has not met its promise. Accessing water through land which is dominant in rural Africa will become far more difficult if current trends continue.

With the exception of South Africa we have found that in the catchments where we have carried out our research no special consideration has been given as to how women might be accorded greater access and control of water, and to seek means to support those that do.[27] IWRM does not, on the surface at least, appear to challenge current gender divisions of labour with respect to the multiple uses and flows of water, the stereotypes that underlie them, and most importantly the power relations that guide decision making about water.

Policy strategies aimed to achieve efficiency and sustainability in water use, in order to enhance women's equitable access to water, should be grounded in an understanding of gender relations and unequal power hierarchies as experienced by women in specific local contexts. The knowledge about how people access, use and control water resources should not be based on stereotypical assumptions about roles, responsibilities and relations, but derived from the social contexts of women's lives and livelihoods; and the changing social, economic and ecological conditions under which resources are accessed.

Acknowledgements

This chapter is based on research from a Norwegian Research Council-funded project, Flows and Practices: The Politics of IWRM in Africa. We are grateful to the Norwegian Research Council for the generous support. We thank the anonymous reviewers and Barbara van Koppen, Lyla Mehta and Kristi Denby for their comments.

References

Alba, R. 2013. Travelling with IWRM. The articulation of water permits and payments for water in policies and practices in Limpopo river basin, Mozambique. MSc thesis. Earth System Science Group. Wageningen University, Wageningen, the Netherlands.

Aliber, M.; Maluleke, T.; Manenzhe, T.; Paradza, G. and Cousins, B. 2011. *Livelihoods after land reform: Trajectories of change in Limpopo Province*. Bellville: PLAAS.

Arora, D. 2015 Gender differences in time poverty in rural Mozambique. *Review of Social Economy* 73(2): 196-221.

AMCOW (African Ministers' Council on Water). 2011. Policy and strategy for main-

27 The Water Allocation Reform Programme in South Africa, which, despite poor implementation, has a target for putting water into the hands of black women.

streaming gender in the water sector in Africa. Dakar: Senegal.

www.amcow-online.org/images/Resources/24%20June%20AMCOW%20Eng.pdf (accessed January 14, 2016)

Anderson, A.; Karar, E. and Farolfi, S. 2008. Synthesis: IWRM lessons for implementation. *Water SA* 34(6): 665-669.

Claassens, A. 2015. Law, Land and Custom, 1913-2014: What is at stake today? In Cousins, B. and Walker, C. (Eds), *Land divided, land restored: Land reform in South Africa for the 21st Century*, pp. 68-84. Auckland Park, SA: Jacana.

Cleaver, F. and Toner, A. 2006. The evolution of community water governance in Uchira, Tanzania: The implications for equality of access, sustainability and effectiveness. *Natural Resources Forum* 30(3): 207-218.

Cornwall, A.; Harrison, E. and Whitehead, A. (Eds). 2007. Introduction: Feminisms in development: Contradictions, contestations and challenges. In Cornwall, A.; Harrison, E. and Whitehead, A. (Eds), *Feminisms in development: Contradictions, contestations and challenges,* pp. 1-20. *London:* Zed Books.

De Jong, E.; Sagardoy, J.A. and Sisto, I. 2012. *Passport to mainstreaming gender in water programmes: Key questions for interventions in the agricultural sector.* Rome: Food and Agriculture Organization, United Nations.

Denby, K. 2014. Institutional integration and local level water access in the Inkomati water management area, South Africa. MSc thesis. Norwegian University of Life Sciences, Aas, Norway.

Department of Water Affairs, South Africa. 2012. *Development of a Reconciliation Strategy for the Luvuvhu and Letaba Water Supply System: Water Conservation and Water Demand Management Strategy and Business Plan Report Prepared by: Willem Wegelin* WRP Consulting Engineers, Report No. P WMA 02/B810/00/1412/6 www.dwa.gov.za/Projects/Luvuvhu/Documents/Web%20Doc%20CD2/WCWDM%20Strategy%20and%20Business%20Plan_Mopani.pdf (accessed September 1, 2016)

Folbre, N. 2004. *Who pays for the kids? Gender and the structures of constraint.* London: Routledge.

GoZ (Government of Zimbabwe). 2012. *National water policy.* Harare: Ministry of Water Resources Development and Management (now the Ministry of Environment, Water and Climate).

GoZ. 2013. *National water Policy*. Harare, Zimbabwe: Ministry of Water Resources and Development.

GWP (Global Water Partnership). 2006. Gender mainstreaming: An essential component of sustainable water management. Policy Brief No. 3. Stockholm, Sweden: Global Water Partnership.

Hellum, A. and Derman, B. 2005. Negotiating water rights in the context of a new political and legal landscape in Zimbabwe. In von Benda-Beckmann, F.; von Benda-Beckmann, K. and Griffiths, A. (Eds), *Mobile people, mobile law: Expanding legal relations in a contracting world*, pp. 177-198. Aldershot and Burlington, VT: Ashgate.

Hellum, A.; Ikdahl, I. and Kameri-Mbote. 2015a. Turning the tide: Engendering the human right to water and sanitation. In Hellum, A.; Kameri-Mbote, P. and van Koppen, B. (Eds), *Water is life: Women's human rights in national and local water governance in Southern and Eastern Africa*, pp. 32-80. Harare: Weaver Press.

Hellum, A.; Kameri-Mbote, P. and van Koppen, B. 2015b. The human right to water and sanitation in a legal pluralist landscape: Perspectives of Southern and Eastern African women. In Hellum, A.; Kameri-Mbote, P. and van Koppen, B. (Eds), *Water is life: Women's human rights in national and local water governance in Southern and Eastern Africa*, pp. 1-31. Harare: Weaver Press.

Hepworth, N. 2009. A progressive critique of IWRM in sub-Saharan Africa: Beyond capacity towards self-determined regulatory personality. PhD thesis. University of East Anglia, UK.

Jimenez, A. and Perez-Foguet, A. 2010. Building the role of local government authorities towards the achievement of the human right to water in rural Tanzania. *Natural Resources Forum* 34(2): 93-105.

Kissikwe, K. 2008. Irrigation-based livelihood challenges and opportunities: A gendered technography of irrigation development intervention in the Lower Moshi irrigation scheme in Tanzania. PhD thesis. Wageningen University.

Lankford, B.; Bakker, K.; Zeitoun, M. and Conway, D. (Eds). 2013. *Water security: Principles, perspectives, and practices*. London: Routledge.

Lecoutere, E. 2012. Sharing scarce common resources: Local water governance in semi-arid sub-Saharan Africa. PhD thesis. Ghent: Ghent University.

Lein, H. and Tagseth, M. 2009. Tanzanian water policy reforms – Between principles and practical applications. *Water Policy* 11(2): 203-220.

Masungu, T. 2007. Allocation and Use of Water for Domestic and Productive Purposes: An Exploratory Study from The Letaba River Catchment. MSc thesis. PLAAS, University of Western Cape, Bellville, South Africa.

Meinzen-Dick, R. and Zwarteveen, M. 1998. Gendered participation in water management: Issues and illustrations from water users' associations in South Asia. *Agriculture and Human Values* 15(4): 337-45.

Movik, S. 2011. *Fluid rights: South Africa's water allocation reform*. Cape Town: HSRC Press.

Nkonya, L.K. 2008. *Rural water management in Africa: The impact of customary institutions in Tanzania*. Amherst, NY: Cambria Press.

Nyabeze, W.R.; Mallory, S.; Hallowes, J.; Mwaka, B. and Sinha, P. 2007. Mainstreaming integrated water resources management in the development process: Determining operating rules for the Letaba river system in South Africa using three models. *Physics and Chemistry of the Earth Parts A/B/C* 32(15-18): 1040-1049.

O'Reilly, K. 2008. Insider/outsider politics: Implementing gendered participation in water resource management. In Resurreccion, B.P. and Elmhirst, R. (Eds), *Gender and natural resource management,* pp. 195-212. London: Earthscan.

Praagman, E. 2013. The political arenas of water management in the Limpopo Basin, Mozambique: Stakeholder participation at different policy levels. MSc thesis. Wageningen University, Wageningen, the Netherlands.

Prabhakaran, P. 2013. Gender invisibility in global water discourses: A feminist critique of Integrated Water Resources Management (IWRM). Master thesis. University of Sussex, IDS, Brighton, UK.

Rathgber, E. 2003. *Dry taps... Gender and poverty in water resource management.* Rome: Food and Agriculture Organization, United Nations.

Republic of Mozambique. 2005. *Gender strategy for the agricultural sector*. Maputo: Ministry of Agriculture

Republic of Mozambique. 2014. Beijing+20 Mozambique Report on the Implementation of the Declaration and Platform of Action. Maputo: Ministry of Women and Social Action.

RSA (Republic of South Africa). 1998. National Water Act. Act No. 36 of 1998. Government Gazette 19182. Cape Town: Government Printers.

RSA. 2013. *National water resource strategy: Water for an equitable and sustainable future*. Pretoria: Government Printers.

RSA. n.d. A gender perspective for water allocations. https://intertest.dwa.gov.za/war/war_website_docs/edition_6/final_documents/extra_reading/a_gender_perspective_for_water_allocations.pdf

Ribeiro, N. and Chauque, A. 2010. *Gender and climate change: Mozambique case study*. Cape Town: Heinrich-Boll Foundation.

Rullia, M.R.; Savioria, A. and D'Odoricob, P. 2013. Global land and water grabbing. *Proceedings of the National Academy of Sciences* (PNAS) 110(3): 892-897.

Rust, U. and Hanise, B. 2009. *The impact of gender in the rural water services environment of South Africa*. Water Research Commission Report No. TT 407/409. Pretoria: Water Research Commission. www.sadc.int/files/8713/5292/8364/Protocol_on_Gender_and_Development_2008.pdf

SADC (Southern African Development Community). 2006. *Regional water strategy*. Maseru: SADC.

SADC. 2008. SADC protocol on gender and development. www.sadc.int/files/8713/5292/8364/Protocol_on_Gender_and_Development_2008.pdf (accessed on January 16, 2016)

Seager, J. 2010. Gender and water: Good rhetoric, but it doesn't 'count'. *Geoforum* 41(1): 1-3.

Sitko, N.J. and Jayne, T.S. 2012. *The rising class of emergent farmers: An effective model for achieving agricultural growth and poverty reduction in Africa*? Food Security Collaborative Working Papers, Working Paper 140907. Michigan State University: Department of Agricultural, Food, and Resource Economics.

http://ideas.repec.org/p/ags/midcwp/140907.html (accessed on 30 September 2014)

South Africa Human Rights Commission. 2014. *The right to access sufficient water and decent sanitation in South Africa*. Pretoria: South African Human Rights Commission.

Tanner, C. 2010. Land rights and enclosures: Implementing the Mozambican land law in practice. In Anseeuw, W. and Alden, C. (Eds), *The struggle over land in Africa: Conflicts, politics and change*, pp. 105-130. Cape Town: HSRC Press.

TAWASANET (Tanzania Water and Sanitation Network). 2012. Does the water sector development program (WDSP) realize water and sanitation rights for marginalized groups? Dar es Salaam. www.tawasanet.or.tz/files/Equity%20report%202012.pdf (accessed May 5, 2015)

Tremblay, H. 2014. A clash of paradigms in the water sector? Tensions and synergies between integrated water resources management and the human rights-based approach to development. http://lawschool.unm.edu/nrj/volumes/51/2/Tremblay.

pdf (accessed on 1 June 2014)

URoT (United Republic of Tanzania). 2002. *National water policy.* Ministry of Water and Lands, Dar es Salaam.

United Nations. 1979. Convention on the Elimination of All Forms of Discrimination Against Women (CEDAW). www.un.org/womenwatch/daw/cedaw/text/econvention.htm#article5 (accessed January 15, 2015)

van Eeden, A. 2014. Whose waters: Large-scale agricultural development in the Wami-Ruvu River Basin, Tanzania. MSc thesis. Norwegian University of Life Sciences, Aas, Norway.

van Houweling, E. 2013. Gender, water and development: the multiple impacts and perspectives of a rural water project in Nampula, Mozambique. PhD dissertation. Blacksburg, VA: Virginia Tech.

van Houweling, E. 2016. A good wife brings her husband bath water: Gender roles and water practices in Nampula, Mozambique. *Society and Natural Resources* 29(9): 1065-1078.

van Koppen, B.; Sokile, C.; Hatibu, N.; Lankford, B.; Mahoo, H. and Yanda, P. 2004. *Formal water rights in rural Tanzania: Deepening the dichotomy?* IWMI Working Paper, Colombo, Sri Lanka: International Water Management Institute.

van Koppen, B.; Khumbane, T.; de Lange, M. and Mohapi, N. 2006. Gender and agricultural productivity: Implications for the revitalization of smallholder irrigation schemes program in Sekhukhune District, South Africa. In Lahiri-Dutt, K. (Ed), *Fluid bonds: Views on gender and water,* pp. 115-130. Stree, Calcutta.

van Koppen, B.; Smits, S. and Rumbaitis del Rio, C. 2014. *Scaling up multiple use water: Accountability in public water sector performance for health and wealth.* Rugby: Bourton on Dunsmore; United Kingdom: Practical Action Publishing.

van Koppen, B.; Derman, B.; Schreiner, B.; Durojaye, E. and Mweso, N. 2015. Fixing the leaks in women's human rights to water: Lessons from South Africa. In Hellum, A.; Kameri-Mbote, P. and van Koppen, B. (Eds), *Water is life: Women's human rights in national and local water governance in Southern and Eastern Africa,* pp. 457-507. Harare: Weaver Press.

Walsh, C. 2015. Life, nature and gender otherwise: Feminist reflections and provocations from the Andes. In Harcourt, W. and Nelson, I. (Eds), *Practicing feminist political ecologies: Moving beyond the 'green economy',* pp. 72-92. London: Zed Books.

Xie, H.; You, L.; Wielgosz, B. and Ringler, C. 2014. Estimating the potential for expanding smallholder irrigation in Sub-Saharan Africa. *Agricultural Water Management* 131(1): 183-193.

15

Viewpoint – IWRM and I: A Reflexive Travelogue of the Flows and Practices Research Team[1]

Alex Bolding

Rossella Alba

ABSTRACT: This viewpoint chapter critically discusses how IWRM travelled to each of the researchers of the Flows and Practices team, through which networks they personally engaged with IWRM, what opportunities the IWRM saga offered these researchers and how they tried to translate the concept and policy idea of IWRM into something more aligned with their concerns. By providing this self-reflection we aim to apply the conceptual framework used for the study of the travel and transformation of IWRM as a policy idea to ourselves, as a group of water professionals, realising that we ourselves have actively attempted to influence, transform, promote or resist the IWRM policy agenda. The viewpoint calls for enhancing transparency, self-reflection and appreciating the role (and power) of researchers and practitioners both as individuals and groups in shaping concepts and ideas.

KEYWORDS: IWRM, policy articulation, policy networks, translation, personal reflection

Introduction

What makes Integrated Water Resources Management, or IWRM as we know it for short, special? Besides the fact that it enhances one's status as a water professional, the I in IWRM can yield one lots of status as a parent amongst teenage offspring as well – iPod, iPhone, iTunes, iCloud and iWRM constitute an interesting list. Such was at least the experience of the lead author of this self-reflexive chapter on IWRM and I. Contrary to what readers may expect, the aim of this contribution to this book is not about the different types of integration that may be alluded to by the I of IWRM, but rather to reflect on the role of IWRM in the lives and careers of the core researchers making up the Flows and Practices: The Politics of Integrated Water Resources Management (IWRM) in Africa project team (hereby referred also as 'Flows and Practices' team, F&P).

1 First published in *Water Alternatives* 9(3): 664-680.

The 'Flows and Practices' project investigated the travel of IWRM ideas as framed in a global policy arena, and their translation into narratives and practices in five countries in sub-Saharan Africa. The articulation of IWRM was analysed by focusing on three key moments/episodes: the flow and spread of IWRM as an idea, the *translations, adoptions and transformations* of IWRM in national policies and the practices or the implementation of IWRM in local contexts (Mehta and Movik, 2014). As analysed in the articles included in this book, the project critically looked at when, with whom, and how IWRM ideas have travelled across countries and river basins. We analyse the politics of the policy process and the outcomes in terms of distribution and access to (water) resources (Mehta et al., 2014). The study insisted on exploring the role of key policy actors, or champions, such as researchers, consultants, state bureaucrats, experts, donors and NGOs in fostering and/or altering the spread of IWRM (Mehta and Movik, 2014). Soon we realised that we ourselves were not impartial observers of this odyssey, but were very much part and parcel of the network of water professionals that contributed to the emergence of, responded to or engaged with IWRM. Hence we ourselves have been articulating, translating and diverting the content and policy journey of IWRM.

With this in mind, we turn our attention to the participants of the F&P project and attempt a self-analysis and critique of our role in the journey. The travelogue provided in this viewpoint is reflexive in the sense that it applies the conceptual framework used for the study of the travel and transformation of IWRM as a policy idea to ourselves, as a group of water professionals and researchers. We propose a reflection on how we have actively attempted to influence, transform, promote or resist the IWRM agenda. This viewpoint complements the other chapters included in this book as it illustrates who the members of the Flows and Practices team are and how they have engaged with IWRM in their work and during their careers.

Eventually, this chapter provides a space for discussing and reflecting on our knowledge and experiences as researchers and professionals in the water sector – including our own ideational 'power'. The direct voices of the participants of the 'Flows and Practices' project, their thoughts, aspirations and dilemmas emerge throughout the chapter. Following Levine et al. (2013: 148) we believe this is relevant for two reasons: first, much of this knowledge is often hidden and "lost after the retirement of key actors of the water sector"; and second, the chapter offers a space for self-criticism and reflection on the ethical and personal dilemmas we have encountered in the everyday practice of critical water studies. In this way, we aim at contributing to the discussion on the 'voices of water professionals' which first began in the pages of *Water Alternatives*' (Special Issue 'Voices of Professionals: Shedding Light on Hidden Dynamics in the Water Sector' – 2013).

In the remainder of this contribution we first of all discuss the methodology used for this self-study. Thereafter we use as a guide five questions we posed during interviews with members of the F&P team. We first analyse when people were confronted with IWRM as a concept and what formed our initial responses and engagements. Next we analyse in which networks people operated when they engaged with IWRM and what opportunities were offered as a result of this engagement. We also try to assess what role IWRM played in our respective careers. Next we delve into the attempts of various members of the group to resist, transform or translate certain elements of IWRM as a policy idea. Finally, we explore the question of what comes next – is there life after IWRM and, if so, what would it look like?

Methods of self-studying the Flows and Practices team

The Flows and Practices project brought together fifteen researchers. Of these, eight are male and seven female, a composition which renders the group unrepresentative for the water world which tends to be dominated by men. In terms of nationality the group is diverse with representatives from Austria (1), Canada (1), France (1), India (1), Italy (1), the Netherlands (2), Norway (1), South Africa (1), Tanzania (3), United Kingdom (1), United States of America (1), and Zimbabwe (1). Most of the participants have working and research experience in sub-Saharan Africa, particularly in the five so-called case study countries included in the F&P project: South Africa, Zimbabwe, Mozambique, Tanzania and Uganda. All group members have been engaged in academia or other research organisations either as a professional or as a student, with the exception of one member who worked for an international NGO in Uganda at the time of the research (but who had a research background). The group is composed of six young, five mid-career and four senior professionals, with four professors in our midst. In terms of disciplinary background, the group is split between six people with a background in applied or water engineering while the remaining nine have a social science background that ranges from economics and water management to anthropology and development studies.

The project came about as a result of three attempts to secure funding of which only the last was successful. First, and key to the genesis of group was an attempt at securing European Union funding, coordinated by Bill Derman and Lyla Mehta at the Norwegian University of Life Sciences (in 2013 the acronym changed from UMB to NMBU with the addition of the veterinary school) in Norway.2 In December 2009, representatives from the Institute of Development Studies (IDS), Wageningen University, International Water Management Institute (IWMI), the Water Research Commission of South Africa, University of Zimbabwe, and the University of Malawi (Chancellor College) were invited by UMB to spend a week together to develop an EU FP7 research project proposal on the Travel of IWRM to Africa. The resulting proposal was submitted for a call on Africa and Natural Resources Management, but was ultimately turned down by one reviewer who did not see how our research project would help spread IWRM in Africa, failing to appreciate the critical nature of our proposed study. A second attempt at securing funding for a 'dumbed down' version of the original EU proposal brought a smaller group together around a similar study on the travel of IWRM with an

2 By 2009, Norway as a non-EU country was allowed entry for the first time into bidding for EU funding for research.

application to the European Science Foundation's 'European Collaborative Research Projects' scheme which sought co funding from Norwegian, British and Dutch research councils. Despite some very strong and constructive comments by the reviewers, one reviewer felt insulted by the lack of respect and attention to the EU Water Framework Directive, which sunk the whole proposal. When this second attempt at securing funding had also failed, an even further focused and financially modest proposal was written for exclusive Norwegian funding by The Research Council of Norway. The third attempt proved successful. By then the team had become even smaller still, coalescing around initially four African countries, viz. South Africa, Zimbabwe, Mozambique and Tanzania (later expanded to five, by including Uganda).

Of the 15 core researchers associated with the Flows and Practices project, 12 were interviewed for this chapter. The interviews were performed in English by the two lead authors in person, mostly during a project workshop held in Brighton (UK) in May 2014, with some follow-up in July 2014, and three interviews by Skype later on. One researcher answered our questions by Email. The interviews were guided by the five questions listed below.

1. When did you first hear about IWRM? Did it appeal to you?
2. What was your first personal engagement with IWRM (where, when)?
3. Did IWRM play a big role in your career? Did it provide opportunities that you would not have had without IWRM?
4. When and how did you develop a critical standing toward IWRM?
5. How are you engaging with IWRM today?

First engagement with IWRM

We started our interviews by asking the interviewees to recall their first encounter and engagement with IWRM. Soon we noticed a clear distinction between young and senior researchers: while the former studied IWRM and its critique, the latter heard about IWRM in the 1990s when the concept was in its initial stage of development carrying a promising agenda. Secondly, despite differences in age and experience, most of the interviewees did not relate the emergence of IWRM with the endorsement of the so-called Dublin Principles during the International Conference on Water and the Environment held in Dublin in 1992 (ACC/ISGWR, 1992). The multiple engagements with IWRM are further outlined below.

Constructing critical perspectives

Three of the M.Sc. students involved in the project learned about IWRM during their university studies and engaged with the concept while writing their Masters thesis within the F&P project. Two students interviewed commented:

> *I heard about IWRM for the first time during my first degree studies in Environmental Science. IWRM was just mentioned during*

> *a course. I didn't pay much attention to it. (...) My first real engagement with IWRM was with my MSc thesis in the context of the F&P project.*[3]

> *I heard about IWRM during my MSc study in International Land and Water Management in Wageningen (...) I have been critical of IWRM even before I heard of it properly – first I had the critique and then I engaged with the concept.*[4]

Some of the senior researchers in the group were rather optimistic when they first encountered IWRM. For instance, Emmanuel Manzungu explained:

> *I heard of IWRM towards the end of my PhD. The concept seemed to reconcile land and water, and promote integration. I then wrote a five pager jointly with Alex [Bolding] and Pieter van der Zaag arguing in favour of IWRM as a new approach in a book on water for agriculture in Zimbabwe, published in 1999* (Manzungu et al., 1999). *IWRM promised to be more encompassing/holistic than just irrigation.*[5]

Alex Bolding first heard about IWRM in the 1990s while working on his PhD on water management at field, irrigation scheme and catchment levels in Zimbabwe (Bolding, 2004) and contributed to the book Emmanuel mentioned above:

> *I heard of IWRM in mid-1998 when finishing a book on water in Zimbabwe that came out in 1999. It made a lot of sense – we made our own definition of IWRM at the time in contrast to the IUCN [International Union for the Conservation of Nature] definition. The concept opened up a much-needed agenda – holistic, how to engage with different types of water use. (...) For my PhD I thought that certain indigenous water allocation and distribution practices I had observed were in line with IWRM as I wanted to promote it. I linked IWRM very much with river basin management and Tennessee Valley Authority style holistic natural resources management.*[6]

In contrast, if IWRM was initially an appealing concept for some, the experience of the senior social and political scientists of the Flows and Practices group proved different as Bill Derman noticed:

> *The concept did not appeal to me as such, I was not coming from the water world (...) I was looking at it [water] from the point of view of resource use and property relations.*[7]

---

3 Skype interview with Aurelia van Eeden by Alex Bolding and Rossella Alba, 27 May 2014.

4 Interview with Rossella Alba by Alex Bolding, Brighton, 1 May 2014.

5 Interview with Emmanuel Manzungu by Alex Bolding and Rossella Alba, Brighton, 2 May 2014.

6 Interview with Alex Bolding by Rossella Alba, Wageningen, 28 May 2014.

7 Interview with Bill Derman by Alex Bolding and Rossella Alba, Brighton, 2 May 2014. Bill Derman entered water through the observations of Zambezi Valley farmers who were disturbed by changes in river flows due to irrigation on the plateau. Calvin Nhira (then Director of the Centre for Applied Social Sciences at the University of Zimbabwe)

He noticed that when he started researching the impact of newly introduced water laws in Zimbabwe, in the mid-nineties, the focus was on water resources management (WRM) not IWRM. Thus, he first engaged with water resources management and only later on with Integrated Water Resources Management as an approach.

A more critical approach towards IWRM was embraced by a part of the researchers within F&P since their first encounter with the concept. For instance Alan Nicol highlights:

> *I heard about IWRM in 1993 at the Nile 2002 conference in Aswan, Egypt. Seemed to me to be an anti-politics concept – technical, boring and policy blind.*[8]

However, most of the researchers in the F&P project soon embraced a critical position towards IWRM. Indeed, the first enthusiasm towards IWRM and its potential was soon replaced by mounting criticism and disillusion. Alex Bolding noticed:

> *By 2000, IWRM was the only game in town and I wrote a critical paper about it for a research conference – in the paper we (Bolding et al., 2000) argued for a politicised IWRM and wondered about five possible meanings of the I in IWRM.*[9]

The limits of IWRM were highlighted also by Barbara van Koppen, who actively participated in defining it, for the Global Water Partnership (GWP):

> *IWRM was soon like a mantra in the GWP. Over time I got frustrated with GWP and IWRM. In 2003 I published a critical paper on IWRM in Africa. IWRM brought a 'paralysis of analysis' and many important issues (water development, poverty alleviation) were side-lined by it. However, GWP just wanted to push one generic agenda for the whole world.*[10]

I and the 'Dublin Principles'

Even though the idea of integrated management of water resources has a long history, IWRM gained increased attention during the 1990s (Biswas, 2004; Conca, 2005; Cherlet, 2012; Mehta and Movik, 2014). The International Conference on Water and the Environment held in Dublin in 1992 represents a turning point in the debate surrounding IWRM (ACC/ISGWR, 1992). The conference led to the endorsement of the so-called 'Dublin Principles' that soon became the guiding principles for the implementation of IWRM worldwide to the point that for many IWRM is conflated with the 'Dublin Principles'. Interestingly, despite differences

formulated a research strategy to examine water as property, and the impacts of Zimbabwe's new water laws.

8 Skype interview with Alan Nicol by Rossella Alba, 5 June 2014. Note: The Nile 2002 conference refers to a series of conferences that took place in the 1990s focusing on 'Comprehensive Water Resources Development of the Nile Basin'.

9 Interview with Alex Bolding by Rossella Alba, Wageningen, 28 May 2014.

10 Interview with Barbara van Koppen by Alex Bolding and Rossella Alba, Brighton, 1 May 2014.

in age and experience, most of the interviewees, if not all, did not relate the emergence of IWRM with the endorsement of the so-called Dublin Principles.

> *[IWRM] Had nothing to do with Dublin in my perception – I only got to know the Dublin Principles through the F&P project.*[11]

Andrew Tarimo learned about IWRM almost ten years before the endorsement of the Dublin Principles, when he started working as Irrigation Manager in the Morogoro Region in Tanzania. Rather than relating IWRM with the Dublin Principles, he first heard about IWRM when the Tanzanian Government introduced a River Basin Management approach and established nine river basins in the country.[12]

Nevertheless, the discussion surrounding the recognition of water as an economic good (Principle No. 4) played a big role in the debate, as Synne Movik, Jeremy Allouche and Lyla Mehta mentioned:

> *I think I first heard of IWRM in 2002 at a conference on FMIS [Farmer-Managed Irrigation Systems] in Kathmandu. The big issue then was water as an economic good, meaning that water would be pushed out of agriculture which of course was perceived as a threat to FMIS. I did not really relate to IWRM at the time (...) IWRM sounded reasonable but it was a water thing – it was about hydrological boundaries, river basins, etc. Dublin Principles did not really connect with it, in my mind.*[13]

> *In 1999 I was doing research on privatisation in the water services sector, and I came across the IWRM concept in a World Bank paper on water reforms in Morocco. During subsequent interviews in Washington at the World Bank I became aware of the so-called Dublin Principles, which pushed IWRM. Actually the reform agenda pushing privatisation and decentralisation had started with a World Bank paper in 1993 on WRM (World Bank, 1993), but it actually happened in the water services sector.*[14]

> *I only picked up on IWRM in the 2000s, when critical papers about it came out from the early to mid-2000s. I also recall a DFID meeting of water professionals where it was debated and many critical views were put forward. Prior to that, I had always been critical of Dublin Principle No.4 that largely focused on private good/economic aspects of water, as opposed to taking a more multifaceted approach.*[15]

Concluding, the discussion above reveals different responses to our first question. First, the age and the experience of the participants seem to shape their opinions on IWRM. Second, at the time of the Flows and Practices project most

11 Interview with Alex Bolding by Rossella Alba, Wageningen, 28 May 2014.

12 Email personal communication with Andrew Tarimo, 8 May 2015.

13 Interview with Synne Movik by Alex Bolding and Rossella Alba, Brighton, 2 May 2014.

14 Interview with Jeremy Allouche by Alex Bolding, Brighton, 7 July 2014.

15 Interview with Lyla Mehta by Alex Bolding, Brighton, 8 July 2014.

of the researchers were critical towards IWRM, but some were not when IWRM entered the water policy scene. Often, these early believers were directly involved in the water sector as engineers or PhD researchers. They first welcomed IWRM as a new approach and it was only through experience and over time that they developed a critical stand towards it. Nevertheless, the advent of IWRM provided opportunities for all the interviewees to converge around the Flows and Practices project and the chance to work together. We further elaborate on this in the following section.

Networks and opportunities

One of the key characteristics of IWRM as a concept and policy idea is that it offered many opportunities for networking – opening doors to different ideas, bringing together people from many different disciplines. This is also one aspect of IWRM that has been emphasised by many of the interviewees. Barbara van Koppen enthusiastically reflected on her term with the Steering Committee and later Nomination Committee of the Global Water Partnership:

> *We met once or twice a year. In Costa Rica we had one of our first regional meetings. There I had the chance to meet a lot of people, like Sunita Narain and Anil Agarwal and many others. We exchanged lots of ideas and had a nice time together. That time was really exciting. People from all over the world, 'the brightest brains from all countries' including civil society organisations were involved in the meetings at the GWP. It was a 'toolkit for learning'.*[16]

Hence if the concept of IWRM can stake one undisputed claim to fame, it must be that it enabled people and ideas to navigate networks, different profession(al)s to meet and opportunities to be offered. So it is legitimate to ask what role IWRM played in the careers of the Flows and Practices team members and what networks and opportunities the concept and its flow offered to the team members.

Below the three most common reactions are presented in more detail. One can summarise them as IWRM providing (1) a stepping stone; (2) a focus point to articulate criticism while making a career in the water world; (3) a sideshow to real issues and a no-brainer which featured in the background. Besides discussing the role IWRM played for the participants, the opportunities offered by the F&P project are also outlined. All the interviewees emphasise that the F&P project has offered them opportunities, for some in the shape of MSc thesis projects, for others temporary research assistant positions, and for others an opportunity to get to know other critical water academics and provide further exposure to critical studies on 'policy travel'.

IWRM as a stepping stone

While most of us stress that working together in the F&P project has been nice

16 Interview with Barbara van Koppen by Alex Bolding and Rossella Alba, Brighton, 1 May 2014.

and inspiring, many would say like Synne Movik that their engagement with IWRM did not offer tremendous opportunities, neither in terms of career nor in fostering IWRM or water in general, during their career, before engaging with Flows and Practices. However, Synne discovered that after moving to a Norwegian consultancy firm:

> *I am working on the EU-WFD [European Union – Water Framework Directive] in Norway today and it's all about IWRM. My colleagues do wonder why I'm so critical of the IWRM concept – it does sound very logical to pursue it.*[17]

In contrast, the critical engagement with IWRM through the Flows and Practices project has provided a stepping stone for many of the younger members of the F&P team. Yet, rather than IWRM per se, the F&P project brought them several opportunities, as Aurelia van Eeden illustrates:

> *IWRM as such did not play a big role in my career, it just happened to be around. At the start I found it boring, redundant and a distraction from the real issues.*[18]

The interviewees readily acknowledge IWRM as the key focus point of the research project, offering opportunities to critically engage with IWRM in thesis work, providing a formative experience and allowing them to learn, and engage with critical water studies and develop research skills. The project also yielded tangible benefits like jobs as research assistants, participation in three conferences and a first publication in a scientific journal (Mehta et al., 2014). Moreover, the opportunity to accumulate knowledge and insights on different dimensions of IWRM helps in engaging with ongoing debates in the water world, like the new Water Act in British Columbia, Canada.

IWRM as a focus point to articulate criticism

The second most prevalent response stresses the role of IWRM as a focus point for articulating critical positions while developing a career. This reaction was particularly prevalent amongst those already occupying a job in the water world as an engineer at the time IWRM became a dominant idea in the water sector. IWRM provided opportunities to further develop their career as critical thinkers/academics/consultants galvanising their agenda and critically engaging with different dimensions of IWRM like decentralisation, stakeholder management, privatisation and water pricing. Although critical towards IWRM as a concept, for those involved in the water sector, IWRM appears as a set course as it was (and still is) a catalyser for funding and project opportunities.

For Alex Bolding, the IWRM proliferation helped in finding research funds:

> *IWRM did provide opportunities – it was a hegemonic concept in the water world, no way around it and it put things on the agenda – like reserving water for the environment, concerns with democratising water management, decentralisation, and water pricing.*

17 Interview with Synne Movik by Alex Bolding and Rossella Alba, Brighton, 2 May 2014.

18 Skype interview with Aurelia van Eeden by Alex Bolding and Rossella Alba, 27 May 2014.

> *IWRM released quite some funds including those associated with my post-doc research on water governance at river basin level. It also generated a lot more knowledge. But more than IWRM it was the idea of River Basin Management that helped me in my career as a researcher.*[19]

For Emmanuel Manzungu, the funded spread of IWRM in the SADC region provided a living:

> *It allowed me to pursue a career by criticising it, definitely not by promoting it. I was part of a team that was in charge of a mid-term review about IWRM implementation in SADC countries; we physically travelled to many countries. I travelled to South Africa, Malawi, Zambia, Lesotho and Swaziland in addition to talking to Zimbabwean officials. They initially asked us for a 100-page report. I prepared a 30-page report. The document focused on IWRM, infrastructure development and water resources development. It was around 2004-2005. The greater part of the content of that 30 pages later became part of the SADC strategy on Integrated Water Resources Development and Management.*[20]

For Andrew Tarimo, IWRM offered the opportunity to work closely with former colleagues and strengthen his professional network:

> *In 1995, the Government [of Tanzania] made a review of the Water Policies following an earlier advice by the World Bank and Danida and, in 1996, the World Bank financed an inter-ministerial project titled River Basin Management and Smallholder Irrigation Improvement Project (RBMSIIP). The RBM component was hosted by the ministry responsible for water, while the SIIP component was lodged with the Ministry of Agriculture. It is at this stage that I developed a real interest in IWRM because the head of the RBM was my former university classmate and the head of SIIP used to be my colleague in the Ministry of Agriculture. By then I was already employed by Sokoine University of Agriculture and therefore I had an opportunity to work with them more closely.*[21]

For Barbara van Koppen operating in the IWMI southern Africa regional office, her earlier-mentioned involvement with IWRM through the GWP helped her establish a reputation:

> *It helped me in my professional career – to become visible, though mainly as a troublemaker (…). I find this work on vague concepts that hide an anti-poor agenda boring. Though I must admit that my exposure to the networks associated with GWP helped me to gain recognition. It has probably also been effective in obtaining my present senior position.*[22]

19 Interview with Alex Bolding by Rossella Alba, Wageningen, 28 May 2014.

20 Interview with Emmanuel Manzungu by Alex Bolding and Rossella Alba, Brighton, 2 May 2014.

21 Email personal communication with Andrew Tarimo, 8 May 2015.

22 Interview with Barbara van Koppen by Alex Bolding and Rossella Alba, Brighton, 1 May 2014.

Alan Nicol who worked for the Overseas Development Institute (ODI) critically engaging with IWRM (Nicol, 2000), before joining the World Water Council in Marseille for a two year stint indicated that:

> *IWRM provided an idea to count on, providing researchable issues, helping me to establish a position and its critique helped to reinforce the debate on politics and power.*[23]

IWRM as a sideshow

Yet in a third response, particularly prevalent amongst those engaging from a social science perspective, IWRM was at the fringe of their main concerns, and only became part of a main course through the F&P project. Virtually all more-senior social science researchers engaging with the water world involved in the F&P project have been critical of Dublin Principle No.4 – whereby the water privatisation debates provided them with a bigger impetus to their careers both intellectually and politically. For instance, for political scientist, Jeremy Allouche:

> *IWRM was always a side dish, never the main course. It didn't mean a lot in terms of fostering my career; as a policy engagement it wasn't offering opportunities and as claim to fame? Not sure. There is only one element of IWRM, treating water as an economic good that is heavily contested and inspires debate...*[24]

The same applies to social scientists, Bill Derman and Lyla Mehta. Bill Derman indicated that:

> *IWRM just happens to be the dominant narrative and as such it needs to be unravelled. Nobody ever explained to me the beauty of IWRM, so it didn't really feature for me, until such time that we as a team started to develop the EU proposal.*[25]

Translating and aligning IWRM with a home-bred agenda

As already alluded to above, many of the researchers of the F&P team have engaged critically with one or two dimensions of the IWRM idea and used the advent of the concept as a key element in critiquing hegemonic discourses in the water world and as a means to foster their own (policy or research) agenda. In that sense, the F&P team members did not treat the concept differently from other policy actors – running with some aspects and actively trying to translate or transform other parts of the concept to align it with their own agenda. A number of translations and diversions feature prominently and are treated in more detail below.

Many of us in our careers initially saw IWRM as something benign and neutral – a good idea, containing all the necessary elements – though it was on the fringe

23 Skype interview with Alan Nicol by Rossella Alba, 5 June 2014.

24 Interview with Jeremy Allouche by Alex Bolding, Brighton, 7 July 2014.

25 Interview with Bill Derman by Alex Bolding and Rossella Alba, Brighton, 2 May 2014.

of the research or policy concerns of many team members of the F&P project before the start of the project. There is a general feeling that there is nothing wrong with the concept as such or with the network of advocacy organisations promoting its spread, like the Global Water Partnership and the World Water Council. The concept makes (hydrological) sense, and the extent to which we can ascribe negative effects to it is debatable. Perhaps by focusing exclusively on its flow into Africa in the context of a research project one is tempted to overestimate its (negative or positive) effects.

Against privatisation and water grabbing, but pushing water as a human right

What some of the team members have issues with are some of the underlying Dublin Principles. It seems that principle No. 3 on women's role in water supply was added as an afterthought at the end of the Dublin conference. While Principle No. 4 on treating water as an economic good has triggered huge debates and is profoundly contested. As Jeremy Allouche highlighted:

> *If I want to be very critical of IWRM I would just observe that IWRM is a spiel of a little clique of consultants. Yet one must also admit that through different gatherings IWRM has been opening up new possibilities. The initial push behind the concept came from environmentalists and the anti-dam movement, and I must admit that I'm not against this dimension of the IWRM 'movement' – it has made engineers rethink about the potential impacts of their infrastructure. (...) We have difficulties in pinning down exact criticism on the concept. People are puzzled by IWRM – it is a vague concept, it contains some good elements. IWRM has failed to deliver, that's what our case studies show. But the principles behind it remain. Water as an economic good, has a much stronger appeal and potential to be criticised than IWRM as such.*[26]

The last point indicates the direction of the most notable and vehement resistance to IWRM: against promoting Dublin Principle No. 4 seeking to treat water as an economic good. Associated with this resistance is the pushing of an alternative agenda that treats water as a human right. As Bill Derman indicated "I've always engaged whatever water reform from the perspective of human rights".[27] Similarly, Lyla Mehta has always been critical of attempts to push for water privatisation and the role of IWRM inspired policy discourse in institutionalising Dublin Principle No.4. For Alex Bolding the second World Water Forum in The Hague (2000) provided an eye-opener in this respect:

> *I thought 'hey, the IWRM crowd is the wrong crowd, this is the private sector'. It was also the time of the peak of privatisation and cherry picking. French companies were involved in promoting 'packaged water' and making a profit out of it, before even im-*

26 Interview with Jeremy Allouche by Alex Bolding, Brighton, 7 July 2014.

27 Interview with Bill Derman by Alex Bolding and Rossella Alba, Brighton, 2 May 2014.

proving the public service.[28]

Aurelia van Eeden has studied how IWRM and its emphasis on water as a private good has affected the ongoing land and water grab on the African continent:

> *I was always critical of IWRM, but in the context of this project I've been trying to see what it does for the ongoing land and water grab in Africa. IWRM has different meanings in each context. When you focus on access to water and water rights, water grabs become an important issue and how IWRM discourse facilitates access by companies. I'm more cynical than critical. At the start, IWRM seemed a wonderful idea, but lots of unforeseen stuff has happened so I cannot accept IWRM with open arms anymore. I'm critical to some aspects of IWRM like the definition of water as an economic good, which implies in terms of water rights that the flow of money and commodification of water work towards skewed access.*[29]

Translating IWRM from management to water development and access

The second most felt point of criticism on IWRM focuses on its purported role in sidelining a pro-poor development agenda for Africa, by redirecting attention towards water management issues rather than towards water development. As Alex Bolding indicated:

> *In the case of Africa, it was a way to stop development of water resources and focus on management, while lack of access to water still remains a big issue together with a lack of development of water infrastructure.*[30]

Barbara van Koppen readily explained how she became critical of the concept over time. Of course, it was Asit Biswas who famously declared the concept dead in 2004 to the shock of some of the Stockholm Water Week attendants (Biswas, 2004). The Tushaar Shah paper (co-authored with van Koppen, 2006) provided a tipping point for van Koppen in criticising the concept. The GWP itself started to get disillusioned by 2009-10.

> *I also fought hard in the GWP to include a poverty eradication and water development component to IWRM. Mike Muller really managed to get more attention for the 'D' for Development within the GWP.*[31]

Pivotal in that transformation of the IWRM agenda into one dealing with water development as well was the work of Emmanuel Manzungu, who has already related above what his role was in formulating the second SADC regional strate-

28 Interview with Alex Bolding by Rossella Alba, Wageningen, 28 May 2014.

29 Skype interview with Aurelia van Eeden by Alex Bolding and Rossella Alba, 27 May 2014.

30 Interview with Alex Bolding by Rossella Alba, Wageningen, 28 May 2014.

31 Interview with Barbara van Koppen by Alex Bolding and Rossella Alba, Brighton, 1 May 2014.

gic action plan (2005-10), which explicitly adds a water development agenda to the customary IWRM recipe book:

> *It was the time of Bruce Lankford's renewed focus on irrigation adaptation and infrastructure development; the African Development Bank was focusing also on irrigation; and the Blair Commission for Africa was active. Hence infrastructure development became a key element of SADC's strategy for IWRM despite resistance by a French lady who insisted on removing dams from the agenda.*[32]

Bringing water allocation back in – multiple use services as IWRM-light

The third stream of criticism raised against IWRM took issue with its GWP-inspired discourse on the trade-off between efficiency, equity and environmental sustainability (GWP, 2000) which helped to depoliticise water allocation debates. Synne Movik was already a doubting Thomas with regard to the benefits of IWRM, but it was not until 2004 with the Biswas speech at the Stockholm water week (Biswas, 2004) and a Tony Allan article (Allan, 2003) that she got really critical:

> *IWRM allows you to see in it and get from it what you like. The Allan article made me realise that water allocation debates were stifled by its apolitical conception in IWRM discourse. It made me realise that allocation issues were really missing from it – that was too political. Contestations did not feature in the concept of IWRM. I started thinking about getting politics back in water governance, and how IWRM helped to keep politics out.*[33]

Barbara van Koppen shared these sentiments but got really disillusioned when IWRM was next used in newly adopted southern African water legislation to promote the issuing of water permits, detrimentally affecting water-allocation debates, by depriving the poor of customary water rights. However, the talk of integration did help to pave the road for the MUS concept – Multiple Use Services (MUS, see www.musgroup.net):

> *I remember well that we presented MUS at the World Water Forum in Istanbul in 2009 as an IWRM-light. That was an active attempt to translate IWRM into something else by promoting a new MUS perspective. Redirecting IWRM towards community water development.*[34]

---

32 Interview with Emmanuel Manzungu by Alex Bolding and Rossella Alba, Brighton, 2 May 2014. Manzungu refers to the irrigation chapter of the Commission for Africa, written by Bruce Lankford (2005).

33 Interview with Synne Movik by Alex Bolding and Rossella Alba, Brighton, 2 May 2014.

34 Interview with Barbara van Koppen by Alex Bolding and Rossella Alba, Brighton, 1 May 2014.

Against centralisation, pro participation

A closely affiliated critique to the points raised above takes issue with the propensity of the IWRM discourse to paradoxically promote centralised, expert-driven institutions that are at base anti-democratic, under the cloak of decentralised user management of water in newly established stakeholder-based institutions (Wester et al., 2009). This phenomenon has been called 'the ghost of TVA' (Tennessee Valley Authority; see Miller and Reidinger, 1998). Alex Bolding became really critical of IWRM in the context of writing a paper on the three waves of River Basin Management – whereby IWRM featured as an anti-democratic ghost of TVA (see also Iyer, 2004):

> *Of course, in 2000 presenting a paper at a Dutch water conference, my co-authors and I were the only ones critical of IWRM – we feared that IWRM would only help reinforce the water engineers' position as so-called experts.*

Interviewer: Why were you critical?

> *Because IWRM is anti-democratic, experts use it for claiming their role, and the bureaucracies to propagate themselves. Instead of opening up the sector, it closed it up.*[35]

Yet it is also readily acknowledged by many of the F&P project team members that IWRM contains certain elements worth fighting for, the most mentioned of which is its emphasis on stakeholder participation in water resources management (Dublin Principle No. 2). As Rossella Alba indicated:

> *I was critical of IWRM before I got to know the concept in a proper manner. (…) Over time I got more critical of various aspects of the concept, like that it is a-political and that it includes the element of seeing water as an economic good. Yet its emphasis on stakeholder participation can be quite useful.*[36]

Similarly, Kristi Denby thought IWRM was a good idea in theory putting together environmental, gender, economics and participation concerns. However, she became very critical of certain aspects of the IWRM policy idea and questioned IWRM's usefulness in practice through engaging with this project.

IWRM morphing into something else…

Finally, it is salient to observe that IWRM is prone to morphing into something else, as indicated above by Barbara van Koppen who started promoting MUS based community development as 'IWRM-light'. Two other emerging guises or interpretations of IWRM, are climate-smart agriculture and the resilient call for adaptive water management in the face of global climate change. IWRM has been used and abused both for 'good' and 'bad' causes – like WaterNet offering accessible research funding for practitioners in the African water sector (through WARFSA) and capacity building programmes in African universities scrutinising ques-

35 Interview with Alex Bolding by Rossella Alba, Wageningen, 28 May 2014.

36 Interview with Rossella Alba by Alex Bolding, Brighton, 1 May 2014.

tions of politics and equity under the banner of IWRM. Alex Bolding observes that

> *At the same time GWP and affiliated advocacy groups like the Netherlands Water Partnership has been using IWRM to shamelessly promote the sale of expert knowledge. So, in principle, there is nothing wrong with IWRM – as a concept it opened up questions (on groundwater management, ecosystem integrity and issues of integration) that are relevant to teach about.*[37]

Alan Nicol, however, never liked the idea:

> *I think engineering and economics provide incomplete solutions. I remember a dinner with the GWP group in London, where I criticised IWRM for not working in practice. (...) [a senior GWP member] acted as if I had insulted his mother. IWRM espouses true believers. The F&P project provides a nice opportunity to articulate our critique on the concept but ultimately IWRM is out-dated – its high point was in 1999-2000 at the second WWF. Since then it has been subject to criticism and has fallen victim to Climate Change and a different set of post 9-11 geopolitical interests. We need to go beyond IWRM. I'm presently involved in water-smart agriculture which is a kind of IWRM at micro-scale though I prefer to avoid the IWRM term.*[38]

IWRM AND OUR FUTURE

So is there a future for IWRM or will the water world switch and bet on a different horse or set of horses? We discussed this question both with our interviewees and in a group discussion during our project conference in Brighton in May 2014.

Interviews revealed different opinions on this amongst the team members, with basically three responses. First there are those of us, who despite levelling criticism against different elements of the IWRM policy idea, believe it is there to stay in its original guise or differently as Adaptive Water Resources Management (AWRM) in response to Climate Change. Second, some interviewees highlighted that some aspects of IWRM were actually quite useful, like the principle of emphasising stakeholder participation, but that it just needs deepening to become more inclusive. A final and third response was that IWRM has done enough damage and needs to be replaced by a human right to water approach.

Within the first category of being critical of IWRM but believing in another lifeline yet, Alex Bolding stressed that the a-political GWP definition of IWRM needs to be unpacked so people realise they have to make choices – you can't have it all. He also believed the Dublin Principles to be fatally flawed:

> *The mention of women is useless in the principles; it doesn't say anything about gender. The definition of water as a private good is abused to promote pricing and profit-making. It is nice that they mention stakeholder participation, but they only say 'at the appropriate level' without specifying. Am I still fascinated by IWRM?*

37 Interview with Rossella Alba by Alex Bolding, Brighton, 1 May 2014.

38 Skype interview with Alan Nicol by Rossella Alba, 5 June 2014.

> *Yes, I am fascinated because I understand where it comes from. I understand the hydrological perspective. And I think it is there to stay. For example, look at the ICID [International Commission on Irrigation and Drainage]; it is a club of traditional engineers purporting to solve political distribution problems with technical, supply-side solutions. But they are still organising their meetings. They even organised the first Irrigation World Water Forum (in Turkey, 2014). For some of them, IWRM is still a revolutionary, innovative concept!*[39]

Jeremy Allouche concurred with the last point, while not expecting to have another project involving IWRM, though many of the issues raised under the banner of IWRM will continue to feature in studies/debates engaging with the water-food-energy nexus (Allouche et al., 2015). He continued by stressing that:

> *[T]he literature on IWRM never really inspired me. Most of it seems to comprise boring case studies of bad quality that contain IWRM in their title. (…) The problem seems to be that IWRM was never really defined as a sexy topic from a social science perspective. (…) It is also important to realise that IWRM can reconfigure itself as adaptive WRM in the face of Climate Change. Thus it can garner a new lease of life.*[40]

A second set of responses were informed by an equally critical perspective on IWRM, but stressed the fact that the concept for its ills had brought something worthwhile as well. Synne Movik stressed that in her new job as a consultant operating in the EU water world, her colleagues frown at her critical perception of IWRM. Yet:

> *[D]espite me being very critical of IWRM, my present work with the EU-WFD (…) points at the issue of stakeholder participation being tabled. IWRM helps to bring different stakeholders together and to talk with each other and debate issues. That did not happen before. Of course, we need to deepen the inclusiveness and type of participation involved.*[41]

In a similar vein, Emmanuel Manzungu stressed that the decentralised stakeholder management of water in so-called Catchment Councils is probably there to stay:

> *Today, there are elements of IWRM in Zimbabwe that are difficult to get rid of. For instance, Catchment Councils – I'm presently engaged in action research that tries to link the work of the Catchment Council to the grassroots level, providing bottom-up feedback loops to improve the quality and depth of stakeholder participation. IWRM still plays a key role in securing funding in the SADC Region.*[42]

39 Interview with Alex Bolding by Rossella Alba, Wageningen, 28 May 2014.

40 Interview with Jeremy Allouche by Alex Bolding, Brighton, 7 July 2014.

41 Skype interview with Alan Nicol by Rossella Alba, 5 June 2014.

42 Interview with Emmanuel Manzungu by Alex Bolding and Rossella Alba, Brighton, 2 May 2014.

Finally, a third set of responses engages with the purported 'damage done' by IWRM and the need for a radically different approach that emphasises a human right to water, explicitly discarding the depoliticising rhetoric of IWRM. As mentioned earlier, the GWP has provided a platform to meet interesting people and ideas, but attempts to push a pro-poor development agenda in GWP have led to naught. Barbara van Koppen stressed the role that the GWP are still playing in agenda-setting in the water sector for SADC, and she acknowledged her critical approach towards IWRM:

> *My engagement nowadays with IWRM is only focused on criticising it. I have a problem because I'm passionate about a human rights approach to water, but hardly any of my colleagues are.*[43]

Lyla Mehta wishes to continue the struggle by engaging with critical research on the successor to IWRM, whether that is the nexus (water-food-energy), the politics of land and water grabs as well as the promise and challenge of integrating human rights around water, food and land issues. Bill Derman emphatically believes the latter comprises the future:

> *I critique water reforms with regard to their inadequacy with human rights. I still do not critique it from an IWRM perspective. I think there was and is no capacity in terms of institutional reach and human resources to do IWRM in countries like Zimbabwe. The key issue of the future in the water sector is the human right to water.*[44]

The discussion about 'the future of IWRM' continued during our project conference where we raised a vote on what's next. The guiding question was: "What is the successor to IWRM as a hegemonic concept or will IWRM simply morph into adaptive water resources management and earn a new lease on life?" We differentiated regionally between the European Union (EU) and sub-Saharan Africa (SSA). First, we addressed the question of what you would wish the next hegemonic concept (the heart) to be that would succeed or displace IWRM.

It was striking to note that only one person in our midst believed and hoped that IWRM would continue to drive the minds and hearts of the water world both in Africa and the EU, albeit possibly in a different guise as adaptive water resources management in the face of climate change mitigation. Water as a human right took an overwhelming lead as a wish for the future, emphasising access to water for all and countering the Dublin Principle that sees water as an economic good. Second placed were the water-food-energy nexus and the Green Growth Economy in the context of the European Union – realising that the greening of the economy may be a powerful alternative discourse for growth in an otherwise stagnant economic zone.

Next we asked the same question about the successor of IWRM but then focusing on what people would suspect the discourse of the day (the gut) will be rather than what they would wish themselves. Gut feelings on what would become the

43 Interview with Barbara van Koppen by Alex Bolding and Rossella Alba, Brighton, 1 May 2014.

44 Interview with Bill Derman by Alex Bolding and Rossella Alba, Brighton, 2 May 2014.

hottest concern in the water world were quite different from the vote cast from the heart. A much more prevalent role for the nexus on water-energy-and food is foreseen both in Europe and Africa, and hardly any for the water as a human right movement. The key geopolitical challenges around energy in the wealthy West and the competition between food and biofuel production in Africa under the rubric of the ongoing land (and water) grab (Mehta et al., 2012) would warrant attention to the nexus (see also Allouche et al., 2015). On the other hand, people expect the Green growth economy to play a major role in EU water debates, while IWRM or its successor AWRM is expected to play a role in sub Saharan African water debates and funding which is heavily tainted by climate-change concerns. On the other extreme, some people expect venture capitalism to rise both in the EU and Africa.

Thus, if we are a barometer for experience and direction, where might IWRM go next (or has gone already)? Discussing the future of IWRM is outside the scope of this chapter and the survey presented above is rather speculative and idiosyncratic. A systematic research by means of discursive analysis of water-related scientific articles and web-based surveys on key words is required for this purpose. Nevertheless, the answers of the interviewees and the group show again how personal beliefs, ideas and knowledge influence the unfolding of concepts.

Conclusion

This chapter has attempted to reconstruct the travel of IWRM within the ranks of the Flows and Practices research team. Our journey started from different places, disciplines and different perspectives as described in the first section. The chapter follows the researchers through their careers and documents how the team members engaged, transformed and used IWRM. The F&P project brought the team together and contributed to further develop the critique not only towards IWRM, but more in general towards dominant concepts, the hidden agendas behind the concept and the power of IWRM-related ideas to divert attention from key societal problems.

The engagement with IWRM has enabled people and ideas to navigate networks, shape and engage policies related with water resources management in different countries – what we referred to as flow. For some of the interviewees, IWRM acted as a stepping-stone, a focus point to build a career and/or a research focus, for others as a sideshow to more pertinent issues (water development and access). While several aspects of the IWRM package received critiques – namely the definition of water as an economic good, the side-lining effect of IWRM in relation to a pro-poor development agenda and the a-political character of IWRM; (most of) the F&P researchers tried to transform IWRM following their personal interests and research agendas. Eventually, we point at some of the personal struggles of the researchers and the tensions between the 'need' to engage with IWRM (if only for increasing one's chances of receiving funding), the increased recognition of the critiques of the concept, and the difficulties in putting forward a different perspective – i.e. the translating of IWRM towards the acknowledgment of water as a human right and water for development.

This points at appreciating the key role and transformative power that researchers and practitioners have in crafting new concepts, shaping the unfolding and translation of ideas. Such processes are deeply influenced by the personal experiences, knowledge systems, beliefs and opportunities that academics and professionals have. This recognition calls for enhancing transparency and self-reflection in research projects.

The fortune of IWRM resides in its ability to encompass multiple meanings, morph into something else while still being defined in one way, for example, the title of an Italian book, is at the same time one, no one and multiple.[45] With this chapter, we attempt to clarify our positions and beliefs, and outline the origin of our understanding and critical approach towards IWRM as a group of researchers.

At heart, we researchers and practitioners are not different from the policy actors, bureaucrats and stakeholders we have been studying under the banner of the F&P project. This insight provides a final and necessary plea for self-reflexive work by scientists, political activists and academics operating in the water field. More subjectivity in research, both in its process and how its findings are constructed/performed, does not make science 'weaker' or more prone to contestation. Rather it shows, in typical symmetrical fashion (Bloor, 1976 cited in Latour, 1987), that water 'experts' and researchers are capable of exerting the same kind of agency as their objects of study, for good or for worse.

Acknowledgements

The chapter draws on ongoing research from a Norwegian Research Council-funded project, Flows and Practices: The Politics of Integrated Water Resources Management (IWRM) in Africa. We would like to thank all the participants to the project for their comments to the previous versions of this chapter and the interviewees for sharing their personal and professional experiences. We thank the three anonymous reviewers for their constructive comments.

References

ACC/ISGWR (United Nations Administrative Coordination Council/Inter-Secretariat Group on Water Resources). 1992. The Dublin statement and report of the conference. Proceedings of the International Conference on Water and the Environment: Development Issues for the 21st Century. Dublin, 26-31 January 1992.

Allan, J.A. 2003. Integrated water resources management is more a political than a technical challenge. In Aisharhan, A.S. and Wood, W.W. (Eds), *Water resources perspectives: Evaluation, management and policy*, pp. 9-23. Amsterdam: Elsevier Science.

Allouche, J.; Middleton, C. and Gyawali, D. 2015. Technical veil, hidden politics: Interrogating the power linkages behind the nexus. *Water Alternatives* 8(1): 610-626.

Biswas, A.K. 2004. Integrated water resources management: A reassessment. *Water International* 29(2): 248-256.

Bloor, D. 1976. *Knowledge and social imagery*. London: Routledge & Kegan Paul.

Bolding, A. 2004. In hot water. A study on intervention models and practices of wa-

45 'One, no one, one hundred thousand' (in Italian, *Uno, Nessuno, Centomila*) is the title of a famous Italian novel written by Luigi Pirandello.

ter use in small-holder agriculture, Nyanyadzi catchment, Zimbabwe. PhD thesis. Wageningen University, Wageningen, the Netherlands.

Bolding, A.; Mollinga, P. and Zwarteveen, M. 2000. Interdisciplinarity in research on integrated water resources management: Pitfalls and challenges. Paper presented at the UNESCO-WOTRO International Work Conference on Water for Society, Delft, the Netherlands, 8-10 November 2000.

Cherlet, J. 2012. Tracing the emergence and deployment of the 'Integrated Water Resources Management' paradigm. 12th EASA Biennial Conference, Nanterre, 10-13 July 2012, France. Unpublished document.

Conca, K. 2005. Growth and fragmentation in expert networks: The elusive quest for integrated water resources management. In Dauvergne, P. (Ed), *Handbook of global environmental politics*, pp. 432-470. Cheltenham, UK: Edward Elgar Publishing.

GWP (Global Water Partnership), 2000. Integrated Water Resource Management. Technical Advisory Committee (TAC). TAC Background Paper No. 4. Stockholm: Global Water Partnership.

Iyer, R.M. 2004. *IWRM carries the seeds of centralisation and gigantism*. Water Front, Stockholm International Water Institute (SIWI) No. 4, pp. 10-11.

Lankford, B. 2005. *Rural infrastructure to contribute to African agricultural development: The case of irrigation*. Report for the Commission for Africa, ODG. Norwich, UK: University of East Anglia.

Latour, B. 1987. *Science in action. How to follow scientists and engineers through society*. Cambridge, Massachusetts: Harvard University Press.

Levine, G.; Solanes, M. and Dikito-Wachtmeister, M. 2013. Introduction – Voices of water professionals: Shedding light on hidden dynamics in the water sector. *Water Alternatives* 6(2): 148-153.

Manzungu, E.; Bolding, A. and Senzanje, A. 1999, Towards integrated water resource management. A conceptual framework. In Manzungu, E.; Senzanje, A. and van der Zaag, P. (Eds), *Water for agriculture in Zimbabwe*, pp. 254-64. Harare: University of Zimbabwe Publications.

Mehta, L.; Alba, R.; Bolding, A.; Denby, K.; Derman, B.; Hove, T.; Manzungu E.; Movik, S.; Prabhakaran, P. and van Koppen, B. 2014. The politics of IWRM in Southern Africa. *International Journal of Water Resources Development* 30(3): 528-542.

Mehta, L. and Movik, S. 2014. Flows and Practices: Integrated Water Resources Management (IWRM) in African Contexts. IDS Working Paper No. 438. Brighton: Institute of Development Studies.

Mehta, L.; Veldwisch, G.J. and Franco, J. 2012. Introduction to the Special Issue: Water grabbing? Focus on the (re)appropriation of finite water resources. *Water Alternatives* 5(2): 193-207

Miller, B.A. and Reidinger, R.B. 1998. *Comprehensive river basin development. The Tennessee Valley Authority*. World Bank Technical Paper No. 416. Washington: World Bank.

Nicol, A. 2000. Adopting a sustainable livelihoods approach to water projects: Implications for policy and practice. Working Paper No. 133. London, UK: Overseas Development Institute.

Shah, T. and van Koppen, B. 2006. Is India ripe for integrated water resources management? Fitting water policy to national development context. *Economic and Political Weekly* August 5: 3413-3421.

Wester, P.; Rap, E. and Vargas-Velázquez, S. 2009. The hydraulic mission and the Mexican hydrocracy: Regulating and reforming the flows of water and power. *Water Alternatives* 2(3): 395-415.

World Bank. 1993. *Water resources management. A World Bank policy paper*. Washington, DC: World Bank.

www.ingramcontent.com/pod-product-compliance
Lightning Source LLC
Chambersburg PA
CBHW060022030426
42334CB00019B/2143

* 9 7 8 1 7 7 9 2 2 3 1 4 2 *